EBBETS FIELD

GREAT, HISTORIC, AND
MEMORABLE GAMES FROM
BROOKLYN'S
LOST BALLPARK

EDITED BY
GREGORY H. WOLF

ASSOCIATE EDITORS
LEN LEVIN, BILL NOWLIN,
AND **CARL RIECHERS**

Society for American Baseball Research, Inc.
Phoenix, AZ

Ebbets Field: Great, Historic, and Memorable Games in Brooklyn's Lost Ballpark
Copyright © 2023 Society for American Baseball Research, Inc.
Edited by Gregory H. Wolf
Associate Editors: Len Levin, Bill Nowlin, and Carl Riechers

ISBN 978-1-960819-17-8
(Ebook ISBN 978-1-960819-16-1)
Library of Congress Control Number (LCCN) 2023919014

Book Design: David Peng
All photographs are part of the SABR-Rucker Archive,
and used with permission.

Society for American Baseball Research
Cronkite School at ASU
555 N. Central Ave. #416
Phoenix, AZ 85004
Phone: (602) 496-1460
Web: www.SABR.org
Facebook: Society for American Baseball Research
Twitter: @SABR

TABLE OF CONTENTS

EBBETS FIELD

GREAT, HISTORIC, AND MEMORABLE GAMES IN BROOKLYN'S LOST BALLPARK:

AN INTRODUCTION

by Gregory H. Wolf

Ebbets Field: Great, Historic, and Memorable Games in Brooklyn's Lost Ballpark evokes memories and the exciting history of the celebrated ballpark through stories of about 100 games played there and several feature essays. Named after Charles Ebbets, majority owner of the Brooklyn baseball club from 1902 until his death in 1925, Ebbets was the home of the Dodgers from 1913 until their relocation to Los Angeles after the 1957 season. Whether they were called the Superbas, the Robins, after skipper Wilbert Robinson, or the Dodgers, the club played in excess of 3,400 games at Ebbets Field, as well as 28 World Series games in nine different postseasons. The games included in this volume reflect every decade in the ballpark's history, from the inaugural regular-season game, against the Philadelphia Phillies on April 9, 1913, to the last one, against the Pittsburgh Pirates, in front of just 6,702 spectators on September 24, 1957.

Unlike its contemporaries, such as Forbes Field in Pittsburgh and Griffith Stadium in Washington, Ebbets Field was never the permanent, primary home of a Negro League team. The one exception was the Eagles, owned by Abe and Effa Manley, who played at Ebbets Field in 1935 before their relocation to Newark the following season. In addition to an insightful feature essay exploring the Manleys' club in Flatbush in 1935, we've included a story about the team's inaugural game at the ballpark on May 18, against the Homestead Grays, as well the first night game in the ballpark. The Cincinnati Reds' Johnny Vander Meer no-hit the Dodgers on June 15, 1938, in what is often considered the first night game at Ebbets Field; however, the first night game at Ebbets Field actually took place almost three years earlier, on September 11, 1935, under portable lights as the Negro League Dodgers played the House of David.

Ebbets Field hosted 28 World Series games and you can read about each one of them in this volume. Uncle Robbie's pitching-dominant teams from 1916 and 1920 captured Brooklyn's first NL pennants since 1899-1900, though no World Series took place after those seasons. After almost two decades, often floundering in the second division, skipper Leo Durocher led

Located in the Crown Heights section of Brooklyn, Ebbets Field was the home of the Dodgers from 1913 through the 1957 season, after which the team relocated to Los Angeles. (Photo: SABR-Rucker Archive)

the Dodgers back to prominence and the pennant in 1941, losing to the Yankees. The Dodgers and Yankees: What sounds more like a World Series than those words? The two teams squared off in the fall classic six times in a 10-year stretch (1947, 1949, 1952, 1953, 1955, and 1956), with the Dodgers capturing their elusive World Series title in 1955. Read about the heroes, like pinch-hitter Cookie Lavagetto and his walk-off double, the Dodgers' only hit of the game, to win Game Four in 1947; Carl Erskine's then World Series record 14 punchouts in Game Three in 1953, as well as what might be the most important game in Ebbets Field history: Johnny Podres' shutout in Game Seven to lead Dem Bums to the promised land in 1955. There was plenty of heartache, too. Catcher Mickey Owen's dropped third strike with two outs in the ninth inning cost the Dodgers a series-tying victory in Game Four in 1941. The Dodgers returned to Flatbush with two chances to capture the title in 1952, yet lost Game Six, 3-2, and Game Seven, 4-2, as 20-year-old Mickey Mantle spanked a pivotal home run in each game. After Clem Labine hurled a classic 10-inning complete game to beat the Yankees, 1-0, in Game Six in 1956, the Dodgers were on the cusp of back-to-back titles. In Game Seven, 27-game winner, NL MVP, and major-league Cy Young Award winner Don Newcombe was bombed for five runs in three innings as Johnny Kucks went the distance in a soul-crushing 9-0 victory, in what proved to be the last World Series game at Ebbets Field.

Some of the games of this volume have historical significance, like Jackie Robinson's debut as a Dodger on April 15, 1947; the first and only All-Star Game at Ebbets Field, in 1949, as well as the first game played in the ballpark, an exhibition with the New York Yankees, on April 5, 1913, four days before the first regular-season game. Other games recall memorable or milestone feats, including Gil Hodges hitting four home runs on August 31, 1950, and the Milwaukee Braves' Joe

Adcock smashing four on July 31, 1954. Babe Herman became the first Brooklyn player to hit for the cycle at Ebbets, on May 18, 1931, and Dem Bums won the pennant on the final day of the 1956 season. We also present some improbable comebacks and some high-scoring slugfests, such as the Dodgers' 22-run outburst on September 6, 1930; a 23-run eruption on July 10, 1943, when the Dodgers twice scored 10 runs in an inning; and the club's 15-run first-inning explosion on May 21, 1952.

For those who want pitching, *Ebbets Field: Great, Historic, and Memorable Games in Brooklyn's Lost Ballpark* contains some of the greatest mound feats at the ballpark's history. We've included no-hitters by Dodgers Dazzy Vance (1925), Ed Head (1946), and a pair by Carl Erskine (1952 and 1956); and by opponents Paul Dean of the Cardinals (1934) and Johnny Vander Meer's historic no-no, his second straight, in the first Dodgers night game at Ebbets Field, in 1938. Fred Frankhouse's abbreviated seven-inning no-hitter from 1937 is included, too. Additional games recount marathon pitching or dominant performances by hurlers, such as Jeff Pfeffer's 18-inning complete game in 1919, Karl Spooner's 15-strikeout gem in his big-league debut in 1954, and 19-year-old Sandy Koufax's two-hit shutout with 14 punchouts for his first big-league win, in 1955.

Ebbets Field: Great, Historic, and Memorable Games in Brooklyn's Lost Ballpark is the result of the tireless work of dozens of members of the Society for American Baseball Research. SABR members researched and wrote all of the essays in this volume. These uncompensated volunteers are united by their shared interest in baseball history and a resolute commitment to preserving that history. Without their unwavering dedication, this volume would not have been possible.

I am indebted to the associate editors and extend to them my sincerest appreciation. Bill Nowlin, the second reader, fact-checker

Carl Riechers, and copy editor Len Levin read all the essays and made numerous corrections to language, style, and content. Their attention to detail has been invaluable. It has been a pleasure to once again work on a book project with such professionals. What a team we have!

I thank all of the authors for their contributions, meticulous research, cooperation through the revising and editing process, and finally their patience. It was a long journey from the day the book was launched to its completion, and we've finally reached our destination. We did it! Please refer to the list of contributors at the end of the book for more information.

This book would not have been possible without the generous support of the staff and Board of Directors of SABR, SABR Publications Director

Cecilia Tan, and designer David Peng. We express our thanks and gratitude to SABR and its photo archives, especially the Rucker Archives for the majority of the photos in the volume.

And finally, I wish to thank my wife, Margaret, and daughter, Gabriela, for their support of and endless patience with my baseball pursuits.

We invite you to sit back, relax for a few minutes, and enjoy reading about the great games and the exciting history of Ebbets Field.

GREGORY H. WOLF
May 1, 2023

EBBETS FIELD

by John Zinn

On an October afternoon in the 1950s, while the Dodgers prepared for the first game of the World Series, an elderly man walked into Ebbets Field. On the surface it seemed like business as usual; Brooklyn had dominated the National League throughout the decade with regular appearances in the fall classic. Sadly, however, this time nothing was the same. Not only was the game being played in Chicago, the Dodgers, on October 1, 1959, called Los Angeles home. Little is known about this Dodgers fan, other than that he appeared to be about 70 and came to Ebbets Field regularly to sit and stare at the iconic, but now superfluous scoreboard.[1] If, however, the man was a lifelong Dodgers fan, he had witnessed a lot of the club's history including watching the 1899 and 1900 championship teams play at the club's home field – Washington Park.

By late 1911, however, our somewhat imaginary Dodgers fan had little reason for optimism. Not only was it over a decade since the Dodgers' last pennant-winning season, Brooklyn fans had endured nine consecutive second-division finishes.

And if the team's performance offered little incentive to attend games, Washington Park itself was no longer a state-of-the-art ballpark. Beginning with Shibe Park in Philadelphia in 1909, Dodgers fans could only read and dream about a new generation of ballparks being built throughout the major leagues. Little did they know that Dodgers owner Charles Ebbets was about to give them and Brooklyn one of baseball's most beloved ballparks.

Unlike the fans, however, the media knew the Squire of Flatbush was up to something. In their holiday mail was an invitation to a January 2, 1912, dinner at which, according to a line highlighted in red, "A very important piece of news" was to be announced.[2] While some speculated that Ebbets would announce improvements to Washington Park, reporters from Brooklyn's four daily newspapers correctly concluded that his announcement was about a new ballpark.[3] Recognizing that the people of Brooklyn had loyally supported a losing team, the Dodgers owner told his audience the fans were "entitled to the new park."[4] While the news wasn't a surprise to the reporters, William

Granger of the *Brooklyn Citizen* claimed "not one [guess about the location] was even close."[5]

Ebbets declared that he had found the right location on 5.7 acres in the southwest part of Crow Hill in the Flatbush section of Brooklyn which was previously known as the Pigtown garbage dump. While the area was described as "farmlike" with few buildings, it was also home to the Brooklyn Institute of Arts and Sciences (now the Brooklyn Museum) as well as the Consumer Park Brewery and the Hygienic Ice Company. It took a few years, but a surge in housing construction that lasted through the 1920s would bring families with children to the area.[6] Bounded by Bedford Avenue, Cedar Place, Montgomery Street, and Sullivan Place, the site was reportedly so accessible by mass transit that the *Brooklyn Daily Eagle* jokingly claimed, "Even a bigamist could ask no more avenues of escape or approach."[7] Just acquiring the land was no small accomplishment. Ebbets had to buy 25 to 30 parcels in great secrecy because if word got out, the prices would have been driven up well beyond his limited financial means.[8]

On this site, Ebbets intended to build a standard Deadball Era ballpark with a double-deck steel and concrete grandstand running from the right-field corner to third base, supplemented by concrete bleachers from third to the left-field foul pole. Although the original plans included bleachers in center field which would have increased the seating capacity to 30,000, no seats were built in fair territory, reducing total seating to about 24,000.[9] While the trapezoid shape of the land mandated a short 301-foot right-field fence, left (419 feet) and center (507 feet) would have the standard dimensions of the period. Of special note was the rotunda, intended as the primary entrance to the park (although congestion would quickly lead to the opening of two additional entrances). Made of marble, the rotunda featured a chandelier with 16 lights "representing so many baseballs," all "suspended from arms in the shape of bats."[10] Before Ebbets could turn his attention to building his new ballpark, however, it had to have a name. While Ebbets Field was suggested from the outset, the Brooklyn owner wisely left the decision to the sports editors of the four Brooklyn daily newspapers. In what may have been a preordained process, they chose Ebbets Field and so it remained throughout its existence.[11]

Brooklyn fans, however, were probably more concerned about when the dream ballpark would become a reality. Understandably caught up in the excitement, Ebbets hoped for an already "doubtful" Flag Day (June 14), but was "positive" fans would enjoy games there by August 27, the anniversary of the Revolutionary War Battle of Brooklyn.[12] However, any even slightly objective observer who visited the site would have concluded that a 1912 opening was unlikely. Not only was there a large hole described as either "the subway to China," or "a Miniature Grand Canyon," the Bedford Avenue side was as much as 16 feet higher than the Sullivan Street side.[13] Clearly significant site work was necessary; it depended on the weather, something Ebbets couldn't control, and brutal cold delayed site preparation until early March.[14]

These delays were only the beginning of the problems Ebbets encountered building his new ballpark. Unforeseen issues like a new sewer, more bad weather, and labor problems doomed any possibility that the ballpark would open in 1912.[15] Far more ominous, however, was that due to Ebbets' poor financial planning, he was in danger of running out of money long before the ballpark was finished. By August 1912, the Brooklyn owner was reduced to asking for loans from his fellow owners, most of whom were not receptive. With no alternatives left, Ebbets faced the inevitable and sold 50 percent of the Dodgers (and Ebbets Field) to Steve and Ed McKeever in order to finish the project.[16] Equal ownership meant decision-making by consensus, which seems to have worked so long as all three men were alive,

A visionary sports executive, Charles Ebbets was the majority owner of the Brooklyn Dodgers from 1897 until his death in 1925 and served as club president from 1898 to 1925. (Photo: Library of Congress)

but not so well afterward. Such problems were, however, well in the future and finally, in April of 1913, some 15 months after the announcement, Ebbets Field was ready to host its first game.

Since just building Ebbets Field was more than a little complicated, it was only fitting that scheduling the opener was also difficult. Under the National League's rotating schedule, created by Ebbets himself, the Dodgers were to open the 1913 season on the road. Thanks, however, to the efforts of Tom Rice of the *Eagle* and the somewhat grudging consent of Ebbets's fellow owners, Brooklyn was awarded a special opener on April 9. By that point, however, Ebbets had preempted the National League opener with two exhibition games against the New York Yankees.[17] If fans needed any further encouragement to attend the April 5 exhibition game, it was provided by "one of the nicest little Spring days the oldest inhabitant of Flatbush could remember."[18] The combination of a new ballpark, a new season, and a nice day produced a vast throng that packed subway and trolley lines. Nor was mass transit the sole means of access. So many came by auto that some of the more sheltered local residents thought "[t]here ain't that many machines [cars] made."[19] If the limited parking that hampered Ebbets Field's future was a problem the day it opened, no mention was made in the media.

After enduring packed subway cars and seemingly endless traffic, fans anxious to see the new ballpark encountered further delays getting to the ticket booths in the rotunda. Once up the ramps, however, they saw the field for the first time, anticipating thousands who never forgot their first view of Ebbets Field. Less fortunate were the estimated 5,000 to 10,000 potential ticket buyers who couldn't get in, missing not only a first look at the new ballpark, but also a dramatic Brooklyn win in the bottom of the ninth.[20] The media heaped praise on the new ballpark, with the *Brooklyn Daily Times* claiming that "Nothing but praise was heard for the new

stadium," while the *Eagle* gushingly proclaimed it "the greatest ball park in these United States."[21] Those who attended the opening made a wise choice since four days later, only 10,000 braved 37-degree temperatures to witness a 1-0 loss to Philadelphia in a blessedly short 90 minutes.[22] The frigid conditions did not, however, stop the chorus of praise for the new ballpark, which the *Philadelphia Inquirer* called "an athletic inclosure second to none."[23]

Although the 1913 Dodgers were destined for another second-division finish, the new ballpark attracted over 100,000 more admissions.[24] Attendance fell over the next two seasons, however, primarily because of head-to-head competition with the Federal League's Brooklyn franchise (even though the Dodgers were finally becoming competitive). By 1915 Brooklyn had not only reached the first division, Ebbets Field hosted its first pennant race. The team's third-place finish sparked plenty of optimism about 1916, which was richly rewarded with the Dodgers' first pennant since 1900 and the team's first appearance in the modern World Series. Unfortunately for Charles Ebbets, the on-the-field success didn't consistently translate into ticket sales, and some important September games drew "pitifully small" crowds of 2,000 to 3,000.[25]

Probably trying to recover the lost revenue, Ebbets unwisely raised prices for World Series tickets, which led to crowds well under capacity for both games played at Ebbets Field.[26] Dodgers fans might have been more understanding had they known that unlike Boston Red Sox owner Joseph Lannin, Ebbets did not pursue a suggestion to shift Brooklyn's home games to a larger ballpark like the Polo Grounds.[27] Those who did attend the first World Series game at Ebbets Field saw a Dodgers victory, but the following day, the Red Sox quickly overcame an early Brooklyn lead to win the game and take control of the Series.

Before the Dodgers had a chance to defend their 1916 National League pennant, the United

States entry into World War I wreaked havoc with major-league baseball. The Dodgers felt the full effect in 1918 when, although the club finished fifth, it was dead last at the box office, drawing under 84,000 fans, a decline of over 80 percent from 1916.[28] Facing the government's work-or-fight order, the owners ended the season early and by mid-September, Ebbets Field was a storehouse for war-related material.[29] While it appeared there would be no 1919 season, the November 11 Armistice restored not only peace, but major-league baseball. There was so much uncertainty about the coming season, however, that the owners chose to play an abbreviated 140-game schedule.[30] Even though fewer games were played at Ebbets Field that season, the big news was that some were played on Sunday.

Ever since the team's founding in 1883, Dodgers fans whose only day off was Sunday were prevented from attending games by the so-called "blue laws," which prohibited baseball games with an admission charge on the Sabbath. From 1904 to 1906, Charles Ebbets unsuccessfully tried various ploys to get around those restrictions.[31] When the wartime environment facilitated reopening the issue in 1917, Ebbets tried again, only to be arrested and convicted of breaking the Sunday baseball laws.[32] Finally in April of 1919, legislative action removed the prohibition, and less than a week later, Ebbets Field hosted its first Sunday game, the first of 13 that season. Although there was little advance sale, about 22,000 attended, more than either of the 1916 World Series home games.[33] Finally baseball at Ebbets Field was available to everyone in Brooklyn.

Nor was the large Sunday crowd a one-time thing, helping 1919 attendance reach almost 361,000, the second highest in the ballpark's brief history. A year later, Ebbets Field hosted 19 Sunday games, which, along with a pennant-winning team, drove attendance to an unprecedented 809,000, second best in the

National League.[34] However, not everyone who passed through the Ebbets Field turnstiles in 1920 was an unquestioning loyalist. As the pennant race headed into September, Tom Rice of the *Eagle* claimed that the team played better on the road because of "a certain sort of Brooklyn fans," who were relentlessly critical without ever offering "a word of encouragement." Hard as it may be to believe, both Ebbets and manager Wilbert Robinson agreed with Rice, warning the not-so-faithful that they could cost Brooklyn the pennant.[35]

But sufficient fans mended their ways and Ebbets Field hosted its second World Series, against the Cleveland Indians. Fortunately, there was no repeat of the dispute over ticket prices and large crowds saw their Dodgers win two of the first three games before being swept at Cleveland in the next to last best-of-nine fall classic. Although the team's performance fell off during the next three seasons, Brooklyn fans continued to flock to the ballpark for the rest of Charles Ebbets' tenure. By 1924 the Dodgers were once again in the heat of the pennant race and finished a close second before record-setting attendance of almost 819,000.[36]

Attendance mattered more in Ebbets Field's early years because owners had few sources of revenue beyond ticket sales. One way of generating additional revenue was hosting other events, athletic and otherwise, when the Dodgers were not playing at home. Even before he started renting his ballpark, however, Ebbets opened the new facility rent-free for a field day for orphans and later admitted local students at no cost to watch their peers compete at baseball and track. Although the events netted Ebbets no revenue, they gave the community a greater sense of ownership of the new ballpark. However, Ebbets also wasted little time in renting his ballpark for other events. College baseball was played there during the inaugural season, followed two years later by boxing and eventually soccer, which actually outlasted the Dodgers. Nonsporting events included opera in 1925 and a 1926 wedding of two orphans sponsored as a fundraiser for a local hospital.[37]

One of the earliest alternative sources of revenue was football, probably because Ebbets had rented out Washington Park for the same purpose. College football was played at Ebbets Field as early as 1917 and continued through the 1940s. The most important college game at Ebbets Field was the 1923 Army-Notre Dame game, played in Brooklyn because the World Series was at the Polo Grounds. Professional football got started at Ebbets Field in 1926 and continued through 1948 with the aptly-named Brooklyn Dodger football teams enjoying only limited success. More historically significant was the first televised football game in 1939, only a year after Ebbets Field hosted a similar milestone for major-league baseball. Far more important to the story of the Brooklyn ballpark, however, were the more than 200 high-school football games played there over a period of 40 years beginning in the ballpark's inaugural season. Featuring at least a dozen schools including historical rivalries like Erasmus-Manual (they played 41 times at Ebbets Field), these games gave countless players, cheerleaders, and band members the chance to perform on the same field as their baseball heroes.[38] The shared experience was yet another link between Brooklyn and Ebbets Field.

By 1925 the Dodgers and Ebbets Field were "one of the most valuable properties in baseball."[39] It was a testament to Charles Ebbets' years of hard work, but sadly those accomplishments would not long survive Ebbets' death on April 18, 1925. Standing in a cold rain at the funeral, Ed McKeever caught a cold that turned into pneumonia and he, too, was dead by month's end.[40] Suddenly 75 percent of the Dodgers and Ebbets Field were owned by the Ebbets (50 percent) and Ed McKeever (25 percent) estates. Far more serious, however, was the fact that this was not simply a transfer of ownership from one generation to the next. Instead it was a sea change from owners engaged in baseball as a business to heirs/investors whose primary concern was receiving regular dividend payments. Ebbets' ownership interest was divided into 15 parts while Ed McKeever, although he was childless, had supported so many relatives that his estate had even more (18).[41] It was a situation ripe for disaster, exacerbated even further by Steve McKeever's ongoing feud with manager Wilbert Robinson.[42]

While these problems were probably not the sole cause, the club dropped to the second division in 1925 and stayed there for the next four seasons. Attendancewise, however, the team continued to draw well, but with so many mouths to feed, dividends quickly exceeded profits. From 1925 to 1929, the Dodgers earned net profits of just over $474,000, but paid out $684,000 in dividends.[43] Not only was there less money to acquire players, there were also little or no funds for repairs and renovations at Ebbets Field, not to mention expanding the park's limited seating capacity. Steve McKeever raised this concern as early as 1928, but said the rest of the board "seemed reluctant" to take any action, a stalemate that continued until the 1930 season finally forced the issue.[44]

Perhaps the worst nightmare of pre-TV-era owners was inadequate seating capacity, which became a major problem in Brooklyn in 1930 when the Dodgers contended for the pennant all season long before finishing fourth. The good news was that the team drew over a million fans for the first time and realized a profit of almost $427,000, exceeding dividends paid for the first time since 1926.[45] The bad news was that on at least a dozen occasions, 5,000 to 10,000 fans couldn't buy tickets because of the limited seating capacity.[46] Every one of those lost admissions would have gone straight to the bottom line, available, among other things, to help pay for the sorely needed expansion. Although still stymied on that front,

Steve McKeever made one badly needed (according to him) improvement – the-20-foot screen on the top of the right-field wall. According to the *Eagle*, McKeever "has been worrying all summer lest a Brooklyn line drive descend abruptly on the bonnet of some elderly lady across that famous thoroughfare Bedford Avenue."[47]

The possibility of adding more seats was facilitated when the "Warring factions" on the board reached some compromises, including adding a neutral fifth board member appointed by National League President John Heydler to break deadlocks.[48] In this improved environment, the expansion of Ebbets Field moved forward, but at a slow pace. Key to Steve McKeever's plan, which would supposedly have expanded the seating capacity to 50,000 to 60,000, was getting New York City to move Montgomery Street (behind the left-field wall) to the other side of the current thoroughfare onto land owned by the Dodgers. This would have facilitated the construction of a new triple-decker stand in left field while maintaining the original outfield dimensions.[49] In spite of rumors that the expanded ballpark would be renamed Brooklyn Stadium, McKeever insisted that it would continue to be called Ebbets Field.[50] Sadly, the city refused to cooperate and the new stands, now reduced to two levels, had to be built on the existing site, encroaching into the outfield, moving deepest center field over 100 feet closer to home plate. Over the years the distance down the left-field line would be decreased to 343 feet while the distance to center field would also be reduced a little bit more. The revised plans added only about 9,000 new seats, not the 25,000 to 35,000 envisioned by McKeever in 1928. According to Philip Lowry in *Green Cathedrals*, Ebbets Field's seating capacity would peak at 35,000 in 1937 and drop to just under 32,000 during the ballpark's last season.[51]

Even with the obvious financial advantages and the approval of 80 percent of the shareholders, the project became bogged down in legal issues.

At the root of the problem was not opposition by the various heirs, but the fact that 75 percent of the stock was owned by estates, some of whose beneficiaries were infants represented by guardians.[52] In the end, approval was sought from the surrogate's court, which ruled that the real issue – mortgaging the property, not the expansion itself, was a business decision, not a legal issue.[53] Armed with that somewhat less than definitive support, the club simultaneously broke ground and began construction on February 16, 1931, on a project estimated to cost $450,000.[54] Unlike the original construction, the expansion proceeded more or less on schedule, and all of the new seats were available by the last weekend in May.[55] Since these were the years of the "Daffiness Boys," it was probably appropriate that the first player to reach the new center-field seats was the club's leading eccentric, Babe Herman.[56]

But the timing of the expansion couldn't have been worse. In a twist worthy of a Dickens novel, as soon as the seating capacity was increased, it was no longer needed.[57] The Dodgers on-the-field performance declined; along with the Depression this sent attendance plummeting by over 344,000 in 1931. Nor was that the end of the downturn as attendance dropped below 500,000 in 1934 and stayed there through 1937.[58] Unsurprisingly, regular profits became regular losses, further exacerbated by the payment of $125,000 in dividends. From 1932 to 1937, the team lost $667,000 and by the end of the period, the ballclub was deeply in debt and at risk of having the National League take over the franchise and Ebbets Field.[59] Naturally the ballpark also suffered and by the late 1930s Ebbets Field badly needed painting and repairs, while the beloved rotunda was "covered with mildew."[60]

But even though it wasn't obvious in 1938, better days were coming, beginning with the arrival of future Hall of Fame members Leo Durocher and Larry MacPhail. Although Durocher came first, acquired in a late 1937 trade, it was MacPhail who had the most immediate impact beginning in early 1938.[61] Described as having "a large and speckled reputation," the flamboyant Dodgers leader was a breath of fresh air, and Ebbets Field, which had become "a monument to peeling paint and mildew," was the immediate beneficiary.[62] After persuading the Brooklyn Trust Company to lend over $300,000 to the already debt-burdened club, MacPhail spruced up the inside of the ballpark and installed lights for night games. A year later, the Brooklyn executive began broadcasting Dodgers games on the radio, a step magnified even further by hiring the soon to be legendary Red Barber as broadcaster.[63]

MacPhail also improved the on the field product by upgrading the roster and hiring Durocher as manager for the 1939 season.[64] Perhaps climbing more rapidly than might reasonably have been expected, the Dodgers moved from seventh place in 1938 to third in 1939 and then won the club's first pennant in over two decades in 1941. And the Dodgers faithful responded to the club's rapid rise, driving 1941 attendance to 1.2 million, almost double that of 1938. Even more impressively, Brooklyn led the major leagues in attendance in both 1941 and 1942, outdrawing both the Yankees and Giants.[65]

Although Dodgers fans were disappointed by the 1941 World Series loss to the Yankees, things were clearly looking up at Ebbets Field. Among those attracted by the team's newfound success were some of the Dodgers' legendary fans, beginning with a "plump, pink-faced woman with a mop of stringy gray hair" named Hilda Chester.[66] After Chester's constant yelling contributed to a heart attack, she substituted banging a ladle on a frying pan until the Dodgers players gave her the famous cow/school bell as a somewhat less grating alternative.[67] Nor was Hilda content to limit herself to cheering from the sidelines; she famously used Pete Reiser to deliver a note recommending a pitching change to Durocher, a missive the Dodgers skipper mistakenly attributed to Larry MacPhail.[68]

Even though she was unaccompanied, Chester probably held her own in the noise department with the Dodgers' most famous group act, the Brooklyn Sym-Phony. Although the band played at Ebbets Field as early as 1937, they didn't attract media attention until the 1941 pennant race.[69] Although not noted for the quality of their music, the group earned praise from Pulitzer Prize-winning historian Doris Kearns Goodwin for their "very creative" song selection intended to annoy opposing players and umpires.[70] In addition to disturbing the opposition and fans who just wanted to watch the game, the band also ran afoul of Local 802 of the American Federation of Musicians in 1951, resulting in a temporary ban on their performances. To fill the void, Walter O'Malley, although not noted for his sense of humor or generosity, gave free admission to any fan bringing an instrument to an August 13 game. Over 2,400 participated, including seven men who dragged/pushed a piano. According to Milton Bracker of the *New York Times*, the so-called musicians "tooted, fiddled, banged, boomed, squeaked, tinkled and clanged" to the point that the evening might better have been labeled "music depreciation night."[71] Also providing musical accompaniment, but of far better quality, was Gladys Goodding, who began playing the organ at Ebbets Field in 1942.[72]

As with all ballparks, advertising was a regular feature at Ebbets Field, from the Bull Durham tobacco ad to the Schaefer Beer sign on top of the scoreboard. Most famous of all was the Abe Stark sign, which actually took two different forms. The original replaced a Bull Durham tobacco advertisement and covered about 150 feet of the right-field wall from top to bottom. Stark, the operator of a Brooklyn clothing store, offered a free suit to any player who hit it with a batted ball. Reportedly many did, prompting Stark to opt for a smaller version when the new scoreboard was installed during the 1931 expansion. With the sign located below the scoreboard and only three feet high, but 30 feet long, fewer players achieved the feat, beginning with Mel Ott that very first season. Later Carl Furillo stood in front of the sign, saving Stark countless free suits to the point that Ralph Kiner and his teammates joked that Stark should have given Furillo a free suit in gratitude.[73]

While Dodgers fans enjoyed another good season in 1942, the United States' entry into World War II eventually took its toll. The on-the-field product became substandard and attendance declined by almost 400,000 admissions from 1942 to 1943 and stayed below 700,000 through 1945.[74] Wartime rationing also limited repairs to Ebbets Field itself, which was graphically illustrated on August 6, 1944, when a Boston Braves home run went through a hole in the right-field screen that hadn't been repaired because of a shortage of building materials.[75] Far more significant, however, were some leadership changes. Not long after the 1942 season, Larry MacPhail left the Dodgers and was replaced by Branch Rickey. Although far less flamboyant, Rickey was even more competent, but was also, according to John Drebinger of the *New York Times*, "a man of strange complexities, not to mention downright contradictions."[76] Also on the scene was Walter O'Malley, an attorney representing the Brooklyn Trust Company, which lent the team money and also was the trustee for the Ebbets and McKeever heirs.[77]

In spite of the wartime problems, the Dodgers' financial situation had improved sufficiently for new ownership to finally buy out the heirs of Charles Ebbets and Ed McKeever. The latter group went first in late 1944, followed by the Ebbets heirs in August of the following year. Naturally, since it was the Dodgers, it was a complicated transaction, but once the ink was dry, Rickey, O'Malley, and the less well-known, but wealthier, John Smith were majority owners of the Dodgers. Still remaining in a minority position were Steve McKeever's heirs.[78]

During the five years or so that O'Malley and Rickey ran the Dodgers, the latter concentrated on baseball operations and gradually built the legendary lineup fondly remembered as the Boys of Summer. Of that group, one made history at Ebbets Field, not just baseball history, but American history. When Jackie Robinson ran out to first base on April 15, 1947, he not only became the first African American to play major-league baseball in the twentieth century, but also ushered in a new phase in the civil rights movement. If, however, the local media realized they were witnessing history, they had little to say about it. Arthur Daley of the *New York Times* called Robinson's debut "quite uneventful" while the *Eagle* and the *Daily News* paid little attention. Nor was the event a hot ticket as the crowd fell short of a sellout. Noteworthy, however, were the African Americans, who made up somewhere between one-third and one-half of the crowd and didn't need to be told something special was going on.[79] Any perceived indifference to the significance of Robinson's joining the Dodgers would quickly fade as those who witnessed his "dignity" in the face of regular abuse had, in the words of Pulitzer Prize-winning biographer Robert Caro, "to think at least a little about America's shattered promises."[80]

While Robinson was the first African American to wear a Dodgers uniform, he was hardly the first to play at Ebbets Field. That distinction went to the Bacharach Giants, who called the Brooklyn ballpark home from 1919 to 1921. After 1921, it wasn't until 1935, when Abe Manley and his wife, Effa, arranged for the Brooklyn Eagles to play there, that another professional Black baseball team called Ebbets Field home. Although the Eagles were the sole Black club to have a major-league ballpark for their home field, the arrangement was unsuccessful largely due to competition not only from New York's major-league clubs, but also from Brooklyn's many semipro teams. The Eagles left Brooklyn after one season, shifting to Newark, where they enjoyed so much success that in 2006 Effa Manley became the first woman inducted into the Baseball Hall of fame. Professional Black baseball returned to Ebbets Field briefly in the postwar years, only to be supplanted by Rickey and Robinson.[81]

When Ebbets Field was built, Charles Ebbets took special pains to have a high-quality playing surface.[82] He was clearly successful, since years after his death many players, both Dodgers and the opposition, had good memories of the field.[83] They also remembered the limited foul territory which, according to Carl Erskine, meant the players could hear almost everything said in the stands. So close were the fans that Randy Jackson said batting practice could be dangerous for fans who didn't pay attention.[84] Visiting players were less appreciative of disgruntled fans who sometimes sprayed ink on the clothing of players who didn't respond positively to an autograph request.[85]

The transition to the great ballclub of the postwar era began with the 1946 return of Pee Wee Reese from military service and the debut of Carl Furillo that same season. In addition to Robinson, Duke Snider and Gil Hodges played for the Dodgers in 1947, followed a year later by Roy Campanella, Billy Cox, Carl Erskine, and Preacher Roe. Further bolstering the pitching staff were the additions of Don Newcombe (1949), Clem Labine (1950), Joe Black (1952), and Johnny Podres (1953). Also playing an important role in the Dodgers' success were Andy Pafko (1951) and Jim Gilliam (1953). Leo Durocher was the manager at the beginning of the postwar period before running afoul of Commissioner Happy Chandler and Rickey. Burt Shotton filled in for Durocher in 1947 and became his permanent replacement in 1948. When Walter O'Malley bought out Rickey after the 1950 season, he replaced Shotton with Charlie Dressen before turning to Walter Alston in 1954.[86]

At some level the manager may not have mattered, since fans at Ebbets Field enjoyed one successful season after another. In the 12 seasons from 1946 to 1957, Brooklyn won six National League pennants and finished second four times, twice after tying for the regular-season lead. The worst performances were two third-place finishes, the last in 1957, the team's final season at Ebbets Field. The six pennants led to 20 World Series games in Brooklyn in which the Dodgers compiled an 11-9 record, including winning 8 of the last 10 Series games played at Ebbets Field. The team was far less successful in the two playoff series, losing both games played in Brooklyn. During this period Ebbets Field also hosted the 1949 All-Star Game, won by the American League, but more significantly the first time African American players took part. Although the Dodgers' on-the-field success was overshadowed by the Yankees' World Series dominance, Bill James believes only the 1906-10 Cubs and the 1942-46 Cardinals "accomplished more [in the National League] than the Dodgers of 1952-56." Over that five-year period, the team averaged 97 wins per season, finished first four times and second once.[87]

Understandably, this is the same period when fans enjoyed so many unforgettable experiences at Ebbets Field. For some it began when they came out of the subway to the aroma of fresh-baked bread from the local Bond Bread factory. As fans followed the crowd to the ballpark, the smell of beer, cigars, peanuts, and hot dogs blended with the bread and produced a unique and memorable Ebbets Field aroma.[88] While there were multiple entrances to the ballpark, the famed rotunda stood out to many.[89] The rotunda was also important for access to the ramps that gave fans their first view of the field. Former NYU President John Sexton believes the rotunda was "a critical threshold" that "connected the profane and ordinary with the sacred and the transcendent."[90] Even though it was a small ballpark, Doris Kearns Goodwin remembered the field as "the largest green space [I] had ever seen."[91] Testifying to the impact of televising every home game since 1947 was the experience of some young fans who were surprised that the field wasn't the black and white they remembered from television.[92] Television coverage was further enhanced in 1950 when O'Malley hired another legendary redheaded broadcaster, Vin Scully.[93] Young fans also enjoyed Happy Felton's Knothole Gang, where after a brief workout a Dodgers player chose a lucky Little Leaguer to come back and interview his favorite Dodger.[94] Overall the atmosphere was reminiscent of a "carnival" or "a country fair."[95]

Unfortunately, however there weren't as many fans enjoying the experience in person. Although attendance exceeded 1 million in each of the final 12 seasons, it peaked at 1,807,000 in 1947 and ranged from 1 million to 1.3 million from 1950 on. Attendance was slightly over 1 million in the 1955 championship season and from 1953 to 1957 the team never led the league in attendance, although it won three pennants and a World Series.[96] Vividly illustrating the new and disturbing reality was the failure to sell out Games Six and Seven of the 1952 World Series, especially 5,000 empty seats at Game Six.[97] In retrospect, it seems the increased availability of games on television was the major cause of the decline in attendance, since the Dodgers broadcasts attracted twice as many viewers as the Giants and "half again as many as the Yankees."[98] Simply put, it was far easier for the average fan, deterred by the aging ballpark, very limited parking and the lack of "major arterial highways" to watch the game from his living room.[99]

All of this might have been tolerable had it been business as usual in the National League, but Boston's 1953 move to Milwaukee turned one of the worst drawing franchises into one of the best. After attracting 1,826,000 fans their inaugural season in Wisconsin, the Braves topped the 2 million mark each of the next four seasons, close to doubling Brooklyn's attendance.[100] The declining attendance did not, however, impact the Dodgers' bottom line. During the same five-year period (1952-56), the Dodgers made more money than any other team in baseball thanks to other sources of revenue.[101]

The Dodgers were obviously not in financial difficulty but the attendance issues were worrisome, a problem that beginning in 1950 was the responsibility of just one man, Walter O'Malley. Given the strong personalities involved, it's no surprise that conflicts developed between O'Malley and Rickey in the late 1940s, especially over the rising expenses of the club's extensive farm system and the new training facility at Vero Beach. Concern over these costs was magnified even more by "Rickey's biggest management blunder," the Brooklyn Dodgers football team, whose financial losses came close to "the team's normal annual profit."[102] Rickey decided to leave Brooklyn in the summer of 1950 and with some skillful maneuvering drove the price of his shares to over $1 million. By early November O'Malley, along with John Smith's widow, met the price and when Mrs. Smith dropped out shortly thereafter, Walter O'Malley, for better or for worse, was the majority owner of the Dodgers.[103]

Initially the shift of control benefited the fans at Ebbets Field. At the time baseball owners did little, if any, marketing, but O'Malley changed that, eliminating separate-admission doubleheaders, dramatically increasing community nights, expanding the Knothole Gang, and offering autograph days. At one point *Newsweek* magazine claimed the Brooklyn owner was "probably the most promotion-minded man in the game."[104] Although O'Malley had no complaints about the on-the-field product, the venue was another matter. Termed a "dirty, stinking old ballpark" by the club's legendary radio and television voice Red Barber, Ebbets Field was clearly showing its age. Even more of a concern was the limited seating capacity and the even more limited parking.[105] While the surrounding neighborhood remained middle or working class through the Dodgers' departure, the migration of fans to the suburbs meant a more difficult trip to a ballpark where "rowdyism" was beginning to be considered all too common. At a time when family outings were becoming the norm, Ebbets Field didn't seem to offer that kind of experience.[106]

It would have been irresponsible for any competent owner to avoid dealing with the future of Ebbets Field, and regardless of how one feels about Walter O'Malley, it's hard to question his competence. Board meeting minutes from 1945 and 1946 confirm not just O'Malley's concern about the issue, but his sense that the current site was not the solution.[107] In 1953 the Brooklyn owner used the *Eagle* to inform the public that "Ebbets Field has never been considered" as the location for a new ballpark. Less publicly, O'Malley also began his vain effort to seek assistance from New York City government in the person of Robert Moses.[108] The controversial story of the failed effort to build a new ballpark in Brooklyn and the team's move to Los Angeles has been told many times and the debate will doubtless go on forever. It is beyond the scope of this essay, however, because even if the Dodgers remained in Brooklyn, they were going to leave Ebbets Field. The point of no return was reached on October 31, 1956, with the announcement that O'Malley had sold the ballpark to real estate developer Marvin Kratter for $3 million to be developed into apartments.[109] Had the Dodgers stayed in Brooklyn, the 1960 demolition of the ballpark would have been delayed but not prevented.[110]

The question remains, however, whether renovating or rebuilding Ebbets Field was a practical alternative, especially since two contemporary ballparks, Fenway Park and Wrigley Field, continue to be two of baseball's most popular venues. Certainly a lack of parking has not been a problem in Boston or Chicago. It has also been claimed that the small site (5.7 acres) made it impossible to expand the seating capacity but again the difference in Boston (6.3 acres) and Chicago (6.7) doesn't seem to support so quick a decision that the solution wasn't to be found on property O'Malley's already controlled.[111] Even if the neighborhoods surrounding Fenway Park and Wrigley Field were more stable, it can still be argued that the existing site didn't get sufficient attention.[112]

In the end, it's all speculation, and the Dodgers played their final game at Ebbets Field on September 24, 1957, before a crowd of 6,702. It is remarkable that over 60 years later so many people still have so many fond memories of the Brooklyn ballpark. The reason may be found in the title of Philip Lowry's classic work about baseball stadiums: *Green Cathedrals*. The characterization resonates because it captures the sacred moments experienced by so many in those special places. In most cases, however, the old ballpark was either replaced with a new one or a team left town because it no longer had a critical mass of fans. At Ebbets Field, however, although ticket sales were down, attendance of over a million a year left many who never forgot their days and nights at the ballpark on Flatbush Avenue. The atmosphere at that final 1957 game has been described as wake-like, but it couldn't have been a wake.[113] A wake means someone died, and while the Brooklyn Dodgers and Ebbets Field are gone forever, they will never die.

SOURCES

In addition to the sources cited in the Notes, the author accessed Retrosheet.org, Baseball-Reference.com, and SABR.org.

NOTES

1 Bob McGee, *The Greatest Ballpark Ever: Ebbets Field and the Story of the Brooklyn Dodgers* (New Brunswick, New Jersey: Rutgers University Press, 2005), 11.

2 *Brooklyn Standard Union,* January 3, 1912: 11.

3 *Brooklyn Daily Eagle,* January 2, 1912: 22; *Brooklyn Citizen,* January 3, 1912: 5; *Brooklyn Daily Times,* January 3, 1912: 12.

4 *Brooklyn Daily Times,* January 3, 1912: 12.

5 *Brooklyn Citizen,* January 3, 1912: 5.

6 Ron Selter, *Ballparks of the Deadball Era: A Comprehensive Study of Their Dimensions, Configurations and Effects on Batting, 1901-1919* (Jefferson, North Carolina: McFarland & Co., 2008), 42; McGee, *Greatest Ballpark,* 39-40, 76, 108.

7 *Brooklyn Daily Eagle,* January 3, 1912: 22.

8 *New York Tribune,* January 3, 1912: 8; *Brooklyn Daily Eagle,* January 3, 1912: 22.

9 Selter, 42; Brooklyn *Daily Eagle,* January 3, 1912: 21-22.

10 Selter, 42; *Brooklyn Daily Times,* April 5, 1913: 17; McGee, 68.

11 *Brooklyn Citizen,* January 3, 1912: 5; *Brooklyn Standard Union,* January 5, 1912: 14; *Brooklyn Daily Times,* January 3, 1912: 12; January 5, 1912: 12.

12 *Brooklyn Daily Eagle,* January 3, 1912: 22.

13 *Brooklyn Daily Eagle,* January 4, 1912: 20; January 7, 1912: 62, *Brooklyn Citizen,* January 3, 1912: 5.

14 *Brooklyn Daily Eagle,* January 10, 1912: 23; February 10, 1912: 1; February 19, 1912: 19; March 5, 1912: 21.

15 *Brooklyn Daily Eagle,* March 20, 1912: 1; July 18, 1912: 17; August 15, 1912: 2; October 21, 1912: 20; *Brooklyn Citizen,* August 16, 1912: 1; *Brooklyn Daily Times,* September 21, 1912: 8.

16 John Zinn, *Charles Ebbets: The Man Behind the Dodgers and Brooklyn's Beloved Ballpark* (Jefferson, North Carolina: McFarland & Co., 2019), 126-127, 131-132.

17 Zinn, *Charles Ebbets,* 134-135.

18 *New York Times,* April 6, 1913: 31.

19 *Brooklyn Daily Times,* April 5, 1913: 1.

20 Zinn, *Charles Ebbets,* 136-138.

21 *Brooklyn Daily Times,* April 5, 1913: 1; *Brooklyn Daily Eagle,* April 6, 1913: 1.

22 Zinn, *Charles Ebbets,* 138.

23 *Philadelphia Inquirer,* April 10, 1913: 10.

24 John Thorn, Pete Palmer, Michael Gershman, and David Pietrusza, *Total Baseball: The Official Encyclopedia of Major League Baseball, Sixth Edition* (New York: Total Sports, 1999), 106.

25 *Brooklyn Daily Eagle,* September 22, 1916: 22; Thorn, *Total Baseball,* 106.

26 Zinn, *Charles Ebbets,* 164; *Brooklyn Daily Eagle,* October 11: 1916, 24; October 12, 1916: 18.

27 Joseph Lannin to Ban Johnson, September 25, 1916, Box 89, Folder 10, August "Garry" Herrmann Papers, BA-MSS 12, National Baseball Hall of Fame Library, Cooperstown, New York.

28 Thorn, 106.

29 *Brooklyn Daily Eagle,* September 14, 1918: 16.

30 *New York Times,* January 16, 1919: 10.

31 Zinn, *Charles Ebbets,* 82-84.

32 Zinn, *Charles Ebbets,* 174; *Brooklyn Daily Eagle,* July 6, 1917: 1; September 24, 1917: 1.

33 Zinn, *Charles Ebbets,* 176-178; *Brooklyn Daily Eagle,* May 5, 1919: 18.

34 *Brooklyn Daily Eagle,* February 11, 1920: 18; Thorn, 106.

35 *Brooklyn Daily Eagle,* August 31, 1920: 18.

36 Thorn, *Total Baseball,* 106.

37 John Zinn and Paul Zinn, *Ebbets Field: Essays and Memories of Brooklyn's Historic Ballpark, 1913-1960* (Jefferson, North Carolina: McFarland & Co., 2013), 101-102, 106-107, 118-120.

38 Zinn and Zinn, *Ebbets Field,* 101, 108-109, 111, 113-117.

39 *New York Times,* May 20, 1925: 18.

40 Zinn, *Charles Ebbets,* 205-206.

41 *Brooklyn Daily Times,* May 6, 1925: 1; Andy McCue, *Mover and Shaker: Walter O'Malley, The Dodgers and Baseball's Westward Expansion* (Lincoln: University of Nebraska Press, 2014), 30.

42 McCue, 30-31.

43 Organized Baseball, Hearings Before the Subcommittee of the Judiciary, House of Representatives, 82nd Congress, 1st Session, Serial, No. 1, Part 6, (Washington: Government Printing Office, 1952), 1600-1601.

44 *Brooklyn Daily Eagle,* February 14, 1928: 24.

45 Thorn, 106; Organized Baseball Hearings, 1600-1601.

46 *Brooklyn Daily Times,* January 8, 1931: 13.

47 *Brooklyn Daily Eagle*, September 1, 1930: 8.

48 *Brooklyn Daily Eagle*, February 5, 1930: 22.

49 *Brooklyn Daily Eagle*, February 14, 1928: 24; February 20, 1928: 22; May 15, 1930: 25.

50 *Brooklyn Citizen*, May 15, 1930: 8.

51 *Brooklyn Daily Eagle*, October 23, 1930: 26; December 22, 1930: 20; Philip J. Lowry, *Green Cathedrals: The Ultimate Celebration of Major League and Negro League Ballparks* (New York: Walker Publishing Co., 2006), 38–39.

52 *Brooklyn Daily Eagle*, December 22, 1930: 20; February 5, 1931: 24; February 13, 1931: 1.

53 *Brooklyn Citizen*, January 15, 1931: 6; *Brooklyn Daily Times*, February 13, 1931: 1.

54 *Brooklyn Daily Eagle*, February 17, 1931: 3; *Brooklyn Daily Times*, February 13, 1931: 1.

55 *Brooklyn Daily Eagle*, June 1, 1931: 20.

56 *Brooklyn Daily Eagle*, August 26, 1931: 20.

57 *Brooklyn Daily Eagle*, December 7, 1931: 26.

58 Thorn, 107.

59 Organized Baseball Hearings, 1600; McCue, 33.

60 McCue, 32.

61 McGee, 136.

62 McCue, 33, 35.

63 McGee, 136-137, 141.

64 McGee, *141.*

65 Thorn, 107.

66 Peter Golenbock, *Bums: An Oral History of the Brooklyn Dodgers* (Chicago: Contemporary Books, 2000), 44.

67 McGee, 166.

68 Golenbock, 45-46.

69 McGee, 126-127, Zinn and Zinn, 69.

70 Zinn and Zinn, 191.

71 Zinn and Zinn, 77; McGee, 220-221.

72 McGee, 165.

73 McGee, 111-112; Zinn and Zinn, 147.

74 McGee, 164-165; Thorn, 107.

75 Zinn and Zinn, 71.

76 Drebinger quoted in McCue, 37; McGee, 168.

77 McCue, 42-43.

78 McGee, 174, 181; McCue, 45, 47-48.

79 *New York Times*, April 16, 1947: 32; *Brooklyn Daily Eagle*, April 16, 1947: 19; *New York Daily News*, April 16, 1947: 66-67; McGee, 196; Zinn and Zinn, 72.

80 Robert Caro, *Lyndon Johnson: Master of the Senate* (New York: Alfred A. Knopf, 2002), 694.

81 Zinn and Zinn, 83-88, 90, 94-99.

82 Zinn, *Charles Ebbets*, 130.

83 Zinn and Zinn, 141, 144-145,160, 166, 173.

84 Zinn and Zinn, 142, 151, 155, 160, 165, 167.

85 Zinn and Zinn, 140, 143, 148, 156, 158, 160.

86 McGee, 188-192, 194, 209-210, 233; McCue, 86-88.

87 Michael D'Antonio, *Forever Blue: The True Story of Walter O'Malley, Baseball's Most Controversial Owner, and the Dodgers of Brooklyn and Los Angeles* (New York: Riverhead Books, 2009), 195.

88 Zinn and Zinn, 176, 189, 215-216.

89 Zinn and Zinn, 183, 189-190, 204.

90 Zinn and Zinn, 190, 199, 218.

91 Zinn and Zinn, 190,

92 Zinn and Zinn, 189, 212, 215; McCue, 55.

93 D'Antonio, 118-119.

94 Zinn and Zinn, 191, 201.

95 Zinn and Zinn, 178, 209.

96 Thorn, 107.

97 McCue, 121; D'Antonio, 163.

98 McCue, 124.

99 McCue, 124-125.

100 Thorn, 107.

101 D'Antonio, 164.

102 McCue, 69-73.

103 McCue, 77-81.

104 McCue, 84, 86, 91, 114-115.

105 McCue, 56, 121, 124.

106 McGee, 163, 240, 276-277; D'Antonio, 110-111, 218.

107 McCue, 56-57.

108 McCue, 129; *Brooklyn Daily Eagle*, December 11, 1953: 18.

109 McGee, 263.

110 McGee, 13, 15.

111 D'Antonio, 91; Selter, 32, 44, 67.

112 McCue, 123.

113 Zinn and Zinn, 212.

INAUGURAL EXHIBITION GAME

April 5, 1913

by Rory Costello

On September 20, 1912, Brooklyn team president Charles Ebbets gave up hope that his new stadium could open before that season's end. Construction had gotten a boost from the experience of his new co-owners, Steve and Ed McKeever. Yet too much work remained undone. The field was game-ready, but the stands were far from complete. Thus, they decided to aim for an opening in the spring of 1913.[1]

That same day, Ebbets raised his stake in the Newark Indians of the International League to a controlling interest.[2] At some point before 1912 ended, Brooklyn scheduled a game against Newark for April 5, 1913. It was to be the first professional match at Ebbets Field.[3]

Meanwhile, another big New York baseball story had broken on December 12. The Chicago Cubs released future Hall of Famer Frank Chance, freeing him to negotiate with the Yankees to become their new manager.[4] "The Peerless Leader" signed a three-year deal on January 8, 1913.[5]

Soon thereafter, Ebbets canceled the Newark game and one against Yale University slated for April 7. Instead, he booked two games against the Yankees, knowing their debut in the city under Chance, then one of the sport's biggest names, would be a big attraction.[6]

Tickets went on sale on March 3, as manager Bill Dahlen's Superbas (the team's dominant name in 1913) made their way to training camp in Augusta, Georgia.[7] Advance sales were indeed brisk. By mid-March, Ebbets' worries about the stadium's readiness had eased enough to enable a much-needed vacation to New Orleans. Steve McKeever oversaw a field inspection on March 17.[8] A crowd estimated at no less than 20,000 turned out just for that event, and before the end of March, all the reserved seats and boxes for the first Yankees game had been sold.[9] Ebbets announced that to provide unobstructed views, no emergency portable seats would be put on the ground.[10]

Ebbets had good box office instincts. "The amount of interest in Frank Chance and his team must have surprised even [Yankees] President Frank Farrell and Chance himself… a tremendous outpouring of rabid Manhattan cranks…

began wildly dashing for tickets a couple of days before the game and could not get enough to satisfy them."[11]

The morning of April 5 was gloomy – but gave way to "rattling fine baseball weather." Even before noon, fans were already en route to the game. Some 50 city policemen – on foot, horseback, and bicycle – were controlling the crowd, but a 100-strong reinforcement was summoned.[12] The stadium's focal point, its marble rotunda, was occupied by numerous floral arrangements which got in the crowd's way.[13]

By 2:00, all 25,000 seats were filled. Ebbets halted ticket sales – two scalpers were arrested – and a reported 10,000 more people were turned away. Thousands took up viewpoints on hills overlooking the stadium; one entrepreneur had put up a temporary grandstand on "McKeever's Bluff" and collected 50 cents a head.[14] Ebbets intimated that he would soon block those vistas.[15]

Shannon's 23rd Regiment Band entertained the crowd. Ebbets' youngest daughter, Genevieve, threw out the first ball. Ed McKeever's wife, Jennie, had the honor of raising the American flag in center field, accompanied by her husband and Ebbets. However, a groundskeeper had to fetch Old Glory from the office first.[16]

Finally, at around 3:30, it was time to play ball. The Superbas' starting pitcher – their ace, Nap Rucker – faced Bert Daniels.

The Yankees lineup provided a notable subplot. In Chicago, Chance had developed one of the finest team defenses ever with himself at first base.[17] He was in decline as a player, though, and had appeared just twice in 1912. Also, the Yankees' starting first baseman for the past eight seasons, Hal Chase, was another marquee name then. Chase's brilliant fielding at first base is still the best ever in the view of many, such as baseball historian Bill James.[18] Chance declared, shortly after the report that he'd come to New York, that he was through as a first baseman and that he'd manage from the bench, not the field.

Yet apparently fans were already speculating that Chase would shift to second base, even though he threw left-handed.[19] Indeed, Chase had played there in the past, including brief stints in 1911 and 1912.

But Chance soon changed his mind, stating that he expected to play, alternating with Chase.[20] In February, he reiterated that he'd take the field again.[21] Thus, Chase worked out at second during spring training in Bermuda, although an ankle injury hampered him. Chance considered holding Chase out of the game at Ebbets Field to avoid aggravating the injury.[22]

Chance too was ailing, with a bad back.[23] Yet on April 5, both Chase (batting fifth and playing second) and the skipper (batting sixth and manning first) were in the lineup. As it developed, Chase wasn't tested in the field, handling just one chance, a pop-up.[24] However, Chance removed "Prince Hal" for a pinch-runner at a key ninth-inning juncture.

Brooklyn won that afternoon, 3-2. Rucker threw five scoreless innings, benefiting from first baseman Jake Daubert's leaping grab of a fifth-inning liner by catcher Ed Sweeney that looked like a potential triple. For the Yankees, Ray Caldwell went six, allowing two runs.

In the bottom of the fifth, Brooklyn scored the game's first run on Casey Stengel's inside-the-park homer. Yankees center fielder Harry Wolter accidentally kicked the ball further toward the wall, allowing Stengel to come all the way around.[25] Wolter was not charged with an error, though, and Stengel got credit for a four-bagger.

In the sixth inning, the Superbas made it 2-0 on another inside-the-park homer to deep center field. Contrary to Ebbets Field's reputation as a "bandbox" for much of its existence, when it opened, the distance to straightaway center was an enormous 507 feet.[26]

The batter, Daubert, described his battle with Caldwell. "I watched Caldwell's style, and when

The first baseball game in Ebbets Field was an exhibition between the Brooklyn Superbas and New York Yankees that drew a sellout crowd of 25,000 while an estimated 10,000 fans were turned away. (Photo: Library of Congress)

I went to bat the first time, I held the stick way out on the end for a free swing against his low speedy shoot. But Ray is a student of the game as well as myself, and he put it high and inside. I could not have hit it with a board. The next time up I 'choked' the bat for a close one, and he crossed me again with his low, fast ones on the outside. The third time up was when [cleanup hitter Zack] Wheat and I tried the hit and run. I again figured he would put it over on the inside, and choked my bat, but he pitched out, and Sweeney caught Wheat trying for second. That got my goat and I changed my tactics. I choked the bat again as if I were expecting that insider, but when Caldwell started his windup, I let the bat slip and guessed him exactly right, for the ball was low and on the outside, just the right place to be caught flush on the nose for the wallop that got me a home run."[27]

The Yankees tied it in the ninth against Frank Allen, who'd replaced Rucker. Chase led off with a walk and Chance followed with a single. On Sweeney's sacrifice, Allen threw wildly. Ezra Midkiff, running for Chase, and Chance both scored.

Yet the Superbas fans went home happy that afternoon. Leading off was Wheat, whose supposed Native American descent was a feature of game stories.[28] He swung for the fences but topped a little grounder toward third. The unintended "swinging bunt" became a scratch single.[29] Sweeney's wild throw sent Wheat to second, though no error was charged. After Daubert sacrificed, Carlisle "Red" Smith's sharp single brought in the winning run. Ray Fisher took the loss.

As the fans filed out, there was commotion – few if any knew how to exit. The aisles were jammed; private security and firemen had to direct the throngs.[30] Crowd control was a serious issue in Ebbets Field's early days.[31]

POSTSCRIPT #1
SUPERBAS-YANKEES REMATCH
OF APRIL 7:

A cold front held attendance down to just 1,000 or so. Though New York won, 8-4, the cold likely contributed to both Yankees starter Jack Warhop's sore arm and Frank Chance's leg injury while running the bases. Chance was out until April 22; he played just 12 games all season. Hal Chase got many fielding opportunities at second and looked good.[32] Yet after five regular-season games, the experiment with Chase at the keystone was over – and Chance traded the divisive star on June 1.

The frigid Monday also caused fatal illness for Gerhard Tidden, baseball editor of the *New York World*. Tidden (a.k.a. "George" or "Roger") wasn't in good health but insisted on covering the game.[33] It prefigured the death from pneumonia of Ed McKeever, contracted at Charles Ebbets' funeral in April 1925.[34]

POSTSCRIPT #2
ANNUAL TRADITION

This started a long-running series of Yankees preseason visits to Ebbets Field, continuing in 1914 and carrying through 1957, the Dodgers' last year in Brooklyn.[35]

SOURCES

For the box score of the game, see "Ebbets Field Is Formally Dedicated with a Pleasing Victory," *Sporting Life*, April 12, 1913: 5.

Many aspects of this game – especially the new stadium's description, the crowds, and the preliminary festivities – are covered at greater length in previous book-length histories of Ebbets Field:

Joseph McCauley, *Ebbets Field: Brooklyn's Baseball Shrine* (Bloomington, Indiana: AuthorHouse, 2004)

Bob McGee, *The Greatest Ballpark Ever* (Piscataway, New Jersey: Rutgers University Press, 2005).

John G. Zinn and Paul G. Zinn, editors, *Ebbets Field: Essays and Memories of Brooklyn's Historic Ballpark, 1913-1960* (Jefferson, North Carolina: McFarland & Co., 2013)

NOTES

1   "Brooklyn Club's New Park," *New York Times*, September 21, 1912: 9.

2   Thomas S. Rice, "Ebbets and McKeever Get Newark Club Stock," *Brooklyn Daily Eagle*, September 21, 1912: 18.

3   "Building of Ebbets Field," *Brooklyn Daily Eagle*, December 29, 1912: 53.

4   "Yankees Get Chance, [Joe] Tinker to Lead Reds," *New York Times*, December 12, 1912: 14.

5   "Frank Chance Manager of New York Yankees," *St. Petersburg* (Florida) *Independent*, January 9, 1913: 6.

6   "Giants to Play 25 Games in South," *New York Times*, January 15, 1913: 14. Yale game was mentioned in "Dodges Predictions," *New York Times*, January 1, 1913: 19.

7   Abe Yager, "Brooklyn Bits," *Sporting Life*, March 8, 1913: 7. The "Dodgers" label jockeyed with "Superbas" in the press (along with a tertiary label, "Infants"). When Wilbert Robinson became manager in 1914, "Robins" came to the fore, but it was not unanimous – both Dodgers and Superbas were still visible in press coverage. Only in 1932 did the team become known for good as the Dodgers.

8   Abe Yager, "Brooklyn Budget," *Sporting Life*, March 22, 1913: 8.

9   Abe Yager, "Brooklyn Bits," *Sporting Life*, March 29, 1913: 6.

10 "No Seats on Ebbets Opening," *Brooklyn Daily Eagle*, March 13, 1813: 22.

11 "Brooklyns Show Great Finishing Powers By Beating Yankees in the Ninth," *Brooklyn Daily Eagle*, April 6, 1913: 58.

12 Superbas Win, 3-2, in Opening Game at Ebbets Field," *Brooklyn Daily Eagle*, April 6, 1913: 1, 5.

13 "Entire World Centers on Brooklyn Tomorrow," *Brooklyn Daily Eagle*, April 8, 1913: 20.

14 "Superbas Win, 3-2, in Opening Game at Ebbets Field."

15 Abe Yager, "Beatific Brooklyn," *Sporting Life*, April 12, 1913: 5.

16 "Superbas Win, 3-2, in Opening Game at Ebbets Field."

17 Chris Jaffe, *Evaluating Baseball's Managers*, Jefferson, North Carolina: McFarland & Company (2010): 83.

18 Bill James, *The New Bill James Historical Abstract*, New York: Free Press (2001): 467.

19 "To Manage from Bench," *Louisville Courier-Journal*, December 12, 1912: 9.

20 "Chance to Play First Base," *New York Times*, January 15, 1913: 14.

21 "Frank Chance Here; To Play First Base," *New York Times*, February 11, 1913: 14.

22 Harry Dix Cole, "New York News," *Sporting Life*, April 5, 1913: 6.

23 Harry Dix Cole, "New York News," *Sporting Life*, March 29, 1913: 5.

24 Harry Dix Cole, "New York News," *Sporting Life*, April 12, 1913: 6.

25 "Superbas Win, 3-2, in Opening Game at Ebbets Field."

26 Ronald M. Selter, "Ebbets Field by the Numbers," *Ebbets Field: Essays and Memories of Brooklyn's Historic Ballpark*: 127.

27 Thomas S. Rice, "Daubert Would Give $500 To See Brooklyn Do Well," *Brooklyn Daily Eagle*, April 7, 1013: 20.

28 See Rory Costello, "Zack Wheat: Native American?" SABR BioProject (https://SABR.org/bioproj/topic/zack-wheat-native-american/).

29 "Brooklyns Show Great Finishing Powers By Beating Yankees in the Ninth."

30 "Superbas Win, 3-2, in Opening Game at Ebbets Field."

31 "Fans, in Near Riot, Mob Ebbets Field," *Brooklyn Daily Eagle*, April 27, 1913: 1.

32 "Yankees Win Costly Game in Brooklyn – Manager Chance, Warhop, and Derrick Injured Playing in Cold Atmosphere," *New York Times*, April 8, 1913: 11.

33 "George Tidden Dead after Long Illness," *Pittsburgh Press*, July 3, 1913. In a 1937 retrospective, Thomas Rice of the *Brooklyn Eagle* wrote that Saturday, April 5, was the cold day – contradicting the stories that were written at the time.

34 "Dodgers Owners: The Timeline," *Los Angeles Times*, October 11, 2003.

35 Research on newspapers.com shows such games taking place during the 1920s, 1930s, and 1940s as well, though whether the sequence of years was unbroken remains open to question.

First regular-season game at Ebbets Field

April 9, 1913

Philadelphia Phillies 1, Brooklyn Superbas 0

by Rory Costello

Brooklyn got a day's head start on the rest of the majors in the 1913 season. Opening Day for the other 14 big-league teams came on April 10 that year, but the *Brooklyn Eagle* newspaper campaigned successfully for the spotlight to shine on the borough's brand-new ballpark: Ebbets Field. As *Eagle* sportswriter Thomas S. Rice later recalled, "The opening was a civic as well as a sporting event and we of the *Eagle* wanted all the baseball owners, managers, players, past stars, public officials and as many other persons of note as could be rounded up to be there with no responsibility for attending openers elsewhere."[1]

As that story was developing, Rice also covered it for *The Sporting News*. The early-opening plan originated with his boss, *Eagle* sporting editor Abe Yager. Yager had originally hoped for Brooklyn to play against the archrival New York Giants, but he withdrew that idea because it would have taken the shine off the Giants' opener at the Polo Grounds on April 10. He then proposed that Brooklyn play the Philadelphia Phillies in a home-and-home series.[2]

For unclear reasons, National League President Thomas Lynch scoffed at the idea. However, Giants President Harry Hempstead was "for it with both feet."[3] Soon thereafter, Jim Gaffney – owner of the Boston Braves, who were to play the Giants – announced that he was on board, as did Barney Dreyfuss of the Pittsburgh Pirates and Charles Murphy of the Chicago Cubs.[4] When the National League held its meeting in February, the change passed unanimously, despite Lynch's ongoing effort to block it.[5]

As the new season got under way, a sign of the times was visible at Ebbets Field. *The Sporting News* wrote, "[A]utomobilists are to get more attention. At the new park that Charles H. Ebbets has built in Brooklyn a system of numbered checks is to be used similar to that operated by theaters. Fans attending in automobiles are to be assigned a waiting room, from where their cars will be called after the game."[6] This was a striking development in the borough whose trolleys gave the team its enduring name, the Dodgers.

It's worth noting that there was no consistent naming convention at that time. The "Dodgers" label jockeyed with "Superbas" in the press (along with a tertiary label, "Infants"). When Wilbert Robinson became manager in 1914, "Robins" came to the fore, but it was not unanimous – both Dodgers and Superbas were still visible in press coverage. Only in 1932 did the team become known for good as the Dodgers. For the purposes of this article, Superbas (the dominant name in 1913) is in effect.

Actually, the first games between big-league teams at the new ballpark were a pair of exhibition matches against the New York Yankees on April 5 and 7. The weather had been springlike on Saturday the 5th, but on Monday the temperature turned wintry.[7] On Wednesday, Opening Day, it was still cold, with a raw wind.[8] "Polar blasts whistled through the huge new stands at Ebbets Field and chilled the enthusiasm of the comparatively small crowd."[9] Perhaps also because it was a weekday, only 12,000 or so were in attendance against the Phillies, whereas the first Yankees game drew an overflow crowd. It's not known how many of the luminaries the *Eagle* had hoped to attract turned up.

Sporting Life made a sly allusion: "But for the generosity of C. Hospitable Ebbets in furnishing the fluid that warms and cheers, the boys in the press box, both local and visiting, would have been frostbitten." Yet despite the conditions, both teams paraded across the field, headed by a band. Brooklyn Borough President Alfred E. Steers threw out the first ball.[10] There were also testimonials to Brooklyn's manager, Bill Dahlen, and first baseman Jake Daubert. Both were presented with floral horseshoes, and Daubert also received a gilded bat.[11]

The game started at 1:30. Nap Rucker, who'd also started the first exhibition game against the Yankees, threw the first pitch. Just 93 minutes later, it was over.[12] The only run was scored in the top of the first, and it was unearned. The Phillies might have had more, because leadoff man Dode Paskert singled but was thrown out trying to stretch his hit into a double.[13] Otto Knabe then doubled. Hans Lobert came to the plate, and rookie right fielder Benny Meyer lost his foul fly in the sun. Center fielder Casey Stengel overcame that misplay by making a sensational catch of Lobert's long drive, but Meyer promptly made his second error of the inning, dropping Sherry Magee's fly and allowing Knabe to score.[14] Philadelphia might have scored again when Cozy Dolan singled, but Stengel threw out Magee at the plate.[15]

The sun in right field was indeed strong. Magee, Meyer's opposite number in right field, made sure that he was wearing smoked glasses. Thus equipped, he handled his two chances cleanly. Meyer had a special pair of glasses made, which reportedly had a prescription in addition to being tinted.[16]

Phillies pitcher Tom Seaton got the first of his 27 victories that season, which led the National League. He went all the way and gave up just six hits, all singles. He walked only one while striking out six. The only Superba to get more than one hit was catcher Otto Miller. Seaton was helped by the glove work of shortstop Mickey Doolin, who made a number of good plays on hard-hit balls. The most notable came in the fifth inning, when he grabbed a drive by Brooklyn's cleanup hitter, Zack Wheat. Daubert followed with a single, and according to *Sporting Life*, a run would have scored. Doolin also turned back a Brooklyn threat in the eighth when he fielded a hard smash by Leo Callahan, pinch-hitting for Rucker. There were two Superbas on base, and the tying run would apparently have scored.[17] By another account of the game, Callahan hit into a force play and Doolin's stop denied Stengel a hit.[18]

Phillies catcher Red Dooin also stood out on defense. He threw out three Dodgers attempting to steal second.[19]

Rucker worked eight innings for Brooklyn, allowing eight hits and also walking just one. As *Sporting Life*'s account put it, "No one can say that

Seaton outpitched Rucker. Nap was hit oftener, but he was there with the tightening-up stuff when danger threatened."[20] Pat Ragan came on in the ninth.

"I remember the game well," said Otto Miller nearly 47 years later.[21] That quote came in much more somber circumstances. On February 23, 1960, Miller joined Roy Campanella, Carl Erskine, Ralph Branca, Tommy Holmes, and 200 fans to bid their old home adieu as the demolition of Ebbets Field started. Lee Allen, historian of the Baseball Hall of Fame in Cooperstown, was also on hand. Allen was presented the key,

mounted on red velvet, that Charles Ebbets had used to open the doors to his ballpark on April 9, 1913. Walter O'Malley used the same key to close the doors after the Dodgers' finale on September 24, 1957.[22]

Miller, who by then was aged 70, was a Brooklyn resident – his home was less than two miles from Ebbets Field.[23] He'd played his entire 13-year big-league career with the same team and added 11 more seasons as a coach for the Robins and Dodgers. The old catcher had tears in his eyes that day when he said to a companion, "A lot of guys are afraid to cry. Not me. I'm not ashamed."[24]

The iconic main entry of Ebbets Field was located at the intersection of Sullivan Place and Cedar Street (later renamed McKeever Place). (Photo: SABR-Rucker Archive)

NOTES

1   Thomas S. Rice, "Rice Recalls Special Opening of Ebbets Field April 9, 1913," *Brooklyn Daily Eagle*, April 25, 1937.

2   Thomas S. Rice, "Blunder by Lynch," *The Sporting News*, January 9, 1913: 1.

3   Rice, "Blunder by Lynch."

4   Thomas S. Rice, "Votes for Ebbets," *The Sporting News*, January 16, 1913: 3.

5   "Many Moguls but Few Items in Gotham Baseball Meets," *The Sporting News*, February 20, 1913: 2.

6   "Holding the Automobile Fans," *The Sporting News*, April 10, 1913: 4.

7   In his 1937 retrospective, Thomas Rice conflated the two games into one and wrote that Saturday, April 5, was the cold day – contradicting the stories that were written at the time.

8   "The Special Opening," *Sporting Life*, April 19, 1913: 8.

9   Thomas S. Rice, "In the Band Wagon," *The Sporting News*, April 17, 1913: 2.

10 "The Special Opening."

11 "Brooklyn Budget," *Sporting Life*, April 19, 1913: 7.

12 "The Special Opening."

13 "Brooklyn Budget."

14 "The Special Opening."

15 "Recruit Loses First Game for Brooklyn," *Richmond* (Indiana) *Item*, April 10, 1913.

16 "Brooklyn Budget."

17 "Brooklyn Budget."

18 "Phillies Win Opening Game," *Montreal Gazette*, April 10, 1913.

19 "Brooklyn Budget"; Seamus Kearney and Dick Rosen, *The Philadelphia Phillies* (Charleston, South Carolina: Arcadia Press, 2011).

20 "Brooklyn Budget."

21 "Ebbets Field Has Quiet, Dignified Wake," *St. Cloud* (Minnesota) *Times*, February 24, 1960.

22 Dana Mozley, "Wreck-Ball Caps Ebbets Rites," *New York Daily News*, February 24, 1960.

23 "The Dodgers' Otto Miller Dies in Fall," *New York Daily News*, March 30, 1962.

24 "Miller Cried When Wreckers Took Over Old Ebbets Field," *The Sporting News*, April 11, 1962: 52.

Robinson's team wins pennant as McGraw throws himself out of the game

October 3, 1916

Brooklyn Robins 9, New York Giants 6

by Mark S. Sternman

Proximate geographies, shared histories, and personal relations drive great sporting rivalries. The race for the 1916 National League crown had all three of these essential elements. The neighboring boroughs of Brooklyn and Manhattan make up part of New York City. Wilbert Robinson and John McGraw spent years together on the Baltimore Orioles and New York Giants. And Brooklyn spent more than a decade chasing New York in the race for senior circuit supremacy.

The Giants had a made a record-breaking charge with a 26-game winning streak to draw close to the Robins in the 1916 campaign, but with just three days to go in the season, New York had been eliminated, while Brooklyn needed just one win and two losses by Philadelphia, which had won the pennant in 1915, to clinch its first postseason berth since 1890.

Lefty Sherry Smith started for the Robins and was hit hard at the start. Speedy George Burns had a leadoff squib to Smith and reached second when the hurler threw the ball wildly to first. Buck Herzog bunted to Smith, who mishandled the ball. Smith had two errors all season before the start of this game and doubled that total after just two batters. "The Brooklyn pitcher seemed to be doing all he could to keep the pennant away from Flatbush," commented the *New York Times*.[1]

With runners on the corners, Dave Robertson singled in Burns to put New York up 1-0. Herzog advanced to third, and Robertson went to second on the throw from Zack Wheat in left. Heinie Zimmerman hit the third ball of the inning to Smith, and more madness ensued. On Smith's toss to Jake Daubert at first to retire Zimmerman, Herzog sought to score only to retreat "to third, where he found Robertson. The latter started … to second, and Herzog [left] third to distract attention from Robertson. This proceeding did not put the Superbas in a very favorable light, but … Herzog was finally trapped between third and home and was out, Robertson taking third."[2]

The DP went 1-3-6-8-2; the fact that Brooklyn center fielder Hi Myers earned an assist gives a good idea of the epic nature of this odd rundown, which seemed to unnerve Smith rather than the

Giants as Art Fletcher hit just his third home run of the year to put New York up 3-0.

Southpaw Rube Benton, on a five-game winning streak, started for New York. He shut down the Robins in the first but gave up a run in the second on Mike Mowrey's double and Ivy Olson's single. Smith immediately gave the run back in the top of the third. With one out, Herzog singled, went to third on Robertson's single, and scored on the play thanks to a throwing error by Myers.

Brooklyn rallied with four in the bottom of third to take its first lead. Jimmy Johnston had an infield single and went to second on Daubert's single. After a force out at second left Myers at first, Johnston scored when Wheat had an RBI single to Benton. George Cutshaw drove in Myers with a single to cut the New York lead to 4-3. The hit knocked Benton out in favor of righty Pol Perritt, who had won his last four decisions. Perritt brought no relief for the Giants as Mowrey singled Wheat home to tie the game. Olson hit a chopper to third; Zimmerman threw him out, but Cutshaw scored to put the Robins up 5-4.

Jeff Pfeffer took over for Smith to start the fourth. Usually a starter, Pfeffer had not pitched more than three innings in relief for Brooklyn in 1916, but special players do special things in special games like a potential pennant-clincher. Pfeffer held New York in the fourth, but the Giants tied the game in the fifth. Bad baserunning prevented a bigger inning for New York. Perritt and Burns both singled, but Pol committed a cardinal sin by making the first out at third base on a throw from Johnston in right. Burns took second on the throw. After Pfeffer struck out Herzog, Robertson had his third hit of the day to plate Burns and even the score, 5-5. The Giants ran into another out when Robertson was caught stealing.

The opportunistic Robins regained the lead for good in the bottom of the frame. With two outs, Perritt plunked Mowrey and then threw a wild pitch that chased him all the way to third. Olson's clutch single gave Brooklyn a 6-5 edge.

In 1916 Pfeffer represented something of a two-way threat as he excelled at pitching and batted .279. He singled in the fourth but did not score. In the sixth, he doubled. Robinson played the percentages and batted for Johnston with left-handed-hitting Casey Stengel, who like Robinson and McGraw would play a key role in the storied history of Gotham big-league ball. Stengel doubled to right; Pfeffer, unsure of whether Robertson would catch the blow, initially held up at second and only got to the third on the two-bagger. On this play, Pfeffer overestimated Robertson's range; on the next, Pfeffer underestimated Robertson's arm. Daubert flied to right, and Robertson threw out Pfeffer at the plate to complete a twin killing. Stengel advanced to third on the play and scored on a single by Myers to put the Robins up 7-5.

Brooklyn never sleeps. Cutshaw led off the seventh with a single and stole second with Perritt pitching from a full windup.[3] Mowrey knocked him in and Perritt out of the game with a single that put Brooklyn up 8-5. George Smith came on to pitch for New York.

The Robins added a final run in the eighth. Stengel walked, advanced to third on Smith's pickoff error, and scored on Daubert's squeeze bunt. The Giants got a meaningless run in the ninth to make the score 9-6. With two outs, Burns flied to Wheat. After making the catch, Wheat "tossed the ball among his friends in the bleachers and took it on the run for the clubhouse. He had to hustle to keep ahead of a thousand or more fans, whose ambition it was to carry him across the field."[4]

Soon after this game ended, Boston completed a doubleheader sweep of Philadelphia to bring a joyous Brooklyn to rhythmic heights: "The town is madly happy from the bridge to Coney Island," the *Brooklyn Eagle* exulted. "Aged folks are feeling snappy; young ones greet you with a

In his third season as Brooklyn's skipper, Wilbert Robinson (left) led the club to the pennant in 1916, its first since 1900, and faced player-manager Bill Carrigan's reigning World Series champion Boston Red Sox. (Photo: Library of Congress)

smile. Brooklyn maids are gaily beaming as they raise a Dodger cheer. Brooklyn youths are wildly screaming loud enough to bust your ear."[5]

Did New York players lay down for their beloved Uncle Robbie, who had coached many of them under McGraw's tutelage? McGraw certainly thought so and ditched his team temporarily in the fourth inning and then for good in the fifth. McGraw later griped that his team's "baseball disgusted me, and I left the bench. I do not like indifferent playing of this kind after the hard work we have had this season. I refused to be connected with it."[6]

Unsurprisingly, Robinson saw the situation differently: "It's ridiculous even to suggest that the Giants were not trying to beat us this afternoon. It looked to me like they were trying pretty hard when they scored three runs in the first inning. At that time I felt like quitting the bench myself."[7]

Regardless of the motivations behind the men who played this game, Brooklyn had cause to celebrate a quartet of surprising heroes. Cutshaw, Mowrey, and Olson hit fifth, sixth, and seventh for a reason – they all played key infield positions but had below-average batting records. On this day, the unheralded trio went 7-for-11 with four runs scored and six RBIs. The best player on the Robins all season, Pfeffer, probably expected to watch as he had just two days of rest after a 10-inning performance against Philadelphia. But Pfeffer, although on the bench at the start of the game, not only pitched, but twirled six sterling relief innings to win his 25th of the year and to put Brooklyn into the World Series thanks to a controversial win over its crosstown rivals.

NOTES

1 "Superbas Capture National Pennant," *New York Times*, October 4, 1916: 12.

2 Thomas S. Rice, "Pennant at Last, After Sixteen Long Years!" *Brooklyn Eagle*, October 4, 1916: 21. Play-by-play accounts of this game come from this article except where otherwise noted.

3 "McGraw Casts Unwarranted Slur Upon His Ball Team," *Brooklyn Eagle*, October 4, 1916: 21.

4 "Victorious Superbas Celebrate Victory," *Brooklyn Eagle*, October 4, 1916: 22.

5 W.R. Hoefer, "The Man of the Hour," *Brooklyn Eagle*, October 4, 1916: 21.

6 "McGraw, 'Disgusted,' Says Team Disobeyed His Orders – Leaves Field in Fifth Inning," *New York Times*, October 4, 1916: 12.

7 "Ridiculous! Says Robinson," *Boston Globe*, October 4, 1916: 1.

ROBINS STAVE OFF RED SOX COMEBACK, CLIMB BACK INTO SERIES

October 10, 1916

Brooklyn Robins 4, Boston Red Sox 3 | Game Three of the World Series

by Mike Lynch

After one-run wins against the Brooklyn Robins in Games One and Two of the 1916 World Series, the Boston Red Sox held a 2-0 lead going into Game Three at Ebbets Field in Brooklyn. Playing at Braves Field in Boston, whose capacity was almost twice that of Fenway Park, the Red Sox had hung on for a 6-5 win in Game One in front of 36,117 fans.[1] Boston took a 6-1 lead into the ninth thanks to five extra-base hits and four Brooklyn errors, but the Robins finally solved Boston starter Ernie Shore in the top of the ninth and scored four runs before Carl Mays got the final out to preserve the win.[2]

Game Two featured an epic pitchers' duel between Red Sox southpaw Babe Ruth and Robins lefty Sherry Smith, both of whom threw more than 13 innings in a 2-1 Boston win. The crowd of 47,373 watched Ruth allow a run in the first inning when center fielder Hi Myers circled the bases for an inside-the-park home run and Brooklyn was up 1-0 after only three batters. That was all the Robins would muster off Ruth, who allowed only five more hits over his final 13⅓ innings before the Red Sox plated the winning run in the bottom of the 14th for a hard-fought 2-1 victory.[3]

Brooklyn's Game Three hopes rested on the shoulders of Colby Jack Coombs, former Philadelphia Athletics star hurler who went 59-21 with a 2.39 ERA for the A's in 1910-1911, and then went 4-0 with a 2.49 ERA in five fall classic starts to help Philadelphia cop back-to-back championships.[4] He won another 21 games in 1912, but almost died of typhoid fever in 1913 and had to miss almost all of the 1914 season while he recovered. Philadelphia released Coombs in 1915 and he signed with Brooklyn, for whom he came back with a 15-10 season followed by a 13-8 mark in 1916 with a 2.66 ERA in 159 innings.

Red Sox manager Bill Carrigan countered in Game Three with right-handed submariner Carl Mays, who had gone 18-13 with a 2.39 ERA in 44 games. Mays faced two batters in the top of the ninth in Game One and earned a save, but Game Three would mark his first postseason start.[5] According to the *Boston Post*, Mays was "the very man whom the experts selected as the most baffling problem that the Brooklyn batters would be called upon to solve."[6] Some felt lefty Dutch Leonard should have gotten the start, but Carrigan preferred to save his second-best hurler from pitching in a "cold raw atmosphere" with a "chilling wind."[7]

Harry Hooper almost homered to lead off the game, but a stiff wind blew his drive to right field foul just before it cleared the wall, and he flied out to left on the next pitch. After Hal Janvrin grounded out, Chick Shorten singled to center and Dick Hoblitzell singled to right, but right fielder Casey Stengel threw Shorten out at third to end the inning.

Mays hit Myers to begin the bottom of the first, Jake Daubert laid down a bunt that Mays misplayed into a hit, Stengel sacrificed the runners to second and third, and Mays intentionally walked Zack Wheat to load the bases. George Cutshaw grounded to first and Hoblitzell fired to catcher Pinch Thomas to force Myers at home, and then Mays struck out Mike Mowrey to end the threat. In the Red Sox second, Coombs set down Duffy Lewis, Larry Gardner, and Everett Scott, the latter driving a ball that Wheat hauled in after a long run; Mays had an equally easy inning, getting Ivy Olson to ground to Scott, fanning Otto Miller on three pitches, and coaxing another grounder to Scott by Coombs.

Coombs allowed a two-out single to Hooper in the top of the third, but Miller threw Hooper out trying to steal second. Brooklyn took a 1-0 lead in the bottom of the frame when Daubert singled to right, Stengel poled a hit to left, and Cutshaw's single to right plated Daubert. The Red Sox continued to be aggressive in the fourth. Shorten followed Janvrin's fly to Stengel with a hit to left and tried to steal second, but Miller gunned him down and Coombs got Hoblitzell on a fly to Myers to end the inning.

The Robins doubled their lead in the bottom of the fourth and went up 2-0. Olson dropped a bunt toward third to lead off the inning. Gardner fielded the ball cleanly, but threw wildly to first

and Olson advanced to second on the error. Miller sacrificed Olson to third and Coombs helped himself out with a run-scoring hit to right. Myers bunted Coombs to second before Daubert grounded out to Scott to send the game to the fifth.

Coombs continued his mastery over Red Sox batters in the fifth and set down Lewis on a liner to left, Gardner on a popup to third, and Scott on a grounder to the mound. The Robins added two more runs in the bottom of the frame on free passes to Wheat and Mowrey, the latter of which had Carrigan argue with umpire Hank O'Day to no avail, and a long two-run triple by Olson that just missed going out of the park. Mays retired Miller on a grounder to Scott, but that marked the end of his day. "The story of Mays' transgressions is a rather gloomy one to Boston fans," wrote the *Boston Post*'s Paul Shannon. "In contrast with yesterday's game this contest was a big disappointment."[8]

Boston finally broke through with two runs in the top of the sixth to cut Brooklyn's lead in half. Hitting for Mays, Olaf Henriksen drew a one-out walk. Hooper followed with a tremendous drive to right-center field that went for a triple and Shorten singled Hooper home with the second run to make the score 4-2. Carrigan turned to 14-game winner Rube Foster to start the sixth and the right-hander found himself amid controversy almost immediately. He retired Coombs and Myers on a lineout and pop fly, respectively, but Daubert lashed a drive down the left-field line that rolled to the fence 400 feet from home plate.

He rounded the bases and headed for home. Lewis recovered the ball and fired to Scott, who threw to Thomas just in time for Thomas to apply the tag, but O'Day called Daubert safe. Thomas immediately called attention to his blocking of the plate and Daubert's positioning that showed he could not have touched the plate, and O'Day reversed course and called Daubert out. The

Hall of Famer Zack Wheat played for Brooklyn for 18 years (1909-1926) and more than a century later still held Dodgers career records for most hits (2,804), total bases (4,003), doubles (464), and triples (171). (Photo: Library of Congress)

crowd erupted in boos as the Robins surrounded O'Day in protest, but the arbiter held his ground and the score remained 4-2.

That lost run loomed large when Gardner belted a Coombs offering over the right-field wall with one out in the seventh to bring Boston to within one at 4-3. Coombs signaled to manager Wilbert Robinson that he was through for the day and Brooklyn's skipper called on ace hurler Jeff Pfeffer, who had won 25 games and pitched to a 1.92 ERA during the regular season, and pitched one inning of relief in Game One.

Pfeffer was brilliant and retired all eight batters he faced, striking out three to earn a save in Brooklyn's 4-3 win. Foster wasn't as dominant but equally effective with three innings of scoreless work, albeit in a loss that pulled the Robins to within one game of tying the series at two games apiece.

"The bright colors of the Boston Red Sox champions were lowered by National League men from Brooklyn this afternoon," waxed T.H. Murnane after the game, "and the fans of Ebbetsville are a happy lot tonight, for they hardly hoped to see their team win even one game from the skillful men from Boston."[9]

SOURCES

In addition to the sources cited in the Notes, the author accessed Retrosheet.org, Baseball-Reference.com, and SABR.org.

NOTES

1   Braves Field had a listed capacity of 45,000 while Fenway Park's was 24,000.

2   Shore might have gotten out of the ninth unscathed when he coaxed a one-out bases-loaded grounder out of Mike Mowrey that Red Sox second baseman Hal Janvrin turned into a two-run error instead of getting at least one out and possibly a double play.

3   Sherry Smith allowed the winning run with one out in the bottom of the 14th and finished the contest with 13⅓ innings pitched.

4   Coombs was excellent in Game Five of the 1911 World Series, allowing only one run through 8⅔ innings, and could have had his fifth career postseason win had he been able to retire either Josh Devore or Doc Crandall with Art Fletcher at third. But Devore doubled in Fletcher, who had doubled and moved to third on a groundout, and Crandall drove in Devore with a single to tie the game at 3-3 before catcher Chief Meyers threw out Devore trying to steal. The Giants completed their comeback in the bottom of the 10th inning with a walk-off sacrifice fly off Eddie Plank, who took the loss.

5   Mays went 6-5 with a 2.60 ERA in 38 games in his 1915 rookie campaign, and paced the American League with 27 games finished and 7 saves (retroactively calculated), but didn't appear for Boston in the 1915 World Series against the Philadelphia Phillies.

6   Paul H. Shannon, "Brooklyn Wins Third, Mays Easy for Robins," *Boston Post*, October 11, 1916: 13.

7   Shannon, "Brooklyn Wins Third."

8   Shannon, "Brooklyn Wins Third."

9   T.H. Murnane, "Brooklyn Won Third Game, 4-3," *Boston Globe*, October 11, 1916: 6.

Larry Gardner's three-run homer deflates Robins in Boston win

October 11, 1916

Boston Red Sox 6, Brooklyn Robins 2 | Game Four of the World Series

by Mike Lynch

With a Game Three win under their belts, the Brooklyn Robins were "bubbling over with enthusiasm" and insisted a second straight victory would give them so much "pep" going into Game Five that the Red Sox wouldn't recognize them.[1] Boston manager Bill Carrigan's hunch to start left-hander Dutch Leonard under better conditions came to fruition when the weather turned warmer for Game Four. The slightly higher temperature brought more fans to Ebbets Field and higher tension when Boston's Royal Rooters disrupted ticket lines and almost caused a riot.[2]

When they learned the Rooters had purchased tickets in advance and would be entering the park to parade across the field, some fans rushed the gate, and mounted police were called on to keep the peace.[3]

Carrigan and Brooklyn skipper Wilbert Robinson tried to outbluff each other by warming up multiple pitchers prior to the game. When Leonard was passed over for Carl Mays in Game Three, the Robins thought the Red Sox southpaw wasn't "right" and might not appear in the series.

Carrigan played that up by having Game One starter Ernie Shore warm up next to Leonard. Robinson took it a step further and had Larry Cheney, Jeff Pfeffer, and Rube Marquard get loose before the game.

When Marquard took the mound, he "received a mighty cheer that increased in volume as he disposed of three men in order. ..."[4] Marquard fielded Harry Hooper's grounder and threw him out at first, then struck out Hal Janvrin and Tillie Walker in the top of the first inning. Robins hitters jumped on Leonard immediately and scored two runs in the bottom of the first to go up 2-0. Leadoff man Jimmy Johnston hammered Leonard's first pitch to the center field fence for a triple and Hi Myers singled to right to give Brooklyn a 1-0 lead.

Fred Merkle walked and Zack Wheat grounded to third for what should have been a double play had Janvrin not been slow getting to second base, resulting in a late throw to first that Wheat just beat.[5] Boston forced Merkle at second, but Myers advanced to third, and Wheat went to second when Leonard threw a wild pitch with

36

George Cutshaw at the plate. Cutshaw grounded to Janvrin, who made his second blunder of the inning when he failed to field the grounder and Myers scored on the error.

Wheat and Cutshaw attempted a double steal with Mike Mowrey at the plate, but the Red Sox got a break when Wheat started for home, then had second thoughts and retreated to third. Janvrin took Carrigan's throw at second and fired to third to cut down Wheat for the second out of the inning. Leonard fanned Mowrey to end the frame. After an easy first, Marquard ran into trouble in the bottom of the second. He walked Dick Hoblitzell on six pitches to begin the inning, then fell behind Duffy Lewis before surrendering a double to the right-field fence that put Red Sox on second and third with Larry Gardner coming up.

Gardner worked the count to 3-and-2 and fouled a couple off before slamming a drive to center field, the longest hit in the series to that point, and raced around the bases for a three-run inside-the-park homer that gave Boston a 3-2 lead. According to Grantland Rice, Brooklyn's chance to win the Series all but died when Gardner crossed the plate. "That one blow, delivered deep into the barren lands of center field," Rice wrote, "broke Marquard's heart, shattered Brooklyn's wavering defense and practically closed out the series."[6]

It also broke Robins fans' confidence in Marquard and when Everett Scott lined to left and reached second when Wheat muffed his fly ball for a two-base error, calls for Marquard's removal from the game grew louder. Carrigan sacrificed Scott to third, but Marquard fanned Leonard and got Hooper to ground to first to end the inning.

Leonard faced four batters in the bottom of the second and walked Chief Meyers, but he couldn't get past second; Marquard allowed an infield single to Walker in the top of the third, but he was caught stealing with two outs and the game went to the bottom of third. Leonard

continued his rebound from his poor first inning and set down Myers, Merkle, and Wheat on a fly out to center, a popup to short, and a fly out to left, respectively.

"The game had now settled down to real business," wrote T.H. Murnane. "Leonard was on his feet, working with his magic spell curves, and the home team commenced to realize that the Fresno pet was all that he had been advertised."[7] In the top of the fourth, Boston began adding insurance runs. Lewis started the inning with a hard liner to left that "singed Mowrey's hand" before landing safely for a hit, and went to second when Gardner sacrificed.[8] Scott grounded to third and Lewis had to hold his ground, but Carrigan rapped a single that scored Lewis and gave the Red Sox a 4-2 lead.

Leonard walked, but ran Boston out of the inning when he tried to go to second on a pitch to Hooper that got away from Meyers, noticed that Carrigan was firmly planted on the base, tried to go back to first, then reversed course when Meyers fired the ball to Merkle at first. Carrigan had no choice but to try for third, but Leonard was an easy out when Merkle tossed to Cutshaw at second.

Brooklyn started the bottom of the fourth with a minor rally when Cutshaw led off with a double and Mowrey walked. Ivy Olson tried to move the runners up with a bunt, but popped out to Hoblitzell. Meyers battled through nine pitches, fouling off three straight, before popping up to Scott for the second out. Pfeffer, hitting for Marquard, took two balls before Leonard struck him out with his next three offerings, "the last of which broke two feet in front of the plate."[9]

Rather than send Pfeffer to the mound in the fifth inning, Robinson called on spitballer Larry Cheney, an 18-game winner who led the National League in fewest hits and most strikeouts per nine innings and tied Pfeffer for sixth in ERA at 1.92.[10] Cheney got off to a rough start and walked Hooper on five pitches. Janvrin attempted a bunt

Rube Marquard played for parts of six seasons (1915-1920) for the Robins, posting a 56-48 record and helping the club to pennants in 1916 and 1920. The ace of New York Giants' three straight pennant winners (1911-1913), Marquard won 19 straight decisions to begin the 1912 season. (Photo: Library of Congress)

but fouled it off, took three balls, then swung at the next two and struck out. But Hooper stole second and the Red Sox had a runner in scoring position.

After Walker popped out to Olson, Hoblitzell hit a shot past Mowrey for a double and the Red Sox increased their lead to 5-2. Cheney struck out Lewis to end the inning but, essentially, the game was over. Brooklyn made one last attempt to plate another run when Merkle and Wheat poled singles with two outs in the bottom of the fifth, but Cutshaw flied to left to end the threat. That was Brooklyn's last hit.

The Red Sox tacked on another run in the seventh when Janvrin came around to score on a wild play that included a hit by Hoblitzell and a throwing error by Cheney. Hooper led off with a single but Janvrin forced him at second when he grounded to third on an attempted bunt. Janvrin went to second when Olson robbed Walker of a hit and threw him out. Hoblitzell topped a grounder to Cheney's right and, though he had no chance to throw out Hoblitzell, the desperate hurler threw to Merkle anyway, but the ball hit the runner in the back and rolled far enough away for Janvrin to score.[11]

Nap Rucker replaced Cheney in the top of the eighth and threw two scoreless innings, allowing only a single to Hooper in the ninth. From the fifth inning on, Leonard set down 11 straight Brooklyn batters before walking Olson with one out in the ninth inning, then retired Meyers and pinch-hitter Gus Getz to close out Boston's 6-2 win.

SOURCES

In addition to the sources cited in the Notes, the author accessed Retrosheet.org, Baseball-Reference.com, and SABR.org.

NOTES

1   "Can Dodgers Tie Up Series? Fans Flock Again to Game," *Brooklyn Standard Union*, October 11, 1916: 1.

2   "Can Dodgers Tie Up Series?"

3   "Can Dodgers Tie Up Series?"

4   T.H. Murnane, "Larry Gardner's Mighty Circuit Drive Puts Robins All but Out of the Running," *Boston Globe*, October 12, 1916: 1, 6.

5   Murnane.

6   Grantland Rice, "Only Question Now Is When," *Boston Globe*, October 12, 1916: 6.

7   Murnane.

8   "Detailed Account of Game by Innings," *New York Times*, October 12, 1916: 12.

9   "Detailed Account."

10 There was method to Robinson's madness when he sent Pfeffer to hit for Marquard but didn't have him pitch. Pfeffer was Brooklyn's best hitter off the bench and Robinson was saving his ace to start Game Five.

11 "Detailed Account."

"Some game!" Twenty-two innings of heartbreaking baseball

August 22, 1917
Brooklyn Robins 6, Pittsburgh Pirates 5 (22 innings)

by Luis A. Blandon Jr.

On a sultry Wednesday afternoon at Ebbets Field, the Robins and Pirates played for 4 hours and 15 minutes in the first game of a doubleheader.[1] A "paltry 1,500 'bushers' were on hand to appreciate" the longest game in the 41-year history of the National League.[2] A Brooklyn newspaper account noted that "forty-seven safeties, one hundred fifty-nine 'at bats,' one hundred and thirty-one putouts, sixty-nine assists and thirty-eight left on bases were employed in the conduct of this diversion."[3]

The 1916 National League champion Robins were managed by Wilbert Robinson.[4] Expectations ran high, but disintegrated as the season progressed. On August 22 the Robins were 53-58, in sixth place, 18 games behind the first-place New York Giants. Rube Marquard was a valuable pitcher with a 12-8 record. Left fielder Jim Hickman was considered the faster runner in baseball, a former college sprinter who held "many minor records to his credit."[5] The starting pitcher was 25-year-old rookie curveballer Leon Cadore. Due to injuries, the team was short of infielders who were "as scarce as kind-hearted U-Boat captains."[6]

The last-place Pirates were an abysmal 36-76, 35½ games behind the Giants. The team was on its third manager of the year, Hugo Bezdek.[7] The football coach in Bedzek "instilled into the motley crew he has gathered … never-say-die-spirit."[8] Fresh from setting the Pirates record for ERA in 1916, southpaw control artist Wilbur Cooper took the mound.[9] Unheralded rookie Jake Pitler manned second.[10]

Cooper had previously dominated the Robins, but seemed to feel the effect of his 14-inning "grind with the Quakers" in his last start.[11] The Robins "found Cooper easy and the Pirates defense [sic] shaky" over the first three innings as they jumped to a 5-1 lead.[12] In the first, the Robins scored on a single to center by Ivy Olson, a sacrifice by Jake Daubert, and Casey Stengel's RBI single into left.

Cooper's struggles continued in the second. Hickman singled to center and advanced on Frank O'Rourke's sacrifice. Shortstop Chuck Ward booted Otto Miller's grounder. Cadore singled to center, scoring Hickman as Miller was thrown out at third by Max Carey. Cadore took second on the throw and scored on Olson's double over third base.

The Pirates answered with a run in the third when Carson Bigbee singled to center and Cadore "winged Carey."[13] Bigbee went to third on Tony Boeckel's fly to Stengel in right and scored on Ward's infield out. The Robins responded with two runs in the bottom of the third. Hi Myers reached base with a scratch hit. Stengel singled to center. They advanced by Jimmy Johnston's sacrifice.[14] Hickman's "timely thump" drove the runners home to make it 5-1.[15]

In the sixth inning, curveballer Elmer Jacobs relieved Cooper, who in his five innings pitched gave up 11 hits and "five sounds."[16] Jacobs pitched 16⅔ innings, facing 66 batters and giving up 17 hits with three walks and one strikeout. A fluke play cost him the game.

Cadore appeared sharp, "settled beyond the slightest doubt."[17] But Bezdek's Pirates fought back to tie the game as Cadore's precision abandoned him. The Pirates scored four runs as the "Buccaneers pounced on the booty exposed by Cadore's carelessness."[18] In the sixth with one out, Pitler and Bill Wagner singled to center and right respectively. After Cooper fouled out, Charlie Jackson walked to load the bases. Bigbee's "slow grounder took a funny hop[,]" bouncing over Johnston's head at second for a single.[19] Pitler and Wagner scored on the play.

The Pirates added tying runs in the seventh. Boeckel started the rally with a Texas Leaguer over second base. He was forced at second by Ward. After Ray Miller struck out, Ward went to second on a muffed pickoff play. Pitler doubled, scoring Ward, and Wagner drove in Pitler with a single to left. The score was 5-5. For the next 13 innings, no one scored.

Relieving Cadore, spitballer Larry Cheney[20] "joined the embroglio" in the eighth, pitching 13 innings with no runs on nine hits, one walk, and seven strikeouts.[21] Each team was "kept from scoring by clever pitching and spectacular fielding

of both nines."[22] In the 13th, with Bigbee on first, Honus Wagner made one of his last appearances, pinch-hitting for Boeckel. Cheney grabbed his bunt and tossed to Myers at second, forcing Bigbee.[23] Hickman squandered an opportunity to end the game in the 14th. With the bases loaded and one out, he hit a soft grounder to pitcher Jacobs, who turned a 1-2-3 double play.

In the 17th Hickman beat out a hit to third and reached second on third baseman Boeckel's errant toss to first. With one out, Hickman advanced on Miller's groundout to short. With Cheney at the plate, Hickman attempted to steal home. Umpire Bill Klem ruled that Hickman had been tagged out on the foot by catcher Bill Wagner.[24] Hickman "vociferously maintained" that he missed the bag and got up to touch the plate.[25] The Robins dugout let Klem hear their disapproval. Klem called time, approached the Robins bench and "banished every soul except your Uncle Wilbert Robinson and the bat boy" to the "outer darkness under the stand."[26]

In the 20th, Cheney singled through the box with one out.[27] On Olson's grounder to second baseman Ward, Cheney "had victory in mind and made a head-first slide for the bag" to break up the double play.[28] While turning the double play, Ward collided with Cheney's head as "he came plunging into second and stretched out cold. Larry was brought around, but was so badly shaken up that he had to retire."[29] Marquard came in relief and yielded "a hit and a pass in his two innings administration."[30]

In the top of the 22nd, Marquard struck out Jacobs and Lee King. Bigbee singled but Carey fouled out to Miller to end the frame. When Jacobs came up, the sparse crowd "were quick to realize the exceptional merit of Jacobs' slabwork. ... [H]e received a tribute which he always will remember."[31]

In the bottom of the inning with one out, Hickman received one of the three walks issued by Jacobs and went to second on O'Rourke's single to left. Otto Miller hit a hard grounder to Adam DeBus at third who tossed to Pitler, forcing the sliding O'Rourke. Without hesitation, "at the crash of the blow, Hickman dug in his spikes into the ground and was at third before O'Rourke was expunged."[32] Hickman turned the corner around third, stopping "just a fraction of a second to look over his shoulder at the play at second base," and kept going.[33] Pitler "calmly held the ball in his hand."[34] Pitler saw Hickman rounding third, froze as he "evidently thought that Hickman would not attempt to make home and deliberated whether to throw to first."[35] The hesitation allowed Hickman to slide safely home, beating Pitler's wild throw to catcher Walter Schmidt. The Robins' win resulted from "five seconds of hesitancy by Pitler."[36] Pitler's lapse "lost the battle, and Jacobs deserves reams of praise."[37] Hickman forced the issue by "the exceptional celerity with which he went from second to third."[38]

As Hickman scored, "a tall, bronzed Bronzed Brooklynite who was warming up in right field, tossed his cap in the air and let his roar mingle with the exulting paeans of the fans."[39] Jack Coombs was relieved, as the game was "getting all too close for comfort to his own world's long distance record game of twenty-four innings."[40]

The team played "twenty-two innings of heartbreaking baseball" as the National League record "for long-distance games was shattered to smithereens."[41] Jacobs was tagged with his 16th loss against four wins. Marquard earned his 13th win of the season. The game broke the record of the July 17, 1914, Pirates-Giants 21-inning marathon.[42]

Umpire Klem ordered the second game to start to at 5:56 P.M. Twilight burgeoned as two scoreless innings were completed. Klem surveyed the skies and "stentatoriously announced that Flatbush had a surfeit of the national pastime for one afternoon."[43] Klem called the game, "evidently conscience-stricken with the realization that the teams had already put in a day's work."[44] It was considered his first decision that was met with approval.

Marquard added to his list of records as winning pitcher in the longest National League game ever played to date.[45] The two teams had played 35 innings before the game was decided, breaking the previous record of 26 innings.[46] The Pirates established the major-league record for consecutive innings played in a given period with 59 in four games, breaking the mark of 43.[47]

The game was the first for 8-year-old Irving Piken. The memories diminished with the passage of time. In 2017, at the age of 108, he noted, "… I don't recall too much about the proceedings."[48]

SOURCES

In addition to the sources cited in the Notes, the author consulted Baseball-Reference.com, Retrosheet.org, and MLB.com.

NOTES

1 The series started on Monday with a Pirates 10-inning 1-0 win followed by a 13-inning 3-3 tie called on account of darkness, resulting in the doubleheader being scheduled.

2 Charles A. Taylor, "Robins Set Extra Frame Record in Real National League Thriller," *New York Tribune*, August 23, 1917: 13.

3 "Record Dodger-Pirate Struggle Replete with Unusual Features," *Brooklyn Daily Times*, August 23, 1917: 6; The game featured 160 putouts, 70 assists, and 40 left on base.

4 From 1914 to 1931, one of Brooklyn's nicknames was Robins, after the team's longtime manager Wilbert Robinson. They were also called the Superbas and the Dodgers.

5 Rice, "Superbas Winners in 22 Innings and Break League Record," *Brooklyn Daily Eagle*, August 23, 1917: 14. [The *Eagle* identified the writer only as "Rice." It was likely longtime *Eagle* sportswriter Thomas S. Rice.]

6 "Record Dodger-Pirate Struggle Replete with Unusual Features."

7 Bezdek is the only person in history who coached both a professional football and a baseball team. He coached the NFL's Cleveland Rams in 1937-1938. During his baseball career he also worked as a college football coach. He was 105-46-13 at Arkansas, Oregon, and Penn State. In 1918 he coached the Mare Island Marines to victory in the 1918 Rose Bowl, then known as the Tournament East-West Football Game. He managed the Pirates through 1919, compiling a 166-187 record.

8 Taylor, "Robins Set Extra Frame Record."

9 Cooper holds the franchise single-season record for ERA (1.87 in 1916) and the all-time records for victories (202) and complete games (263).

10 Pitler played in 111 games, mostly at second base, for the Pirates in 1917 and 1918. His career batting average was .232; of his 89 hits, only 13 were for extra bases, and none were home runs. After playing two games in 1918, he was sent down to Jersey City. On his way to New Jersey, he took a side trip to play in an "outlaw" baseball league in Pennsylvania. As a result, he incurred a nine-year ban from playing for a major-league farm team. Pitler later became a minor-league manager for the Brooklyn Dodgers and was a Dodgers coach from 1947 to 1957.

11 Charles J. Doyle, "Dodgers Beat Pirates 6-5," *Pittsburgh Post-Gazette*, August 23, 1917: 8.

12 George Underwood, "Superbas Triumph in Twenty-Second," *Sun* (New York), August 23, 1917: 11.

13 Underwood; in 11 at-bats, Bigbee accounted for six of the Pirates' 19 hits.

14 The Robins had seven sacrifice hits in the game.

15 Underwood.

16 Doyle, "Dodgers Beat Pirates 6-5."

17 Taylor.

18 "Record Dodger-Pirate Struggle Replete with Unusual Features."

19 Ed F. Balinger, "Pirates Lose 22-Inning Game to Dodgers," *Pittsburgh Daily Post*, August 23, 1917: 8.

20 Over a three-year span, 1912-1914, Cheney was one of the National League's most durable and effective pitchers, racking up more than 300 innings each season.

21 "Record Dodger-Pirate Struggle Replete With Unusual Features."

22 Taylor.

23 At 43, Honus Wagner was in his last season, a part-time player.

24 Balinger.

25 "Klem Went on a Rampage When Hickman Stole Home," *Brooklyn Daily Eagle*, August 23, 1917: 14.

26 "Klem Went on a Rampage."

27 In the 18th inning, Cheney struck out. He was the only Robin to strike out in the game.

28 Doyle, "Dodgers Beat Pirates 6-5."

29 Underwood, "Superbas Triumph in Twenty-Second."

30 Underwood.

31 Doyle.

32 "Dodger' Victory Sets New League Record," *Brooklyn Standard Union*, August 23, 1917: 10.

33 "Robins Make New Long-Game Record," *New York Times*, August 23, 1917: 15.

34 "Jimmy Hickman's Steal Home Wins Record Game for Game for Robins," *New York Evening World*, August 23, 1917: 12.

35 "Robins Make New Long-Game Record."

36 "Dodger' Victory Sets New League Record."

37 Taylor.

38 "Rice."

39 Underwood.

40 Underwood. The longest game at the time was the September 1, 1906, 24-inning contest in which the Philadelphia Athletics defeated the Boston Americans, 4-1. Coombs was the winning pitcher.

41 "Robins Make New Long-Game Record." The Robins played in the longest game in major-league baseball on May 1, 1920. Cadore was the starting pitcher against the Boston Braves. Cadore and Braves starter Joe Oeschger each pitched the entire game before it was called for darkness tied at 1-1 after 26 innings.

42 Larry Doyle hit a two-run home run in the 21st inning to give the Giants a 3-1 win. Marquard pitched a complete-game victory.

43 "Record Dodger-Pirate Struggle Replete with Unusual Features."

44 "Robins Make New Long-Game Record."

45 Winning pitcher Marquard held the record for the most consecutive games won in a season, tied with Tim Keefe at 19; and the most consecutive wins from the start of the season.

46 The Robins and Pirates played three extra-inning games in a row for a total of 45 innings.

47 "Feature Facts of Record Game," *New York Tribune*, August 23, 1917: 13. Pitler set a record for putouts in extra-inning games by a second baseman (15). Bigbee set a record with 11 at-bats in a game.

48 Rachel Marcus, "Oldest Living Dodgers Fan, 108, Always Excited To See Jackie Robinson," ESPN. com, April 15, 2017. https://www.espn.com/mlb/story/_/id/19136234/oldest-living-dodgers-fan-going-strong-favorite-player-jackie-robinson, accessed December 10, 2019; Jennifer Karmarkar, "111-year-old Laguna Woods resident was the oldest man in U.S.," Orange County Register (Anaheim, California), March 10, 2020. https://www.ocregister.com/2020/03/10/oldest-man-111-dies-in-laguna-woods/, accessed May 4, 2020. At 111, Irving Piken was believed to be the oldest man in the United States, according to the Gerontology Research Group. He died on February 23, 2020.

GRINER LOSES NO-HITTER WITH TWO OUTS IN THE NINTH

May 6, 1918

Brooklyn Robins 2, Philadelphia Phillies 1

by J.G. Preston

Dan Griner's last major-league win was his best one: he came within one out of pitching a no-hitter.

The son of a Confederate soldier, Griner joined the St. Louis Cardinals in August 1912, his first professional season, making the jump from the Class D Appalachian League. In his first full season in the majors, 1913, he led major-league pitchers in losses and runs allowed. After he also posted losing records in 1914 and 1915 – and got into fistfights with three teammates in 1914, sending one to the hospital – the Cardinals let him go early in the 1916 season. But after he spent two seasons with St. Paul of the American Association, he got another shot at the big leagues in 1918 with the Brooklyn Robins, who were hard up for pitching after losing two starters to the military and World War I during the offseason.[1]

However, the Robins didn't seem so hard up for pitching as to actually use Griner. He worked only seven innings in the team's first 15 games, all in relief and all in losses. His light workload may have been in part because of an ankle injury he suffered in spring training.[2] Then on May 6,

Brooklyn manager Wilbert Robinson gave Griner the ball to face the Philadelphia Phillies at Ebbets Field. He was still so little known in Brooklyn that the *New York Times* story about the game referred to him as "Dave" Griner.[3]

"It is not knocking to say that Griner had not made any sort of a favorable impression up to yesterday," said the account of the game in the *Brooklyn Daily Eagle*, "and the 1,200 or so fans present groaned aloud when he was announced."[4]

The Phillies had started the season with seven wins in their first nine games, including a three-game sweep of Brooklyn in Philadelphia in which they scored 19 runs, before their bats went cold. They entered the May 6 game with a five-game losing streak and had been shut out in four of them, and their bats stayed cold against Griner, as he retired the side in order in each of the first four innings, striking out three.

Meanwhile the Robins put up two runs in the first inning against Philadelphia's Joe Oeschger. Ivy Olson led off with a Texas League single behind second base, and Ollie O'Mara followed with a similar hit to the same spot, putting runners on first and second. Jake Daubert laid down a bunt, but Phillies first baseman Fred Luderus dropped Oeschger's throw. "The bobble so upset Luderus that he clutched the ball while Olson ran home," according to the *Philadelphia Inquirer*.[5] O'Mara went to third on the play and scored when cleanup hitter Hy Myers singled to right. Daubert was thrown out by Gavvy Cravath while trying to advance to third. Myers took second on the throw and advanced to third when Jimmy Johnston grounded out to short. Jim Hickman followed with a walk and stole second, but Oeschger got out of the inning by retiring Ray Schmandt on a groundball to third.

The Phillies finally put a man on base with one out in the fifth inning, when Luderus reached on an error by second baseman Schmandt, who fumbled a groundball. Irish Meusel walked, bringing Harry Pearce to the plate.

At that point Brooklyn catcher Mack Wheat (the younger brother of his Hall of Fame teammate Zack Wheat) made the defensive play of the game. "Pearce raised a foul which dropped a few feet from the screen," Al C. Palma wrote in the *Brooklyn Citizen*. "Wheat misjudged the ball and overran it. As it came down he reached for it. The ball hit his glove and he toppled over. Just as the sphere was hopping out, Mack made another lunge and hugged it tight."[6]

The runners advanced to second and third after the catch – Wheat nearly threw out Luderus trying to take third, but third baseman O'Mara mishandled the throw – and Griner walked Bert Adams intentionally to load the bases for the pitcher Oeschger, who was retired on a foul pop to Daubert at first to end the inning.

Philadelphia went down in order in the sixth and seventh. Pearce led off the eighth with an easy fly ball to right that Hickman lost in the sun and dropped for an error, Pearce taking second. Possum Whitted, batting for Adams, hit a line drive to Daubert, who caught it and then doubled off Pearce. Oeschger struck out, and Griner took a no-hitter into the ninth. The score was still 2-0, as the Robins had managed just two hits, both singles, after the first inning. Brooklyn did miss out on a scoring opportunity in the bottom of the eighth when, with one out, Olson singled, stole second, and moved to third on a passed ball. But O'Mara popped out and Daubert flied out to end the inning.

Mike Fitzgerald, leading off the ninth, was retired on a fly ball to left. Dave Bancroft then worked the count to 3-and-2. "There was no question but that the next ball delivered by Griner was over the plate," Palma wrote. "However, [umpire Bill] Klem called it a ball and the assumption is that he thought it too low."[7]

Milt Stock followed with a groundball to short. Olson threw to Schmandt to get the second out of the inning, but when Bancroft went into second base standing up, Schmandt was unable to make the relay to first. While some accounts opined that Bancroft prevented a game-ending double play, Palma was not convinced the Robins would have gotten the out at first because the groundball was a slow one. In any event, if strike three had been called on Bancroft, the game would have been over.

But it was not, and Cravath, the Phillies' slugging cleanup hitter (he had already led the National League in home runs four times and would do so twice more), went to the plate as the tying run. He "swung wildly at the first ball pitched to him and the sphere sped on a line over second base," according to the *New York Tribune*'s Charles A. Taylor, with Stock taking third on the single.[8]

Griner had lost his no-hitter, but he still had a game to win, with the tying run on base. The next batter, Luderus, swung at the first pitch and hit a groundball to O'Mara at third, who threw to Schmandt at second, retiring pinch-runner Patsy McGaffigan to end the game and give Griner his seventh major-league shutout. There would not be a no-hitter at Ebbets Field until Dazzy Vance threw one against the Phillies in 1925.

Exterior view of Ebbets Field's iconic brick and arches, circa 1918. Outfield bleachers were constructed in 1926. (Photo: SABR-Rucker Archive)

Griner's pitching in the game was described in the *Brooklyn Daily Eagle*: "His principal assets were a slow ball and a fast drop. He had both working to perfection, and the heady change of pace he put over was the principal cause of the Phillies' collapse. Daniel mixed in other assorted shoots here and there, but the teaser and the quick drop were the tricks that stood the Phils on their heads."[9]

The one-hitter was the second Griner pitched in the major leagues. He lost the first one. On July 30, 1914, pitching for the Cardinals, Griner allowed a leadoff single to Les Mann in the third inning; Mann came around to score on a sacrifice, a groundout and an error. The game was tied 1-1 going into the bottom of the ninth, when Braves pitcher Lefty Tyler reached on an error to lead off the inning, moved to second on a sacrifice, took third on a groundout, and scored when Cardinals third baseman Zinn Beck fumbled Rabbit Maranville's grounder.[10]

Griner went on to start five more games for Brooklyn in May 1918, losing them all. In June, facing the prospect of being drafted by the military, he left the team to work at a munitions plant and pitched for the plant's team in a shipyard league. He returned to Organized Baseball in 1919, pitched for St. Paul's American Association champions in 1919 and 1920, and kicked around the minors as a pitcher and sometime manager through 1924.

Griner finished his major-league career with a record of 28-55 – but he was just one out away from a place in the history books.

SOURCES

Gregory H. Wolf's biography of Griner in the SABR Baseball Biography Project is the definitive source for biographical information on Griner. Game accounts were accessed via Newspapers.com.

NOTES

1   Gregory H. Wolf, "Dan Griner," Society for American Baseball Research Baseball Biography Project, https://SABR.org/bioproj/person/f05dd83a.

2   "Robby Looks for Dodgers to Finish in the First Division," *Brooklyn Daily Times*, May 7, 1918: 8.

3   "Phillies at Mercy of Griner's Shoots," *New York Times*, May 7, 1918: 10.

4   Rice, "Superbas Off on Long Tour After Cleaning Up Phillies," *Brooklyn Daily Eagle*, May 7, 1918: 20. (Rice was the sportswriter's byline.)

5   "Cravath Spoiled Dan Griner's Dream," *Philadelphia Inquirer*, May 7, 1918: 12.

6   Al C. Palma, "One Uncontrolled Pitch Beat Griner Out of No-Hit Game," *Brooklyn Citizen*, May 7, 1918: 5.

7   Al C. Palma, "One Uncontrolled Pitch Beat Griner Out of No-Hit Game."

8   Charles A. Taylor, "Cactus Sticks Dan Griner for Lone Hit in Shut-Out," *New York Tribune*, May 7, 1918: 12. Several newspaper accounts of the game indicated that, under the apparent baseball etiquette of the time, Cravath should not have tried to get a hit with two out in the ninth inning of a no-hitter. "Gavvy Cravath, a player with a record that is spotless, with a reputation as a sportsman and a gentleman, brought shame upon himself by violating the first rule of baseball ethics. He made a base hit when he should not have done so." Hugh S. Fullerton, "Different Complexion on American League Race," *New York Evening World*, May 7, 1918: 13. "When a twirler has gone the route without having a hit charged against him and the last man comes to bat he does not exert himself in trying to spoil the proudest record a pitcher may hope to have in baseball." "Cravath Robs Griner of a No-Hit Game," *Brooklyn Daily Standard Union*, May 7, 1918: 10. In that same newspaper: "Bancroft asked Cravath when he walked back to the bench with his chin resting on his chest, 'Why did you do it?' [Cravath] replied, 'I swung wildly. The ball hit the bat. It's too bad to spoil that kid's no-hit game.'" "Notes of the Game," *Brooklyn Daily Standard Union*, May 7, 1918: 10.

9   Rice, "Superbas Off on Long Tour After Cleaning Up Phillies."

10 Glen L. Wallar, "Griner, Beaten, Gives One Hit," *St. Louis Daily Globe-Democrat*, July 31, 1914: 10.

BROOKLYN'S PFEFFER TOSSES 18-INNING COMPLETE GAME

June 1, 1919

Philadelphia Phillies 10, Brooklyn Robins 9 (18 innings)

by J.G. Preston

Brooklyn's Jeff Pfeffer (not to be confused with his brother, Big Jeff Pfeffer[1]) was the National League's hottest pitcher to start the 1919 season. He won each of his first seven starts, pitching a complete game in each (one of them going 11 innings), with an ERA of 1.38. His winning streak came to an end on May 28, when he pitched another complete game – this time going 13 innings – but was defeated by the Cardinals, 7-5.

Four days later he went the distance again. This time the distance was quite a bit farther.

Pfeffer faced the Philadelphia Phillies at Ebbets Field on June 1, 1919.[2] His mound opponent was former Columbia University star George Smith, who had been Pfeffer's Brooklyn teammate the year before. Smith was traded to the Giants after the 1918 season and then dealt to the Phillies two weeks before this game.

Both pitchers got off to rocky starts. The Phillies used consecutive singles by Cy Williams, Irish Meusel, Fred Luderus, and Gavvy Cravath in the top of the first to score two runs, then the Robins tied the game in the bottom of the inning.

After Ivy Olson and Tommy Griffith singled, Zack Wheat drove Olson in with a single to right, and when right fielder Cravath let the hit go through him, Griffith came around to score.

Brooklyn took a 3-2 lead in the fourth inning when Wheat doubled, moved to third on a sacrifice by Hy Myers, and scored on Ed Konetchy's single. Pfeffer held onto the lead until the sixth, when the Phils tied it on a two-out walk to Luderus followed by singles by Cravath and Doug Baird.

Williams put the Phillies on top in the seventh inning with a two-out, two-run homer over the right-field wall, scoring Bert Adams, who had singled.[3] The Phils made it 7-3 in the eighth inning. Baird reached on a two-out infield single and went to third on a single by Harry Pearce. With Adams at the plate, the Phillies attempted a double steal. Catcher Ernie Krueger's throw went through to shortstop Olson, who then threw back to home to try to retire Baird. Olson's throw was high, Baird scored, and when the ball went into the grandstand, umpire William "Lord" Byron allowed Pearce to score as well.[4]

Jeff Pfeffer was a rugged right-hander who anchored Uncle Robby's pitching staff at the end of the Deadball Era. In parts of nine seasons (1913-1921) with Brooklyn, he went 113-80, including 25 wins in 1916 and 23 in 1914. (Photo: Library of Congress)

But Smith couldn't hold onto the lead, and the Robins batted around in the bottom of the eighth to tie the game. Olson led off with a single to right and went to second when Cravath fumbled it for his second error of the game. Lee Magee beat out an infield hit, Olson going to third, and Griffith walked to load the bases. Wheat followed with a single off second baseman Possum Whitted's shoe to score Olson, and Myers brought Magee and Griffith home with a single. Konetchy advanced the runners to second and third with a sacrifice, then Clarence Mitchell, making his first appearance of the season pinch-hitting for third baseman Lew Malone, walked to load the bases.[5] Wheat scored the tying run when Krueger hit a groundball to short, Mitchell being forced out at second. With the go-ahead run on third, Brooklyn manager Wilbert Robinson allowed Pfeffer to bat for himself, and he struck out to end the inning.[6]

Both teams were scoreless in the ninth and 10th innings, with Milt Watson coming in to pitch for the Phillies in the ninth after Smith was removed for a pinch-hitter in the top of the inning. Then Philadelphia scored in the 11th, with the help of two Brooklyn errors. Adams doubled, went to third when Wheat muffed Watson's fly ball to left, and scored when second baseman Magee fumbled Meusel's grounder. Watson also tried to score on the play, but right fielder Griffith scooped up the loose ball and made a perfect throw to the plate to retire him.[7] The Robins kept the game going when Magee tripled in the bottom of the inning and Griffith brought him home with a sacrifice fly.

The game was scoreless through the next four innings, but the Robins missed an opportunity to win the game in the 14th. Griffith led off with a walk and went to third on Wheat's single to right.[8] Myers hit a groundball that went off the hand of third baseman Baird; shortstop Pearce picked it up and threw to first to retire Myers, with Griffith holding at third. "Tommy could easily have scored the winning run then and there," in the view of the *Brooklyn Daily Eagle*.[9] Konetchy was intentionally walked to load the bases. Ray Schmandt then hit a tapper that catcher Adams grabbed with his foot on home plate to force out Griffith, then threw to first to retire Schmandt, who had made no attempt to run, thinking it was a foul ball. The Robins protested, but to no avail, and the inning was over.[10]

In the top of the 16th, with Pfeffer still on the mound, Whitted singled, advanced to second on Williams's sacrifice, and scored on Luderus's two-out base hit. Brooklyn wasn't done yet, though. In the bottom of the inning, Griffith and Wheat singled. Myers bunted, and Watson's throw to third was too late to retire Griffith, leaving the bases loaded with none out. Konetchy hit a groundball back to the box; Watson threw home to retire Griffith, but Adams's throw to first attempting to retire Konetchy was off target and Wheat scored the tying run on the error.[11] The Robins still had the winning run in scoring position, but Schmandt was retired on a short fly ball to left and Pfeffer popped out to third. (Pfeffer didn't hit a ball out of the infield in eight trips to the plate in the game.[12])

In the top of the 18th, Williams – batting for the ninth time – singled to right with one out, went to second on Meusel's groundout to Pfeffer,

and scored when Luderus doubled to right-center, his fourth hit of the day. The Robins had already come from behind to tie the game four times, but this time they had no answer; Watson retired the side in order in the bottom of the inning, striking out Myers and Konetchy for the final outs – the only batters Watson fanned in his 10 innings of work – and the Phillies came away with a 10-9 victory.

Pfeffer faced 77 batters in his 18 innings of work, allowing 23 hits. It wasn't his longest outing in the major leagues; on June 17, 1915, he pitched 18⅔ innings at Chicago before the Cubs won in the bottom of the 19th.[13]

This wasn't the longest game the Robins and Phillies played against each other in 1919. On April 30 in Philadelphia, the teams played a 9-9 tie that was called on account of darkness after 20 innings. Both starting pitchers went all the way in that game, Burleigh Grimes for the Robins and Joe Oeschger for the Phils, facing 84 and 82 batters, respectively.[14] Two weeks later, the Phillies traded Oeschger to get George Smith.

SOURCES

In addition to the sources cited in the Notes, the author accessed Retrosheet.org, Baseball-Reference.com, SABR.org, and *The Sporting News* archive via Paper of Record.

NOTES

1   Jeff Pfeffer's given name was Edward; Big Jeff's given name was Francis. One researcher says both got their nicknames from their supposed physical resemblance to heavyweight boxing champion Jim Jeffries. John Bennett, "Jeff Pfeffer," Society for American Baseball Research Baseball Biography Project. https://SABR.org/bioproj/person/25b464c2. But another researcher found no evidence that the nickname was connected to Jeffries. Bill Lamb, "Big Jeff Pfeffer," Society for American Baseball Research Baseball Biography Project. https://SABR.org/bioproj/person/fa863125. Lamb found that Francis Pfeffer was usually referred to in newspapers as "Frank" – the name he called himself – and was seldom referred to as "Big Jeff." Different newspaper accounts of the June 1, 1919, game refer to Edward Pfeffer as Ed, Jeff, and Big Jeff.

2   This game would be a rare one-game series, making up a game that was rained out on May 7. Brooklyn had a rare Sunday offday originally scheduled for June 1. Their next series was to be against Boston, where Sunday games weren't allowed until 1929.

3   Home runs were still relatively rare in 1919; only 22 were hit in 70 games at Ebbets Field. Williams finished the year with nine homers, third-most in the National League.

4   "Robins Wage Futile Fight Against Philadelphia Through Eighteen Innings," *New York Times*, June 2, 1919: 18.

5   Mitchell was normally a pitcher – he won 125 games in the major leagues – but he was frequently used as a pinch-hitter and had a .252 career batting average. He also started 61 games at first base and 12 in the outfield in his major-league career.

6   In fairness, Pfeffer was a decent hitter for a pitcher, finishing his major-league career with a .206 batting average. He even started a game in right field and batted seventh when the Robins had a number of injured players in 1917. Even though Pfeffer had already given up seven runs, Robinson was in no hurry to take him out

of the game, as the Robins had six games scheduled in Boston over the next three days and their pitching staff would be stretched thin. Brooklyn played consecutive doubleheaders at Boston on June 2, 3, and 4 to make up three games that were postponed by weather on April 24, 25, and 26. George B. Underwood, "Luderus' Double Downs Dodgers in 18th Inning," *New York Sun*, June 2, 1919: 17. The *Sun* and *Philadelphia Inquirer* referred to Brooklyn's team as the Dodgers; the *Brooklyn Daily Eagle* called them the Superbas. Other sources called them the Robins, the nickname commonly used during Wilbert Robinson's managerial tenure.

7   "Robins Not Getting the Utmost from Their Consecutive Hitting," *Brooklyn Daily Times*, June 2, 1919: 8.

8   Al C. Palma, "Playing Long Games Becoming a Habit with the Robins," *Brooklyn Citizen*, June 2, 1919: 5.

9   "Hitting 'Em Out," *Brooklyn Daily Eagle*, June 2, 1919: 2.

10 "Phillies Down Dodgers in Grand 18-Inning Battle, Score 10 to 9," *Philadelphia Inquirer*, June 2, 1919: 14.

11 "A Long, Sad Story, Mates; Just 18 Innings of It," *Brooklyn Daily Eagle*, June 2, 1919: 18.

12 Al C. Palma, "Playing Long Games Becoming a Habit with the Robins."

13 That was the game in which the Cubs' George Washington "Zip" Zabel set the major-league record that still stands, pitching 18⅓ innings in relief after starting pitcher Bert Humphries was injured in the first inning.

14 Oeschger is best remembered for another game he pitched against Brooklyn, when he was with the Boston Braves, going all the way in a 26-inning 1-1 tie on May 1, 1920. He faced 90 batters in that game, six fewer that Brooklyn's Leon Cadore, who also went the distance.

Covelski goes the distance to win Series opener

October 5, 1920

Cleveland Indians 3, Brooklyn Robins 1 | Game One of the World Series

by Joseph Wancho

The Cleveland Indians were making their initial appearance in the World Series in 1920. Tris Speaker's club finally broke through to finish atop the American League after finishing a close second to Boston in 1918, and then to Chicago in 1919. Their opponents, the Brooklyn Robins, were making their second trip to the fall classic, and were hoping for a better outcome than their last appearance. In that World Series, in 1916, they were disposed of in five games by the Boston Red Sox. (Three of the five games were decided by a single run.)

While the Indians were in the midst of a tight pennant race with New York and Chicago, the news broke out of the Windy City that seven current members of the White Sox had allegedly conspired to lose the 1919 World Series to Cincinnati. (An eighth player allegedly involved, Chick Gandil, had retired after the 1919 season). The players were subsequently suspended for the final series of the season. Without many of their key personnel, the White Sox lost two of three to the St. Louis Browns. The Yankees could not close a three-game gap to catch Cleveland.

The Robins were in a pennant race themselves with their archrival New York Giants. On September 25 Brooklyn held a four-game advantage over John McGraw's crew. Both teams were headed for a five-game series at Ebbets Field. Brooklyn took three of the five, icing their second NL pennant.

A gray and breezy day at Ebbets Field was the site for Game One of the World Series. The Indians wore black armbands in remembrance of Ray Chapman, who was killed when he was beaned by Yankees pitcher Carl Mays on August 16. The starting pitcher for the visiting Indians was Stan Coveleski, who posted a 24-14 record during the regular season. Toeing the rubber for Brooklyn was Rube Marquard. The tall left-hander was 10-7 during the season, but had not pitched since September 26, when he bested the Giants. The Robins' manager, Wilbert Robinson, felt that Marquard, a Cleveland native, would be the ideal hurler to neutralize player-manager Tris Speaker and the other left-handed batters in the Indians' lineup. Of course, Spoke stacked his lineup with right-handed batters to counter the strategy.

The 1920 best-of-nine World Series opened on October 5 at Ebbets Field, where temporary bleachers were erected on the outfield. In a tight pitching duel featuring just five hits by both teams, the Cleveland Indians' Stan Coveleski emerged victorious, 3-1. (Photo: Library of Congress)

The series was a best five-of-nine format, with the games going 3-4-2 between the two cities. The series was supposed to start at Cleveland's Dunn Field (renamed League Park in 1928). However, Indians owner James Dunn wanted to add more seating with temporary stands in center field and in right field in front of the bleachers. Construction was taking a bit longer than anticipated, so the first three games were transferred to Brooklyn.

The breezy conditions that made it a bit chilly for the fans was not uncommon. Ebbets Field was located in a sort of pocket that took in all the cold drafty weather of Flatbush. The Game One crowd was 23,573, a couple of thousand under capacity. In Cleveland, fans gathered on East 6th Street between Rockwell and Superior Avenues to get as close as they could to the action. An electric scoreboard relayed the action by telegraph to let the throng know what was going on 465 miles to the east.

Cleveland scored first against Marquard. First baseman George Burns hit a high pop just past the infield between first and second base. Ed Konetchy, the Robins' first baseman, and Pete Kilduff, the second baseman, gave chase. However, the wind blew the ball toward short left field, where it fell out of Konetchy's reach. Burns, hustling all the way, motored toward second base. Konetchy corralled the baseball and threw to second in hopes of cutting down the baserunner. But Brooklyn shortstop Ivy Olson was not covering the bag. Konetchy's heave rolled across the diamond to the field boxes in back of third base. Burns dashed home with the first tally of the game.

After Larry Gardner grounded out, Smoky Joe Wood walked. Joe Sewell singled Wood to third. Steve O'Neill ripped a double to left field, scoring Wood and sending Sewell to third. The next batter was Coveleski, who hit a grounder toward first base. Konetchy fielded the ball cleanly, stepped on first base and fired home to catcher Ernie Krueger, who tagged Sewell to complete the unorthodox twin killing and keep the score at 2-0, Cleveland.

The Cleveland defense was at the forefront in the Robins' half of the second inning. Speaker snared a drive by Zack Wheat a long run and Wood backed up to the wall to haul in a long drive off the bat of Hi Myers. Still, Coveleski was masterful with his curve, keeping the Robins off balance and off the scoreboard. Cleveland added a third run in the top of the fourth on another RBI double by O'Neill.

The Indians weren't the only team making plays in the field. In the fifth inning Speaker sent a line drive to right field that looked certain to be a round-tripper. But rightfielder Tommy Griffith leapt at the wall and snared the baseball with his left (gloved) hand to preserve the 3-0 deficit.

Brooklyn scored its lone tally in the seventh inning when Wheat led off with a double to right-center field, went to third on a groundout by Myers, and scored when Konetchy grounded out to first. The home team looked as if it might have something brewing in the eighth inning when Krueger led off with a smash toward left-center, but Speaker made a shoestring catch for the first out. Clarence Mitchell, pinch-hitting for reliever Al Mamaux, sent a single to the right-field foul line. Krueger would have certainly scored, showing the value of Speaker's running catch. Coveleski retired the next two batters.

Game One went to the Indians, 3-1. Coveleski went the distance, scattering five hits and striking out three. Marquard, who pitched six innings, gave up all three Indians runs and all five of their hits, striking out four. Marquard did not start another game, pitching in relief in Game Four.

The Indians' skipper was all smiles after the victory. "The result of the game goes to show that I was not boasting when I contended that Cleveland would display just as good pitching as Brooklyn," Speaker said. "They would have us believe that Brooklyn has the real pitching market

cornered. It is my belief that the pitching in the American League is every bit as good as that in the National and that our batting average of .302 was deservedly earned.

"Coveleski pitched excellent ball today. With the wind blowing as hard as it was, he worked under a handicap, but he delivered in the pinches, and that is what counts. He never was nervous. It was just a ballgame with him. He pitched a typical Coveleski game."[1]

Zack Wheat penned a column for the Cleveland Plain Dealer that gave Cleveland fans a view from the opposition. "Of course a post mortem on the game reveals that we made one mistake in judgment," wrote the Brooklyn captain." This is when O'Neill came up the second time. This was in the fourth inning with Wood already on second base. We should have passed O'Neill and nailed the pitcher. Instead O'Neill was allowed to get a two-base hit and brought Wood home. Gardner and Sewell were already out and of course we were reasonably sure to strike out Coveleski. That is the only flaw I can pick in our game. The rest was pure luck."[2]

SOURCES

In addition to the sources cited in the Notes, the author accessed Retrosheet.org, Baseball-Reference.com, and SABR.org.

NOTES

1   "Speaker Praises Indians Pitching," *New York Times*, October 6, 1920: 10.

2   Zack Wheat, "Indians Had All Luck, Says Wheat," *Cleveland Plain Dealer*, October 6, 1920: 17.

GRIMES THROWS WORLD SERIES SHUTOUT

October 6, 1920

Brooklyn Robins 3, Cleveland Indians 0 | Game Two of the World Series

by Bob LeMoine

Fans in Brooklyn lined up outside Ebbets Field for tickets to the World Series on Monday, October 4, 1920. For $1 or $2 they could get a ticket to see their hometown heroes the Dodgers, Brooklyns, Superbas, or Robins play in the World Series against the Cleveland Indians. It didn't matter which nickname a fan chose for the team because, more important, these devoted followers "pay the bills, do the shouting, bait the umpire and keep the National Pastime on its feet," wrote the *Brooklyn Daily Eagle*. Keeping the game on its feet was maybe the most important contribution the fans made at that time. Baseball had been rocked by scandal and the World Series of 1919 would be forever remembered for gamblers and crooked play, which left a stain on the game. How would fans react, since a grand jury was currently exploring this Black Sox scandal? In Brooklyn, the line of fans waiting for tickets was never less than 500 during the day. Some fans made an entire day out of it anyway, "hanging about in the neighborhood, patronizing transient hot dog-geries and this and that to while away the time."[1] They were ready.

A 20-5 September helped propel Wilbert Robinson's Brooklyn club to the National League pennant. Pitching was the main reason the team was in the World Series. Brooklyn's pitching staff had the best ERA (2.62) and the most strikeouts (553) in the NL. Burleigh Grimes led the way with a 2.22 ERA and a 23-11 record. But their hitting wasn't bad, either, led by Zack Wheat, Hi Myers, and Ed Konetchy, all .300 hitters.

While fans in Brooklyn stood in line during the day, the Cleveland Indians hopped the train that night heading east. "We can hit them all," one player optimistically remarked about the Brooklyn pitching.[2] The Indians had survived a tight pennant race all season, and their 20-6 mark in September helped them outlast the emerging Yankee dynasty and the scarred White Sox franchise. Six Cleveland starters batted over .300, giving the team a .303 average. Three starting pitchers won a total of 75 games: Jim Bagby (31 wins), Stan Coveleski (24), and Ray Caldwell (20).

Game One at Ebbets Field drew 23,573 fans who were disappointed when their home team couldn't muster any offense against Coveleski.

Brooklyn starter Rube Marquard was knocked for three runs in a 3-1 loss. Game Two was Grimes vs. Bagby before a smaller crowd of 22,559. A highly experienced crew of umpires handled the Series: Tommy Connolly, Hank O'Day, Bill Dinneen, and Bill Klem.

After a scoreless top of the first, Brooklyn put a run on the board in the bottom of the inning. With one out, Jimmy Johnston bounced a grounder to deep shortstop. Joe Sewell stopped it on the grass but his throw was low and hit the bag, bouncing straight up in the air. Johnston was safe. Johnston stole second and, after a groundout, scored on a hit by Wheat, who stretched it into a double with some fine sliding around Sewell. "Sewell's lack of experience was responsible for his failure to make the out," wrote Thomas S. Rice in the *Brooklyn Daily Eagle*.[3] "Little Joe did not shine with any undue amount of brilliance today," remarked Henry P. Edwards in the *Cleveland Plain Dealer*.[4]

Many at Ebbets Field were probably thinking the same thing: Ray Chapman would never have let that happen. Chapman, the Indians' young shortstop, had been hit in the head by a pitch from the Yankees' Carl Mays on August 16. The blow to the left side of his skull resulted in emergency surgery, but Chapman died the next day. The Indians were playing the Series in his memory.

Grimes put a man on base in each inning from the second through the fourth. In the second, it was Larry Gardner, who pulled a double down the left-field line. Gardner was caught in no man's land on Doc Johnston's bouncer to the mound and was tagged out. In the third, after two were out on comebackers to the box, Charlie Jamieson singled to center. In the fourth, player-manager Tris Speaker drew a walk. Both Jamieson and Speaker were left on base.

In the bottom of the third, Grimes helped his own cause by hitting a single to center. Ivy Olson laid down a bunt and on Bagby's wild throw to second, both runners were safe. Grimes was spiked by Sewell on the play as he leapt over Sewell and

went headfirst into the bag. Grimes spent a few minutes trying to walk it off while Al Mamaux warmed up the bullpen. He stayed in the game but limped noticeably throughout. Johnston tried to bunt them over but popped up. Tommy Griffith doubled to right to send in Grimes and make the score 2-0. Wheat was intentionally walked to load the bases. The Indians played the infield in. Myers grounded to Gardner, who threw to the plate. Catcher Steve O'Neill got the force play at home but his throw to first hit Myers in the back. Seeing this, Griffith took off for home, but quick-thinking first baseman Doc Johnston (brother of Jimmy) threw him out at the plate. Cleveland avoided further damage and Brooklyn held a 2-0 lead.

Grimes had a one-two-three inning in the fifth and "Grimes' spitball appeared to have the Indians badly puzzled," wrote the *Plain Dealer*.[5] Brooklyn added its final tally in the bottom of the inning. With Ivy Olson on second, Griffith grounded over the middle. Sewell was in front of it, but the ball caromed off his knee for a single and Olson trotted home to give Brooklyn a 3-0 lead. Sewell was again mentioned for his less-than-stellar fielding. In the sixth, Grimes worked around a Speaker double and held the Indians scoreless again.

In the seventh, Gardner smashed a liner through the box which was knocked down by Pete Kilduff, but he had no play on Gardner. Johnston's grounder forced Gardner at second. Sewell's drive sent Griffith to the wall in right field to haul it in. O'Neill singled, and the tying run came to the plate. Jack Graney, 6-for-13 as a pinch-hitter during the regular season, came up to hit for Bagby but struck out on three pitches.

George Uhle pitched for Cleveland and retired the side in order in the seventh. Grimes showed some fatigue in the eighth, issuing back-to-back walks to Jamieson and pinch-hitter George Burns. Speaker's grounder moved the runners up. Elmer Smith, fifth in the AL with 12 home runs (a far cry from Babe Ruth's league-leading 54), popped out to the catcher. Gardner drew a walk, Grimes' third of the inning. The faithful at Ebbets Field breathed a sigh of relief when Johnston grounded into a force play. Grimes and Brooklyn had survived the threat.

Pinch-hitter Les Nunamaker singled in the ninth inning with two out but Jamieson flied out to Wheat to end the game. Despite seven hits and four walks, Grimes made the pitches when he had to and held on for the complete-game shutout. The Indians had their chances with 10 men left on base. "The Brooklyn pitcher's control was none too good at times," wrote Edwards, "but in the pinches he could make the ball behave perfectly and with flawless support he was able to swing the whitewash brush with effect."[6] Grimes threw 130 pitches in all, 25 in that precarious eighth inning when 14 of them were wide.[7]

SOURCES

Besides the sources cited in the Notes, the author relied on the following:

Baseball-Reference.com

Retrosheet.org

Rice, Thomas S. "The Game in Detail," *Brooklyn Daily Eagle*, October 6, 1920: 1.

NOTES

1   "Crowd at Ebbets Field to Purchase Tickets for Series," *Brooklyn Daily Eagle*, October 4, 1920: 1.

2   "Tribe, Confident, Leaves for Fray," *Cleveland Plain Dealer*, October 5, 1920: 17.

3   Thomas S. Rice, "Superbas Play Better in World Series Than in League," *Brooklyn Daily Eagle*, October 7, 1920: 22.

4   Henry P. Edwards, "Robins' Star Pitcher Holds Indians When They Get Dangerous," *Cleveland Plain Dealer*, October 7, 1920: 20.

5   "Details of Cleveland's Whitewash," *Cleveland Plain Dealer*, October 7, 1920: 20.

6   Edwards, "Robins' Star Pitcher Holds Indians When They Get Dangerous."

7   "Day's Pitching is Analyzed," *Cleveland Plain Dealer*, October 7, 1920: 20.

SHERRY SMITH STYMIES THE CLEVELAND BATS

October 7, 1920

Brooklyn Robins 2, Cleveland Indians 1 | Game Three of the World Series

by Bob LeMoine

A crowd of just over 25,000 filed into Ebbets Field in Brooklyn for Game Three of the 1920 World Series. Others piled onto the rooftops of nearby houses along Bedford Avenue and Montgomery Street.[1] "The fans turned out in droves," wrote the *New York Times*, "and long after the game started thousands were left outside the gates waiting for a chance to elbow through the portals which led to the bleacher and pavilion seats. The aisles of the grandstand were jammed."[2]

The fans were passionate about their hometown Dodgers (or Superbas, Brooklyns, or Robins), champions of the National League, who had tied the best-of-nine series with the American League champion Cleveland Indians the day before. Cleveland's bats had been silenced by the far from dominating yet solidly precise pitching of Burleigh Grimes, who shut out the Indians, 3-0. Cleveland's astounding hitters (a .303 team batting average in the regular season), led by player-manager Tris Speaker, had batted a meager .190 (12-for-63) so far, leaving 10 runners on base in Game Two.

Brooklyn manager Wilbert Robinson's team had played to its strengths. Brooklyn's pitching staff had the best ERA (2.62) and most strikeouts (553) in the NL. Grimes led the way with a 2.22 ERA and 23-11 record. Led by Zack Wheat, Hi Myers, and Ed Konetchy, they could also hit with the best of them.

In Game Three, Sherry Smith (11-9, 1.85 ERA) took the hill for Brooklyn, while Ray Caldwell (20-10, 3.86) was a curious choice of Speaker. Despite a career-high 20 victories, Caldwell's ERA was 4.97 from September on, while the newly reacquired Duster Mails went 7-0 down the stretch. But Caldwell had the experience while Mails was unpredictable, and Speaker went with the experience.

Hank O'Day, Bill Dinneen, Bill Klem, and Tommy Connolly were the umpires for the Series.

Despite walking Bill Wambsganss, Smith threw a scoreless first inning. It was a short day for Caldwell. He walked Ivy Olson "and some of the balls sailed so wide out that [catcher Steve] O'Neill had to jump on the infield carpet," wrote Harry Cross of the *Cleveland Plain Dealer*.[3] Jimmy

Johnston sacrificed Olson to second. Shortstop Joe Sewell was playing in the shadow of the popular Ray Chapman, who had been killed after being hit in the head by a pitch from the Yankees' Carl Mays on August 16. Sewell had struggled so far in the Series, and another "perilous moment," Cross wrote, was upon "the little shortstop who has jumped from the bush league right into the nervous strain of the world's series."[4] Sewell booted a grounder from Tommy Griffith, and Olson made it to third. Wheat singled to left, scoring Olson. Myers looped a hit off the glove of a leaping George Burns at first and Griffith scored. Speaker was impatient and jogged in from center to take out his starter. "Caldwell was a sorry figure as he walked to the bench," Cross wrote. "The greatest chance of his baseball career had come and he had failed." He lasted just one-third of an inning, and in came the lefty Mails, "one of those eccentric left-handers who is chock full of confidence."[5]

Ed Konetchy popped up to second. Pete Kilduff launched a long fly ball in foul ground in "the deepest wildness of right field," where a sprinting Smoky Joe Wood made a nice running catch.[6] The former Red Sox pitching ace had reinvented himself as a dependable utility outfielder for Speaker, his old teammate. Mails had put out the fire in the first.

Smith didn't allow a Cleveland hit through three innings and was the beneficiary of excellent defensive play by right fielder Tommy Griffith. In the second, Larry Gardner lined hard to right, but Griffith nabbed it on the run. Wood smashed one to deep right by the foul line and Griffith again ran it down. Griffith showed why he finished in the top 10 in fielding percentage, assists, putouts, and range factor for right fielders throughout his career. When the inning ended, Griffith ran to the bench amid the cheering fans who acknowledged his defensive prowess.

Mails walked leadoff man Otto Miller to begin the second. When Smith attempted to bunt Miller over, he popped it up and Mails did a whirling dance to snag it and whip a throw to first to double up Miller. Olson singled to center but was caught stealing to end the inning.

Robinson made a curious move in the bottom of the third by lifting defensive guru Griffith to avoid a lefty-lefty matchup with Mails. He sent up right-hander Bernie Neis to pinch-hit. Neis was no slouch defensively either, and had blazing speed. The percentages didn't work this time and Neis grounded out. Mails surrendered a single to Wheat, but nothing further.

Smith benefited from yet another dazzling defensive play. In the fourth, Wambsganss rocketed a shot that third baseman Johnston was unable to spear going to his left. Shortstop Olson backed him up, picking the ball off the outfield grass and nailing the runner with a pinpoint throw. It was even more significant because of what happened next. Speaker launched a drive to left that Zack Wheat got in front of, but the ball took a weird bounce, went through his legs, and rolled into foul territory. Speaker made it all the way around the diamond in what was scored a double and an error on Wheat. The Indians would take it, considering that this was the first hit they managed against Smith.

With one gone in the fifth, Sewell walked. O'Neill singled to center and it looked as if Cleveland finally was getting to Smith. Mails ripped a liner to Olson, who flipped to second baseman Kilduff. Kilduff's relay was wild but Konetchy laid flat out for the ball, keeping one toe on the base, to the roar of the crowd. "Man, sir," exclaimed Thomas S. Rice of the *Brooklyn Daily Eagle*. "That was a heap of a play!"[7] The Dodgers got out of the jam. The crowd was equally appreciative of glovework by the opposition, applauding George Burns of Cleveland. In the sixth, the first baseman chased a foul popup near the box seats and "reached his hand over the heads of a box full of Brooklyn Society folk and nabbed the ball," wrote the *Plain Dealer's* Cross.[8] Myers singled, but Mails was helped by another double play.

The best defensive play of the game may have come in the eighth inning. Mails had done his job for Tris Speaker with 6⅔ scoreless innings of relief and only three hits allowed. With one out and O'Neill at first, Speaker sent pinch-hitter extraordinaire Les Nunamaker to the plate. Nunamaker was a career .391 hitter in that role (36-for-92) but only 3-for-15 in 1920. He sent a sizzling grounder to Johnston at third, who started a perfect double play to Kilduff and "Koney" at first. "There's the flashiest double play that the Dodgers ever executed," someone in the crowd boasted as the multitudes were on their feet roaring yet again.[9] "That play," wrote Rice, "had not only to be without a flaw, but had to be put through without wasting time enough to blink an eye. It is safe to say that not one fan in ten at the diamondside thought Kilduff would get the ball to Koney in time."[10]

George Uhle came out of the bullpen for Cleveland in the bottom of the eighth, just as he had in Game Two. He again pitched a scoreless frame.

Smith retired Cleveland in the ninth on three groundballs and put the finishing touches on a World Series masterpiece. He allowed only one run, which was unearned, and he had forced 18 batters to ground out. So far in the World Series, Cleveland's mighty batting attack had been stymied by Brooklyn pitchers, who had allowed only one earned run. Cleveland now had a two-games-to-one lead in the series. The roar of the crowd at Ebbets Field was matched across the East River at the electronic scoreboard in Times Square, where an estimated 12,000 folks "solidly packed up to Forty-Fourth Street, and jammed both the east and west corners of Broadway."[11]

At 9 o'clock that night, diehard Brooklyn fans turned out at Grand Central Station to send best wishes to their team on its journey to Cleveland. Fans were enthusiastic, believing their Dodgers would bring Brooklyn its first World Series title. "The cheers that answered the toots of the locomotive as it pulled out with the train conveying the Superbas made the spacious station appear to tremble," wrote James J. Murphy in the *Brooklyn Daily Eagle*.[12]

The rest of the World Series would be much different in Cleveland, however, and those screaming fans would get used to uttering the phrase at Ebbets Field, "Wait 'til next year."

SOURCES

Besides the sources listed in the Notes, the author relied on statistical information from Baseball-Reference.com and Retrosheet.org.org.

NOTES

1   Al C. Palma, "Robins Outplay Indians in All Departments of Game," *Brooklyn Citizen*, October 8, 1920: 4.

2   "Robins Win Third Game When Smith Baffles Indians," *New York Times*, October 8, 1920: 1.

3   Harry Cross, "Brooklyn Drives Ray Caldwell from Box; Wins in First Inning," *Cleveland Plain Dealer*, October 8, 1920: 19.

4   "Brooklyn Drives Ray Caldwell from Box; Wins in First Inning."

5   "Brooklyn Drives Ray Caldwell from Box; Wins in First Inning."

6   "Brooklyn Drives Ray Caldwell from Box; Wins in First Inning."

7   Thomas S. Rice, "Superbas Rule Favorites as They Speed to Cleveland," *Brooklyn Daily Eagle*, October 8, 1920: 24.

8   "Brooklyn Drives Ray Caldwell from Box; Wins in First Inning."

9   "Brooklyn Drives Ray Caldwell from Box; Wins in First Inning."

10 "Superbas Rule Favorites as They Speed to Cleveland."

11 "12,000 Watch Scoreboard," *New York Times*, October 8, 1920: 15.

12 James J. Murphy, "Will Be Back with the Title, Say Superbas Traveling West," *Brooklyn Daily Eagle*, October 8, 1920: 1.

Pittsburgh's Dave Robertson "runs gamut of hits" as first player to hit for the cycle at Ebbets Field

August 30, 1921

Pittsburgh Pirates 8, Brooklyn Dodgers 2

by Mike Huber

With a little more than a month left in the 1921 regular season, the Pittsburgh Pirates "were determined to break the sustained slump which has threatened their possession of first place."[1] Before a three-game series with the Brooklyn Robins, the Pirates had lost six straight games and had seen their lead over the New York Giants shrink to 2½ games. Brooklyn had lost six of nine games before the Pirates arrived, sinking into fifth place in the National League standings.

The two teams split the first two games of the series. The third and final game took place at Ebbets Field on a Tuesday afternoon before a crowd of 5,000 fans who "sweltered in weather that sent the mercury soaring skyward."[2] To break up the tension that might have been keeping his team from playing what he considered their normal game, Pirates manager George Gibson "tried a new experiment which turned the batting practice into a burlesque."[3] Instead of the usual batting practice, the infielders pitched to the batters and each pitcher "took a few turns with the stick."[4]

A pair of right-handers started the game. Whitey Glazner "did mound duty for the Buccaneers,"[5] opposed by Brooklyn's Leon Cadore. Glazner, in just his first full season in the majors, was making his sixth appearance against Brooklyn, sporting a 1-1 record against the Robins. Cadore was likewise making his sixth appearance against Pittsburgh, with a 3-2 mark.

Pittsburgh threatened in the first frame, as both Max Carey and Rabbit Maranville singled. With two outs and Dave Robertson batting, the Pirates tried a double steal, and Carey was caught stealing third for the third out. Ivy Olson and Tommy Griffith had singles for Brooklyn in their turn at bat, but Olson was caught stealing and the Robins went away empty-handed.

Two innings later, Pittsburgh's Carson Bigbee bunted his way to first and advance to third on two groundouts. George Cutshaw then "pasted the ball through deep left"[6] for a triple, driving in Bigbee. Robertson then sent an "over-the-garden wall wallop"[7] over the wall in right-center for a two-run homer. Clyde Barnhart doubled on a ball hit to the fence in right field. Charlie Grimm brought him home with a single up the middle. By the time Cadore retired Walter Schmidt for the third out, the Pirates had a team cycle, garnering a homer, triple, double, and two singles and four runs. Brooklyn manager Wilbert Robinson lifted Cadore for a pinch-hitter in the bottom of the third, and Johnny Miljus replaced him on the mound.

In the fifth, Robertson stroked a two-out double "on a fast sprint which beat [Hy] Myers' throw."[8] He scored when Barnhart singled. The score was now 5-0. In the home half, walks to Ray Schmandt and Ernie Krueger put two men on with one out. Robinson sent Bernie Neis to pinch-hit for Miljus, but he grounded into a double play.

Sherry Smith, who started his career as a Pirate, became the third Robins pitcher. Smith "was on the hill three frames and received a drubbing."[9] In the sixth, Carey reached on an error when Zack Wheat dropped Carey's liner to left. With Maranville batting, Smith "caught Carey balanced toward second and nailed him off first."[10]

In the top of the seventh, the Pirates got to Smith. Cutshaw hit a one-out single, which second baseman Pete Kilduff knocked down with his bare hand. Robertson singled, as did Barnhart, whose hit drove in Cutshaw. After Grimm forced Robertson at third, Schmidt singled, plating Barnhart. Pittsburgh had extended its lead to 7-0.

Meanwhile, Glazner was in top form. After yielding two singles to the Robins in the first frame, he kept them hitless until the seventh, when Wheat led off the inning with a single to center, a Texas Leaguer over second base. Myers also singled, sending Wheat to third. An out later, Kilduff sent a grounder to Barnhart at third, who forced Myers at second, but Wheat scored Brooklyn's first run.

In the top of the eighth, Cutshaw singled with two down. Robertson then sent Smith's offering to the gap in right-center and legged out a triple, driving in Cutshaw. The three-bagger gave Robertson a "gamut of hits,"[11] as he became the first player to hit a single, double, triple, and home run in the same game at Ebbets Field.

Dutch Ruether became Brooklyn's third pinch-hitter of the game when he batted for Smith in the bottom of the eighth. But he and the Robins went quietly, three up and three down. The Robins made one last offensive attempt in the bottom of the ninth. Wheat singled to right with one out. Myers singled to center. On the next play, Wheat was forced at third for the second out. Kilduff sent a single into left for his second run batted in of the game, as Myers scored, but that was all the Robins could muster against Glazner. Pittsburgh won, 8-2.

The first-place Pirates "played like pennant winners against the Robins at Ebbets Field."[12] With his 4-for-5 performance at the plate, Robertson "led in this savage attack on Uncle Wilbert's four flingers."[13] His batting average rose 17 points to .358, and his slugging percentage jumped 54 points to .577 since his arrival on the Pirates. In addition to Robertson's hitting, Cutshaw had a triple and two singles, while Barnhart added a double and two singles. Every Pittsburgh position player had at least one hit. In total, the Pirates banged out 16 base hits. Glazner allowed two runs on just seven hits, all singles, proving to be "a puzzle to the Dodgers all the way."[14]

Interestingly, the *Brooklyn Daily Eagle* reported to its readers that "not one of the four Brooklyn pitchers lasted long enough to get to bat."[15]

On this day, Robertson was the offensive star for the struggling Pittsburgh team. Oddly enough, he had started the 1921 season with the Chicago Cubs. The Cubs traded Robertson to the Pirates on July 1 for Elmer Ponder, a relief pitcher who had made only eight appearances for Pittsburgh, gaining a 2-0 record with a 2.19 earned-run average. The Cubs made Ponder a starter, but he didn't fare well in the season's second half, going 3-6 with a 4.74 ERA in 16 games. As for Robertson, he played in 22 games for the Cubs before the trade, batting only .222 with eight hits (five singles and three doubles). The Pirates gave him a chance to play every day, and he paid them back with a .322 batting average, 6 home runs and 48 runs batted in.

Although the Pirates played .600 baseball in August (18-12), they struggled down the stretch, finishing the season by winning only 12 of 28 games (with a tie) in September/October. They dropped to second place in the pennant race on September 9, never to return to first. Robertson's crew finished four games behind the New York Giants, who went on to defeat the New York Yankees in an eight-game World Series. The Brooklyn Robins won 12 of their final 25 games and never rose out of fifth place in the standings.

Ebbets Field opened in 1913, and Robertson became the first major leaguer to hit for the cycle at the iconic ballpark. The first Brooklyn player to cycle at Ebbets Field was Babe Herman, who did so on May 18, 1931, against the Cincinnati Reds.

Robertson's accomplishment was the sixth by a Pittsburgh player in franchise history,[16] coming nine seasons after Honus Wagner's cycle on August 22, 1912. Robertson was also the fourth player to hit for the cycle in 1921, following the New York Yankees' Bob Meusel (May 7 against the Washington Senators), the New York Giants' Dave Bancroft (June 1 against the Philadelphia Phillies), and the St. Louis Browns' George Sisler (August 13 against the Detroit Tigers).

SOURCES

In addition to the sources mentioned in the Notes, the author consulted Baseball-Reference.com, MLB.com, Retrosheet.org.org and SABR.org.

https://www.Retrosheet.org.org/boxesetc/1921/B08300BRO1921.htm

https://www.Baseball-Reference.com/boxes/BRO/BRO192108300.shtml

NOTES

1   Charles J. Doyle, "Pirates Win Slugfest from Dodgers, 8-2," *Pittsburgh Post-Gazette*, August 31, 1921: 9.

2   Edward F. Balinger, "Robertson's Bat Helps Glazner Win in Eastern Finale," *Pittsburgh Daily Post*, August 31, 1921: 9.

3   Balinger.

4   Balinger.

5   "Pirates Vent Ire on Dodger Hurlers," *New York Times*, August 31, 1921: 9.

6   "Pirates Close Eastern Trip with Victory," *Pittsburgh Press*, August 31, 1921: 20.

7   Doyle.

8   "Pirate Game in Detail," *Pittsburgh Post-Gazette*, August 31, 1921: 9.

9   Balinger.

10 "Robertson Runs Gamut of Hits as Pirates Take Last Game," *Brooklyn Daily Eagle*, August 31, 1921: 20.

11 "Robertson Runs Gamut of Hits as Pirates Take Last Game."

12 "Pirates Vent Ire on Dodger Hurlers."

13 "Pirates Vent Ire on Dodger Hurlers."

14 Doyle.

15 "Robertson Runs Gamut of Hits as Pirates Take Last Game."

16 The first five cycles in Pittsburgh history were accomplished by Fred Carroll (May 2, 1887), Fred Clarke (July 23, 1901, and May 7, 1903), Chief Wilson (July 3, 1910), and Honus Wagner (August 22, 1912).

BIGBEE'S BIG DAY BUSTED BY BOOTS

June 21, 1922

Brooklyn Robins 15, Pittsburgh Pirates 14 (10 innings)

by Ken Carrano

It takes a great deal of effort to secure 25 hits in a baseball game and manage to lose it. In the case of the Pittsburgh Pirates in their game in Brooklyn on the damp afternoon of June 21, 1922, it was a poor defensive effort that contributed to their demise at the hands of the Robins, who managed "only" 19 hits, blew three separate leads, and gave up eight runs in the final three innings, and still secured the victory. According to Edward Balinger of the *Pittsburgh Post*, "It was more like taffy pulling (than baseball). Each side seemed to vie with the other to see which could gum up the most plays."[1]

The Pirates started Hal Carlson to face the Robins on this day. Carlson's last start did not instill confidence in manager George Gibson: He had surrendered seven runs in 3⅓ innings across town at the Polo Grounds against the New York Giants. Robins skipper Wilbert Robinson chose Leon Cadore to face the Pirates. Cadore had lost his last start as well, a 4-2 10-inning loss on June 15 to the St. Louis Cardinals. Cadore, best known for pitching 26 innings on May 1, 1920, against the Boston Braves, had a 4.98 ERA entering the game. The game on this day would not help that statistic.[2]

The Pirates got to Cadore for a run in the first inning with singles by Rabbit Maranville, Carson Bigbee, and Clyde Barnhart scoring Maranville for a lead that lasted a half-inning. In the Robins' first, singles by Jimmy Johnston, Zack Wheat, Hi Myers, and Clarence Mitchell gave the Robins a 2-1 lead, which was also short-lived. In the second inning, three singles and a double by Bigbee gave the Pirates a 4-2 lead. Bigbee was in the middle of what was perhaps his best major-league season; he entered the game hitting .359 and had hit safely in 14 of his last 17 games.[3]

In the Robins' second, Carlson, perhaps undone due to a trip around the basepaths in the top half of the inning, allowed a double to Hank DeBerry and walked Cadore. Gibson brought in Johnny Morrison to replace Carlson. Andy High greeted Morrison with a bunt that he beat out when Barnhart fell trying to field it, loading the bases. Johnston's fielder's choice scored DeBerry, and Tommy Griffith tied the game with a slow single to short that Pie Traynor threw away,

Cadore scoring. Wheat's groundout scored Johnston, giving Brooklyn back the lead at 5-4.

Cadore started his next inning after scoring in the same manner as Carlson, allowing a double to Traynor and a walk to Ray Rohwer, but he got out of the inning unscathed. The Robins continued to score in the third. Mitchell led off the frame with a single, DeBerry tripled Mitchell home, and Cadore's single scored DeBerry to jump the Robins' advantage to 7-4.

Robinson's men would be excused for thinking that they were in good shape for a victory – Cadore threw the first one-two-three inning of the game in the top of the fourth, and the team increased its lead in the bottom half. Griffith led off the inning with a single but was forced at second on Wheat's grounder. Then came consecutive singles by Myers, Mitchell, and Ivy Olson and a 9-4 advantage. Cadore's streak of five consecutive outs was shattered in the top of the fifth with consecutive singles by Bigbee (hit number three) and Barnhart. Traynor popped to second, but Rohwer walked to load the bases. Charlie Grimm's sacrifice fly scored Bigbee and Johnny Gooch's single scored Barnhart, and the Pirates had trimmed their deficit to 9-6. Gibson brought in Earl Hamilton to keep the Bucs in the game and he gave the Pirates their first one-two-three inning in the bottom of the fifth.

If the fielding gods had been holding things together to that point, they started to falter in the sixth. Hall fumbled a groundball off Maranville's bat to start the sixth, but Cadore was able to pitch around that. Hamilton was not as lucky. Wheat walked with one out and moved to second when Traynor fumbled Myers' grounder. After Mitchell's popup, Olson singled to plate Wheat and push the Robins' lead back to 10-6. Traynor made his second error of the inning (and third of the game) when he dropped DeBerry's grounder to load the bases, but was able to handle Cadore's bouncer to force DeBerry and end the inning.

The seventh inning was the only one of the game in which neither team scored, but any boredom felt by the estimated 3,500 spectators after that was abated by what followed. Cadore retired the first two hitters on groundouts, but Max Carey's single and Bigbee's fourth hit of the game, a double to right, put two runners in scoring position, and Barnhart's single put two runs across the plate and Cadore in the dugout. Uncle Robbie brought in Al Mamaux to preserve the lead, but his stay was short: He allowed singles to Traynor and Rohwer that scored Barnhart. Robbie then tried to end the rally with Sherry Smith, but Smith allowed a game-tying single to Grimm, it was 10-10, and the Pirates had back. Chief Yellow Horse was able to keep the Robins at bay in the bottom of the eighth, and so the chaos would continue.

Smith's ninth inning started innocently enough. He retired the first two Pirates, but Carey singled, Bigbee tripled (hit number 5), Barnhart singled, and the Pirates had their first lead since the second inning, 12-10. It could have been worse, but Barnhart was thrown out at third trying to advance on Traynor's single. Robinson's men, now needing two to tie the game, started strongly with Bert Griffith's pinch-hit double off Chief Yellow Horse, but he was thrown out trying to go to third on Dutch Ruether's bunt. Johnson's single put the tying runs on and Yellow Horse on the bench, as Gibson brought in the veteran Babe Adams to save the game. Adams could not, allowing a double to Tommy Griffith that scored Bernie Neis, running for Ruether, then intentionally walked Wheat to load the bases. The strategy nearly worked, but Myers' fly ball sent Johnston home to tie the game again and send it to extra innings.

Robinson brought in Burleigh Grimes to slow the resurgent Pirate bats, but Rohwer had other ideas, launching a shot to right, the only home run of the game, to give the lead back to the Pirates. Grimes gave the Pirates an insurance run when his wild pitch allowed Gooch, who had singled and moved to third on an Adams single and Maranville groundout, to score. In the bottom of the inning, Adams had a chance to close out the game that Yellow Horse couldn't an inning earlier, but by now the fielding gods had completely given up. Olson launched a long fly to right that Rohwer had in his glove, but the force of hitting the wall dislodged the ball and Olson got to second. Otto Miller then reached on an error by third baseman Barnhart, with Olsen staying at second. Grimes, the next batter, bunted. Adams tried to force Olson at third. His throw instead evaded Barnhart and went down the third-base line. Bigbee retrieved the ball and tried to throw out Miller, but his throw was cut off by Adams, whose relay to Gooch instead found the Brooklyn dugout and the game was tied again. Grimes, who had continued his run down the first-base line unaware of what was happening, was awarded third. Consecutive walks to Hal Janvrin and Johnston set up a force at any base, but Tommy Griffith found the outfield with a long fly to Rohwer, who had no chance to throw out Grimes.

The win elevated the Robins to third place ahead of the Pirates, who perhaps traveled back to Pittsburgh contemplating what could have been a great come-from-behind victory. Instead, the Robins had secured one of the wilder games of 1922.

SOURCES

In addition to the sources listed in the Notes, the author accessed Retrosheet.org and Baseball-Reference.com, as well as the Brooklyn Daily Eagle, the Pittsburgh Gazette, and the Pittsburgh Post at newspapers.com

NOTES

1   Edward F. Balinger, "Bucs Lose to Dodgers in Weird Game, 15-14, Drop to Fourth Place," *Pittsburgh Post*, June 22, 1922: 10.

2   Cadore was 42-40 with a 2.99 ERA during the 1919-1921 seasons but entering this game his record sat at just 2-4 with an ERA of 4.98.

3   Bigbee would be known better for his scoring the winning run in the 1925 World Series for the Pirates, and for being the first player to have 11 at-bats in one major-league game. The second time a batter had 11 at-bats in a game was in the game Cadore threw on May 1, 1920.

A Rube awakening: Brooklyn bats bombard Boston's Marquard

July 2, 1925

Brooklyn Robins 20, Boston Braves 7

by Mark S. Sternman

Good-looking matchups on paper sometimes fail to deliver anywhere close to anticipated results. Two pitchers who would wind up among baseball's immortals squared off in an early summer game. One would hurl a complete-game win, while the other would fail to retire a single batter.

Burleigh Grimes and Rube Marquard had faced each other in Brooklyn earlier in the 1925 season. On April 26 Marquard had blanked Boston for eight innings in a 3-0 win. Ten weeks later, a far different game unfolded.

In the top of the first, the Braves could not touch Grimes and his signature grandfathered spitter.[1] While two Braves reached via walks and one advanced on a wild pitch, Grimes escaped unscathed.

In sharp contrast, Marquard was bombarded, although he could have sued William Marriott for nonsupport. Leadoff hitter Dick Cox reached on third baseman Marriott's throwing error. Milt Stock singled. Zack Wheat, the biggest name in the batting order for either team, grounded to Marriott, who booted it to load the bases. Could this have constituted the key play of the

game? Had Marriott got one out (or two), might the veteran Marquard have settled down into a groove?

More than a century after this baseball game, these questions recall an anecdote told by a columnist after the 1940 NFL championship game: "Wide open on the Bears' 4-yard line, Charley Malone dropped a Sammy Baugh pass. Some folks would fantasize that had Malone scored to tie the game at 7 it would have been a different kind of contest. 'Yes,' Baugh was reported to have commented, 'it would have been 73-7 instead of 73-0.'"[2]

Marquard faced three more batters and yielded a trio of singles. The first, by Jack Fournier, "was the longest ever made at Ebbets Field. It hit the wall near the exit gate in right center. The way [Bernie] Neis went after the ball bluffed Wheat into thinking he was going to catch it. [Wheat] hugged first and then moved to second when the ball caromed off the wall."[3]

Since Marquard could not get anyone out, this lucky break failed to help him. Marquard left trailing 4-0 with two men on base. "Bill Vargus, a fledgling left-hander from Boston College, followed the veteran southpaw to the box," the *New York Times* reported. "It developed that among the things not included in the curriculum at old B.C. is a course in how to pitch to big league batters."[4]

Vargus got the first out of the day for the Braves via a fly ball that extended the Robins' lead to 5-0. Zack Taylor hit a foul pop, but his opposite number, backstop Mickey O'Neil, dropped the ball for the third Boston error of the inning. Given new life, Taylor squibbed a ball for a single that Vargus threw away for the fourth error of the frame. A lifetime .248 hitter who batted over .300 twice, Grimes hit an RBI single to give Brooklyn a 6-0 lead. After a groundout, the Robins hit four consecutive singles to get into double figures and close the first with a 10-0 lead. "If one of those much-advertised California earthquakes were to do its stuff in Flatbush, pick up the 101st Cavalry Army, a few blocks away from the ball park, and set it down in center field, it could not have loomed up much larger than that gigantic, 10-run half inning,"[5] which featured 10 hits, four errors, and two men left on base. The competitive portion of the game had seemingly ended after the initial inning.

The Braves scored a run in the sixth on two singles, a grounder, and a fly ball. Facing Vargus for the final time, Brooklyn put up five in response in the bottom of the sixth. Oscar Siemer, who had replaced catcher O'Neil in the second (suggesting that Boston player-manager Dave Bancroft[6] blamed both halves of his battery for the first-inning malfunctions), mimicked his predecessor by likewise committing an error, although this one took place on a throw from Neis to the plate as Cox scored to put Brooklyn up 11-1. Cox scored from second base on a single, illustrating that the Robins sought to score as many runs as possible. Had Siemer made the play, Taylor would not have hit in the sixth with two on and two out. Since Siemer did not hold onto the ball,

Taylor got to hit and tripled in two runs to put Brooklyn up 15-1.

Jimmy Welsh homered in the seventh to make the score 15-2. Against Boston's Foster Edwards, Fournier hit a sacrifice fly to plate Cox in the bottom of the frame as the Robins restored a 14-run bulge at 16-2.

Brooklyn piled on in the bottom of the eighth against the ineffective Edwards. With one out, Hod Ford walked, Taylor singled and Grimes reached on an error by shortstop Bob Smith (the sixth miscue by the Braves) to load the bases. Cox hit a sacrifice fly for one run, Wheat doubled in a pair, and Fournier singled in one more. It was 20-2.

Fans of defensive indifference would have really enjoyed the top of the ninth. Doubtless relaxing, Grimes gave up five hits. Having played errorless baseball to that point, the Robins made two errors. Boston also took six extra bases on indifference before the game mercifully ended with the gridiron-like score of 20-7.

All nine Brooklynites scored and drove in runs. Only Ford failed to have a hit. With a career-high seven RBIs, Fournier had the most impressive box-score line, 5-2-4-7, but many Robins had prime days at the dish, including Cox, who also set a career high with four runs scored. Brooklyn went an impressive 14-for-22 with runners in scoring position.

Marquard completed his Hall of Fame career in 1925. He never won another game in the majors and made his next and final start on August 29. (He gave up six runs and lost.) Marquard pitched his second-to-last game in relief at Ebbets Field on September 6 in the second game of a doubleheader. He gave up a run in an inning. Marquard had fonder Brooklyn memories as a member of the 1916 and 1920 NL champion Robins, but on July 2, 1925, Brooklyn showed that he could no longer effectively pitch against big-league hitters.

SOURCES

In addition to the sources cited in the Notes, the author accessed Retrosheet.org, Baseball-Reference.com, SABR.org, and *The Sporting News* archive via Paper of Record.

NOTES

1   After the 1920 spitball ban, Grimes was one of 17 pitchers allowed to keep throwing it until retirement.

2   Shirley Povich, "In Football History, 73-0 a Score of Infamy," *Washington Post*, December 7, 1990.

3   "The Boston Massacre," *Boston Globe*, July 3, 1925: 9.

4   M.W. Corum, "20 Robin Markers Heaped on Braves," *New York Times*, July 3, 1925: 9.

5   Thomas Holmes, "Robins Mistreat Braves in Unrestrained Biffing Orgy, Garnering 22 Hits," *Brooklyn Eagle*, July 3, 1925: 16.

6   Bancroft, the best player on the below-average Boston team, missed this game after fouling a ball off his foot the previous day. "Dodgers' First Nets 10 Runs," *Boston Globe*, July 3, 1925: 9.

VANCE TIES NL RECORD WITH 17 STRIKEOUTS AND KNOCKS IN GAME-WINNER IN 10TH

July 20, 1925
Brooklyn Robins 4, St. Louis Cardinals 3

by Gregory H. Wolf

Hard-throwing Dazzy Vance was in agony. Brooklyn sportswriter Thomas W. Meany reported that Vance suffered from serious inflammation in his right shoulder caused by warming up too quickly six days earlier against the Pittsburgh Pirates.[1] According to Robins beat reporter Thomas S. Rice, Vance's right arm was "blue from the rupturing of a blood vessel," which gave rise to rumors that the reigning National League MVP might be lost for an extended period.[2] Shrugging off the stinging pain, Vance surprisingly took the mound and "reached the very pinnacle of his brilliant career," gushed the *Brooklyn Standard Union*, in a heroic performance that "approache[d] closely the limit of human achievement."[3]

Vance's courageous hurling occurred at an opportune time for the Robins, who were one of the majors' biggest disappointments this far in the 1925 season. Following their surprise second-place finish in 1924, the Robins had got out to a fast start in '25, but had since lost 24 of their last 39 games to fall to 42-43, though they occupied fourth place. The rubber match of a three-game series against the St. Louis Cardinals as part of

a 21-game homestand also marked the return to the dugout of beloved skipper Wilbert Robinson, the club's namesake. According to the *Brooklyn Eagle*, the 61-year-old manager had turned over the day-to-day "management" of the team to star player Zack Wheat in mid-June and spent most of his time in the press box.[4] "[I returned] merely to cheer up the team," said Uncle Robbie. "We have had darned hard luck."[5]

Robinson called on his ailing ace to get the team back to .500. A 34-year-old pitching marvel, Vance laid claim as the NL's best hurler. After cups of coffee in 1915 and 1918, Vance caught on with the Robins in 1922 and had posted a 64-33 slate in his first three seasons with the club. In 1924, he won the pitching Triple Crown, leading the league with 28 wins, a 2.16 ERA, and 262 strikeouts, the third of seven consecutive seasons in which he led the NL in punchouts. He was 12-6 and paced the majors with 120 strikeouts thus far in '25, but had been pummeled in his last start, yielding 11 hits and eight runs (six earned) in just four innings in a loss to the Pirates. More troubling was Vance's aching right shoulder. Should Vance not be able to pitch after warming up, reported the *Standard Union*, swingman Tiny Osborne would take his place.[6]

On a warm, 80-degree Tuesday afternoon, 3,500 spectators were on hand at Ebbets Field for the 3:30 start time against the St. Louis Cardinals.[7] A half-game behind the Robins, the fifth-place Redbirds (42-44) had taken the first two games of the series.

Looking wobbly as the game commenced, Vance walked the first two batters. It was an ideal situation for the league's most potent one-two punch, Rogers Hornsby, batting .413 and slugging .777, and Jim Bottomley, who checked in at .374 and .623. The Rajah, who had taken over for Branch Rickey as manger just a month earlier, fanned swinging, then Sunny Jim looked at a called strike. Vance dispatched Chick Hafey on an outfield fly to end the threat.

Toeing the rubber for the Cardinals was 30-year-old journeyman southpaw Duster Mails. Back in the majors after a two-year stint winning 47 combined games for Oakland Oaks in the Pacific Coast League, Mails had pitched briefly for the Robins in 1915 and 1916. Just three days earlier, Mails had tossed a four-hitter to beat the New York Giants, even his record at 2-2, and improve his career slate to 27-19. After leadoff hitter Hod Ford walked, Milt Stock reached base on Mails' throwing error to second base. Wheat grounded into a 5-3 double play and Jack Fournier popped up to kill the rally.

Vance had fanned two batters in each of the first three innings but got into another jam in the fourth. Bottomley and Hafey connected for consecutive singles to short right field with no outs. After Specs Toporcer bunted the runners over, Les Bell drove them in on a single to center. Vance seemed to be on the ropes, but got some help from his batterymate, Hank DeBerry, who threw out Bell attempting to steal before Bob O'Farrell walked. Mails fanned looking for the third out.

Eddie Brown led off the fifth with the Robins' second hit of the game. After Brown was forced by DeBerry's one-out grounder, weak-hitting Vance (5 hits in 58 at-bats) pounded a home run into deep left field to tie the game, 2-2.

In an exciting pitchers' duel, both pitchers mowed down their opponents. "[Mails'] curve and change of pace were corkers and he had all the speed," opined Rice.[8]

Vance continued to pile up the strikeouts, the product of "uncanny pitching, which came as a result of tremendous speed and a lightning curve," St. Louis sportswriter Martin J. Haley wrote admiringly.[9] Vance fanned two in the seventh, then struck out the side in the eighth, pushing his total to 14, while also yielding hits to Max Flack and Hornsby. Vance mesmerized the high-powered Redbirds with a "bewildering assortment of hooks and benders in addition to his 'sway-back' fast ball," exclaimed Meany.[10]

A brouhaha erupted in the eighth after Vance led off with a single and was forced by Ford. Former Cardinal Milt Stock doubled down the left-field line. Just as Ford rounded third, Hafey fumbled the ball, according to Haley.[11] Hafey whipped the ball to Toporcer at short, who threw home. Catcher Bob O'Farrell courageously "threw down his hand to meet the crushing spikes" of Ford, wrote Cardinals beat reporter J. Roy Stockton.[12] "O'Farrell had the ball before Ford started his final desperate leap," opined Stockton, but umpire Peter McLaughlin called Ford safe.[13] The Cardinals erupted in protest, but to no avail. "[T]he decision at the plate looked very bad," admitted Rice,[14] while Robinson supposedly told Hornsby the same thing after the game.[15]

The Cardinals tied the game in the top of the ninth on Toporcer's leadoff triple and Bell's single. After Mails executed a two-out sacrifice bunt, Vance intentionally walked Max Flack, who had already collected two hits and drawn a free pass. That strategy worked when Ralph Shinners popped up to second.

The game went into extra innings when Mails set down the Robins one-two-three in the ninth.

Vance began the 10th by fanning Hornsby and Bottomley for the third time each to increase his strikeout total to 17. Hafey gave the Redbirds a glimmer of hope by singling and stealing second. Unperturbed by baserunners, Vance repeated the same strategy from an inning earlier and walked Toporcer on Robinson's order, despite bringing the more dangerous hitter Bell to the plate. Bell, who had knocked in all three Cardinals runs, popped up to second baseman Stock.

DeBerry led off the bottom of the 10th with a double and was replaced by pinch-runner Johnny Mitchell. After two unsuccessful attempts to execute a sacrifice bunt, Vance connected for his third hit of the game, a solid single to center that easily drove in Mitchell for the winning run, ending the game in 2 hours and 10 minutes.

Newspapers around the country raved about Vance's strikeout total. He punched out a batter in every inning and two in an inning five times, including fanning the side in the eighth. Of his 17 strikeouts, 6 were looking and 11 swinging.[16] Vance fanned every Cardinals starter except the bespectacled Toporcer, who "sees as through a pair of glasses, darkly," quipped sportswriter James M. Gould.[17] Vance permitted 15 baserunners, including nine hits. By contrast, Mails allowed nine baserunners, including one walk.

Vance's 17 strikeouts equaled the mark set by the Chicago Cubs' Jack Pfiester in a 15-inning complete-game loss, 4-2, to the Cardinals in the first game of a doubleheader on May 30, 1906. Charles Sweeney of the NL Providence Grays fanned 19 in 1884 when the distance from the front of pitcher's box to home plate was 50 feet. Jack Coombs of the Philadelphia Athletics held the modern record. He fanned 18 twice: on September 1, 1906 in a 24-inning, 4-1 complete-game victory against the Boston Americans and then in a 16-inning 0-0 tie with Big Ed Walsh and the Chicago White Sox on August 4, 1910. The Cardinals' Dizzy Dean matched Vance's record in a nine-inning, 8-2 complete-game victory in the first game of a doubleheader over the Cubs on July 30, 1933. Pfiester, Vance, and Dean co-owned the NL record until the Boston Braves' Warren Spahn punched out 18 in a 15-inning complete-game loss to the Cubs on June 14, 1952.

Vance's dominance was even more impressive given the context of pitching in his era. In 1925 big-league teams averaged only 2.8 strikeouts per game compared with 8.9 in 2019. For the entire 1925 season, a pitcher recorded 10 or more strikeouts in game only 10 times (including once in the World Series), and more than 10 only twice. Vance recorded four of those games. The first three came in three consecutive starts in May when he whiffed 10, 10, and 13.

Vance finished the season as the NL leader in wins (22) and strikeouts (221) while the Robins slumped to sixth place (68-85).

SOURCES

In addition to the sources cited in the Notes, the author accessed Retrosheet.org, Baseball-Reference.com, SABR.org, and *The Sporting News* archive via Paper of Record.

NOTES

1   Thomas W. Meany, "Vance's Strikeout Records, Under Present Pitching Rules, Remarkable," *Brooklyn Times*, July 21, 1925: 14.

2   Thomas S. Rice, "Vance Whiffing of 17 in 10 Innings Best Stunt in Modern Times," *Brooklyn Eagle*, July 21, 1925: 2A.

3   "'Dazzy' Vance Reaches Pinnacle in Career in Striking Out Seventeen," *Brooklyn Standard Union*, July 21, 1925: 14.

4   Thomas S. Rice, "Uncle Robbie Goes Back to Bench and Will Shake Up Batting Order," *Brooklyn Eagle*, July 20, 1925: 2A.

5   "Uncle Robbie Goes Back to Bench and Will Shake Up Batting Order."

6   "Southpaw Twirling Again Proves Puzzle to Robins – Lose Third Straight," *Brooklyn Standard Union*, July 20, 1925: 10.

7   "The Weather," *Brooklyn Standard Union*, July 21, 1925: 18.

8   Thomas S. Rice, "Vance Whiffing of 17 in 10 Innings Best Stunt in Modern Times."

9   Martin J. Haley, "Vance Whiffs 17 Cardinals as Robins Take 10-Inning Game, 4-3," *St. Louis Globe-Democrat*, July 21, 1925: 11.

10 Meany.

11 Haley.

12 J. Roy Stockton, "Vance Fans 17, Drives In 3 Out of 4 Runs to Beat Cardinals," *St. Louis Post-Dispatch*, July 21, 1925: 9.

13 Stockton.

14 Thomas S. Rice, "Vance Whiffing of 17 in 10 Innings Best Stunt in Modern Times."

15 Stockton.

16 Haley.

17 James M. Gould, "Rogers Hornsby and Bottomley Strike Out Three Times," *St. Louis Star and Times*, July 21, 1925: 10.

Dazzy Vance tosses first no-no in Ebbets Field history and extends hitless streak to 17 $^1\!/_3$ innings

September 13, 1925

Brooklyn Robins 10, Philadelphia Phillies 1 | First Game of Doubleheader

by Gregory H. Wolf

The Brooklyn Robins were winding down a disappointing season. Widely considered to be a challenger for the NL pennant in 1925, owing to its strong second-place (92-62) finish the year before, the club had "slumped badly," opined the *Brooklyn Eagle*.[1] Skipper Wilbert Robinson's squad (65-68) was in fourth place, 17½ games behind the Pittsburgh Pirates. The pitching staff was expected to be its strength, but it had under-performed, and would finish the season with the league's second highest ERA (4.77), more than a run worse than the previous campaign. The exception to the club's dismal performances was Dazzy Vance, whom Robinson called his "only consistent winner we have had this season."[2]

Vance laid claim to being the big leagues' best and most overpowering pitcher. After several cups of coffee in the 1910s, the 6-foot-2, 200-pound right-hander finally caught on as a 31-year-old with the Robins in 1922 by "propel[ling] baseball's fastest ball," cooed Brooklyn's *Times Union*.[3] Two

years later he won a major-league-most 28 games, led baseball with a 2.16 ERA, and was named the National League MVP. Described by the *Eagle* as the "master of the cyclonic delivery and deceptive curvist," Vance also captured his third straight strikeout crown, fanning 262, the most in the NL since Christy Mathewson's 267 in 1903.[4] With less than three weeks to go in the 1925 regular season, Vance once again sat atop the NL leader-boards with 21 wins and 204 strikeouts.

Vance took the mound against the tail-end Philadelphia Phillies (58-77) in the opener of a Sunday doubleheader, which had been originally schedule on Labor Day Monday, but was postponed by inclement weather. As the crowd estimated at 20,000 at Ebbets Field settled into their seats, Vance walked the first batter he faced, Heinie Sand. Two quick punchouts followed and a tapper to the hill ended the frame.

The Robins attacked the Phillies' starter, 34-year-old journeyman spitballer Clarence

Mitchell, who entered the game with a 10-15 slate and was 69-83 in parts of 11 seasons. Johnny Mitchell doubled to right, moved to third on a passed ball, and scored on Milt Stock's single. After Jimmy Johnston tripled to drive in Stock, Philadelphia skipper Art Fletcher pulled Mitchell and sent in Art Decatur, whom the Robins knew well. He had been their swingman in the previous three seasons until his trade to the Phillies in late April. Dick Cox doubled to make it 3-0 with no outs. Two batters later, Cox scored on Charlie Hargreaves' groundout.

The first-inning offensive outburst provided more than enough runs for the Robins on this fateful day, but Uncle Robbie's men kept pounding the tater. In the fifth, they victimized Decatur for four more runs on five hits. Stock's single drove in two and Johnston's single accounted for another. After Dick Cox's single put runners on first and third, Johnston tallied the fourth run on a daring delayed double steal, swiping home under the tag of Jimmie Wilson. The Johnston and Stock tag-team continued in the sixth. Stock drew a walk off the Phillies third and final hurler, Huck Betts, and subsequently scored on Johnston's single for the Robins' ninth run. In the seventh Hank DeBerry's sacrifice fly to plate Hargreaves accounted for the team's 10th and final run.

Notwithstanding Brooklyn's bashing, this game was about Vance, who had come close to throwing no-hitters in two of his last four starts, both of which came in the opener of twin bills in front of the home faithful in Flatbush. And in each game Lady Luck had forsaken him. On August 23 Vance blanked the Chicago Cubs, but surrendered what Brooklyn newspapers called two scratch hits. In his last outing, Vance had run roughshod over Phillies on September 8, yielding only an infield hit to Chicken Hawks with one out in the second, fanning six and walking none.

Dame Fortune was not entirely on Vance's side in this game either. Hawks led off the second

with a routine fly to left fielder Jimmy Johnstone, who had started because Zach Wheat was suffering from "stomach trouble."[5] According to sportswriter Richards Vidmer, the ball "struck in [Johnston's] outstretched hand," caroming to the ground for an error.[6] Wheat "could have caught [the ball] in his watch pocket," continued the longtime New York Times scribe. The Eagle was more forgiving, suggesting that the "miscue was rather excusable" because the sun was in left field, causing Johnston to misjudge the ball's arc.[7] Johnstone's poor throw to the infield resulted in his second error and enabled Hawks to reach third. Bernie Friberg's sacrifice to center, drove in Hawks. The Phillies' run, wrote the Eagle was a "crime," yet few in Ebbets Field could have surmised what would unfold over the next seven innings.[8]

"Inning after inning the Phils swung hard, but futilely," gushed Brooklyn's Standard Union.[9] After Hawks reached safely, Vance retired 24 consecutive batters. Vance "had all of his speed," remarked the Eagle, noting that the burly right-hander "used an abundance of fast curves and considerably more changes of pace and slow curves than usual."[10] The Philadelphia Inquirer described Vance as "superb and invulnerable."[11]

Vance was "picture of perspiration after each inning," wrote Charles Segar in the Brooklyn Citizen.[12] It was a hot afternoon with temperatures in the mid-80s and especially humid.[13] The rugged, stubbly-faced Vance continually brushed the sweat from his brow, yet seemed impervious to the "burning rays of sunshine" that had spectators continually fanning themselves.[14]

With two outs in the fifth, Wilson smashed what the Standard Union called a "wicked grounder" directly to Hargreaves at first.[15] A backup catcher, Hargreaves was playing his first big-league game at first base, replacing star Jack Fournier, who was ill. Hargreaves made routine stop, then executed a "perfect peg" to Vance end the inning.[16]

After cups of coffee in 1915 and 1918, Dazzy Vance emerged as one of baseball's best pitchers as a 31-year-old with Brooklyn in his first full season in 1922. He led the NL in strikeouts his first seven seasons and was the 1924 National League MVP with a big-league-best 28 wins and a 2.16 ERA. (Photo: SABR-Rucker Archive)

Vance took the mound in the ninth "encased in tattered and sweat begrimed shirtsleeves," wrote Brooklyn sportswriter Thomas W. Meany.[17] Vance whipped two quick strikes to Lew Fonseca, pinch-hitting for Betts. Fonseca popped up Vance's third offering. Hargreaves "had it in his hands," noted the *Times*.[18] However, the inexperienced first sacker fumbled the ball and it dropped into foul territory for an error. One can only imagine what Vance thought, but he suppressed his emotions to "curve over a fourth successive strike" to punch out Fonseca.[19] The next batter, pinch-hitter Wally Kimmick, fanned on three straight pitches.[20] Then Freddy Leach swung at Vance's first pitch, and his eighth of the inning, connecting for the Phillies' second hard drive of the game. The low liner rocketed straight to Johnstone, who atoned for his earlier miscue that resulted in the Phillies only run. He made a routine running catch, securing Vance's no-hitter and ending the game in 1 hour and 45 minutes. Vance's teammates from the field and dugout rushed to the mound to congratulate the popular and well-liked player for his accomplishment.

Vance's dominance was "so thorough that not even brilliant fielding was required," opined the *Eagle*.[21] He faced the minimum 27 men, struck out nine and walked one. In authoring the big leagues' only no-hitter of the 1925 season, and the first in the history of Ebbets Field, Vance extended his hitless streak to 17⅓ innings. (It ended after two outs in the first inning of his next start.) He became the second pitcher in big-league history to toss a no-hitter and one-hitter in successive starts, joining Howard Ehmke,

who accomplished the feat for the Boston Red Sox in 1923. (Max Scherzer of the Washington Nationals joined that select group in 2015; only the Cincinnati Reds' Johnny Vander Meer tossed consecutive no-hitters, in 1938.) Vance's no-hitter was Brooklyn's first since Nap Rucker turned the trick against the Boston Braves on September 5, 1908, and the fourth in franchise history.[22]

With Brooklyn en route to a dismal sixth-place finish, Vance was shut down after his next start and did not pitch in the season's final two weeks. Nonetheless, he led the NL with 22 wins, tied for the lead with four shutouts, won his fourth straight strikeout title, and finished second in complete games (26).

The Phillies avenged their loss to the Robins, 7-3, in the second game of the doubleheader. The game was marred by an ugly scene between the Phillies' George Harper and Hargreaves at first base in the seventh inning. The two players almost came to blows after a shoving match and had to be restrained by teammates. When Harper took his position in left field to begin the eighth, spectators pelted him with bottles, forcing the game to be delayed by several minutes as the grounds crew cleaned the field.

SOURCES

In addition to the sources cited in the Notes, the author accessed Retrosheet.org, Baseball-Reference.com, SABR.org, and *The Sporting News* archive via Paper of Record.

NOTES

1. "Dazzy Vance Finally Lands Nice in Hall of Fame," *Brooklyn Eagle*, September 14, 1925: 20.

2. "Stock's Homer With 2 On Makes Jess Petty Winner; Why Vance Did Not Play," *Brooklyn Eagle*, September 13, 1925: D1.

3. Tomas W. Meany, "Vance Achieves Chief Ambition by Hurling No-Hit Game Against Phillies," *Brooklyn Times Union*, September 14, 1925: 26.

4. "Dazzy Vance Finally Lands Nice in Hall of Fame," *Brooklyn Eagle*.

5. "Dazzy Vance Finally Lands Nice in Hall of Fame."

6. Richards Vidmer, "No Hits Off Vance, but Phils Get Run," *New York Times*, September 14, 1925: 23.

7. "Dazzy Vance Finally Lands Nice in Hall of Fame."

8. "Dazzy Vance Finally Lands Nice in Hall of Fame."

9. "No-Hit Game by Vance Is Fitting Climax to Season of Brilliant Effort," *Brooklyn Standard Union*, September 14, 1925: 12.

10. "Dazzy Vance Finally Lands Nice in Hall of Fame."

11. "Johnston's Error Spoils Shut-Out Win," *Philadelphia Inquirer*, September 14, 1925: 12.

12. Charles Segar, "Dazzy Vance's No-Hit Ambition Is Finally Realized," *Brooklyn Citizen*, September 14, 1925: 8.

13. "The Weather," *Brooklyn Standard Union*, September 14, 1925: 16.

14. Vidmar.

15. "No-Hit Game by Vance Is Fitting Climax to Season of Brilliant Effort," *Brooklyn Standard Union*.

16. "No-Hit Game by Vance Is Fitting Climax to Season of Brilliant Effort."

17. Meany.

18. Vidmer.

19. Vidmer.

20. Vidmer.

21. "Dazzy Vance Finally Lands Nice in Hall of Fame."

22. The first no-hitter in Brooklyn franchise history was by Tom Lovett on June 22, 1891, against the New York Giants. Mal Eason pitched one on July 20, 1906, against the St. Louis Cardinals.

BILL TERRY HITS FOR THE CYCLE WITH GRAND SLAM

May 29, 1928

New York Giants 12, Brooklyn Robins 5

by Mike Huber

Two months into the 1928 season, the National League had a tight race for the top spot. While the Cincinnati Reds held first place (28-16),[1] four other teams were within striking distance. The third-place New York Giants (21-15) traveled to Brooklyn to take on the fourth-place Robins (22-17) at Ebbets Field. A week earlier, the Giants had split four games with the Robins (the games were also played in Brooklyn). This game was the first of a five-game series.[2] For the visiting Giants, Fat Freddie Fitszsimmons was named for mound duty, making his sixth start of the season. The home team countered with Jesse Petty. These were the same two hurlers as in the last game of the previous series.

In that May 24 match-up with New York, Petty had tamed the Giants' bats, allowing just three hits in a complete-game 3-0 victory. Fitzsimmons also pitched a complete game, allowing six hits. Two of the Brooklyn runs were unearned. However, on this occasion, Petty "took an unmerciful pasting"[3] from the Giants. The *Daily News'* Sam Schnitzer wrote, "It was truly a sad afternoon for some 10,000 Brooklyn folk."[4] He added,

"[T]he Polo Grounders reared up at Ebbets Field and socked the employees of [Dodgers manager] Wilbert Robinson 12 to 5."[5]

Giants first baseman Bill Terry played a major role in the game, hitting for the cycle. Coming into this contest, though, Terry was in a slump, batting .264, with only two hits and one RBI in his last 28 at-bats.

Both pitchers were on form in the early stages of the game. Petty breezed through the first, getting three straight groundouts. In the second, Les Mann led off with a single for the New Yorkers, and Terry followed with an infield single. Travis Jackson laid down a successful sacrifice bunt. Petty then walked Andy Cohen to load the bases, and the Giants looked poised for a rally. However, Petty induced Bob O'Farrell to ground into an inning-ending double play.

Fitzsimmons had allowed a single to Harvey Hendrick in the first but pitched a three-up, three-down second. In the bottom of the third, Petty started things with a one-out single off his counterpart. Jigger Statz lined a double, with Petty advancing to third. Hendrick stroked a single to left, driving in both runners, and the Robins had taken a 2-0 lead.

Petty retired the first two batters in the top of the fourth before Terry tripled. Terry should have been stranded when Jackson hit a grounder to third, but Brooklyn third baseman Hendrick threw the ball away and Terry scored. (The run was unearned.) An inning later, the Giants took the lead. Fitzsimmons helped his own cause with a leadoff single into the hole at short. Fitzsimmons was forced at second on Andy Reese's grounder. Freddie Lindstrom singled to left. Reese rounded second and kept going, drawing a throw from left fielder Rube Bressler. Reese was safe, and in a heads-up play, Lindstrom took second on the throw. Mel Ott slashed a two-run single, and the score was now 3-2 in favor of New York. Each pitcher was laboring; both teams put runners on in every time at bat.

In the bottom of the sixth, the Robins put together a rally, getting two runners aboard with two outs (Dave Bancroft and Butch Henline had each singled). Instead of pinch-hitting for Petty, the Brooklyn manager let his pitcher bat, and Fitzsimmons sent Petty back to the dugout after three straight strikes. That decision would come back to haunt Robinson and the Dodgers.

Petty returned to the pitching mound to face the Giants in the top of the seventh, with the top of the New York batting order due up. Reese opened the frame with an infield hit to short. Bancroft fielded the slow roller but could not get the ball to first in time. Petty then walked Lindstrom. Ott bunted and reached base safely. According to the *Brooklyn Daily Eagle*, "Petty ran away from the [bunted] ball instead of toward it."[6] That meant that the bases were loaded and the Giants had not hit the ball out of the infield. Mann grounded a ball to Robins third baseman Hendrick, who fired home for the force out on Reese, but the bases remained filled. Terry then not only hit the ball out of the infield but he smacked it out of Ebbets Field for a grand slam. Thomas Holmes

of the *Brooklyn Daily Eagle* had some fun with his account of the game, writing, "Terry's ball dodged between the traffic of Bedford Ave. for approximately 10 minutes."[7]

Terry's clout was followed by Jackson's solo home run, a shot into the bleachers beyond the left-field fence. Those two round-trippers knocked Petty out of the game. Ray Moss entered to finish the seventh. After walking Cohen, Moss retired both O'Farrell and Fitzsimmons. Moss also pitched the eighth, but he let the game get out of hand. Lefty O'Doul, pinch-hitting for Reese, singled to start the inning. Lindstrom forced O'Doul at second, and then Ott drove a hit to center. Statz misplayed the ball, and Lindstrom motored to third. With runners on the corners, Jimmy Welsh batted for Mann and drew a free pass. For the second consecutive inning, Terry was batting with the bases loaded. He launched an offering from Moss into deep center for a two-run double. The ball "bounced off the center field exit gate."[8] Jackson followed with a sacrifice fly to left, plating Welsh. The Giants had built an 11-2 lead. Bill Terry had hit for the cycle.

Lou Koupal pitched the ninth, mainly as mop-up duty. He allowed a walk to O'Farrell and a single to O'Doul. (Fitzsimmons struck out in-between.) With Lindstrom batting, the Giants pulled off a double steal, which proved opportunistic, as Lindstrom then lifted a fly ball to center and O'Farrell scored Run Number 12 for New York.

Down by 10 runs, Brooklyn rallied in its half of the ninth. Jake Flowers (pinch-hitting for Bancroft) and Henline hit back-to-back singles. Babe Herman, batting for Koupal, singled, scoring Flowers, and Henline ended up on third (Herman advanced to second) after an error by Giants catcher O'Farrell. Statz connected for the fourth straight single of the inning, plating Henline. Hendrick grounded into a 6-3 double play, but Howard Freigau (who was pinch-running for Herman) scored, cutting the New York lead to 12-5. Fitzsimmons finally retired Ty Tyson on a fly ball to center to end the game. Much was written in the Brooklyn papers the next day second-guessing Robinson's decision to let Petty bat in the sixth. Had he inserted Herman as a pinch-hitter then, which seemed "a most logical spot for the southpaw to be removed,"[9] would the outcome have changed? Petty had been tagged for 12 hits and eight runs (seven earned).

For New York, Terry came out of his slump with a vengeance. He drove in half of the Giants' runs, as both his home run and double came with the bases loaded. Terry's batting average jumped 23 points, and his slugging percentage shot up 69 points. Ott and Cohen also "proved exceedingly obstreperous," according to the *Daily News*.[10] Ott laced three singles in the contest, while Cohen added a double, single, and two walks. Fitzsimmons earned his fourth win of the season, despite allowing 11 hits and five earned runs.

The two teams met again the next day in a doubleheader, with the first game beginning at 10:30 in the morning, "for the benefit of early risers."[11] New York won the opener, 9-1, but the second game (which was not scheduled to start until 3:00 P.M.) was called after six innings due to darkness, with the score tied 2-2. The two teams split the final two games of the series, but New York had climbed a notch in the standings, while the Dodgers had dropped to fifth place.

Terry's collection of a single, double, triple, and home run marked the 11th time a Giants player had hit for the cycle.[12] His accomplishment came six years after Ross Youngs (April 29, 1922). Teammates Mel Ott and Freddie Lindstrom joined the Hit-for-the-Cycle Club in the next two seasons; Ott did so on May 16, 1929, and Lindstrom did so on May 8, 1930. Another New Yorker, the Yankees' Bob Meusel, hit for the cycle in 1928 (July 26), setting a record as the first American League player to hit for the cycle in three different games. Terry and Meusel accounted for the only two cycles hit in 1928.

SOURCES

In addition to the sources mentioned in the Notes, the author consulted Baseball-Reference.com, MLB.com, and Retrosheet.org.

Baseball-Reference.com/boxes/BRO/BRO192805290.shtml

Retrosheet.org/boxesetc/1928/B05290BRO1928.htm

NOTES

1   The Reds faded in the standings, finishing the season in fifth place. The St. Louis Cardinals won the pennant, ending up two games ahead of the Giants.

2   The first three games of the series were played at Ebbets Field (May 29-30), while the last two were at the Polo Grounds (June 1-2).

3   Sam Schnitzer, "Giants' Big Clubs Clip Robins' Wings," *New York Daily News*, May 30, 1928: 25.

4   Schnitzer.

5   Schnitzer.

6   Thomas Holmes, "Giants Show Proclivity for Big Innings Against Robins," *Brooklyn Daily Eagle*, May 30, 1928: 18.

7   Holmes.

8   Holmes.

9   Holmes.

10 Schnitzer.

11 Schnitzer.

12 MLB.com/news/players-who-hit-for-the-cycle/c-265552018.

A NEW "DEAD" BALL?
WILD NINTH INNING TOTALS
11 RUNS IN ROBINS' VICTORY

July 12, 1929
Brooklyn Robins 8, St. Louis Cardinals 7

by Doug Feldmann

When Ebbets Field locker-room attendant Dan Comerford arrived at work on the morning of July 12, 1929, several packages were waiting for him at the clubhouse door. The five boxes – each containing a dozen new baseballs – had been sent from the office of National League President John Heydler. Seeing the parcels did not surprise Comerford, as it was his routine every morning to rub the shine off the new pearls for each game. Yet, these baseballs were different; they were experimental in design, having been directed by Heydler for trial use in the battle that afternoon between the Brooklyn Robins and the St. Louis Cardinals. For the first time in Comerford's recollection, the balls were covered with a more rugged horsehide instead of the usual slick, glossy finish. The official reasoning from the league was that they would be easier for pitchers to grip. "Naturally, the players were curious about the new balls," wrote Thomas Holmes of the *Brooklyn Eagle* of the Robins as they got into their uniforms. "Before the game they stood around while the pellets were being unwrapped. They looked at them, felt of them and still continued to wonder."[1]

A better grip was not achieved, however, by one of the day's hurlers. "Ironically enough," Holmes wrote, "Sylvester Johnson, the St. Louis right-hander, proceeded to give the wildest exhibition any pitcher has provided at Ebbets Field this year."[2]

Meanwhile, it had been a long time since Dazzy Vance, the Brooklyn ace twirling for the Robins against Johnson this afternoon, had picked up *any* type of baseball for a significant length of time. In making his first start in 12 days while resting a sore arm, Vance got ready to face the Cardinals with a nondescript 5-4 record. Arguably the most dominant moundsman in the National League over the preceding decade, Vance had led the circuit in strikeouts in each of the past seven seasons and was anxious to get back to work toward claiming another crown. His Robins, led by manager Wilbert Robinson, entered the day in fifth place at 34-41, a full 15 games behind the front-running Pittsburgh Pirates. The Brooklyn club was on a massive homestand which, save for a one-day trip across town to the Polo Grounds, would stretch for nearly a month from June 27 to July 21.

The Cardinals sat just ahead of Brookyln in fourth place at 39-38 under first-year manager Billy Southworth, who had appeared in his last game as a player three days earlier, on July 9. His team busted out of the gate with a 26-15 mark to open the season (including a 6-0 individual run by Johnson) but swooned in recent weeks, losing eight of 11 on their current road trip after dropping four games at Sportsman's Park at the hands of the Chicago Cubs.

Johnson and Vance had previously locked horns in Ebbets Field two months earlier, on May 10, and the result was a 4-0 shutout for Johnson as part of a three-game sweep by the Cardinals. And when home-plate umpire Edward McLaughlin rolled one of the new baseballs out to the mound for Vance to begin play, another pitching duel started to unfold.

The game remained scoreless heading into the top of the fifth, when a barrage of hits – and a grounder that skidded through the legs of Brooklyn center fielder Johnny Frederick for an error – added up to a 2-0 Cardinals advantage. After 15 scoreless innings woven by Johnson against them in their home park, the Robins finally broke through in the bottom of the seventh, when Babe Herman lofted a long home run over the right-field fence to even the battle.

The 2-2 score held until the ninth, when an explosive final inning rarely seen in the annals of the game took flight.

After the Cardinals loaded the bases with one out, pinch-hitter Frankie Frisch was seen "hobbling up to the plate practically on one foot in nursing a lingering ankle injury," wrote Holmes.[3] Frisch, batting for Charley Gelbert, incurred the sprain in Philadelphia, the Cardinals' last stop. Despite the immense pain, Frisch cleared the bags with his 24th double of the season after which Eddie Delker ran for him. Taylor Douthit continued the Cardinals merry-go-round with a single to score Delker while Carey Selph, starting at second base in the place of Frisch, followed

with a RBI hit to plate Douthit. Johnson went into the bottom of the ninth with a 7-2 lead. Nonetheless, several of the men who contributed to the onslaught would fail the Cardinals on the defensive side.

Perhaps complacent with the newfound big lead, Johnson became "wilder than a Borneo bad man," wrote Martin Haley of the *St. Louis Globe-Democrat*.[4] After getting Frederick to tap an easy grounder to first baseman Jim Bottomley to start the Robins' last chance, Johnson allowed two hits and two walks – a collapse aided by interspersed errors by Douthit in center and Delker at short. Harold Haid, succeeding Johnson on the mound, walked two more men after his first hitter, Jake Flowers, also reached on a bobbled groundball by the second baseman Selph. And when Haid allowed his second free pass, unable to find the strike zone against 5-foot-9 pinch-hitter Val Picinich (batting for Vance), the tying run was forced across the plate, unearned.

Fred Frankhouse was then summoned by Southworth as the last line of defense to pitch to Frederick, batting for the second time in the inning. Frederick atoned for his error in the top half of the ninth (and his leadoff out in the bottom half) by stroking a hard single to right. Flowers crossed the plate with yet another unearned run, resulting in a stunning 8-7 triumph for Brooklyn – which had abandoned 13 men on base over the course of the afternoon.

Except for the home run by Herman (who also walked four times, leaving him with one official at-bat in the game), few hard hits were witnessed. Holmes wrote that "the [new] ball, according to some of the players, had a different sound when hit with a bat. ... The question before the house is whether the balls have any less 'rabbit' in them than the balls previously used in the league this season."[5] Instead of an improved grip, it was speculated by Holmes and other writers covering the game (including J. Roy Stockton of the *St. Louis Post-Dispatch*[6]) that the ball had been ordered to be deadened by Heydler in response to the record number of home runs seen in Organized Baseball in the past year. With a total of 11,730 round-trippers having departed minor- and major-league ballparks in 1928,[7] the reformed pill was perhaps an effort to bring the offensive game back inside the outfield walls. Haley cited other evidence from the afternoon. "Two of the doubles, one for each team, resulted when fly balls were lost in the sun, one by [Ernie] Orsatti and one by Herman."[8]

Overall, Wally Gilbert led the offensive attack for the Robins with three hits and two runs scored, while on the St. Louis side, Chick Hafey ran his hitting streak to 11 games by muscling a broken-bat single to left field in the fifth inning. The loss for the Cardinals left them with a dismal 5-20 mark since June 15, and Southworth did not survive the team's midsummer free-fall. He was fired on July 21, but would return to much greater heights as the St. Louis skipper in the 1940s.

Understandably, the Robins' last-minute offensive heroics wound up echoing throughout an Ebbets Field that had largely emptied from hopelessness by the time Flowers scored. "A Brooklyn fan bet his casual neighbor $10 on the result of the game," sportswriter Holmes observed. "At the end of the first half of the ninth, he paid and walked out of the park."[9]

SOURCES

In addition to the sources cited in the Notes, the author accessed Retrosheet.org, Baseball-Reference.com, SABR.org, and *The Sporting News* archive via Paper of Record.

NOTES

1   Thomas Holmes, "Heydler's New Consignment of Baseballs to Robins Seems Less Lively," *Brooklyn Eagle*, July 13, 1929.

2   Holmes.

3   Holmes.

4   Martin Haley, "Cardinals Donate Robins 6 Runs in Ninth," *St. Louis Globe-Democrat*, July 13, 1929.

5   Holmes.

6   J. Roy Stockton, "Dodgers Overcome Five-Run Lead of Birds in 9th," *St. Louis Post-Dispatch*, July 12, 1929.

7   Stockton.

8   Haley.

9   Holmes.

BROOKLYN SCORES SEASON-HIGH 22 TO IGNITE WIN STREAK

September 6, 1930
Brooklyn Robins 22, Philadelphia Phillies 8

by Chris Rainey

The schedule-makers did not do Brooklyn any favors in the summer of 1930. From August 6 through September 2 the team played only two home games. During that stretch the Robins fell from first place into fourth. Their travels had ended "ignominiously" when they were shut out by Boston's Ed Brandt, "a five-and-ten" pitcher.[1] The road-weary players were given a three-day break to recoup and prepare for the final month of the campaign.

The last-place Philadelphia Phillies were coming to town with the worst pitching numbers in the National League; they closed the season with an all-time worst team ERA of 6.71. Rested bats facing an incendiary pitching staff suggested that Saturday's game could become a slugfest. After all, the two franchises had a recent history of high-scoring affairs. Brooklyn had scored 14 in the previous meeting of the teams, on August 31. Earlier in the season the Robins had dropped a 16-15 decision to the Phillies. In 1929 the two teams combined for 36 runs on May 18 in the Baker Bowl.

Les Sweetland had started the August 31 game for Philadelphia and surrendered 11 earned runs. He was slated to start the September 6 game. Despite that poor showing, Sweetland had been something of a jinx to the Robins. The big lefty had opened the season with a nifty 1-0 victory over the Brooklynites. Entering the game, he had only six victories, but three of them were against manager Wilbert Robinson's squad.

The Robins sent Cuban Adolfo Luque, "baseball's first major Latino star," to the mound to open the game.[2] The Phillies went quietly on two grounders to shortstop Glenn Wright and a fly ball. Brooklyn center fielder Johnny Frederick led off with a single to right; second baseman Eddie Moore followed with a single to left. This brought up slugging right fielder Babe Herman who launched a drive over the right-field screen to give Brooklyn a 3-0 lead. Sweetland regrouped and escaped the inning without further damage.[3]

Philadelphia's pitching in 1930 was certainly suspect, allowing a franchise-high 1,199 runs. They tried to offset that deficiency with a powerful offense led by lefties Chuck Klein and Lefty O'Doul, who were both in the top five of the league in batting average coming into the game.

Heavy hitters for the 1930 Brooklyn Robins (L to R): RF Babe Herman (35-130-.393), CF Johnny Frederick (17-76-.334), 2B Jake Flowers (2-50-.320), 1B Del Bissonette (16-113-.336), and C Al Lopez (6-57-.309). (Photo: SABR-Rucker Archive)

The team would plate 944 runs in 1930, the most by a Phillies team in the modern (since 1901) era. The Robins caught a break as Bernie Friberg subbed for O'Doul in the game.

The Phillies offense responded in the top of the second. Klein singled and first baseman Don Hurst followed with a double to left. Third baseman Pinky Whitney doubled to right to score the pair. Then catcher Spud Davis drove a ball into the left-field bleachers to put the Phillies up 4-3. Luque composed himself and closed out the frame.[4]

Sweetland committed a cardinal sin to open the second by walking Luque. Frederick followed with a home run to recapture the lead. Manager Burt Shotton sent Sweetland to the showers. He was replaced by right-hander Earl "Hap" Collard. "The newcomer was treated no better than his predecessor."[5] Hap faced seven batters and surrendered five hits and a walk. His only out came

on a Wright grounder that forced a man at the plate. Collard was replaced by Hal Elliott.

Elliott faced Luque with the bases loaded and coaxed a fly ball to short center; Fred Brickell proceeded to muff the catch. Klein backed up the play and "was on the ball like a cat."[6] He relayed to second base for a force out while the Robins' sixth run of the inning crossed the plate. Then the Phillies completed an odd 8-7-4-5[7] double play by catching runner Wally Gilbert at third to end the inning.

Down 9-4, the Phillies added a run in the third on a single, a walk, and an RBI double by Davis. Elliott, a 6-foot-1-inch righty who had attended the University of Michigan, slowed the Robins attack but still yielded two singles and two triples to make the score 12-5 after three innings. The players caught their breath in a scoreless fourth inning and Luque retired the Phils again in the fifth.

"In the fifth (the Robins) laid into Elliott for a cool eight, totaling three bases on balls, five singles and a triple."[8] Herman launched the triple with two out and two on. Left fielder Friberg nearly robbed Herman but the ball squirted from his grasp. Herman was running with reckless abandon and was cut down at the plate for the third out.

The Phillies brought in rookie Albert "Buz" Phillips in the sixth. Shortstop Wright greeted him with his 19th home run of the season, into the seats in right-center. Phillips "did comparatively well" after that.[9] He surrendered a double to Ike Boone (subbing in left field) in the ninth for the last Brooklyn tally.

Boone, shortstop Gordon Slade, and catcher Hank DeBerry entered the game for the Robins in the seventh. Friberg and Klein singled to open the stanza and set the stage for Hurst's three-run blast to pull the Phils within a baker's dozen. The Phillies managed only two singles after that.

Luque was never "called upon to show his best, twirling just well enough to protect the big lead."[10] The win pushed his record to 13-7. (The 1930 season was the last in which he reached double-digit wins.) At the plate he went 2-for-4 with an RBI and two runs scored. Not bad for a player who was a month past his 40th birthday.

Sportswriter Thomas Holmes noted that there were only "about six thousand customers … which indicates that the fans of Flatbush are ready to call it a season, on the assumption that the Robins did that little thing a few weeks ago."[11] His postmortem was premature. The victory sparked a resurgence by the Robins, who won their next 10 games and returned to the top of the standings. Included in that streak was a masterful 6-0 shutout win by Luque over the Chicago Cubs.

The St. Louis Cardinals came to town on September 16 trailing Brooklyn by a single game. The Cardinals swept the three-game series and sent the Robins into a tailspin that saw them end the season in fourth place.

The 22 runs by the Robins on September 6 were their season high. They had twice tallied 19 runs, the Giants and Pirates being their victims. The Robins scored their 22 runs on 24 hits. They had recorded a season-high 28 hits in the win over Pittsburgh on June 23. Brooklyn's explosive but erratic offense reached double digits in runs 25 times during the 1930 season. But they also suffered through 25 games in which they either scored only once or were shutout.

ACKNOWLEDGMENTS

Baseball Reference and Retrosheet were invaluable in creating this game story.

NOTES

1   Henry Richards, "Flock to Encounter Phillies Saturday in Effort to Climb," *Brooklyn Standard Union*, September 3, 1930: 8.

2   Peter Bjarkman, https://www.lavidabaseball.com/adolfo-luque-first-latino-superstar/, accessed September 4, 2019.

3   "Herman Hits Homer with 2 on in First," *Brooklyn Daily Times*, September 6, 1930: 15.

4   The *Brooklyn Times Union*, in an article that covered the first two innings of the game, said that Hurst's double scored Klein. Like many evening papers in major-league cities, the *Times Union* covered as much of the game as deadlines allowed.

5   William McCullough, "Dodgers Wallop Phillies by 22-8," *Brooklyn Times Union*, September 7, 1930: 14.

6   Thomas Holmes, "Four Phillie Pitchers Fail to Halt Flock's Bats in 22-8 Slugfest," *Brooklyn Daily Eagle*, September 7, 1930: 35.

7   Center fielder to left fielder to second baseman to third baseman. One runner was put out at second on a force play and the other at third.

8   Holmes.

9   Holmes.

10 McCullough.

11 Holmes.

As Robins rout Reds, Babe Herman becomes first Brooklyn player to hit for the cycle at Ebbets Field

May 18, 1931
Brooklyn Robins 14, Cincinnati Reds 4

by Mike Huber

The 1931 Cincinnati Reds started the season with a dismal 2-17 record and after only 10 games found themselves in last place in the National League, a position they would hold for the rest of the season. On May 18 the Reds (6-18) played the final game of a three-game series against the seventh-place Brooklyn Robins (10-16). The Robins weren't much better, having won two of their first 12 contests. They were having trouble scoring; in their last six games, which included two victories, Brooklyn had managed only 17 total runs and had been "winging along weakly since the season's opening."[1]

So, on a Monday afternoon game at Ebbets Field, approximately 5,000 fans turned up,[2] probably expecting to see a low-scoring game. However, according to the *Brooklyn Times Union*, "The Brooklyn Robins did most of the hitting in the National League when they bombarded four Cincinnati pitchers for 16 hits and a 14 to 4 victory."[3] Surprisingly, the Reds also banged out 12 hits.

Sloppy Thurston, a journeyman who had pitched for four teams, made his third start of the year for the Robins. In his previous start (April 25), against the Boston Braves, he faced only four batters and "the Hub team cashed in twice."[4] Through 4⅔ innings pitched in his three appearances (one in relief), Thurston had allowed 14 hits and 12 runs, bad enough for a 19.29 earned-run average. Opposing Thurston was Cincinnati's Al Eckert. Virtually a rookie (he had appeared in only two games in 1930), Eckert was making his first and only start of the year. He had also pitched only 4⅔ innings so far in the season, allowing two earned runs, for a 3.86 ERA. Reds manager Dan Howley was giving his regular rotation a break.

Cincinnati's Edd Roush began the game with a single, but the next two batters flied out. Harvey Hendrick then smacked a long drive to left. Brooklyn's Lefty O'Doul ran back, "jumped to the sphere as it was about to sail over his head[,]"[5] and made a one-handed catch against the wall, saving at least one run and securing the third out.

In the bottom of the first, the Robins "wasted no time in indicating that they were on the warpath."[6] Fresco Thompson doubled to left and took third on a wild pitch. One out later, Babe Herman greeted Eckert "with a prodigious home run into the stands in left center."[7] The *New York Daily News* said the ball left the field "over the razor blade sign"[8] and landed in the 10th or 12th row of seats. After Eckert retired Del Bissonette, he walked Glenn Wright, and Johnny Frederick followed with his own blast over the wall, making it 4-0.

In the second, Ownie Carroll was now twirling for the Reds. He had spent parts of the previous season with three teams (the Tigers, Yankees, and Reds). Thurston led off with a single to left. With Thompson batting, Carroll had Thurston picked off but threw the ball away and Thurston ended up at third base. With two down, Herman blasted a triple over Roush's head in deep center. The ball bounced off the exit gate and Thurston scored easily. Bissonette poked a single up the middle, driving in Herman. Carroll then walked Wright and Frederick, loading the bases. Wally Gilbert laced a single to left, and two more Robins crossed the plate. By the time Carroll retired Ernie Lombardi for the final out of the inning, nine Brooklyn batters had come to the plate. The Robins gave Thurston an eight-run lead after two innings, so the big right-hander had to just "go through the motions for nine innings."[9]

Cincinnati finally answered in the third. Clyde Sukeforth led off with a single and moved to second on Carroll's base knock to left. Roush then singled to right field, but Carroll was thrown out. Sukeforth had stopped at third and Herman's throw to shortstop Wright caught Carroll running too far off second. Cliff Heathcote rolled a grounder to first, which was misplayed by Bissonette, and Sukeforth scored. Joe Stripp bounced into a double play, but the Reds had ended the shutout.

The game settled down until the bottom of the fifth. Back-to-back doubles by Frederick and Gilbert gave Brooklyn its ninth run of the game and Howley made another pitching change, bringing on Biff Wysong, who became the next victim of the Brooklyn bats. Wysong was a rookie making just his fifth major-league appearance. In the sixth, O'Doul reached on an error by second baseman Tony Cuccinello. Herman then "completely fooled the Cincinnati infield."[10] The Reds were playing Herman deep, completely on the outfield grass, probably anticipating a double-play groundball. Herman laid down a perfect bunt and beat it out for his third hit of the game. But on the play, O'Doul raced toward third base and was thrown out. Herman promptly stole second base and scored when Wright singled off Wysong. His run made it 10-1 in favor of the home team.

Cincinnati added a solo tally in the top of the seventh on doubles by Cuccinello and Sukeforth. However, in the bottom half, Brooklyn kept up the attack. Gilbert walked and Lombardi singled to right. Thurston struck out, and both runners advanced on a successful double steal with Thompson batting. This caused Wysong to walk Thompson, loading the bases for O'Doul, who was the only Brooklyn batter not to get a hit in the game. He lifted a sacrifice fly to right, and Gilbert scored. Herman then slammed a double to center field, driving in two more runs. Herman himself scored on Bissonette's second single of the afternoon. Eight men batted and four of them scored, leading the *Cincinnati Enquirer* to tell its readers, "Having biffed everybody else, the brutal Robins biffed Biff with consistent vigor."[11] Herman's double gave him a single, double, triple, and home run; he had hit for the cycle.

Thurston was touched for single runs in each of the last two innings. Wally Roettger's RBI double drove Hendrick home in the eighth. In the ninth, Sukeforth singled with one out. Red Lucas pinch-hit in the pitcher's spot and Sukeforth advanced to second and then to third on defensive indifference with Lucas at the plate. Lucas then flied out to center, deep enough for a sacrifice, scoring Sukeforth. When Thurston retired Estel Crabtree on a weak grounder to first for the final out of the game, the fans cheered the Robins' 14-4 victory.

This was "the first time this season that the Dodgers really demonstrated their real hitting prowess."[12] To soften the blow, the *Cincinnati Enquirer* reported that the Robins faced "second-string pitchers on the Red side."[13] Nonetheless, Brooklyn had knocked out 16 hits, including six for extra bases. With his 4-for-5 performance, Herman had also scored four runs and driven in five. Gilbert had a 3-for-3 day with two walks and three runs batted in. Thurston helped his own cause at the plate, going 2-for-5 with a run scored. With the complete-game win, Thurston's ERA dropped 10 full runs, to 9.22. Including the last three innings of their May 17 game against the Reds, the Robins had made 23 hits and scored 19 runs in just 11 innings.

National League President John Heydler watched the first two innings of the game and "then departed for his home in Garden City, having seen at least one or two good reasons why the Reds are in last place."[14]

The *Brooklyn Citizen* described Herman as the "elongated outfielder [who] whaled the tar out of the horsehide."[15] The 27-year-old outfielder had batted .381 in 1929 and .393 in 1930. Like his teammates, he had struggled until this game, batting only .301 in Brooklyn's first 26 games. By hitting for the cycle, Herman upped his average to .324 and raised his slugging percentage to .611.[16] He became just the second Brooklyn player (since

1901) to hit for the cycle, after Jimmy Johnston (May 25, 1922, against the Philadelphia Phillies), and the first to do so at his home ballpark of Ebbets Field.

Herman's feat was the first cycle of 1931. Phillies slugger Chuck Klein accomplished the rare event on July 1, against the Chicago Cubs. Then, three weeks after Klein and only 67 games after his first, Babe Herman cycled again, becoming the ninth major leaguer to hit for the cycle twice in his career.[17] This second time (July 24), he did it at Forbes Field against the Pittsburgh Pirates. Two seasons later, on September 30, 1933, Herman hit for the cycle for a record-tying third time, as a member of the Cubs. As of the beginning of the 2021 season, he remained one of only four players in history to hit for the cycle three times in his career, joining John Reilly, Bob Meusel, and Adrian Beltre.

SOURCES

In addition to the sources mentioned in the Notes, the author consulted Baseball-Reference.com, MLB.com, Retrosheet.org, and SABR.org.

https://www.baseball-reference.com/boxes/BRO/BRO193105180.shtml

https://www.retrosheet.org/boxesetc/1931/B05180BRO1931.htm

NOTES

1   Roscoe McGowen, "Robins on 16 Hits Subdue Reds, 14 to 4," *New York Times*, May 19, 1931: 39.

2   Box score, *New York Daily News*, May 19, 1931: 42.

3   Dixon Stewart, "Babe Herman on Rampage as Flock Collects 16 Hits," *Brooklyn Times Union*, May 19, 1931: 17.

4   Lee Scott, "Robins Lose, 5-4," *Brooklyn Citizen* (Brooklyn, New York), April 26, 1931: 11.

5   Lee Scott, "Dodgers Hope to Knock Cardinals Out of First Place," *Brooklyn Citizen*, May 19, 1931: 6.

6   Jack Ryder, "Robins Slam Red Reserves From Here to Kingdom Come," *Cincinnati Enquirer*, May 19, 1931: 9.

7   Scott, "Dodgers Hope to Knock Cardinals Out of First Place."

8   Pat Robinson, "It's Great Trick, Even for Robins," *New York Daily News*, May 19, 1931: 42.

9   Scott, "Dodgers Hope to Knock Cardinals Out of First Place."

10   "Dodgers Hope to Knock Cardinals Out of First Place."

11   Ryder.

12   "Dodgers Hope to Knock Cardinals Out of First Place."

13   Ryder.

14   Ryder.

15   "Dodgers Hope to Knock Cardinals Out of First Place."

16   Herman finished the 1931 season batting .313.

17   The previous eight were John Reilly (who cycled three times in his career), Tip O'Neill, Pete Browning, Mike Tiernan, Jimmy Ryan, Fred Clarke, George Sisler, and Bob Meusel (who also cycled three times in his career).

Hack Wilson's pinch-hit, walk-off grand slam sends Dodgers home victorious

May 14, 1933
Brooklyn Dodgers 8, Philadelphia Phillies 6

by Doug Feldmann

A steady rain was pouring down on Ebbets Field in the bottom of the ninth inning. His team clinging to a 6-4 lead, Philadelphia Phillies pitcher Fidgety Phil Collins loaded the bases with four erratic pitches to the Brooklyn Dodgers' Johnny Frederick, prompting Phillies manager Burt Shotton to come to the mound. Shotton's struggling Phillies (8-16) were sitting in last place in the early-season National League standings, and in facing the beatable Dodgers (9-11) of manager Max Carey, he did not want another one to get away.

Shotton called upon submarining reliever Ad Liska from the bullpen to face the next Brooklyn batter, Jake Flowers. As he made his way toward home plate, however, the 0-for-3 Flowers suddenly reversed his steps. Emerging from Carey's dugout to take his place was another player – an unmistakable, portly figure. The pinch-hitter's physique could only belong to one person, a body once described by a newspaperman of the day as being "shaped like a beer keg, and not unfamiliar with its contents."[1]

As the man waddled toward the batter's box, the cheer quickly grew from behind the Dodgers' dugout. "What a spot for the Hack!!!"[2]

Lewis "Hack" Wilson, tipping 200 pounds despite being all of 5-feet-6-inches tall, more resembled a lineman on a small-town high-school football team than a major-league baseball player. Three years removed from his amazing 191-RBI season with the Chicago Cubs, Wilson – batting a mere .167 (6-for-36) with no home runs to start 1933 – had recently been benched by Carey, and had appeared only in a pinch-hitting role twice in the past week. Nonetheless, everyone on the Flatbush premises – including Carey, the Dodger fans, and perhaps even Wilson himself – sensed that a turnaround was imminent in the next moment.

The decisive moment about to transpire was the climax to a back-and-forth, muddy struggle all afternoon long.

With rookie Frank Pearce making his third major-league start for the Phillies, the game stood even at 3-3 in the bottom of the sixth. In that inning, the Dodgers edged in front on a

93

fly ball to center by Del Bissonette that scored Flowers. The Phillies tied it again in the seventh, on Dick Bartell's clutch two-out single to center field off Dodgers relief pitcher Joe Shaute (who had replaced starter Walter "Boom-Boom" Beck in the third and threw nearly five innings). Bartell's hit plated Brooklyn native Neal Finn, who had singled and taken second on a hit by Chick Fullis.

After the Phillies added two more in the eighth for a 6-4 advantage, a frustrated Brooklyn manager Carey was ejected by home-plate umpire Cy Pfirman in the bottom half "for real or alleged remarks on the subject of called balls or strikes."[3]

Shortly thereafter, the rain could no longer be ignored, and a 15-minute delay hit the game. "There was a squall in every inning," Harold Parrott of the *Brooklyn Eagle* wrote of the unabated rain, "and Pfirman at the plate was like a man standing up in a row boat."[4] Aptly named for the inclement environment, Brooklyn pitcher Hollis "Sloppy" Thurston, in his final major-league season, held the Phillies in check in the top of the ninth to set the stage for the drama.

Before giving the free pass to Frederick, Collins permitted a single to Danny Taylor and walked Lefty O'Doul. (He would be sent across town to the New York Giants a month later.) The downpour then resumed; but as Flowers made his U-turn back toward the Brooklyn bench and Wilson came out, Pfirman and his crew remained intent on finishing the battle.

It would not last much longer. "Wilson swung on Liska's first and last pitch," wrote Parrott, "and bulged the wire mesh above the fence in right center."[5]

The grand slam touched off a puddle-splashing celebration among the Dodger faithful in the neighborhood – both outside Ebbets Field and within. "Round, little Wilson hit that one as he used to sock 'em for the Cubs," said the *Philadelphia Inquirer*, "wading through the mud in the wake of three other fellows. He [then] had to fight his way through the wild-eyed fans to get off the field."[6]

The water-logged homers by Wilson and fellow Dodger Joe Stripp were the only extra-base hits anyone was able to drive through the day's precipitation. Stripp, Taylor, and Tony Cuccinello had stroked two hits apiece for Brooklyn while Don Hurst and Finn, the latter back in his home borough, knocked two singles for the Phillies and Spud Davis contributed two RBIs. Collins, in relief of Snipe Hansen and a strong, six-inning effort from Pearce, was charged with the loss while Thurston picked up the win.

Carey's Dodgers finished the 1933 season in the second division, marking his final stint as a manager. Fourteen 14 years later, the losing skipper Shotton returned to Brooklyn full-time and manage the Dodgers to a pennant in 1947, guiding his revolutionary team through perhaps the most transformational season baseball had ever seen.

SOURCES

In addition to the sources cited in the Notes, the author accessed Retrosheet.org, Baseball-Reference.com, SABR.org, and *The Sporting News* archive via Paper of Record.

NOTES

1   Doug Feldmann, *Dizzy and the Gas House Gang* (Jefferson, North Carolina: McFarland, 2000), 114.

2   Harold Parrott, "'What a Spot for the Hack' Was Cry and Smashing Home Run Was Echo," *Brooklyn Eagle*, May 15, 1933.

3   "A's Drop Twin Bill; Phils Lose," *Philadelphia Inquirer*, May 15, 1933.

4   Parrott.

5   Parrott.

6   "A's Drop Twin Bill; Phils Lose."

ARKY VAUGHAN HITS FOR THE CYCLE AND GOES 5-FOR-5

June 24, 1933
Pittsburgh Pirates 15, Brooklyn Dodgers 3

by C. Paul Rogers III

The Pittsburgh Pirates were nursing a four-game losing streak heading into a Saturday-afternoon contest against the Brooklyn Dodgers on June 24, 1933. Pittsburgh had finished in second place in 1932, just four games behind the pennant-winning Chicago Cubs, and had high hopes for a pennant in 1933. The team had shot out of the gate by winning seven out of eight and was in first place almost continually through the end of May before faltering and losing 14 of 23 thus far in June. With their current losing streak, the Pirates had slipped to third place with a 33-29 record and had fallen to a season-high five games off the pace. The Dodgers, coming off a third-place finish in 1932, were in fifth place, six percentage points ahead of the sixth-place Cincinnati Reds, and were four games below .500 for the year.

Prospects for a Pirates win looked pretty good considering right-hander Bill Swift was toeing the rubber for Pittsburgh. Swift, who had just turned 25 and was in his second year in the big leagues, already had eight wins for the season and sported an outstanding 2.91 earned-run average. He was opposed by 34-year-old Sloppy Thurston, who was on the downside of a nine-year big-league career. As a spot starter and reliever, the right-handed Thurston was 4-2.[1]

Both hurlers retired the side in order in the first inning, giving promise of a pitchers' duel. In the top of the second, Pirates shortstop Arky Vaughan hit his sixth home run of the year when he "pasted a drive into the right field chicken wire" with one out and no one on to break the brief scoring drought.[2] After Swift retired the Dodgers in their half of the second on three fly balls, the Pirates extended their lead to 2-0 on a one-out double to left field by Adam Comorosky that drove in Freddy Lindstrom, who had reached on a bunt single.[3] Paul Waner hit a comebacker to Thurston, who caught Comorosky in a rundown for the second out as Waner reached on the fielder's choice. Pie Traynor singled to left to put runners on first and second and Vaughn loaded the bases with an infield single to first. But Thurston induced Gus Suhr to ground out to second baseman Tony Cuccinello on a 3-and-0 pitch to avert further damage.[4]

The Dodgers closed the gap to 2-1 in the bottom of the third on singles to left field by Al Lopez and Danny Taylor followed by a two-out single to center by Johnny Frederick to score Lopez and send Taylor to third. Swift regrouped to retire Joe Stripp on a fly ball to Waner in right to end the threat. After a scoreless, hitless fourth, the Pirates extended their lead to 4-1 in the top of the fifth, all with two outs and no one on. Paul Waner worked what seemed like a harmless walk, but Traynor made Thurston pay with a ringing double to left that plated Waner from first. The lefty-swinging Vaughan followed with his third hit of the game, a single to right to drive in Waner with the Pirates' fourth run of the day.

Neither team threatened for the next inning and a half, heading into the top of the seventh. Through six innings Swift had allowed only three singles, all in the third inning, and showed no signs of weakening. After the Pirates batted in the seventh, however, it was largely academic, as they scored four runs to extend their lead to 8-1. Comorosky tagged Thurston for a one-out solo home run, his first of the season, and after Waner grounded out to Jimmy Jordan at shortstop for out number two, Traynor kept the inning alive with a bloop single behind second base. That brought up the firecracker-hot Vaughan, who promptly laced his fourth hit of the day, a double to right to score Traynor from first.

With that, Dodgers manager Max Carey came out to get Thurston and waved in veteran southpaw Fred Heimach. As things turned out, Carey should have reconsidered. Heimach immediately gave up run-scoring singles to Suhr and Tommy Thevenow before retiring the side on a comebacker from Hal Finney. Cuccinello reached Swift for a solo home run, his team-leading eighth round-tripper of the season, in the bottom of the seventh to bring the score to 8-2 heading into the eighth.

Heimach's shaky performance in the seventh presaged a complete pounding by Pirates bats in the eighth as they scored seven more runs from a total of three triples and five singles. Seven of the hits were consecutive with two outs and included Vaughan's cycle-completing two-run triple, his fifth hit of the game in five at-bats. Manager Carey left Heimach in to finish the inning and take one for the team. His ugly totals were 10 hits and eight runs allowed, all earned, in 1⅓ innings.[5] Heimach's earned-run average from the outing jumped more than three runs, to 8.69.[6]

In the bottom of the eighth, Swift, after retiring pinch-hitter Chink Outen on a popup to second baseman Thevenow, was touched for another solo home run, this time by Taylor, to bring the score to 15-3. In the top of the ninth Vaughan batted with two out against reliever Rosy Ryan with a chance for his sixth hit of the day, but settled for a walk. In the bottom half, Swift retired Hack Wilson on a foul pop to Finney behind the plate and got Sam Leslie on a fly ball to Lindstrom in center field before allowing a double to Cuccinello. But Lopez flied harmlessly to center to seal Swift's complete-game victory in a brisk hour and 55 minutes.

Swift, in running his record to 9-5, allowed six hits and did not walk a batter. For the afternoon, the Pirates manufactured 21 hits and 36 total bases, which included eight extra-base hits. The 21-year-old Vaughan was in just his second big-league season. In addition to going 5-for-5 and hitting for the cycle, he reached base all six times, drove in five runs, and scored three. After batting .318 as a 20-year-old rookie in 1932, he finished the 1933 season with a .314 batting average and was well on his way to a Hall of Fame career. He again hit for the cycle on July 19, 1939, again going 5-for-5, this time against the New York Giants in the Polo Grounds.

Vaughan's best season was with the Pirates in 1935 when he was batting .401 in mid-September before tailing off slightly to .385 to lead the league. He also led in walks (97), on-base percentage (.491), and slugging percentage (.607) while reaching career highs in home runs (19) and runs batted in (99). In 14 major-league seasons, Vaughan compiled a .318 batting average, making the National League All-Star team nine times. Tragically, he was killed in a boating accident in Northern California in 1952 when he was just 40 years old.[7]

The 1933 Pirates, despite having five future Hall of Famers in their lineup including Vaughan,[8] again finished in second place, this time five games behind the Giants. The excitement of a second consecutive pennant race must have been a nice diversion for the people of Pittsburgh from the depths of the Great Depression, but the team drew only 288,747 fans, fifth best in the National League.[9]

NOTES

1 Thurston had won 20 games with the Chicago White Sox as a 25-year-old in 1924 but had not come close to replicating that success. His career record was a respectable 89-86.

2 Harold Parrott, "Pirates Beat Dodgers 15-3," *Brooklyn Daily Eagle*, June 25, 1933: D1.

3 According to the *Brooklyn Eagle*, Comorosky was playing left field because Lloyd Waner had come down "with a spell of the grippe." Parrott: 36.

4 Not surprisingly, Suhr's swinging on a 3-and-0 pitch with the bases loaded resulted in "a call down" from Pirates manager George Gibson. Parrott: 36.

5 One news report called Heimach "a good, game chap by standing up under 10 hits in pitching only one and one-third innings." "Pirates Stop Losing Streak, Win 15-3," *Pittsburgh Press*, June 25, 1933: Sports Section 1. The *Brooklyn Eagle* was not so charitable. Its subheading for the game read, "Heimach, Massacred in Relief Role, Gives Up Eight Hits in One Inning." A subheading in the middle of the game story read, "Heimach Luckily Escapes With Life," *Brooklyn Daily Eagle*, June 25, 1933: D1.

6 Heimach's next outing, on July 17 also against the Pirates, was even worse. Relieving in the eighth inning of a game the Dodgers were losing 5-2, he gave up nine earned runs in one-third of an inning. At 32 he was at the end of the line of a journeyman career that spanned 13 seasons. Pitching for four teams, he finished with a lifetime record of 62-69 and an earned-run average of 4.46.

7 Ralph Moses, "Arky Vaughan," SABR Bioproject: sabr.org/bioproj/person/4e00be9b.

8 The others were Pie Traynor, Freddie Lindstrom, Paul Waner, and Lloyd Waner.

9 That figure means that the Pirates averaged about 3,750 fans a game without taking into account doubleheaders for which the Pirates charged only one admission. The Pirates had drawn almost the exact same number of fans (287,262) to their second-place finish in 1932.

DAFFY DAZZLES WITH NO-HITTER

September 21, 1934

St. Louis Cardinals 3, Brooklyn Dodgers 1 | Second Game of Doubleheader

by Gregory H. Wolf

"We're just a couple of natural born pitchers from down Texas way," bantered Paul "Daffy" Dean about himself and his famous brother Dizzy. "Two good natured ordinary fellers who God gave perfect pitchin' bodies."[1] After Dizzy worked on a no-hitter for 7⅓ innings in the first game of a doubleheader, Daffy upstaged his loquacious older sibling by tossing a no-hitter to complete the St. Louis Cardinals' shutout sweep of the Brooklyn Dodgers. "There's little you can add when writing about the Deans," quipped Brooklyn sportswriter Tommy Holmes. "Superlatives are useless."[2] But that didn't prohibit sportswriters from trying. Daffy's remarkable performance, praised scribe George Smith of the *Brooklyn Citizen*, "overshadows all of the miracle feats of the pitcher's mound in the last twelve years"; he considered it the best-pitched game since Charlie Robertson tossed a perfect game in 1923.[3]

The Redbirds were surging at just the right time. The rough-and-tumble Gas House Gang had won 11 of its last 14 games, all on the road as part of a grueling a 23-game, 3½-week road swing. Suddenly catapulting themselves back into the pennant race, the Cardinals (86-56) had erased a seven-game deficit on September 6 and trailed the NL-leading New York Giants by 3½ games with just 11 games to play. Player-manager Frankie Frisch called on the Dean boys to start the doubleheader, their second in two days.

While Dizzy Dean, in his third full season, had captured the attention of the baseball world with his down-home aphorisms and braggadocio, as well as his exploits on the mound, rookie Paul was much less talkative. He had emerged as a star the previous season with the Columbus Red Birds in the American Association, winning 22 games, including a no-hitter. Upon Paul's arrival on the big-league club, Dizzy predicted confidently that the duo would win 45 games. Few sportswriters had any reason to doubt him. But Paul struggled as the season commenced, yielding eight earned runs in his first six innings in three rough outings. Then he caught fire, winning his next eight straight starts. The press dubbed the 21-year-old right-hander Daffy, but he despised the moniker, which neither he nor his teammates used. But it nonetheless stuck. Unlike his brother, Paul was reserved and cut a less imposing figure on the mound. At 6-feet 2 and 170 pounds, Paul looked "more like a drug clerk than a famous athlete," jested Dodgers beat writer George Smith.[4]

An estimated 20,000 spectators at Ebbets Field took in the Friday afternoon twin bill, needed to make up two games canceled by inclement weather two weeks earlier.[5] Holding court at the team's hotel on the morning of this game, Dizzy bragged that the Dodgers "will be pitching against one-hit Dean and no-hit Dean today."[6] He was almost right. In the first game Dizzy held the sixth-place Dodgers (65-77) hitless for 7⅓ innings, settling on a three-hit shutout behind a 17-hit, 13-run Cardinals barrage to record his NL-best 27th victory.

Dizzy was a tough act to follow under any circumstances, but Paul was pitching the best ball in his career. He was coming off two extra-inning complete games, both in high-leverage contests against the Giants at the Polo Grounds, tossing a 12-inning shutout on September 13 and an 11-inning, 3-1 victory three days later, pushing his slate to 17-9 (3.70 ERA).

The game unfolded as a scoreless pitchers' duel through five innings. Paul didn't look sharp in the first inning. After leadoff hitter Buzz Boyle fanned, Lonnie Frey smashed what Lee Scott of the *Brooklyn Citizen* considered a sure hit, but left fielder Ducky Medwick made a spectacular grab.[7] Dean walked the next batter, Len Koenecke, on a 3-and-2 count. "I pitched low and outside to Lennie," explained Paul, "and low and outside it went."[8]

The Dodgers' 32-year-old right-hander Ray Benge was pitching just as well. A dependable workhorse, Benge had averaged 221 innings his previous six season and was enjoying his best campaign (14-11). He yielded just one hit – a single to Dean in the third.

The Cardinals scored the game's first run in the sixth. Dean stroked a one-out double to

center. (A capable hitter, Dean batted .241 on 20 hits in 1934.) Pepper Martin followed with another two-bagger to drive him home. The Redbirds tallied their second run in the seventh on Ripper Collins's single to plate Medwick, who had doubled. The offensive star of the game, Medwick tripled in the eighth and scored the Cardinals' third and final run on Collins's groundout.

Staked to the lead, Dean mowed the Dodgers down. "My curve was breaking good and as the game went along I felt looser and better," he said.[9] With two outs in the seventh, Dean and his rookie batteyrmate, Bill DeLancey, met on the mound to discuss their approach to Sam Leslie.[10] The Dodgers cleanup hitter, Leslie began the day hitting a team-high .326, and had lofted two deep fly balls against Dean in this game. Leslie connected for another one and Dean immediately thought it was gone. He "slammed a fast ball to left center that looked like a home run," said Paul.[11] Medwick, considered among baseball's best left fielders, raced back and made a running catch to end the inning.

With palpable tension in the last several frames, the crowd was firmly on Dean's side, cheering and clapping after each batter he retired in his quest for a no-hitter. Dodgers first-year skipper Casey Stengel made Dean earn it. To start the ninth, Casey played matchups, calling on left-handed-hitting rookie Jim Bucher to hit for Al Lopez. Dean rung him up for his sixth strikeout. Casey sent in another left-handed-hitting pinch-hitter, September call-up Johnny McCarthy. He lofted a high popup that second baseman Frankie Frisch secured, eliciting another round of applause. An out away from a feat his Hall of Fame brother would never accomplish in the majors, Dean faced Boyle, who lined a chopper to shortstop Leo Durocher. "The ball was so sharply hit that it struck Leo in the chest," remarked sportswriter Bill McCullough in the *Brooklyn Times Union*, adding, "There wasn't a heart in the ball park that wasn't in the mouth."[12]

The feisty Durocher, who would later become a star player and notorious manager of 'Dem Bums, recovered quickly. He retrieved the ball in the dirt and rifled a shot to first baseman Ripper Collins to retire the speedy Boyle, ending the game in 1 hour and 38 minutes and securing Dean's no-no.

Pandemonium broke out. Dean's teammates mobbed him on the mound and fans poured onto the field. During the economic hardship of the Great Depression, the Deans had touched a nerve among baseball fans and were wildly popular wherever they played. A police escort was finally required to help Paul and his teammates retreat to the dressing room.

In a dominating performance, Paul Dean retired the last 25 batters he faced. "Everything went my way," he stated in his subdued, modest manner. "I was always ahead of the hitters."[13] The big leagues' only no-hitter in 1934, Dean's gem was the first no-hitter in 1,140 days, breaking the longest no-hitter drought in history (as of 2021 still the longest).[14] Bobby Burke of the Washington Senators was the last to turn the trick, holding the Boston Red Sox hitless on August 8, 1931. Dean's no-no was the first in the NL since the Giants Carl Hubbell beat the Pittsburgh Pirates on May 8, 1929. The previous Cardinals hurler to author a no-hitter was Jesse Haines, who held the Boston Braves hitless on July 17, 1924.

The Cardinals' doubleheader shutout sweep cut the Giants lead to three games. Paul lost his next two outings, then tossed a complete game to put the Cardinals into sole possession of first place, on September 29. The next day Dizzy tossed a shutout on two days' rest to win his 30th game and capture the pennant on the final day of the season.

Paul Dean finished the season with a 19-11 slate (3.43 ERA, 123 ERA+) and led the majors by striking out 5.8 batters per nine innings. The Gas House Gang etched its name in baseball lore by winning the World Series in seven games over the Detroit Tigers. And once again it was the Dean Brothers' show. Dizzy won two games, but Paul proved to be even more dazzling, tossing two complete games, yielding just one earned run in each.

SOURCES

In addition to the sources cited in the Notes, the author accessed Retrosheet.org, Baseball-Reference.com, SABR.org, and *The Sporting News* archive via Paper of Record.

NOTES

1 Ray J. Gillespie, "Paul Dean Only Rookie to Pitch No-Hit Contest," *St. Louis Star and Times*, September 22, 1934: 11.

2 Tommy Holmes, "Dean Brothers Bubbling Over with Fame," *Brooklyn Eagle*, September 22, 1934: 6.

3 George Smith, "Paul Dean Not Greatly Excited Over the Doings of the Dean Brothers," *Brooklyn Citizen*, September 22, 1934: 6.

4 Smith.

5 Smith.

6 Roscoe McGowen, "Paul Dean, Cards, Hurls No-Hit Game, *New York Times*, September 22, 1934: 8.

7 Lee Scott, "Brooklyn Fans Thrilled as Younger of Dean Boys Pitches No-Hitter; They Have Won 45 Games," *Brooklyn Citizen*, September 22, 1934: 6.

8 Bill McCullough, "No-Hit, No Run Game by Paul Highlights Star Performance," *Brooklyn Times Union*, September 22, 1934: 13.

9 J. Roy Stockton, "Paul Dean First St. Louis No Hit Pitcher Since 1924," *St. Louis Post-Dispatch*, September 22, 1934: 1B.

10 Gillespie.

11 Gillespie.

12 McCullough.

13 McCullough.

14 "Ebbets Field No-Hitter," NoNoHitters.com, https://www.nonohitters.com/ebbets-field-no-hitters/.

THE 1935 NEGRO NATIONAL LEAGUE BROOKLYN EAGLES

by Alan Cohen

On July 30, 2006, Effa Manley was inducted into the Baseball Hall of Fame. She and her husband, Abe Manley, had been at the helm of one of the great Negro League teams, the Newark Eagles. But every baseball story has a beginning, and the baseball journey of Abe and Effa Manley began with the Brooklyn Eagles. On November 13, 1934, a bit more than a year after their marriage, the Negro National League awarded a franchise to the Manleys.[1] Ben Taylor was hired as manager and, by early December, the team had two star pitchers and a team bus.[2]

The team played at Ebbets Field in 1935.

Owner Manley outfitted his players in fine attire for the season. Per the *New York Age*, "The home uniforms are of a light shade with the letters 'Eagles' written across the chest."[3]

After starting the season on the road, the Eagles played their first home game at Ebbets Field on Saturday, May 18, in front of 2,500 spectators. Mayor Fiorello LaGuardia of New York threw out the first pitch, and home runs by Clarence "Fats" Jenkins and Herbert "Rap" Dixon gave the Eagles a 4-1 first-inning lead.

After that, it was pretty much all downhill for the Eagles. They were outslugged by the Homestead Grays, 20-7. The Pittsburgh contingent had four homers, and each member of the Grays' lineup scored at least one run. All but veteran third baseman George Scales hit safely. The game was broken open by a grand slam off the bat of Jerry Benjamin in the fifth inning. Joe Strong started on the mound for the Pittsburgh team but left the game in the second inning when Brooklyn took its last lead, 6-5. The win went to Willie Gisentaner, who came on with one out in the second inning and pitched the rest of the game. Willie helped his cause with a home run. Ted "Double Duty" Radcliffe took the loss. He was able to pitch only into the second inning. Elbert Williams came in with two outs in the inning and exited the game after Benjamin's grand slam in the fifth. Gavin, whose appearance was so brief that his first name is not known, hit Gisentaner with a pitch. James Reese completed the game for the Eagles, allowing the final six Grays runs. Their star slugger, Buck Leonard singled and doubled in the game.[4]

The teams split a doubleheader on May 19. In the first game, Ray Brown was the starting pitcher for the Grays and pitched the first five innings, leaving with a 6-5 lead. The Eagles, down 9-7 going into the bottom of the eighth, rallied for 11 runs and won the game 18-9. Leon Day pitched the first seven innings for Brooklyn. Ted "Double-Duty" Radcliffe finished up and was credited with the win. In the second game, the Grays won 4-2 as Louis Dula, who started the game with four no-hit innings, bested Radcliffe.[5] The Eagles won the final game of the series, 4-3. Brown and Bill Jackman waged a pitchers' duel for the first five innings. Jackman, a submarine-style pitcher, went all nine innings for the win, allowing five hits. At the plate, he was 2-for-4 with two RBIs. The Eagles, who had 10 hits, all singles, broke the ice in the sixth inning with the bases loaded and two out when Rap Dixon stole home. He was poised halfway between third base and home and made a mad dash home when the catcher returned a pitch to the mound. Later in the inning, the Eagles' lead was extended to 3-0 on Jackman's single. Leonard tripled home a run in the seventh and scored on a fly ball, but the Grays did not get any closer.[6]

Before the Eagles played at Ebbets Field again, Taylor was released as manager and replaced by first baseman George Giles. Taylor, upset with this development, sued the Eagles.[7]

The Eagles did not get off to a good start under Giles, losing a doubleheader to Chicago on May 25. In the opener, which the Eagles lost 8-2, the American Giants had 13 hits, including homers by Willie Wells and George "Mule" Suttles. Turkey Stearnes went 2-for-5 with an RBI for Chicago. After the Eagles tied the second game at 5-5 in the ninth inning, the teams played on until the 12th, when the game was decided by a grand slam off the bat of Suttles, his second homer of the doubleheader.[8] The 9-5 loss brought the team's record at Ebbets Field to 2-4. The next day, the Eagles' fortunes changed, and they swept the American Giants. The opener went 10 innings

and the Eagles won 6-5. They had tied the game with a pair of runs in the ninth inning. In the 10th, Rap Dixon doubled home Harry Williams with the winning run. Jackman, who came on to pitch the 10th inning, was awarded the victory. In the second game, things did not start well for the Eagles. Starting pitcher James Reese allowed the first two batters to reach base. Jackman came on in relief and allowed one run. The Eagles retaliated with nine first-inning runs and cruised to a 14-4 win. Among the 17 Eagles hits were a homer by manager Giles and two hits, including a triple, by pitcher Jackman.[9]

On Memorial Day, the Eagles hosted the New York Cubans and split the doubleheader. In the opener, the Eagles won 6-5 with Elbert Williams pitching a complete game, scattering 13 hits. The Cubans won the nightcap, 4-0, in a game highlighted by a homer off the bat of Alejandro Oms and the pitching of Luis Tiant.[10] Crowd estimates varied, but the *New York Age* reported that the Eagles had drawn 7,500 on Thursday, far more than the 6,000 drawn by the Dodgers the following Sunday.[11]

Rain washed away the games scheduled in June at Ebbets Field, including the first-ever Ebbets Field night game scheduled for June 4, and the Eagles didn't return home until July. They finished the first half of the season in fourth place with a 15-15 record.

On July 7, the team opened the second half of the season, splitting a doubleheader with the Philadelphia Stars at Ebbets Field. Manager Giles was the batting star for the Eagles with two doubles in each game. In the opener, the Stars won 6-5, their offense sparked by Jake Dunn, who went 3-for-4 with a homer. Ted "Double-Duty" Radcliffe pitched the Eagles to a 6-5 win in the nightcap, contributing two of his team's nine hits.[12]

A week later the Crawfords of Pittsburgh came to town. They played four games over two days. On Saturday, July 13, the teams split a doubleheader with 8,000 fans looking on. The

Crawfords won the opener, 7-3, as Josh Gibson went 3-for-4, Judy Johnson doubled, and Sam Bankhead went 2-for-4. The Crawfords tallied four eighth-inning runs off Eagles starter Elbert Williams to overcome a sixth-inning solo homer by Giles that had given the Eagles a 3-2 advantage. Rosey Davis pitched the complete-game win for the Crawfords. In the second game, the Eagles turned the tables, scoring three runs in the sixth inning off pitcher Bill Harvey to win 4-3. The key hit in the rally was a two-run double by Javier Perez, who went on to score the third run of the inning on an errant throw from left field. Once he had the lead, pitcher Leon Day shut down the Grays with one hit over the last three innings.[13]

The next day Josh Gibson homered to lead the Crawfords to a 5-3 win in the opener, as Leroy Matlock pitched a six-hitter for the winners. The Eagles were kept in the game by a superlative play by outfielder Fats Jenkins with one run in and two runners on in the ninth inning. His fielding gem secured the third out, but the Eagles were unable to make up the deficit. Brooklyn won the nightcap, 12-6, and got to see a hit by the legendary Oscar Charleston. Charleston, then 38 years old, was the player-manager of the Crawfords and, after going 0-for-4 in the opener, inserted himself as a pinch-hitter in the nightcap, singling off Jackman in the eighth inning. James "Cool Papa" Bell had a hit in each game for the Crawfords. The batting star for the Crawfords in the second game was Curtis Harris, who went 3-for-4 with two doubles and a homer. Jenkins, after flashing his glove in the opener, went 3-for-5 with a sacrifice and a stolen base in the nightcap for the Eagles. The aptly named Crush Holloway homered for the Eagles.[14] Holloway had signed on with the Eagles earlier in July and his name, which was not a nickname, came from the fact that, at the time he was born, his arrival prevented his father from attending the Texas Railroad Exposition. At the Exposition, locomotives tried to crush each other. Hence the unlikely first name.[15]

The next weekend brought the Elite Giants to town. Calling Detroit, Columbus, and Nashville home at times during the 1935 season, they were, on the weekend of July 20-21, known as the Nashville Elites. The Eagles won on Saturday, 4-1, in a game abbreviated by rain. The game was decided when the Eagles scored three runs in the third inning. The opportunistic Eagles used a walk, three singles, a fly out and an errant throw to take the 4-1 lead. The rains came after the sixth inning.[16] The Eagles fell prey to the Elites by scores of 13-8 and 10-0 on Sunday with Zollie Wright homering in each game. Nashville's Andy Porter was the pitching star of the day. He stopped the damage when the Eagles scored four runs in the fifth inning of the opener and pitched the entire second game.[17]

On August 3 and 4, the Dodgers played at Ebbets Field – the Newark Dodgers, that is. The Eagles won the doubleheader on Saturday by scores of 4-2 and 8-2. In the opener, a two-run fourth-inning homer by Bert Johnson gave Newark a 2-1 lead, but the Eagles came from behind for the win. Once again, the Dodgers claimed the lead in the second game, this time on a first-inning homer by James Williams. But the Eagles tied it on a Giles homer and went on to win easily behind the pitching of Leon Day. Young Ray Dandridge of Newark went 5-for-9 in the doubleheader.[18] Cheers turned into tears the next day as the Dodgers took advantage of opportunities in each game to sweep the Eagles, 9-5 and 14-12. In the opener, with the score tied at 5-5 in the top of the seventh inning, Jack McCoy's bases-loaded double proved decisive. The teams combined for 41 hits in the nightcap and the Eagles had a 12-10 lead until a bases-loaded triple by Jim Lindsay propelled the Dodgers to their second come-from-behind win of the day. In each case the pitcher victimized by the winning hit was Jackman.[19]

The Eagles were well represented at the East-West Game at Chicago's Comiskey Park on August 11. Manager-first baseman George Giles, left fielder Clarence "Fats" Jenkins, shortstop Bill Yancey, right fielder Ed Stone, and young pitcher Leon Day were named to the squad, although Yancey did not get to play in the game. Day was in the early stages of a career that would take him to Cooperstown.[20]

The team spent the balance of August on the road and returned to Ebbets Field to face the Newark Dodgers in a doubleheader on September 1. The Eagles slugged their way to a win in the opener. They broke things open with an 11-run eighth inning and won 19-8. Pitcher Jackman went 3-for-5 with a homer to aid his own cause and center fielder C.B. Griffin contributed a homer as well. Third baseman Javier Perez had three singles. In the nightcap the Eagles made the most of six hits, including a two-run third-inning double from Perez, winning 9-4 for pitcher Elbert Williams.[21]

After their Negro National League season ended, there was the Crispus Attucks Community Council charity doubleheader featuring, the Eagles, the Pittsburgh Crawfords, the Philadelphia Stars, and the New York Cubans. The doubleheader took place on September 8 and the record crowd of 10,000 fans got a preview of postseason activity because the Cubans and Crawfords were scheduled to face each other in the league championship series. The Cubans and Stars played in the opener and the Crawfords and Eagles played in the nightcap.[22] The original plan was for pitcher Martin Dihigo to play all nine positions for the Cubans, but he played the entire game at third base.[23] The Cubans and Stars played to a 2-2 tie before the Crawfords, with Josh Gibson going 2-for-4, defeated the Eagles 12-3. Leroy Matlock pitched the complete-game win for the Crawfords. Leon Day started for the Eagles but was victimized when the Crawfords broke open the game with a total of eight runs in the seventh and eighth innings.

The dominance of the Crawfords was capsulized in the *Philadelphia Tribune*: "The devastating machine that the Pittsburgh Crawfords are so proud of moved its powerful way across the diamond and when the game was over the Brooklyn Eagles were just a small spot in the sod."[24]

Night baseball came to Ebbets Field for the first time on September 11, 1935, when the Eagles took on the House of David in an exhibition. Pitching for the bearded crew was none other than Grover Cleveland Alexander. The lights were provided by the visitors as the Dodgers had yet to install lights at Ebbets Field.[25] Alexander, at age 48, pitched the first inning for the House of David, yielding a hit to Fats Jenkins, who was left stranded. Terrence "Elmer the Great" McDuffie pitched the entire game and struck out 10 for the Eagles, who won 6-1. Five of the Eagles' 11 hits were triples.[26]

The Eagles concluded their season at Ebbets Field on September 15 with a doubleheader against a minor-league all-star team. A quick scan of the box scores indicates that the all-stars were little more than legends in their own minds. The teams split the two games with the Eagles losing the opener 6-5 before coming back to win the nightcap 10-9. In the game, scheduled to go seven innings, the Eagles came from behind to tie the game with three seventh-inning runs and pushed across the game-winner in the eighth when the all-stars' center fielder dropped a fly ball.[27]

The Eagles had played their last game in Brooklyn. In November it was announced that the team was moving to Newark, New Jersey. Owner Abe Manley announced that he had lost $10,000 during the team's year in Brooklyn.[28] As the Newark Eagles, Manley's team would enjoy great success culminating in a Negro League World Series win in 1946.[29]

SOURCES

In addition to Baseball-Reference.com and the sources cited in the Notes, the author used:

"Grays Win 2, Lose 2 to Brooklyn," *Pittsburgh Courier*, May 25, 1935: 16.

"Mayor to Start League Game at Ebbets Field," *New York Amsterdam News*, May 18, 1935: 11.

Lewis, Teddy. "Brooklyn Promenade," *New York Age*, May 18, 1935: 7.

Von Wilkinson, Eric. "Mayor LaGuardia and Prominent City Officials Attend Opening of Negro Nat'l League in B'klyn," *New York Age*, May 25, 1935: 5.

NOTES

1   "Brooklyn Granted N.N. League; Bankhead Goes to Grays in Trade," *Pittsburgh Courier*, November 17, 1934: 15.

2   "B'klyn Eagles Buy Players," *New York Age*, December 8, 1934: 5.

3   "Mayor LaGuardia to Throw Out First Ball at Negro Nat'l Opening at Ebbett's [sic] Field Brooklyn, Sunday," *New York Age*, May 18, 1935: 5.

4   "Pittsburgh Nine Thumps Eagles in Opener, 20-7," *New York Daily News*, May 19, 1935: 82; "Grays Put Damper on Eagles' Opener," *Pittsburgh Press*, May 19, 1935: Sports Section – 2.

5   "Eagles in Even Break Against Pittsburgh Grays," *Brooklyn Daily Eagle*, May 20, 1935: 11.

6   "Black Eagles Have New Ace," *Brooklyn Times Union*, May 21, 1935: 3A; Lew Zeidler, "New Teeth Put Life in Dixon's Diamond Work," *Brooklyn Daily Eagle*, May 21, 1935: 21; "Grays Bow to Eagles," *New York Age*, May 25, 1935: 5.

7   "Sues Brooklyn Eagles," *Baltimore Afro-American*, July 13, 1935: 16.

8   "Homer Subdues Eagles in 12th," *Brooklyn Times Union*, May 26, 1935: 2A.

9   "Brooklyn Eagles Score Double Win," *Brooklyn Daily Eagle*, May 27, 1935: 12; "Jackman Stars on Slab Against Chicago Tossers," *Brooklyn Times Union*, May 27, 1935: 3A.

10 "New Feud Born as Eagles Split with Cubans," *Brooklyn Times Union*, May 31, 1935: 3A.

11 Lewis E. Dial, "The Sport Dial," *New York Age*, June 8, 1935: 8.

12 "Manager Giles Stars with Bat Against Philly," *Brooklyn Times Union*, July 8, 1935: 3A.

13 "Crawford Club Wins and Loses," *Pittsburgh Press*, July 14, 1935: Sports Section, 5; "Eagles, Crawfords Split Twin Bill," *Brooklyn Times Union*, July 14, 1935: 3A; "Crawfords Break Even," *Pittsburgh Sun-Telegraph*, July 14, 1935: 2-5.

14 "Jenkins Shines for Eagles' Nine," *Brooklyn Times Union*, July 15, 1935: 3A.

15 "Brooklyn Eagles Sign Holloway, Outfielder," *New York Age*, July 20, 1935: 8.

16 "Brooklyn Eagles Trounce Nashville," *Brooklyn Times Union*, July 21, 1935: 2A.

17 "Eagles Defeated by Strong Rivals," *Brooklyn Times Union*, July 22, 1935: 3A.

18 "Eagles Triumph in Double-Header," *Brooklyn Times Union*, August 4, 1935: 3A.

19 Eagles Subdued in Doubleheader," *Brooklyn Times Union*, August 5, 1935: 3A; "Newark Dodgers Humble Eagles," *Brooklyn Daily Eagle*, August 5, 1935: 10.

20 "West Nine Wins Colored Classic," *Brooklyn Times Union*, August 12, 1935: 3A.

21 "Perez Stands Out for Eagles with Hard Hitting," *Brooklyn Times Union*, September 2, 1935: 3A.

22 "Gibson, Oms Set for Benefit Bill," *Brooklyn Times Union*, September 5, 1935: 2A.

23 Irwin N. Rosee, "Dihigo to Play Every Position in Benefit Game," *Brooklyn Times Union*, September 7, 1935: 3A.

24 "10,000 Watch Cubans Tie Stars in N.Y.," *Philadelphia Tribune*, September 12, 1935: 11.

25 "First Night Fray at Ebbets Field," *Brooklyn Times Union*, September 11, 1935: 3A.

26 "M'Duffie Shines in Night Opener," *Brooklyn Times Union*, September 12, 1935: 3A.

27 "Eagles Rally to Gain Even Break," *Brooklyn Times Union*, September 16, 1935: 3A.

28 "Eagle Tossers Quit Brooklyn," *Brooklyn Times Union*, November 12, 1935: 2A.

29 See Frederick C. Bush and Bill Nowlin, eds., *The Newark Eagles Take Flight: The Story of the 1946 Negro League Champions* (Phoenix: SABR, 2019). https://sabr.org/latest/sabr-digital-library-newark-eagles-take-flight-story-1946-negro-league-champions.

Negro League Brooklyn Eagles
Play Inaugural Home Opener at Ebbets Field

May 18, 1935

Homestead Grays 20, Brooklyn Eagles 7

by Gregory H. Wolf

Few names are as synonymous with the development of Negro League baseball as Abe and Effa Manley. The couple is most commonly associated with the Newark Eagles, which they owned from 1936 until they disbanded the club in 1948, one year after Jackie Robinson integrated the White major leagues, thus signaling the end of the biggest and arguably most important predominantly Black-owned business enterprise in the United States. The couple's foray into professional baseball, however, began with the Brooklyn Eagles.

In November 1934 the Manleys were awarded an expansion team in the second incarnation of the Negro National League.[1] Since its revival in 1933, the NNL was plagued by the financial instability of its member teams, exacerbated by the effects of the Great Depression on American society. The NNL viewed the Manleys, a wealthy couple residing in Harlem, as a means to help stabilize the league, which had been without a club in New York City. The NNL also added the New York Cuban Stars, owned by influential Alex Pompez, which further legitimized the league.[2]

The Manleys systematically built their team from scratch. Their initial task was hiring Ben Taylor, whom the *Brooklyn Eagle* described as "one of the best colored managers in baseball."[3] Taylor had spent two decades as a first baseman and manager in the Negro Leagues and had established his reputation with the Indianapolis ABCs, owned by his brother, C.I. Taylor. In 1934 he had managed a White team in Stapleton, on Staten Island.[4]

By the time the owners of the Negro League clubs conducted their business meeting, led by league Commissioner W. Rollo Wilson, on January 11 and 12 in Harlem, the Manleys had already secured the arrangements to play their home games at Ebbets Field in Brooklyn when the Dodgers were on the road.[5]

While Taylor spent the offseason combing the country for talent, the Manleys engaged a prolific and well-known sportswriter to drum up interest in their club and locate prospects. James Estes Gardner, known as Chappy, was a former Negro Leaguer, football player, and college coach, with contacts throughout the world of Black baseball.[6] The Eagles took 28 players to their training camp in Jacksonville, Florida; however, Taylor anticipated keeping a roster of 17 for the regular season while assigning the others to two minor leagues in the South (Southern League and Texas League).[7]

Manley spared no expense putting together his roster. The "Eagles definitely have a good club," opined the *Brooklyn Times Union*,[8] while the *New York Age* described the team as a "balanced squad" with an "alert, hard-working line-up."[9] Among the top signees were 32-year-old right-hander Ted Radcliffe, who had acquired the moniker "Double Duty" for his ability to catch the first game of a twin bill and then pitch the second contest; 37-year-old Clarence "Fats" Jenkins, whom Stephen V. Rice described in the player's SABR BioProject entry as an "athletic marvel" and "dynamic hitter," as well as an exceptional basketball player in nascent professional leagues;[10] and 18-year-old Leon Day, the future Hall of Famer who developed into one of the greatest Negro League pitchers of his generation.

The Eagles home opener took place on Saturday, May 18, as part of a four-game series with the Homestead Grays over three days. "[I]t is likely to crackle all over the field tomorrow as the Eagles feel for the first time the warm enthusiasm of a home crowd," predicted Brooklyn sportswriter Irwin N. Rose.[11]

It was an especially festive day at Ebbets Field, despite cool temperatures in the low 60s and gray, overcast skies. A crowd of 2,500 was on hand for the 3 P.M. start time [For purposes of comparison, the Dodgers averaged 6,111 spectators per home game, which ranked fourth among the eight NL teams.]

The pregame celebration began with "impressive ceremonies," noted the *Brooklyn Times Union*.[12] The ballpark was adorned with special bunting and decorations. Set up in the infield was the Brooklyn Colored Elks Band, which provided musical entertainment. In an especially

exhilarating moment, the Eagles raised their pennant up the flagpole instead of the Dodgers flag.

A large group of dignitaries viewed the festivities from box seats. In addition to police, city officials, and pastors, the most prominent in the group were Samuel Leibowitz, a nationally renowned New York attorney who had defended nine Black men in the infamous Scottsboro, Alabama, trial,[13] and Harlem Alderman Conrad Johnson.

Mayor Fiorello LaGuardia, a New Deal Republican, threw out the ceremonial first pitch. The *New York Age*, the city's most influential African American newspaper, opined that LaGuardia's symbolic act "definitely puts the young circuit on a par with its well-established contemporaries," and noted that the mayor had thrown out the first pitch for the Giants and Yankees, but not the Dodgers.[14]

The Eagles and Grays entered the game with identical 3-3 records. The Eagles began the season by defeating the Newark Dodgers twice, then losing three of four games to the reigning NNL champion Philadelphia Stars. Manger Cum Posey's Homestead squad, named for the steel town on the Monongahela River, seven miles southeast of Pittsburgh, welcomed the return of its two best players, wrote the *Pittsburgh Post-Gazette*.[15] Slugger and future Hall of Famer Buck Leonard, whom the paper called "Flash" and was later known as the "Black Lou Gehrig"; and Vic Harris, described as the "heart and soul" of the club.[16]

The Eagles took the field "equipped as a big-league club," boasted the *New York Age*.[17] They wore uniforms of a "light shade" with "Eagles" written across the chest, reported the paper. (The road uniforms were darker with "Brooklyn" across the front.)

The game itself was a laugher. "A cool breeze seemed to affect the players of both teams from the start," submitted the *New York Age*, "as the game was loosely played."[18]

After the Grays scored a run in the opening frame, the Eagles erupted for four runs in the first off starter Joe Strong. The big blows were Jenkins' leadoff home run and a round-tripper by cleanup hitter Rap Dixon, a five-tool ballplayer and dangerous slugger whose best seasons came with the Harrisburg Giants and the Baltimore Black Sox in the 1920s.[19]

By the end of the second inning, both starting pitchers had been knocked from the box. The Grays stormed back with four runs and the Eagles answered with two more to retake the lead, 6-5.

The Eagles' lead was fleeting. The Grays pounded three relievers, Roy S. Williams and an unnamed Gavin (also referred to as Galvin) in what appears to be their only appearance in an NNL game, and Sleeky Reese. The Eagles erupted for four runs in the third to take a 9-6 lead. "I never saw so many home runs in my life," recounted Effa Manley. "I went home in the third inning and had my first drink of whiskey."[20] The Grays continued their barrage in the fifth, adding five more runs. The "most lethal blow," wrote the *Pittsburgh Press*, was Jerry Benjamin's grand slam.[21]

While the Grays were racking up a 14-6 lead, Willie Gisentaner took over in the second and shut down the Eagles. Known as Three Finger for his mangled index finger on his pitching hand, the southpaw pitched the final 7⅔ innings, yielding just six hits and one additional run (in the fifth).[22]

The Grays tacked on three runs in both the seventh and eighth innings for an eventual 20-7 victory. Posey's squad racked up 23 hits, led by Matt Carlisle's four safeties. They smashed 12 extra-base hits, including four home runs, with Benjamin, Buddy Burbage, Harris, and Gisentaner connecting. The Grays collected 11 hits; three of the five extra-base hits were home runs (Jenkins, Dixon, and Clarence Palm).

The doubleheader the following day was "far more exciting and thrilling," opined the *New York Age*.[23] In front of 5,000 spectators, the Eagles won the first game, 18-9, and lost the second 4-2, which was called after six innings because of darkness. The Eagles lost the Monday matinee, 4-3, to wrap up their first and only season-opening home series in Brooklyn.

In the offseason, the Manleys purchased the Newark Dodgers. They combined the rosters of both teams and renamed the club the Newark Eagles.

SOURCES

In addition to the sources cited in the Notes, the author accessed Retrosheet.org, Baseball-Reference.com, Seamheads.com SABR.org, and the following articles:

Sylvester, Harry. "Negro Big Loop Ball Team for Brooklyn," *Brooklyn Eagle*, January 9, 1935: 23.

"Eagles Getting Ready for Their Opening Day on Saturday," *Brooklyn Citizen*, May 15, 1935: 35.

"Grays Swamp Brooklyn, 20-7," *Pittsburgh Sun-Telegraph*, May 19, 1935: 20.

"Major Colored League Opens Season Today," *Brooklyn Citizen*, May 18, 1935: 6.

"Taylor Sign Players for Brooklyn Nine," *Brooklyn Eagle*, January 17, 1935: 25.

NOTES

1   James Overmyer, *Queen of the Negro Leagues: Effa Manley and the Newark Eagles* (Lanham, Maryland: Scarecrow Press, 1993), 33.

2   Brian Mckenna, "Alex Pompez," SABR BioProject, https://sabr.org/bioproj/person/alex-pompez/.

3   Harry Sylvester, "Negro Big Loop Ball Team for Brooklyn," *Brooklyn Eagle*, January 9, 1935: 23.

4   Sylvester.

5   "N.Y. and Brooklyn Get Franchise in National Association of Negro Baseball Clubs at Meeting Here," *New York Age*, January 19, 1935: 5.

6   Sylvester.

7   "Taylor Takes a Squad of 28 South," *Brooklyn Eagle*, March 1, 1935: 2.

8   Irvin N. Rose, "Brooklyn Ready for First Peek at Black Eagles," *Brooklyn Times Union*, May 17, 1935: 10.

9   "Mayor LaGuardia to Throw Out First Ball at Negro Nat'l League Opener at Ebbets Field, Brooklyn, Sunday," *New York Age*, May 18, 1935: 5.

10   Stephen V. Rice, "Fats Jenkins," SABR BioProject https://sabr.org/bioproj/person/fats-jenkins/.

11   Rose.

12   Brooklyn Eagles Beaten in Opener," *Brooklyn Times Union*, May 19, 1935: 14.

13   "The Scottsboro Defense Attorney," American Experience PBS. https://www.pbs.org/wgbh/americanexperience/features/scottsboro-defense-attorney-samuel-leibowitz/.

14   "Mayor LaGuardia to Throw Out First Ball at Negro Nat'l League Opener at Ebbets Field, Brooklyn."

15   "Crippled Grays Open Series in Brooklyn," *Pittsburgh Post-Gazette*, May 17, 1935: 22.

16   Charlie Fouche, "Vic Harris," SABR BioProject. https://sabr.org/bioproj/person/vic-harris-2/.

17   "Mayor LaGuardia to Throw Out First Ball at Negro Nat'l League Opener at Ebbets Field, Brooklyn."

18   Eric von Wilkinson, "Mayor LaGuardia and Prominent City Officials Attend Opening of Negro Nat'l League in B'klyn," *New York Age*, May 25, 1935: 5.

19   "Grays Put Damper on Eagles' Opener," *Pittsburgh Press*, May 19, 1935: 16.

20   John Holway, Voices from the Great Black Baseball Leagues (New York: Dover Publications, 2012), 320.

21   "Grays Put Damper on Eagles' Opener."

22   "Grays' Three-Fingered Star," *Pittsburgh Courier*, August 31, 1935: 14.

23   Wilkinson.

THE LIGHTS GO ON AT EBBETS FIELD

September 11, 1935
Brooklyn Eagles 6, House of David 1

by Alan Cohen

"Oh, I'm not really great. I'm just good, darn good."

– Terris "Elmer the Great" McDuffie,
  August 14, 1935.[1]

Night baseball came to Ebbets Field for the first time on September 11, 1935, when the Brooklyn Eagles of the Negro National League took on the House of David in an exhibition. Pitching for the bearded crew was their manager, none other than Grover Cleveland Alexander. The House of David, taking on all comers, had amassed a record of 81-11 in 1935 after winning the Denver Post championship in 1934. At one point in the 1935 season, they had won 27 straight games, and they had shut out the opposition in 33 games.[2]

The House of David team played in front of big crowds, and one of those big crowds, estimated to be as large as 20,000, had seen Alexander matched up with another future Hall of Famer, Dazzy Vance, at nearby Dexter Park on Sunday, September 8. Alexander pitched two shutout innings, but the 44-year-old Vance pitched six scoreless innings and his Bushwicks prevailed, 6-0.[3]

At that time, there were several teams crisscrossing the country as the "House of David." This particular group was known as the Western House of David. All they seemed to have in common with the other House of David teams was an abundance of facial hair. And there was a bit of confusion. On September 10, the newspaper in Lead, South Dakota, said that the very same House of David team would be playing the Kansas City Monarchs in the South Dakota town on September 11 at 4:30 P.M.[4] The folks got to see the Monarchs defeat House of David, 8-1, and perhaps they got to see Satchel Paige. They did not get to see Grover Cleveland Alexander. Perhaps it was an actor posing as Alexander.

Twice before in 1935, the Eagles were scheduled to take on the House of David but on each occasion the rains came, and the event was postponed. They were initially scheduled to play under the lights on June 4. Rain resulted in the game being rescheduled for June 10. Another night of rain pushed the date out for another three months.

On September 11 in Brooklyn, the festivities got underway at 9:00 P.M. The lights were provided by the visitors as the Dodgers had yet to install lights at Ebbets Field.[5] Alexander, at age 48, pitched the first inning for the House of David, yielding a hit to Fats Jenkins, who was left stranded. Walter Laufer came on in the second inning, pitched the balance of the game for House of David, and was the losing pitcher in the 6-1 contest.

Terris "Elmer the Great" McDuffie pitched the entire game for the Eagles, striking out 10 and walking only one batter. McDuffie allowed only six hits, three of which came in the sixth inning when the House of David scored its only run of the night, tying the game. Five of the Eagles' 11 hits were triples.[6] McDuffie had joined the Brooklyn Eagles on August 14, 1935. He had spent most of the season pitching for the New York Black Yankees and had an 11-4 record, per the *Brooklyn Eagle*. One of his wins had been a no-hitter against House of David.[7]

Jenkins was the batting star of the game, accounting for three of his team's hits including one of the five triples.

The game was tied at 1-1 going into the bottom of the sixth inning, when the Eagles scored three runs to take the lead for good. They took the lead on a triple by shortstop Bill Sadler, who had two hits in the game.

Hitting triples for the Eagles, in addition to Jenkins and Sadler, were manager George Giles, right fielder Ed Stone, and catcher Fred "Tex" Burnett.

Between the fifth and sixth innings, the House of David put on an entertaining display of their "pepper game."

The House of David squad often matched up against Negro League teams and next on their agenda was a stop at Paterson, New Jersey, against the New York Black Yankees on September 12. Then there was a matchup with the Pittsburgh Crawfords in Altoona, Pennsylvania, on September 16.[8]

The night game had the approval of the front office of the Brooklyn Dodgers. Business manager Bob Quinn and club President Steve McKeever, according to the *New York Post* in a pregame report, were said to be equally interested in the possibilities of night baseball at Ebbets Field, feeling that a successful trial "may spur them to install permanent arcs next season for the use of the Eagles as well as the Dodgers."[9] This prediction was premature. The Eagles would play only once more in Brooklyn (a doubleheader against a group of minor-league all-stars on September 15) before relocating to Newark in 1936. As for the Dodgers, they did not play their first night game at Ebbets Field until June 15, 1938 – but that is another story.

Terris McDuffie hung around a while, pitching from 1930 through 1954, but is largely forgotten. He pitched in three Negro League East West All-Star games. He tried out with the Brooklyn Dodgers on April 7, 1945, but did not impress Branch Rickey.[10] McDuffie was still hurling in 1954 for the Eagles, at age 44, but it was for the Dallas Eagles in the Texas League. On July 17, 1954, he hurled his last complete game, defeating Bobby Locke of San Antonio, 5-1. On August 3, 1954, almost 19 years after he arrived at Ebbets Field to pitch with the Brooklyn Eagles, McDuffie pitched Dallas to a 6-5 win over Shreveport.[11] It was his last professional win. He was released on August 13.

One last note about that workout in 1945. Catching him that day was 43-year-old Clyde Sukeforth, a Dodgers coach who was pressed into service as a wartime replacement player in 1945. He had last played in 1934 and played through June 7 in 1945. He then was pressed into duty as a scout. On August 24, 1945, after a Negro League game at Chicago's Comiskey Park, Sukeforth introduced himself to the Kansas City shortstop – Jackie Robinson.

SOURCES

In addition to Baseball-Reference.com and the sources shown in the Notes, the author used the following sources:

"First Night Game at Ebbets Field: Western House of David to Meet Eagles Tomorrow," *Brooklyn Times Union*, September 10, 1935: 3-A.

"Eagles Trim House of David," *Brooklyn Daily Eagle*, September 12, 1935: 21.

NOTES

1   Lew Zeidler, "Just Below the Majors," *Brooklyn Daily Eagle*, August 14, 1935: 17.

2   "House of David Team Tackles Black Yanks at Stadium Tonight," *Paterson* (New Jersey) *Evening News*, September 12, 1935: 23.

3   William J. Granger, "Dazzy Vance and Grover Alexander Draw 16,000 Fans to Dexter Park; Bushwicks Score Two Easy Wins," *Brooklyn Citizen*, September 9, 1935: 6.

4   "Monarchs and Davids Play Here Tomorrow," *Lead* (South Dakota) *Daily Call*, September 10, 1935: 1.

5   "First Night Fray at Ebbets Field: Eagles Tackle Alexander's Bearded Clan in Arc Inaugural Tonight," *Brooklyn Times Union*, September 11, 1935: 3A.

6   "M'Duffie Shines in Night Opener: Eagles' Ace Pitcher Hero in Victory Over Alexander's Club," *Brooklyn Times Union* (Four Star Edition), September 12, 1935: 3A.

7   Zeidler.

8   "Another Big Baseball Game for Altoona Fans," *Altoona* (Pennsylvania) *Tribune*, September 10, 1935: 9.

9   "Eagles Play Night Game," *New York Post*, September 11, 1935: 15.

10 Jack Smith, "Dodgers Try Out Negro Players," *New York Daily News*, April 8, 1945: 71.

11 United Press, "Beaumont Downs Cats; Tulsa Drops Game to Houston," *Sapulpa* (Oklahoma) *Herald*, August 5, 1954: 6.

FRANKHOUSE TOSSES RAIN-SHORTENED NO-HITTER

August 27, 1937

Brooklyn Dodgers 5, Cincinnati Reds 0 (seven innings)

by Gregory H. Wolf

In the midst of the best game of his career, the Brooklyn Dodgers' Fred Frankhouse was just four outs away from every pitcher's dream – a no-hitter – when Mother Nature intervened. Pacing in the clubhouse, "fuming with impatience," reported the *New York Times*, Frankhouse wondered if he'd get the chance to etch his name into the record books.[1]

It was no surprise that a paltry crowd of 2,818 paid customers had showed up for ladies day at Ebbets Field for a Friday-afternoon twin bill necessitated by the postponement of the previous day's scheduled game because of rain.[2] With the nation still firmly in the grip of the Great Depression, a battle between perennial second-division clubs provided little diversion from stark economic realities. Heading to their worst season in two decades, first-year skipper and former Dodgers pitching great Burleigh Grimes's squad was slumping. They had lost 13 of their last 18 games and sat in the NL cellar (44-67), a result of season-long pitching woes and weak bats. Their opponent, the sixth-place Reds (45-64), hadn't enjoyed a winning season in nine years.

Grimes called on his "curve-ball specialist" Frankhouse to start the opener.[3] The 33-year-old right-hander had toiled as an undistinguished swingman in his first six years in the big leagues until he fell under the tutelage of renowned pitching guru Bill McKechnie, skipper of the Boston Braves, in 1932. "[McKechnie] changed my style of pitching," explained Frankhouse, "from sidearm to overhand. The result has been better control and more stuff on the ball. My curve ball especially is more effective."[4] Frankhouse developed one of the best curves in the NL, according to *Who's Who*.[5] Sportswriter Clifford Bloodgood wrote that Frankhouse's "curve ball is still definitely wicked to even curve ball hitters."[6] The effectiveness of his career-altering pitch resulted from an unorthodox grip. "My curve is fashioned by the snap of my wrist and the position of my fingers on the ball," explained Frankhouse. "My middle fingers are bent under, pressing the cover."[7]

Harnessing the control of his breaking pitches, Frankhouse emerged as a dependable workhorse, earned an All-Star berth in 1934, and had averaged 14 wins and 236 innings pitched the previous four seasons (1933-1936). Acquired by the Dodgers in a trade prior to spring training in 1936, Frankhouse entered the game tied with Luke Hamlin for the team lead with eight victories (seven defeats), pushing his career slate to 101-84.

The game started sloppily. Frankhouse walked leadoff hitter Hub Walker, then second baseman Jim Bucher threw wildly after scooping up Ival Goodman's routine double-play grounder. Frankhouse and his batterymate, Babe Phelps, completed a nifty strike out-throw out twin killing, fanning Chick Hafey and catching Walker attempting to swipe third. Frankhouse, however, was still fighting with his bender. After he walked Les Scarsella, Buddy Hassett made what sportswriter Lou Smith of the *Cincinnati Enquirer* called a "sweet stop" on Gilly Campbell's drive down the foul line and tossed quickly to Frankhouse covering the bag to end the inning.[8]

Toeing the rubber for manager Chuck Dressen's Reds was 29-year-old swingman Al Hollingsworth. In his third season, the southpaw was 9-8 and 24-31 in his three-year career. After walking Hassett in the first, Hollingsworth was tagged for a run in the second. Cookie Lavagetto led off with a single, stole second as Phelps struck out, then raced home when Gibby Brack's roller went through shortstop Buddy Myer's legs. What should have been the Reds' first of a series of miscues was ruled "magnanimously" a hit, quipped sportswriter Lou Smith.[9]

The Dodgers tacked on another run in the third and again in the fourth, both coming with two outs. In the third, Hassett beat out a high bounder to short. Heinie Manush's grounder in almost the exact spot should have ended the frame, but Myers fumbled the ball and threw wildly to first, enabling Hassett to reach third. Lavagetto's single made it 2-0. In the fourth, Bucher's single drove in Johnny Cooney, who had doubled, the game's only extra-base hit, for a 3-0 lead.

With one out in the sixth, three successive infield grounders loaded the bags for the Dodgers. Cooney singled just out of the reach of second baseman Alex Kampouris; Bucher's hopper went through third baseman Lew Riggs's legs for an error on what should have been an inning-ending double play; and then Hollingsworth slipped and fell trying to field Hassett's grounder. Heinie Manush, the 35-year-old longtime AL star with the Detroit Tigers, St. Louis Browns, and Washington Senators, in his first season in the NL, plated Cooney on a force-play grounder. Lavagetto's third straight hit, yet another grounder, drove in Bucher for the Dodgers fifth and final run.

After a shaky first, Frankhouse kept bending pitches over the plate. Even though he lacked his normal control, he had "plenty on the pill," observed sportswriter Kevin Jones in the *New York Daily News*.[10] He issued one walk in four of the next six innings, but required "no spectacular fielding play," opined Dodgers beat reporter Tommy Holmes to erase the Reds.[11] The most difficult fielding play came in the third. Goodman connected for a fly to deep right, which Manush snared on the run against the scoreboard.[12]

Frankhouse almost lost his no-hitter on a fluke with two outs in the fifth. Hub Walker tried to get out of the way of a high inside pitch, but as he did do, the ball hit his bat. Cookie Lavagetto "hovered over the ball," reported the *Daily News*, as it rolled down the third-base line.[13] He made no attempt to pick it up, knowing that he had no play at first, and the ball slowly drifted into foul territory.

Staked to a 5-0 lead, Frankhouse took the mound in the top of the eighth just six outs away from a no-hitter. The sunny skies on a warm afternoon had gradually given way to the gray clouds that had blanketed Brooklyn the previous days. Frankhouse fanned Walker for the first out. "His curveball was completely baffling," cooed Holmes.[14] And Frankhouse kept throwing benders and batters knew what to expect.

"[Frankhouse] throws curves, and then more curves" wrote syndicated New York sportswriter Daniel M. Daniel.[15] Goodman pounded a curve in the dirt to Bucher at second base for the second out. Before Frankhouse tossed his first pitch to Hafey, a "sudden cloudburst descended," reported sportswriter Lee Scott of the *Brooklyn Citizen*.[16]

The rain came down in such a torrential outburst that home-plate umpire Lee Ballanfant immediately ordered players off the field.[17] Per major league rules, Ballanfant was required to wait for 30 minutes to call the game, which was beyond the requisite five innings to make it official. By that time, however, Ebbets Field had become a "lake," reported Roscoe McGowen of the *New York Times*.[18] Ballanfant called the game, as well as the second contest of the twin bill.

Frankhouse walked six and fanned three in 7⅔ innings in what proved to be the closest he ever came to an official no-hitter. He tossed a complete game and yielded just two earned runs in his next outing, but lost 4-2 to the Cubs. It was the first of six defeats to finish the season 10-13 with a 4.27 ERA, which was well above the league's 3.91 average.

SOURCES

In addition to the sources cited in the Notes, the author accessed Retrosheet.org, Baseball-Reference.com, SABR.org, and *The Sporting News* archive via Paper of Record.

NOTES

1   Roscoe McGowen, "Reds Subdued by Frankhouse, 5-0; Rain Halts Play in Eighth Inning," *New York Times*, August 28, 1937: 10.

2   Kevin Jones, "No-Hitter for Frankhouse," *New York Daily News*, August 28, 1937: 25.

3   Lou Smith, "Redlegs Held Hitless by Fred Frankhouse in 7⅔ Inning Tussle," *Cincinnati Enquirer*, August 28, 1937: 11.

4   Clifford Bloodgood, *Baseball Magazine*, March 1932, quoted from Bill James and Rob Neyer, *The Neyer/James Guide to Pitchers* (New York: Fireside, 2004), 210.

5   Bill James and Rob Neyer, *The Neyer/James Guide to Pitchers*.

6   Clifford Bloodgood, *Baseball Magazine*, March 1932, quoted from Bill James and Rob Neyer, *The Neyer/James Guide to Pitchers*.

7   Clifford Bloodgood, *Baseball Magazine*, March 1932, quoted from Bill James and Rob Neyer, *The Neyer/James Guide to Pitchers*.

8   Smith

9   Smith.

10 Kevin Jones, "No-Hitter for Frankhouse."

11 Tommy Holmes, "Frankhouse No-Hitter May Not Reach Books," *Brooklyn Eagle*, August 28, 1937: 14.

12 Smith.

13 Jones.

14 Holmes.

15 Daniel M. Daniel, *Baseball Magazine*, September 1937, quoted from Bill James and Rob Neyer, *The Neyer/James Guide to Pitchers*.

16 Lee Scott, "Frankhouse First Brooklyn Hurler to Pitch No-Hit, No-Run Game Since 1925," *Brooklyn Citizen*, August 28, 1937: 6.

17 McGowen.

18 McGowen.

VANDER MEER TOSSES SECOND STRAIGHT NO-HITTER IN FIRST MAJOR LEAGUE NIGHT GAME AT EBBETS FIELD

June 15, 1938

Cincinnati Red 6, Brooklyn Dodgers 0

by Gregory H. Wolf

It's never been duplicated in the majors or minors and might be baseball's most unbeatable record. In just his 21st big-league start, the Reds Johnny Vander Meer recorded his second consecutive no-hitter, holding the Dodgers hitless in the first major-league night game at Ebbets Field.[1] New York sportswriter Hy Turkin hailed the accomplishment as the "greatest pitching feat in the 100-year history of baseball."[2]

Vander Meer and the Reds were the talk of baseball when they arrived in Brooklyn to commence a three-game series on the front-end of a 16-game road swing. The perennial also-rans hadn't finished in the first division since 1926, but new skipper Bill McKechnie had the club in third place (25-21), 5½ games behind the New York Giants. Wire service sportswriter George Kirksey described the Reds' unanticipated success as "one of the most important developments" in baseball,[3] while Reds beat reporter Lou Smith opined that the club had recently made "tremendous strides" to compete for the pennant.[4] The Reds shored up their slugging department by acquiring long-ball threat Wally Berger from the Giants on June 6.

A week later they picked up durable workhorse Bucky Walters from the Philadelphia Phillies. Walters was scheduled to make his Reds debut in the opener against the Dodgers on June 14; however, the game was postponed because the Dodgers' train from Grand Rapids, Michigan, where they had played an exhibition, arrived five hours late in the City of Churches.[5] Walters would have to wait a few extra days,[6] though, as McKechnie did not want to alter the rhythm of his prized young hard-throwing southpaw, Johnny Vander Meer.

Vander Meer was in the midst of a dominating stretch. He had won his previous four starts, yielding just 13 hits and three runs in 37 innings, culminating with his no-hitter against the Boston Braves at Crosley Field on June 11. Since his days as a high-school prodigy, Vander Meer had been touted as one of baseball's hardest throwers. He participated in the Dodgers spring training as an 18-year-old in 1933, but his lack of control turned off club brass. Current Dodgers vice president Lee MacPhail could only wish he still had the hurler; two years earlier as Reds VP, MacPhail had acquired Vander Meer, who was named *The Sporting News* Minor League Player of the Year after winning 19 games and fanning 295 for the Durham (North Carolina) Bulls in the Class B Piedmont League in 1936.

Vander Meer's stunning transformation from a wild hurler who walked 69 batters in 84⅓ innings as a rookie in 1937 to one of baseball's most overpowering pitchers was directly related to his skipper. A renowned whisperer to pitchers, McKechnie helped Vander Meer alter his pitching motion from a side-arm to a straight overhand delivery during spring training.[7] In addition, the Deacon increased his pitcher's workload (he was making his fifth start in 19 days) to improve his control.[8] Vander Meer also credited the Boston Red Sox' Lefty Grove for helping him during spring training to polish his mechanics.[9]

It was an historical moment for skipper Burleigh Grimes' seventh-place Dodgers (21-28) who were inaugurating an 18-game homestand at Ebbets Field, the club's 26-year-old ballpark in the Flatbush neighborhood of Brooklyn. Beat reporter Tommy Holmes described the festivities for the first big-league night game in New York City history as an "after-dark diamond circus."[10] (Crosley Field in Cincinnati was the only other major-league ballpark with lights.) Among the capacity crowd of 38,748 were Vander Meer's parents, as well as a contingent of 500 fans from his home town of Midland, New Jersey, about 30 miles from Brooklyn.[11] At 8:35 P.M. the newly installed lights were activated to the awe of the spectators, who were entertained by the Brooklyn Edison Legion Band and drum and fife corps from Manhattan and East Orange.[12] Jesse Owens, the four-time gold medalist from the 1936 Summer Olympics in Berlin, put on a track-and-field exhibition, including a 100-yard dash against the Reds' Lee Gamble and the Dodgers' Ernie Koy.[13] After going through ground rules with both teams, home-plate umpire Bill Stewart finally yelled "Play Ball!" at 9:45 P.M.[14]

Vander Meer breezed through the first and second innings, walking one. His mound opponent, Max Butcher, a 27-year-old right-hander with a 21-23 career slate (4-2 thus far in '38), struggled in the opening frame, yielding a single and a walk to two of the first three batters he faced, then came undone in the third. With two outs, six consecutive batters reached, beginning with a single by Berger, who advanced to second on third baseman Cookie Lavagetto's errant throw. After Ival Goodman walked, former Dodgers farmhand Frank McCormick brought both runners home on a home run to left field. After a walk to Ernie Lombardi and Harry Craft's single, Lew Riggs laced a run-scoring single to send Butcher to the showers. Tot Pressnell replaced Butcher and fanned Billy Myers to end the threat.

The Reds tacked on two more runs. With one out in the seventh, Goodman's screecher back to the mound hit Pressnell in the right kneecap. Writhing in pain, Pressnell left the game on a stretcher and was replaced by Luke Hamlin. Lombardi, batting .359, was intentionally walked to bring up Craft, whose third single of the game made it 5-0. Vander Meer himself scored the game's last run with one out on the eighth. Red-hot Berger collected his 9th hit in 18 at-bats with the Reds, a triple to deep center to plate Vandy.

Staked to an early 4-0 lead by his teammates' high-octane offense, Vander Meer unleashed his blazing fastball and knee-buckling curve on Dodgers hitters, whom he had mesmerized 14 days earlier with a five-hitter. "I was much faster tonight than last Saturday," said Vander Meer, who fanned four and walked three against the Braves in his first no-hitter. "My curve ball was breaking sharper."[15]

Vandy breezed through the third inning through the sixth, issuing two walks, both to wily 39-year-old veteran Kiki Cuyler. "I realized after the fifth that I had a splendid chance to turn another no-hitter," he said.[16] The pressure intensified for Vander Meer, who might have also showed the fatigue of pitching on just three days' rest or less for the third time in his last six starts. (One of those was on two days' rest.)

In the seventh Vander Meer faced his first test. He issued consecutive one-out walks to Lavagetto, who entered the game leading the NL with a .360 batting average, and Dolph Camilli. Vander Meer escaped the jam by fanning Koy and inducing Leo Durocher to ground weakly to second.

By the end of the seventh, Vander Meer's quest for baseball immortality had won over the fans, who vigorously applauded after each out he recorded.[17] After pushing his way through photographers located in foul territory hoping to capture a glimpse of history, Vander Meer breezed through the eighth, registering his sixth and seventh strikeouts.[18] Nonetheless, he admitted, "I felt a little tired in the last two [innings]."[19]

In the dramatic final inning, Vander Meer was a "trifle wild," noted Lou Smith, though not as wild as he was when he faced the Dodgers exactly one year earlier, walking 11.[20] The stakes, however were different in this game. Vandy was a pitch away from walking Buddy Hassett before he induced a weak grounder down the first-base line that he fielded himself for an unassisted out. Vander Meer walked the next three batters, Babe Phelps, Lavagetto, and Camilli, on 18 pitches to load the bases.[21] The capacity crowd went silent.

McKechnie motioned for Bucky Walters to warm up quickly and sauntered to the mound to have a conversation with his young pitcher and infielders while the crowd chanted to leave Vander Meer in the game.[22] The Deacon, whose Hall of Fame credentials were built on his handling of pitchers, did just that. On Vandy's second pitch, Koy hit a slow roller to third baseman Riggs. The All-Star was "so careful in making the throw home," observed sportswriter Roscoe McGowen,

that catcher Lombardi had no time to whip the ball to first for a double play.[23] The Reds fielded flawlessly the entire game and needed no "spectacular plays," reported Turkin.[24] With the count 1-and-1, Durocher sent a scorching liner down the right-field foul line. It appeared as though it might be a grand slam, reported Tommy Holmes, but it curved foul.[25] Durocher lifted the next pitch to center field, where Craft easily corralled it to end the game in 2 hours and 23 minutes.

"[B]edlam broke loose," reported Smith; fans rushed the field to celebrate Vander Meer's feat. An overpowering Vander Meer overcame eight walks and yielded just five outfield fly outs to extended his hitless streak to 18⅓ innings and scoreless streak to 26 innings. (Those streaks eventually reached 21⅓ and 33 innings, respectively.)

Vander Meer's consecutive no-hitters are among baseball's most romantic and mythologized accomplishments. They catapulted the 23-year-old pitcher into instant national stardom and intensified expectations of greatness, both of which took an enormous psychological toll on the pitcher. He finished with an impressive 15-10 slate in '38, but struggled the next season (5-9) and was demoted to the minors in 1940. "Double No-Hit" never authored another no-no and finished his 13-year career with a 119-121 record.

SOURCES

In addition to the sources cited in the Notes, the author accessed Retrosheet.org, Baseball-Reference.com, SABR.org, and the following newspaper articles:

"Here's How Vandy Mowed 'Em Down," *Cincinnati Enquirer*, June 16, 1938: 14.

"Trading Time Is Over with No Red Deals Made," *Cincinnati Enquirer*, June 16, 1938: 17.

NOTES

1   The Dodgers-Reds game was the first game to be played under permanent lights at Ebbets Field; however, it was not the first game to be played under lights at the ballpark. On September 11, 1935, the Negro National League Brooklyn Eagles hosted the House of David in an exhibition at Ebbets Field that was illuminated by temporary lighting. "First Night Game at Ebbets Field: Western House of David to Meet Eagles Tomorrow," *Brooklyn Times Union*, September 10, 1935: 3-A.

2   Hy Turkin, "Vandy's 2nd No-Hitter Eclipses Dodgers, 6-0, in 1st Night Game," *New York Daily News*, June 16, 1938: 50.

3   George Kirksey (United Press), "Reds' Rise Is Feature of Majors," *Cincinnati Enquirer*, June 15, 1938: 12.

4   Lou Smith, "Pennant Aspirations Develop in Minds of Reds," *Cincinnati Enquirer*, June 15, 1938: 12.

5   Lou Smith, "Pennant Aspirations Develop in Minds of Reds."

6   Walters debuted in the makeup game, the second game of a doubleheader on June 17.

7   Associated Press, "'Who Taught Vander Meer to Control Ball?' Baseball Seems to Think It Is a Mystery," *Cincinnati Enquirer*, June 18, 1938: 18.

8   George Kirksey, "Reds' Rise is Feature of Majors."

9   "'Who Taught Vander Meer to Control Ball?' Baseball Seems to Think It Is a Mystery."

10 Tommy Holmes, "Vandy's 2d No-Hitter Eclipses MacPhail's Lights," *Brooklyn Daily Eagle*, June 16, 1938: 16.

11 Harold Parrott, "Boro Notables in Baseball Throngs as Floodlights Inaugural Proves Social and Financial Success — Babe Ruth Cheers," *Brooklyn Daily Eagle*, June 16, 1938: 17.

12 Lee Scott, "Vander Meer Makes Baseball History in Brooklyn's First Night Game," *Brooklyn Citizen*, June 16, 1938: 16.

13 Scott.

14 Louis Effrat, "Fans Jam Stands Long Before Game," *New York Times*, June 16, 1938: 27.

15 Lou Smith, "Vander Meer in Second No-Hitter; Reds Defeat Brooklyn, 6 to 0," *Cincinnati Enquirer*, June 16, 1938: 1, 14.

16 "Vander Meer in Second No-Hitter; Reds Defeat Brooklyn, 6 to 0."

17 "Vander Meer in Second No-Hitter; Reds Defeat Brooklyn, 6 to 0."

18 "Vander Meer in Second No-Hitter; Reds Defeat Brooklyn, 6 to 0."

19 "Vander Meer in Second No-Hitter; Reds Defeat Brooklyn, 6 to 0."

20 "Vander Meer in Second No-Hitter; Reds Defeat Brooklyn, 6 to 0."

21 George Kirksey (United Press), "Nerve," *Cincinnati Enquirer*, June 16, 1938: 14.

22 "Nerve."

23 Roscoe McGowen, "40,000 See Vander Meer of Reds Hurl Second No-Hit, No-Run Game in a Row," *New York Times*, June 16, 1938: 27.

24 Turkin.

25 Holmes.

MUNGO TO THE RESCUE IN WILD ONE AT EBBETS FIELD

August 7, 1938
Brooklyn Dodgers 11, Cincinnati Reds 10 | First Game of Doubleheader

by Alan Cohen

"Crazier than the guy sitting next to the railing of the upper stands and throwing peanut shells down on the fans below."[1]

The Cincinnati Reds entered the Sunday doubleheader at Brooklyn having won each of the seven prior encounters between the Dodgers and Reds at Ebbets Field in 1938, and the Dodgers needed to reverse the trend if they wanted to escape the second division. They entered the games in sixth place, 1½ games behind the fifth-place Boston Braves and nine games behind the fourth-place Chicago Cubs. The Reds, meanwhile, were fighting for their first pennant since 1919. They started the day in third place, six games behind the league-leading Pittsburgh Pirates.

The first game of the doubleheader which began with a steady drizzle and ended in sunshine, akin to the fortunes of the home team, featured 21 runs, 26 hits, two singing ballplayers, a come-from-behind Dodgers win, and a winning pitcher who would be memorialized in song more than 30 years after the fact (along with the game's starting battery for Cincinnati) – something for everyone – except for Reds manager Bill McKechnie, who saw his 52nd birthday celebration ruined.

A crowd of 18,138 was assembled at the home of the Dodgers, and they saw their heroes fall behind 7-0 in the opener. Bill Posedel started for the Dodgers and manager Burleigh Grimes pulled him from the game in the first inning. Johnny Vander Meer of no-hit fame started for the Reds and held the Dodgers hitless in the first inning. He walked two.

The Reds scored five first-inning runs off Posedel. Lonny Frey, batting leadoff for the Reds, walked. Wally Berger then singled for Cincinnati and with two runners on, Dusty Cooke hit one back through the box that bounded off Posedel's knee in the direction of the Dodgers bullpen, down the first-base line. Frey scored on the play, and the Reds had runners at second and third. Frank McCormick then singled home the two runners, making the score 3-0. After Ernie Lombardi grounded out, Harry Craft hit a two-run homer that gave Cincinnati the five-run lead. The homer also gave Posedel the rest of the day off. Dodgers manager Grimes summoned Van Lingle Mungo from the bullpen, and the Carolinian got the Dodgers out of the inning without further damage.

Mungo was hit hard in the second inning by the top of the Reds order, yielding a pair of runs. Singles by Frey, Berger, Cooke, and McCormick did the damage.

Vander Meer showed a wild streak. Adding to his pair of first-inning walks were two more passes opening the second; this resulted in his removal. Bucky Walters came on in relief, and the first thing he did was walk another batter. A two-run single by Mungo was followed by a run-scoring single by Johnny Hudson, and the Dodgers had shaved three runs off the Cincinnati lead. Walters, with runners on second and third with one out, escaped further harm by getting Buddy Hassett to ground into a force play and Dolph Camilli to ground out.

The Dodgers crept closer with a run in the third inning. Kiki Cuyler singled and came home on a triple by Leo Durocher.

In the fourth inning, Brooklyn scored another run. Goody Rosen reached on a throwing error by shortstop Billy Myers and went station to station on a single by Hudson and a walk to Hassett. With the bases loaded, the Reds made their second pitching change of the game, bringing in Lee Grissom to face Camilli. Camilli's fly ball to right field was not deep enough to do any damage and the bags were still loaded with one out. Cookie Lavagetto hit a fly ball to deep left field and all three runners tagged up. Rosen scored and Hudson made it safely into third base.

However, Hassett was caught between first base and second base. The throw from left fielder Berger was cut off by third baseman Lew Riggs, who threw the ball across the infield. Hassett was ruled out for running out of the baseline, interfering with the throw from Riggs to first baseman McCormick. Dodgers first-base coach Babe Ruth

disagreed with the call, argued with umpire Beans Reardon, and was ejected from the game. It was Ruth's first ejection since he joined Brooklyn in late June and resulted in the fans in the left-field stands showering the field with debris.

The Reds reestablished a four-run lead with single runs in the seventh and eighth innings. In the seventh, with one out, Lombardi singled to center field and went to second on a wild pitch. After Riggs was intentionally walked, Lombardi scored on a single by Myers. In the eighth inning, Frey walked, stole second, advanced to third on a groundout, and scored on a single by McCormick.

The Dodgers, trailing 9-5, bounced back in their half of the eighth inning. Brooklyn had only nine hits in the game but made them count. Cincinnati's Grissom was humming along and hadn't allowed a hit since he entered the game in the fourth inning. In the eighth inning with one out, the Cincinnati reliever walked Merv Shea, who came out of the game for pinch-runner Ernie Koy. Mungo's grounder to shortstop to Myers resulted in an errant throw to first base (his second miscue of the game), and the Dodgers had runners on first and third. After Rosen walked to fill the bases, Grissom was gone, relieved by Gene Schott. Schott was ineffective. One run scored on a fielder's choice and two came home on a double by Hassett. Croonin' Joe Cascarella came on to strike out Camilli and end the inning. The score was 9-8 after eight innings.

As if there had not been enough of the exciting and unusual in one game, the ninth inning was the icing on the proverbial cake.

Cincinnati extended its lead with a run in the top of the inning, by which point each batter in the Reds lineup, with the exception of the pitchers, had at least one base hit. Craft singled to lead off the inning and was forced at second by Riggs. Myers then slammed a triple to the wall in left-center field, scoring Riggs, but was gunned down when he tried to make it an inside-the-park homer, the relay throw coming from second

After concluding his 22-year major-league career with the Boston Braves in 1935, Babe Ruth had a brief coaching career with the Brooklyn Dodgers, debuting as first-base coach on June 19, and served through the remainder of the season. (Photo: SABR-Rucker Archive)

baseman Hudson on the throw from left fielder Hassett. The top of the ninth ended with the score 10-8 in favor of the visitors.

Cascarella went back to the mound in the bottom of the inning. With one out, Cuyler walked. After Durocher popped to second, the roof fell in. Gilly Campbell singled and Tuck Stainback, batting for Mungo, drove in Brooklyn's ninth run with a single. Rosen delivered the tying and winning runs with a triple off the big scoreboard in right field.

Mungo, who pitched the final 8⅔ innings of the game, was rewarded with his fourth win of the season and his first since June 30, when he hurled a one-hitter against Boston. The once promising flamethrower, who averaged 16 wins per season from 1932 through 1936, led the league in shutouts in 1935, and struck out a league-leading 238 batters in 1936, was in the midst of a bad season in which he went 4-11.

Cascarella took the loss, bringing his record to 3-7. He was in the last year of a five-year big-league career. He went 4-7 in 1938 and finished his career with a 27-48 record. He was noted for his singing as early as 1928, when he sang on the radio in New York. He was a tenor and sang opera.[2]

The other singer in the game was Hassett of Brooklyn, whose ninth-inning throw kept the margin at two runs. Hassett batted .292 with 1,026 hits during his seven-year big-league career. Known as the Bronx Thrush, he would sing "When Irish Eyes Are Smiling" at the drop of a leprechaun.[3]

Brooklyn, after winning the second game of the doubleheader, 6-3, finished the day in sixth place, 16 games behind the league leaders. But their "Daffiness Boys" tag still intact, they finished the season in seventh place. It was their sixth straight second-division finish, and they were still looking for their first pennant since 1920.

Cincinnati fell into a third-place tie with Chicago, eight games removed from the league lead with 52 games left to play. They weren't able to make up the difference, finishing the season in fourth place, six games behind the first-place Cubs.

Cincinnati's top player in 1938 was Lombardi who had gone 1-for-5 with a single in the seventh inning on August 7. He batted .342 for the season and was selected the league's Most Valuable Player. He was inducted into the Hall of Fame in 1986.

In 1939, Cincinnati won the pennant and Brooklyn, with new manager Leo Durocher, freed itself of the daffiness tag, finishing in third place with an 84-69 record.

SOURCES

In addition to Baseball-Reference.com and the sources shown in the Notes, the author used:

Scott, Lee. "Dodgers Display Plenty of Grit in Double Victory over Cincinnati Team, *Brooklyn Citizen*, August 8, 1938: 6.

Holmes, Tommy. "Flock Earns Even Break Against West in Rout of Reds," *Brooklyn Daily Eagle*, August 8, 1938: 12.

McGowen, Roscoe. "Reds Bow 11-10, 6-3, as Dodgers Rally," *New York Times*, August 8, 1938: 16.

Smith, Lou. "Brooks Deal Crushing Blow to Reds, Grabbing Double Bill," *Cincinnati Enquirer*, August 8, 1938: 11-12.

NOTES

1 Hy Turkin, "Dodgers Conquer Reds, 11-10, 6-3," *New York Daily News*, August 8, 1938: 31.

2 Bill Nowlin, "Joe Cascarella," SABR BioProject, https://sabr.org/bioproj/person/73544a94.

3 Warren Corbett, "Buddy Hassett," SABR BioProject https://sabr.org/bioproj/person/bd0ce416.

Brooklyn's bats heat up in a wacky win over the Phillies

May 1, 1939
Brooklyn Dodgers 13, Philadelphia Phillies 12

by James Forr

Nine games into his managerial career and Leo Durocher already had the Brooklyn Dodgers feeling, for the first time in years, relevant.

General manager Larry MacPhail vowed that Durocher would instill some much-needed "up-and-at-'em fight" in the moribund Dodgers franchise, and people took him at his word.[1] Preseason predictions were cautiously optimistic and early attendance figures suggested fans were buying in, too.

Brooklyn came into the afternoon with a 4-4 record. Nothing ailed them that a little more offense couldn't help. Two major offseason acquisitions, Gene Moore and Tony Lazzeri, hadn't done much, nor had the 1938 rookie wonder Ernie Koy. However, as was often the case in this era, Philadelphia pitching provided a potent tonic for a hitting malaise.

To be fair, the Phillies had looked uncharacteristically respectable to that point, with wins in four of their first nine games, including back-to-back walk-off victories over Brooklyn back home at Shibe Park. "Give me another good pitcher and

a fellow on first who can tag that ball and I'll give the fans of Philadelphia a real ball club," boasted new manager Doc Prothro.[2] He never got either of those things, really, and even if he had, he needed a lot more than that. But for the moment, it appeared that he might be onto something.

The two starting pitchers had hooked up in a classic duel 10 days earlier, a game that ended in a 2-2 tie called due to darkness. Philadelphia's Claude Passeau struck out 11 over eight innings, while the Dodgers' Vito Tamulis went the distance, surrendering just five hits, despite a scary moment when he was overcome by a sharp pain near his heart. It turned out to be a ruptured blood vessel in his chest, which must have been less dire than it sounded because he pulled himself together and finished the game. This was his first appearance since then.

Neither starter lasted long. The Dodgers attacked Passeau in the first inning. With the bases loaded and one out, Moore, who was hitting .103, doubled in a pair. Then Dolph Camilli slid home just ahead of Passeau's throw on Lazzeri's fielder's choice, and Al Todd drove in a run on a groundout. Just like that, it was 4-0, and Passeau was through.

The Phillies got two back off Tamulis in the top of the second, thanks to Les Powers' RBI triple and a single from George Scharein that plated Powers. Brooklyn extended the lead to 5-2 in the third against Elmer Burkart when Camilli scored on an error, but Philadelphia replied immediately. Run-scoring hits by Burkart and Heinie Mueller chased Tamulis and narrowed the Dodgers edge to 5-4. Undeterred, Brooklyn tallied four times in the bottom of the fourth to stretch the lead back to 9-4, as Moore again delivered a big blow with a two-run single.

It was 11-5 heading to the ninth and it didn't appear that Philadelphia had much hope against knuckleballer Tot Pressnell, who had been stellar in his season debut, surrendering one run on three hits in relief of Tamulis. However, it proved "a crazy ninth inning that had all the spectators dizzy."[3]

Pressnell took care of the first man, but then everything fell apart. Mueller removed the first bolt with a solo home run over the right-field scoreboard. After a walk to Hersh Martin and a double by LeGrant Scott, Dodgers third baseman Cookie Lavagetto booted Morrie Arnovich's groundball, which let in Martin and cut the lead to 11-7. Pinky May walked to load the bases, and then Powers finally chased Pressnell with a sharply hit single to left that scored Scott and made it 11-8.

Durocher walked in from his shortstop position and summoned freshly minted Dodger Whitlow Wyatt. After nine years of luckless toil in the American League, Wyatt returned to the minors, learned how to throw a slow curve, and became a new man in Brooklyn. He had shut out the Phillies two days earlier and sported an ERA of 0.95, but Durocher called on him too soon. He had thrown only about five pitches in the bullpen before entering to face dangerous pinch-hitter Chuck Klein with the bases still loaded.[4]

Klein greeted Wyatt with a long smash that barely eluded the reach of a leaping Goody Rosen and clattered off the exit gate in center field. The double brought home Arnovich and May and the lead was down to 11-10. Philly tied it a moment later when Wyatt unleashed a wild pitch that scored Powers. Then after a walk to pinch-hitter Bill Atwood, Wally Millies lifted a popup into shallow center. As Lazzeri made the catch, Klein broke for the plate and barely beat Lazzeri's weak throw. It was a seven-run ninth inning, and the Phillies had grabbed a 12-11 lead.

Philadelphia's mop-up man, Jim Henry, entered to finish it off, but the job was too big. Durocher was flipping switches all over the place. First, he lifted himself for a pinch-hitter, Fred Sington, who walked. Van Lingle Mungo ran for Sington. Oris Hockett, batting for Wyatt, dumped a single into center field, which advanced the tying run into scoring position. For reasons lost to time, Durocher then sent out Tuck Stainback to run for Mungo. "A pinch-runner for a pinch-runner is a wrinkle entirely new in baseball, but anything can happen when the Phillies and Dodgers meet," mused the *Philadelphia Inquirer.*[5]

Durocher ordered Rosen to bunt. After two failed attempts, his groundball to second served the purpose, moving the runners to second and third for the erstwhile goat, Lavagetto, whose error in the top half had led to two unearned runs. After a long conference at the mound, the Phillies decided to pitch to him. Lavagetto erased his blunder with a line drive up the middle, his third hit of the day. The blow scored Stainback and Hockett and gave Brooklyn a wild 13-12 victory.

The 3-hour 2-minute marathon triumph was the Dodgers' fourth straight win and moved them into a fourth-place tie. Lavagetto knocked in four runs, after coming into the day with just one RBI through the first eight games. The struggling

Moore stroked two hits and matched a career-high with five RBIs. Lazzeri's three hits raised his average 100 points.

The Dodgers weren't a great team yet, maybe not even an especially good one. They hovered around .500 for most of the season before a hot streak in September boosted them into third place. They were never in serious contention, but for the first time, Brooklyn led the major leagues in per-game attendance. Something felt different. This peculiar and spirited come-from-behind victory was a small, early hint that Durocher would deliver on MacPhail's promise.

SOURCES

In addition to the newspaper sources cited in the Notes, the author used Baseball-Reference.com and Retrosheet.org for play-by-play and other information:

https://www.baseball-reference.com/boxes/BRO/BRO193905010.shtml

https://www.retrosheet.org/boxesetc/1939/B05010BRO1939.htm

The author also reviewed the following sources:

Effrat, Louis. "Hit by Lavagetto Stops Phils, 13-12," *New York Times*, May 2, 1939: 30.

Holmes, Tommy. "Dodgers Ready for Ten-Game Western Invasion," *Brooklyn Daily Eagle*, May 2, 1939: 14.

NOTES

1   Tommy Holmes, "No Miracles Expected from New Manager of Flatbush Flock," *Brooklyn Daily Eagle*, October 13, 1938: 20.

2   "Phils Show Teeth for Dentist Pilot," *The Sporting News*, May 4, 1939: 3.

3   Lee Scott, "Dodgers Win Crazy Game and Move Into Tie for Fourth Place," *Brooklyn Citizen*, May 2, 1939: 6.

4   Scott.

5   "Dodgers Grab 13-12 Verdict in Last Frame," *Philadelphia Inquirer*, May 2, 1939: 21.

CAMILLI'S BLAST HELPS EXTEND DODGERS LEAD OVER CARDS TO TWO GAMES

September 6, 1941

Brooklyn Dodgers 4, New York Giants 1

by Peter Seidel

It had been over two decades since the Dodgers won the 1920 National League pennant. Most of those years were spent in the second division. By 1937 the Dodgers were in dire straits financially. They were $700,000 in debt to their bank, the Brooklyn Trust Company, "$470,000 on a refinanced mortgage for Ebbets Field. (The club) had lost $129,140 in 1937 and hadn't turned a profit since 1930."[1] The Dodgers' phone service had been disconnected for nonpayment and Ebbets Field was in disarray with broken seats and mildew in the rotunda, and badly needed a fresh coat of paint.

National League President Ford Frick suggested that the owners hire a strong executive to manage the struggling club. Frick recommended Branch Rickey, who in turn recommended Larry MacPhail. MacPhail, a brilliant executive for the Cincinnati Reds, was available after the 1937 season, having left the Reds because of his heavy drinking and loutish behavior. Given the Brooklyn job, MacPhail wasted no time rebuilding the Dodgers. In March 1938 he acquired slugging first baseman Dolph Camilli from the Phillies for

light-hitting Eddie Morgan and $45,000. Morgan would never play another game in the major leagues while Camilli led the National League in home runs (34) and RBIs (120) en route to a Most Valuable Player Award in 1941. That trade is widely regarded as one of the worst in Phillies history. MacPhail also stole Pete Reiser from the St. Louis Cardinals in 1938; Reiser also went on to star for the Dodgers.

In 1939 MacPhail hired Leo Durocher to manage the team, claimed Dixie Walker off waivers, and hired Red Barber to announce the games on the radio. In 1940 MacPhail added rookie Pee Wee Reese at shortstop and acquired outfielder Joe Medwick and pitcher Curt Davis for four players and $125,000 in a trade with St. Louis.[2]

By 1941 the Dodgers were engaged in a ferocious season-long battle for the National League pennant with the Cardinals. Brooklyn player-manager Durocher lamented before a September weekend series against their crosstown rival New York Giants, "There aren't any tough clubs for us any more or any easy ones. It's just as though we were playing the Cardinals every day. The only way to win a pennant is to win more games than any other club and it doesn't matter who we beat as long as we have gained more decisions than St. Louis at the finish. And of course, to wind up with fewer defeats."[3]

On September 6, the Dodgers hadn't played since the 3rd. Meanwhile, the Cardinals had lost two straight games to the Cubs and fallen into second place. Going into this game against the Giants, the Dodgers (85-47) and Cardinals (83-47) were tied in the loss column, but the Dodgers had played and won two more games than St. Louis, giving them a precarious one-game lead in the National League standings. So important was this game to Durocher that he suited up and played shortstop to give slumping Reese a much-needed day off. Reese was having a rough time after breaking his ankle in August 1940 and seeing his rookie season end early. He began the 1941 season with a brace on his ankle and even though he managed to play in 152 games, he finished the season with a .229 batting average. Going into this game, Reese had been hitless in the Dodgers' previous two series against the Phillies and the Braves and had only three hits in his previous 28 at-bats.

Bill Terry's Giants were ready to remind Durocher that not only were there indeed six other teams in the National League, but that nothing would delight Terry more than to knock their intracity rivals out of first place.

Taking the hill for Brooklyn was 37-year-old Curt Davis, Durocher referred to Davis as a "great clutch pitcher."[4] Davis won seven of his last nine decisions to close out the 1941 season and he didn't beat himself as he led the National League with only 1.6 walks per nine innings. Considered a throw-in when he was acquired from the Cardinals, Davis had a stellar 1939 season, winning 22 games and making the All-Star team. As he started against the Giants, he was 10-6 with a 3.14 ERA.

After breezing through a one-two-three top of the first, Davis surrendered a leadoff single to Babe Young to start the second inning. However, Davis enticed the next batter, Jo-Jo Moore, into a 1-6-3 double play. Gabby Hartnett smacked a two-out single, but Billy Jurges' fly ball to center field ended the Giants threat.

Brooklyn drew first blood in the bottom of the second as slugger Dolph Camilli crushed a Bill McGee fastball well over the scoreboard in right field for a 1-0 lead. It was Camilli's 30th round-tripper of the season, making him only the second Dodger have a 30-home-run season. (Babe Herman hit 35 in 1930.) Camilli's wallop also ensured that he would win a Bulova watch for leading Brooklyn in homers that year. Lew Riggs and Jim Wasdell followed with singles to right field. Giants center fielder Johnny Rucker dropped Durocher's fly ball in right center and Riggs scored, making it 2-0. Mickey Owen worked the count to 3-and-0 but smacked into a double play. Davis looked at strike three to end the Dodgers rally.

The game settled down until the Dodgers' sixth. Walker led off with a single but was thrown out attempting to steal second. Billy Herman worked a walk off McGee and scored on a bloop double by Pete Reiser that landed just past Giants shortstop Jurges and skipped by left fielder Moore, who overran it. It was now 3-0, Dodgers. McGee intentionally walked Camilli. The Giants outfield then flashed some serious leather to keep the game close. Riggs launched a McGee offering to deep center field that Rucker caught on the run crashing into the center-field fence. Then Wasdell smacked a shot to deep right that Mel Ott tracked down, also crashing into the fence.

In the Giants' seventh, Billy Herman bobbled Babe Young's leadoff grounder and Moore singled, putting runners on the corners with no outs. Hartnett's groundout plated Young, and the unearned run made the score 3-1, Dodgers. Davis wild-pitched Moore to third, but retired the next two batters.

With Ace Adams pitching for the Giants, Reiser led off the bottom of the eighth with a triple to left field and Camilli ripped a line-drive single past Adams, easily scoring Reiser and giving the Dodgers a 4-1 lead. Davis gave up a one-out single to Hartnett in the ninth, but got two more outs to claim his 11th victory.

The Giants outhit the Dodgers 9-7, but were 0-for-7 with runners in scoring position.

The Dodgers got some help from Reds pitching ace Johnny Vander Meer, who hurled a two-hit shutout over the Cardinals, striking out 14 in the process. The Dodgers victory paired with the Cardinals loss gave Brooklyn a two-game lead over St. Louis. The next weekend, the Dodgers would travel to St. Louis and take two out of three games from the Cardinals. After winning a hard-fought National League pennant, the Dodgers lost the World Series to the Yankees in five games. Bill James referred to the 1941 Brooklyn Dodgers as "one of the greatest teams that never was."[5] Their roster featured four Hall of Famers (Herman, Medwick, Reese, and Paul Waner); the top two MVP candidates (Camilli and Reiser); and two 22-game winners (Kirby Higbe and Whitlow Wyatt).

SOURCES

In addition to the sources cited in the Notes, the author consulted Baseball-Reference.com, Retrosheet.org, and BackToBaseball.com.

NOTES

1   Andy McCue, "Los Angeles/Brooklyn Dodgers Team Ownership History," Retrieved from SABR.org: https://sabr.org/research/los-angeles-brooklyn-dodgers-team-ownership-history.

2   Ralph Berger, "Larry MacPhail," Retrieved from SABR BioProject: https://sabr.org/bioproj/person/1b708d47.

3   Tommy Holmes, "Well-Rested Giants Threat to Dodgers," *Brooklyn Daily Eagle*, September 6, 1941: 7.

4   Bill James, *The New Bill James Historical Baseball Abstract* (New York: Free Press, 2001).

5   James.

DODGERS SWEEP GIANTS IN TWIN BILL AS SEASON-ENDING 17-GAME ROAD TRIP LOOMS WITH PENNANT ON LINE

September 7, 1941

Brooklyn Dodgers 13, New York Giants 1 | Game One
Brooklyn Dodgers 4, New York Giants 3 | Game Two

by Jack Zerby

The 1941 Brooklyn Dodgers got their season started on the wrong foot – and to add insult, it had been at home and against their archrival New York Giants. The Giants swept Brooklyn at Ebbets Field in a three-game series beginning April 15. But the Dodgers got back on track. They were 12-8 against New York as the mundane Giants (62-67, fifth place, 22 games out) visited Ebbets Field on September 7. On tap was a doubleheader that would wrap up the teams' head-to-head meetings for the season.[1]

A month earlier, on August 6, Brooklyn had moved into a first-place tie with the St. Louis Cardinals, aptly enough with a 3-1 win over the Giants at the Polo Grounds, as Kirby Higbe outdueled Carl Hubbell. Although Brooklyn was 22-10 for the month of August, the Cardinals were very much in the hunt; the Dodgers bounced between first and second throughout the month and were a half-game back of St. Louis when September dawned. By the end of play on September 6, though, Brooklyn had a two-game lead over the Cardinals with the Giants' twin bill on the agenda, capping a Saturday-Sunday three-game series.

Another month earlier, as baseball took its annual break for the All-Star Game in early July, Giants manager Bill Terry, in verbiage possibly polished by the reporting sportswriter, had predicted from his home in Memphis, "If that strong-arm trio of mound aces, Whitlow Wyatt, Kirby Higbe, and Hugh Casey, continue at top form, it appears the Dodgers will march in easily."[2] Terry's club, then 39-32 and 9½ games out in third place, was fulfilling its part of that prophecy; from July 10 through their 4-1 loss in the first game of the Brooklyn series on Saturday afternoon, New York had gone 23-35 and sunk out of the pennant race. The Dodgers weren't running away as easily as Terry had predicted – they had been in and out of the lead from July 25 through September 1 – but there were three weeks left in the season.

Terry was right about the three right-handed pitchers he singled out. They were indeed as advertised. Higbe and Wyatt, slated to start the Sunday games, each had 19 wins going in. Casey had 11 wins as a starter and, most recently, manager Leo Durocher's bullpen stopper.[3]

131

Terry had been a member of the Giants since 1923 and their player-manager since June 4, 1932, when he replaced an ailing John McGraw.[4] Terry had ended his playing career with the 1936 season but continued to manage. Durocher, after a playing career that began ever so briefly in 1925, had broken in as a player-manager with Brooklyn in 1939.[5] He was 35 in 1941 and still playing sparingly.[6]

The morning action around Ebbets Field was frenzied on what became a hot Sunday afternoon as summer eased into autumn.[7] While some fans "slept on the sidewalk all night for the privilege of paying to sit in the sun-scorched bleachers for six hours," the gates opened at 9 A.M. with 25,000 unreserved seats available; they were gone by 10:30. Then, $1.10 standing-room tickets went on sale. Dodger management had closed off about 1,500 seats in center field to improve the batting background, causing many of those unable to get into the ballpark to climb to apartment building roofs, then "strain their eyes through field glasses for hours, watching a ball game three-quarters of a mile away."[8]

By game time, 34,361 were either sitting or standing in the ballpark, the Dodgers' third largest home crowd of the season. The turnout bumped Ebbets Field attendance to 1.19 million for the season.[9]

Higbe got Durocher's nod in the first game. The 26-year-old South Carolinian had been the losing pitcher against New York in a relief appearance the week before, but the "grateful refugee" from the Philadelphia Phillies had rebounded with a win, his 19th of the season, on September 2 against the Boston Braves.[10] Terry sent out lefty screwballer Hubbell, pitching in the 14th of the 16 seasons he toiled for the Giants en route to the Hall of Fame. The elder statesman, 38, was a respectable 10-7 so far for a club going nowhere. He had a 1-2 record and a no-decision in four previous 1941 starts against Brooklyn.

With Durocher settling himself in at short-stop for only his ninth start of the season, Higbe yielded a one-out single to Johnny Rucker in the top of the first but was easily out of the inning with groundball outs by Mel Ott and Babe Young. In the Brooklyn half, Hubbell got himself in a quick hole by walking Dixie Walker and Billy Herman, the first two batters he faced. Pete Reiser moved them up a notch with a sacrifice before Hubbell got Joe Medwick on a groundout to third base on which Walker couldn't advance. But Cookie Lavagetto, next up, "lashed a first-pitch single to center and the two runs romped to the platter."[11]

Brooklyn nicked Hubbell for two more runs in the third inning on doubles by Herman and Medwick and a single by Dolph Camilli.[12] The lefty got through the fourth without further damage, but was gone when Gabby Hartnett pinch-hit for him in the top of the fifth with one out and Odell Hale on first base after a walk. Hartnett kept things going with a single that moved Hale to third base – Dick Bartell scored him with a fly ball; it was 4-1, Brooklyn.

Bob Bowman took over on the mound for New York in the fifth. He got off to a decent start, picking Medwick off first base after a leadoff single. But he was back in trouble with a walk to Lavagetto. Next up, Camilli – on his way to the 1941 National League MVP award – "with three balls and no strikes against him, rocketed homer No. 31 over the right field fence."[13]

With a now-five-run lead, Higbe pitched around Durocher's error and a two-out single to avoid damage in the sixth. Just to be sure of their cushion, the Dodgers worked over Bowman for five more runs in their half, capped by another two-run homer by Camilli. Durocher, up next but apparently satisfied with the margin, retired to the shade of the dugout at that point, replacing himself with Pee Wee Reese, 22 and in his first full season with Brooklyn.[14]

Terry's third pitcher, Johnny Wittig, gave up two more runs in the eighth inning as Brooklyn's

Acquired in an offseason trade with the Philadelphia Phillies, hard-throwing Kirby Higbe tied teammate Whit Wyatt for the NL lead in wins (22) to help lead the Dodgers to the NL pennant in 1941. (Photo: SABR-Rucker Archive)

total mounted to 13. Higbe cruised the rest of the way – "an easy afternoon" – to a 13-1 win, his 20th win of the season.[15]

Offensively, Camilli's three hits included his 31st and 32nd home runs of the season. He drove in five runs. Medwick's four hits produced three runs batted in, and Lavagetto chipped in with three more RBIs. Even Higbe, with a career .172 on-base percentage, reached base twice in four trips, with a single and a walk.

In St. Louis that afternoon, the second-place Cardinals and Cincinnati – standing third but 13 games out – also played a doubleheader. St. Louis won the first game; as St. Louis and Brooklyn moved to their respective second games on September 7, the Dodgers maintained a two-game lead in the pennant race.

Durocher, benching himself in favor of Reese for the second game in Brooklyn, tabbed Wyatt as his starter. Wyatt was 33 years old and had pitched himself out of the majors in the American League before a comeback year with the Double-A Milwaukee Brewers in 1938 resuscitated his career and caught Larry McPhail's eye in Brooklyn.[16] There, the Georgian had become a dominant pitcher and stood 19-9 as he took on the Giants, trying to match Higbe's 20 wins.

His mound opponent was a lanky, big-eared lefty from the Blue Ridge Mountains of western North Carolina. Cliff Melton, now 29, had won 20 games as a rookie with the 1937 Giants and started two games in that year's World Series against the Yankees. As Hubbell's teammate, he had tried to learn the screwball; the experiment never worked, and Melton never achieved the same success he had had as a rookie. Each spring training from 1938 onward, writers and fans looked for great things from him, but he tended to fall just short even in his best starts and gained the reputation of a "tough-luck loser."[17] And once again, as he faced the Dodgers this afternoon attempting to avoid a sweep, his gritty competitiveness would not quite be enough.

Wyatt and Melton traded effective goose eggs through the first four innings. And while no runs were involved, a literal dustup in the Dodgers' fifth inning riled the crowd. With two outs and the bases empty, home-plate umpire Tom Dunn called a third strike on Camilli. It disturbed Camilli enough for him to take exception, but the volatile Durocher was enraged. "He stormed out of the dugout, kicked up clouds of dust and finally held his nose in a gesture of disgust. That earned him a trip to the showers." As Durocher continued to remonstrate, the crowd, eager for some action, directed "a shower of pop bottles, beer cans, and fruit" at Dunn.[18] And whether it happened then, while Durocher was playing in the first game, or possibly back in the clubhouse as a banished Durocher presumably continued a solitary kicking tirade, "the Skipper left the ball park with a painful charley horse and very thoughtful about playing against the Cardinals in the series starting Thursday."[19]

New York, mathematically eliminated from the pennant race by losing the first game,[20] found some life against Wyatt in the top of the seventh and the game still scoreless. Rucker reached first base on Reese's boot of his groundball. Brooklyn missed a double play on Ott's grounder to second. Wyatt got to 3-and-2 on the next hitter, Young, and Young lifted Wyatt's next pitch over the right-field screen for a two-run homer. Jo-Jo Moore followed with a double off the same screen and scored on Hartnett's single. The remaining Dodgers brain trust, Red Corriden, Chuck Dressen, and George Pfister, stuck with Wyatt down 3-0, but Billy Jurges doubled Hartnett to third with one out. That finished Wyatt. The happenstance triumvirate brought in Johnny Allen, who intentionally walked Hale to load the bases and get to Melton. Melton wasn't the worst-hitting pitcher in baseball and managed 32 RBIs in his eight-year career; but when Allen had a chance to increase the lead and give himself more breathing room, he prevailed. Melton dribbled the ball back to the mound; Allen started a classic 1-2-3 double play to end the half-inning.

Yet, the Giants had a lead. Brooklyn chipped away with three singles against Melton in their seventh with Reiser scoring on yet another Camilli RBI. Melton rallied to close out the Dodgers without a baserunner in the eighth, and took the 3-1 lead into the ninth.

There, he ran into real trouble. Herman singled, leading off. Second baseman Hale butchered Reiser's groundball for a two-base error, putting the tying runs on second and third with no outs. Medwick, 4-for-5 in the first game but hitless to this point against Melton, rifled a sharp opposite-field single down the first-base line to bring home Herman and Reiser. The fans, with little to cheer about since the first game, erupted: "There never had been such a scene in Ebbets Field as was unfolded in the ninth following Medwick's game-tying hit. Seemingly every fan present rose and all began sending a storm of paper onto the field. It came in cascades of torn bits as well as whole newspapers and score cards."[21] The "snowstorm" of paper "almost concealed the Giant outfielders from the stands" and was accompanied by a "terrific volley of sound."[22]

Umpire Dunn immediately had the field announcer inform the crowd that unless they stopped throwing paper the game would not proceed. It took 10 minutes for "the regular ground crew and every available usher from the lower stands" to clear the field. When the game resumed, Lavagetto sacrificed Medwick to second. Terry had stuck with Melton after Medwick's hit and the delay, and the lefty gutted his way out of the inning without further scoring, retiring the dangerous Camilli and Reese on groundballs with the potential winning run on second base.

Casey, one of the Dodgers pitching stalwarts singled out by Terry back in July, had come on to replace Allen in the top of the ninth and had retired New York in order. He did the same in the 10th. Even then, with the pitcher's spot the

Giants' only hope with two outs, Terry allowed Melton to bat; this time he got more bat on the ball than he had in the seventh but still grounded out to second base.

Back on the mound, the ill-fated southpaw was immediately in a hole when Mickey Owen, leading off the Brooklyn 10th, singled. Casey sacrificed him to second, but Melton retired Walker on a fly ball to center field for the second out. To get to a lefty-on-lefty matchup, the Giants intentionally walked Herman, bringing up Reiser, although he was leading the National League in batting average.[23] The second-guessable strategy didn't work; Reiser responded as he had all season, belting Melton's 3-and-2 pitch "into deep left field," scoring Owen.[24]

This time, "the noise was puny compared with the earlier din, when telegraphers couldn't hear their instruments click."[25] "The bugs poured out on the diamond, hundreds of them forming behind that utterly screwy band from Greenpoint, which headed for the dugout of the departed Giants [with] their rendition of Chopin's funeral march, then around the ball park blaring forth tunes of victory."[26]

Casey got the dramatic 4-3 win; Melton went 9⅔ tough innings only to absorb another loss.

Out west, Cincinnati won the second game in St. Louis, boosting Brooklyn to a three-game lead in the pennant race. But the vicissitudes of scheduling at a time when ballclubs traveled by train had left the Dodgers facing a 17-game road trip that took them to every other National League ballpark – except the nearby Polo Grounds. The trip started in Chicago on September 10 and ended in Boston on September 27. In between, the Dodgers had stops in St. Louis, Cincinnati, Pittsburgh, and Philadelphia. The Dodgers wouldn't be back to Ebbets Field until September 27 and a two-game series against Philadelphia.

Brooklyn started the trip in potentially disastrous fashion by losing both ends of a doubleheader to the Cubs at Wrigley Field on

September 10; the twin loss cut their lead to a single game going into a crucial series in St. Louis. But there, they regrouped to win the first game in 11 innings and two of three, increasing their edge to two games.[27] Over the rest of the trip, Brooklyn showed its mettle, winning nine of 12 games against the lesser lights of the National League to keep the Cardinals at bay.

St. Louis stayed close, but through the long trip the Dodgers' lead was never smaller than a game, never more than 2½ games – their season-ending edge over the Cardinals. The team their writers and fans lovingly called "the Bums" didn't "march in easily," as Bill Terry had predicted at the All-Star break, but with Camilli, Reiser, Medwick, Higbe, Wyatt, and Casey leading the way they persevered to win 100 games for the first time since 1899 and their first National League pennant since 1920.[28]

EPILOGUE

Some might have had forebodings, but none of the jubilant Dodgers fans assembled that Sunday afternoon in Ebbets field knew that exactly three months later, December 7, 1941, the Japanese attack on Pearl Harbor would draw the United States into World War II – altering their lives, the lives of the players they watched that afternoon, and lives all around the world.

SOURCES

In addition to the sources cited in the Notes, the author accessed the Baseball-Reference.com, Retrosheet.org, and Baseball Cube.com websites for play-by-play details and box scores, and for season, team, and player pages and daily batting and pitching logs.

https://www.baseball-reference.com/boxes/BRO/BRO194109071.shtml

https://www.retrosheet.org/boxesetc/1941/B09071BRO1941.htm

https://www.baseball-reference.com/boxes/BRO/BRO194109072.shtml

https://www.retrosheet.org/boxesetc/1941/B09072BRO1941.htm

NOTES

1   A single game was originally scheduled for September 7. The rainout of a Giants-Dodgers doubleheader scheduled for July 4 moved one of those games to August 12, also as part of a doubleheader. The other rainout game was moved to September 7. https://www.baseball-reference.com/teams/BRO/1941-schedule-scores.shtml.

2   Associated Press, "Terry Picks the Dodgers," *New York Times,* July 10, 1941: 24. At the close of play on July 6 for the 1941 All-Star break, Brooklyn had a three-game lead over St. Louis in the National League.

3   Russell Wolinsky, "Hugh Casey," SABR Baseball Biography Project. https://sabr.org/bioproj/person/312ca33d.

4   Jimmy Powers, "Bill Terry Replaces M'Graw," *New York Daily News,* June 4, 1932: 28.

5   Durocher, 19, had one plate appearance with the 1925 New York Yankees. He was back with them in 1928 for 102 games (385 plate appearances) at second base and shortstop.

6   Durocher gave himself 43 plate appearances in 18 games during the 1941 season. He played shortstop and second base and hit .286.

7   Jack Smith, "Flock Wins 13-1, 4-3," *New York Daily News*, September 8, 1941: 34.

8   Hy Turkin, "25,000 Dodger Seats Sold in Hour and Half," *New York Daily News,* September 8, 1941: 35.

9   Roscoe McGowen, "Bottle Shower at Ebbets Field," *New York Times,* September 8, 1941: 18. The Dodgers finished 1941 with attendance of 1.21 million, leading the National League for the third straight season. They continued that string through 1943.

10 The Dodgers acquired Higbe from the moribund Phillies during the 1940-41 offseason for three players and $100,000. *New York Daily News* writer Jack Smith dubbed him "a grateful refugee." Jack Smith, "Dodgers Blast Giants in 1st Game, 13-1," *New York Daily News*, September 8, 1941: 34.

11 Smith, "Dodgers Blast Giants."

12 Camilli's single driving in Medwick gave him an even 100 RBIs for the season. Smith, "Dodgers Blast Giants."

13 Smith, "Dodgers Blast Giants."

14 Durocher left the game hitting .300. He played in only two more games in 1941, going hitless in two at-bats.

15 Smith, "Dodgers Blast Giants." Higbe was the first NL pitcher to reach 20 wins in 1941. McGowen, "Bottle Shower at Ebbets Field." By season-end, Higbe had 22 wins, matched by his teammate Whitlow Wyatt. Bob Feller of the AL Cleveland Indians led the major leagues in 1941 with 25 wins.

16 Jack Zerby, "Whit Wyatt," SABR Baseball Biography Project. https://sabr.org/bioproj/person/107fef7b.

17 Jack Zerby, "Cliff Melton," SABR Baseball Biography Project. https://sabr.org/bioproj/person/4beba279.

18 Jack Smith, "Dodgers Blast Giants."

19 Tommy Holmes, "Giant-Dodger Season Series Set a Record," *Brooklyn Daily Eagle*, September 8, 1941: 13.

20 Holmes, "Giant-Dodger Season Series Set a Record."

21 McGowan, "Bottle Shower at Ebbets Field."

22 Tommy Holmes, "Dodgers Off on Last Junket to 'Badlands,'" *Brooklyn Eagle*, September 8, 1941: 13.

23 Smith, "Flock Wins." Reiser went into the September 7 doubleheader hitting .335 and went on to win the batting title at .343. He led the 1941 National League in runs scored, triples, batting average, slugging, total bases, and hit by pitches, and tied with Johnny Mize of the Cardinals in doubles. He finished second to Camilli in the 1941 NL MVP voting. https://www.baseball-reference.com/players/r/reisepe01.shtml.

24 Smith, "Flock Wins."

25 McGowan, "Bottle Shower at Ebbets Field."

26 Holmes, "Dodgers Off." The band was presumably the Dodger Sym-Phony. https://historicgreenpoint.wordpress.com/2014/04/26/the-dodger-sym-phony-band/.

27 Brooklyn won the first game in St. Louis on a two-run single by Walker in the top of 11th. Freddie Fitzsimmons had pitched the first 10 innings and got the win. Casey closed out the Cardinals with a clean inning. Camilli had a crucial three-run homer in the fourth, with Reiser, who had been hit by a pitch, one of the runners on base when he hit it.

28 The Brooklyn franchise dates from 1884 and had several names. In 1899, the Brooklyn Superbas won 101 games to top the 12-team National League. The Dodgers name appeared for the first time in 1911 was used again in 1912, but when the team won the 1920 National League pennant, it was known as the Brooklyn Robins. The Brooklyn Dodgers appeared again in 1932; the franchise has carried that name through the present time — in Brooklyn through 1957 and in Los Angeles thereafter.

Fitzsimmons's injury, Casey's blunders and Russo's pitching lead Yankees

October 4, 1941

New York Yankees 2, Brooklyn Dodgers 1 | Game Three of the World Series

by James Forr

Brooklyn's Freddie Fitzsimmons knew nothing but hard luck on the big stage.

He had started three World Series games for the New York Giants and lost them all. In 1933 he lost a shutout in which he got no support. In 1936 he lost a pitchers' duel in which he was brilliant. Later in that Series he lost a blowout in which he was terrible. He had lost in every way imaginable. But his most shattering October disappointment was yet to come.

With the Yankees and Dodgers tied at a game apiece, the 1941 World Series shifted to Ebbets Field. After a rainout on Friday, Saturday dawned sunny and steamy, more like July than October. Flatbush hadn't seen a World Series in 21 years and the park was humming. An usher compared the frenzied fans to the residents of a nearby asylum. The *New York Times* observed, "An astonishing number of alcoholics roamed through the bleacher section."[1] Yankees starter Marius Russo was practically a neighbor, Brooklyn-born and residing just five miles away, but as he warmed up, the fiery crowd hollered and heckled him all the same.

The Game Three pitching matchup was a study in contrasts. Russo was a quiet, self-effacing left-hander, a conventional-looking athlete with conventional stuff. And then there was the colorful Fitzsimmons, with his gelatinous belly and dancing knuckleball. The veteran right-hander was something to behold. "He would turn his back completely to the batter as he was winding up, wheel back around and let out the most god-awful grunt as he was letting the ball go – rrrrrhhhhhooooo!" recalled his manager, Leo Durocher. "[He sounded] like a rhinoceros in heat."[2]

Now 40 years old and clearly at the end of the line, Fat Freddie was the oldest pitcher to start a World Series game. He pitched in constant pain, his elbow ballooning after every appearance, but he still could be effective in the right spots. Durocher gave him a start once every week or two throughout the season – half of those against Pittsburgh. Fitzsimmons responded with a 6-1 record and an ERA of 2.07 in 12 starts, including a critical win over St. Louis in mid-September. His Game Three start was his first action in 16 days.

Russo had sat in the bleachers at Ebbets Field as a kid but now he was starting a World Series game there – a very different situation. He looked out of sorts at the beginning. He walked two men in the first two innings, was consistently behind hitters, and worked slowly. "To tell you the truth, I was nervous," Russo admitted. "So, I took it easy, cooled down, and tried to work on myself."[3] The early walks didn't hurt, and after that the Dodgers didn't know what to do with him. He didn't allow a hit until Joe Medwick's roller up the third-base line with two out in the fourth, and through six innings no Dodger advanced past first base.

Fitzsimmons was nearly as dominant, surrendering four hits through six innings. The Yankees' only serious chance came in the fifth, when Joe Gordon, who had reached base successfully in all eight plate appearances in Games One and Two, tripled high off the wall in left-center field. After an intentional walk to Phil Rizzuto, Fitzsimmons struck out Russo to extinguish the threat.

Everything changed in the seventh. Gordon reached again, this time on a walk, and was on second base with two outs for Russo, a man who could handle himself at the plate. On a 1-and-1 pitch, he smashed a low liner up the middle. Fitzsimmons was an excellent fielder and much nimbler than he looked, but he didn't react quickly enough. The drive struck him on the knee and ricocheted about 20 feet into the air to shortstop Pee Wee Reese, who squeezed it. "One of the hardest balls I ever hit," Russo recalled. "It would've scored a run if Fitzsimmons hadn't got in the way."[4]

That play ended both the inning and Fitzsimmons's day. As his wife, seated behind the dugout, brought her hand to her face and broke into tears, Fitzsimmons limped off, supported by his teammates and muttering obscenities with every agonizing step. X-rays were negative. It turned out to be just a severe bruise, but the pain was too much. "Leaving that game was the disappointment of

my career because I felt sure I could have won it. … I wanted to win that one more than any game I pitched."[5]

In the top of the eighth, Durocher summoned relief ace Hugh Casey, who proceeded to undo Fitzsimmons' masterpiece in a matter of minutes with a bewildering sequence of mental blunders. The first mistake occurred as he prepared to enter the game. His warm-up pitches were slow and casual, almost as if he assumed Fitzsimmons was fine. Dodgers President Larry MacPhail was sitting alongside one of his scouts, Ted McGrew, and was dumbfounded. "[W]hen we watched Casey just lobbing the ball up in the bullpen we both relaxed, feeling sure Fitzsimmons would be back. We both almost fell out of our seats when we saw Casey called in."[6]

With one out, Red Rolfe singled, and then on a hit-and-run Tommy Henrich slapped one to the right side, just beyond the reach of first baseman Dolph Camilli. Second baseman Pete Coscarart darted to his left and made the play right behind Camilli, but when he looked up there was no one to throw to. Casey was late covering first and everyone was safe. (Casey claimed he initially broke toward the bag but stopped once the ball eluded Camilli, figuring it would get through to the outfield.[7])

Next came American League MVP Joe DiMaggio, who was 1-for-10 in the Series but in the midst of arguably the greatest season of his career. Durocher called for a pickoff play. Coscarart sneaked in behind Rolfe, who was leaning toward third, and had Casey made the throw, Rolfe probably would have been out. Instead, he held the ball.

Then he made the same mistake again, only worse. With the count full on the ninth pitch of the at-bat, Coscarart again slipped behind Rolfe, but instead of firing to second, Casey came home. DiMaggio rifled the pitch through the hole that Coscarart had vacated and into right field, bringing home Rolfe with the first run of the game.

Led by MVP Dolph Camilli, the Dodgers staved off a fierce challenge from the St. Louis Cardinals to capture the pennant in 1941, winning 100 games for skipper Leo Durocher. (Photo: SABR-Rucker Archive)

Brooklyn Dodgers — 1941 National League Champions

TOP ROW, LEFT TO RIGHT— CASEY, P. CAMILLI, I.B. PFISTER, C. WASDELL, O.F. FRANKS, C. SPENCER, C. COSCARART, I.F. FITZSIMMONS, P. GALAN, O.F. WALKER, R.F.
MIDDLE ROW. MEDWICK, L.F. DAVIS, P. DRAKE, P. FRENCH, P. WYATT, P. ALBOSTA, P. HAMLIN, P. KIMBALL, P. HERMAN, 2B. ALLEN, P.
BOTTOM ROW. WILSON, TRAINER. LAVAGETTO, 3.B. REESE, S.S. REISER, C.F. CORRIDEN, COACH. DUROCHER, MGR. DRESSEN, COACH. HIGBE, P. OWEN, C. RIGGS, 2.B. BORDER, BATBOY.

Charlie Keller followed with another single, which scored Henrich and made it 2-0.

Casey is best remembered for throwing a curveball that eluded catcher Mickey Owen and led to the game-winning run in Game Four, but the botched pickoffs, though less dramatic, were themselves a major turning point. When Durocher confronted him in the clubhouse, Casey didn't offer much of a defense. "I don't know what happened to me, Skip. I wanted to throw the ball but I just froze."[8] Durocher replied, "Casey, that's just like you coming in here telling me there was $1,000 laying on second base today but you walk in here without picking it up!"[9]

Several years later Casey put part of the blame for DiMaggio's hit on Coscarart. He was filling in for Billy Herman, who had exited in the fifth inning with a pulled muscle in his side. "I didn't work out any signs with Coscarart the way I always did with Herman," Casey contended. "It was a three-and-two pitch and I think Billy would have been where the ball was hit."[10]

Russo faltered a bit his third time through the order. The Dodgers wasted Pete Reiser's double to start the seventh, but cashed in on Dixie Walker's leadoff double in the eighth as Reese delivered a two-out RBI single.

Brooklyn finally may have been figuring Russo out, but manager Joe McCarthy was committed to his starter and Russo knew it. "Oh, yeah. Even though we had Johnny Murphy, one of the best relievers ever. McCarthy had so much confidence in me, even if I wasn't sure I could make it."[11] He rewarded his manager's faith, setting down the heart of the Brooklyn lineup in order in the ninth, preserving the 2-1 victory and giving New York a two-games-to-one lead in the series.

The Dodgers were sparing in their praise for their conqueror. "Was Russo that good? I've seen him a lot faster," snapped Cookie Lavagetto.[12]

Durocher didn't sound overly impressed either. "It's just that we're not hitting the ball at all."[13]

Meanwhile, bouquets piled up at Fitzsimmons's feet from all directions. "Gosh, he pitched great ball. He had marvelous stuff. Everything he threw had a sharp break to it," said DiMaggio.[14] "It was great to win, but I'm sincerely sorry Fitz had to lose his chance of winning that way."[15]

Sorry didn't begin to describe the emotions the Dodgers were experiencing. Durocher felt the anguish as keenly as anyone. "We would have won, 1-0, if Fitz could have stayed in there. There isn't the slightest doubt of that in my mind."[16]

SOURCES

In addition to the sources cited in the Notes, the author used the Baseball-Reference.com and Retrosheet.org websites for pertinent information, including play-by-play and box scores:

https://www.baseball-reference.com/boxes/BRO/BRO194110040.shtml

https://www.retrosheet.org/boxesetc/1941/B10040BRO1941.htm

The author also reviewed the following sources for play-by-play and other information:

"Third Series Game in Detail," *Brooklyn Eagle*, October 5, 1941: 2C.

Drebinger, John. "Four-Hitter by Russo," *New York Times*, October 5, 1941: 8-9.

Rennie, Rud. "8th Inning Attack Wins 4-Hitter for Russo After Fitzsimmons Is Injured," *New York Herald Tribune*, October 5, 1941: Sec. 3, 1.

The author also would like to thank Jack Zerby for his assistance.

NOTES

1 Meyer Berger, "Brooklyn Frenzy Hits a New High," *New York Times*, October 5, 1941: 9.

2 Leo Durocher and Ed Linn, *Nice Guys Finish Last* (Chicago: University of Chicago Press, 2009), 145.

3 Lou Cohen, "Russo Didn't Have All His Stuff, Says Gordon," *Brooklyn Eagle*, October 5, 1941: 2C.

4 Bill Madden, *Pride of October: What It Was to Be Young and a Yankee*, (New York: Grand Central Publishing, 2008), Kindle e-book, in chapter "Echoes of the Iron Horse, Cro, and Fat Freddie Fitzsimmons."

5 Joe King, "Diamond Dossier: Fitzsimmons," *The Sporting News*, April 23, 1952: 11.

6 "McPhail Is Dissatisfied," *New York Times*, October 5, 1941: 8.

7 "1941 10 08 World Series Game 4 Yankees at Dodgers Radio Broadcast," *YouTube*, uploaded by Classic Baseball on the Radio, December 10, 2016, https://www.youtube.com/watch?v=UKI46b0RdZ8. (Casey comment about covering first base occurs during the pregame at 10:44.)

8 Durocher and Linn, 161.

9 Harold Parrott, "Both Sides," *Brooklyn Eagle*, December 1, 1941: 15.

10 Bill Roeder, "Baseball," *New York World-Telegram*, September 6, 1947, cited in Lyle Spatz, *Hugh Casey: The Triumphs and Tragedies of a Brooklyn Dodger* (Lanham, Maryland: Rowman & Littlefield, 2016), 89.

11 Madden.

12 Harold Parrott, "Casey Fails Fitz in Clutch, Blowing Two Plays," *Brooklyn Eagle*, October 5, 1941: 1-2C.

13 "Casey Fails Fitz in Clutch."

14 Peter J. DeKever, *Freddie Fitzsimmons: A Baseball Life* (Bloomington, Indiana: AuthorHouse: 2013), 259.

15 "Gossip of Third Game," *The Sporting News*, October 9, 1941: 7.

16 "Casey Fails Fitz in Clutch."

Owen's dropped third strike costs Dodgers Series-tying win

October 5, 1941

New York Yankees 7, Brooklyn Dodgers 4 | Game Four of the World Series

by Don Zminda

It was, without question, one of the wildest ninth innings in postseason history. The Brooklyn Dodgers, holding a 4-3 lead over the New York Yankees in Game Four of the 1941 World Series, were one strike away from evening the Series at two games apiece. Dodger reliever Hugh Casey, who had pitched scoreless ball since entering the game with two out in the top of the fifth inning, had retired Johnny Sturm and Red Rolfe on groundouts to open the frame. With a 3-and-2 count on Yankees right fielder Tommy Henrich, Casey threw a pitch that broke sharply, and Henrich swung and missed. The Ebbets Field crowd erupted. Dodgers win! Series tied!

But wait. ... Henrich was running toward first base, and Dodgers catcher Mickey Owen was chasing after the ball, which was rolling toward the backstop. The game was about to turn upside down.

Up to then, it had been a very competitive series. The Yankees, winners of the four of the last five World Series (1936-39), had won Game One at home behind Red Ruffing, 3-2. After Whitlow Wyatt and the Dodgers evened the Series with a 3-2 victory of their own, the Yankees took the Series lead with a 2-1 victory at Ebbets Field. Casey had been the Dodgers goat in Game Three, taking the loss after surrendering both Yankee runs in the top of the eighth to break a scoreless tie.

Dodgers manager Leo Durocher selected right-hander Kirby Higbe, 22-9 in the regular season, to start Game Four; Joe McCarthy, skipper of the Yanks, countered with right-hander Atley Donald, who had posted a 9-5 record. The Yankees quickly took the lead in the top of the first; Rolfe singled with one out, Joe DiMaggio drew a walk one out later, and Charlie Keller singled past Brooklyn first baseman Dolph Camilli to drive in Rolfe.

The Yankees made it 3-0 in the top of the fourth. After New York loaded the bases to open the inning on double by Keller, a walk to Bill Dickey, and Joe Gordon's single, Higbe seemed poised to escape the jam when Phil Rizzuto hit into a third-to-home force out and Donald struck out on three pitches. But Sturm singled to center, driving in Dickey and Gordon and moving Rizzuto to second. With left-handed hitters Rolfe and

Henrich up next, Durocher replaced Higbe with lefty Larry French. When one of French's pitches landed in the dirt and got away from Owen, the runners tried to advance, but Owen was able to grab the ball quickly and throw to third; Rizzuto was tagged out in a rundown to retire the side.

The Dodgers responded with two runs in the bottom of the fourth. After retiring the first two hitters, Donald walked Owen and Pete Coscarart. Jimmy Wasdell batted for French and "sliced a fly that landed less than two feet inside the left-field foul line deep in the corner for a double, scoring Owen and Coscarart."[1] The Yankees threatened to score again in the fifth, loading the bases with two out against Johnny Allen, who had taken over from French. But Casey relieved Allen and got Gordon to fly out to end the inning. The Dodgers took the lead in the bottom of the frame. After Dixie Walker doubled, (according to the *Los Angeles Times* play-by-play) Pete Reiser "hit the first pitch over the scoreboard in right field for a home run, scoring behind Walker. The scoreboard is about 40 feet high and 350 feet from home plate. The crowd went wild over the Dodgers taking the lead, and Donald stalked off the mound as [Marv] Breuer, another right-hander, came in to pitch for the Yankees."[2]

Reiser's home run gave the Dodgers a 4-3 lead, and it remained that way until the top of the ninth, with Casey shutting down the Yankees and Breuer (three scoreless innings) and Johnny Murphy (a one-two-three eighth) doing likewise against the Dodgers. Then came the fateful ninth, and the two-strike pitch that got away from Owen after Henrich swung and missed.

"With two strikes on Henrich," wrote Henry McLemore, "Casey throws a perfect curve that cuts the middle. As Henrich swings and misses, the crowd jumps to its feet to applaud its heroes. Policemen run around the field to guard the diamond. For a split second, Brooklyn has won the game and the series is tied at 2-all. Then – for reason that only the fates who pull the strings

on us humans know – the ball spins out of the hands of Catcher Mickey Owen and rolls toward the stands."[3]

Henrich was able to reach first safely before Owen could retrieve the ball and retire him at first, and the Yankees were still alive. The turn of events seemed to rattle Casey. With Joe DiMaggio at bat, Paul Zimmerman wrote, "The unnerved Casey put one right in the groove and DiMag smashed it into left field a clean hit. Up came Charlie Keller, who had already enjoyed three hits today. He tore into one of Hughie's offerings and planted it high against the barrier in right field for two bags, easily chasing Henrich and DiMaggio home. …" Keller's double gave the Yankees a 5-4 lead. "Casey, thoroughly upset now, walked Bill Dickey and Joe Gordon drove in the other two runs with a double against the left field wall" to make it 7-4.[4] Casey walked Rizzuto before finally ending the half-inning by retiring Yankee pitcher Johnny Murphy on a groundout. Murphy retired the Dodgers in order, with no ball leaving the infield, in the bottom of the ninth to preserve the victory. Instead of being tied two games apiece, the Yankees now held a three-games-to-one series lead and were one victory away from their fifth World Series championship in the last six seasons.

"I really can't tell you how it happened, fellows," Owen told reporters after the game, "because I don't know. It was a good pitch, maybe the best curve ball Casey threw all afternoon. It squirted out of my glove somehow. Why, I don't know. I DO know I'm a better catcher than that!"[5]

As for the ball that got away from Owen, many observers contended that Casey's 3-and-2 pitch to Henrich was not a curveball, but an illegal spitball. Casey himself told conflicting stories. Several years after he had left the Dodgers, he told J.G. Taylor Spink, "I give you my word it was not a spit ball. It was a crazy sinker. Sometimes that pitch looks like a spitter. I don't pitch spitters."[6] But then he changed his story. "Years later," wrote sportswriter Tommy Holmes, "Casey admitted his third strike to Henrich had been a spitball, which may explain why Owen didn't handle it."[7]

Writing about the alleged spitter in his 1975 autobiography, *Nice Guys Finish Last*, Casey's manager, Leo Durocher, wrote, "It just isn't true, though. Hugh Casey didn't even know how to throw a spitball."[8] And in a 1988 *New York Times* interview of Owen and Henrich by Dave Anderson, Owen contended that "if Casey threw a spitball, he threw it on his own. … It never looked like a spitball to me. It was a curveball. That's what I called for." Henrich agreed. "That's right," he told Anderson. "Spitballs drop down. I swung at a big breaking curveball."[9]

Spitball or curve, the ball got away from Owen, and the Dodgers had shockingly lost a game they thought they had won. The next morning's *New York Times* featured a parody of "Casey at the Bat" entitled "Casey in the Box – 1941," by *Times* newsman Meyer Berger. The poem concluded:

> *Oh somewhere North of Harlem the sun is shining bright*
>
> *Bands are playing in The Bronx and up there hearts are light.*
>
> *In Hunts Point men are laughing, on The Concourse children shout.*
>
> *But there is no joy in Flatbush. Fate had knocked their Casey out.*[10]

In Game Five that afternoon (October 6), the Yankees wrapped up the Series with a 3-1 victory. Mickey Owen, sadly, joined the ranks of players best remembered for letting a crucial victory get away. When Owen died in 2005, nearly 64 years after the dropped third strike, the headline of his *New York Times* obituary was, "Mickey Owen Dies at 89; Allowed Fateful Passed Ball."[11]

SOURCES

In addition to the sources cited in the Notes, the author consulted Baseball-Reference.com, Retrosheet.org, and the following:

Spatz, Lyle. *Hugh Casey: The Triumphs and Tragedy of a Brooklyn Dodger* (Lanham, Maryland: Rowman & Littlefield, 2017).

NOTES

1   "Here's Play-by-Play on Yanks' 7-4 Win," *Los Angeles Times*, October 6, 1941: 18.

2   "Here's Play-by-Play."

3   Henry McLemore, "McLemore Saw It, but He Doesn't Believe It," *Los Angeles Times*, October 6, 1941: 20.

4   Paul Zimmerman, "Lucky Break Gives Yankees 7-4 Victory," *Los Angeles Times*, October 6, 1941: 1.

5   Harold Parrott, "Both Sides," *Brooklyn Daily Eagle*, October 6, 1941: 15.

6   J.G. Taylor Spink, "Looping the Loops," *The Sporting News*, September 28, 1949: 6.

7   Tommy Holmes, *The Dodgers* (New York: Macmillan, 1975), 89.

8   Leo Durocher with Ed Linn, *Nice Guys Finish Last* (New York: Simon & Schuster, 1975), 162.

9   Dave Anderson, "Owen, Henrich Say Casey Threw a Curve," *New York Times*, June 12, 1988: 453.

10 Meyer Berger, "Casey in the Box – 1941," *New York Times*, October 6, 1941: 20.

11 Richard Goldstein, "Mickey Owen Dies at 89; Allowed Fateful Passed Ball," *New York Times*, July 15, 2005. https://www.nytimes.com/2005/07/15/sports/baseball/mickey-owen-dies-at-89-allowed-fateful-passed-ball.html (accessed October 14, 2019).

THE DODGERS SUBMIT QUIETLY TO TINY BONHAM AND THE YANKEES

October 6, 1941

New York Yankees 3, Brooklyn Dodgers 1 | Game Five of the World Series

by James Forr

At the start of Game Three, Brooklyn fans draped a large banner from the railing of the center-field bleachers that read, "We waited 21 years, don't fail us now." The sheet proclaimed its message proudly throughout Games Three and Four. But by late in Game Five, the banner was sagging and unreadable, an apt metaphor for the fate of the Dodgers, who wilted in submission to the relentless Yankees machine.

Brooklyn and its fans seemed understandably deflated after a crushing defeat in Game Four, when a potential game-winning third strike got away from catcher Mickey Owen and opened the door to a four-run ninth-inning Yankees rally. The fans didn't hold it against Owen. They gave a him a rousing ovation when he was introduced in Game Five. However, although attendance was a tick higher than it had been for the previous two games, the park was unusually subdued. New York's stunning comeback had brought mortality into clear focus.

The Dodgers went with their best to try to keep the Series alive. Veteran Whitlow Wyatt, the winning pitcher in Game Two, tied for the National League lead with 22 victories that summer. Meanwhile, Yankees manager Joe McCarthy turned to his fifth different starter of the Series, the ironically nicknamed Tiny Bonham, a hulking product of the Oakland, California, shipping docks who approached his assignment with the eagerness of a puppy: "When McCarthy told me I was going to pitch the fifth game I was so thrilled that tears came to my eyes. It was what I had always wanted to do."[1]

New York threatened in the first, putting men at first and second for Joe DiMaggio, but on a 3-and-2 pitch, Wyatt struck out the American League MVP and Owen cut down Red Rolfe at third on the front end of an attempted double steal. Brooklyn mounted a challenge of its own in the bottom half, but after Pete Reiser's two-out triple, NL home-run champ Dolph Camilli, suffering through a miserable Series, popped harmlessly to short.

Charlie Keller began the Yankees' second with a walk, and Bill Dickey followed with a single up the middle. Reiser had a good chance to catch Keller advancing to third, but his perfect one-hop

145

throw from center skipped through the legs of third baseman Lew Riggs. Wyatt was backing up, which temporarily saved the day, but next came the irrepressible Joe Gordon, who was 6-for-11 in the Series so far with four RBIs. On his second pitch, Wyatt uncorked a wild one that sailed way over Owen's head and allowed Keller to score the first run. Then Gordon singled to right, driving in Dickey and giving New York a 2-0 lead.

The Dodgers showed a fluttering pulse in the bottom of the third. Wyatt, a dangerous hitter, led off with a double high off the left-field wall, advanced to third two batters later when Riggs singled off Bonham's foot, and then came home on Reiser's fly out. That perked up the crowd until the fifth, when Tommy Henrich took Wyatt deep, hammering his first pitch over the wall in right, just fair but well gone. "When last seen from the high press box," Shirley Povich wrote in the *Washington Post*, "the ball was being pursued by a posse of boys down a street two blocks from the park."[2]

Henrich's blow put the Yankees up 3-1, and seemed to take the energy out of everyone on the Brooklyn side except for Wyatt. He brushed back the next hitter, DiMaggio, with a couple of fastballs before retiring him on a long fly to center. On his way back to the dugout, DiMaggio had a few words for the Dodgers right-hander. "I didn't like how a couple of pitches came at my head," DiMaggio admitted. "When I passed him, I said, 'The Series is over, kid, so take it easy.'"[3] When Wyatt, the former Sunday school teacher, offered a profane rejoinder, DiMaggio lost his characteristic cool and spun back toward the mound to have it out.

Immediately the benches cleared to keep the two men away from each other. No punches were thrown and apparently no feelings were too badly bruised. When DiMaggio returned to his position in center field in the bottom of the fifth, the bleacherites booed lustily and one fan whipped an apple at him, but for Wyatt, it was all in the game.

"It's just one of those things that happens in the heat of battle," he shrugged. "Joe is a great player and I like him."[4]

The rest of the way was as easy as breathing for Bonham. "You know, it may sound [strange], but I wasn't as nervous out there as I have been for some league games," he said.[5] Bonham was known for his forkball, but he claimed he threw it only twice, instead relying almost entirely on fastballs. He wasn't overly deceptive, but he was extremely effective. He allowed just two baserunners from the fourth inning onward, retiring the side on four pitches in the sixth and three pitches in the seventh. Were it not a World Series game, it would have been a monstrously dull way to spend an afternoon. *The Sporting News* described the crowd as "still as a morgue."[6] The only real excitement in the late innings came when a fan in the upper deck in left field carelessly discarded a cigarette and caught a piece of red, white, and blue bunting on fire.

With two outs in the ninth, pinch-hitter Jimmy Wasdell lifted a routine fly ball to DiMaggio, an anticlimactic end to a tightly fought World Series. New York took the game, 3-1, and the Series four games to one. The Yankees weren't new to this. It was their fifth title in six years, but they celebrated as if they had never won before. Indeed, it had been a challenging season – they dropped 16 of their first 31 games and then saw their beloved erstwhile first baseman, Lou Gehrig, die in June. They had earned the right to cut loose.

Coach Art Fletcher danced on a trunk in the clubhouse as the team sang its traditional victory song, "The Sidewalks of New York." McCarthy was late coming in from the field, but when he arrived, his guys belted out another rendition just for him. DiMaggio pushed his way through the madness to hand the baseball to Bonham, who kissed it for the benefit of photographers before giving McCarthy a back ride around the room, with the rest of the team pummeling them every step of the way. As the *New York Times* described it, "Punches were flying, bodies were swaying, trunks were being banged around, benches were pushed out of place, towels flew through the air. And the noise was terrific."[7]

Brooklyn manager Leo Durocher was ostensibly gracious, ducking into the Yankees' celebration in his underwear to shake hands with McCarthy and give Bonham a congratulatory slap on the cheek. Back in his own clubhouse, though, he was somewhat less tactful. "[W]e made their pitching look good because we weren't hitting," he groused. "No pitcher like that Tiny Bonham today, who was throwing fastballs all afternoon because he does not own a curve, should make us look so bad."[8] He also sought out home-plate umpire Bill McGowan after the game to remind him of Brooklyn's displeasure with the veteran arbiter's strike zone.

His players struck a similar tone. Camilli was bellyaching about Brooklyn's bad luck. "If we'd just got half the breaks, not all of 'em, the Series right now would be no worse than three games to two in our favor."[9] Teammate Dixie Walker called the champs "the luckiest club that ever stepped onto a ball field."[10]

McCarthy heard some talk like this from the writers gathered in his clubhouse and was having none of it. "What the hell?" he exploded. "The Dodgers were lucky to win a game. Those Dodgers are a great team. You can't take that away from them, but don't expect me to sit here for hours praising them. I have a great bunch of ballplayers of my own."[11]

The degree of the Yankees' October dominance is nearly incomprehensible. Since 1927, they had appeared in 36 World Series games. They won 32. McCarthy surpassed the Athletics' Connie Mack and became the first manager to win six World Series titles. Brooklyn was still waiting for its first. Its fans, though, were undeterred. A man named Mike Rinaldi spoke the mantra that would be repeated incessantly in the borough over the next decade and a half, when he told a reporter, "It's in the bag for next year."[12]

SOURCES

In addition to the sources cited in the Notes, the author used the Baseball-Reference.com and Retrosheet.org websites for pertinent information, including play-by-play and box scores.

The author also reviewed the following sources for play-by-play and other information:

Drebinger, John. "Yankees Win Series as Bonham Beats Dodgers, 3-1," *New York Times*, October 7, 1941: 1, 28.

Vaughan, Irving. "Yankees Win Eighth World Series Title Since 1927," *Chicago Tribune*, October 7, 1941: 21.

"Yanks Get to Wyatt in Second to End Series at Ebbets Field," *New York Times*, October 7, 1941: 29, 31.

NOTES

1   Robert B. Cooke, "Staid Yankees Stage Wild Dressing Room Scene as Though Series Crown Were Novelty," *New York Herald Tribune,* October 7, 1941: 29.

2   Shirley Povich, "Whit Wyatt Bows Before 34,072 Fans," *Washington Post,* October 7, 1941: 18, 21.

3   Henry McLemore, "Gordon: Ace of the Series," *St. Louis Post-Dispatch,* October 7, 1941: 1-2B. Some newspaper accounts claimed DiMaggio hollered at Wyatt, "It isn't over yet;" however, given the Yankees' lead in the game and commanding advantage in the series, it seems more logical that DiMaggio would have taunted Wyatt by saying the Series *was* over, which is the version of the story that he told McLemore.

4   Billy Goodrich, "Farley, Ever the Politician, Sits Behind Dodgers, Roots for Yanks," *Brooklyn Eagle,* October 7, 1941: 11.

5   Cooke.

6   "Bonham's Four-Hit Pitching Stifles Dodgers in Clincher," *The Sporting News,* October 9, 1941: 8.

7   James P. Dawson, "Punches, Towels Fly in Profusion," *New York Times,* October 7, 1941: 28.

8   Harold Parrott, "Gordon Good But He's No Frisch – Leo," *Brooklyn Eagle,* October 7, 1941: 11.

9   Roscoe McGowen, "Bombers Lauded by Dodger Scout," *New York Times,* October 7, 1941: 28.

10   "Gossip of the Fifth Game," *The Sporting News,* October 9, 1941: 8.

11   Lou E. Cohen, "Dodgers Lucky to Win One Game, Says McCarthy," *Brooklyn Eagle,* October 7, 1941: 11.

12   "'Wait Till Next Year,' Dodger Fans Chant," *Brooklyn Eagle,* October 7, 1941: 1, 3.

Kurowski's home run lifts Cardinals into first-place tie with Dodgers

September 12, 1942
St. Louis Cardinals 2, Brooklyn Dodgers 1

by Stephen V. Rice

Oh, pass the biscuits, Mirandy,
I'm a-gonna load up my gun.
I'll use your biscuits for bullets,
I'll put them varmints on the run.

— from the song "Pass the Biscuits, Mirandy,"
  by Spike Jones and His City Slickers, 1942

The Brooklyn Dodgers won the 1941 National League pennant by a 2½-game margin over the second-place St. Louis Cardinals. On August 15, 1942, the Dodgers were again in first place, and with a 9½-game lead over the second-place Cardinals, appeared to be shoo-ins to win another pennant. But the improbable happened. Over the next 27 days, the Dodgers posted a pedestrian 15-12 record while the Cardinals went on a 24-4 tear. The Brooklyn lead had shrunk to a single game when the archrivals met at Ebbets Field on Saturday, September 12, 1942. "Every nook and corner" of the ballpark was filled by a crowd of 27,511 who came to see "a real-life drama unsurpassed by anything in fiction."[1]

"The Cardinals deserve credit" for their "gallant uphill fight against seemingly unsurmountable odds," wrote Lee Scott of the *Brooklyn Citizen*.[2] "The psychological edge is now with the Cardinals."[3] The team reveled in "Pass the Biscuits, Mirandy," a hit song the players adopted as their anthem.

The starting pitchers on September 12 were both southpaws named Max: stocky Max Lanier for the Cardinals and lanky Max Macon for the Dodgers. Lanier's season record was 12-7 with a 2.96 ERA; Macon was 5-2 with a 2.07 ERA since his call-up from the minors in July. The Maxes knew each other; they were teammates on the pennant-winning 1937 Columbus (Ohio) Red Birds of the American Association.

To face these tough left-handers, Cardinals manager Billy Southworth and Dodgers skipper Leo Durocher put extra right-handed hitters in their starting lineups. In left field, Southworth replaced Stan Musial, a brilliant 21-year-old rookie and left-handed batter, with journeyman Coaker Triplett. Durocher replaced two left-handed-hitting stars, Pete Reiser and Dixie

Walker, with Frenchy Bordagaray and Johnny Rizzo in center and right fields, respectively. The lineups were nonetheless star-studded. Four Cardinals (Jimmy Brown, Walker Cooper, Terry Moore, and Enos Slaughter) and five Dodgers (Billy Herman, Joe Medwick, Mickey Owen, Pee Wee Reese, and Arky Vaughan) were members of the 1942 NL All-Star team.

The Cardinals were retired in order by Macon in the top of the first inning. Bordagaray led off the bottom half by singling up the middle and promptly stole second base. But he was easily thrown out when he tried to steal third. His attempt was "ridiculously reckless," declared the *New York Daily News*.

With one out in the top of the second, Cooper singled to left field. Up to the plate stepped George "Whitey" Kurowski, the 24-year-old son of Polish immigrants.[4] Kurowski was the Cardinals' rookie third baseman and a right-handed batter. After fouling off several pitches, he turned on an inside pitch and pulled it down the left-field line. His drive landed in the lower left-field seats, barely fair, for a two-run home run. The Dodgers got one back when they scored a run in the bottom of the second, on Dolph Camilli's single and Reese's double to deep left-center field.

After Cooper drew a walk with two outs in the top of the fifth, Kurowski "took a vicious cut at the ball and there was a dangerous streak of white lightning down to third," said the *Daily News*. "It looked like a sure hit – but [third baseman] Vaughan claimed it to end the inning."

In the bottom of the seventh, controversy erupted over a close play at first base. Owen led off by grounding the ball toward the hole on the right side of the infield. First baseman Johnny Hopp went for it and couldn't get to it, but Brown, the second baseman, was able to grab it. He threw to Lanier, covering first, who got there just in time. Owen was out, according to first-base umpire Al Barlick. Chuck Dressen, the Dodgers first-base coach, and Durocher argued vociferously with

Barlick, and both were ejected from the game as angry Brooklyn fans threw debris onto the field in protest.

Later in the inning, Vaughan drew a walk from Lanier. Augie Galan, pinch-hitting for Macon, sent a grounder up the middle, which shortstop Marty Marion reached with a diving stop. Marion tossed to Brown at second base for a force out, but Brown dropped the ball. Now with Vaughan on second base and Galan on first, Lanier uncorked a wild pitch in the dirt. As Cooper, the catcher, ran to the backstop to retrieve the ball, Vaughan raced around third and headed home. It was a desperate attempt to tie the game. Cooper fired the ball to Lanier covering home plate, and Vaughan was out by a yard.

Billy Herman drew a walk from Lanier with one out in the bottom of the eighth. Rizzo sent a long drive to right field, which Slaughter caught on the run for the second out. Medwick singled to right field (his 2,000th major-league hit), and Herman advanced to second base. Now Camilli, the NL MVP in 1941, stepped to the plate with a chance to knock in the tying run. Lanier got him to ground the ball weakly to Brown for the third out. Camilli simultaneously "broke his bat and the fans' hearts," said Dick McCann of the *Daily News*.

Lanier went the distance. In the bottom of the ninth, Slaughter made another fine running catch, on Owen's drive to right-center field. Reese's "hot grounder" was handled by Kurowski for the second out. And Vaughan popped out meekly to Hopp for the third out.

The final score was Cardinals 2, Dodgers 1. The Cardinals were now tied with the Dodgers atop the NL standings.

The Dodgers went 10-4 in the remaining games of the season, but the Cardinals did even better, winning 12 of 14 games to capture the pennant. The Cardinals' 106 victories in 1942 were the most by a NL team since the Pittsburgh Pirates won 110 in 1909.

The Cardinals defeated the Yankees in five games in the 1942 World Series. Kurowski was again a hero; his ninth-inning home run off Red Ruffing provided the margin of victory in Game Five. In celebration, Kurowski and his teammates sang, "Pass the Biscuits, Mirandy."

"That Cardinal team never stopped hustling, not for one minute," said Billy Herman years later. "When a team has got that kind of fire, you can just feel it in the clubhouse before a game. It's like electricity."[5]

SOURCES

Game coverage in the September 12 and 13, 1942, issues of the *Brooklyn Eagle*, *New York Daily News*, *St. Louis Post-Dispatch*, and *St. Louis Star-Times*.

NOTES

1   Tommy Holmes, "Flock Faces Loss of Lead in Tilt Today," *Brooklyn Eagle*, September 12, 1942: 1; Judson Bailey (Associated Press), "Two Maxies Due to Pitch in Brooklyn," *Boston Globe*, September 12, 1942: 6.

2   Lee Scott, "Rest May Prove Advantageous to Dodgers as Jittery Cards Play Phils," *Brooklyn Citizen*, September 14, 1942: 6.

3   Lee Scott, "Dodgers in Last-Ditch Stand Must Halt Cardinals in Today's Big Game," *Brooklyn Citizen*, September 12, 1942: 6.

4   1930 US Census.

5   Donald Honig, *The Man in the Dugout* (Chicago: Follett, 1977), 253.

DODGERS DOUBLE DOWN IN ROUT

July 10, 1943
Brooklyn Dodgers 23, Pittsburgh Pirates 6

by Kevin Larkin

"Four Pirate pitchers bent like reeds in the fury of the Dodger attack," quipped Brooklyn sportswriter Tommy Holmes writing of the Dodgers' offensive outburst against visiting Pittsburgh.1 For the first time in franchise history, the Dodgers scored at least 10 runs in an inning twice in a game.

Entering the game, the Dodgers were in second place, four games behind the first-place St. Louis Cardinals, while skipper Frankie Frisch had his Pirates in third place 7½ games behind St. Louis.

Leo Durocher was in his fifth year of managing the Dodgers and the team had finished no worse than third (Durocher's first year at the helm, 1939). The team was led by second baseman Billy Herman, third baseman Frenchy Bordagaray, outfielder Dixie Walker, and former Pirates outfielder Paul Waner, all of whom batted .300 or better in 1943.

This was the third game of a five-game series; the teams had split the first two. Durocher's choice for a starting pitcher was 10-year veteran Curt Davis, a 39-year-old right-hander who entered the contest with a record of 4-5 and an ERA of 1.58. Pittsburgh's starter, righty Johnny Podgajny, entered the game with a record of 4-7 and a 2.11 ERA.

Smoldering in the shadow of dissension in their clubhouse at game time the previous day, the Dodgers half-heartedly called off their general rebellion and their frustrated anger and burst into full flame against the Pirates. Arky Vaughan was on a personal strike after Durocher had suspended Bobo Newsom for berating catcher Bobby Bragan for missing a third strike, according to the New York Daily News.2

Durocher said that the trouble had started out in the third inning of the game played the previous day. After the Pirates had scored a run, they had a runner on third base with two out. Bragan missed a third strike which allowed Elbie Fletcher to reach first base.3

Later, on the bench, Bragan told Durocher he had called for a fastball, but Newsom threw something else. Bragan thought it might have been a knuckler, but said it could have been a spit ball because there was a wet spot on the ball when he picked it up.4

Newsom said indignantly it was a fast ball, although the Brooklyn benchwarmers, including Durocher, thought it was a breaking pitch.[5]

Durocher was quoted as saying, "I am sick and tired of Newsom acting as though the only thing that matters is whether he wins or loses. It isn't right that he (Newsom) is trying to blame the kid" (Bragan).[6]

Durocher also added, "he's suspended." Branch Rickey, the front office generalissimo of the Flatbush forces said he would stick by his manager.[7]

The revolt in the playing ranks threatened the cancellation of the next game. Minutes before game time Vaughn had agreed to play and the Dodgers trotted out on the field.[8]

This was the latest in the baseball fortunes in Brooklyn, as Vaughn was upset over Newsom's punishment and appeared at Durocher's office door in the clubhouse a half hour before game time. He said to Durocher, "Here's another uniform you can have." Durocher leaped to his feet and said, "I don't know what it's all about, Arky, but if that's the way you feel about it, take it off."[9]

Durocher called off infield practice and held a meeting with his players with the newspapermen in attendance. He said that Newsom's suspension had nothing to do with the Bragan incident, and wanted the suspension to last longer than three days. Durocher then said that the suspension resulted when he questioned Newsom on how he had pitched to Vince DiMaggio when DiMaggio doubled to left field. Newsom said high and inside. I told him it wasn't far enough inside and he virtually told me I was a liar.[10]

Durocher denied suspending Vaughn although he had said to him following the altercation, "You're suspended too." Durocher said Vaughn quit and turned in his uniform. Vaughn and Newsom then watched the game from the rightfield stands near the bullpen. However, it was later announced by Secretary Mel Jones that Vaughn was back in uniform and on the bench.[11]

Davis allowed the Pirates' leadoff hitter, Frankie Gustine, a single but then retired Johnny Barrett (fly ball to center field), Jim Russell (groundout that advanced Gustine to second), and Bob Elliott (fly ball to left field) to send the Pirates into the field of play and the Dodgers to bat.

Podgajny got Al Glossop to fly out to Vince DiMaggio in center field and then allowed the next six batters to reach base: Paul Waner singled, Walker doubled, and Augie Galan walked to load the bases. Billy Herman, the Dodgers second baseman, doubled to score all three runners and give Brooklyn a 3-0 lead. A walk to Dolph Camilli and a single by Bragan loaded the bases again. Manager Frisch replaced Podgajny with another right-hander, Harry Shuman, who gave up a single to Red Barkley that scored Herman and Camilli and sent Bragan to third base. Barkley stole second base with Davis at bat. Davis flied out to Barrett in right field for the second out of the inning. The runners held as Glossop, who had led off the game, singled to load the bases a third time. Third baseman Elliott's error on Waner's grounder allowed Bragan and Barkley to score and gave Brooklyn a 7-0 lead.

Walker reached base for the second time in the inning on a walk that loaded the bases for the fourth time in the inning. Brooklyn's Galan hit a bases-clearing triple to give the Dodgers a 10-0 lead. After a walk to Herman, Frisch went to the mound a second time and replaced Shuman with left-hander Johnny Gee, who got Camilli to fly out to center field and end the carnage.

It was a one-two-three inning for Davis in the second and while Gee allowed consecutive one-out singles to Barkley and Davis, Glossop grounded into an inning-ending double play. Waner led off the bottom of the third for Brooklyn with a single and after Walker lined out to shortstop, Galan doubled, putting left Dodgers at second and third. A single by Herman scored both runners and the Dodgers' lead grew to 12-0.

With two outs in the top of the fourth inning, Elbie Fletcher, the Pirates' first baseman, walked. DiMaggio singled; Fletcher scored when Dodgers right fielder Waner let the ball get past him and catcher Bragan fumbled Waner's belated throw home. DiMaggio wound up at second. After a walk by Al Lopez, Pete Coscarart's double scored DiMaggio. A triple by pitcher Gee scored two runs and made the score 12-4, Brooklyn.

Brooklyn posted its second 10-run inning in the fourth inning. Barkley began it by drawing a walk. With one out, Glossop also walked. A single by Waner loaded the bases. Barkley scored on a single by Walker. Galan walked to force in a run, and Herman's single scored Waner and Walker. Galan scored on Camilli's single and the fourth walk of the inning, this one to Bragan, loaded the bases again. Gee gave up a double to Barkley to score Herman and Camilli, and was yanked in favor of Bill Brandt. Brandt gave up a fly ball to Davis that scored Bragan and a home run to Glossop to score two more and give the Dodgers a 22-4 lead. Waner walked again, but Walker's fly out ended the inning.

With Brandt still on the mound in the bottom of the fifth inning, Camilli worked a two-out walk. A single by Bragan advanced Max Macon (pinch-running for Camilli) to third base. With Barkley at the plate, Macon stole home to give the Dodgers a 23-4 lead.

The scoring ended in the top of the eighth inning. The Pirates' Bob Elliott singled off Davis. Tommy O'Brien flied out to left field and after a walk to Johnny Wyrostek, Bill Baker's single scored Elliott and sent Wyrostek to third base. The 29th and last run of the game came in as Wyrostek scored on Coscarart's force-play grounder to third.

Despite all the time spent baserunning, the game ended in a tidy 2 hours and 10 minutes.

SOURCES

In addition to the game story and box-score sources cited in the notes, the author consulted the Baseball-Reference.com and Retroshett.org websites.

NOTES

1   Tommy Holmes, "Dodgers Crush Pirates, 23-6 with Two 10 Run Outbreaks," *Brooklyn Eagle*, July 11, 1943: 21.

2   "Dodgers Smother Pirates, 23-6,with Two 10 Run Innings, *New York Daily News*, July 11, 1943: 162.

3   Tommy Holmes, "Newsom Winds Up in Doghouse After Clubhouse Spat With Lippy", *Brooklyn Daily Eagle*, July 10, 1943:6.

4   "Newsom Winds Up in Doghouse After Clubhouse Spat With Lippy"

5   "Newsom Winds Up in Doghouse After Clubhouse Spat With Lippy"

6   "Newsom Winds Up in Doghouse After Clubhouse Spat With Lippy"

7   "Newsom Winds Up in Doghouse After Clubhouse Spat With Lippy"

8   Roscoe McGowen, "Dodgers Revolt Against Durocher, Then Play and Win Game, 23 to 6", *New York Times*, July 11, 1943:1

9   *New York Times*

10 *New York Times*

11 *New York Times*

BROWN DEBUTS FOR DODGERS AS A 16-YEAR-OLD SHORTSTOP

August 3, 1944
Chicago Cubs 6, Brooklyn Dodgers 2 | Game One of Doubleheader

by Bill Pearch

Leo Durocher, manager of the eighth-place Brooklyn Dodgers, refused to accept excuses from his new shortstop, Tommy Brown. Brown arrived at Ebbets Field fresh off an all-night train ride that brought him to the big leagues from the Newport News Dodgers of the Class-B Piedmont League. Thinking a 16-year-old shortstop would make a difference for the Dodgers seemed a stretch. The Dodgers' on-field product was decimated with many key players, including regular shortstop Pee Wee Reese, having answered the call of the military for service in World War II. Reese, who joined the US Navy after the 1942 season, left a hole in the middle of the infield.[1] General manager Branch Rickey and Durocher tested 26-year-old Bobby Bragan's skills at shortstop in Reese's absence. Bragan instead demonstrated his lead legs and lack of mobility.[2] Brooklyn's brain trust remembered Brown, whom Durocher had sarcastically nicknamed "Buckshot," from spring training earlier in the year.[3]

"I don't think Leo Durocher will use you for a couple of days at least," Rickey said, attempting to settle the teenager's nerves. "However, he's the manager of the team and don't be surprised if he decides to play you sooner than expected."[4]

Thanks to rain one week earlier, the Dodgers had a doubleheader lined up against the Chicago Cubs on August 3, 1944. Durocher did not hesitate to insert Brown, one of the youngest infielders ever to make a major-league roster, into the Dodgers' starting lineup for the first game of the twin bill.[5] With a record of 38-59, the Dodgers had nothing to lose except sole possession of the National League's cellar.

Brown was the product of an unconventional upbringing in Brooklyn's Bensonhurst neighborhood. He never knew his father and the youngster's aunt and uncle served as guardians during his formative years.[6] By the time he turned 12 years old, Brown left school to earn an honest wage alongside his uncle unloading barges on New York's docks.[7] When the youngster was not working the docks, he passed his time playing baseball on Brooklyn's cobblestone streets or on one of the borough's Kiwanis club teams.[8]

In 1943 one of Brown's friends persuaded him to participate in the Dodgers' open tryouts with

2,500 other aspiring ballplayers at the Parade Grounds. An avid Dodgers fan, Brown attended the tryouts without his own spikes or glove, but survived the three-day workout. Team management assured Brown that his performance distinguished himself from the others and he would rank among the handful of players who would hear from the team at a later date.[9] That winter, Brown received news that he should report to the Dodgers' spring-training camp at Bear Mountain, New York.[10]

After spring training the Dodgers assigned Brown to the franchise's farm team in Newport News, Virginia. By the end of July 1944, he had 91 minor-league games under his belt.[11] Brown was batting just shy of .300 and pacing the Piedmont League with 11 triples when he received news that the Dodgers expected him to report to Ebbets Field. Reluctant to leave a situation in which he excelled, Brown informed his manager, Jake Pitler, that he was not interested.[12] Despite the protest, Pitler said, "No, you've got to leave now."[13] He made sure Brown packed and boarded a train headed for Brooklyn.

Heavy rains drenched Ebbets Field and its 6,146 spectators just minutes prior to the game, but the inclement weather would not wash away Brown's debut.[14] During pregame warmups, Durocher noted Brown's erratic defense and wildness. After fielding groundballs, the young shortstop consistently missed his mark and heaved the ball beyond first baseman Howie Schultz's glove.[15] Durocher shook his head and remembered the nickname, "Buckshot," that he gave to Brown during spring training.[16] Once the game started, Brown fielded his position and watched as Chicago's Dom Dallessandro belted a two-run homer in the top of the first inning giving the Cubs a 3-0 lead.

Brown's first trip to the plate came in the bottom of the second inning against the Cubs starting pitcher, Bob Chipman. Eddie Stanky singled with one out and stood on first base. Brown reached first safely after grounding into a fielder's choice. Pitcher Curt Davis ended the inning on a fly ball to Bill Nicholson in right field.

Cubs third baseman Stan Hack challenged Brown's defense leading off the third inning. Brown misjudged Hack's high bounder, the ball rolled up his arm, and by the time he secured the ball, his throw was too low and too tardy.[17] The runner was safely on first base.[18] The young shortstop found vindication as Hack attempted to swipe second base. With Phil Cavarretta at the plate, catcher Bragan fired a strike to Brown, who applied the tag on Hack.

Brown's nervousness continued as the Cubs held a 5-0 lead in the top of the fourth inning.[19] With two outs and Mickey Kreitner on first, Chipman tapped an easy groundball to short. Brown allowed the grounder to trickle through his legs; he was charged with an error. The youngster dodged a bullet when Hack squashed the Cubs' rally with a groundout to first base.

With Brooklyn still trailing 5-0, Schultz started the Dodgers' fourth inning with a double. Bragan and Stanky failed to bring him home. Brown found himself batting with a runner in scoring position. He popped up to third baseman Hack, who ranged into foul territory to retire the side.

With two outs and the bases empty in the top of the seventh inning, Brown steadied his nerves in the field. He cleanly gloved shortstop Roy Hughes' grounder and fired a strike across the infield to Schultz, retiring the side.

The Cubs maintained their comfortable five-run lead heading into the home half of the seventh. Brown stepped to the plate with no outs and an opportunity for damage. Stanky, who had led off the inning with a walk, stood on first base. Brown smashed a Chipman pitch into left-center field, but Stanky applied the brakes at third and the rookie stopped at second with a double. The kid from Brooklyn notched his first major-league base hit. Just as they had been doing since Brown took the field at the start of the game, the Dodgers fans applauded the feat.[20]

With Stanky at third and Brown at second, Mickey Owen entered the game as a pinch-hitter for the pitcher Davis. Owen hit a fly ball to Dallessandro in left field and sent Stanky racing home to put Brooklyn on the scoreboard. Frenchy Bordagaray, the Dodgers' center fielder, grounded a pitch back to Chipman, but first baseman Cavarretta made a wild throw to third base and was charged with an error.[21] Brown took advantage of the miscue, rounded third and charged home. Within moments, his inaugural base hit resulted in his first run and trimmed the Cubs' lead to 5-2.

In the top of the eighth inning, the Cubs added an extra run to extend their lead to 6-2. In the home half of the frame, Bragan singled with one out. Hoping to start a late rally, Durocher sent Paul "Big Poison" Waner in to pinch-hit for Stanky. He promptly popped out to Dallessandro in foul territory. The crowd began to rumble as Brown returned to the plate, but he hit a grounder to Hack at third base, who hurled the ball across the field and ended the inning.

Both teams hung zeroes on the scoreboard in the ninth inning. Brown did not get another opportunity to hit or drive in a run, but the 16-year-old shortstop finished his first major-league game batting 1-for-4. He ended with a double, one run scored, and an error. Neither Brown nor his teammates had much time to celebrate as the second game of the doubleheader was about to start.

SOURCES

In addition to the sources cited in the Notes, the author accessed Retrosheet.org, Baseball-Reference.com, and SABR.org.

NOTES

1   C. Paul Rogers III, "Tommy Brown," SABR BioProject; https://sabr.org/bioproj/person/7913ae6c.

2   Hy Turkin, "Cubs, Flock Offer Only Local Game," *New York Daily News*, August 3, 1944: 36.

3   Lyle Spatz, ed., *The Team That Forever Changed Baseball and America: The 1947 Brooklyn Dodgers.* (Lincoln and London: University of Nebraska Press, 2012), 125.

4   Lee Scott, "Kid Plays Well as Dodgers Lose Twice," *Brooklyn Citizen*, August 4, 1944.

5   Harold C. Burr, "Brown's Major Baptism Due Against Chi Cubs," *Brooklyn Daily Eagle*, August 3, 1944: 17.

6   Spatz, 125.

7   Bill Traughber, "Tommy Brown Recalls His Career," SABRgraphs.   http://www.multibriefs.com/briefs/sabr/TommyBrown.php

8   "Kiwanis Ball Project Spreads to Groups," *Brooklyn Daily Eagle*, April 11, 1944: 13.

9   Spatz, 125.

10 Traughber.

11 Skip Nipper, "Nashville Volunteer Tommy Brown and His Place in Baseball History," *Baseball in Nashville*, June 5, 2019. https://baseballinnashville.com/main/f/nashville-volunteer-tommy-brown-and-his-place-in-baseball-history.

12 Traughber.

13 Rogers.

14 Dick Young, "Cubs Rout Dodgers, 6-2, 7-1," *New York Daily News*, August 4, 1944.

15 Young.

16 Spatz, 125.

17 Young.

18 Burr.

19 Scott.

20 Young.

21 Irving Vaughan, "Cubs Gain Fourth Place by Defeating Dodgers, 6-2, 7-1," *Chicago Tribune*, August 4, 1944.

DIXIE WALKER HITS FOR THE CYCLE AS DODGERS CLIMB OUT OF LAST PLACE

September 2, 1944
Brooklyn Dodgers 8, New York Giants 4

by Mike Huber

The 1944 Brooklyn Dodgers were struggling. They played .167 baseball in July, winning just five of 30 games. They had completed a 20-game road trip from August 9 to 27. After winning the first three games against the Chicago Cubs, they went 3-14, including losing both ends of three doubleheaders, and they dropped into last place in the National League, 45 games behind the St. Louis Cardinals. Now that the dreadful road trip was over, the Dodgers had won their first three home games back at Ebbets Field.

A modest crowd of 12,441 showed up on Saturday, September 2, to see the Dodgers compete with their rivals, the New York Giants. The Giants had also played on the road for 17 games in mid-August, losing 13 straight before winning the final three. The Giants had gone 4-3 since, and they came into Brooklyn in fourth place in the NL standings, 10 games ahead of the Dodgers.

Right-hander Curt Davis started for Brooklyn. He was five days shy of his 41st birthday and had been used as both a starter and reliever by manager Leo Durocher. Bill Voiselle did the twirling for the Giants. The 25-year-old righty had been called up in each September of the previous two seasons, making only six total appearances. In 1944, his first full season with New York, he made 43 total appearances, and he led the American League in games started (41), innings pitched (312⅔), home runs allowed (31), and strikeouts (161). Before this game, he had beaten the Dodgers five times in six starts.[1]

The Dodgers began clubbing Voiselle in the bottom of the first inning. Frenchy Bordagaray started things with a single. Voiselle, in an attempt to pick him off, threw the ball away for an error, and Bordagaray scampered to second. Augie Galan walked, and then Dixie Walker poked an RBI single, plating Bordagaray with the game's first run. An inning later, Tommy Brown walked with one away. Davis sacrificed him to second, and Brown scored when Bordagaray grounded a ball to third. Third baseman Nap Reyes fielded the ball and threw the ball past first baseman Phil Weintraub for the second error in as many innings. Brown scored and Bordagaray again scampered to second. After two innings, New

York had made two costly errors and Brooklyn had a 2-0 lead.

In the third, "Brooklyn fell on Bill Voiselle with wild Neanderthal cries and chased him" from the field. Walker led off with a home run that "cleared the right field wall and went on into Bedford Avenue through an opening in the screen."[2] The ball had not gone over the screen; it had gone through it! Luis Olmo and Howie Schultz then hit back-to-back doubles, and New York player-manager Mel Ott pulled Voiselle. Rookie Jack Brewer came out of the bullpen in relief. Eddie Stanky sacrificed Schultz to third before Brown grounded out. Then, with Davis batting, Schultz attempted to steal home and was tagged out, but the Dodgers had doubled their advantage.

Davis had been tagged for three singles in the first three innings, but with one out in the top of the fourth, Ott "doubled to left and gimped home on Weintraub's triple off the center field wall."[3] Weintraub's three-bagger came a great price, though. He jammed his ankle at third base and had to be carried off of the field on a stretcher.[4] Hal Luby ran for Weintraub. (He later played third base and Reyes moved from third to first.) An out later, Buddy Kerr bashed a double, scoring Luby. Reyes was intentionally walked, bringing up the pitcher. Ott sent Billy Jurges in as a pinch-hitter for Brewer, and Jurges produced, driving in the third New York run of the inning with a single.

The Giants had made the game close, bringing them within a run of the Dodgers, but Brooklyn "stepped right out again and fattened their advantage with three runs in their fourth."[5] Ace Adams became the third New York pitcher, and he quickly retired the first two batters he faced. Then, however, he lost some control and walked both Mickey Owen and Galan, bringing up the hot-hitting Walker, who drove an Adams offering to the center field exit gate. The ball bounced off the screen and Walker made it to third base with

a triple. Olmo singled in Walker, and suddenly the Dodgers had those three runs back.

Stanky led off the home half of the fifth with a walk. Brown bunted him to second, and Bordagaray brought him home with his third single of the afternoon. The Dodgers had "scored steadily for the first five innings,"[6] and now led the Giants, 8-3.

Davis yielded a pair of two-baggers to Kerr and Johnny Rucker in the sixth. Rucker's "towering shot hit the top rail of the high screen but instead of going on over bounced back on the field, so Johnny was held to a double."[7] Kerr had scored but Rucker was stranded, and the Giants still trailed by four runs.

The game settled down. Walker hit a one-out double in the bottom of the sixth (his 30th double of the season), but his teammates could not bring him home, and the Dodgers did not muster any more threats. On the mound, Davis was touched for four more hits through the final three innings, but New York could not cross the plate with a runner. Behind Davis's complete game, Brooklyn had won 8-4. The Dodgers ran their modest winning streak to four games and lifted themselves out of the National League basement.

Davis, dubbed "Ol' Dan'l Boone,"[8] allowed 14 hits to the Giants, three more than all five of the New York hurlers combined. The difference was that Davis "tighten[ed] up in the pinches to leave [11] Giant runners stranded on the bases."[9] The Dodgers left only seven men on base. Bordagaray had another single to open the eighth and finished the game with a 4-for-5 day at the plate (all singles). For the Giants, Kerr was 3-for-4 with two doubles and two runs scored.

In the Brooklyn victory, "the people's choice [Walker] belted a single, double, triple and home run for a perfect day."[10] He had driven in four runs and scored two. He raised his average 6 points to .361 and his on-base plus slugging percentage (OPS) to .980. Dixie Walker became the fifth Brooklyn franchise batter to hit for the cycle, joining Oyster Burns (August 1, 1890, against the Pittsburgh Alleghenys), Jimmy Johnston (May 25, 1922, against the Philadelphia Phillies), and Babe Herman (who hit for the cycle twice – on May 18, 1931, against the Cincinnati Reds and again on July 24, 1931, against the Pittsburgh Pirates).

Walker's accomplishment of the rare event was the third cycle of the 1944 season, coming after two Boston Red Sox players: Bobby Doerr's cycle on May 17 (against the St. Louis Browns)[11] and Bob Johnson's cycle on July 6 (against the Detroit Tigers).

For the month of September, the two teams headed in opposite directions. Brooklyn won 14 and lost 14. This game was a high point for the Dodgers and especially for Walker, who led the National League in batting average with a .357 mark. Meanwhile, New York lost 18 of 27 contests, including 15 of its final 19 games of the season. After Walker's star turn, the Giants lost the next game to the Dodgers, too, but for the season, New York had the edge, taking 12 of 22 in the rivalry series. Despite the loss, Mel Ott remained on the field after the game, as he "spent ten minutes giving autographs to a group of wounded soldiers who saw the game."[12]

SOURCES

In addition to the sources mentioned in the Notes, the author consulted baseball-reference.com, MLB.com, Retrosheet.org and SABR.org.

https://www.baseball-reference.com/boxes/BRO/BRO194409020.shtml

https://www.retrosheet.org/boxesetc/1944/B09020BRO1944.htm

NOTES

1 Voiselle's loss to the Dodgers came in a night game played on May 23 at Ebbets Field. According to the *Brooklyn Eagle*, "there was a great confusion in the Giant outfield over a fly ball that fell safe, allowing two Dodgers runners to score the winning runs with two out in the ninth inning." In reality, an error had been charged to Johnny Rucker, making both runs unearned. See Harold C. Burr, "Dodgers Rout Giants, 8-4, as Walker Stars," *Brooklyn Eagle*, September 3, 1944: 15.

2 Roscoe McGowen, "Walker's 4 Blows Help Dodgers Trim Giants Again, 8 to 4," *New York Times*, September 3, 1944: S1.

3 Hy Turkin, "Walker Clouts for Cycle as Dodgers Rap Giants, 8-4," *New York Daily News*, September 3, 1944: 48.

4 The papers reported that the x-rays revealed no break, but Weintraub did have a bad sprain.

5 Turkin.

6 Burr.

7 McGowen.

8 McGowen.

9 "Walker Glitters in Brooklyn Win," *Rochester* (New York) *Democrat and Chronicle*, September 3, 1944: 16.

10 McGowen.

11 This was Doerr's first time hitting for the cycle. His second time came on May 13, 1947, against the Chicago White Sox.

12 Burr.

ED HEAD'S NO-HIT GAME

April 23, 1946
Brooklyn Dodgers 5, Boston Braves 0

by Lyle Spatz

For the first time since 1941, the 1946 baseball season opened with the United States at peace. Fans, who had endured subpar baseball for the previous three years would turn out in record numbers this season. In Brooklyn, the Dodgers would shatter their previous attendance record, drawing just under 1.8 million. An early indication of what was to come was the near-capacity crowd of 26,787 that showed up at Ebbets Field on April 23 for a Tuesday afternoon game against the Boston Braves. Weekday afternoon games, particularly in the spring, were typically not well attended. But the Dodgers had gotten off to a 5-1 start and pennant fever was already being felt in Brooklyn.

On the mound for the Dodgers was Ed Head, a 28-year-old right-hander, who was making his first major-league appearance since 1944. After two years in the Army's Tank Destroyer Corps at Fort Hood, Texas, he had made the team out of spring training, though his arm was still sore from absorbing the recoil from a 57-millimeter antitank gun.

That Head had ever made it to the major leagues was a miracle in itself. In 1935, when he was 17, Head was a left-handed pitcher for a semi-pro team in Louisiana. One afternoon he was on a bus for scheduled game against another team. He and his girlfriend, who accompanied him, were seated on the left side of the bus; Head in the aisle seat and the girl in the window seat. As teenage boys typically do, Head had his left arm draped over her shoulders.

Unfortunately, they were seated almost directly in the path of another bus that rammed theirs. Head was knocked unconscious. When he awoke, he saw his girlfriend was dead and his left arm, wrenched loose from its socket, was "a mass of shattered bone and mangled flesh."[1] The local doctor told him he would have to amputate the arm.

Head argued against amputation and pleaded to have his uncle, who had the only fluoroscope in the area, to come look at the injury. His uncle, a doctor, determined that he could save the arm, which he did following many hours of surgery.

For several days Head's life had been in danger and the thought of his ever pitching again had been dismissed. His lifetime goal had always been to be a major-league pitcher, but with his left arm nearly useless, that would be impossible. At that point, Head realized there was only one way he could reach his goal, by throwing right-handed. The dedication and effort needed to make this happen would have discouraged most people, but Head worked and practiced until he succeeded.

The day before Head's return to baseball, his wife, Johnnie Mae, had given birth to their second son, whom they named Rickey. So before he took the mound, he was handing out cigars in the clubhouse. When he did take the mound, he pitched the game of his career, a 5-0 no-hitter. Head had flirted with a no-hitter once before. On May 29, 1942, he retired the first 18 New York Giants before walking Bill Werber, ending the possibility of a perfect game. The no-hitter ended when Harry Danning led off the eighth inning with a single.

Head was not overpowering this afternoon, striking out only two, but he used an assortment of fastballs, curveballs, sliders, and changeups to keep the opposing batters off stride. The Braves had only four baserunners, three walks, and a fifth-inning error by shortstop Pee Wee Reese, while Brooklyn's defense turned two double plays. Reese's error was clearly a bobble, with no controversy on the scoring.

The Dodgers used four straight hits to take a two-run lead in the third inning. They added two more in the fifth on a two-run double by Ed Stevens. Ferrell Anderson's solo home run in the sixth accounted for Brooklyn's fifth run.

Meanwhile, Head kept getting easy outs. He had only two close calls, one in the seventh inning and one in the eighth. Tommy Holmes led off the seventh with a long drive to right center field that rookie center fielder Carl Furillo ran down and caught in front of the exit gate. In the eighth Whitey Wietelmann slashed a line drive between Reese and third baseman Pete Reiser that Reiser was able to grab with his glove hand.

This was a knowledgeable crowd, aware of what was happening. They were silent when Chuck Workman, batting for Boston pitcher Mort Cooper, led off the ninth with a walk. But they rose in joy when, as Connie Ryan was striking out, catcher Ferrell Anderson threw to first baseman Stevens to double up Workman. Johnny Hopp made the final out on a groundball to second baseman Billy Herman as the crowd erupted in cheers.

In true baseball tradition, none of the other Dodgers mentioned to Head that he was throwing a no-hitter. Herman said he hadn't realized it until the later innings when the crown began loudly cheering every putout. Reese and Stevens claimed they first learned about it when they reached the dressing room.

"Boy, what a day, what a day," Head said in the Dodgers clubhouse after the game. "First I celebrate the birth of my son and then I pitch a no-hitter. And would you believe it," he added, "I knew I was going to do it all the time. I felt great right from the start. I threw only one bad pitch all game – that one to Holmes – I meant to keep it on the outside. You can bet I was saying to myself, 'Come on Furillo.'"[2]

Head said he did not think he had anything extra, but just threw harder and harder as the game progressed. "All I used was my fastball, curve, slider, and change of pace. The slider is the only thing I didn't have before the war."[3]

Head's no hitter was the first by a Dodger since Tex Carleton's at Cincinnati on April 30, 1940. It was the first in Brooklyn since June 15, 1938, when Johnny Vander Meer of the Reds pitched his second consecutive no-hitter in the first night game at Ebbets Field.

A few weeks after the no-hitter, Head reinjured his arm, ending his major-league career.

NOTES

1   Tom Meany, "Fluoroscope Helped to Avoid Amputation; Youth, Now a Dodger, Then Learned to Throw With Other Hand," *PM*, April 30, 1942.

2   Joseph M. Sheehan, "Head Of Dodgers Wins No-Hitter, 5-0," *New York Times*, April 24, 1946.

3   Sheehan.

BROOKLYN AGAINST THE WORLD - 1946

EBBETS FIELD WELCOMES YOUNG STARS FROM ACROSS THE COUNTRY AND BEYOND

August 6, 7, 8, 1946

by Alan Cohen

The *Brooklyn Eagle*, beginning in 1946, staged its "Brooklyn Against the World" competition at Ebbets Field. The main forces behind the game were Branch Rickey of the Dodgers and Lou Niss, the sports editor of the Brooklyn Eagle.

Players from around the United States, Canada, and Hawaii were brought to Brooklyn as part of the "World" team for a three-game series that was played August 7, 8, and 9 at Ebbets Field. Most of them were sponsored by newspapers. Vic Marasco, a player representing the *Los Angeles Times*, had the time of his life: "Those people from the *Brooklyn Eagle* and the Brooklyn Dodgers didn't spare the horses when it came to taking us around." He summed it all up by saying, "I think I learned more on this trip than all the time I was in Fremont High and I just want to congratulate the kid who makes it next year. He's in for the biggest treat of his life."[1] The "fence-denting" Marasco had family in Brooklyn and thus had a built-in cheering section for the series.[2] He signed with the Dodgers, spent 10 seasons in the minor leagues and put up some pretty good numbers,

but Triple A was as far as he would get. He retired after the 1958 season.

Marasco came a long way, but 130-pound pitcher Henry Kiyoshi Tominaga came an even longer distance – from Honolulu, complete with a shirt with "Hawaii – 49th State," across his chest. He was accompanied by Wilfred Rhinelander of the *Honolulu Star Bulletin*.

The BAW contests had topflight managers. Brooklyn was managed by Leo Durocher, who brought along Chuck Dressen, Dixie Walker, and Johnny "Red" Corriden as coaches. The World was managed by Hall of Famer George Sisler, who had as his coaches Andy High, Fresco Thompson, and Clyde Sukeforth. The "World" players were housed at the St. George Hotel.

The *San Francisco Chronicle, Los Angeles Times, New Orleans States, Toronto Star, Buffalo Courier-Express, Mobile Register,* Montreal Newspapers, *Charleston Gazette, Boston Post, Spokane Spokesman-Review, Indianapolis Star, Charlotte Observer, Wichita Eagle, Cleveland News, Philadelphia Record,* St. Paul Amateur Baseball Association, *Fort Worth Star-Telegram, Chicago Daily*

News, Honolulu Star Telegram, and Bridgeport Post sent players to Brooklyn.

Jimmy Murphy and Tommy Holmes of the *Brooklyn Eagle* chronicled the games. Murphy was a champion of sandlot ball and the youth of Brooklyn looked forward to seeing their names in his articles. The "World" players started arriving in town in late July and had their first practices on Thursday August 1. The dream agenda was printed in the *Eagle* on July 28.

On August 1 the players worked out at Ebbets Field and Erasmus High School and witnessed the finale of a three-game series between the Dodgers and St. Louis Cardinals. Later that day, they went to a show at Radio City Music Hall, which included the movie *Anna and the King of Siam* with Rex Harrison and Irene Dunne.[3] On the way to and from the theater, coach Art Dede acted as tour guide, pointing out the sites along the way. On August 2 the teams traveled up the Hudson River to West Point and went on to Bear Mountain, where they practiced and had a steak dinner at the Bear Mountain Inn.

The climax of their day was seeing welterweight boxers Willie Joyce and Danny Kapilow lace up their gloves in a bout at Madison Square Garden. The following day, after practice and dinner, they saw the Dodgers play the Cincinnati Reds at Ebbets Field and took in *Ice-Time* at the Rockefeller Center Theater in Manhattan. On Sunday, August 4, there was no practice, but the boys were kept busy. They were back at Ebbets Field to see the Dodgers and Reds in the afternoon. That was followed by a trip to Jones Beach, where they had a seafood dinner and witnessed the water show, which featured the Magic Water Ballet, diving exhibitions, clowning and a water polo match. After that players Henry Tominaga, Lenny Yochim, Roger Breard, Alex Romanchuk, and Joe Della Monica appeared on the *We the People* broadcast on CBS radio.[4] A group of players dined at Jack Dempsey's Restaurant in Manhattan.

There were a couple of days left until the series was to begin, and the kids continued to practice hard, eat well, and be entertained as they had never been in their lives. Next up was a Monday trip to see *Oklahoma!* at the St. James Theater. After the performance, the boys went backstage to visit members of the cast. Beatrice Lynn, who hailed from Flatbush, posed with Chris Kitsos and Joe Torpey of the Brooklyn squad.[5]

On August 6 the boys were off to Coney Island and its famous Steeplechase amusement park, dinner at Bossert's Marine Roof with its majestic view of the New York skyline, and a trip to the Polo Grounds to see the Dodgers play the Giants. The next morning, they were up early for deep-sea fishing.[6]

During the series, there was even more sightseeing scheduled. From the Brooklyn Museum and nearby Botanical Gardens at the northeast end of Prospect Park to the zoo in the park, the kids saw all that Brooklyn had to offer, including a trip to the Brooklyn Navy Yard on August 8, where they toured the aircraft carrier USS *Kearsarge*.

National League umpire-in-chief Bill Klem worked the series at first base. Klem was no longer an active umpire, and he felt that the plate required the services of an active umpire. Butch Henline was chosen for the task. Klem's reasoning was, "It will be a great series for the boys, and I want to make certain that the game is not spoiled by incompetent officiating. That's why Henline has been assigned for all three games."[7]

The games were broadcast on WHN radio by Dodgers announcers Red Barber and Connie Desmond.

On August 7, the date of the first game, Tommy Holmes introduced the starting Brooklyn nine to his readers.[8] All of the boys were heroes. Fifteen of the Brooklyn players, including each of the starting nine, were signed by big-league teams. Two of the boys on the Brooklyn roster made it to the majors, one all the way to Cooperstown.

The boys woke up to cloudy skies and rain on August 7. As afternoon turned into evening the rain stopped. Before heading to Ebbets Field on August 7, the players dined in Sheepshead Bay and were joined by baseball's Clown Prince, Al Schacht. Brooklyn Borough President John Cashmore threw out the first ball, and Brooklyn legend Gladys Gooding sang the National Anthem.[9] Also in attendance was Hilda Chester, the most vociferous fan of the Dodgers. Hilda was hard to miss. She came to each game equipped with her cowbells and heckled the opposition with an unmatched fervor. The young "World" players were not spared.[10]

The opening game was won by Brooklyn. The score was 4-2, and the game was completed in 97 minutes. Al McEvoy, a lefty who starred at Brooklyn Prep, pitching three no-hitters during his time there, had a complete-game victory for the Brooklyn team, striking out 13, allowing only five hits and no earned runs. McEvoy went to Holy Cross, going 7-0 in his freshman year, before signing with the Yankees. He went 11-4 in two minor-league seasons. At the end of the 1949 season he pitched very briefly at the Triple-A level and went no further.

New Orleans' Lenny Yochim was almost as good as McEvoy in his BAW appearance. In 4⅓ innings of work, he allowed four hits, only two of which left the infield, and struck out eight. He was signed by Pittsburgh and made it to the majors for brief visits in 1951 and 1954, appearing in 12 games with a 1-2 record. In 10 minor-league seasons, many of them spent with the Bucs' Double-A club in New Orleans, Yochim compiled a 100-68 record. After his playing days, he became a well-respected scout for the Pirates.

An unsung coach working with the Brooklyn youngsters was Art Dede. Thirty years earlier, Dede had played with the Brooklyn Robins – for one game on October 4, 1916, in the team's second-to-last game of the season.[11] He had one plate appearance and was unable to reach base safely.

In 1946 Dede was working with Brooklyn first baseman Arnold Wallis. He taught him a play in which the first baseman, with runners on first and second and none out, a definite bunt situation, would charge toward the third-base line and toss the ball to third base for the force play. He worked the play in the first Brooklyn Against the World game. (In his playing days "World" manager Sisler, a top first baseman of his day, had often used this play, as did first baseman Hal Chase.)[12]

In the second game, Vernon Frantz of Wichita and Rickey Rowe of Fort Worth handled Brooklyn, as the World won 4-3 in front of 10,222 spectators. Brooklyn's pitcher was Artie Raynor of Rockville Center, Long Island. Raynor had played right field in the first game. Playing right field in the second game was Ed Ford of Astoria, Queens, and Aviation High School in Manhattan. Ford had played his sandlot ball with a group of his friends in Astoria, Queens. They called themselves the 34th Avenue Boys.[13] Raynor pitched brilliantly, allowing no hits and no runs in four innings, but the pitchers who followed him to the mound did not enjoy as much success.

Frantz ran into misfortune in top of the fifth inning when Brooklyn scored twice without the benefit of a hit. Angelo Palmieri replaced Raynor in the bottom of the inning and relinquished the lead. The World loaded the bases without a hit. Chicago's Art Sepke, pinch-hitting for Frantz, ended Brooklyn's no-hitter with a single, chasing two of the runners home. An inning later the World went out in front with another unearned run. Brooklyn tied the game in the seventh inning. The game was decided in the eighth inning when the World scored another unearned run, this time off pitcher Bob Cowherd, who was tagged with the loss.

Frantz signed with the Dodgers and was in their organization from 1947 through 1951. He was out of baseball at age 22.

In the finale, Brooklyn's Bill Mackel, from the University of Pennsylvania, and Bob Kunze, who had overcome a childhood battle with infantile paralysis, shut down the World by 5-1 to win the series for Brooklyn, defeating Dick Baptista of San Francisco. Mackel pitched the first six innings, striking out nine, and yielding but two singles. The World's only run was unearned.

Mackel signed with the Giants in 1949 and fashioned a 16-7 record for Bristol in the Class-D Appalachian League. In 1950 the dream ended at age 22. After college, Kunze played with unaffiliated minor-league teams through 1952. As no major-league organization was interested in his services, he called it a career at the age of 23. Baptista did not play in Organized Baseball.

Brooklyn used six Brooklyn pitchers in the three games. None made it to the majors. Ed Ford, who played in only the second game and played in right field, was signed by scout Paul Krichell of the Yankees as a pitcher. He did return to Ebbets Field as a player on October 3, 1953, in the fourth game of the 1953 World Series. Along the line, he had become known as Whitey Ford and, although he did not have success on October days at Ebbets Field in 1953 and 1956, he did have a Hall of Fame career with the Yankees.

Chris Kitsos of Brooklyn's James Madison High School played his sandlot ball with the Sheepshead Bay Boy's Club. BAW coach Art Dede encouraged Kitsos to try switch-hitting. He signed with the Dodgers and spent five seasons in their minor-league system.

He made seven stops in the Dodgers organization, and then he got noticed. He batted .334 in 1951 with Asheville in the Tri-State League. He led his league in runs scored (134), doubles (43), and stolen bases (30). Next stop – Brooklyn? Not quite.

The Dodgers infield was populated by fellows named Robinson, Reese, and Cox, and their minor-league system had an abundance of talent. Kitsos was expendable and was drafted by the Chicago Cubs. The Cubs called the shortstop up in 1954, and on April 21, he was inserted as a defensive replacement in the eighth inning after a struggling Ernie Banks had been pulled for a pinch-hitter. He handled two groundballs flawlessly, returned to the dugout, and never reemerged. His major-league career was over.

Art Sepke, who was chosen to go to the game by Rogers Hornsby and represented the *Chicago Daily News*, was a man of many positions and talents. He batted .405 (17-for-42) in his senior year at Schurz High School and hurled his team to five wins as well.[14] Sepke signed with the Yankees and his dream of a big-league career ended after a poor performance in 1949. He continued in baseball and served as an area scout for the Kansas City Royals.

The *Spokane Sportsman-Review* sponsored the Inland Empire All-Star Baseball Game, featuring the best 30 players from Washington, Montana, and Idaho, on July 10. Players were observed by the committee headed by longtime Dodgers scout Howie Haak.[15] Selected to go east was Lou Damman of Leiston, Idaho, who went 3-for-4 with a sensational catch on a ball hit between shortstop and third base.[16]

Damman was accompanied east by writer Denny Spellecy. In the first game of the series, he batted second, and went 1-for-3 with an RBI while handling four chances at third base.[17] He banged his head coming through the hatch on the tour of the *Kearsarge* on August 8 and wound up "with a bad headache, a feeling of loginess, and a slight fever"[18] that caused him to miss the final two games of the series. Damman signed with the Dodgers and played in the minors from 1947 to 1954.

From the Twin Cities came the St. Paul Amateur Baseball Federation's representative, Alex Romanchuk who had completed his first year at St. Thomas College, where he went 5-0. In his five years of playing amateur ball in the Twin Cities, Romanchuk had gone 60-18.[19] Romanchuk received an offer to sign with the Dodgers, but his Russian-born mother wanted her sons to be engineers. Professional baseball was not an option, and he went on to complete his studies at the University of Minnesota. Although Romanchuk did not play in Organized Baseball, he was sought after by amateur teams in Minnesota and was a fixture in the Independent North Star League.

The chief beneficiary of the three games in Brooklyn was sandlot baseball. The monies raised, $22,371 in all, went to a foundation with the goal of providing greater opportunities for youngsters to play baseball and stay out of mischief. Over the coming years, boys from Brooklyn and Long Island would find their way to new fields with new equipment in any number of leagues.

SOURCES

In addition to Baseball-Reference.com and the sources cited in the Notes, the author used:

Barrouquere, Peter. "A Scout on Honor: 50-Year Baseball Love Affair Spiced with Grief, Rewards," *New Orleans Times Picayune*, April 16, 1995.

Gould, Ben. "Ed Ford Second Grad of Brooklyn vs. World to Reach Big Leagues," *Brooklyn Daily Eagle*, July 12, 1950: 22.

Gould, Paul. "Brooklyn Crowned 'World' Series King," *The Sporting News*, August 21, 1946: 32.

Holmes, Tommy. "As Brooklyn Moved One Up on the World," *Brooklyn Daily Eagle*, August 8, 1946: 15.

Peterson, Armand, and Tom Tomashek. *Town Ball: The Glory Days of Minnesota Amateur Baseball* (Minneapolis: University of Minnesota Press, 2006)

Correspondence:

Steve Romanchuk (son of Alex Romanchuk)

Sheryl Sepke Hart (daughter of Art Sepke)

NOTES

1   Al Wolf, "Sportraits," *Los Angeles Times*, August 15, 1946: 9.

2   Whitney Martin, "Baseball World Against Brooklyn," *Altoona Tribune*, August 7, 1946: 8.

3   James J. Murphy, "Sisler Tales Over as Pilot of World All-Star Combine," *Brooklyn Daily Eagle*, August 1, 1946: 15.

4   "Boro, World Pilots Announce Starting Lineups Tomorrow," *Brooklyn Daily Eagle*, August 5, 1946: 10.

5   "Brooklyn Born and Bred," *Brooklyn Daily Eagle*, August 6, 1946: 13.

6   "Thrilling Program of Entertainment Awaits All Stars," *Brooklyn Daily Eagle*, July 28, 1946: 21.

7   "Big League Umps to Work Star Tilt," *Brooklyn Daily Eagle*, July 27, 1946: 6.

8   Tommy Holmes, "Eagle All-Stars Face the World," *Brooklyn Daily Eagle*, August 7, 1946: 17.

9   James J. Murphy, "Brooklyn All-Stars Seek 2nd Win Tonight," *Brooklyn Daily Eagle*, August 8, 1946: 1, 15-16.

10 "Array of Notables See Brooklyn Triumph," *Brooklyn Daily Eagle*, August 8, 1946: 15.

11 "Superba Rookies Beaten by Giants," *Brooklyn Daily Eagle*, October 5, 1916: S2.

12 Tommy Holmes, "Clinical Notes as the World Got Even," *Brooklyn Daily Eagle*, August 9, 1946: 12.

13 Fay Vincent, *We Would Have Played for Nothing* (New York, Simon and Schuster, 2008), 149-150.

14 "Chicago Selects a Handy Man for World All-Stars; Sepke Plays Infield, Hurls — Hornsby Among Experts Making Choice," *Brooklyn Daily Eagle*, July 24, 1946: 15.

15 "Spokane to Choose Player for World Team vs. Eagle: Game Among Stars of 3 States to Aid in Selecting Athlete," *Brooklyn Daily Eagle*, June 6, 1946: 15.

16 Danny Spellecy, "Brooklyn Jaunt to Lou Damman: Lewiston Boy named as Outstanding Young Player," *Spokane Spokesman-Review*, July 12, 1946: 1, 14.

17 Danny Spellecy, "Brooklyn Stars Top World Nine," *Spokane Spokesman-Review*, August 8, 1946: 10.

18 Danny Spellecy, "Damman Bumps Head, Misses Chance to be Pinch Hitter," *Spokane Spokesman-Review*, August 9, 1946: 16.

19 "World Grabs College Ace: St. Paul 'Star' Picks Romanchuk, Unbeaten 17-Year-Old Hurler," *Brooklyn Daily Eagle*, July 26, 1946: 10.

VANDER MEER'S TIRELESS 15 INNINGS END IN FUTILITY

September 11, 1946
Cincinnati Reds 0, Brooklyn Dodgers 0 | 19 innings

by Richard Cuicchi

Cincinnati's Johnny Vander Meer had experience in momentous games at Ebbets Field prior to the Reds' contest on September 11, 1946. Eight years earlier, he had etched his name in history with his second consecutive no-hitter.[1] However, this time the southpaw's magnificent outing wasn't as much about limiting the number of hits by the opposing Brooklyn Dodgers as it was about his part in the longest game in major-league history to end in a scoreless tie. Vander Meer incredibly logged 15 out of the game's 19 innings; but unlike the no-hitter, his effort went all for naught, since the game ended in a scoreless tie.

The 1946 season was turning into the latest chapter of an ongoing story about pennant competition between the Dodgers and St. Louis Cardinals. With the Dodgers trailing the Cardinals by two games, they were in a fierce battle for first place, so every game down the September stretch was important to each team. The race was reminiscent of the Dodgers' run at the National League pennant against St. Louis in 1942 when they wound up finishing the season two games behind the Cardinals. When the Dodgers won their last pennant, in 1941, the Cardinals were the runners-up.

The Reds had been out of contention since the end of June, and the team continued to plummet in the standings, falling to 27½ games out of first place by September 11. They were a team of contrasting extremes, possessing the worst offense in the league while also featuring one of the best pitching staffs.

All major-league teams were recovering from the effects of World War II in 1946. The regular players, including most of the game's stars, who had gone into military service returned to the sport.

Thirty-one-year-old Vander Meer missed the 1944 and 1945 seasons while serving in the US Navy. He understandably struggled to return to his pre-service form, when he had put together three seasons that resulted in 49 wins and a 2.71 ERA. His first five games of the 1946 season resulted in three losing decisions and a 5.47 ERA. After going 2-5, he seemed to get on track with six consecutive wins between June 28 and July 25, but then lost five of his next six decisions.

Pee Wee Reese and Pete Reiser made their major-league debuts at age 21 for the Dodgers in 1940, became All-Stars, then missed three full seasons (1943-1945) during World War II. While injuries derailed Reiser's promising career, Reese became the emotional leader of the team and a Hall of Famer. (Photo: SABR-Rucker Archive)

Manager Leo Durocher's Dodgers were led by outfielder Dixie Walker, who was among the league leaders in batting average and RBIs. Pete Reiser, Pee Wee Reese, and Cookie Lavagetto were among the servicemen returning to the Dodgers. On September 11, Hal Gregg drew the starting assignment against Vander Meer. He had been the ace of the Dodgers' staff in 1945, claiming 18 wins. He was 5-3 coming into the September 11 game but his last six starts included two losses and four no-decisions.

The Reds wasted no time trying to get on the scoreboard. Dain Clay led off the game with a walk. He was thrown out by left fielder Reiser trying to go from first to third on Benny Zientara's single to left. Clay would take another aggressive baserunning chance in the 19th inning with the same result.

The next play exhibiting excitement occurred in the top of the fifth inning when the Reds' Eddie Lukon was thrown out at the plate as he tried to stretch a triple into a home run. His smash off the right-center-field wall eluded outfielders Walker and Carl Furillo. Reiser chased down the ball and relayed it to Eddie Stanky, who threw to catcher Bruce Edwards for the tag on Lukon.[2]

Vander Meer was in control through the first 10 innings, allowing runners to reach second base only twice. He yielded five hits and a walk, and struck out 11. Gregg was equally effective in his 10 frames, giving up five hits and two walks and striking out six.

Gregg was relieved by Dodgers relief ace Hugh Casey to start the 11th inning. Casey was also stingy with Reds batters, giving up only two hits in his five innings.

Vander Meer breezed through five more innings, yielding only two more hits and walking one. Before he exited, he allowed a double to Lavagetto and intentionally walked Bruce Edwards in the 15th inning. Facing Joe Medwick, who was pinch-hitting for Casey, Vander Meer got out of the jam by inducing a groundout to end the inning.

Art Herring started the 16th inning for the Dodgers and ran into trouble when he gave up two singles, including one to Vander Meer. But then he retired the next two batters without a score.

Reds catcher Ray Mueller informed manager Bill McKechnie that his batterymate was tiring, and McKechnie wisely decided to lift Vander Meer for Harry Gumbert in the bottom of the 16th.[3] Gumbert finished the game by holding the Dodgers to one hit.

With darkness approaching, Dodgers reliever Hank Behrman started the top of the 19th by walking Clay. A sacrifice bunt by Zientara moved Clay to second. Behrman intentionally walked Lonny Frey to face Bert Haas. When Clay attempted to score on Haas's single, Dixie Walker made an accurate throw to Edwards, who blocked the plate and tagged out Clay. Clay protested the call, but umpire George Barr wasn't entertaining his argument.[4]

The Dodgers momentarily thought they had salvaged the game when Reese led off the bottom of the 19th with a long fly ball to left-center, but the wind brought it back from the wall and it was caught by Max West.[5] Gumbert retired Reiser and Walker to end the inning.

The game was called because of darkness after 4 hours and 40 minutes. The 19 scoreless innings approached a record set on August 1, 1918, between the Pittsburgh Pirates and Boston Braves that involved 20 innings without a score before the Pirates wound up winning the game in the 21st inning. The longest previous scoreless tie in the National League was a 16-inning contest on June 13, 1916, between Boston and Cincinnati.[6]

In another marathon game on September 11, the Chicago Cubs and Boston Braves played to a 3-3 tie after 17 innings.

Vander Meer's performance extended his scoreless-innings streak against Brooklyn to 24. He tied a personal-best record of 14 strikeouts in a game, although his other two performances occurred in nine-inning games in 1941 and 1943.

About his decision to replace Vander Meer with Gumbert to start the 16th inning, McKechnie said, "Johnny wanted to continue, but I would never forgive myself if I would have permitted him to go on and something would have happened to his arm." He added, "No one game is worth risking a pitcher's future to win."[7]

A victory would have moved the Dodgers to within one game of the Cardinals, who lost to Philadelphia that day, but they had to settle for a half-game improvement. The game was replayed on September 20. Vander Meer got the start again for the Reds, but this time he lasted only five innings and wound up with his ninth loss of the season.

The Dodgers eventually caught up with St. Louis, and the two teams wound up in a tie at the end of the regular season. The Cardinals defeated Brooklyn in a tiebreaker series to win their fourth pennant in five years. The Reds franchise wouldn't be relevant again until 1956, when they won 91 games for a third-place finish.

Vander Meer finished the season with a 10-12 record, a 3.17 ERA, 11 complete games, and four shutouts. He pitched three more seasons for the second-division Reds, winning 17 games in 1948. He is most remembered for his consecutive no-hitters in 1938, but his 15-inning shutout performance ranks right behind them as a personal best.

SOURCES

In addition to the sources cited in the Notes, the author consulted Baseball-Reference.com and the following:

Holmes, Tommy. "Dodgers Open Crucial Card Series: Great Opportunity Lost by Failure to Defeat Reds," *Brooklyn Eagle*, September 12, 1946: 12.

Lichtman, Paul. *The Dutch Master: The Life and Times of Johnny Vander Meer*" (New York: Vantage Press, 2001).

NOTES

1   Vander Meer pitched his consecutive no-hitters on June 11, 1938, in Cincinnati and June 15, 1938, at Ebbets Field.

2   Roscoe McGowen, "Dodgers Battle to 19-Inning Scoreless Tie With Reds; Cards Lose to Phils," *New York Times*, September 12, 1946.

3   Lou Smith, "Reds and Brooks Scoreless in 19 Innings," *Cincinnati Enquirer*, September 12, 1946: 1.

4   McGowen.

5   McGowen.

6   Harold Burr, "Six Help Tie Longest Zero Knot in Majors," *The Sporting News*, September 18, 1946: 13.

7   Lou Smith. "Deacon Saves Vandy; Too Good to Abuse," *Cincinnati Enquirer*, September 12, 1946: 16.

CARDINALS FINISH TIE-BREAKER SWEEP, ADVANCE TO WORLD SERIES

October 3, 1946

St. Louis Cardinals 8, Brooklyn Dodgers 4
Game Two of National League Tie-Breaker Series

by Don Zminda

In 1946, for the first time in history, a major-league pennant race ended in a tie when the Brooklyn Dodgers and St. Louis Cardinals ended the 154-game season with identical 96-58 records. National League rules specified a best-of-three playoff; the winner of a coin toss could choose to either open the series at home, which would mean playing Games Two and (if needed) Three on the road, or opt for Game One on the road with home-field advantage if the series went the three-game limit. Given the right to call the toss, Cardinals owner Sam Breadon picked heads, but it came up tails; Dodgers manager Leo Durocher elected to open the series in St. Louis. "The Lip," wrote Robert Weintraub, "wanted to have the deciding game played at home, so he agreed to head to Missouri for the opener, then host Games Two and Three, should a third game be necessary."[1]

It was perhaps fitting that the regular season had ended in a deadlock between Brooklyn and St. Louis, as there were many "family ties" between the teams. Dodgers President and general manager Branch Rickey had held the same position with the Cardinals from 1917 to 1942, and Durocher had played for the Redbirds from 1933 to 1937. Much of the St. Louis roster consisted of players signed during Rickey's Cardinal tenure; St. Louis manager Eddie Dyer had begun his major-league playing career when Rickey managed the club, and then got his start as a manager in Rickey's Cardinal farm system. There was even a pair of brothers opposing each other in the playoff series: Dixie Walker for the Dodgers, Harry Walker for the Cardinals.

The series opened at St. Louis's Sportsman's Park on Tuesday, October 1, with Howie Pollet (20-10) of the Cardinals facing Ralph Branca (3-0) of the Dodgers. The game was tight, but Pollet threw a complete-game eight-hitter for a 4-2 Cardinals victory while battling a shoulder injury and an oblique strain. Veteran center fielder Terry Moore and rookie catcher Joe Garagiola each had three hits for St. Louis.

After a day off for travel – the train trip from St. Louis to New York City took over 20 hours – the series resumed at Brooklyn's Ebbets Field on Thursday, October 3. Dodgers rookie left-hander

174

Joe Hatten (14-10) took the hill against the Cardinals' Murry Dickson (14-6) before a packed house of 31,437. The *Brooklyn Eagle* reported that at 9:30 A.M., over 10,000 fans were lined up to buy tickets, and that the queue had grown to twice that number by noon. "Many of the fans," the paper reported, "had been waiting in line since midnight."[2] Scalpers were charging $25 for tickets with a face value of $1.75.

"If [Eddie Dyer] leads with Murry Dickson, a righthander," Durocher had stated in his ghost-written "Durocher Says" column the morning of the game, "we will stack our lineup with lefthanded power, playing [Augie] Galan at third and [Dick] Whitman in the outfield. We figure to get a hatful of runs in our own ballyard. Dickson should be no puzzle."[3] His assessment appeared to be correct when Dodgers left-handed hitters broke through against Dickson in the bottom of the first (after Hatten had set down the Cardinals in top half). With two out Galan reached first on an infield hit, lefty swinger Dixie Walker drew a walk, and another left-handed hitter, Ed Stevens, drove in Galan with a single to center. But Dickson retired Carl Furillo to end the threat and then took command, not permitting another Dodgers hit until the bottom of the ninth. Fred Lieb wrote that "in the intervening seven innings, [the Dodgers] were as helpless before Murry Dickson, little St. Louis righthander, as so many Erasmus High School boys."[4] Over that seven-inning span, Dickson allowed only one ball past the infield. "Dickson was using his knuckler and had great control on his curve, and his fastball was sinking in," Dyer commented after the game. "That was why those Dodgers were hitting into the dirt around second base."[5]

The Cardinals wiped out Brooklyn's 1-0 lead in the top of the second. With one out Erv Dusak tripled to left; the Dodgers protested that Galan had tagged Dusak before his foot touched third, but third-base umpire Beans Reardon stood by his call. (Photos in the next morning's *Brooklyn*

Eagle indicated that Dusak should have been called out.) Marty Marion, the next hitter, drove in Dusak with a fly ball to center field. Clyde Kluttz then singled to center, and Dickson gave himself the lead with a triple to center field. It was the first triple of Dickson's major-league career, which had begun in 1939.

It was still 2-1 in the top of the fifth when the Cardinals put together another rally. After Stan Musial doubled with two out, Durocher elected to intentionally walk right-handed-hitting Whitey Kurowski to set up a lefty-lefty matchup between Hatten and Enos Slaughter. Slaughter spoiled the strategy with the Cardinals' third triple of the game, scoring Musial and Kurowski. Dusak then singled to plate Slaughter with the Cardinals' third run of the inning. St. Louis scored another run in the seventh on two walks, a sacrifice, and a beautiful squeeze bunt by Marion, and twice more in the eighth when Kurowski singled with the bases loaded.

With an 8-1 lead entering the bottom of the ninth and Dickson looking invincible, the Cardinals were preparing to sip the champagne. But the Dodgers weren't quite ready to surrender. Galan opened the frame with a double off the right-field wall ("the first Brooklyn hit in roughly two and a half hours," wrote Robert Weintraub[6]), and scored one out later when Stevens tripled. Furillo singled to score Stevens, and when Dickson threw a wild pitch to move up Furillo and then walked Pee Wee Reese, Dyer replaced Dickson with left-hander Harry Brecheen. The first batter he faced, Bruce Edwards, singled to drive in Furillo, and suddenly it was 8-4. When pinch-hitter Cookie Lavagetto drew a walk, the bases were loaded with the tying run coming to the plate, and still only one out.

Brecheen retired Eddie Stanky on a called third strike for the second out, and 6-foot-6 Howie Schultz, who had homered in the first game of the tiebreaker series, advanced to the plate as a pinch-hitter. Dyer came to the mound and told Brecheen, "Forget about the home run. Just get the ball in there." Brecheen took Dyer's advice, and, wrote Weintraub, "Schultz whacked it down the left-field line. It landed in a cloud of dirt … just foul. An inch to the right, and three runs would have scored." With the count 3-and-2, Brecheen surprised Schultz by throwing a screwball. "I almost fell down swinging at it," Schultz, known as "The Leaning Tower of Flatbush," said later. He missed it by nearly a foot, and the Cardinals were heading to the World Series to face the Boston Red Sox.[7]

"In my opinion this is the last time the St. Louis ball club will be that close to us," proclaimed Durocher the next day. "I told our boys yesterday they have some big years ahead of them. We will all be riding high with the players already here plus the sensational kids Branch Rickey has been getting ready at Montreal, Fort Worth and Mobile."[8] Durocher proved to be an accurate prophet: Over the next 10 seasons, the Dodgers would win six National League pennants, the Cardinals none … thanks in good part to a group of "sensational kids" led by Jackie Robinson, who would arrive in Brooklyn the next year.

SOURCES

In addition to the sources cited in the Notes, the author consulted Baseball-Reference.com, Retrosheet.org, and the following:

Drebinger, John. "Cards Win Pennant, Defeating Dodgers Again for Two-Game Play-Off Sweep," *New York Times*, October 4, 1946: 17.

"He Done Us Wrong" (photos with caption), *Brooklyn Daily Eagle*, October 4, 1946: 15.

NOTES

1   Robert Weintraub, *The Victory Season: The End of World War II and the Birth of Baseball's Golden Age* (New York: Little, Brown and Company, 2013), 308.

2   "Ebbets Field Stormed by 20,000 Rabid Fans," *Brooklyn Daily Eagle*, October 3, 1946: 1.

3   "Durocher Says: We're Set to Trump 'Em On Our Own Field Today," *Brooklyn Daily Eagle*, October 3, 1946: 16.

4   Fred Lieb, "Cards Hold Mastery Over Dodgers to End," *The Sporting News*, October 9, 1946: 8.

5   Sid Feder, "Cards' Celebration Like A-Bomb Bursting," *St. Louis Globe-Democrat*, October 4, 1946: 19.

6   Weintraub, 315.

7   Weintraub, 315.

8   "Durocher Says: We'd Have Given Sox Better Fight Than Cards," *Brooklyn Daily Eagle*, October 4, 1946: 15.

Jackie Robinson's debut with the Dodgers

April 15, 1947

Brooklyn Dodgers 5, Boston Braves 3

by Lyle Spatz

Jackie Robinson's major-league debut was more than just the first step in righting an historical wrong. It was a crucial event in the history of the American civil rights movement, the importance of which went far beyond the insular world of baseball.

The Dodgers signed Robinson to a major-league contract just five days before the start of the 1947 season. Baseball people, especially those in Brooklyn, were still digesting the previous day's news of manager Leo Durocher's one-year suspension (for conduct detrimental to baseball), when the story broke of Robinson's promotion from the Montreal Royals of the International League. He would be the first Black American to play in what were then designated the major leagues since catcher Moses Fleetwood Walker played for the Toledo Blue Stockings of the American Association back in 1884.

Robinson had played second base for the Royals in 1946, but on orders from the Dodgers he had been working out at first base all spring. He played the position in Brooklyn's final three exhibition games against the Yankees, and again two

days later when the Dodgers opened the season at Ebbets Field against the Boston Braves. Rumors of a sellout may have discouraged some fans from attending, but whatever the reason, a crowd of only 26,623 saw Robinson's debut, including "an estimated 14,000 black fans."[1]

In his *New York Times* column the morning of the game, Arthur Daley credited the Dodgers for doing a "deft" job of paving the way for Robinson, but added, "Yet nothing can actually lighten that pressure, and Robbie realizes it full well. There is no way of disguising the fact that he is not an ordinary rookie and no amount of pretense can make it otherwise."[2]

Robinson made the game's first putout, receiving the throw from fellow rookie Spider Jorgensen on Dick Culler's ground ball to third base. Dodgers left-hander Joe Hatten started the game for Brooklyn. Hatten gave up a single and a walk in the first, but no Braves scored.

Interim manager Clyde Sukeforth had Robinson batting second, so after Eddie Stanky grounded out, the rookie first baseman stepped in against Johnny Sain for his first major league

Jackie Robinson debuted with the Dodgers on April 15, 1947, after a fantastic season with the Montreal Royals of the Triple-A International League. He led the circuit with a .349 batting average and tied for the lead with 113 runs in 124 games while leading the Royals to the league title. (Photo: SABR-Rucker Archive)

at-bat. Sain, the National League's winningest right-hander in 1946, retired him easily on a bouncer to third baseman Bob Elliott. After flying out to left fielder Danny Litwhiler in the third inning, Robinson appeared to have gotten his first big-league hit in the fifth. But shortstop Culler made an outstanding play on his ground ball and turned it into a well-executed 6-4-3 double play.

When he next batted, in the seventh, Brooklyn was trailing, 3–2. Stanky was on first, having opened the inning by drawing Sain's fifth walk of the afternoon. It was an obvious bunt situation, and Robinson laid down a beauty, pushing the ball deftly up the right side. The *Brooklyn Daily Eagle*'s Harold C. Burr wrote that Robinson had "sacrificed prettily."[3]

Boston's rookie first baseman, Earl Torgeson, fielded it, but with Robinson speeding down the line, he "made a hurried throw in an effort to get Robinson but hit him on the shoulder blade and the ball caromed into right field, allowing Jackie and the other runner to advance to second and third."[4] Pete Reiser's double scored both runners and finished Sain. Stanky scored the tying run, and Robinson scored the go-ahead run – which by game's end proved the winning run. Reiser later scored on Gene Hermanski's fly ball off reliever Mort Cooper as the Dodgers won, 5–3.

When the Dodgers took the field in the ninth inning, Robinson remained on the bench as veteran Howie Schultz took over at first base. Sukeforth had inserted Schultz as a defensive measure, but the Dodgers soon realized that Robinson needed no help. Schultz played in only one more game before Brooklyn sold him to the Phillies. Ed Stevens, the team's other first baseman, played in just five games before he was sent back to the minors.

Hal Gregg, in relief of Hatten, got the win, and Hugh Casey got the first of his league-leading 18 saves.[5] Sain bore the loss.

The popular Reiser, coming back from yet another injury, clearly had been the star of the game, and it was he, not Robinson, who was the focus of the story in the next day's *New York Times*. Roscoe McGowen's game account mentioned Robinson only in relation to his play, leaving columnist Arthur Daley to take note of his debut, which he called "quite uneventful."[6]

He wrote that Robinson "makes no effort to push himself...and already has made a strong impression," and then quoted Robinson as saying "I was nervous in the first play of my first game at Ebbets Field, but nothing has bothered me since."[7]

In retrospect, it would be easy, and fashionable, to attribute the writers' casual treatment of this history-making game to racism. It is perhaps more charitable, and accurate, to think that they handled it in this way because it took place at a time when baseball reporters believed that that's what they were: baseball reporters, men who felt their sole duty was to report what took place on the field. Red Barber and Connie Desmond, the Dodgers' radio broadcasters, did the same.

Rachel Robinson has written about this Opening Day game: "In 1947, as Jack took his place in the batter's box in Ebbets Field, and Rickey watched from the owner's box, the meaning of the moment for me seemed to transcend the winning of a ballgame. The possibility of social change seemed more concrete, and the need for it seemed more imperative. I believe that the single most important impact of Jack's presence was that it enabled white baseball fans to root for a black man, thus encouraging more whites to realize that all our destinies were inextricably linked."[8]

Robinson's first base hit came in the season's second game, on April 17 against the Braves. His first run batted in came against the New York Giants on April 18. By season's end, he had hit for a .297 batting average (with a .383 on-base percentage), with a league-leading 29 stolen bases. He scored 125 runs, and drove in 48. His

28 sacrifice hits led both leagues. Robinson was the overwhelming choice in voting for Rookie of the Year, the first player ever accorded Rookie of the Year honors, at a time before voters honored a separate rookie in each league.

SOURCES

This article is adapted from the author's "Jackie Robinson on Opening Day, 1947-1956." Joseph Dorinson, and Joram Warmund, eds. *Jackie Robinson: Race, Sports, and the American Dream* (Armonk, New York: M. E. Sharpe, 1998.)

In addition to the sources cited in the Notes, the author also consulted Baseball-Reference.com and Retrosheet.org.

NOTES

1 Jules Tygiel, *Baseball's Great Experiment: Jackie Robinson and His Legacy* (New York: Oxford University Press, 1983), 178.

2 Arthur Daley, "Play Ball!," *New York Times*, April 15, 1947: 31.

3 Harold C. Burr, "'Old' Reiser, 'New' Hernanski Stars of Dodgers' Opening Day Triumph," *Brooklyn Daily Eagle*, April 16, 1947: 19. Left fielder Hermanksi also had a run batted in.

4 Carl Rowan with Jackie Robinson, *Wait Till Next Year* (New York: Random House, 1960), 179.

5 Nobody had ever heard of "saves" in 1947, and Casey died never knowing that he had twice been the National League leader.

6 Arthur Daley, "Opening Day at Ebbets Field," *New York Times*, April 16, 1947: 32.

7 "Opening Day at Ebbets Field."

8 Rachel Robinson, with Lee Daniels, *Jackie Robinson: An Intimate Portrait* (New York: Abrams, 2014), 66.

9 Compiled from data furnished by Dr. David W. Smith of Retrosheet.

JACKIE ROBINSON'S BATTING AND FIELDING RECORD ON OPENING DAY[9]

		AB	H	2B	3B	HR	BB	SB	SAC	R	RBI	PO	A	E
April 15, 1947 vs BOS	1B	3	0	0	0	0	0	0	1	1	0	11	0	0
April 20, 1948 at NY	2B	5	1	1	0	0	0	0	0	1	2	2	3	0
April 19, 1949 vs NY	2B	5	3	0	0	1	0	0	0	2	1	6	6	0
April 18, 1950 at PHI	2B	4	2	1	0	0	0	0	0	1	0	2	1	0
April 17, 1951 at PHI	2B	4	2	0	0	1	0	0	0	1	2	8	1	0
April 17, 1952 at BOS	2B	3	1	0	0	0	1	0	0	0	0	2	0	0
April 17, 1953 vs PIT	3B	3	2	0	0	0	0	0	0	2	0	0	2	0
April 13, 1954 at NY	LF	4	1	0	0	0	0	0	0	0	0	2	0	0
April 13, 1955 vs PIT	3B	4	2	1	0	0	0	0	0	1	1	0	3	0
April 17, 1956 vs PHI	LF	3	0	0	0	0	0	0	1	0	1	1	4	1
TOTAL		38	14	3	0	2	1	0	2	9	7	34	23	1

THE DODGERS STRIKE BACK

October 2, 1947

Brooklyn Dodgers 9, New York Yankees 8 | Game Three of the World Series

by Thomas J. Brown Jr.

The Dodgers were in a hole after losing the first two games of the World Series to their crosstown rivals the Yankees. But now the Series was headed to Ebbets Field and the Dodger faithful were confident that their team could bounce back.

"Now that we've got the Yanks in our own backyard, they can't hurt us anymore" was the feeling throughout Brooklyn. Alfred Salerno of the *Brooklyn Daily Eagle* wrote: "The result of today's game was clear in their minds. We were going to win. And everything would turn out for the good."[1]

The Dodgers sent Joe Hatten to the mound. Manager Burt Shotton originally planned to start Ralph Branca. But he had been forced to use Branca in the first game of the Series and didn't think he would be ready on just two days' rest.

But Shotton had good reason to feel confident in Hatten, who had been used as a starter and reliever throughout the season. Hatten had finished with a 17-8 record that included 11 complete games. After the poor performance by Dodgers pitchers in the first two games, their fans hoped Hatten would restore confidence in the Brooklyn pitching staff.

Hatten looked good through the first two innings. Although the Yankees got a single in each inning, Hatten kept their bats in check and the Yankees scoreless.

Bobo Newsom started for the Yankees. The 17-year veteran had been purchased by the Yankees in midseason. He played a key role in their pitching staff down the stretch, finishing with a 7-5 record and a 2.80 ERA.

Newsom "was lucky to escape unscathed right from the start"[2] when two Dodgers baserunners were caught stealing. Jackie Robinson singled. He stole second on a wild throw by the catcher but was tagged out after overrunning the base. Pete Reiser, next up, also walked. He was also caught stealing. Reiser twisted his ankle on the hard slide but stayed in the game.

Newsom's luck did not last. After Phil Rizzuto raced in to grab Dixie Walker's hopper and make a quick throw to George McQuinn for the first out, he struggled, starting when he walked Gene Hermanski.

Bruce Edwards then doubled to left field. Lindell dived for the ball as it bounced off the wall but missed. By the time Joe DiMaggio ran it down, Hermanski had crossed the plate with the Dodgers' first run.

Pee Wee Reese followed with a single to center, scoring Edwards. Spider Jorgensen flied out to DiMaggio for out number two and it appeared the Yankees might get out of the inning. But Hatten singled and a passed ball allowed both runners to advance.

Yankee fans began to wonder when Yankees manager Bucky Harris might pull Newsom. Harris later said that he "didn't think that [Vic] Raschi was sufficiently warmed up in the pen at the time" and that Newsom still "had good stuff."[3]

But Eddie Stanky doubled off the right-field wall and both runners scored, and Newsom was finally sent to the showers. A "sobered" Newsom later said, "I thought I was fast and had my stuff but they just hit me."[4]

Raschi went to the mound to get the final out. When Robinson's single left runners at the corners, it was clear that Raschi might not have been warmed up. As Reiser's ankle continued to swell, Shotton was forced replace him with Carl Furillo.

Furillo had been kept on the bench because "he supposedly can't hit right-handed pitching."[5] He promptly exploded off the right-handed Raschi for a double that sent Stanky and Robinson across the plate. The Dodgers were finally retired after Walker grounded out for the second time in the inning. But the Dodgers had grabbed a six-run lead

The Yankees may have been in a hole but they quickly began to dig out of it with some help from Hatten. Sherm Lollar led off the third with a single. The Dodgers hurler then walked pinch-hitter Allie Clark.

Hatten bore down to get the next two outs. But Lindell and DiMaggio followed with singles that scored one run apiece, leaving the Dodgers with a four-run lead at 6-2.

"Sensing that Hatten was going to need all the help he could get,"[6] the Dodgers scored another run in their half of the third. Karl Drews was on the mound for the Yankees and he was wild from the start. He clipped Hermanski on the leg and then moved him to second on a wild pitch. Edwards' groundout pushed Hermanski to third. He came home on Jorgensen's single down the left-field line.

The Dodgers expanded on their lead in the fourth against Spud Chandler, the Yankees' fourth pitcher. After Chandler walked two of the first three batters he faced, singles by Walker and Hermanski plated two runs, pushing the Dodgers' total to nine. It was the most any Dodgers team had scored in a World Series game.

But Hatten continued to struggle, surrendering two more runs in the fourth. He walked leadoff batter Johnson, who came home on Lollar's double. Snuffy Stirnweiss's two-out single brought home Lollar, giving the Yankees four runs for the game.

Hatten got himself in trouble again in the fifth when he let the leadoff man get on base for the fourth time. DiMaggio then "teed off to present a customer in the upper left-center deck with a Series souvenir."[7] Although Hatten got the next batter out, Shotton replaced him with Branca.

Branca got through the frame unscathed but got himself in trouble in the sixth. Pinch-hitter Bobby Brown got things started with a blast that "caromed off the screen atop the fence in right field and which [the Yankees] maintained should have been ruled a home run."[8]

Brown ended up on third and advanced to third when Stirnweiss grounded out to short. Tommy Henrich then hit a line drive that bounced off Stanky's glove into short right field. Brown scored and Henrich ended up on second. The score was now 9-7. Walks to DiMaggio and McQuinn loaded the bases. With two outs and the count 3-and-1 on Billy Johnson, most in attendance expected that Johnson "would be ordered to take the next pitch."[9] He wasn't and swung hard but raised a soft pop fly to Stanky for the third out.

Harris later said, "I let Johnson hit that 3-and-1 pitch against Branca in the sixth because I had confidence in his ability to smack one. He popped up. What else is there to say? We won the pennant taking chances and I had to play the game the same way."[10]

The Dodgers were scoreless in the sixth. With one out in the seventh, Branca faced pinch-hitter Yogi Berra. Berra was hitless in the Series so far and Harris had benched him. Berra hit the third pitch over the scoreboard, "which barely missed knocking the clock off Ebbets Field."[11] The home run cut the Brooklyn lead to just one run at 9-8. It was the first pinch-hit home run in World Series history.

After Berra's homer, Shotton brought in Hugh Casey to replace Branca. Casey retired the Yankees but got into trouble in the eighth. He walked leadoff batter Henrich. Lindell singled. DiMaggio stepped to the plate.

DiMaggio tried to check his swing but wasn't fast enough. The ball cracked off his bat for a grounder to Stanky, who scooped up the ball, tagged Lindell, and made a quick toss to first to complete the double play. McQuinn grounded to Robinson for the third out, and the Yankees were still trailing by one run.

After the game Lindell insisted that Stanky had never touched him, and Harris "backed his player."[12] "I'm not dishonest and I don't kick unless I'm on the level," Lindell said. "I didn't feel any kind of a tag and I'm certain I ran past him as he swiped at me."[13] American League umpire Bill McGowan, who made the call, was not swayed.

After the Dodgers were scoreless in the eighth, Casey retired the Yankees in order in the ninth. Jackie Robinson grabbed Johnson's leadoff groundball to Robinson and flipped it to Casey for the first out. Rizzuto flied out to right field. With two outs, Berra hit a line drive up the middle. Casey "had the presence of mind to throw up his glove and deflect Berra's smash to Stanky,"[14] who threw Berra out at first, and the game was over.

After the game, DiMaggio was inconsolable about his eighth-inning at-bat, saying, "I tried to check myself on a slider, topped it and lost a ball game."[15]

Casey was credited with the win. The *Brooklyn Daily Eagle's* Tommy Holmes wrote "Ordinarily, a pitcher preserving a one-run lead for two and two-thirds innings does not become a hero to name your children after. But these are not ordinary times. And this was not an ordinary ball game."[16]

SOURCES

In addition to the sources cited in the Notes, I used the Baseball-Reference.com and Retrosheet.org websites for box-score, player, team, and season pages, pitching and batting game logs, and other pertinent material.

https://www.baseball-reference.com/boxes/BRO/BRO194710020.shtml

https://www.retrosheet.org/boxesetc/1947/B10020BRO1947.htm

NOTES

1   Alfred Salerno, "Bleacher Fans Defy Yanks in All-Night Vigil," *Brooklyn Daily Eagle*, October 3, 1947: 1.

2   Dick Young, "Flock Wins 9-8, Casey Halts Yanks," *New York Daily News*, October 3, 1947: C19.

3   Young.

4   James Dawson, "Several Incidents Rouse Bombers Ire," *New York Times*, October 3, 1947: 33.

5   Young.

6   Young.

7   Young.

8   Dawson.

9   Young.

10   Joe Trimble, "2 Gambles Cost Yanks Possible Win: Bucky," *New York Daily News*, October 3, 1947: C17.

11   Young.

12   Dawson.

13   Trimble.

14   Tommy Holmes, "The Innkeeper Draws One for the Dodgers," *Brooklyn Daily Eagle*, October 3, 1947:16.

15   Dawson.

16   Holmes.

LAVAGETTO'S WALK-OFF DOUBLE SHOCKS YANKEES

October 3, 1947

Brooklyn Dodgers 3, New York Yankees 2 | Game Four of the World Series

by Thomas J. Brown Jr.

When the New York Yankees won the first two games of the 1947 World Series, many fans started calling it the "worst World Series in history."[1] After Brooklyn beat the Yankees 9-8 in Game Three, Dodgers fans showed up at Ebbets Field hoping to see their team even the Series. History-minded Brooklyn fans might have recalled former National League President Harry Pulliam's words about "taking nothing for granted in the game of baseball."[2] Their recollection was perfect. The World Series game on October 3, 1947, proved that. The Dodgers were held to one measly hit by Yankees pitcher Bill Bevens, and didn't get it until the ninth inning: But the hit, by seldom-used Cookie Lavagetto, plated the tying and winning runs.

Harry Taylor was given the nod as Brooklyn's starter. The right-hander finished the season with a 10-5 record but struggled late in the season after he tore a tendon in his right elbow. Taylor failed to pitch more than two innings in his final two starts of the season, leading many to wonder how he would perform in the Series.

Taylor got in trouble immediately. Snuffy Stirnweiss and Tommy Henrich led off with singles. Yogi Berra then hit a groundball to first, and when shortstop Pee Wee Reese couldn't handle the throw to second for a force out, the bases were loaded.

Taylor then threw four straight balls to Joe DiMaggio and the Yankees were up by a run. "Taylor was through; he had been a losing gamble," opined sportswriter Dick Young.[3] Dodgers manager Burt Shotton was forced to go to his bullpen for Hal Gregg.

Gregg got George McQuinn to pop out to short, and Billy Johnson to hit into a double play that left the Yankees with just one run on the scoreboard. That lone run "was all the Yanks made out of their flying start" due to Gregg's efforts.[4]

The Yankees had an opportunity to add to their lead in the third. With two outs, Gregg walked DiMaggio. McQuinn hit a tapper in front of the plate. Catcher Bruce Edwards grabbed it and threw wild to first. DiMaggio and McQuinn were running on contact. Rounding third, DiMaggio "was waved on by the usually cold calculated [coach] Chuck Dressen, who miscued this time. Out in right Dixie Walker collared the ball and fired it to the plate in ample time for the third out."[5]

The Yankees did add another run in the fourth when Johnson led off with a triple and came home on Johnny Lindell's double to right field. That made the score 2-0.

Meanwhile, the Yankees' starter, right-hander Bill Bevens, owner of a 7-13 season record, kept the Brooklyn bats "silent as a tomb"[6] for the first eight innings as he held the Dodgers lineup hitless. Bevens was far from perfect on the mound. He walked eight through the first eight innings. But Bevens, even with his wildness, kept Brooklyn from scoring until the fifth.

In that inning, the first two batters, Spider Jorgensen and pitcher Gregg, walked, Eddie Stanky sacrificed them into scoring position. Reese followed with a groundball to short that allowed Jorgensen to score and narrow the Yankees' lead to one run.

Although Bevens was never able to tame his wildness, he received outfield support that kept the Dodgers in check. Gene Hermanski was robbed of hits twice. In the fourth inning DiMaggio made a running catch over his shoulder of a drive by Hermanski. In the eighth, Henrich robbed him of another hit when he caught Hermanski's smash by "climbing up the scoreboard in right."[7]

Hank Behrman took over from Gregg in the eighth. He held the Yankees in that inning but got in trouble in the ninth. A pair of singles and a fielder's choice on a bunt loaded the bases, putting New York in a position to blow the game open.

Shotton rushed Hugh Casey in from the bullpen. Casey had pitched the final 2⅔ innings the day before. He was credited with the Dodgers' win, in large part because his "million-dollar serve"[8] had forced DiMaggio to hit into a double play at a crucial moment.

This time, with the bases loaded, Casey faced Henrich, who "slapped the first pitch right back

into Casey's hands. [Casey] fired to Edwards at the plate for one out and Edwards winged it to Robinson at first for the double play."[9] Once again, the Yankees saw an opportunity slip away.

After that it was the Dodgers' ninth. They were down to their final three outs. Bruce Edwards led off and hit a fly ball that Lindell caught with a leap against the front of the left-field bleachers. Bevens then walked Carl Furillo, his ninth free pass.

Spider Jorgensen fouled out to first baseman McQuinn and Bevens needed just one more out to become the first pitcher to throw a no-hitter in a World Series.

Shotton now sent into the game as a pinch-runner.

Manager Shotton sent Pete Reiser up to bat for Casey and Al Gionfriddo in to run for Furillo. With the count 2-and-1, Gionfriddo broke for second. Berra's throw was high and Gionfriddo slid head-first into second. "For the briefest moment, all mouths snapped shut and all eyes stared at umpire Babe Pinelli. Down went the umpire's arms signaling that the [Dodgers] had stolen base no. 7 on the weak-winged Yankee backstop corps," noted a sportswriter.[10]

With the count 3-and-1, Yankees manager Bucky Harris ordered Bevens to walk Reiser, who had a sore ankle. Many in the stands were amazed at the move, which "seemed a direct contradiction of one of baseball's fundamental precepts which dictates against putting the 'winning' run on base in such a situation."[11]

Shotton countered by sending Eddie Miksis to run for the hobbled Reiser. With no left-handed hitters left on the bench, Shotton sent Cookie Lavagetto, "a wiry baseball veteran at 34, an almost forgotten figure while the Dodgers were driving to the pennant,"[12] to bat for Stanky.

Lavagetto swung at the first pitch – a fastball – and missed. Bevens threw another fastball. Lavagetto swung and connected, sending the ball toward the right-field wall. Over raced Henrich but he could not reach the ball and it sailed over his head.

Henrich desperately tried to grab the ball as it bounced off the wall but the sloping fence made that difficult and the ball caromed under his legs. Finally he grabbed the ball and while off-balance hurried a throw into McQuinn who relayed it to the plate.

But Gionfriddo and Miksis had already crossed home. Miksis landed on the plate "with a sitting slide. A big grin on his puss, [Miksis] sat right on home plate like an elated kid. He was home with the winning run and he didn't want to get up."[13]

Meanwhile Lavagetto trotted into second. "For a moment everyone on the field seemed stunned," noted sportswriter Tommy Holmes. "Then there was a mad rush from the Dodger bench. They almost pulled Cookie apart and Cookie was almost hysterical himself."[14]

As the Dodgers celebrated, Bevens walked silently off the field. "In a matter of seconds, a priceless no-hit victory had been wrenched from his grasp and converted into a galling one-hit defeat."[15]

It was the third World Series one-hitter and the first one the pitcher lost. Eddie Reulbach threw one for the Cubs in 1906 and another Cubs pitcher, Claude Passeau, threw the other one in 1945.

Bevens also entered the World Series record book by giving up 10 walks. It was one more than the previous record, set by Jack Coombs of the Philadelphia Athletics in 1910. But, as with his loss, "[Bevens] will never reflect upon that [record] with any feeling of gratification," observed the *New York Times*'s John Drebinger.[16]

While Bevens took the loss, Hugh Casey earned the win. "Just one pitch and he's the winning pitcher of a World Series game. That's wonderful," said Dodgers general manager Branch Rickey.[17] Casey had lost two games in succession to the Yankees in the 1941 World Series. Now he had won two straight.

Lavagetto said Shotton "had to tell me twice before I realized that he wanted me to go up and pinch-hit for Stanky. And he couldn't have found a better man, chimed in Stanky from a nearby locker."[18]

Harris justified his decision to walk Reiser because he was a "dangerous home run hitter." Shotton, meanwhile, "played his cards perfectly in the ninth," opined the *Brooklyn Daily Eagle*'s Harold Burr.[19]

Burr added that the game "left the 33,343 fans with fallen arches, weak knees and thumping hearts, hardly able to stand, let alone grope their way to the subway. It was Alice in Wonderland, Walt Disney and Frank Merriwell all in one ball park."[20]

SOURCES

In addition to the sources cited in the Notes, I used the Baseball-Reference.com, and Retrosheet.org websites for box-score, player, team, and season pages, pitching and batting game logs, and other material.

NOTES

1   Dick Young, "Cookie Hit with Two Out in Ninth Spoils Bevens' No-Hitter," *New York Daily News*, October 4, 1947: 24.

2   Tommy Holmes, "Lavagetto Breaks Up Game of Games," *Brooklyn Daily Eagle,* October 4, 1947: 3.

3   Young.

4   John Drebinger, "Dodgers' Only Hit Beats Yankees 3-2," *New York Times*, October 4, 1947: 1.

5   Drebinger.

6   Drebinger.

7   Harold Burr, "Miracle Strikes Flatbush," Brooklyn Daily Eagle, October 4, 1947: 1.

8   Young.

9   Drebinger.

10 Young.

11 Drebinger.

12 Holmes.

13 Young.

14 Holmes.

15 Drebinger.

16 Drebinger.

17 Young.

18 Burr.

19 Burr.

20 Burr.

SPEC SHEA'S PITCHING IN PUTS YANKEES ON VERGE OF TITLE

October 4, 1947

New York Yankees 2, Brooklyn Dodgers 1 | Game Five of the World Series

by Thomas J. Brown Jr.

Brooklyn fans could barely believe what they were seeing. After losing the first two games of the 1947 World Series, their team rebounded to win the next two games at Ebbets Field. The fifth game, the last one to be played in Flatbush for the Series, was packed with fans hoping to see the Dodgers take the lead in the Series.

Brooklyn manager Burt Shotton surprisingly picked Rex Barney to start. Barney had last started on July 4 and didn't last through the second inning. Shotton's starters had struggled throughout the Series, with none lasting more than four innings.

Tommy Holmes wrote in the *Brooklyn Daily Eagle* that "while it was obvious that Shotton was in a bad way for pitchers, no one thought he'd dig deep enough in the barrel to come up with Barney."[1]

Barney immediately made the Brooklyn faithful wonder if Shotton had made a mistake. He walked leadoff batter Snuffy Stirnweiss, who ended up on third when the next batter, Tommy Henrich, doubled. Then Barney walked Johnny Lindell to load the bases "with nobody but the great [Joe] DiMaggio at bat."[2]

Pitching coach Clyde Sukeforth "dashed to the mound for a steady-down confab with the jittery starter and whatever he said should be recorded for posterity, observed sportswriter Dick Young. "Suddenly, erratic [Barney] was transformed into a confident phenom."[3]

Barney struck out DiMaggio on a fastball. Then he grabbed George McQuinn's comebacker and threw home to get Stirnweiss. Finally, Barney struck out Billy Johnson for the third out.

Dick Young wrote in the *New York Daily News*: "There's nobody like [Barney] to keep the crowd and the game in a constant state of commotion. He puts them on and then he blows them over."[4]

After Bill Bevens lost a one-hitter the previous day on Cookie Lavagetto's pinch-hit double in the bottom of the ninth, Yankee starter Spec Shea told Bevens that he "would get even." Later he said, "I wanted to square what they did to [Bevens] yesterday. That [loss] hurt me almost as much as it did him."[5]

Rookie Shea started for the Yankees four days after he pitched five innings and earned a win in the Series opener. Shea showed that he meant to make up for the previous day's loss by shutting down the Dodgers through the first five innings.

Pee Wee Reese was the first Brooklyn baserunner when Shea walked him in the fourth. But two quick outs left Reese stranded on first as Shea maintained his no-hitter.

Barney continued to pitch wild over the next two innings, walking three batters and throwing a wild pitch to give the Yankees several opportunities to score. In the third he managed to get out of another jam when DiMaggio grounded into a double play.

The Yankees finally took advantage of Barney's wildness in the fourth. With two out, he walked Aaron Robinson and Rizzuto. With Shea coming to bat, Brooklyn fans probably felt that Barney could get out of one more jam.

But Shea "pulled far into the bucket on a curve ball and his bat sweeping around had the good fortune to be grooved in the path of the ball."[6] After Shea pulled into first with a single that brought Robinson home with the Yankees' first run, he "looked somewhat astonished himself."[7]

Barney walked the next batter, Stirnweiss, to load the bases but retired Henrich on a groundout to prevent any more scoring by the Yankees.

DiMaggio batted for the third time in the fifth, and "[t]he sight of 10 Yankees getting on base in the first four frames with only one run resulting must have annoyed [the] old pro."[8] DiMaggio hit a blast into the upper left-field seats that provided the second Yankees run.

DiMaggio later said, "I hit a fast ball for that one. I would have like a couple of others instead of those double play grounders. But Shea made up for our hitting shortcomings."[9]

When Barney walked Billy Johnson, "Shotton's nerves couldn't stand it any longer."[10] Joe Hatten was called in from the bullpen and Barney

left with nine walks, barely missing the record set by Bevens the previous day.

Shea kept the Dodgers hitless into the fifth, when Gene Hermanski hammered a single to right field with nobody out.[11] But Shea retired the next three batters.

Not so in the sixth. Al Gionfriddo, pinch-hitting for Hatten, walked to lead off the inning. Shea struck out Eddie Stanky, then walked Reese. Jackie Robinson stepped to the plate. He had gone hitless in his last eight at-bats but chose this one to break out of his slump.

Robinson hit a single up the middle that "barely grazed Shea's leaping glove-tips as it flew over the middle, then squeezed through the converging gloves of Rizzuto and Stirnweiss and bounded into center."[12]

Gionfriddo scored and Reese ended up on third, arriving barely ahead of DiMaggio's throw, and Robinson ended up at second. The Dodgers suddenly had an opportunity to tie the score and grab the lead. But Dixie Walker fouled out to third baseman Johnson and Hermanski hit an easy fly ball to DiMaggio for the third out.

After pulling Barney, Shotton relied on his bullpen down the stretch. The Dodgers relievers, Hatten, Hank Behrman and "the inevitable Hugh Casey, held fast, with the Bombers getting just two blows in the last four innings."[13]

Behrman got into trouble in the seventh after a leadoff single by Henrich, a walk, and a passed ball put two runners in scoring position. But he struck out McQuinn and retired Johnson on a groundball back to the mound.

The Dodgers had another chance to catch up to the Yankees in the seventh. Bruce Edwards led off with a walk but Carl Furillo failed to move him forward when he "was unable to deliver a vital bunt."[14] With two outs, Arky Vaughan doubled. The Dodgers had runners at second and third. If Furillo had succeeded in his bunt attempt, the score would have been tied.

After pinch-hitter Pete Reiser was intentionally walked and Ed Miksis ran for him, Reese, who had walked twice after flying out in the first, came to bat. Shea buckled down and quickly got two strikes on him. Then "Reese stood at attention and let Shea curve him with that called third strike."[15]

Casey kept the Yankees from scoring in the final two innings but had to work out of trouble twice. Shea hit a two-out double in the eighth and moved to third on a passed ball but never made it home after Casey struck out Stirnweiss.

In the ninth Henrich reached when Miksis couldn't handle his groundball, and Casey hit Lindell on the right arm to put a Yankee in scoring position with no outs.

But Casey got DiMaggio to hit a double-play grounder to shortstop. Henrich reached third but he was thrown out when he tried to score on a wild pitch as a result of Edwards's "cat-like pursuit of the ball" after Casey threw wild.[16]

Yankees manager Bucky Harris stayed with Shea in the ninth even though he had his best reliever, Joe Page, ready in the bullpen. Edwards led off with a single that had the Dodgers fans anticipating another comeback.

Vic Lombardi ran for Edwards. Furillo stepped into the batter's box with a second opportunity to push a runner forward. His sacrifice bunt was successful this time and the Dodgers had a runner in scoring position.

After Jorgensen flied out to right field, Shotton sent the previous day's hero, Lavagetto, to bat for Casey. The Dodgers faithful were on their feet in hopes that he might repeat his previous day's heroics.

With the count 3-and-2, Shea "threw that Sunday curve over the plate. Lavagetto wasn't cheated. He swung with all his power, pulling for the left field fence. But he missed."[17] Observed sportswriter Tommy Holmes: "The gods of baseball fortune will only take just so much."[18]

Shea had allowed just four hits and Harris told his young pitcher afterward, "You pitched a swell game." Then he told reporters gathered in the clubhouse: "I don't want any more like that. Going down to the last pitch is too much wear and tear on the nerves. But it's great to win those kind."[19]

As the Series moved back to Yankee Stadium for the sixth game, Henrich left these parting words for his teammates: "We have said our farewell to Brooklyn for 1947. Now we'll try to give them something to remember in the Bronx tomorrow."[20]

SOURCES

In addition to the sources cited in the Notes, I used the Baseball-Reference.com and Retrosheet.org websites for box-score, player, team, and season pages, pitching and batting game logs, and other material.

https://www.baseball-reference.com/boxes/BRO/BRO194710040.shtml

https://www.retrosheet.org/boxesetc/1947/B10040BRO1947.htm

NOTES

1   Tommy Holmes, "Yankees Nip Dodgers 2-1 as Shea Stars," *Brooklyn Daily Eagle*, October 5, 1947: 23.

2   Holmes.

3   Dick Young, "Shea's 4-Hitter Beats Dodgers 2-1," *New York Daily News*, October 5, 1947: 96.

4   Young.

5   James Dawson, "Youthful Hurler Mobbed by Mates," *New York Times*, October 5, 1947: 170.

6   Holmes

7   Holmes.

8   Dawson.

9   Dawson.

10 Young.

11 Young.

12 Young.

13 John Drebinger, "Shea Wins in Box," *New York Times*, October 5, 1947: 169.

14 Young.

15 Holmes.

16 Holmes.

17 Holmes.

18 Holmes.

19 Dawson.

20 Dawson.

ROBINSON'S FIRST GRAND SLAM WINS IN A WALKOFF

June 24, 1948

Brooklyn Dodgers 6, Pittsburgh Pirates 2

by Bill Nowlin

The Dodgers hosted the Pittsburgh Pirates for a Thursday afternoon doubleheader at Ebbets Field, with the Pirates only one game behind the Boston Braves in the National League standings. They'd been in third place for most of the season, but had tied for first for one day, June 16. The second game was a makeup for a rainout on the 22nd. The Dodgers were in sixth place, 7½ games back. They hadn't seen the first division since May 15. Two right-handers opposed each other as starting pitchers: Harry Taylor for Brooklyn and Bob Chesnes for Pittsburgh. Taylor had been 10-5 in 1947, his official rookie year.[1] Chesnes, a rookie, was undefeated and riding a three-game win streak.[2]

After five innings the Pirates held a 2-0 lead and Taylor was out of the game, replaced by pinch-hitter Marv Rackley in the bottom of the fifth. The runs had come on a third-inning single by third baseman Frankie Gustine and a fifth-inning triple by center fielder Johnny Hopp. He drove in Chesnes, who had walked.

Left-hander Paul Minner threw three scoreless innings for Leo Durocher's Dodgers.[3]

After seven innings, the score remained 2-0. But Brooklyn tied it in the bottom of the eighth. The two runs scored on what the *Pittsburgh Press* characterized as "one hit and some shoddy fielding."[4] Chesnes walked pinch-hitter Bruce Edwards and second baseman Billy Cox, with a groundout in between.[5] First baseman Jackie Robinson singled to shallow left, loading the bases. (The *Press* put "single" in quotation marks; the ball had tipped off Hopp's glove.)[6] Carl Furillo lifted a fly ball to his Pirates counterpart in center field. Edwards tagged up and scored – and so did Cox, when second baseman Danny Murtaugh committed an error. Chesnes intentionally walked Pee Wee Reese, and got Gene Hermanski to ground out and end the inning.

In the ninth, reliever Willie Ramsdell set down the Pirates in order.

Chesnes walked the leadoff batter in the bottom of the ninth, catcher Gil Hodges.[7] Tommy Brown, who had come into the game to play third base, sacrificed Hodges to second. Pirates manager Billy Meyer turned to his bullpen and summoned Mel Queen. Preston Ward pinch-hit for Ramsdell, and Queen walked him intentionally, setting up a potential double play. Then he got Dick Whitman to foul out to third base. But he walked Cox on four pitches, loading the bases and bringing up Robinson, the Rookie of the Year in 1947.

Robinson watched two pitches go by, a strike and then a ball. He swung at the third pitch and hit a grand slam to win the game, "a drive that went deep into the left-field stands."[8] The *Times* added, "The customers went a bit off their trolleys when they saw the ball going into the stands, and Robinson wasn't unhappy about it, either. 'It's the first time in my life that I ever hit a grand-slam homer anywhere.'"[9]

It was Robinson's third home run of the season. With four runs batted in, he now had 27.

As in the eighth inning, the Dodgers' runs all scored on one base hit. Vince Johnson of the *Pittsburgh Post-Gazette* grumbled a bit about the grand slam: "A single would have done just as well," Tell that to the 24,745 fans from Flatbush.[10]

Ramsdell, of course, got the win. Chesnes bore the defeat. The time of game was 2:49.

The Bums saw their team sweep the Pirates. And they saw more hitting from Robinson in the second game.

The Associated Press game story declared, "Jackie Robinson went on a batting rampage today, banging out seven hits including six in a row."[11] He had two doubles and two singles in the second game, called on account of darkness after 7½ innings; the Dodgers outscored the Pirates, 8-6, and leapfrogged the Phillies into fifth place. Robinson was 4-for-4, was the lead runner in a first-inning double steal after singling Arky Vaughan home with the first run of the game

and moving to second when Furillo was hit by a pitch. Robinson scored three runs, and drove in a pair. The late-June steal was his first stolen base of the year. He'd reported to spring training 25 pounds overweight.[12]

In the doubleheader, Robinson was 7-for-9 with six RBIs and four runs scored. The "ebony clouter" boosted his batting average from .280 to .306.[13]

At the end of his sophomore season, Robinson had driven in 85 runs to the 48 RBIs he had in 1947. His batting average was one point lower, at .296. He hit 12 homers in 1947 and 12 in 1948. He scored 108 runs, 17 fewer than the 125 he had scored the year before. He'd led the league with 29 stolen bases in 1947; in 1948, he stole 22. In 1949 he was named the National League's Most Valuable Player.

Of Robinson's 137 career home runs, nine were hit in the ninth inning and six were hit in extra innings. Fifty were hit with two outs. Seventy-seven of them were hit at Ebbets Field. Jackie Robinson hit only one other grand slam in his career. It came precisely two years later – on June 24, 1950. It was also hit late in an Ebbets Field game, against the same Pittsburgh Pirates team, this time off Vic Lombardi. The Dodgers won that game, 21-12.

SOURCES

In addition to the sources cited in the Notes, the author consulted Baseball-Reference.com and Retrosheet. org. Thanks to Gregory Wolf for assistance.

NOTES

1   He had appeared in four games without a start or a decision late in 1946. His 10-5 record in 1947 was accompanied by a 3.11 earned-run average. He had a very good 2.82 ERA before the June 24 game, but a record of 1-3.

2   Chesnes finished the 1948 season with a 14-6 (3.57 ERA) record. His only other two years in the majors saw him go 7-13 (5.88) in 1949 and 3-3 in just nine appearances in 1950 (5.54 ERA).

3   Minner had appeared in four major-league games as a reliever, three in 1946 and just one to this point in 1948. Most of his career was spent with the Cubs (1950–56). The 1948 season was his best for ERA; he was 4-3 with a 2.44 ERA. In 1952, he won 14 games for the Cubs.

4   Lester J. Biederman, "Pirates Right Back Where They Started," *Pittsburgh Press*, June 25, 1948: 30.

5   Cox had started the game playing third base, but moved to second in the top of the eighth.

6   Biederman. The *Post-Gazette's* Vince Johnson, though, acknowledged that Hopp had only gotten to the ball "after a hard run." Vince Johnson, "Robinson's Batting Big Factor in Bums' Double Triumph," *Pittsburgh Post-Gazette*, June 25, 1948: 20.

7   Hodges had caught in 24 of his 28 games in his first season, 1947. In 1948 he caught in 38 games and played first base in 96. By 1949, he was the Dodgers' full-time first baseman (and an All-Star for seven seasons in succession).

8   Roscoe McGowen, "Dodgers Defeat Pirates, 6-2, 8-6, As Robinson Drives Home 6 Runs," *New York Times*, June 25,1948: 30.

9   McGowen.

10   The *New York Times* reported attendance of 28,835. The *Post-Gazette* had the lower figure. The *Brooklyn Daily Eagle* counted 10 fewer attendees than the *Times*: 28,825.

11   Associated Press, "Jackie Robinson on Spree as Dodgers Top Bucs Twice," *Standard-Speaker* (Hazleton, Pennsylvania), June 25, 1948: 29.

12   Jackie Robinson, *I Never Had It Made* (New York: Ecco, 1995), 71.

13   The phrase was used by James J. Murphy, "Lip Smiles Again as Dodgers Come Alive Against Bucs," *Brooklyn Daily Eagle*, June 25, 1948: 16.

DODGERS FOURTH OF JULY FIREWORKS

July 4, 1948

Brooklyn Dodgers 13, New York Giants 12

by Paul E. Doutrich

The 28,770 holiday fans who filed into Ebbets Field on the Fourth of July in 1948 came to watch the Brooklyn Dodgers play their crosstown rival, the New York Giants. Some may have planned to watch fireworks that evening after the game. Little could they have suspected that they were about to see an early fireworks exhibition that afternoon.

The first two innings provided only a hint of what was in store for fans later in the game. With two outs in the bottom of the first inning, Dodgers center fielder Gene Hermanski laced a triple to center field but was stranded when the next hitter, George Shuba, popped out to the Giants catcher. The Dodgers added two more singles in the second, but again were unable to score. The best the Giants could do during those opening frames was a walk in each inning.

The Giants got the scoring started in the third. Struggling with his control, Dodgers pitcher Harry Taylor added three more walks to his account in the third. The first, to pitcher Ray Poat, came with one out. First baseman Whitey Lockman followed the second out with another

free pass. With two runners on and two out, Les Layton drove a triple to right field that plated both baserunners. Playing in his only major-league season, Layton was filling in for Bobby Thomson, the Giants' regular left fielder. Layton had been used exclusively as a pinch-hitter until three days earlier, when he replaced Thomson. After five more consecutive starts, Layton would start only a half-dozen more games at the end of the season. In 1949 he was back in the minor leagues, where his professional baseball career ended six years later.

Pee Wee Reese led off the Dodgers third with a double to left field and was bunted to third base by Jackie Robinson. With Reese lurking off the base, the Giants pitcher, Poat, balked while delivering his first pitch to Hermanski. The pitch drilled the Dodgers center fielder in the hip. The balk brought Reese in with the Dodgers' first run. Misinterpreting the call, Dodgers manager Leo Durocher leaped out of the dugout ready to do verbal battle with home-plate umpire Scotty Robb until he recognized that the call had gone in his favor. Instead, Giants catcher Walker Cooper complained about the balk call with no success. When the inning ended the Giants' two-run lead had been cut in half.

The top of the fourth looked like the top of the third. Dodgers pitchers again walked three and gave up a triple. This time, however, the triple came after the first walk. A groundout and another walk later, Taylor was lifted in favor of southpaw Paul Minner, who issued the third free pass of the inning before getting the third out.

As the game began to heat up, the Dodgers' rookie catcher, Roy Campanella, came to the plate in the fourth with Carl Furillo, who had singled, on first and two outs. Campanella had started the season in Brooklyn but was sent back to the Dodgers' Triple-A affiliate in St. Paul in late April. Branch Rickey had hoped to make an outfielder out of Campanella and, ostensibly, sent him to the minors to learn the position. However, the underlying reason for the move was to integrate the St. Paul team. Rickey promised Campanella and Durocher, who was not happy about the arrangement, that Campy would return to the Dodgers sometime in midseason. That time had come two days earlier, on July 2. Since then the Dodgers' new starting catcher had been pounding the ball. In eight official trips to the plate, he had seven hits, including a second-inning single. His onslaught continued in his second at-bat. This time it was his first major-league home run, a two-run shot to left field that tied the game.

The Giants wasted little time in retaking the lead. Johnny Mize led off the fifth with a bunt single and Walker Cooper followed with a single to right. Mize moved to third on a groundout, and scored on Sid Gordon's line-drive out to left field. Shortstop Jack Conway followed with a single that plated the second Giants run of the inning. Conway, who was filling in for the Giants' regular shortstop, Buddy Kerr, went to second when left fielder Shuba misplayed the ball. Two days earlier, Kerr had been hit in the left cheekbone on a throw by Campanella during a steal attempt.

The throw knocked Kerr out, but there were no broken bones (though Kerr still suffered from nausea on this day). Conway's base hit ended the day for Minner, who was replaced by knuckleballer Willie Ramsdell.

The bottom of the fifth began with the end of Durocher's day. Unhappy with home-plate umpire Robb's strike zone, Durocher, who had been barking at the umpire throughout the game, confronted him while leadoff hitter Reese was at the plate. A few minutes later, the Dodgers manager was gone. After Durocher's exit, Poat set down the three Dodgers batters he faced.

The Giants added three runs to their lead in the top of the sixth. They scored after three more walks, a muffed tag by Reese on a steal attempt, and a bases-loaded triple by Willard Marshall, the Giants' third three-bagger of the day. Now up by five runs, Poat, in the bottom of the inning, again cut through the Dodgers hitters, giving up only a double to Bruce Edwards.

An inning later, Poat was not as successful. With two outs, the Giants pitcher gave up singles to Reese and Robinson. Hermanski followed with a double that scored Reese. Andy Hansen replaced Poat on the mound and on his first pitch, Robinson stole home on the front end of a double steal. Giants catcher Walker Cooper recognized that he could not get Robinson, so instead threw to third to get Hermanski. The throw caught third baseman Sid Gordon by surprise and the ball bounded into left field, enabling Hermanski to score the Dodgers' third run of the inning. A single and a walk later, Hansen turned the ball over to Larry Jansen, who got the third out.

Hank Behrman, the Dodgers' fourth pitcher of the day, put down the Giants in order in the top of the eighth. In the bottom of the inning, the Dodgers continued what they had begun the previous inning. Gil Hodges led off with a double and one out later Arky Vaughan, batting for Behrman, doubled Hodges home. Pee Wee Reese followed with a single and Jackie Robinson beat out a bunt to load the bases. Dave Koslo replaced Jansen and walked the tying and go-ahead runs across the plate. Alex Konikowski, the Giants' fourth pitcher, was called in to get the final two outs.

Once again the Giants wasted no time getting the lead back. Ralph Branca, who was given the responsibility for closing out the Giants in the ninth inning, served up a game-tying home run to the first hitter he faced, Willard Marshall. One out later, Jack Conway reached base on a throwing error by third baseman Eddie Miksis. Bobby Thomson, batting for the pitcher, followed with a single to center. Bill Rigney then stepped to the plate and smacked a three-run shot deep into the left-field stands. It was Branca's last pitch of the day. Erv Palica got the Dodgers out of the inning.

Giants reliever Monty Kennedy took over for Konikowski in the bottom of the inning. With their team again down by three runs, some Dodgers fans left for home and missed the afternoon's explosive grand finale. Gil Hodges led off with a single to left. The next hitter, catcher Campanella, worked the count full, then unloaded his second home run of the day, pulling the Dodgers within a run of the Giants. Sheldon Jones replaced Kennedy on the mound and was greeted with a sharp single by right fielder Dick Whitman. Jones then walked Reese and gave up a perfectly placed bunt single to Robinson to load the bases. The next scheduled hitter was pitcher Palica, but he was pulled in favor of Pete Reiser, the 37th player in the game. The Reiser who faced Jones was not the same one who six years earlier had established himself as one of the best players in the game. Broken bones, badly sprained and torn muscles, and at least three concussions from chasing fly balls into outfield walls had drained much of the greatness out of Reiser. Only a day earlier, he had visited the hospital for treatment on two badly sprained ankles. Used primarily as a pinch-hitter in 1948, he came to the plate hitting below .200. After fouling off three pitches, Reiser drilled a bullet into right field. Whitman easily scored the tying run with Reese and the winning run right behind him.

After Reiser's game-winner, exhausted fans headed home. As they left, some anticipated another fireworks celebration that night, but they all remembered the fireworks they had seen that afternoon.

SOURCES

The author consulted Baseball-Reference.com, Retrosheet.org, SABR.org, and the following:

Lanctot, Neil. *Campy: The Two Lives of Roy Campanella* (New York: Simon and Schuster, 2011).

McGowen, Roscoe. "Dodgers Count Four Times in 9th to Overcome Giants," *New York Times*, July 5, 1948: L-10.

Young, Dick. "Dodgers Edge Giants, 13-12, with 4 in 9th," *New York Daily News*, July 5, 1948: 41-42.

"MUSCLES" WESTLAKE HITS FOR THE CYCLE AS PIRATES DOUBLE UP DODGERS

July 30, 1948
Pittsburgh Pirates 10, Brooklyn Dodgers 5

by Mike Huber

The 31,278 fans who came through the turn-stiles at Ebbets Field on July 30, 1948, saw something to always remember from the unlikeliest of hitters. Pittsburgh's Wally Westlake hit for the cycle against the Brooklyn Dodgers.[1] Westlake had gone 2-for-24 (two singles) in his previous seven games, a stretch that had seen his batting average drop 20 points. Yet on this day, he joined the ranks of those who had accomplished the rare feat of getting a single, double, triple, and home run in a game.

Westlake had played four seasons in the minors (from 1940 to 1942 and in 1946 – his career was interrupted by World War II service) before signing with the Pittsburgh Pirates. He batted .273 in his rookie 1947 season, playing all three outfield positions. In 1948 the outfielder had a steady place as the fifth batter in the Pirates' lineup. He started the season strong, and by June 19 was batting .350. A little over a month later, on July 29, his average had slipped to .295.

The Pirates had only won five of 15 games since the All-Star Game, dropping from second to fifth in the standings. They came into Ebbets Field having lost all three games of a recent series with the Boston Braves. Further, this was the Pirates' first trip to Ebbets Field since Leo Durocher was replaced by Burt Shotton as manager of the Dodgers.[2] Pittsburgh's situation was the inverse of Brooklyn's. The Dodgers had gone 13-4 since the All-Star break and, dating back to July 2, had vaulted up in the National League standings from seventh place to second. Now, after sweeping a three-game series at home from the St. Louis Cardinals, Brooklyn was hosting the Pirates.

According to the *Pittsburgh Post-Gazette*, the Pirates "had their lineup revamped for the fourth time in as many games."[3] Manager Billy Meyer was searching for a spark that would ignite his offense. Stan Rojek once again was the leadoff batter, after three days in the seventh spot. After five straight games as a pinch-hitter, Frankie Gustine batted second, followed by ex-Dodger Dixie Walker, who had started the season as the Pirates' cleanup hitter. Rookie right-hander Bob Chesnes took the mound for the Bucs. His previous start (in the first game of a doubleheader on July 25) was also against the Dodgers, when he pitched into the eighth inning, allowing six runs (five earned) in a 7-6 loss at home.

For the Dodgers, Ralph Branca, also a righty, was seeking his 13th win of the season. He had faced the Pirates earlier in the week (in the second game of the July 25 doubleheader) and had been unlucky. Although Branca had allowed only three runs in six innings pitched, Rex Barney had come on in relief in the seventh and gave up a grand slam to Danny Murtaugh after which the game was ended by the Sunday curfew.[4]

In the first inning, Chesnes made an error that set the stage for a Brooklyn offensive outburst. Marv Rackley hit a routine grounder to first baseman Max West. Chesnes ran over to cover the base and dropped the throw from West. Jackie Robinson walked, and Gene Hermanski reached safely on a bunt single to the pitcher. Still with none out, Dick Whitman grounded a ball to West and beat him to the bag. Rackley scored the unearned run. Roy Campanella also singled, plating Robinson. But the Dodgers came away with only those two runs, as Tommy Brown lined into a double play and Gil Hodges flied out.

Pittsburgh's offense got going in the top of the second. Ralph Kiner singled and took third when Westlake doubled. West connected on an offering by Branca and "hammered the ball over the right field wall"[5] for three runs and the lead. The score remained 3-2 until the fourth, when, with one out, Westlake "drove a 400-foot homer into the stands in dead center"[6] for his 11th home run of the season. After West grounded out, Danny Murtaugh singled to left and Clyde Kluttz hit his third homer of the season. Pittsburgh had doubled its run total. After Kluttz's blast, Branca exited the game. He had allowed three homers in this contest and had served up 20 round-trippers in 25 appearances to this point in the season.[7]

Rojek led off the top of the fifth with a double to left-center. Gustine blooped a single to right-center, driving home Rojek. With two outs, Westlake "rifled one off the concrete above

Hermanski's head and made three bases when the ball bounced swiftly back over Gene's head."[8] No other outfielder was close enough to cut off the ricochet, so Westlake raced around the bases with a triple. West clubbed a fly ball to center, and Rackley misplayed the ball; Westlake scored easily and West made it to second. The Pirates had added three more tallies and now led 9-2.

Brooklyn answered in the bottom half with three runs of their own, when Hermanski hit his seventh home run of the season off Chesnes with pitcher Paul Minner[9] and Robinson aboard. However, after the fifth inning, Chesnes was "master of the situation."[10] He held the Dodgers hitless from the end of the fifth until the ninth, when Robinson stroked a two-out single, his third hit of the game

In the top of the seventh, Kiner lined a two-out single into left field, and Westlake followed by grounding a single up the middle, giving him the last hit necessary for the cycle. Neither runner scored, but Westlake was now 4-for-4 with three runs scored. In the top of the eighth, rookie Monty Basgall, who had entered the game as a pinch-runner for Murtaugh in the fourth inning and then stayed on to play second base, belted a Hugh Casey 2-and-0 pitch over the wall for his second homer of the season. After that, the last two frames went by without much action. Westlake batted one last time in the top of the ninth. He swung at Casey's first offering and grounded to third baseman Brown, who threw to second to force out Kiner.

The final score was Pittsburgh 10, Brooklyn 5. The Pirates pounded out 14 base hits as they snapped their losing streak, and those "fourteen socks totaled thirty bases."[11] Chesnes went the distance, scattering eight hits and earning his sixth win. He had walked five Dodgers batters, but only two of those runners scored. Branca failed again to pick up win number 13; instead, he was tagged with his seventh loss. Half of the six hits he allowed had left the ballpark.

Westlake was the star of Pittsburgh's offense. He drove in two runs and scored three. Noted the *Pittsburgh Press*, "The power in Wally Westlake's bat, which is as unpredictable as which way the wind will blow tomorrow, was turned on again last night."[12] His batting average jumped to .305, and his slugging percentage increased by 29 points. Rojek contributed two hits to the offensive outpouring, giving him 99 base hits for the season (leading the team).

Pittsburgh and Brooklyn squared off again the next day, and Pirates skipper Meyer inserted the exact same lineup against the Dodgers (with Basgall starting this time for Murtaugh). The result was a 5-2 victory for the visitors. Westlake was 1-for-3 with two runs batted in. Rojek was 2-for-5 at the top of the batting order. Pittsburgh batted around in the top of the ninth, plating four runs to seal the win.

Westlake's feat marked the 14th time in Pittsburgh franchise history that a batter had hit for the cycle.[13] Westlake's accomplishment was the second cycle of the 1948 season, joining New York Yankees star Joe DiMaggio, who had hit for the cycle for the second time in his career on May 20. A month after Westlake, Dodgers star Jackie Robinson became the third and final player of the 1948 season to hit for the cycle, doing so on August 29.

Westlake only had 33 extra-base hits in 1948,[14] collecting three in this game. He became the first player in 1949 to hit for the cycle (June 14, 1949), again going 4-for-5, but this time with three runs batted in and two runs scored. Coincidentally, the home run in the 1949 game was also his 11th circuit clout of the season.

SOURCES

In addition to the sources mentioned in the Notes, the author consulted Baseball-Reference.com, Retrosheet.org, and SABR.org.

https://www.baseball-reference.com/boxes/BRO/BRO194807300.shtml

https://www.retrosheet.org/boxesetc/1948/B07300BRO1948.htm

NOTES

1   Chester L. Smith, "Westlake Restores Waning Popularity with Meyer," *Pittsburgh Press*, July 31, 1948: 6.

2   Durocher managed the Dodgers through the first half of the 1948 season. He even managed the National League squad in the All-Star Game, However, when the second half of the 1948 campaign started, Shotton was at the helm.

3   Vince Johnson, "Bob Chesnes Hurls Seven Hitter as Westlake Gets Four," *Pittsburgh Post-Gazette*, July 31, 1948: 8.

4   *See* retrosheet.org/boxesetc/1948/B07252PIT1948.htm.

5   Johnson.

6   Johnson.

7   Branca allowed 24 home runs in 1948, fourth-most in the majors.

8   Roscoe McGowen, "Brooks Toppled by Chesnes, 10-5," *New York Times*, July 31, 1948: 11.

9   Minner had relieved Branca in the fourth inning.

10   McGowen.

11   McGowen.

12   Smith.

13   Westlake joined Fred Carroll (May 2, 1887), Fred Clarke (July 23, 1901, and May 7, 1903), Chief Wilson (July 3, 1910), Honus Wagner (August 22, 1912), Dave Robertson (August 30, 1921), Pie Traynor (July 7, 1923), Kiki Cuyler (June 4, 1925), Max Carey (June 20, 1925), Arky Vaughan (June 24, 1933, and July 19, 1939), Bob Elliott (July 15, 1945) and Bill Salkeld (August 4, 1945), as Pittsburgh players who had hit for the cycle.

14   Westlake had 10 doubles, six triples and 17 homers in 1948.

Hermanski first Dodger to whack three home runs in Brooklyn as Erskine goes distance in first career start

August 5, 1948

Brooklyn Dodgers 6, Chicago Cubs 4

by Gregory H. Wolf

Gene Hermanski's name will forever be etched in the long history of professional baseball in Brooklyn, dating back to the city's teams in the National Association (1872-1875), American Association (1884-1889), and the National League beginning in 1890. Despite hitting only 46 home runs in his nine-year career, spent primarily as a reserve with three different teams, Hermanski was the first Brooklyn player to clout three round-trippers in front of his home crowd.

The Dodgers' 1948 season was as disappointing as the 1947 was exciting. The reigning NL pennant winners stumbled from the outset under skipper Leo Durocher, who returned to the club after his one-year banishment by Commissioner Happy Chandler for a series of controversial incidents. In mid-July Leo the Lip suddenly bolted the team, languishing in fifth place with a losing record (35-37), and took over the helm of the New York Giants. Sixty-three-year-old Burt Shotton, who had taken the reins in the previous season in Durocher's absence, once again came to the rescue even though he had claimed he

would never manage again. Already beginning to heat up, the Dodgers responded to Shotton's deft touch and much less antagonistic approach to managing.

Heading into a doubleheader with the cellar-dwelling Chicago Cubs (40-58), necessitated by a rainout earlier in the series, 'Dem Bums' had won 14 of 21 games under Shotton to move into third place (49-44), just 4½ games behind the front-running Boston Braves.[1] One of the major reasons for the Dodgers' recent success was Hermanski.

The 28-year-old slugger had sipped a cup of coffee with the Dodgers in 1943 before serving in the military for two years. Highly touted, Hermanski was used sparingly in 1946 and then platooned with Pete Reiser in left field in 1947, starting all seven games of the '47 World Series. According to Dodgers beat writer Harold C. Burr, Hermanski's teammates began calling him the "Picture Ballplayer." He seemingly did everything right in practice and had excellent form and technique, but failed to produce the expected results on the field.[2]

Moved to right field in 1948 following the trade of longtime starter Dixie Walker, Hermanski started off slowly, then went on a tear. "[A]s Hermanski goes so go the Dodgers," quipped Associated Press sportswriter Joe Reichler.[3] Since July 4, the Massachusetts native had batted .339 and slugged .600 with five home runs and 25 RBIs in 30 games. His one-out double in the ninth inning would have won the previous game against the Cubs, but Jackie Robinson was cut down at the plate. Instead, Hermanski scored the winning run on Bruce Edwards' single.

On a windy, drizzly Wednesday afternoon, a Ladies Day crowd of 20,352 (15,579 paid) packed Ebbets Field for the midweek twin bill.[4]

Toeing the rubber for the Dodgers was 21-year-old right-hander Carl Erskine, making his first big-league start. Originally signed as a high schooler in 1945, Erskine "skyrocketed" through the Dodgers farm system, noted sportswriter Dick Young.[5] He had joined the Dodgers less than two weeks earlier after posting a stellar 15-7 slate with Fort Worth in the Double-A Texas League, and had thus far thrown 2⅔ hitless innings of relief and picked up two wins.

Erskine breezed through the first, tossing all 11 of his pitches for strikes. A soft-tosser with what Young called a "tricky change-up," Erskine fanned Clarence Maddern looking to end the frame. "[I]t sails to one side or the other," said Erskine of the pitch, which caused havoc for catchers.[6] Through four innings, Erskine had faced the minimum 12 batters. He walked two, both of whom were erased in inning-ending double plays he initiated.

While Erskine moved 'em down, Hermanski knocked 'em out against Cubs starter Ralph Hamner. In the first inning, with Robinson on first via a hit-by-pitch, Hermanski extended his hitting streak to eight games with a smash that "cut its way through the wet headwinds on a buzzing line and barely stayed fair as it whirred over the right screen," wrote Young.[7] It was Hermanski's

eighth home run of the season, one more than his career total of seven, all of which he whacked the previous year.

Two innings later, with Marv Rackley on first after walking, Hermanski sent Hamner's 3-and-2 pitch on a "soaring arc" over the right-field screen and onto Bedford Avenue to give the Dodgers a 4-0 lead.[8]

"[I]t must have been difficult for Erskine to realize that he was up in the majors at all," quipped beat writer Howard C. Burr about the Dodgers' ensuing defensive blunders.[9] Despite tying for the NL lead in double plays accomplished in 1948, the Dodgers were an average fielding team and made six errors in this game, leading to three unearned runs.

Andy Pafko led off the fifth with a chopper that third baseman Tommy Brown threw wildly to first, then moved to third on Bill Nicholson's single. Peanuts Lowrey's single put the Cubs on the board. Pee Wee Reese, acknowledged as the NL's premier defensive shortstop, scooped up Bob Scheffling's hard chopper to start a 6-4-3 double play. Roy Smalley's single drove in Nicholson to cut the Dodgers' lead in half. Erskine fanned Phil Cavarretta, pinch-hitting for Hamner, to apparently end the inning, but Roy Campanella committed a double error when he dropped the third strike and threw poorly to first. With the Cubs threatening to blow the game open, Pee Wee came to the rescue, picking up Emil Verban's grounder and tossing to first to end the inning.

The Dodgers miscues continued in the sixth. Center fielder Marv Rackley misplayed Hal Jeffcoat's fly ball. Jeffcoat moved to third on Pakfo's single and scored on Nicholson's force out to pull the Cubs to within a run.

Campanella gave the Dodgers a 5-3 lead on a one-out single off reliever Bob Rush to drive in Bruce Edwards, running for George Shuba, who had led off the sixth with a single. Campy tried for second when Lowrey threw home, but Scheffing whipped the ball to Smalley, who tagged

Campanella at second. Gil Hodges followed with a single on which Campy might have scored.

Erskine faced another threat in the eighth. Clyde McCullough led off with a single and scored on Lowrey's two-out single. Erskine committed the Dodgers' final miscue when he heaved wildly a relay throw to the plate, allowing Lowrey to reach third. With the Cubs 90 feet away from tying the game, Erskine induced Scheffing to fly out.

Hermanski dug in to lead off the eighth. In his previous at-bat, he walked on five pitches from reliever Doyle Lade. It appeared as if pull-hitting Hermanski might draw another free pass. Reliever Jess Dobernic "tried to keep the ball on the outside," recalled Hermanski, but made a mistake.[10] "It was the best smacked ball of the three, going out on a low trajectory," noted Harold Burr about Hermanski's opposite-field blast into deep left field. "It looked as if it would strike the wall but it had more legs than a Ziegfeld chorus and cleared the parapet."[11] Hermanski's blast gave the Dodgers a 6-4 lead.

Erskine set down the Cubs one-two-three in the ninth to complete the victory in 2 hours and 26 minutes. "He pitched with his heart like a real veteran," said Shotton of Erskine's eight-hitter with five punchouts and two walks.

Notwithstanding Erskine's victory in his first start, Hermanski was the star of the game. Twenty-two years after Jack Fournier became the first Dodgers player to hit three home runs in a game, on July 13, 1926, against the Cardinals in St. Louis, Hermanski, wearing number 22 on his uniform, became just the second Dodgers player do turn the trick and the first ever in Brooklyn. "Ski was a brilliant light in the clammy darkness-inducing drizzle that accompanied the entire game," wrote Young poetically about Hermanski's feat.[12]

"I never hit three homers in a game before, not even with the Bushwicks," said Hermanski, referring to the city's well-known semipro team, for which he had played.[13]

Epilogue: Hermanski enjoyed his most productive season in the majors in 1948, setting career bests in many offensive categories, including home runs (15), RBIs (60), and slugging average (.493), while the Dodgers finished in third place (84-70). Shotton, the last NL skipper to wear street clothes in the dugout, would lead the Dodgers to the pennant in 1949 and a second-place finish in 1950 before retiring. Though it took a few seasons, Erskine developed into an All-Star, won 20 games in 1953, and posted a 122-78 slate in his 12-year career, all with the Dodgers.

By the time the Dodgers relocated from Brooklyn to Los Angeles after the 1957 season, a Dodger had hit at least three home runs in a game five more times, four of which occurred at Ebbets Field. It happened four times in 1950: Duke Snider (and again in 1955), Tommy Brown, Campanella (in Cincinnati), and Hodges, who became just the sixth player in big-league history to club four home runs in a game, smacking a quartet at Ebbets Field in a 19-3 victory over the Braves.

SOURCES

In addition to the sources cited in the Notes, the author accessed Retrosheet.org, Baseball-Reference.com, SABR.org, and *The Sporting News* archive via Paper of Record.

NOTES

1   The second game of the series, on August 3, was rained out and rescheduled as part of a twin bill on August 5.

2   Harold C. Burr, "Picture-Hitter Gene Hermanski Steps Out of Frame for Dodgers," *Brooklyn Eagle*, August 6, 1948: 11.

3   Joe Reichler (Associated Press), "Hermanski's Three Homers Aid Dodgers Climb Into 2d," *Passaic* (New Jersey) *Herald-News*, August 6, 1948: 14.

4   Roscoe McGowen, "Brooks Take 2d Place by Point, Erskine Turning Back Cubs, 6-4," *New York Times*, August 6, 1948: 12.

5   Dick Young, "Hermanski's 3 Homers Turn Back Cubs, 6-4," *New York Daily News*, August 6, 1948: 16C.

6   Young.

7   Young.

8   Young.

9   Burr.

10   Burr.

11   Burr.

12   Young.

13   Burr.

HODGES AND COX COMBINE FORCES ON OFFENSIVE EXPLOSION

June 12, 1949

Brooklyn Dodgers 20, Cincinnati Reds 7

by Richard Cuicchi

The final score of the game between Brooklyn and Cincinnati on June 12, 1949, looked like that of a football game. Gil Hodges and Billy Cox were the offensive stars for the red-hot Dodgers. Except that they weren't scoring or passing for touchdowns; they were hitting home runs and driving in runs in bunches that propelled the Dodgers to a blowout win, 20-7. The duo accounted for 14 runs in routing the Reds, who went through seven pitchers during the game.

Hodges and Cox were part of a skilled infield that included Jackie Robinson and Pee Wee Reese. Dodgers manager Burt Shotton called it "the best in the majors."[1] Dodgers general manager Branch Rickey had assembled a talented squad that he said was "the best team I have ever been associated with."[2] This was a high compliment considering that Rickey had constructed several championship teams in St. Louis during the 1920s, 1930s, and 1940s.

The Dodgers had defeated Cincinnati the day before for their sixth straight win. Brooklyn held a 1½-game lead over St. Louis and the Boston Braves coming into the game. They had been in first place since June 6 as a result of the winning streak. They were riding on the backs of several players during their surge in the standings.

Two years after he integrated White baseball in 1947, Robinson was the best player on the Dodgers team. They had won the NL pennant in 1947, when Robinson was the Rookie of the Year. Veterans Dixie Walker, Pete Reiser, Eddie Stanky, and Cookie Lavagetto had moved on, while Robinson got even better in 1949.

After a poor April, Robinson began May with a .188 batting average and finished the month hitting .360. Opposing pitchers held him hitless in only three games in May as he hit .431 with 6 home runs and 34 RBIs. His slash line coming into the June 12 game was .346/.407/.566. Robinson's hitting practice under the instruction of Hall of Famer George Sisler during spring training was paying off.

Twenty-five-year-old first baseman Hodges was in his second full season with Dodgers. He had been on a tear, including hitting streaks of 19 games and 10 games. On June 12 he was batting .304 with 7 home runs and 35 RBIs.

In his second year with Brooklyn, third baseman Cox was better known for his defense, but he had hit safely in 15 of the first 19 games of the season before going on the injured list with a sprained ankle on May 8. On June 12 he had been back for only five games.

Reese was also part of the Dodgers' hit parade. He was in the midst of an 11-game hitting streak that included nine consecutive multi-hit games. He was sporting a .417 on-base percentage to go along with 8 home runs and 36 RBIs.

Duke Snider and former Negro League player Roy Campanella had joined the team since Robinson arrived and had quickly established themselves as key contributors. Outfielder Carl Furillo was having his best season since joining the Dodgers in 1946.

These players formed the core of Dodgers teams that won five more NL pennants and finished second three times from 1949 to 1956.

The day game at Ebbets Field in front of 24,020 fans was the third game of the series. The Dodgers had won the first two, 10-5 and 11-3. Shotton went with right-hander Rex Barney as his starter, and Reds manager Bucky Walters countered with Herm Wehmeier. Barney, who had led the team in wins (15) in 1948, had been erratic during the 1949 season (2-4 and 5.11 ERA), although he had posted a two-hitter in his last start. Wehmeier was 1-2 in six starts.

The Dodgers mounted a 5-0 lead through the first four innings, chasing Wehmeier in the third inning and reliever Bud Lively in the fifth.[3] Three of the runs came on two home runs by Cox, one each off Wehmeier and Lively. Cox had hit only one home run in his first 24 games. Wehmeier was trying to walk Robinson in the first inning, when he hit a pitchout to drive in the Dodgers' first run.[4] Furillo drove in the other run.

After four scoreless innings pitched, the bottom fell out for Barney in the top of the fifth. The Reds loaded the bases on a single by Virgil Stallcup, a double by Dixie Howell, and a walk to Bobby Adams, then gave up a run-scoring walk to Johnny Wyrostek. Grady Hatton smashed the third grand slam of his career, his fifth home run of the season, to tie the game, 5-5. After walking Danny Litwhiler, Barney was replaced by Paul Minner, who got the Dodgers out of the inning.

The fireworks ignited for the Dodgers with one out in the bottom of the inning. Robinson doubled off Ken Raffensberger and scored on Hodges' single off Harry Gumbert. After a single by Furillo and an intentional walk to Bruce Edwards loaded the bases, Cox cleared the bases with a line-drive double to right field off Howie Fox.

Pitcher Minner sent Cox home with a single. Walks to Gene Hermanski and Snider loaded the bases again, and Robinson's single off Jess Dobernic drove in two more runs for the Dodgers' sixth and seventh tallies of the inning. Hodges made it a 10-run inning with a home run to left field that plated Snider and Robinson and made the score 15-5. A fly out by Furillo ended the inning.

Both teams took a breather in the sixth as both Minner and the Reds' Johnny Vander Meer retired the opposition in order. In the seventh, the Reds punched back with two runs on Litwhiler's homer off Minner that landed in the upper left-field stand.

After retiring Pee Wee Reese leading off the bottom of the seventh, Vander Meer loaded the bases on walks to Hermanski, Snider, and Robinson. Hodges responded with a grand slam, making the score 19-7. A month earlier he had hit his first career grand slam, and he hit 14 during his career.[5]

Remaining on the mound for mop-up duty in the eighth inning, Vander Meer gave up the final run of the game on a wild pitch with Robinson batting that scored Hermanski.

The 20 runs were the most the Dodgers would score in a game in 1949. They battered seven Reds pitchers for 13 hits and 11 walks, including four home runs.

Hodges had a personal best eight RBIs in a game, but he exceeded that with nine a year later. Cox had six RBIs on his two homers and a double. Pee Wee Reese's 11-game hitting streak was ended.

Raffensberger, the first of five Reds pitchers in the fifth inning, threw only two pitches but was charged with the loss. He had also taken the loss in his start the day before. The Reds' use of five pitchers in one inning tied a major-league record with five other teams.[6] Minner, who finished the game throwing 4⅔ innings, got his third win of the season.

Robinson contributed to the football-like score with two hits and three RBIs. If the 20-7 contest had been a football game, the Dodgers would have been well-positioned with Robinson, an outstanding running back with UCLA in 1938 and 1939. He solidified his standing as a Dodgers superstar by winning the National League batting title (.342) and Most Valuable Player Award in 1949.

Brooklyn battled the Cardinals down to the wire, never more than 2½ games behind or 3½ games ahead. The Dodgers finally secured first place on September 29 and held on to win the pennant by one game. Despite having one of the best teams to that point of the franchise's history, they lost to the New York Yankees in five games in the World Series.

SOURCES

In addition to the sources cited in the Notes, the author consulted Baseball-Reference.com and the following:

Burr, Harold C. "Slugging Dodgers Gunning for More Than Standoff in St. Louis Series," *Brooklyn Daily Eagle*, June 13, 1949: 13.

Holmes, Tommy. "What Delayed the Dodgers?" *Baseball Digest*, November 1949: 25-26.

Rampersad, Arnold. *Jackie Robinson: A Biography* (New York: Alfred A. Knopf, 1997).

Smith, Lou. "Bums Murder Reds," *Cincinnati Enquirer*, June 13, 1949: 18.

NOTES

1   Peter Golenbock. *Bums: An Oral History of the Brooklyn Dodgers* (New York: G.P. Putnam's Sons, 1984), 230.

2   Golenbock.

3   Lively was removed for a pinch-hitter.

4   Roscoe McGowen. "Dodgers Crush Reds with 10 Runs in Fifth; Giants Lose to Pirates." *New York Times*, June 13, 1949.

5   As of 2021, Hall of Famer Willie McCovey was the National League leader with 18.

6   McGowen.

THE ALL-STAR GAME
FINALLY COMES TO BROOKLYN

July 12, 1949

American League 11, National League 7

by Lyle Spatz

Brooklyn's Ebbets Field was hosting the All-Star Game for the first time, the last of the major league locations in existence in 1933 to have the honor. Brooklyn was to have hosted the 1942 game, but baseball shifted the contest to the Polo Grounds. The thinking was that the Polo Grounds' larger seating capacity would produce greater attendance, and thus more revenue for the two charitable beneficiaries – the Bat and Ball Fund, which supplied baseball equipment to servicemen, and the Army and Navy Relief Fund.[1]

This game, played through an intermittent drizzle, was a sloppily played slugfest that featured 25 hits, a record 18 runs, and a record six errors, five by the Nationals. Two of those errors came in the first inning and allowed the AL to score four unearned runs. The NL fought back, and despite squandering several scoring opportunities actually went ahead, 5-4, in the third, only to surrender the lead permanently an inning later. Vic Raschi of the New York Yankees, the winning pitcher a year earlier, entered the game in the seventh inning and pitched three scoreless innings to preserve the victory.

For the first time in All-Star play, six umpires were used, with one stationed down the left-field line and one down the right-field line. Yet, oddly, when they made the traditional switch after 4½ innings, NL ump Al Barlick, who'd been behind the plate, departed, resulting in the right field line being uncovered for the remainder of the game.

National League manager Billy Southworth of the Boston Braves chose as his starting pitcher lefty Warren Spahn, who along with Johnny Sain had helped pitch Boston to its first pennant in 34 years in 1948. But Spahn was mainly ineffective in this game, giving up four runs, six hits, and two walks in 1⅓ innings. In fairness, the four runs were unearned and with better luck, Spahn might have retired the Americans in order in the first.

Spahn struck out leadoff hitter Dom DiMaggio and number-three batter Ted Williams, and should have had the number-two batter George Kell. The Tigers' third baseman had bounced a routine grounder to his opposite number, Eddie Kazak of the St. Louis Cardinals, but the rookie's throw handcuffed New York Giants first baseman Johnny Mize, and Kell was safe.[2]

Kell stole second as Williams was striking out, but even there, a better throw by Philadelphia Phillies catcher Andy Seminick might have gotten him. Joe DiMaggio, playing in his 11th All-Star Game, singled to left and the AL had its first run. Then, after walking Philadelphia A's shortstop Eddie Joost, Spahn gave up a single to Washington Senators first baseman Eddie Robinson. DiMaggio scored and Joost went to third.

When Cass Michaels of the Chicago White Sox followed with a bouncer to Brooklyn's Pee Wee Reese, Spahn appeared to have escaped with just the two runs allowed. But the Dodgers shortstop failed to handle the routine groundball. Joost scored run number three and Red Sox catcher Birdie Tebbetts's single to left brought Robinson home with the fourth run. Spahn had struck out the side (all three victims being members of the crosstown Boston Red Sox), but was charged with four unearned runs.

Mel Parnell was the first Red Sox pitcher to start an All-Star Game since Lefty Grove in 1936, and his match-up with Spahn was the first time two pitchers from the same city had squared off since the Giants' Carl Hubbell and the Yankees' Lefty Gomez did so in 1934.

In the home first, Parnell quickly surrendered half the lead. He retired Reese, but then Jackie Robinson slashed a double to left and the Cardinals' Stan Musial, in what was a familiar sight to Brooklyn fans, drove a home run over the wall in right and onto Bedford Avenue.

Robinson, playing in his third big-league season, was the first African American to participate in an All-Star Game. Currently leading the National League with a .362 batting average, he was the league's leading vote-getter (1,891,212) and second overall to Williams (2,087,466). The *Chicago Tribune*, conductor of the poll, announced that the fans had cast 4,637,743 votes, more than half a million higher than in 1948.[3]

To fill out the roster, Southworth and AL manager Lou Boudreau of the Cleveland Indians had selected three additional Black players: Southworth chose pitcher Don Newcombe and catcher Roy Campanella, both of the Dodgers, and Boudreau chose Indians outfielder Larry Doby. (Doby was one of five Cleveland players on the AL team, although none of the defending World Series champions had been elected to start.)

With one out in the AL second, Kell singled and Williams walked. Joe DiMaggio was up next, prompting Southworth to bring in right-hander Newcombe to replace Spahn. Newcombe had made his big-league debut on May 20, less than two months earlier, making the 53 days between his debut and his appearance in an All-Star Game the shortest such span ever. If the rookie was nervous, he didn't show it. He retired DiMaggio on a fly to Pittsburgh's Ralph Kiner in left, and then got Joost on a popup to first baseman Robinson to end the threat.

In the home second, a walk to the Giants' Willard Marshall, a single by Kazak, and a pitch that hit Seminick loaded the bases with no outs and finished Parnell. Boudreau called on Tigers right-hander Virgil Trucks to pitch to Newcombe, an exceptionally good-hitting pitcher. Newcombe, a left-handed batter, drove a ball deep to left field that the overwhelmingly National League crowd thought for a moment might be the first All-Star grand slam. However, the ball got held up in the wind just enough to allow Williams, playing despite a fractured rib, to make an outstanding one-handed catch while crashing into the wall. The blow scored Marshall, but when Reese followed by grounding into a 4-6-3 double play, the NL was forced to settle for just the one run.

"Boy, I thought I had that one," Newcombe said. "I never hit a ball any harder, and I'd caught Williams over in left-center. But he got it. ... It was the biggest day of my life, and I sure wanted to win."[1]

Williams, in turn, paid tribute to the Dodgers pitcher. "Newcombe is as fast as anybody in

Considered one of the best defensive shortstops of his era, Hall of Famer and 10-time All-Star Pee Wee Reese was the quiet yet forceful captain of the postwar Dodgers. (Photo: SABR-Rucker Archive)

our league," he said. "His fast ball was hopping," nodded DiMaggio in agreement.[5]

Another double play prevented the NL from a possible big inning in the third, although the two runs they did push across put them ahead, 5-4. Jackie Robinson, on his way to a batting championship and a Most Valuable Player Award, opened the inning with a walk. He went to third on Musial's single and scored the tying run as Kiner bounced into a double play. However, the Nationals weren't through. Mize singled to right and moved to second on a walk to Marshall. Brooklyn's Gil Hodges ran for Mize and scored when Kazak followed with a single.[6]

When the National Leaguers took the field in the top of the fourth, Hodges was at first base while Campanella had replaced Seminick behind the plate. The new NL configuration had five of the hometown Dodgers in the field, three of whom were Black, including an all-Black battery.

After Newcombe began the inning by getting Boston's Dom DiMaggio to ground out to third baseman Sid Gordon of the Giants, Kell singled and Williams walked. Newcombe got the big second out by again getting Joe DiMaggio, who also grounded out to Gordon, but he couldn't get by Joost. The 11-year veteran, playing in his first All-Star Game, hit a twisting grounder off the end of his bat between first baseman Hodges and second baseman Robinson. Hodges made a barehanded attempt to grab it, but the ball bounced off his hand and into right field as Kell and Williams raced home.

"I hit the ball on the end of the bat," Joost said. "Just call it a well-placed single."[7] The fluke hit put the AL back ahead, 6-5, and would serve to make Newcombe the losing pitcher and Trucks the winner.

George Munger of the Cardinals worked a scoreless fifth, but in the sixth the Americans scored two more off Boston's Vern Bickford to stretch their lead to 8-5. Again the Nationals

came back, scoring two in the home half to once more make it a one-run game. The AL's runs came on Joe DiMaggio's double that scored brother Dom and the Browns' Bob Dillinger, running for Kell. DiMaggio, with three RBIs for the day, left for pinch-runner Doby, making the Cleveland outfielder the first Black to play for the American League in All-Star competition.

Because an injured heel had sidelined him for the first 65 games of the season, DiMaggio's name had not been on the AL ballot. Nevertheless, he'd batted .350 since returning to the Yankees lineup, and Boudreau had named him to start in place of his teammate Tommy Henrich. Unlike 1947 and 1948, the first two years of fan balloting, the outfielders were chosen as a group rather than by individual position. Henrich had finished second behind Williams, but had missed the last week with a knee injury, and though he was on the bench and in uniform, he was unavailable to play.

After an 11-minute rain delay in the home sixth, Kiner blasted a two-run homer off A's left-hander Lou Brissie, who had replaced Trucks in the fourth. They would be the NL's final runs as any hopes for a National League victory ended with the new pitchers chosen to work the seventh inning. For while the Americans jumped on Howie Pollet for a quick three runs, Raschi would hold the Nationals scoreless the rest of the way.

Cleveland's Joe Gordon greeted Pollet with a double, and singles by Dom DiMaggio and Dillinger plus a double by Indians outfielder Dale Mitchell netted three more runs and made the score 11-7. Cincinnati's Ewell Blackwell and Brooklyn's Preacher Roe were the sixth and seventh National League pitchers used. Blackwell set the Americans down in order in the eighth, and Roe did the same in the ninth. Unfortunately for the NL, those fine performances came too late.

Although Raschi, a 13-game winner at the break, was far from invincible – the Nationals had runners on in each of the final three innings – he duplicated his three scoreless innings of the previous year. Two men were on via walks in the seventh, but neither Reese nor Robinson could deliver them. Nor could the Nationals take advantage of Musial's leadoff walk in the eighth or Pafko's two-out single in the ninth. Pafko had taken second when Mitchell mishandled the ball, the AL's only error of the day, but Reese made the final out.[8]

The game, less than crisply played, lasted 3 hours and 4 minutes, the first All-Star Game to exceed the three-hour mark. Records were also set for the most pitchers used by one team (seven by the NL) and by both teams (11), and for the most players used by both teams (42).

DiMaggio's hitting stood out, particularly his double in the sixth, said winning manager Boudreau. "Those were two big runs," Boudreau said, "but the break of the game came in the fourth on Joost's hit. Jackie Robinson didn't think it was a well-played game and he was sorry the NL lost, he said. "But I certainly got a great thrill out of being in it."[9]

Southworth was proud of the pitching job turned in by Newcombe and Blackwell. He'd been criticized for both selections: Newcombe because of his lack of experience, and Blackwell because his sore arm had limited him to just one victory in the season's first half. Critics had claimed that either Robin Roberts or Ken Heintzelman of the Phillies or the Reds' Ken Raffensberger would have been the better choices.

With its 11-7 victory, the American League reached its high-water mark in All-Star competition. The win, the American League's fourth in a row and seventh in the last eight, gave it an overwhelming 12-4 lead in the series. Counting their shutout in 1946, the Nationals had scored a total of just three runs in the last three games.[10]

SOURCES

In addition to the sources cited in the Notes, the author used Baseball-Reference.com, Retrosheet.org, and SABR.org.

This article is adapted from the author's 1949 chapter in David Vincent, Lyle Spatz, and David Smith, *The Midsummer Classic: The Complete History of Baseball's All-Star Game* (Lincoln: University of Nebraska Press, 2001).

NOTES

1 Fifty thousand fans were expected, but rain limited the crowd to 33,694.

2 The official scorers charged Mize with the error, later decided the error should go to Kazak, and several days afterward changed it back to Mize. Sportswriter Roscoe McGowen, the chief scorer, said that the three-man scoring panel had determined that Kazak's throw was not in the dirt and that Mize should have handled it.

3 N.L. Looks to Southworth as Savior in All-Star Game," *Chicago Tribune*, July 10, 1949.

4 Tommy Holmes, "Dodgers Lack Luster in Latest N.L. Fiasco, *Brooklyn Eagle*, July 13, 1949.

5 Harold Burr, "Nat'l Loop Says It with Dodgers," *Brooklyn Eagle*, July 13, 1949.

6 Hodges had finished third in the voting for first basemen, behind Mize and Philadelphia's Eddie Waitkus, but Waitkus had been incapacitated since suffering a gunshot wound on June 15. Waitkus was listed as an honorary member of the team, but for the first time since 1933, neither side had to replace anyone because of last-minute injuries.

7 "Joost's End-of-Bat Hit Big One – Lou," *Washington Post*, July 13, 1949.

8 It was an awful day for Reese. In addition to his costly error, the popular Dodgers captain went hitless in five at-bats.

9 Roscoe McGowen, "Newcombe and Blackwell Silence Critics of National Hurling Staff," *New York Times*, July 13, 1949.

10 The NL scored one run in a 2-1 loss in 1947 and two runs in a 5-2 loss in 1948.

MUSIAL HITS FOR CYCLE
TO LEAD CARDINALS ROUT

July 24, 1949

St. Louis Cardinals 14, Brooklyn Dodgers 1

by Mike Huber

By the middle of June 1949, the National League pennant race came down to two teams, the St. Louis Cardinals and the Brooklyn Dodgers. From that point on, those two battled for the top spot.[1] On July 22, the first-place Dodgers hosted a four-game series against the Cardinals. This wound up a 21-game road trip for St. Louis, who managed to lose half a game in the standings over the first 17 contests. Burt Shotton's Dodgers were completing a 15-game homestand and entered the series with a 2½-game edge over the Cardinals.

The second-place visitors won the first two games of the series, as the Cardinals "had outplayed and outgamed the beloved Bums."[2] Suddenly, Brooklyn held the slimmest of leads, a mere half game, in the senior circuit. A crowd of 34,042 fans turned out to root for the Dodgers on a hot Sunday afternoon, and, according to the *St. Louis Star and Times*, "The place had a World Series game air."[3] This was the fourth largest crowd of the season for the Flatbush faithful (and the first sellout Sunday crowd[4]), but many did not stay to see the final out, as the Cardinals won handily,

14-1. Six-time All-Star and reigning National League Most Valuable Player Stan Musial led all batters by hitting for the cycle.[5]

Howie Pollet, St. Louis' 12-game winner, faced off against Don Newcombe, who was in search of his eighth victory for Brooklyn. Newcombe was forced to wait another day for that win. In fact, he threw only 12 pitches before being lifted for reliever Paul Minner in the top of the first inning. Red Schoendienst and Lou Klein started the game for St. Louis with back-to-back singles. With runners at the corners, Newcombe uncorked a wild pitch, allowing Schoendienst to score. That brought Musial to the plate. He entered the game in a mini-slump, having gone just 8-for-35 (.229) in his last eight games. Musial swung at an offering from Newcombe and smacked a triple to deep center. Klein scored and Newcombe hit the showers. Shotton brought in left-hander Minner to face the Cardinals' cleanup hitter, Enos Slaughter. Slaughter greeted him with an RBI-single and Ron Northey followed with a double to left. Five batters had five hits and St. Louis had an early four-run lead.

Two innings later, the Cardinals sent eleven batters to the plate. Minner only faced the first three. Slaughter doubled, Northey singled, and Rocky Nelson tripled on a line drive to right. The second St. Louis triple of the game brought in the second reliever for the Dodgers, Carl Erskine. The Cardinals put up five more hits, including a single by Musial. With the score 8-0 and runners on first and second, Musial sent a ground ball to right field. Carl Furillo fielded the ball and threw home to catcher Bruce Edwards, whose error then allowed two runners to score, making it a 10-0 ballgame. The Cardinals put together six singles, a double and a triple in the outburst.

The Dodgers had a chance in the first inning to score, putting two runners aboard, but Pollet worked his way out of the jam. In the bottom of the third, however, Pee Wee Reese and Billy Cox hit singles, and after Furillo hit into a double play, Jackie Robinson grounded a single through the infield to left field to plate Reese. That was the lone run Pollet allowed.

In the top of the fifth with two outs, Musial sent a 3-1 Erskine pitch out of the park for a solo home run. The blast "was a perhaps 440-foot smash that cleared the high center field wall toward right, bounding into Bedford [A]ve. and caroming off an automobile agency sign with a bang."[6] Two innings later, he completed the cycle with a double to left-center field, driving in Pollet and Klein. Musial then scored the fourteenth run of the game for St. Louis on a Chuck Diering single.

In his final plate appearance in the top of the ninth inning, "those patrons who remained gave Stan a mighty cheer as he came to bat."[7] With two outs, Musial drew a walk and was stranded when Slaughter grounded to first unassisted. Musial's line for the day was four hits and a walk in five at-bats (he had flied out to the gap in right-center in the second inning), three runs scored and four driven in, although he also accounted for two unearned runs in the third inning. Slaughter added three hits for the Cards, who amassed 16 safeties in the game. Catcher Joe Garagiola was the only starting player for St. Louis without a hit in the game.

Musial became the 10th St. Louis Cardinals batter to hit for the cycle. It had been nine years since Johnny Mize cycled (July 13, 1940) and it took another 11 years before Bill White accomplished this rare feat (August 14, 1960).[8]

Reese and Robinson were the offensive standouts for Brooklyn, each with a 2-for-4 performance, and they are the two players who figured in the Dodgers' lone tally. Erskine pitched seven innings for Brooklyn. He faced 34 batters and allowed seven runs (six earned) on eight hits and four walks. The Cardinals' Pollet, on the other hand, pitched superbly, scattering eight hits in a complete game. In "notching his thirteenth victory of the campaign, [he] never had to fret. Handed four runs before a Cardinal had been retired in the first, the stylish southpaw was able to coast."[9]

In the locker room, Musial remarked, "It's about time I had a good day."[10] In this game alone, Musial used all of Ebbets Field to spray four hits in collecting the hits necessary for the cycle.[11] He raised his batting average to .299 and upped his slugging percentage 22 points, to .523. The next day, Musial went 3-for-4, a home run shy of the cycle, and his batting average rose to .304. He had broken out of the slump; in fact, his average never dipped below .300 for the rest of the season, finishing at .339.

In the four-game series with the Dodgers, Musial had 15 at-bats and connected nine times for hits, including two doubles, two triples, and two home runs. In the nine games played at Ebbets Field to this point in the season, Musial was batting .559 (19 for 34). For the season, Musial hit better against the Dodgers than any other team, going 37-for-90 (.411), with an incredible .523 in 12 games at Ebbets Field.

The Cardinals' victory extended their winning streak to five games (it soon reached nine – with two ties – before a 4-2 loss to Brooklyn in St. Louis). The *Brooklyn Daily Eagle* told its readers that "Musial and the rest of the maddened marauders from across the Mississippi knocked the Dodgers out of first place by making it three in a row over the stumbling Flock."[12] The victory with Musial's cycle put them a half-game ahead of the Dodgers in the National League pennant race. As Musial also told reporters about the St. Louis success, "Cream always comes to the top."[13] However, when the 1949 season ended, the Bums (97-57) finished one game ahead of the Redbirds (96-58), earning the chance to face the New York Yankees.

SOURCES

In addition to the sources mentioned in the Notes, the author consulted Baseball-Reference.com, MLB.com, and Retrosheet.org.

baseball-reference.com/boxes/BRO/BRO194907240.shtml

retrosheet.org/boxesetc/1949/B07240BRO1949.htm

NOTES

1 The Boston Braves held first place in the NL until June 4, but by June 15, the Braves had fallen to third place and finished the 1949 campaign in fourth.

2 "Musial, Pollet Mop Up On Dodgers, 14-1," *St. Louis Star and Times*, July 25, 1949: 16.

3 *St. Louis Star and Times*.

4 *St. Louis Star and Times*.

5 Musial had played in the All-Star Game every year from 1943 to 1949 (except 1945, when he did not play baseball due to military service). He won the NL's Most Valuable Player Award in 1943, 1946 and 1948. Musial also placed second in the MVP voting four times, including three years in a row from 1949-1951.

6 *St. Louis Star and Times*.

7 *St. Louis Star and Times*.

8 As of 2020, there have been 19 cycles in St. Louis Cardinals franchise history, by 17 different players. Tip O'Neill hit for the cycle twice in an eight-day span in 1887, and Ken Boyer also hit for the cycle twice (in 1961 and 1964).

9 Louis Effrat, "Redbirds Defeat Brooklyn by 14-1," *New York Times*, July 25, 1949.

10 *St. Louis Star and Times*.

11 The photograph is an Associated Press Wirephoto, found in both the *St. Louis Star and Times* and the *St. Louis Post-Dispatch*.

12 Harold C. Burr, "Missouri Murder, Inc., Pushes Cards Into First," *Brooklyn Daily Eagle*, July 25, 1949: 13.

13 "Blasting in Best Bat Circles Again," *The Sporting News*, August 3, 1949: 1.

MIZE'S FIRST WORLD SERIES
WAS ALL RIGHT

October 7, 1949

New York Yankees 4, Brooklyn Dodgers 3 | Game Three of the World Series

by Ken Carrano

As pennant races go, the 1949 races in both the American and National Leagues were among the closest in history. In the American League, the New York Yankees trailed the Boston Red Sox by one game with two to play (in Yankee Stadium) and won them both to win the AL title. In the National League, the Brooklyn Dodgers trailed the St. Louis Cardinals by one game on September 28. The next day the Cardinals lost and the Dodgers won a pair. Brooklyn had a half-game lead and hung on to win the pennant by one game.[1]

The first two games of the World Series had been exciting only among those who enjoyed pitchers' duels. The Yankees, hosts of the first two games, won Game One 1-0 with a Tommy Henrich walk-off home run off Don Newcombe. The next day, the Dodgers reversed that score and tied the series behind Preacher Roe. Dodgers fans started lining up for the 2,700 bleacher seats available for Game Three at Ebbets Field hours before Game Two started. A 17-year-old, Matty Segall of Brooklyn, started the line at the Bedford Avenue bleacher gate at 9:00 A.M. on Thursday for the Friday afternoon affair. Abe Stark, he of the famous "Hit Sign, Win Suit" sign at Ebbets, passed out doughnuts to those in line.[2]

Yankees manager Casey Stengel named Tommy Byrne to start the pivotal Game Three. Byrne had been fighting a sore shoulder toward the end of the season but told Stengel he was ready.[3] Byrne had led the American League in fewest hits per nine innings (5.7) and most strikeouts per nine innings (5.9), but also became the fifth AL pitcher since 1901 to walk more than 175 batters in a season.[4] Dodgers manager Burt Shotton chose Ralph Branca over Rex Barney to start Game Three, but was especially confident in his hitters. "I figured we would take care of things in our own orchard. We'll start hitting now and we'll be rougher," Shotton said.[5]

It is impossible to have fewer runs scored in the first two games than this World Series had, surprising for both teams. (Brooklyn led the NL in runs scored, the Yankees were second in the AL.)[6] But both teams were second in their league in fewest runs allowed, and another low-scoring game was a possibility.

Ebbets Field during the 1949 World Series facing the New York Yankees, en route to their first of five straight titles for manager Casey Stengel. Late-season acquisition Johnny Mize runs to first base after stroking a pinch-hit two-run single in the ninth inning of Game Three. (Photo: SABR-Rucker Archive)

Both pitchers had one-two-three first and second innings. The Yankees' Cliff Mapes led off the top of the third inning with a walk. After Jerry Coleman struck out, Byrne got the game's first hit, a single, moving Mapes to third. After Phil Rizzuto's attempt at a squeeze bunt drifted foul, he lifted a fly ball to right field and Mapes scored. Byrne was perfect in the third, but Pee Wee Reese homered to lead off the Dodgers' fourth inning, and the game and Series were tied again.

After Reese's homer, Byrne retired Eddie Miksis, but Carl Furillo singled. To this point, Byrne had been able to keep his wildness in check, but the law of averages kicked in for a man who averaged 0.91 walks per inning in 1949. Byrne

walked Jackie Robinson and Gil Hodges to load the bases, whereupon Stengel called on the best relief pitcher of 1949, Joe Page.[7] Page had led the league with 60 appearances, and had gone 6⅔ innings on October 1, helping the Yankees save their season, and was tasked to go the rest of the way on this day. Page escaped the inning by getting Luis Olmo to foul out and Duke Snider to ground out.

While Byrne found an early shower, the veteran Branca had found the groove that Preacher Roe was in the day before. After allowing a two-out double to Gene Woodling in the fourth inning, Branca retired 12 straight batters from the fifth through the eighth. Page was almost as effective during this stretch, allowing only a walk to Jackie Robinson in the sixth inning and a walk to Reese and single by Miksis in the eighth. He escape the eighth by getting fly outs from Furillo and Robinson.

Branca's mastery extended to the first batter in the ninth but it took a spectacular play by Robinson to get the first out. Yogi Berra had missed Game Two after aggravating a left thumb injury in Game One, but now he coaxed a walk out of Branca. Branca was laboring now too, and after getting Joe DiMaggio to pop out, Bobby Brown singled and Woodling walked to load the bases. Johnny Mize, purchased by the Yankees from the Giants earlier in the year for $40,000, had "an abnormal ability to respond to the most urgent demands."[8] He also owned a lifetime .349 batting average with five home runs off Branca from his days with the Giants. Stengel's decision to have Mize bat for Mapes brought out the hecklers from the Dodgers dugout. "Hey John, Leo's watching you" was the chant from the Dodgers bench.[9] "I could hear them, too," Mize said, "especially that Gene Hermanski. He's got a foghorn in his throat."[10] Leo Durocher watched as Mize clobbered a 2-and-1 pitch against the screen in right field, scoring Berra and Brown. Before facing Mize, Shotton had sent out coach Clyde Sukeforth to talk to Branca. In the dressing room after the game, Reese was asked what Sukeforth had told Branca. "I didn't hear," Reese replied, "but whatever he told him was wrong."[11] One batter too late, Shotton replaced Branca with Jack Banta, who gave up a run-scoring single to Jerry Coleman, giving the Yankees a 4-1 advantage.

Page now needed three outs to give the Yankees a 2-1 Series lead, but he was tiring too.

Olmo and Roy Campanella hit solo home runs to bring the Dodgers within one run with two out, but Page struck out pinch-hitter Bruce Edwards to secure the victory. Shotton was philosophical after the game. "When they get men on bases and then hit it up against the fence, there's gotta be runs," he observed. He consoled Branca, saying, "Ralph Branca got the ball where he wanted it and still Mize hit it. If you had to throw that ball 40 times it would still be right there. Only trouble is, he hit it."[12]

Stengel insisted that he planned to leave Mize in even if Shotton had changed pitchers. "Mize came in at just the right time," said Stengel. "Shotton had Joe Hatten warming up. That's why I waited to see if he were going to change before I took out Mapes. But Mize has been hitting left handers and right handers for years. I wouldn't have changed again. He's like DiMaggio and Henrich and Berra. They hit all kinds of pitching."[13] After the game, Mize said, "This World Series stuff is all right."[14] In his first World Series in 11 major-league seasons (along with three years of military service during World War II), Mize got used to that "all right" feeling as the Yankees won Games Four and Five to win the 1949 Series, and was a big part of the Yankees' run of five straight titles.

SOURCES

In addition to the sources listed in the Notes, the author accessed Retrosheet.org and Baseball-Reference.com, as well as the following:

Anderson, Dave. *Pennant Races – Baseball at Its Best* (New York: Galahad Books, 1994.)

NOTES

1. The only time up to this point that pennant races had been closer was in 1908, when the Chicago Cubs won the title by one game over the New York Giants and Pittsburgh Pirates, and the Detroit Tigers won the pennant by a half-game over the Cleveland Naps.

2. Richard J. Roth, "'Faithful' Pass Loyalty Test in All-Night Vigil," *Brooklyn Daily Eagle,* October 7, 1949: 1.

3. Tommy Holmes, "It'll Be Branca or Barney – Yanks Pick Byrne – And Experts Hear the Bats Booming," *Brooklyn Daily Eagle,* October 7, 1949: 5.

4. Other pitchers who walked 175 or more in a season were Bob Feller (1938, 1941), Bobo Newsom (1938), Bob Harmon (1911), Nolan Ryan (1974, 1976, 1977), Bob Turley (1954, 1955), and Sam Jones (1955).

5. Holmes.

6. The only other World Series to have two 1-0 games was the 1966 Series between the Baltimore Orioles and Los Angeles Dodgers, when the Orioles won Games Three and Four in their Series sweep.

7. The save became an official statistic in 1969 and has been calculated retroactively. Page's 27 saves in 1949 were more than that every other major-league team, and nearly 11 percent of all saves in 1949.

8. Jerry Grillo, SABR BioProject, https://sabr.org/bioproj/person/a7ac6649.

9. The reference was to Leo Durocher, Mize's manager with the Giants.

10. "'Leo's Watching,' Brooks Chant Before Mize Hits," *New York Times,* October 8, 1949: 17.

11. Gene Kessler, "Numbers Game for Mize," *Chicago Sun-Times,* October 8, 1949: 34.

12. Ted Smits (Associated Press), "Burt Shotton Philosophical," *Portland Oregonian,* October 8, 1949: 13.

13. "Mize Proud as Rookie of His Role in Series," *Chicago Tribune,* October 8, 1949: 20.

14. "Mize Proud as Rookie of His Role in Series."

ONE HIGHLY PRODUCTIVE INNING NOT ENOUGH FOR THE BUMS

October 8, 1949

New York Yankees 6, Brooklyn Dodgers 4 | Game Four of the World Series

by John Bauer

They lined up. In the small hours after the New York Yankees won Game Three of the 1949 World Series with a three-run outburst in the top of the ninth that broke a 1-1 tie, the Brooklyn faithful lined up. Solo shots by Luis Olmo and Roy Campanella in the Dodgers half of the ninth made it close, but their efforts only narrowed the loss to 4-3. There were 1,000 fans by 3:00 A.M. for a game that would determine whether the Brooklyn Dodgers would even the 1949 World Series with the New York Yankees or leave the Dodgers on the brink of elimination. With only 2,700 bleacher seats available for the game, the line grew to 3,000 by 7:00 A.M.[1] Brooklyn was turning out to see its Bums. Would the support be enough?

After the Game Three victory, Yankees manager Casey Stengel immediately named Eddie Lopat as his choice to pitch Game Four. Dodgers manager Burt Shotton would wait. His pitching staff appeared surprisingly depleted. Preacher Roe had injured his finger knocking down a line drive in Game Two, and Shotton's choices appeared to be the middling Rex Barney or Joe Hatten. Perhaps

Game One starter Don Newcombe might be able to pitch. Newcombe struck out 11 Yankees in the Series opener, and the only run allowed was a ninth-inning home run by Tommy Henrich that broke (and ended) a scoreless tie. Shotton wanted to see if his young emerging ace would be ready to pitch with two days' rest. Stengel recognized the opportunity of beating Newcombe with Roe likely out for the Series. Stengel said, "If we can beat Newcombe, their best pitcher, we'll be in a pretty good position, don't you think?"[2] Indeed, Shotton handed the ball to Newcombe with the Series likely on the line. Could the fans in the packed Ebbets Field be a difference-maker?

In the top of the first, the Yankees appeared to have kept their bats warm from their late-inning rally in Game Three. Phil Rizzuto and Henrich opened with singles into the Brooklyn outfield. Runners positioned at the corners, Yogi Berra slapped the ball to Eddie Miksis. The third baseman collected the ball and threw to Campanella for a play at home. The Dodgers catcher never tagged Rizzuto, who was called out by umpire Lou Jorda for running outside of the basepath. Meanwhile, Henrich had rounded second, observing the action involving Rizzuto. Henrich mistook Jorda's raised arm for a timeout, and Campanella alertly fired the ball to Jackie Robinson to tag Henrich for the second out.[3] Berra, whose ball started the mayhem, held first base. Newcombe issued consecutive walks to Joe DiMaggio and Bobby Brown to load the bases. With Newcombe's control teetering, Duke Snider claimed Gene Woodling's drive to center field for the third out.

Pee Wee Reese opened the home half of the inning with a double to left-center, but three consecutive groundouts stranded him at second base. Lopat and Newcombe kept the opposition from reaching base in the second and third innings before the Yankees claimed the advantage in the fourth. DiMaggio had struggled offensively during the Series, likely the result of a recent illness,[4] and brought a Series batting average of .091 into Game Four. While he connected with enough power to drive Newcombe's pitch into deep left, Olmo made the catch in front of the advertising on the outfield wall. Brown smacked a double to center ahead of a Woodling walk, setting up Cliff Mapes to break the deadlock. Mapes hit a high fly toward the left-field corner; unlike DiMaggio's ball, Olmo could not gather this one. Mapes's ball landed for a double that scored Brown and Woodling for a 2-0 Yankees lead. Olmo caught Jerry Coleman's fly ball in foul territory before Lopat found the gap between Olmo and Snider for a run-scoring double. Down 3-0, Shotton sent Newcombe to an early shower, calling upon Hatten in relief. Rizzuto singled to left, and third-base coach Frank Crosetti waved his pitcher home. Lopat, however, "was running out of gas as he rounded third and his motor died on his way home."[5] Olmo's throw home accounted for the third out.

Despite being winded to end the top of the fourth, Lopat made quick work of the Dodgers in the bottom of the inning. He allowed only a two-out

walk to Robinson before the Yankees padded their lead in the fifth. Hatten issued a leadoff walk to Henrich, then Berra's belter got past Hodges and into right field. Gene Hermanski was playing right field after Carl Furillo injured his right groin on a throw in Game Three.[6] Although Henrich made no move toward third,[7] Hermanski fired the ball to Miksis. The third baseman muffed the catch, which allowed Henrich to claim third base after all. Hatten loaded the bases by intentionally walking DiMaggio. Brown slammed Hatten's pitch off the right-field wall for a bases-clearing triple. The Yankees proved unable to add to their 6-0 lead despite Brown's presence on third with none out. Fly outs by Woodling and Hank Bauer, the latter replacing Mapes in the lineup, and a ground out by Coleman closed the visitors' fifth.

Brooklyn's bats came alive in the bottom of the sixth. Reese led off with a short fly toward center field. DiMaggio lost his footing on the play, allowing the ball to drop for a single. Shotton selected Billy Cox to pinch-hit for Miksis. Cox topped a grounder back to Lopat, which resulted in a single as the pitcher could not make the play. Snider's grounder to Rizzuto started a double-play that left Reese at third. Snider struggled at the plate during the Series, finishing 3-for-21 with eight strikeouts. In response to a question about whether he should have pinch-hit for Snider at this point in the game, Shotton replied, "I have nobody who is a better hitter than Snider."[8] During the regular season, that may have been true.

It was now Robinson's turn at the plate. Rumors about Robinson's future were the subject of press reports on the day of the game, saying he was apparently headed to the Boston Braves for $250,000 in the offseason. Dodgers co-owner John L. Smith dismissed the report about Robinson as "a piece of flubdub."[9] Smith added, "I think it was an especially bad thing to have been started right now when Robinson and the rest of the Dodgers are fighting to win the World Series."[10]

Robinson smacked Lopat's pitch to left field, scoring Reese for the first Brooklyn run. Robinson's hit was the catalyst for a singles parade that would bring the Dodgers back into the game. Hodges singled to center, advancing Robinson to third. Olmo also singled to center, a play that scored Robinson. 6-2, Yankees. Campanella smacked another single, this one to left, scoring Hodges. Hermanski then slapped the ball to Bauer, his right-field counterpart, which plated Olmo and reduced the deficit to 6-4. Hermanski's base hit, the Dodgers' seventh of the inning, tied a World Series record for the most singles in an inning.

Through the Dodgers rally, Stengel believed Lopat would find the elusive third out. The Yankees skipper stated, "[T]hose things were just ground balls with eyes that were drifting through the infield and I kept feeling that he'd get out of the inning."[11] Although he wanted to hold Allie Reynolds in reserve for Game Five, Stengel brought him to shut down the Brooklyn surge. A "flipping called third strike"[12] on Spider Jorgensen ended the inning. Jorgensen complained later, "I thought it was high and a ball."[13]

For the seventh, Shotton handed the ball to right-hander Jack Banta, who won 10 games for Brooklyn and enjoyed a run of eight straight starts over the final month of the season. Entrusted with keeping the Yankees off the scoreboard so the Dodgers could rally, Banta induced ground-balls from DiMaggio, Brown and Woodling, all of them fielded by Robinson, for an easy three-up, three-down inning before the stretch. Reynolds and Banta traded zeros through the game's final innings. The Dodgers' sixth-inning rally proved fleeting, as Reynolds kept the Dodgers off the bases for game's final three innings. The Dodgers could not muster enough action even to add tension or otherwise excite the sellout crowd in the home ninth. Campanella led off with a grounder to Brown for the first out, and Reynolds struck out Hermanski and Dick Whitman to end the game. Tommy Holmes characterized the game for his *Brooklyn Eagle* readers: "The fourth game produced one highly productive inning and eight disappointing ones for the Dodgers and their constituents."[14]

Shotton faced criticism after the game for his choice of Newcombe, a 17-game winner who pitched an almost flawless Game One, over Barney or Hatten, both of whom had ERAs more than a run greater than Newcombe's. It seemed as if Newcombe's difficulties overshadowed the work of Lopat and Reynolds through eight of nine innings to quiet the Dodgers offense. After the Series, Stengel emerged as a defender of Shotton's Game Four selection. "Pitching Newcombe on Saturday was the proper move. Just as my starting [Vic] Raschi again [in Game Five], with only two days' rest, was the right thing to do."[15] Unlike Shotton, though, Stengel would get the result he wanted in making such a pitching move. Twenty-four hours after this game, New York would complete a sweep of games at Ebbets Field to claim the 1949 World Series.

SOURCES

In addition to the sources cited in the Notes, the author consulted Baseball-Reference.com and Retrosheet.org.

NOTES

1   Tom Schroth, "Fans Keep Vigil in Fog Outside Ebbets Field," *Brooklyn Eagle*, October 8, 1949: 1.

2   Arthur Daley, "Sports of the Times," *New York Times*, October 9, 1949: 5, 2.

3   Harold C. Burr, "Dodgers Bow, 6-4, Must Win Today to Remain in Series," *Brooklyn Eagle*, October 9, 1949: 1.

4   John Drebinger, "Yanks Defeat Dodgers, 6-4, For 3-1 World Series Lead," *New York Times*, October 9, 1949: 5, 1.

5   Burr: 26.

6   Roscoe McGowen, "Dodgers' Clubhouse Picture of Frustration After Third Loss to Yankees," *New York Times*, October 9, 1949: 5, 3.

7   Drebinger.

8   McGowen.

9   Daniel, "Rumored Sale of Jackie to Braves Just 'Flub-dub,'" *The Sporting News*, October 19, 1949: 25.

10   "Sale of Robinson Denied," *New York Times*, October 8, 1949: 17.

11   Holmes, "Three Straight Is All Dodgers Need," *Brooklyn Eagle*, October 9, 1949: 26.

12   Burr: 26.

13   "Shotton Shuns Row Over 'Turning Point,'" *Brooklyn Eagle*, October 9, 1949: 26.

14   Holmes.

15   "Stengel Defends Shotton, Calls Newcombe Right Pick," *The Sporting News*, October 26, 1949: 6.

"DUMBFOUNDED THAT THEY WON IT SO EASILY"

October 9, 1949

New York Yankees 10, Brooklyn Dodgers 6 | Game Five of the World Series

by Eric Enders

As Dodgers fans streamed through Ebbets Field's turnstiles on October 9, 1949, their mood matched the day's weather: warm and sunny. "You could not have a finer day for a baseball game," broadcaster Red Barber said as World Series Game Five began.[1] Brooklynites were optimistic that their team of young sluggers, led by Jackie Robinson, could rebound from the 3-games-to-1 deficit it faced in the fall classic. But almost immediately, the Yankees stormed to a 5-0 lead that effectively ended the game and the season. "A dramatic World Series, which had moved along with the ponderous and measured pace of a Greek tragedy, wound up at Ebbets Field yesterday like a slap-stick comedy," Arthur Daley quipped in the *New York Times*.[2]

The Dodgers' problems began with the controversial decision to start Rex Barney, a wild 24-year-old fireballer, instead of staff ace Preacher Roe, who had twirled a six-hit shutout in Game Two four days earlier. Barney hadn't pitched since the regular-season finale seven days earlier, when he was shelled by the Phillies. According to Barber, Barney hadn't thrown so much as a warm-up

pitch during the interim. "Manager [Burt] Shotton … had a little talk with Preacher Roe," Barber said on the air before the game, "and Roe said no, he didn't think he had enough rest. Roe, during the regular season, never pitched with less than five days' rest, sometimes seven.[3] He's quite slender of physique and quite frail."[4]

Before the game Ebbets Field was its usual festive self, with organist Gladys Gooding singing the national anthem while accompanying herself on her instrument. The Dodger Sym-Phony Band also showed off its famously dubious musicianship, much to the crowd's delight.[5] "To say Ebbets Field was crowded would indeed be putting it mildly," the *Brooklyn Daily Eagle* noted. "They were standing three-deep all around the lower stands, with all runways and aisles of both tiers, offering any form of vantage point, thoroughly occupied."[6]

The Yankees got off to a quick start in the first inning thanks to a botched play by Brooklyn. Trying to field Barney's wild pickoff throw, shortstop Pee Wee Reese collided with umpire Art Passarella, with the ball glancing off Reese's glove into center field. Joe DiMaggio then clobbered a long drive that Duke Snider snagged with a spectacular leaping catch, crashing into the center-field wall at the 399-foot marker. DiMaggio's long fly, followed by a Bobby Brown single up the middle, gave the Yankees a 2-0 lead before the Dodgers even came to bat.

Brooklyn's undoing came early – in the top of the third. Barney began the frame promisingly, retiring Yogi Berra and DiMaggio before his command unraveled completely. "Barney walked everybody in the ball park with the exception of Gov. Thomas E. Dewey," the *Eagle's* Harold Burr snarked.[7] After issuing his fifth and sixth walks of the game, Barney gave up a sharp two-run single to Jerry Coleman, then he was mercifully removed. New York led 5-0 by the time the dust settled, and although the game still had 6½ innings to go, the outcome was never in doubt from then on.

A nice moment for Yankees fans came in the fourth, when DiMaggio batted for the third time. On each of his previous two trips, he'd been robbed in spectacular fashion by Duke Snider – a leaping catch at the wall in the first, and a sprawling grab of a sinking liner in the third. For the Yankee Clipper, it had been a forgettable game, a forgettable World Series (he was 1-for-16 so far), and a forgettable 1949 season. He'd missed the first half of the year with bone spurs in his heel, and as October approached, he contracted a mysterious wasting illness that caused him to lose 18 pounds.[8] Many speculated that his retirement was imminent. "He hung on through the series when he hardly had the strength to get the bat around," the *Eagle* noted. "The question now is whether Joe can come back. The Clipper has been coming apart at the seams too often of late."[9]

DiMaggio had looked better on this day, albeit making two loud outs. Now, on his third try, he launched a blast so far that even Snider couldn't catch it, sending the ball deep into the left-field stands for his first homer since September 10.

The round-tripper provided the weary DiMaggio with some much-needed catharsis. "No home run I've ever hit has given me more satisfaction," he said afterward.[10]

That made the score 6-1, and the game became a laugher in the sixth, when New York plated four more runs to lead 10-1. The Dodgers made a cursory comeback attempt in the seventh, when Gil Hodges launched a three-run homer off tiring Yankees starter Vic Raschi – but the rally was quelled when New York summoned ace reliever Joe Page, who recorded the final seven outs with little difficulty. The performance gave Page nine innings pitched against Brooklyn with only two earned runs, and he was widely hailed as the hero of the Series – though Allie Reynolds pitched much better.

Before the Yankees were crowned champions, there was one more historic moment in store. It had been an unusually long game, and the sky was starting to darken by the top of the ninth. Commissioner Happy Chandler summoned umpires Cal Hubbard and Beans Reardon (who was working the final game of his career) and ordered them to have the ballpark's lights turned on. For the first time in history, a World Series game was played under electric lights. (The first *scheduled* night game in a World Series wouldn't take place until 22 years later, in 1971.) "But the additional illumination, which cast an eerie light in the autumn dusk, was scarcely needed to reveal the disparity between the two teams," John Drebinger remarked in the *New York Times*.[11]

After Hodges struck out to end the game, the Yankees commenced their celebration in the cramped visitors' clubhouse. Players whooped, hollered, and shotgunned beer. DiMaggio embraced his 8-year-old son, Joe Jr. And Charlie Keller, the veteran slugger who'd played the final game of his Yankee career a week earlier before missing the entire Series with a back injury, simply sat quietly in a corner and munched on a sandwich.[12]

Much of the credit for the victory was heaped on New York's new manager, Casey Stengel – a surprise hire before the season started – who had never won more than 77 games in nine previous major-league seasons. The *New York Times* described Stengel, 60, as a "wit and philosopher and regarded by many up to this year as mostly clown."[13] Now he became the toast of the Big Apple for winning a championship with what one writer called "a misfit club… a never-say-die bunch of guys who made up in spirit and aggressiveness what they lacked in talent."[14] It took some chutzpah to describe the Yankees, of all teams, as scrappy underdogs, but that was how the press framed the story. Even Shotton, Brooklyn's manager, agreed. "Not even The Lord could have gotten more out of the Yankees than Casey Stengel," he said.[15]

Dodgers fans, meanwhile, licked their wounds, waited for next year, and complained bitterly that Shotton had left Rex Barney in the game too long. Brooklyn's players appeared shell-shocked. "They really knocked us down and stepped on us," Jackie Robinson admitted. "I still don't see how a team like ours could have been licked by a team like that."[16] Echoed infielder Spider Jorgensen: "I thought we were going to bowl over the Yankees, but we didn't hit. … Rather than being disappointed that the Yankees won the Series, I was dumbfounded that they had won it so easily."[17]

SOURCES

In addition to the sources cited in the Notes, the author accessed Retrosheet.org, Baseball-Reference.com, and SABR.org.

NOTES

1   Red Barber, Radio Broadcast of 1949 World Series Game 5. Published on YouTube channel "Classic Baseball on the Radio," https://youtu.be/JHCQ6Ol09UQ.

2   Arthur Daley, "Champions of the World," *New York Times*, October 10, 1949: 28.

3   While the gist of Barber's statement is accurate, Roe in 1949 actually did start five games on three days' rest or less.

4   Red Barber, Radio Broadcast of 1949 World Series Game 5.

5   Red Barber, Radio Broadcast of 1949 World Series Game 5.

6   Bert Hochman, "That Old Bromide's Here Again as Flock Gets 6 to Yankees' 10," *Brooklyn Daily Eagle*, October 10, 1949: 3.

7   Harold C. Burr, "Shotton Admits Yanks Are Better Club," *Brooklyn Daily Eagle*, October 10, 1949: 11.

8   John Drebinger, "Yanks Win Series, Beating Dodgers in Fifth Game, 10-6," *New York Times*, October, 10, 1949: 27.

9   "DiMaggio Calls Homer in Finale His Best," *Brooklyn Daily Eagle*, October 10, 1949: 12.

10 "DiMaggio Calls Homer in Finale His Best."

11 Drebinger.

12 James P. Dawson, "Victorious Yanks Overwhelmed by Joyous Fans in Riotous Clubhouse Scene," *New York Times*, October 10, 1949: 27.

13 Drebinger.

14 Leo H. Peterson, "Stengel Man of Hour in Yankee Conquest," *Brooklyn Daily Eagle*, October 10, 1949: 11.

15 Burr.

16 Roscoe McGowen, "Shotton Looks Ahead to Next Year and Series Triumph for Dodgers," *New York Times*, October 10, 1949: 28.

17 Danny Peary, *We Played the Game* (New York: Hyperion, 1994), 110.

Rough inning for Cardinals third baseman leads to improbable Dodgers comeback

May 18, 1950
Brooklyn Dodgers 9, St. Louis Cardinals 8

by Brian M. Frank

St. Louis third baseman Tommy Glaviano was having a solid start to the 1950 baseball season. Slotted in as the Cardinals' leadoff hitter, he was hitting .342 with an on-base percentage of .464. He'd made four errors in his 20 games at the hot corner, but no one could have foreseen the disastrous defensive inning that was about to befall him to help finish off one of the biggest comebacks in Brooklyn Dodgers history.

The Cardinals were looking to avoid being swept by Brooklyn, after well-pitched games by Preacher Roe and Don Newcombe led the Dodgers to victories in the first two games of the three-game series. What was about to transpire in the third game, is what Harold Burr of the *Brooklyn Daily Eagle* called "one of those games that might well be the making of one team and the ruination of the other."[1]

A pair of veteran southpaws battled in the series finale, as Brooklyn sent Joe Hatten, 1-2 with a 4.33 ERA, to the mound to face Howie Pollet, 3-3 with a 2.17 ERA, on a chilly, overcast 52-degree day at Ebbets Field.

Events did not go Hatten's way to start the game. Chuck Diering reached on an error by Dodgers third baseman Billy Cox with one out in the top of the first. He advanced to third when red-hot Stan Musial, who entered the game hitting .451, banged one off first baseman Gil Hodges' knee and into the grandstand for a ground-rule double. After Johnny Lindell was intentionally walked and Enos Slaughter popped out, Marty Marion singled Diering and Musial home to give St. Louis a 2-0 lead.

The Cardinals continued to chip away at Hatten as the game progressed. St. Louis scored another run on Diering's RBI double in the second inning. Hatten was fortunate to escape further damage when Slaughter lined out to left field with the bases loaded to end the frame. The Cardinals put together another rally in the fourth inning. Tommy Glaviano led off the inning with a home run. After the Redbirds put runners at first and third, Dodgers manager Burt Shotton pulled Hatten from the game and replaced him with right-hander Erv Palica. The first batter Palica faced, Marty Marion, hit a groundball that looked as though it would be the third out of the inning, but it got through Gil Hodges at first and two runs crossed the plate to put the Cardinals comfortably in front, 6-0.

St. Louis continued the onslaught in the sixth inning when Johnny Lindell blasted a two-run home run off Billy Loes, a 19-year-old reliever making his major-league debut. It was Lindell's first hit as a Cardinal after he had been purchased from the Yankees. The two-run shot gave the Cardinals a seemingly insurmountable 8-0 lead.

Meanwhile, Howie Pollet was making short work of the Dodgers. Through six innings, he'd allowed only two hits and three walks. However, in the seventh he began to show signs of tiring when he gave up singles to Duke Snider and Roy Campanella to start the inning. He was able to retire the next three batters and escape the inning without a Dodger crossing the plate. After seven innings, the Cardinals led 8-0, and as Dick Young wrote in the *New York Daily News*, "[T]he Brooks had nicked Howie Pollet for only four hits. They had looked more miserable than the weather. They hadn't hit, their pitching had been punk, and even their defense, which has been Brooklyn's matchless pride, had been butchered."[2]

The gloomy atmosphere for the Dodgers and their fans was amplified as rain started falling on Ebbets Field to start the eighth inning. Jim Russell led off the eighth with what looked to be a harmless single into left field. Jackie Robinson drilled a double to right and Carl Furillo sent a ball through the raindrops and into the left-field seats to cut the Cardinals' lead to 8-3. The Dodgers faithful rejoiced, as "the 17,579 fans, including Ladies Day guests and Knothole Kids started a mad clamor on a rising crescendo as the runs went clattering impossibly over the dish."[3] Hodges lined out to center field for the first out of the inning. Duke Snider singled and Campanella followed by drilling a ball that was caught by left fielder Lindell. Bruce Edwards, pinch-hitting in the pitcher's spot, lined a single to left and when

the ball was bobbled by Lindell, Snider raced to third. That was the end of the line for Pollet. Dick Young wrote, "Seven straight line drives flew off the Brooks bats. Rarely in his life has Pollet been hit so hard."[4]

The Cardinals' bullpen was shorthanded – as Ted Wilks was out with an elbow injury – so manager Eddie Dyer turned to Gerry Staley, who had a 5.35 ERA in seven games, to try to end the Dodgers' offensive outburst. Pee Wee Reese greeted the new hurler by rapping the ball through the left side of the infield, bringing home Snider and cutting the Cardinals' lead to 8-4. But with runners at first and second, Staley was able to avoid further damage by getting pinch-hitter Gene Hermanski to pop out for the final out of the inning.

Ralph Branca came out of the Dodgers bullpen in place of Rex Barney who'd thrown a shutout eighth, and retired the Cardinals in order in the ninth to keep the deficit at four runs heading into Brooklyn's final at-bat.

Rain was falling steadily as Jim Russell collected his third hit of the afternoon, a double into the right-field corner, to lead off the bottom of the ninth. Jackie Robinson cashed in Russell with another double into the right-field corner to cut the Cardinals lead to 8-5 and cause Dyer to pull Staley in favor of southpaw Al Brazle. Brazle retired Furillo on a popup for the inning's first out. Hodges then hit a bouncer to short and beat Marion's throw to first. Snider, after being behind 1-and-2 in the count, worked a walk to load the bases, and then catastrophe struck the Cardinals, specifically third baseman Tommy Glaviano.

Harold Burr wrote: "Fate decreed that the last three Dodgers should make (Glaviano) their target. It was raining steadily and hard, the ground under his spikes treacherous and the ball slippery, by way of excuse."[5] Roy Campanella stepped up to the plate representing the winning run. He hit a sharp ground ball to Glaviano, who fielded the ball cleanly and fired a wild throw to second base, forcing Red Schoendienst to come off the bag, and all hands were safe as Robinson scored to cut the lead to 8-6. Cloyd Boyer was brought in to replace Brazle and try to finish the game for St. Louis. He seemed to do his job when he induced pinch-hitter Eddie Miksis to hit a "high bouncer right at Glaviano."[6] Rather than throwing to second for what looked like "a certain force out at second and a probable double play," Glaviano fired home to try to force Hodges.[7] But the throw was once again well wide of the mark and catcher Del Rice had to "dive flat on his face for the save" as Hodges crossed the plate.[8]

Pee Wee Reese came up with the tying run at third and Campanella representing the winning run at second. Reese became the third consecutive batter to hit a grounder to Glaviano. Dick Young wrote: "This time, Tommy didn't throw wild. He didn't throw at all, because he never held the ball. He had planned to scoop it up, step on third, and fire to first – but in moving toward third, he let the ball zip through his legs and into left."[9] Ebbets Field erupted as the tying and winning runs crossed the plate. Roscoe McGowen reported in the *New York Times*, "The downpour of torn papers that fluttered down on the field when Campanella raced over the plate with that all-important run turned the drizzle into a snow storm."[10]

The improbable had happened as three straight balls hit to Glaviano ended up as errors, tying a major-league record for errors in a single inning.[11] Cardinals manager Eddie Dyer summed up his team's mood, saying: "That was the most bitter defeat of any I've had in the years I've managed."[12]

Brooklyn had managed only two hits through six innings, and trailed 8-0 through seven, but rallied for nine runs in the final two frames for an improbable victory. An afternoon that began slowly for the Dodgers suddenly changed in the eighth inning and ended with "a deluge of rain, runs, hits, and errors."[13]

SOURCES

In addition to the sources cited in the Notes, the author consulted Baseball-Reference.com and Retrosheet.org.

NOTES

1   Harold C. Burr, "Glaviano Becomes Brooklyn's Man of the Week with 3 Bobbles," *Brooklyn Daily Eagle*, May 19, 1950: 19.

2   Dick Young, "Dodgers Overhaul Cards, 9-8, on 3 Glaviano Errors in 9th," *New York Daily News*, May 19, 1950: C20.

3   Burr.

4   Young.

5   Burr.

6   Young.

7   Bob Broeg, "Glaviano Goat of a Black Day," *St. Louis Post-Dispatch*, May 19, 1950: 10C.

8   Young.

9   Young.

10 Roscoe McGowen, "Dodgers Score 9 Runs in Last 2 Innings to Upset Cards," *New York Times*, May 19, 1950: 33.

11 McGowen.

12 Broeg: 8C.

13 Burr.

A "WEIRD AFFAIR" AND SLUGFEST IN FLATBUSH

June 24, 1950

Brooklyn Dodgers 21, Pittsburgh Pirates 12

by Glen Sparks

The Dodgers and Pirates broke off what *New York Daily News* sportswriter Dick Young called their "weird affair"[1] at just before midnight on June 24, 1950. Brooklyn led, 19-12. A report from the Associated Press boasted, "The crowd of 22,010 was treated to one of the wildest games in Ebbets Field history."[2] And it wasn't over.

Umpires suspended the action with one out in the bottom of the eighth inning. According to the New York state Sunday baseball law, play could not continue – no matter how exciting – after 11:59 P.M. Saturday. When the game picked up on August 1, Brooklyn hitters ripped a few more line drives. One of baseball's brawniest teams won, 21-12. The Dodgers collected 25 hits, including eight for extra bases. Jackie Robinson, Carl Furillo, and Roy Campanella knocked four hits apiece.

The three-game series began on June 23. Brooklyn scored eight times in the seventh inning and won, 15-3. Duke Snider drove home four runs and led a 19-hit attack. Furillo smacked a home run "into the center-field bleachers – that used to be more or less unprofaned ground."[3]

Brooklyn upped its record to 34-22 and led the pennant chase by one game over the Phillies. Pittsburgh dropped to 21-38 and looked up from seventh place, 14½ games from the top.

Young gave Brooklyn batters only so much credit. He wrote that "the Pirate pitching may have had some small part in the one-sidedness of the tilt. Buc bowlers make the good old American game look like cricket, inasmuch as a team may remain at bat against them all night."[4]

Harold C. Burr from the *Brooklyn Eagle* noted that one "sarcastic" fan yelled "Fore!" after Furillo's long blast. That fan, according to Burr, "has been rooting for the return of the old-fashioned pitchers' battle for years." Were the baseballs of 1950 livelier than ones from past seasons? According to Burr, "The manufacturers claim that their baseballs are turned out on the same old machines and that perhaps some of 'em are wound tighter than others." Also, of note, Burr wrote, "Baseball is a perverse game where a famine follows hard after a feast. It's just possible the Flock would like to recall some of those 15 runs tonight."[5]

In the second game, the Dodgers' 24-year-old right-hander Ralph Branca faced 28-year-old lefty Cliff Chambers. Both pitchers took early showers. Pittsburgh scored four runs in the opening frame. Branca, already a three-time All-Star, began by walking Stan Rojek and Ted Beard. Ralph Kiner singled to load the bases. Pittsburgh went ahead, 1-0, when Gus Bell grounded out and Rojek raced home. Danny Murtaugh popped out, and first baseman Dale Coogan ripped a pitch deep into the right-field stands. Coogan, playing his first and only big-league season, never hit another home run.

Branca's day ended after catcher Earl Turner homered to start the second inning. His replacement, the often wild-armed right-hander Rex Barney, retired Pittsburgh in order.

Brooklyn scored its first run in the second inning. Furillo led off with a line-drive single to center field, advanced to second on a Campanella base hit, and made it to third after Pee Wee Reese's grounder forced Campanella at second. Barney drew a walk, which loaded the bases. Chambers also walked Billy Cox, bringing Furillo home.

Dodgers hitters knocked out Chambers in the third. Furillo lined a two-run double that scored Snider and Robinson after both players singled. Gil Hodges, the next batter, doubled Furillo home. Chambers gave way to Murry Dickson, a reliever known as "Tom Edison Jr." "because," according to his SABR biography, "he was always experimenting on the mound."[6]

Dickson, though, could not figure out a way to put down the Brooklyn rally. Campanella greeted him with an RBI single. Reese followed by knocking a base hit into right field. After Barney struck out, Cox singled to fill the bases once again. Pirates manager Billy Meyer pulled Dickson for Mel Queen. Snider greeted the new pitcher with a two-run double, making the score 8-5.

Strong hitting – weak pitching? – kept this game suspenseful. Barney, in the last year of a once-promising career, battled his control once again and walked Turner to lead off the fourth. He got Johnny Hopp, pinch-hitting for Queen, to ground into a double play but issued free passes to Rojek and Beard. Kiner stepped to the plate. The Pirates outfielder had slammed a career-high 54 home runs in 1949 and led the NL in homers for a fourth straight season. Against Barney, Kiner hit his 16th round-tripper of 1950 "into the upper deck in deepest left center,"[7] tying the game, 8-8.

Enter a new reliever for the Pirates, Frank Papish. The left-hander appeared in just four games in 1950 and just once after this contest. With one out, Hodges, the big first baseman and former Marine, blasted a solo home run, one of his 32 round-trippers in 1950.

Brooklyn manager Burt Shotton called on Dan Bankhead in the fifth. Baseball's first African American pitcher, a former member of the Birmingham Black Barons and Memphis Red Sox, Bankhead found himself in quick trouble. The right-hander gave up a two-run double to Nanny Fernandez, along with the lead. Pittsburgh took a 10-9 advantage.

Bankhead began the sixth by walking Beard and Kiner. Dodgers pitchers had now given up 10 bases on balls. Shotton, surely tiring of the gifts, asked Preacher Roe, usually a starter, to end this rally. Wally Westlake, though, greeted Roe with a run-scoring double. Two batters later, Coogan added a run-scoring fly ball. The Pirates now led 12-9. It wasn't enough.

The Dodgers pushed across five runs in the sixth. Bill Werle gave up all of them. Robinson and Furillo singled to open the frame. After Hodges flied out, Campanella and Reese followed with RBI hits. Preacher Roe, a woeful hitter, "laid down a poor bunt to the left of the mound."[8] Werle grabbed the ball and that's when, Young wrote, "the screwiness started."[9] Werle threw wildly to third base while trying to force out Campanella, and the ball sailed into left field. The Brooklyn catcher and Reese easily scored. Kiner

Acquired from the Pittsburgh Pirates after the 1947 season, Preacher Roe went 90-33 over a six-year stretch with the Dodgers (1948-1953), including a 22-3 mark in 1951. (Photo: SABR-Rucker Archive)

threw to the plate, wildly like Werle did. Roe, rounding second, "was waved all the way home on a unique four-base bunt." The Dodgers moved ahead, 14-12.

Roe held the Bucs scoreless over his next two innings. In the bottom of the eighth, Brooklyn added seven more runs. Vic Lombardi, a 5-foot-7-inch left-hander, endured the agony. The former Dodger (1945-47) walked Reese and, after Roe grounded out, gave up a triple to Billy Cox. Jim Russell walked, and Snider singled to fill the bases.

Robinson, with three hits already, stepped to the plate. Exactly two years earlier, he hit a grand slam in the ninth inning to beat the Pirates at Ebbets Field, 6-2. On this day, he boasted a .358 batting average and a robust .447 on-base percentage. The first African American major leaguer of the twentieth century was the reigning National League Most Valuable Player. He topped the circuit in 1949 with a .342 batting average and 37 stolen bases. He also drove home 124 runs and scored 122. The former football and basketball star at UCLA and infielder for the Kansas City Monarchs slammed a pitch "deep into the left-field seats."[10] Pittsburgh sportswriter Charles J. Doyle called that blast "the most sensational moment of the battle."[11]

Furillo singled, and Hodges came to bat. That's when the clocked ticked to 11:59. Young, in his lead the following day, wrote, "Running out of time before the Bucs ran out of pitchers, Brooklyn last night scored 19 runs but still didn't have a victory, for sure." In the following paragraph, he added, "You can bet the 22,010 fans who sat through the dizzy doings will be talking about

it right up to the date of resumption."[12] Doyle called the game up to that point a "sensational affair."[13] Brief rain showers, one in the second inning and another in the third, had stopped the action, though just briefly. Those delays, Young estimated, "added up to only 19 minutes."[14]

By time play resumed, the Dodgers had slipped to fourth place with a 51-40 record. The Phillies, a team with talented young players like Robin Roberts and Richie Ashburn and labeled the Whiz Kids, had moved into first. The Pirates, meanwhile, had dropped into last place, with a 34-60 mark, 22½ games behind their cross-state rival.

More than one month after the game's opening pitch, Campanella drove a one-out double to right field that scored Furillo and Hodges. Reese and Roe grounded out to end the inning. Dick Young wrote, "Brooklyn batters, too accustomed to the extravagance of their own pitchers, weren't satisfied to coast on the seven-run bulge they enjoyed last night."[15] Even so, he added, "They needn't have bothered" to tack on those extra runs. "The game was in good hands, Preacher's left."[16] Roe quickly retired the Pirates in the top of the ninth. Thus ended what the *Pittsburgh Press* back in June, nearly echoing the words of Young, had called "a weird conflict."[17]

SOURCES

In addition to the sources cited in the Notes, the author accessed Retrosheet.org, Baseball-Reference.com, and SABR.org.

NOTES

1   Dick Young, "Dodgers Lead Bucs, 19-12; Suspend at Midnight," *New York Daily News*, June 25, 1950: 421.

2   Associated Press, "Dodgers Leads Bucs, 19-12, as Law Halts Tiff," *Rochester* (New York) *Democrat and Chronicle*, June 25, 1950: 60.

3   Harold C. Burr, "Dodgers Take Turns on Alternate Days of Going from Ridiculous to Sublime," *Brooklyn Eagle*, June 24, 1950: 6.

4   Young, "Dodgers Soak Pirates, 15-3, on 19 Hits, 3 HR," *New York Daily News*, June 24, 1950: 162

5   Burr.

6   Murry Dickson SABR bio, sabr.org/bioproj/person/1bb26f23.

7   Young, "Dodgers Lead Bucs, 19-12; Suspend at Midnight."

8   Young, "Dodgers Lead Bucs, 19-12; Suspend at Midnight."

9   Young, "Dodgers Lead Bucs, 19-12; Suspend at Midnight."

10   Charles J. Doyle, "Bucs Trail, 19-12, as Curfew Stops Game," *Pittsburgh Sun-Telegraph*, June 25, 1950: 31.

11   Doyle.

12   Young, "Dodgers Lead Bucs, 19-12; Suspend at Midnight."

13   Doyle.

14   Young, "Dodgers Lead Bucs, 19-12; Suspend at Midnight."

15   Young, "Flock Cops Buc Encore 21-12, Then Wins, 3-1," *New York Daily News*, August 2, 1950: 194.

16   Young, "Flock Cops Buc Encore 21-12, Then Wins, 3-1."

17   Les Biederman, "Curfew Halts Battle in the 8th Inning; Kiner Clouts No. 16," *Pittsburgh Press*, June 25, 1950: 39.

KINER SCORES 4, DRIVES IN 8, IN HITTING FOR CYCLE AGAINST THE DODGERS

June 25, 1950

Pittsburgh Pirates 16, Brooklyn Dodgers 11

by Mike Huber

"Pitching is called 70 per cent of baseball."[1] The Pittsburgh Pirates knocked 20 hits off 70 percent of the Brooklyn pitching staff, beating the Dodgers in an old-fashioned slugfest, 16-11, before 20,196 fans during a Sunday afternoon tilt at Ebbets Field. Ralph Kiner carried his team to victory, hitting for the and driving in eight runs. This was the final game of a three-game series. The Dodgers entered the game with a record of 34-22, while the Pirates started 14½ games behind Brooklyn, in seventh place at 21-38. In the loss, the "Brooks did some heavy hitting, too, but their efforts were dwarfed and their lead over the second-place Phils was cut to half a game."[2]

Pirates' rookie righty Vern Law started and faced Dodgers' 1949 National League Rookie of the Year Don Newcombe on the mound. From the outset, Newcombe, a 6-foot-4-inch right-hander, was not sharp, allowing a double to Stan Rojek to start the game. Ted Beard then walked, and Kiner followed with a home run, a line drive into the bleachers. Quickly, Newcombe and the Dodgers were down 3-0 before recording an out.

The Brooklyn squad responded quickly. With two outs in the bottom of the first, Duke Snider walked, Jackie Robinson singled, and Carl Furillo doubled both home.

In the Pirates' third, Kiner singled with two outs. Gus Bell also singled, and Danny Murtaugh plated two runs with a double to center. Given the circumstances, Dodgers manager Burt Shotton did not hesitate to use his bullpen, since he had used just one pitcher on Friday, though he followed that with four hurlers on Saturday against the Bucs. He made the call for Joe Hatten to relieve Newcombe, and the southpaw Hatten stemmed the tide, keeping the score at 5-2.

Brooklyn tied the game in the fifth as it appeared that Law had "tired in the terrific heat."[3] Pee Wee Reese bunted safely down the first-base line. George Shuba pinch-hit for Hatten and scorched a double to right, sending Reese to third. Billy Cox walked to load the bases, and Pittsburgh manager Billy Meyer called upon Cliff Chambers to end the threat. Lefty Chambers uncorked a wild pitch, bringing Reese home.

Fly balls by Jim Russell and Snider created two outs, but also brought in two runs, to tie the game, 5-5.

Ralph Branca became the third Dodgers pitcher at the start of the sixth inning. After retiring the Pirates in order, the right-handed veteran ran into trouble in the seventh, walking Rojek and Beard to start the inning. Kiner, who had struck out in the fifth, again came to bat with two runners aboard. He hit a double to center, earning two more RBIs, and Branca was done. Shotton replaced him with right-hander Al Epperly, who had last pitched in the major leagues in 1938.[4] Epperly didn't fare much better than his predecessors, yielding a run-producing double to Bell, walking Murtaugh, and serving up another RBI double to Dale Coogan. Bell scored, but Furillo fielded Coogan's safety and fired the ball to Robinson, whose relay cut down Murtaugh at the plate. Just like that, the Pirates had scored four more times and had a 9-5 advantage. The Dodgers did get back one run, when Snider tripled in the bottom of the seventh and scored on Furillo's fly, but Pittsburgh struck again in the eighth. Beard hit his third home run of the season, a two-run shot, after Rojek's leadoff single, to bump Pittsburgh to an 11-6 lead. Epperly had "an undistinguished Flatbush debut, yielding three runs, four hits, and two walks in one inning."[5] That brought Erv Palica into the game, and the right-hander had to face the hot-hitting Kiner. Pittsburgh's left fielder laced a triple to right, completing the cycle, but the inning ended with Kiner still standing on third.

Brooklyn did not give up. Reese doubled with one out in the bottom of the eighth. Tommy Brown pinch-hit for Palica and tripled to right, bringing in Reese. Cox's fly ball brought home Brown, and after eight innings, the Pirates' lead had been pared to 11-8.

Billy Loes entered the game in the top of the ninth as the sixth Dodgers hurler; however, Loes never recorded an out. Pete Castiglione singled to left and Ray Mueller bunted toward the mound and legged it out. Chambers loaded the bases with a single to left. Shotton had seen enough and motioned once again to his bullpen. After Rex Barney (another right-hander) entered, Rojek greeted him with a two-run single to center field, but Chambers was thrown out at third. Barney then walked Beard. Kiner entered the batter's box and sent a Barney offering into the lower left-field stands for a three-run home run, his second round-tripper of the game. As a result, the Pirates had added five more runs, making the tally 16-8.

Even with an eight-run lead in the ninth inning, Pittsburgh skipper Meyer made a pitching change. Chambers was touched for singles by Snider and Robinson, so Bill Macdonald came on in relief. He managed to get one out before Gil Hodges blasted a three-run home run, his eighth of the season, to make it 16-11. Roy Campanella flied out and Reese struck out to end the game.

For the game, Kiner was 5-for-6, with four runs scored and eight runs batted in. This was the only time in the 1950 season that Kiner had more than three hits in a game. His 14 total bases in a single game rank second on the Pirates' all-time list, behind only Willie Stargell, who had 15 against the Chicago Cubs on May 22, 1968. Kiner's average jumped 15 points to .287 with this feat. Earlier in the season, on May 9, Kiner had also hit two home runs in a contest against the Dodgers, and he had driven in seven runs in that game. Rojek was 4-for-5 with four runs scored, and he had led off in four innings, reaching base three times. Bell also was productive with a 3-for-5 day. The first four batters in Pittsburgh's lineup scored 14 of the Pirates' 16 runs.

In the offensive outburst, the Pirates "walloped three homers, five doubles, and a triple, while the Brooks made one round-tripper, four doubles, and two triples."[6] The three-game series between the Dodgers and the Pirates was, simply put, a display of power. Together, the Pirates and Dodgers scored 76 runs. Brooklyn scored 45 runs and had to settle for one victory, one suspended game, and one defeat. Tommy Holmes of the *Brooklyn Daily Eagle* wrote, "It's plain that right now all batters are stepping in swinging from the handle and batting with all kinds of confidence, while the pitchers, poor wretches, work like terrorized fatalists."[7] Brooklyn had defeated the Dodgers on Friday, June 23, 15-3. Saturday night's game was suspended, because of the 11:59 curfew, with Brooklyn leading 19-12 with one out in the bottom of the eighth inning, just after Jackie Robinson had hit a grand slam and Furillo had singled. It was completed on August 1 with new umpires; during the interval from game suspension to resumption, Coogan and Earl Turner had left the Pirates, so defensive substitutions had to be inserted (the Dodgers eventually won, 21-12).[8] Sunday's game was 16-11, in favor of the Pirates.

The two home runs gave Kiner 18 "official" round-trippers for the season. He had hit one the night before (also off Barney), but the home run did not count until the game was completed in August. Even so, with 18 homers and 54 RBIs, he was leading the National League in both categories.[9]

Kiner's cycle was the 16th to date in Pittsburgh franchise history. He also added a second home run to his cycle. It came a little over a year after Wally Westlake accomplished the feat for the second time and almost one year before Gus Bell. For four consecutive seasons, a member of the Pirates had hit for the cycle: Westlake (July 30, 1948, and June 14, 1949), Kiner (June 25, 1950), and Bell (June 4, 1951).

NOTES

1   Tommy Holmes, "Dodger Pitchers Battered as Slugfest Engagement With Pirates Comes to End," *Brooklyn Daily Eagle*, June 26, 1950: 11.

2   Louis Effrat, "Pirates Overpower Dodgers With 20 Blows; Reds Top Giants Twice," *New York Times*, June 26, 1950: 32.

3   Jack Hernon, "Kiner's Big Bat Subdues Bums, 16-11," *Pittsburgh Post-Gazette*, June 26, 1950: 16.

4   Al Epperly pitched nine games for the Chicago Cubs in 1938, with a record of 2-0, and he did not return to the big leagues until 1950, making his debut in this game. For the season, he pitched in five games (all in relief) and did not record a decision. His final major-league game was on July 7, 1950.

5   Effrat.

6   Effrat.

7   Holmes.

8   retrosheet.org/boxesetc/1950/B06240BRO1950.htm.

9   Kiner finished the 1950 season with 47 home runs, leading the National League for the fifth consecutive year. He continued to be the NL's home-run king through 1952, a string of seven straight seasons. His 118 RBIs in 1950 were 8 behind Philadelphia's Del Ennis.

GIL HODGES HITS FOUR HOME RUNS

August 31, 1950

Brooklyn Dodgers 19, Boston Braves 3

by Thomas J. Brown Jr.

Returning from a road trip on which they won 8 of 11 games, the Dodgers still trailed the league-leading Philadelphia Phillies by 6½ games. Back at Ebbets Field, they hoped to continue their solid playing and gain some ground on Philadelphia. If they could beat the Boston Braves, their first opponent, they could put some distance between themselves and the Braves, who were just 1½ games behind them.

Carl Erskine took the mound for the Dodgers. The right-hander had not pitched well early in the season. After being sent down to the Montreal Royals, he changed his arm motion and won 10 games before he was recalled in August. Erskine entered the game with a 1-3 record. He had struggled in his last outing, surrendering five earned runs in 3⅓ innings.

Erskine started out strong, striking out the first two Boston batters he faced and retiring the first five Boston hitters without allowing a ball out of the infield. But with two out in the second inning, the Braves' Sid Gordon hit a solo blast into the left-field bleachers for his 24th home run of the season. The *New York Times* called Gordon's

smash the "most lonesome home run" of the game in light of the barrage that followed over the next eight innings.[1]

Braves starter Warren Spahn had 16 wins and was 2-3 against the Dodgers so far in 1950. After an easy first inning, the left-hander was tagged for a leadoff single by Carl Furillo. The next batter was Gil Hodges, who sent a fastball into the left-field stands for a home run. Hodges' blast gave the Dodgers a 2-1 lead and they would not look back for the rest of the evening.

Spahn got Roy Campanella on a fly ball, but allowed singles to Billy Cox and Erskine. After Spahn struck out Tommy Brown, Pee Wee Reese doubled to bring Cox across the plate for the Dodgers' third run.

Spahn fared no better in the third. The first two Dodgers he faced singled and Braves manager Billy Southworth pulled his southpaw for Normie Roy. The first batter Roy faced was Hodges, who hit his first pitch, a curveball, into the left-field bleachers. After Roy surrendered hits to Campanella and Erskine, Southworth replaced him with Mickey Haefner.

240

Haefner walked Brown, loading the bases. Reese grounded into a force play at second, but when second baseman Roy Hartsfield, threw wild to first, two runs scored. Then Duke Snider hit his 24th home run of the season, bringing the Dodgers' total for the inning to seven runs. It was the fourth time in the season that the Dodgers had scored that many runs in one inning.2 The home run, Snider's only hit of the game, extended his hitting streak to 18 games.

The Dodgers struck again in the sixth. Bob Hall was now on the mound for the Braves, having replaced Haefner in the fifth. He walked Furillo to lead off the inning. Then Hodges hit a fastball over the left-field fence, his third round-tripper of the game.

Hall gave up three more singles before he could record the first out. One of the singles was by Erskine, his fourth of the game. With the bases loaded, Reese singled in another run and Snider's grounder plated one more. By the time Johnny Antonelli got Robinson to fly out for the third out, the Dodgers led 14-1.

Antonelli, the Braves' fifth pitcher, stayed on the mound for the rest of the game. He gave up three runs in the seventh. Hodges, hoping to hit a fourth home run, had to be content with an infield single. After the game, Hodges said, "I was really gunning for that fourth one. I knew it would tie the record. I got my chance in the seventh but I guess I was too anxious. I swung too soon on a change-of-pace and just beat out a slow roller for a single."3

Trailing 17-1, the Braves picked up two runs in the eighth. Earl Torgeson hit a one-out single off Erskine and Bob Elliott walked. Del Crandall's force-play grounder left runners at first and third. A single by Gordon sent Torgeson home and a double by Willard Marshall scored Crandall.

The Dodgers – and Hodges – responded immediately. With Bobby Morgan on base after a walk, Hodges strode to the plate for the sixth time. With the count 2-and-2, he hit one over 400

feet into the upper left-field stands. Later he said: "I knew it was going for a homer as soon as I hit it. It felt better than the first three and I figured it would be longer. It sure was a great feeling – and what a night to do it with my wife here watching!"4

Hodges' final home run gave him 23 for the season. Hodges set a major-league record for total bases (17) in a game.5

The final home run put Hodges in the record books as the fourth player to hit four home runs in a nine-inning game. Lou Gehrig was the last player to do it, on June 3, 1932. The other two players to achieve the feat were Bobby Lowe in 1894 and Ed Delahanty in 1896.6

When the press caught up with him in the locker room after the game, Hodges was asked about his accomplishment. "Did I think that I was going to hit the fourth one? I didn't think I'd even hit three, and when I did, I didn't figure to come up a sixth time."7

John Griffin, the Dodgers clubhouse custodian, presented Hodges with the ball that he hit for homer number four. "A boy from the Bronx who told me his name was O'Dell Johnson just brought it to the door," Griffin told Hodges. "He was sitting out in Section 33 and retrieved your fourth home run. He thought you might like it. I gave him two new baseballs in exchange." Hodges put the ball on the shelf in his locker and noted, "I'll find a spot for that."8

In the clubhouse after the game, Reese shouted to Hodges, "You know you keep all of us late with all of your monkey business?" His teammate Bruce Edwards also called out to the reporters crowded around Hodges, "What about that double I hit in the eighth? Doesn't anyone want to put my name in the paper? Boy, that ball was hit!"9

But this was Hodges' night. The 14,226 paying customers got their money's worth while the "thousands of Brooklynites who didn't venture out in the August heat regret it today. They missed one of the best one-man shows of the year."10

SOURCES

In addition to the sources cited in the Notes, I used the Baseball-Reference.com and Retrosheet.org websites for box-score, player, team, and season pages, pitching and batting game logs, and other material.

NOTES

1   Roscoe McGowen, "Brooklyn Slugger Ties Major Record," *New York Times*, September 1, 1950: 24.

2   Harold Burr, "Gil Only Living Player to Hit 4 Homers in Game," *Brooklyn Daily Eagle*, September 1, 1950: 16.

3   Norman Miller (United Press), "Hodges Joins 3 Greats With 4 Homers in Game," *Binghamton Press and Sun-Bulletin*, September 1, 1950: 23.

4   Miller.

5   Another Dodger – Shawn Green of the Los Angeles Dodgers – set the record at 19 total bases in 2002.

6   McGowen.

7   Burr.

8   Burr.

9   Burr.

10 Burr.

Tommy Brown's unlikely three homers

September 18, 1950
Chicago Cubs 9, Brooklyn Dodgers 7

by Richard Cuicchi

Tommy Brown first gained notoriety as a 16-year-old for the Brooklyn Dodgers in 1944. His unique opportunity to reach the big leagues at such a young age came about because most of baseball's regular players were serving in the military during World War II. He would be a part-time player during his entire nine-year major-league career that included only 31 home runs. Consequently, his improbable three-homer game on September 18, 1950, was one of the highlights of his career. Yet his feat that day was minimized by the Dodgers' frustration from extending their decline during a race for the pennant.

The way Brown initially got into Organized Baseball was also improbable. The teenager had quit school at a young age to work on the docks in New York City. At the urging of a friend, he attended a tryout with the Dodgers in 1943 without a glove and spikes. The 15-year-old was among a handful of players from a pool of 2,500 hopefuls who were called back by the Dodgers for a further look.[1] He signed a minor-league contract that took him to Class B Newport News for the 1944 season.

There, Brown hit .297 in 91 games and was called up to the Dodgers at the beginning of August. Leo Durocher was the manager of the Dodgers team, whose offense was credible but whose pitching was last in the league. With Pee Wee Reese still in the Navy, Durocher had tried several players at shortstop, including Bobby Bragan, Eddie Stanky, Bill Hart, and Gil English, but none of them had distinguished themselves.

Brown was thrown into the starting lineup right away, making his debut on August 3 and getting a double in four at-bats. He is still the youngest position player (16 years, 241 days) to debut in the majors.[2] The seventh-place Dodgers weren't going anywhere, so Durocher stuck with Brown as his everyday shortstop, even though he was erratic with his fielding (16 errors) and displayed a weak bat (.164) in 46 games.

Brown didn't want to stay with the Dodgers. He said, "I needed schooling and experience. I wanted desperately to go back to the minors. I wasn't ready." He appealed to Branch Rickey to be sent back down, but Rickey obliged him only after the regular players returned from the war.[3]

With Reese firmly entrenched at shortstop, Brown was moved to the outfield during the 1949 season. Manager Burt Shotton used him as one of several outfielders he shifted in and out of the lineup, practically using the left-field position in continuous platooning fashion. Duke Snider and Carl Furillo were everyday starters in the other two outfield positions.

Still only 22 years old in his sixth major-league season in 1950, Brown was referred to by the *Brooklyn Daily Eagle* as the "perpetual rookie,"[4] while the *New York Times* called him the "youngest 'veteran' in the big leagues."[5]

Brown had an odd practice of keeping track of the home runs he hit during batting practice. By his count, he had 170 for the season going into the game on September 18.[6] Yet he seemed to have trouble making contact during actual games, having hit only two home runs for the season. Prior to 1950, he had a total of seven in 650 plate appearances.

The Dodgers were one of the favorites to contend for the National League pennant in 1950 after having fielded one of the franchise's best teams ever when they won the pennant in 1949.

It appeared the Dodgers would fulfill the expectations when they held a slight lead in the standings as late as June 29. However, the surprising Philadelphia Phillies Whiz Kids overtook the Dodgers, and during the first two weeks of July, Brooklyn fell to fourth place behind St. Louis and Boston.

Going into the game on September 18, the Dodgers were in third place after a three-game losing streak and lagged the leading Phillies by 8½ games. Shotton had come under fire for the team's recent lackluster performance.

Before a paid attendance of 2,051, the Dodgers' smallest crowd of the season at that point, the Cubs' Randy Jackson led off the game with a home run against Preacher Roe, an 18-game winner at this point.[7]

Roe was not up to his usual form, and his troubles became more evident in the third inning when he walked three and gave up a single before Mickey Owen doubled in Hank Sauer and Roy Smalley. A third runner, Wayne Terwilliger, was called out at home on a throw from left fielder Brown.

Facing former Dodger Paul Minner in the bottom of the third, Brown hit a home run to left field with Roe on base. It was his third home run of the season, which equaled his career high.

Leading off the Dodgers' fifth with the team losing 3-2, Brown tied the game with his second home run, hit to left off Monk Dubiel, who had replaced Minner in the third.

In the Cubs' seventh, Roe allowed a leadoff double to Hal Jeffcoat, who was sacrificed to third by Preston Ward. After Hank Sauer walked, Andy Pafko singled to break the tie. A walk to Terwilliger loaded the bases, at which point Shotton summoned Dan Bankhead from the bullpen. In a game of chess, Cubs manager Frankie Frisch countered with pinch-hitter Ron Northey in place of Owen, and it paid off. Northey cleared the bases with his ninth homer of the season and the eighth grand slam of his career.

A seemingly comfortable 8-3 lead by the Cubs turned out not to be the case in the bottom of the eighth inning. With one out, Cal Abrams singled off Dubiel, and Brown followed with his third home run to left field. Then Reese singled and scored on Snider's single and a wild throw by third baseman Randy Jackson. With Dutch Leonard in the game relieving Dubiel, Hodges followed with another single that scored Snider. With the score 8-7 and the tying run on base with one out, Leonard retired the side without allowing another run.

The Cubs made it 9-7 in the ninth when Terwilliger hit a solo home run off Billy Loes. Leonard retired the Dodgers in order in the bottom of the ninth.

Despite the loss, Brown had the best performance of his career. He went 4-for-4 with a single and a walk besides his three homers. He drove in five runs. But his amazing outing was overshadowed by Northey's grand slam, and Dodgers pitchers gave up 12 hits and nine walks, including eight by Roe, who took his 11th loss of the season. Dubiel got credit for the win even though he gave up five earned runs in his five innings.

In a dejected clubhouse, Shotton said, "Perhaps there was some way to win a ballgame like that one. But if there was one, I don't know it."[8]

The Dodgers extended their losing streak to four games, putting them nine games behind the Phillies and 1½ games behind Boston. However, they rebounded to win 13 of their last 17 games of the season. With a chance to tie for the league lead in the last two games of the season against the Phillies, the Dodgers came up short by losing the final game in a classic matchup between 19-game winners Robin Roberts and Don Newcombe.

The Dodgers were able to get added power from Pafko in left field and finally gave up on Brown by trading him to the Phillies in June 1951. He also played two seasons with the Cubs in 1952 and 1953, then ironically spent six years in the minors before retiring at age 31 in 1959.

SOURCES

In addition to the sources cited in the Notes, the author consulted Baseball-Reference.com and the following:

"Northey's 4 Run Pinch Homer Helps Cubs Beat Dodgers, 9-7," *Chicago Tribune*, September 19, 1950: 3,1.

NOTES

1   C. Paul Rogers III, "Tommy Brown," SABR BioProject. sabr.org/bioproj/person/7913ae6c.

2   Joe Nuxhall, a pitcher with the Cincinnati Reds in 1944, was the youngest player (15 years, 316 days) in history.

3   Tim Pinacchio, "How It Was During the War Years," *Baseball Digest*, January 1977: 67.

4   Tommy Holmes, "Dodger Slide Dims Brown's 3 Homers," *Brooklyn Daily Eagle*, September 19, 1950: 13.

5   Roscoe McGowen, "Brooks Beaten by Chicagoans, 9-7, Despite Brown's 3 Homers, Single," *New York Times*, September 19, 1950.

6   "Flock Eyes Bucs for Victory Tonic," *Brooklyn Daily Eagle*, September 19, 1950: 13.

7   Roe finished the season 19-11.

8   Holmes.

Kiner's three dingers boost Pirates over the Dodgers

July 18, 1951

Pittsburgh Pirates 13, Brooklyn Dodgers 12

by Thomas Rathkamp

"I was gunning for it, all right," said Ralph Kiner, the Pittsburgh Pirates star left fielder. "I was sure gunning for that fourth home run in the ninth inning yesterday against the Dodgers … You don't get these chances too often."[1]

Although another home run would have nudged Kiner deeper into rare historic company, the three he walloped spearheaded the Pittsburgh Pirates to a 13-12 triumph over the Dodgers in front of 7,083 fans at Ebbets Field. It was the fourth triple-homer game of Kiner's career. A potential fourth homer nestled into Carl Furillo's glove near the stands in deep right-center in the ninth inning.[2]

As with most slugfests, this contest was wrought with blown leads, sloppy fielding, and (quite obviously), shoddy mound work. After the game, the losing pitcher, Erv Palica, was verbally dressed down by his manager, Charlie Dressen, and GM Buzzi Bavasi.

"He's finished," Dressen said. "Here's what's wrong with him." (Dressen clutched his own throat, signaling that Palica choked under pressure.)[3]

"I walked up to him in the clubhouse," declared Bavasi. "And I said – you haven't got a gut in your body. I was hoping he would punch me in the nose. But all he said was, 'I try to do good.'"[4]

Dressen, in his inaugural year as Brooklyn's manager, replaced Burt Shotton, who had apparently been relieved in part because he "bruised the feelings" of his pitchers. It would appear that Dressen wouldn't dare snarl at his hurlers; apparently he had not gotten the memo. Joe King wrote in *The Sporting News*, "Dressen couldn't be trusted doing the same this year. Has a manager ever before been yoked with such a galling handicap?"[5]

The terse rhetoric notwithstanding, Palica was hardly the lone goat on the mound, for either team. In the top of the first, Brooklyn starter Phil Haugstad surrendered Kiner's first blast, a towering grand slam that pushed the Pirates to a 4-0 early cushion, the 10th grand slam of his career. Singles by Pete Castiglione and George Metkovich and a walk coaxed by Gus Bell provided full sacks for Kiner.

Nine Pirates batted in the opening frame, and Haugstad's day finished quickly. (All six batters he faced reached base.) Reliever Dan Bankhead salvaged the inning by recording all three outs. Considerably more anonymous than teammate Jackie Robinson, Bankhead was the first African American pitcher in the major leagues. He and four brothers played in the Negro Leagues. The 1951 season was his last, after a career in the Negro Leagues, Puerto Rico, the Dominican Republic, Mexico, and Canada.[6]

In the bottom of the second, Pirates starter Murry Dickson gave back half the runs, yielding a Roy Campanella two-run homer. The fourth inning through the sixth furnished a staggering 17 combined runs. For the Pirates, Kiner, referred to as "Mr. Slug" by beat writer Jack Hernon, was far from finished. The league leader in home runs at the time was opponent Gil Hodges with 28. Hodges had wrestled the home-run lead from Kiner earlier in the season.

Ralph McPherran Kiner was born in Santa Rita, New Mexico, on October 27, 1922. His father died when he was 4. His mother, who served as a nurse in World War I, took a job in Alhambra, California, near Los Angeles. Growing up in a warmer climate afforded young Kiner ample opportunity to hone his baseball skills. In his rookie year with the Pirates, 1946, a Pittsburgh sportswriter described Kiner in this way: "Kiner can run like a deer, he can throw like a DiMaggio and when his bat clicks nothing but the fences will stop his line drives."[7] Although his throwing arm and speed were often questioned early in his career, few accounts doubted his hitting ability.

After a scoreless third, the Pirates exploded in the top of the fourth. Castiglione opened the inning with a strikeout, then Metkovich singled. Gus Bell's triple plated him. Kiner followed with his second clout of the day, this time into the upper left-field stands, and a 7-2 advantage. One out later, Joe Garagiola homered over the screen in right. The bottom of the order then joined the

fun. George Strickland singled and scored on Monty Basgall's triple.

"Ball players seldom aim deliberately for seats or the fence," said the red-hot Kiner. "We simply try to meet the ball squarely and hope it will carry."[8]

As insurmountable as a 10-2 lead seemed at the time, the combatants were hardly trending in the same direction in 1951. The Dodgers entered the game with a 53-31 mark; the Pirates were 33-50. One glance at the lineup cards might appear to render this an unfair fight – even though the Pirates had triumphed the day before, 4-3. Anchored by four future Hall of Famers, the band from Brooklyn battled back in the very next half-inning. Their efforts were supplemented by some paltry Pirates defense; the chief philanthropist was Pirates shortstop George Strickland, with two errors. (He finished 1951 with 37 errors.)

After Dickson fanned Hodges, Campanella reached when Strickland's throw sailed over Metkovich's glove at first. Don Thompson followed with a single off Metkovich's glove, sending Campanella to third. Billy Cox reached on Strickland's second miscue, a grounder that squirted through the shortstop's legs, preventing a double play.[9] Another Pirates mistake led to the next Dodgers run. With pinch-hitter Hank Edwards at the plate, Dickson balked, sending Thompson home free. Edwards doubled in Cox, then Furillo singled in Edwards. All four Dodgers runs were unearned, and sliced the Pirates' lead in half.

With the Dodgers' starting pitcher recording no outs and their relievers getting knocked around just as badly, the chance of winning this game was predicated on their hurlers reversing course on their performance. The Pirates fifth began with a groundout, but Gus Bell belted a solo shot off Palica for an 11-6 Bucs advantage. The embattled Dodgers reliever retired Kiner and Bill Howerton to stop the bleeding.

The emerging slugfest took a respite in the next two half-innings. Then suddenly, the

Dodgers' bats awoke with a vengeance in the bottom of the sixth. Once again, the lowly Pirates aided the effort with sloppy play. Had the famous Dodgers fan Hilda Chester still been around, it was certain the players would have heard her cowbell, along with the loud shrieks emanating from her homemade noisemaker, a frying pan and a metal spoon.[10]

Dickson walked the first two Dodgers batters in the sixth, Don Thompson and Billy Cox. Palica reached base after Dickson flubbed a sacrifice bunt. The Dodgers knocked Dickson out of the contest after Carl Furillo doubled home Thompson, Cox, and Palica. Mel Queen replaced Dickson, retired Pee Wee Reese, then walked Duke Snider. Jackie Robinson then smashed a home run that gave the Dodgers a 12-11 lead. Queen stopped the scoring there, but a new game had emerged.

The final three frames were much less docile on offense. The ending defied all that had happened before. Kiner led off the eighth with his third home run, tying the score. Erv Dusak followed with a double to right. With two outs, former Dodger Pete Reiser coaxed a broken-bat single, scoring Dusak and giving Pittsburgh the lead for good.

"How about that, said an unidentified player. "Kiner hits three home runs but Pete wins the game with a broken-bat single."[11] Pirates reliever Ted Wilks held the Dodgers scoreless in the final two frames. Despite giving up nine walks, committing four errors, and blowing a 10-2 lead, the Pirates squeaked out a victory. Kiner's final blast was his eighth of the season against Brooklyn; none were as sweet as this game's wallops, which accounted for seven RBIs. A piece in the *Pittsburgh Press* said that the league leader in home runs, Gil Hodges, "must have been glad to see the Bucs go."[12]

"I gave it everything I had when I faced Erv Palica in the ninth (attempting a fourth homer)," said Kiner. "Usually you swing and hope. This time I swung, hoped, and prayed."[13]

SOURCES

In addition to the sources cited in the Notes, the author accessed Retrosheet.org, Baseball-Reference.com, SABR.org, and *The Sporting News* archive via Paper of Record.

NOTES

1   Ralph Kiner, "Kiner's Liners," *Pittsburgh Press*, July 19, 1951: 38.

2   Jack Hernon, "Kiner Smashes in 3, Drives in 7 as Bucks Trim Dodgers, 13-12," *Pittsburgh Post-Gazette*, July 19, 1951: 16.

3   United Press, "Dodgers Might Sell Palica for Choking Up on the Bucs," *Pittsburgh Press*, July 19, 1951: 38.

4   "Dodgers Might Sell Palica."

5   Joe King, "Shotton's Censure of Pitchers Led to Muffler on Dressen, but He Gets His Message Across," *The Sporting News*, July 25, 1951: 16.

6   Rory Costello, "Dan Bankhead," BioProject, Society for American Baseball Research, https://sabr.org/bioproj/person/62db6502.

7   Charles J. Doyle, "California Sun, Buc Pitching Turn Back Clock for Frisch," The Sporting News, February 28, 1946, 8, quoted in Kiner's SABR biography written by Warren Corbett. https://sabr.org/bioproj/person/ralph-kiner/.

8   Kiner.

9   Hernon.

10 Oscar Palacios, "Ebbets Field: Home of the Brooklyn Dodgers," *Ballpark Sourcebook: Diamond Diagrams*, 1988 Stats Inc., 98-99.

11 Hernon.

12 "Dodgers Might Sell Palica."

13 "Dodgers Might Sell Palica."

ROBINSON'S HEROICS HELP DODGERS PULL OUT TWO TENTH-INNING WALK-OFF WINS

August 22, 1951

Brooklyn Dodgers 4, St. Louis Cardinals 3 | 10 innings, Game One of Doubleheader
Brooklyn Dodgers 8, St. Louis Cardinals 7 | 10 innings, Game Two of Doubleheader

by Nathan Bierma

Jackie Robinson was in the heart of the prime of his career. His 1947 rookie season had marked his historic, arduous, and triumphant debut. The 1949 campaign, in which he batted a career-high .342, led the league in stolen bases with a career-high 37, and was named the MVP, stands out in retrospect. And yet, authorized biographer Arnold Rampersad wrote, Robinson "saw the 1951 season as his best yet in the majors."[1]

Even though Robinson would finish a distant sixth in MVP voting that season (with his teammate Roy Campanella winning the honor), the benefit of advanced statistics bears out his perception. Robinson's slash line of .342/.432/.528 and Wins Above Replacement (WAR) of 9.3 in 1949 are virtually identical to his 1951 output of .338/.429/.527 and WAR of 9.7. Beyond the individual stats, Robinson's bat delivered some of the biggest swings of the season, in some of the Dodgers' most desperate moments, to keep his team afloat in a surprisingly close pennant race.

In mid-August the Dodgers wrapped up a homestand at Ebbets Field as victors over Boston and the presumptive pennant winners over the rest of National League. Their lead over their rival Giants reached 13 games on the 11th and stood at 12½ games as they left town two days later.

"The bookies about town set the odds of a New York pennant at 100-1," wrote Joshua Prager. "The season was surely over."[2]

But then the Dodgers crossed boroughs to the Polo Grounds and were swept, and limped out of Boston after splitting a four-game series with the Braves. Just like that, as the Dodgers returned to Ebbets Field, their previously insurmountable lead was down to eight games.

If the Dodgers (74-41) could right the ship against any opponent, it might be the Cardinals (56-56), against whom they'd won their last 12 meetings. On the other hand, such a streak suggested that the Cardinals were overdue to give Brooklyn a battle. As it turned out, they gave them two.

The opening game of the teams' series on August 21 was rained out, setting up a doubleheader the next day. Game one that Wednesday afternoon pitted Cardinals rookie starter Tom Poholsky (4-10) against Preacher Roe, who was enjoying a career year, entering the game with a 16-2 record (en route to a career-high 22 wins). The Dodgers rattled Poholsky quickly. With two outs in the first and no one on, Duke Snider reached on an error and Robinson hit an infield single, claiming second and Snider snatching third after Poholsky's throwing error. It was up to Gil Hodges to deliver on the Dodgers' good fortune, and he hit a line drive to center field to score both runners and put the home team ahead 2-0.

Roe cruised through the early stanzas for Brooklyn and Poholsky settled in for St. Louis for a couple of quiet innings. Then St. Louis struck back in the top of the fourth. After Solly Hemus grounded out to Robinson, Red Schoendienst sent a single to center. Stan Musial strode to the plate and belted a two-run home run to tie the game.

Both teams' bats were quiet until the sixth inning, when the same Cardinals combination struck again. This time Schoendienst led off with a single to left, and Musial doubled him home, though he was thrown out trying to take third. The Cardinals led 3-2. "The Dodgers had a rough time of it beating ... the graceful Cardinal bats-man," the *Brooklyn Daily Eagle* wrote of Musial's day at the plate.[3]

The Dodgers couldn't return fire until the eighth inning. They pressured Poholsky with a leadoff single by Carl Furillo and a bunt single by Pee Wee Reese. After Snider lined out to left, Robinson came up and smacked a line drive to center to score Furillo and tie the game. Reese ended up at third and Robinson at second thanks to an errant throw from center field, but the Dodgers couldn't capitalize and regain the lead. Hodges was intentionally passed to set up a potential double play, and Roy Campanella obliged to end the inning.

Each team managed a walk but nothing else in the ninth, and the game went to extra innings. Taking the mound in the top of the 10th for his third inning of relief was Clyde King, a righty

riding high during a standout season. Originally pressed into service by the Dodgers at age 20 during World War II, King had struggled to keep a steady big-league job in Brooklyn ever since.[4] But now he was red-hot, already tallying a career high 12 wins and enjoying a streak of 11⅔ score-less innings.[5]

King extended his streak, setting down the top of the order with a groundout from Hemus, a line drive from Schoendienst that Furillo extinguished with a fine catch in right field, and a popup to short by Musial, to bring Brooklyn back to bat.[6]

With Poholsky still on the hill for the Cardinals, Furillo led off with a single and Reese sacrificed him to second. Snider, batting third in his second of seven straight All-Star seasons for the Dodgers, was intentionally walked with first base open, and Robinson was retired on a foul popup to the catcher. The batter was Hodges with two on and two outs. He struck a single to left field and Furillo scored from second to end the game. The Dodgers had won, 4-3.

* * *

The nightcap matched two starting pitchers, Gerry Staley (14-12) and Carl Erskine (14-8), with similar records at similar points in their careers; each was in the process of sealing a perennial place in their team's starting rotation; each man's recent 14th win was a career high. Erskine began with ease, making one hitless trip through the Cardinals lineup, before the Cardinals unleashed a rapid rally in the fourth inning to take command of the game. Hemus singled and, after Schoendienst flied out, Musial and Hal Rice walked to load the bases. Enos Slaughter hit a grounder to Reese at shortstop, but Reese erred on his throw to second, and both Hemus and Musial scored. The next batter, Nippy Jones, grounded one right back to Reese, who misplayed it again, and Rice came home to make it 3-0, Cardinals. Billy Johnson's single scored Slaughter and

Jackie Robinson debuted with the Dodgers at age 28 in 1947. Over the course of the next seven seasons, he was arguably the best player in baseball, batting .319 with a .414 on-base percentage. (Photo: SABR-Rucker Archive)

Del Rice's base hit brought home Jones. Erskine was charged with only one earned run because of the mess Reese had made, but with only one out in the fourth and the Dodgers in a gaping 5-0 hole, Dodgers manager Chuck Dressen relieved his starter, bringing in Bud Podbielan. The reliever retired the next two batters to get the Dodgers out of the inning.

Brooklyn put a dent in the St. Louis lead right away. After Snider and Robinson hit singles and Hodges was out on a fly ball to center field in the bottom of the fourth, Campanella and Pafko belted consecutive base hits, each scoring a runner, to make the score a more manageable 5-2.

The Cardinals instantly resumed their attack in the fifth. New Dodgers hurler Johnny Schmitz was greeted with leadoff triples off the bats of Schoendienst and Musial. The latter ran home on Hal Rice's fly ball, and the St. Louis lead was back to five runs, at 7-2.

Again, the Dodgers responded in the bottom half of the inning. After Reese and Snider walked and Dick Bokelmann relieved Staley, Robinson rapped his third straight hit of the game, a single to right that scored Reese and moved Snider to third base. A double-play ball by Hodges ended the inning, with the score 7-3.

Clem Labine was next out of the Brooklyn bullpen, and pitched around a leadoff walk in the top of the sixth inning. Andy Pafko took Bokelmann deep in the bottom of the inning to make it 7-4.

Following three volatile innings, Labine and Bokelmann both hurled two scoreless stanzas, until the Dodgers reached their point of desperation in the bottom of the ninth. Pinch-hitter Don Thompson led off with a hit and snatched second on a wild pitch to Furillo. After Furillo walked and Reese grounded out to second, a single by Snider scored Thompson and moved Furillo to third.

With runners at the corners, one away, and Bokelmann still on the hill for the visitors, up came Jackie Robinson, seeking his fourth hit of the night at the game's most crucial moment. To the exultation of the Ebbets Field faithful, he belted a double over the head of Slaughter in right field to score Furillo and bring the Dodgers within one, at 7-6. Hodges received another free pass to set up a force out, just as in the eighth inning of the first game, but this time Campanella launched a fly ball to center field. He was out, but Snider tagged up to complete the comeback and tie the game. When Cox grounded out to second, the game headed to extra innings for a second time that day.

Dressen brought back Clyde King, the winner of the opener after three scoreless innings of relief, to start the 10th inning for Brooklyn. King suffered only a two-out single by Slaughter before getting Jones to fly out to third. It gave Brooklyn a chance to close it out in the bottom of the 10th for the second time that day.

With the pitcher's spot due up to lead off the 10th, Dressen decided to let King bat. King didn't make contact, but he "cutely let himself get hit by a pitched ball," the *Brooklyn Daily Eagle* commented, to give the Dodgers a baserunner.[7]

Up next, Furillo was nearly the hero of the night, sending a fly ball soaring to deep right-center, but the wind held it up and Musial made the catch at the wall for the first out.[8]

But after that loud out, followed by a single by Reese, Bokelmann's day was done. "It would seem that acting manager Terry Moore kept ... Bokelmann ... in too long," commented the *Daily Eagle*. "But the Red Birds are up against a pitching shortage with three of their stars out of action."[9]

Reliever Al Brazle came in and struck out Snider. With two outs and his pitcher standing on second base, bound to either return to the mound or make it home, Jackie Robinson came to the plate. Robinson was 4-for-5 in the game and his clutch RBI double the previous inning was a big reason the game was still going. He took a ball and a strike from Brazle, then connected one more glorious time on a "slashing ... single down the left field line," as the *New York Times* described it.[10] King rounded third and came home amid a scene of jubilation. To the fans' delirious disbelief, the Dodgers had won it again on another 10th-inning two-out walk-off hit.

Robinson's clutch hits had batted Brooklyn to the doubleheader sweep, while King's pitching and improbable baserunning had earned him two wins for the day. "He bears the name today of young reliable in the hearts of a million Dodger fans," said the *Daily Eagle*.[11]

"The Dodgers looked like a great ball club again in sweeping the Cardinals aside twice to make it 14 in a row over the Missourians," the *Daily Eagle* commented. "They picked up half a length on the streaking Giants and now lead the New Yorkers by eight lengths," after "a long day and night of baseball."[12]

The *Times* agreed the Dodgers had regained their stride, and speculated that the Giants' recent resurgence couldn't last.

"Coming from behind in both contests," the *Times* said, "the Brooks showed that they are too solid an aggregation to remain in a long slump."[13]

SOURCES

In addition to the sources cited in the Notes, the author accessed Retrosheet.org, Baseball-Reference.com, SABR.org, and *The Sporting News* archive via Paper of Record.

NOTES

1   Arnold Rampersad, *Jackie Robinson: A Biography* (New York: Ballantine Books, 1998), 241.

2   Joshua Prager, *The Echoing Green: The Untold Story of Bobby Thomson, Ralph Branca, and the Shot Heard Round the World* (New York: Pantheon Books, 2006), 86.

3   Harold C. Burr, "King for a Day – and a Night – and a Season," *Brooklyn Daily Eagle*, August 23, 1951: 16.

4   James Lincoln Ray, "Clyde King." SABR Bio-Project. Accessed at https://sabr.org/bioproj/person/4f4481b9.

5   Burr, "King for a Day."

6   "King for a Day."

7   "King for a Day."

8   "King for a Day."

9   "King for a Day."

10   Louis Effrat, "Dodgers Trip Cards 4-3 and 8-7, Taking Both Games in 10 Innings," *New York Times*, August 23, 1951: 35.

11   "King for a Day."

12   "King for a Day."

13   Effrat, "Dodgers Trip Cards." Robinson's clutch performance prefigured one on the last day of the season in Philadelphia, when he hit an RBI triple, made a game-saving diving catch in the ninth inning, and hit a home run in the 14th inning to give the Dodgers a 9-8 victory and force a playoff series with the Giants. The Giants, of course, would go on to win that series in one of the most memorable moments in baseball history, perhaps overshadowing some of Robinson's heroics that season.

BRANCA VS. THOMSON, ROUND 1

October 1, 1951

New York Giants 3, Brooklyn Dodgers 1 | Game One National League Playoff

by Andrew Milner

At 9:30 on the evening of September 30, 1951, the New York Giants, having clinched a tie for the National League pennant that afternoon in Boston by winning their seventh straight game, arrived at Grand Central Station to a welcoming crowd of approximately 2,500. Forty minutes earlier the Brooklyn Dodgers, who salvaged a tie for first on the strength of Jackie Robinson's 14th-inning home run at Shibe Park, returned to an estimated 11,000 at Penn Station. A three-game playoff would begin the next afternoon at Ebbets Field. "It's a new season," Giants vice president Chub Feeney said. "We eliminated six teams and now we play for the championship. Just like hockey and basketball."[1]

Giants manager Leo Durocher chose sinker-baller Jim Hearn as his starting pitcher for Game One, adding, "I'll have everybody in the bullpen today except Sal Maglie and Larry Jansen."[2] Durocher's rival manager, Charlie Dressen, chose between youth and age: "It might have been Clem Labine, the youngster, but in the clutch Dressen preferred (Ralph) Branca's experience," observed a sportswriter.[3] Branca had already pitched in

Sunday evening's game, giving up two runs in 1⅓ innings. From August 12, when the Giants' comeback started, Hearn had a 7-2 record, while Branca went 3-9.[4]

Thirteen-year-old Dodger fan Sheldon Goodman got the festivities started in Brooklyn overnight by scaling the Ebbets Field fence and evading the Dodger security.[5] Then, "(t)he girl at the switchboard downstairs said she had to fight her way through a mob to get into the park at 7:45 a.m."[6] Things grew only more hectic later that morning: "Up McKeever Place, down Sullivan Place and along Bedford Ave. the fans pushed and pulled in the obviously doomed attempt to squeeze what some estimated to be 50,000 persons into a ball park designed for fewer than 35,000. Within two hours after tickets went on sale at 9 A.M., all 17,400 reserved seats were sold out."[7] One Dodger rooter from Youngstown, Ohio, said, "Me, I'm the only Dodger fan in town, in the county. Why? Guess it's them (Red) Barber and (Connie) Desmond fellas. They won me over." A Giant fan in line proclaimed, "All year I've been taking a beating, but today is my day. We'll take them in two straight. Then Yankees – look out!"[8]

The Ebbets Field crowd of 30,707 included General and Mrs. Douglas MacArthur, five months after returning to the United States from Asia. The five-star general, who had attended Yankee, Giant and Dodger games throughout the 1951 campaign, said, "I have shooed three teams along this year and here they are all under the wire. I can't lose."[9]

New Yorkers unable to get a ticket could watch the game on WOR-TV, while fans across the United States could watch on the NBC network in a TV milestone. Twelve years after the first major-league baseball game was telecast from Ebbets Field, the Dodgers' ballpark hosted the first coast-to-coast network baseball broadcast as microwave relay and coaxial cables transmitted the first playoff game over the NBC network. "Some of the local frenzy over the Dodger-Giant play-off may rub off on the rest of the country," the *Herald Tribune* predicted.[10]

Prior to the game, the Dodgers physician injected Roy Campanella's right thigh muscle with Novocain. The Brooklyn catcher had injured it during the Phillies game and, according to the *Daily News*, was "limping at a crab's pace."[11]

Robinson, in honor of his previous evening's performance in Philadelphia, received an ovation from the Ebbets Field crowd when he stepped to the plate with two outs in the first – and, when Pee Wee Reese ended the frame by being caught stealing, was given a second ovation when he walked to the plate to complete his at-bat to open the bottom of the second.[12]

The Dodgers got on the board two batters later, with left fielder Andy Pafko's two-out solo home run into the lower left-field stands. It was Pafko's 17th home run for the Dodgers since being traded from the Cubs on June 15.

With one out in the top of the fourth, Branca hit Monte Irvin with a pitch. After Whitey Lockman flied to center, third baseman Bobby Thomson came to bat. In John Drebinger's words, "Thomson arched a powerful drive into the left-field stand and though it was a beautiful Indian summer afternoon the Flatbush horde was plunged into gloom deeper than a moonless night on the Gowanus."[13]

Thomson, Frank Conniff declared in the following afternoon's *Journal-American*, "has suddenly smelled money, or been bowled over by the idea that he can become a big wheel around this town, or been hit over the head by some occult occurrence that finally opened the way to greatness for him."[14]

The Giants extended their lead in the eighth, when Irvin led off with a home run to left, his 24th of the year and his league-leading 121st RBI. When Lockman then reached second on center fielder Duke Snider's error, the Giants threatened to break the game open, but Branca got out of the eighth without giving up another run. The Giants clearly had Branca's number, however – they'd hit 10 of the 18 home runs Branca had surrendered to that point in 1951. After Bud Podbielan relieved him in the ninth, Branca "wandered about the locker room avoiding the waiting newspaper men and muttering to himself, '(O)ne pitch, just one pitch.'"[15]

Hearn held the Dodgers hitless for the final 4⅓ innings, striking out five and walking two over the course of the game. He was assisted by the Giants defense, which pulled off four double plays in the final six innings. "Jim Hearn, whose pitching used to be considered by the Dodgers pretty much in the nature of an extension of batting practice, came back (Monday) to practice a bit of five-hit necromancy," wrote the *Herald Tribune*'s Harold Rosenthal.[16]

Giants coach Herman Franks declared, "For the first time this year, we came through these doors to play the Dodgers confident of winning. Now we got 'em locked up. They're dead."[17]

A Brooklyn bus driver said the following morning, "That loss yesterday was just to lull the Giants into a feeling of over-confidence, false security. We got them just where we want them." When a Giants fan on the bus replied that the Dodgers "shoulda stood in Philadelphia," the driver snapped, "You subversive!"[18]

SOURCES

In addition to the sources cited in the Notes, the author also consulted Baseball-Reference.com.

NOTES

1   Lou Miller, "Giants Over the Shock of That Brook Recovery," *New York World Telegram & Sun*, October 1, 1951: 19.

2   Leonard Shecter, "But Lippy Always Has That Maglie!" *New York Post*, October 1, 1951: 35.

3   Al Buck, "Giants 6 to 5 Choice in Playoff," *New York Post*, October 1, 1951: 36.

4   Baseball-reference.com 1951 season game log pages for Jim Hearn and Ralph Branca.

5   "Fan, 13, Hoists First One Over Ebbets Fence," *New York World Telegram & Sun*, October 1, 1951.

6   Bill Roeder, "MVP Candidates Out in Open; Playoff Is Their Election Day," *New York World Telegram & Sun*, October 1, 1951: 18.

7   Julian Fox and Richard J. Roth, "50,000 Mount Big Push for 35,000 Seats," *Brooklyn Daily Eagle*, October 1, 1951: 1.

8   "Faithful Smash Gates in Ticket Run," *New York World Telegram & Sun*, October 1, 1951: 2.

9   Barney Kremenko, "Reese Happy to Delay Trip to Old Ky. Home," *New York Journal-American*, October 1, 1951: 18.

10 "Playoffs Seen on TV 1st Time Coast-Coast," *New York Herald Tribune*, October 2, 1951: 23.

11 Dick Young, "Hearn's 5-Hitter Chills Dodgers, 3-1," *New York Daily News*, October 2, 1951: 52.

12 Al Laney, "What World Series? Flathush Concerned Only with Giants," *New York Herald Tribune*, October 2, 1951: 24.

13 John Drebinger, "Giant Homers Win from Dodgers, 3-1," *New York Times*, October 2, 1951: 32.

14 Frank Conniff, "Robert Thomson Sees the Light," *New York Journal-American*, October 2, 1951: 19.

15 Ed Sinclair, "Dodger Clubhouse So Quiet One Could Hear Branca Pound Wall," *New York Herald Tribune*, October 2, 1951: 24.

16 Harold Rosenthal, "Giants Beat Dodgers, 3-1, on Home Runs by Thomson and Irvin in First Play-Off," *New York Herald Tribune*, October 2, 1951: 1.

17 Rud Rennie, "Giants Happy and Confident After Opening Victory Over Dodgers in Play-Off Series," *New York Herald Tribune*, October 2, 1951: 24.

18 J.F. Wilkinson, "Loyal Fans Explain That Loss: 'IF—!'" *Brooklyn Daily Eagle*, October 2, 1951: 3.

Dodgers rout Reds with 15-run first inning

May 21, 1952
Brooklyn Dodgers 19, Cincinnati Reds 1

by Steven C. Weiner

In the 1950s, a kid's trip to a Dodgers game at Ebbets Field was a very special occasion and one of unimaginable joy. The atmosphere, the color, the noise, and the food challenged all the senses. The game was an opportunity to see Jackie, Pee Wee, Duke, Campy, and all the others. If you managed to get there a half hour before first pitch and peered deep down the first-base line into the Dodgers bullpen, you could even see the pregame show from a distance.

On this night, watching a game on a small black-and-white television was an opportunity not to be taken for granted and the pregame show, *Happy Felton's Knot-Hole Gang*, was not to be missed. The show brought together Little Leaguers and Dodgers players with Felton, wearing a Dodgers uniform and serving as the host. To begin, he would warm up with three youngsters and introduce a Dodgers player. Each youngster got to ask the player a baseball question.

The guest Dodger would then play catch with the kids and judge their fielding ability, arm, speed, and baseball competence. Every youngster received baseball equipment for appearing on the show. The winner, as selected by the player, would return the following day and have a televised chat with his favorite Dodger.[1] It was entertainment in its simplest form, to which any kid could relate.

The matchup on May 21, 1952, pitted the Dodgers and the visiting Cincinnati Reds. Ewell Blackwell started for Cincinnati. Blackwell was a lanky, 6-foot, 6-inch, side-arming right-hander nicknamed The Whip. Warren Corbett began his SABR biography of Blackwell this way: "Fear. Ballplayers don't like to talk about it. Rarely is a pitcher so fearsome that he can't be ignored. Walter Johnson was one. Bob Feller. Randy Johnson. Ewell Blackwell was one."[2] Blackwell, often in poor health and suffering from shoulder pain, was having a tough season, entering the night with a 1-5 record. However, he enjoyed a solid track record against the Dodgers, including three wins in his stellar 1947 season.[3]

For the Dodgers, Chris Van Cuyk was a young pitcher seeking a regular spot in the starting rotation after brief opportunities in 1950 and 1951. He was the younger brother of Johnny Van Cuyk, a pitcher who had a cup of coffee[4] with the Dodgers in the 1947-49 seasons without any decisions.

Tonight was not going to be Blackwell's night. The bottom of the first inning started innocently when he got out Billy Cox on a groundout to third. After Pee Wee Reese walked and Duke Snider hit his fourth home run of the season, Blackwell would face only three more batters. When George "Shotgun" Shuba knocked in Jackie Robinson with a single to right, that ended Blackwell's night. Bud Byerly came in to pitch to Gil Hodges, and the Reds caught Andy Pafko trying to steal third base. At that point, the Dodgers led 3-0. Five straight Dodgers had reached base, but there were now two outs in the inning. Probably no one could imagine what was about to happen.

Another 14 batters in a row reached base on seven singles, five walks, and two hit batsmen. The Dodgers led 15-0 after facing four Reds pitchers: Blackwell, Byerly, Herm Wehmeier, and Frank Smith. Reese alone reached base three times in the first inning and even Van Cuyk contributed with two singles and two RBIs. Frank Smith struck out Snider looking to end the bottom of the first inning 59 minutes after it began. (Remarkably, it took only 2:26 from start to finish to end the Reds' nightmare.)

In the first inning alone, the Dodgers set six modern major-league records:[5]

- Most runs scored in one inning, 15 (old record 14, by the 1920 Yankees, 1922 Cubs, 1948 Red Sox, 1950 Indians).

- Most runs scored in first inning, 15 (old record 14, by the 1950 Indians).

- Most runs scored with two outs, 12 (old record 11, by the 1942 Pirates).

- Most batters to face pitcher in one inning, 21 (old record 19, by the 1922 Cubs and 1948 Red Sox).

- Most RBIs in one inning, 15 (old record 14, by the 1948 Red Sox).

- Most batters to reach base safely in a row, 19.[6]

"If this had been a boxing match, the referee would have stopped the fight at the opening bell," a pair of authors observed.[7] Blackwell wasn't about to hang around the ballpark. He showered quickly, took a taxicab back to the Commodore Hotel, sat down in the bar for a drink and heard the television announcer blare out that the Dodgers were still hitting in the bottom of the first inning. Blackwell recounted the rest of the tale in an interview with Donald Honig.[8] "Then the next thing I know Bud Byerly comes in and sits down next to me. ... He didn't say anything. 'Don't you want to know what the score is?' I asked. 'Frankly, no,' he said. 'Don't feel so bad,' I said. 'At least they can't blame it all on us.'"[9]

Of course, the game took its full course though the outcome was a virtual certainty. The Dodgers scored two runs in each of the third and fifth innings in an identical manner on singles from Van Cuyk followed by home runs from Bobby Morgan, his first two of the season and his first ones ever at Ebbets Field. Morgan had replaced Cox to begin the second inning. The lone run for Cincinnati came in the fifth inning on Dixie Howell's first home run of the season. For Van Cuyk, a complete-game five-hitter was just one part of the 19-1 Dodgers' victory. His four hits nearly equaled the Reds' total and his two RBIs would have been sufficient for the victory.

The Dodgers' victory put them in first place, a half-game ahead of the New York Giants in the National League race. They held that position for all but six more days on their way to a World Series date with the New York Yankees. Blackwell beat the Dodgers, 7-4, on June 15 in his next start at Ebbets Field. In late August, he was traded to the Yankees and made only four more major-league starts after the 1952 season. On June 14, Van Cuyk pitched another complete-game victory over the Reds, 6-2, at Ebbets Field, but two months later he hurled his last game in the major leagues. But for this night, it was "fifty-nine minutes of sheer ecstasy"[10] and a good night's sleep for any youngster who happened to catch the first inning on TV.

AUTHOR'S NOTE

In the 1950s, Brooklyn Dodgers games were televised on WOR-TV Channel 9 in New York. On a school night for this third-grader, the deal was that I could watch the pregame show, *Happy Felton's Knot-Hole Gang,* and the first inning of the game on the 12-inch Andrea television in the basement of our home. Then I would be off to sleep. On this night, I maintained that a deal is a deal!

SOURCES

In addition to the sources cited in the Notes, the author also accessed Baseball-Reference.com and Retrosheet.org.

NOTES

1   *Happy Felton's Knot-Hole Gang* on June 26, 1956, preceding the Dodgers vs. Cubs game, is provided as an example (youtube.com/watch?v=KsQuqhWhm8o). Jackie Robinson answered questions and conducted the workout. The previous winner had selected Pee Wee Reese for his solo chat and as the show concluded, Pee Wee took him into the dugout to meet other players.

2   Warren Corbett, "Ewell Blackwell," SABR Baseball Biography Project, sabr.org/bioproj/person/63151815.

3   Blackwell led the National League in 1947 with 22 wins, 23 complete games and 193 strikeouts. He finished second to Bob Elliott (Boston Braves) in the voting for the Most Valuable Player Award. Blackwell no-hit the Braves 6-0 on June 18 and was denied a second consecutive no-hitter on June 22 when Eddie Stanky singled with one out in the ninth inning in the Reds' 4-0 win over the Dodgers. Blackwell was a National League All-Star for six consecutive years, 1946-1951.

4   Paul Dickson, *The Dickson Baseball Dictionary*, 3rd Edition (New York: W.W. Norton & Company, 2009), 230. The term means a brief trial in the major leagues by a minor-league player. "The phrase seems to have derived from the observation that a young player's first taste of the major leagues is usually quite short, figuratively just long enough to drink a cup of coffee."

5   Joseph M. Sheehan, "Brooks Set Marks Routing Reds, 19-1," *New York Times*, May 22, 1952: 33.

6   Sheehan. Sheehan commented that there was "no previous listing, but this has to be a record, too."

7   Bruce Nash and Allan Zullo, *Baseball Hall of Shame*, (New York: Simon and Schuster, 1989), 139.

8   Donald Honig, *Baseball Between the Lines: Baseball in the Forties and Fifties As Told by the Men Who Played It* (Lincoln: University of Nebraska Press, 1993), 46-54.

9   Honig, 53.

10 William F. McNeil, *The Dodgers Encyclopedia* (Champaign, Illinois: Sports Publishing Inc., 2001), 367.

ERSKINE TOSSES FIRST NO-HITTER

June 19, 1952

Brooklyn Dodgers 5, Chicago Cubs 0

by Gregory H. Wolf

Some wondered if the game would even start. It was a hot, muggy Thursday afternoon in Brooklyn with temperatures in the mid-80s and rain on the way.[1] The skies were dark and the lights were on at Ebbets Field by the 1:30 game time. When the clouds finally burst open at 2:10, a torrential rainfall with high winds interrupted the game, and the prospect of resuming play did not appear good.

The Dodgers were rolling over their competition. Skipper Chuck Dressen's squad had the best record in baseball (39-15) and a four-game lead over the New York Giants as they prepared to conclude a three-game series with the Chicago Cubs as part of a 19-game homestand broken up by a sole game in the Polo Grounds. As expected, the club's high-powered offense was lighting up the scoreboard; however, its pitching staff proved much stronger than anticipated. Given the loss of ace Don Newcombe, serving in the military, Dressen relied on a group of relatively inexperienced hurlers.

One member of that "Kiddie Corps" was 25-year-old Carl Erskine, a 5-foot-10, 160-pound right-hander. On a team with big personalities, Erskine was unassuming and good-natured, and neither smoked nor drank. "His gentle expression, rosy complexion and general demeanor," opined sportswriter Lorin McMullen, "doubtless caused more than one of his managers to think that he was entirely too nice to make the grade in the rough, tough, dog-eat-dog world that is baseball."[2] Erskine emerged in his fourth season, in 1951, as a dependable swingman, going 16-12 and logging 189⅔ innings. Still battling inconsistencies thus far in '52 (such as tossing his first shutout and also getting bombed in starting and relief assignments), Erskine was 5-1 and 42-23 in his career.

Despite the ominous weather forecast, the Dodgers-Cubs matchup drew a crowd of 13,232 to Flatbush, including an estimated 5,000 knotholers and 500 blind guests.[3] The Cubs were one of the feel-good stories thus far in baseball. Following a last-place finish a year earlier, player-manager Phil Cavarretta's team was in third place (34-23), but on this day was riding a four-game losing streak.

After Erskine breezed through a one-two-three first, the Dodgers took their whacks against Cubs starter Warren Hacker. Biding his time between the minors and the big-league club in the previous four seasons, the 27-year-old right-hander finally caught on in '52. He was coming off two stellar complete-game victories to push his record to 4-1 with a robust 2.68 ERA. Pee Wee Reese got things started by smashing a one-out grounder that took a bad hop, according to the *New York Times*, over shortstop Eddie Miksis's shoulder.[4] After Jackie Robinson popped up, Reese stole second and advanced to third on catcher Toby Atwell's poor throw, then sauntered home when Roy Campanella parked his ninth home run in the lower left-center seats for a 2-0 Dodgers lead. Carl Furillo followed by spanking his sixth home run, which landed in almost the same spot. The Dodgers made it 4-0 on Andy Pafko's solo shot, his 10th round-tripper of the season, with one out in the second. That one sent Hacker to the showers.

Staked to an early lead and seeing the clouds darken, Erskine worked quickly, not wanting to waste his teammates' three round-trippers should the game be called. He dispatched the Cubs in order in the second, and the first two batters in the third. Then Erskine had a hiccup, walking reliever Willie Ramsdell on four straight pitches. "I was in a hurry to get the side out, as the rain was coming," said Erskine. "I was anxious to hurry it up so it would be a legal game. I kept firing balls to Ramsdell and couldn't get one over."[5] Erskine's bugaboo was his control and one of the reasons he had not yet fully established himself as a starter. Nonetheless, he seemed embarrassed by walking a pitcher, a former Dodger whom he described as "the only man who couldn't hit the ball out of the park if I'd teed it up for him."[6] Miksis followed with a rifle smash that looked as if it would fall for a hit, but left fielder Andy Pafko raced over to snare it on the run. Unbeknownst at the time, Pafko's catch was the

first of several stellar plays that helped Erskine make history.

A furious thunderstorm erupted at the top of the fourth, sending players and spectators running for cover. According to the *Brooklyn Eagle*, the Dodgers' grounds crew, led by Eddie Durham, had the infield covered in record time: 1 minute and 20 seconds.[7] Vicious winds swept the park; sportswriter Roscoe McGowen described them as a "twister" that forced the grounds crew to sit on top of the infield tarpaulin to keep it from flying away.[8]

After a 44-minute delay, home-plate umpire Jocko Conlan resumed the game. "I didn't mind the long wait," said Erskine. "I threw six or seven warm-up balls when we got back and seemed to still have my stuff." Erskine made quick work in the fourth, retiring the side on three straight grounders.[9]

Erskine was known to have one of the league's best changeups, but discarded it early in this contest, in favor of his fastballs, curves, and sliders. "I was getting 'em out," he quipped, "so I didn't have to use my change of pace except once."[10]

The Cubs pounded Erskine's breaking ball into the dirt all afternoon which resulted in some slick fielding. With one out in the fifth, Dee Fondy hit a sharp ball back to the mound. Cubs beat writer Irving Vaughan described it as a "cinch hit into dead center,"[11] while Erskine said "it was a do-or-don't play."[12] Instinctively Erskine reached out with his glove hand and made a clean stop and then perfect throw to first for the out. In the sixth, third baseman Bobby Morgan charged Ramsdell's slow chopper and threw to an outstretched Gil Hodges at first in one of the closest plays of the game. The Cubs hit only five balls out of the outfield. NL home run leader (and eventual MVP) Hank Sauer connected for the hardest shots, but right fielder Carl Furillo had it perfectly played and caught it against the scoreboard.

Since replacing Hacker with one out in the second, Ramsdell had shut down the Dodgers' vaunted offense, which eventually led the NL in scoring for the fourth straight season. He retired 17 of 18 batters, yielding only a bunt single to Pafko in the fifth. Dem Bums finally got to the 36-year-old knuckleballer with two outs in the eighth. Reese singled and stole second, then Robinson walked. Campanella's single gave the Dodgers a 5-0 lead.

Erskine entered the ninth just three outs away from his first no-hitter since his high-school days. He also knew a no-hitter could end instantly, and shutouts, too. In the previous summer he retired 21 straight Cincinnati Reds on July 16 at Ebbets Field, only to yield a leadoff single in the eighth to Ted Kluszewski and then lost the shutout three batters later on Virgil Stallcup's two-run home run.

On the other hand, the gods of no-hitters were on the Dodgers' side that June week in 1952. Just two days earlier, two Class D Dodger farmhands twirled no-nos. Anthony Develis of Ponca City (Oklahoma) held Iola hitless and fanned 16 in the Kansas-Oklahoma-Missouri League; Valdosta's Don Terwedow was less spectacular in his seven-walk no-hitter against Moultrie (Georgia) in the Georgia-Florida-League.[13] (Neither of those prospects ever reached the majors.)

Erskine retired Bob Ramazzotti on a grounder that third baseman Morgan charged and threw precisely for the first out of the ninth. Erskine "had a good slider, and a good curve, and a live fast ball that hopped, but we even gave up on that fast ball in the ninth inning," said catcher Roy Campanella. "Didn't want to take a chance with it, even though he was behind on the hitters. We gave 'em sliders and curves."[14] Left-handed-hitting Cavaretta, calling on himself to pinch-hit for Ramsdell, sent a hard smash deep into the right-field stands. The crowd took a collective gasp, but the ball was foul.[15] Erskine dispatched him on a high popup to center fielder Duke Snider. On a 3-and-2 count, Miksis, another former Dodger, grounded to Reese, whose throw to Hodges ended the game in 1 hour and 48 minutes to secure Erskine's no-hitter.

Except for his walk to Ramsdell, Erskine was in control throughout the game, tossing 103 pitches, including 63 strikes. It was the first no-hitter against the Cubs since Fred Toney engaged Hippo Vaughan in an epic hitless duel through nine innings on May 2, 1917, at Weeghman Park (later known as Wrigley Field) and completed the no-hitter in 10 frames. Erskine's gem was the first Dodgers no-hitter since Rex Barney's against the Giants at the Polo Grounds on September 9, 1948 and the first Dodgers no-hitter at Ebbets Field since Ed Head's against the Boston Braves on April 23, 1946. Erskine would also author the Dodgers' next no-hitter, on May 12, 1956, against the Giants at Ebbets Field.

SOURCES

In addition to the sources cited in the Notes, the author accessed Retrosheet.org, Baseball-Reference.com, SABR.org, and *The Sporting News* archive via Paper of Record.

Walter O'Malley, president of the Dodgers, gives Carl Erskine a $500 check for tossing a no-hitter. Also celebrating are (L-R) Carl Furillo, Preacher Roe, Roy Campanella, and skipper Charlie Dressen. (Photo: SABR-Rucker Archive)

NOTES

1   "Daily Almanac," *New York Daily News*, June 20, 1952: 2.

2   Lorin McMullen, "Erskine Shows What Nice Guys Can Do," *Fort Worth Star-Telegram*, June 20, 1952: 15.

3   Harold Burr, "It's Picnic Times for the Erskine Family," *Brooklyn Eagle*, June 20, 1952: 14.

4   Roscoe McGowen, "Erskine Hurls No-Hitter and Misses Perfect Game by One Walk," *New York Times*, June 20, 1952: 28.

5   Burr.

6   Dick Young, "Erskine No-Hits Cubs, 5-0; Walk Costs Perfect Game," *New York Daily News*, June 20, 1952: 64.

7   "Hitless Effort Earns Erskine Bonus," *Brooklyn Eagle*, June 20, 1952: 14.

8   McGowen.

9   Burr.

10 Burr.

11 Irvin Vaughan," Dodgers' Erskine Holds Cubs Hitless, 5-0," *Chicago Tribune*, June 20 1952: 37.

12 McGowen.

13 Bob Gould, "No-Hitters Turned In by 2 Farmhands," *Brooklyn Eagle*, June 19, 1952: 17.

14 Young.

15 McGowen.

DODGERS WIN THE PENNANT!

September 23, 1952

Brooklyn Dodgers 5, Philadelphia Phillies 4 | Game One of Doubleheader
Philadelphia Phillies 1, Brooklyn Dodgers 0 | 12 innings, Game Two of Doubleheader

by Paul E. Doutrich

On September 23, 1952, with autumn in the air, fans filed into Ebbets Field to watch a Dodgers doubleheader against the Phillies. Home-team patrons came to the game anticipating Brooklyn's first National League pennant since 1949. With six games left to play, the Dodgers needed just one more win to clinch the championship, a championship that they deserved. The team had played well all season, climbing into first place on June 1 and remaining there throughout the rest of the season. Returning from a three-game sweep of the Boston Braves, the team was primed to claim the pennant. The championship seemed almost inevitable. Just one more win. However, everyone remembered what had happened the two previous seasons. The specter of the Bobby Thomson blast that completed the Giants' amazing September run the previous year still haunted Dodgers fans. Memories of 1950, when the Dodgers finished a game back of Philadelphia's Whiz Kids, also lingered.

The day began well for the Dodgers. Despite a two-out walk followed by Del Ennis's single, rookie starter Johnny Rutherford kept the Phillies

off the scoreboard. Phillies starter Karl Drews did not do as well. In the bottom of the inning, he walked Duke Snider with two outs, then served up a Jackie Robinson line-drive double to left that scored Snider.

The second inning went about the same as the first for Rutherford. Facing the bottom of the Philadelphia order, he issued a one-out walk to third baseman Willie "Puddin' Head" Jones but otherwise had no problems. In the bottom of the inning his mound counterpart, who was looking for his fifth win over the Dodgers, cruised through the Brooklyn order retiring the side in order.

It was in the third that Rutherford ran into some trouble. With one out, center fielder Richie Ashburn singled up the middle. Bill Nicholson then worked Rutherford for the Phillies' third walk in three innings. With runners on first and second, Del Ennis grounded a potential double-play ball that third baseman Billy Cox muffed to load the bases with one out. Next up was Granny Hamner. The Phillies shortstop smacked Rutherford pitch well over the left-field fence. It was the second grand slam of his career and gave his team a three-run cushion.

In the bottom half of the third inning, Drews needed just three pitches to put down the Dodgers. After years of struggling with his control, the Phillies pitcher used a particularly effective sinker to work his way into a Philadelphia rotation that included Robin Roberts and Curt Simmons. He had already beaten the Dodgers four times in 1952, twice on shutouts. Enjoying what was easily the best year in his major-league career, Drews finished the season with 14 wins while dropping 15, and had a 2.72 ERA. In the top of the fourth it took Rutherford six pitches to match Drews.

In their half of the fourth inning, the Dodgers began chipping away at the Phillies' lead. After retiring nine in a row, Drews served up a pitch that left fielder George "Shotgun" Shuba launched over the scoreboard in right-center field. Shuba had played for Montreal most of the previous season but manager Chuck Dressen brought him up at the beginning of the 1952 season to add bench strength, especially against right-handed pitching. The move turned out well for the Dodgers. After the game Dressen claimed, "There's the difference between last year's club and this – (pitcher Joe) Black and Shuba. We'd have never won the pennant without them."[1]

Well before helping the Dodgers win the pennant, Shuba had already attained a bit of baseball celebrity. On April 18, 1946, while playing for Montreal in a game against Jersey City Giants, Shuba followed Jackie Robinson in the batting order. That day Robinson hit a three-run home run and Shuba, unlike his teammates who had just scored, shook Robinson's hand as he crossed the plate. A photographer snapped a picture, labeled "A Handshake for the Century," which was the first photograph of an interracial handshake in professional baseball history. That handshake has been immortalized by statuary and paintings ever since.[2]

An inning later Brooklyn took the lead. After Rutherford put down the Phillies in order, Gil Hodges led off the Dodgers fifth with a single to left field. Rutherford followed Hodges and laid down a sacrifice bunt that first baseman Ed Waitkus fumbled, putting runners on first and second. The next hitter, Billy Cox, forced Hodges at third, but Pee Wee Reese lined a pitch to center field, scoring Rutherford. Reminiscent of the run-scoring double that he had hit to clinch the pennant in 1949, Duke Snider swatted a double to right-center, pushing both Cox and Reese across the plate.

Now only four innings away from the National League pennant, much of the burden of holding the lead fell on the shoulders of Johnny Rutherford. He got through the sixth and seventh innings giving up only a single to Puddin' Head Jones in the sixth and a walk to Bill Nicholson in the seventh. Meanwhile, Rutherford rapped out the only Dodgers hit during those two innings.

In the eighth the Dodgers hurler ran into some trouble. Granny Hamner led off with a single to right field and went to second on a groundout to first by catcher Smokey Burgess. Jones then collected his third hit of the day, a single that put the tying run on third with only one out. Rutherford escaped the inning when Waitkus grounded sharply to Jackie Robinson at second who scooped the ball up and threw to his keystone partner Pee Wee Reese, who fired to first to complete the double play.

After Drews set down the Dodgers in order one more time, the Phillies came to the plate in the ninth inning with a last chance to prevent the Dodgers from clinching the pennant. As he took the mound in the ninth, Rutherford could not have imagined that this was the last regular-season inning he would pitch in the major leagues. His only other Dodgers appearance came in the eighth inning of Game Four of the World Series. Called in to relieve starter Joe Black, Rutherford

Carl Furillo, Jackie Robinson, Roy Campanella, Pee Wee Reese, Duke Snider, Preacher Rowe, and Gil Hodges were all members of the 1952 NL All-Star team. (Photo: SABR-Rucker Archive)

gave up a triple to Mickey Mantle, who then scored the final run in the Yankees' 2-0 win. Certainly not spectacular, Rutherford's season had been successful by most standards. It was also a numerologist's delight. He had started 11 games and relieved in 11 more. He finished with a 4.25 ERA with five wins and five losses as a starter and two wins and two losses as a reliever. In his 97⅓ innings on the mound, he had given up 97 hits, struck out 29, and walked 29. In this his last regular-season inning in the major leagues, Rutherford brought the pennant back to Brooklyn by getting the three Phillies he faced, Johnny Wyrostek, Connie Ryan, and Richie Ashburn, on routine groundouts.

The final out ignited a brief celebration by Dodgers fans and players alike "although for Brooklyn it was a rather polite demonstration."[3] Several Dodgers faithful jumped onto the field while the players embraced and tossed their hats in the air. Perhaps the most enthused was Jackie Robinson. Amid handshakes and hugs and back pats in the locker room, Robinson told reporters that much of the credit for his team's victorious season belonged to manager Dressen. "I think you've (Dressen) done a tremendous job with the pitching staff. I don't think anybody could have done better. For that matter, I think you've handled the team excellently. And I think everybody should be made aware of it."[4] Of course, the afternoon wasn't over. There was still a second game to be played. The full celebration would have to wait.

Aside from the starting pitchers, the Phillies made only one change from the first-game lineup. Backup catcher Stan Lopata was penciled in for Smokey Burgess. His batterymate would be Curt Simmons, a hard-throwing southpaw who had established himself as one of the better lefties in the National League. Simmons had been the National League's starting pitcher in that year's All-Star Game. Billy Loes took the mound for the Dodgers. In his first full season with Brooklyn, Loes, who threw from the right side, had begun the season in the bullpen but worked his way into the starting rotation. Aside from establishing himself as a fine young hurler, Loes was already becoming known for his zany antics and various eccentricities.

The game immediately became a pitchers' duel. Through the first two innings the only baserunner was the Dodgers' leadoff hitter, Billy Cox, who walked. The game's first hit came in the top of the third when the Phillies' Eddie Waitkus lined a one-out single to center. Simmons followed with a base on balls, but the two runners were stranded as Loes struck out Connie Ryan and got Richie Ashburn to pop up to right.

The Dodgers didn't get their first hits until the next inning. Rocky Bridges, who replaced Pee Wee Reese at shortstop in the top of the inning, singled to left but was caught stealing a batter later. Manager Dressen had begun replacing his starters in third when he substituted Bobby Morgan for Jackie Robinson. By the seventh inning all the Dodgers regulars, except for Cox, who had moved from third to second, were in the clubhouse getting an early start on their championship celebration. Loes remained on the mound.

The two pitchers continued to cut through the opposition. Simmons ran into some trouble in the eighth when the Dodgers' first three hitters singled. Simmons weathered the storm on a force

out at the plate, a strikeout, and a foulout. Loes' challenge came in the next half-inning when the Phillies got a runner to third with one out. Loes struck out the next two hitters.

The duel between Simmons and Loes continued into extra innings. Loes' day ended in the 11th when he was replaced by Jim Hughes, but the duel continued. Finally, in the top of the 12th, the Phillies broke through. With Eddie Waitkus on first and one out, Johnny Wyrostek, pinch-hitting for Simmons, drilled a shot to right field for a double that scored Waitkus. The game ended half an inning later after Kent Peterson, who replaced Simmons, struck out the side to preserve the Phillies' 1-0 victory.

For those Dodgers fans still in Ebbets Field, the loss was a minor flaw in an otherwise happy day. Their team for the second time in four years would finish atop the National League and get another chance to knock off their crosstown rival, the Yankees, in the World Series.

SOURCES

In addition to the sources cited in the Notes, the author accessed Retrosheet.org, Baseball-Reference.com, and SABR.org.

NOTES

1   Ralph Roden (Associated Press), "Brooks Clinch NL Pennant," *Elmira* (New York) *Advertiser*, September 24, 1952: 13.

2   Claire Noland, "Baseball teammate of Jackie Robinson," *Los Angeles Times*, October 1, 2014: 19.

3   Stan Baumgartner, "Dodgers Win NL Pennant, Beat Phils 5-4, Bow 1-0," *Philadelphia Inquirer*, September 24, 1952: 52.

4   "Dodgers Clinch National Flag by Splitting with the Phillies," *Rochester* (New York) *Democrat and Chronicle*, September 24, 1952: 28.

MATHEWS BECOMES FIRST **NL** ROOKIE TO HIT THREE HOME RUNS IN A GAME

September 27, 1952

Boston Braves 11, Brooklyn Dodgers 3

by Bill Pearch

The Brooklyn Dodgers and Boston Braves were two teams headed in opposite directions. Brooklyn, with 96 wins and the National League pennant already clinched, had a World Series date with the New York Yankees. On Saturday, September 27, 1952, Dodgers manager Charlie Dressen gave the ball to pitcher Joe Black as a final regular-season tune-up.[1] Locked in seventh place and the owners of 63 wins, the Braves were a woeful team aspiring to snap a 10-game losing streak. Their lone attraction was a powerful rookie third baseman, Edwin Lee Mathews.[2]

Boston's last taste of victory had come at the Chicago Cubs' expense in the first game of a twin bill on September 14. Johnny Klippstein, the Cubs pitcher, was one out away from sending the scoreless affair into extra innings. After three fruitless at-bats, 20-year-old Eddie Mathews provided ninth-inning heroics and deposited his 22nd career home run into Braves Field's deep left-field seats to win the game, 1-0.

"I was a little surprised when I saw the right fielder backing up for the ball," Mathews said after the game. "I felt sure it was gone when I hit it, and then when I saw [Frank] Baumholtz moving back I was a little worried."[3]

In the 10 games since the Braves' last win, Mathews batted .250, managing a mere 10 hits during his last 40 at-bats with no runs batted in. With the season winding down, he hoped to provide a spark that would end the season-high losing streak when he stepped to plate against the Dodgers with one out in the top of the first inning.

Before Mathews' first at-bat, Braves center fielder Sam Jethroe opened the game with a single to right field. Johnny Logan followed by flying out to center field. Mathews eyed Black and took practice swings as fewer than 5,000 fans watched from the Ebbets Field stands. With the count 2-and-2, Jethroe broke for second. Catcher Roy Campanella gunned the ball to shortstop Pee Wee Reese who successfully applied the tag.

Mathews stepped back in the batter's box with the bases wiped clean, two outs, and the count full. Black coaxed the young lefty into chasing strike three, fanning for his 115th time in the season.[4]

Before the start of the season, Braves players and coaching staff heaped praise upon Mathews. The California native, considered one of the best hitting prospects in the game, accelerated through Boston's minor-league system.[5] Dixie Walker, Mathews' manager with the Double-A Atlanta Crackers, did not hesitate to compare the youth's hitting prowess with that of Babe Ruth and Ted Williams.[6]

"He hits the longest balls I've ever seen," said Jack Daniels, Boston's right fielder. "The funny part of it is that he makes everything look so easy. A twist of the wrists and the ball is out of the park."[7]

"The biggest factor is he doesn't scare," said Tommy Holmes, the former manager of the Braves. Holmes, who was fired early in 1952, added, "He has hitting guts, I wish I had 10 percent of him."[8] This would prove true in Mathews' next trip to the plate.

Duke Snider's first-inning home run gave the pennant winners an earlier 1-0 lead, but Boston answered in the top of the third. Following Daniels' leadoff walk, second baseman Jack Dittmer belted a two-run blast, giving the Braves a 2-1 edge. With two outs and Virgil Jester on second base, Mathews stepped in to face Black for the second time. He worked the count full, then connected with Black's fast curve and sent the ball on a line over Ebbets Field's 30-foot-high fence for a two-run home run. On one bounce, the ball hit a filling station across the street from the ballpark.[9] With his 23rd homer of the year, Mathews extended the Braves' lead to 4-1.

The round-tripper meant Mathews had homered in all eight National League ballparks during his rookie campaign.[10] He launched the first of his career against the Philadelphia Phillies at Shibe Park on April 19. By June 6 he had accomplished the feat at New York's Polo Grounds (April 23), Pittsburgh's Forbes Field (April 30), St. Louis's Sportsman's Park (May 4), Boston's Braves Field (May 10), Cincinnati's Crosley Field (June 1), and Chicago's Wrigley Field (June 6). Only Ebbets Field had eluded him until this game.

In the top of the fifth, Black surrendered a single to Jethroe that plated Dittmer and gave the Braves a 5-2 lead. In the bottom of the inning, Dressen pulled his hurler, who was slated to lead off the bottom of the frame, for a pinch-hitter. Black, who had not worked much down the stretch, realized he was not as sharp as he wished.[11] Brooklyn failed to capitalize and sent Ben Wade to the mound in the sixth.

Leading off the inning, Eddie Mathews swung and missed at Wade's first offering. With his twist of the wrists, he hit the second pitch, a belt-high fastball, over the scoreboard near the 340-foot mark. The rookie sensation extended the Braves' lead to 6-2 and logged his first career multi-homer game.

"If I had to compare him with someone from the past I'd say Charlie Gehringer," said Doc Gautreau, former Braves infielder and team scout, earlier in the season. "Only, this kid has much more power than Gehringer ever did."[12]

Boston added another run in the top of the seventh inning. Wade surrendered a leadoff walk to Daniels. Daniels went to second when Dittmer reached on an error by second baseman Jackie Robinson. Pitcher Jester advanced the runners on a sacrifice. Jethroe's fly ball to center field drove Daniels home to give the Braves a 7-2 advantage.

As he did in the sixth, Mathews again led off in the eighth. Wade, still on the mound, got Mathews to unsuccessfully chase his first offering. He took the second for a ball. Mathews connected on the third pitch and sent another home run over the right-field fence.[13] Then the Braves scored three more runs, two of them unearned because of an error by third baseman Bobby Morgan.

Not only did Mathews tie Sid Gordon for the team lead in home runs with 25, he became the first rookie in National League history to hit three home runs in a game. Mickey Cochrane accomplished the feat as an American League rookie on May 21, 1925. Cochrane, a member of the Philadelphia Athletics, clubbed three solo home runs in a 20-4 rout of the St. Louis Browns at Sportsman's Park.[14] Cleveland Indians rookie first baseman Hal Trosky clubbed three home runs against the Chicago White Sox in the second game of a doubleheader at Cleveland's League Park on May 30, 1934.[15] Jim Tabor, the Boston Red Sox rookie third baseman, matched the feat against the Philadelphia Athletics at Shibe Park in the second game of a doubleheader on July 4, 1939.[16]

When Mathews stepped to the plate in the top of the ninth, the fans wondered if he had a fourth home run in his bat. Brooklyn's new pitcher, Billy Loes, missed the strike zone with his first three pitches. The lefty swung at the fourth pitch and hit a grounder to shortstop Reese, who scooped it up and fired the ball to Gil Hodges at first base.

Mathews (3-for-5, 4 RBIs) powered the Braves to their 11-3 victory. Both managers as well as Mathews' teammates were in awe of his performance.

"It's his wrists and his hips that do it. He's learning to lay off that high ball," said Braves manager Charlie Grimm. "He takes a real swing – no double-hitch – and if he's fooled, he goes through with his swing. With his terrific wrist power, and his speed down the line, he's going to be harder and harder to stop. He has improved so much defensively that – with the exception of Billy Cox – he's the best third baseman in the league right now."[17]

"That kid's going to be tough for everyone next year," said Dressen. "Now that he's learned to lay off the high inside pitch, we'll have to rewrite the book on him."[18]

"He might become one the greatest," said Walker Cooper, the Braves catcher and team captain. "That would be when he learns how they're trying to pitch him – and what. He's not even a good hitter right now."[19]

SOURCES

In addition to the sources cited in the Notes, the author accessed Retrosheet.org, Baseball-Reference.com, and SABR.org.

NOTES

1   Dave Anderson, "Mathews Slams Three Homers in Boston Win," *Brooklyn Daily Eagle*, September 28, 1952: 18.

2   Harold Kaese, *The Boston Braves: 1871-1953* (Boston: Northeastern University Press, 1954), 282.

3   Bob Holbrook. "Home Run Into Wind Provokes Admiration," *Boston Globe*, September 15, 1952: 8.

4   Al Hirshberg, *The Eddie Mathews Story* (New York: Julian Messner, Inc., 1961), 84.

5   David Fleitz, "Eddie Mathews," SABR BioProject, https://sabr.org/bioproj/person/ebd5a210.

6   Bob Holbrook, "Braves' Mathews Classed with Ruth, Ted by Walker," *Boston Globe*, February 2, 1952: 4.

7   Bob Holbrook, "Daniels Says He'll Produce for Holmes," *Boston Globe*, January 23, 1952: 10.

8   Roger Birtwell, "Tribe Shells Black, Beats Dodgers, 11-3," *Boston Globe*, September 28, 1952: 63.

9   Birtwell.

10 Birtwell.

11 Dick Young, "Mathews Hits 3, Dodgers Bow, 11-3," *New York Daily News*, September 28, 1952: 74.

12 Birtwell.

13 Birtwell.

14 "Rookie Hits 3 Homers," *San Francisco Examiner*, September 28, 1952: 41.

15 Edward Burns, "White Sox Beat Indians, 8-7, in 12th; Lose, 5-4," *Chicago Tribune*, May 31, 1934: 19.

16 Gerry Moore, "Tabor Equals Two Home Run Records," *Boston Globe*, July 5, 1939: 7.

17 Birtwell.

18 Hirshberg, 85.

19 Birtwell.

Joe Black and tremendous defense beat Yankees in Series opener

October 1, 1952

Brooklyn Dodgers 4, New York Yankees 2 | Game One of the World Series

by Brian M. Frank

Harold C. Burr gave a tepid review of the Dodgers pitching staff that headed into the 1952 World Series. "Some are pitchers with good arms, some with sore arms, some with tired arms, and some with no arms at all," he wrote. "But it's by this motley corps that the Dodgers must rise or fall with in the World Series."[1]

On paper, Brooklyn's pitchers didn't match up well with the well-seasoned New York Yankees staff, particularly when it came to postseason experience. Dodgers starters had only two career World Series wins. Preacher Roe had one and Ralph Branca, who wouldn't even pitch, had the other. On the other hand, the Yankees' top three pitchers had won 10 games in the fall classic. Their Game One starter, Allie Reynolds, had four wins, while Vic Raschi and Ed Lopat had each won three.

Manager Chuck Dressen's solution to his team's pitching conundrum for Game One was to start a rookie right-hander who had been used as a reliever for most of the season. Joe Black was one of Brooklyn's best pitchers all year, going 15-4 with a 2.15 ERA in 56 games, 54 of which were

in relief. Black's two starts came in his final two appearances of the season. Dressen's logic was that if he threw Black in the first game, he'd have the option of using him in relief or starting him again, depending on how the Series unfolded. "If that guy pitches the way he has pitched all season, our chance is as good as theirs," Dressen said the day before the opener.[2]

The young hurler seemed unfazed by his starting assignment against a team attempting to win its fourth consecutive World Series, and its first since Joe DiMaggio retired. "These aren't the same Yankees I first saw when they had DiMaggio, (Tommy) Henrich, and (Charlie) Keller," Black said. "They're wearing the same letters on their shirts, but I don't believe they frighten anybody." He added, "They're a good ballclub – hope nobody thinks I'm knocking them – but the Dodgers seem to me to be a pretty good ballclub, too."[3]

A huge crowd of 34,861 saw Brooklyn open the scoring in the second inning. Jackie Robinson hit one of Reynolds' sliders "in a long white loop which rode with a tailwind into the

A star with the Negro League Baltimore Elite Giants, Joe Black debuted with the Dodgers at age 28 in 1952 and emerged as baseball's best reliever. He was manager Chuck Dressen's surprise pick to start Game One of the '52 World Series. (Photo: SABR-Rucker Archive)

delighted laps of the distant patrons. They lifted hats, threshed arms, windmill fashion, clasped hands in congratulations or shook fists encouragingly at their hero, who circled the bases at a sedate trot."[4] It was Robinson's first home run in World Series play.

The Yankees answered right back in the top of the third when Gil McDougald led off by hitting one just over the left-field wall. The ball cleared the fence so narrowly that Dodgers left fielder Andy Pafko argued that a fan in the front row had reached over and interfered. His protest came to no avail and the game was tied. Black rebounded from the homer by striking out the next three batters.

The top of the fourth inning was rather eventful, even though the Yankees failed to score. Phil Rizzuto led off with a single. Mickey Mantle bunted up the third-base line and beat Black's throw to first. Yogi Berra hit a groundball to first baseman Gil Hodges, who threw to Pee Wee Reese at second for the force. Mantle's hard slide into second successfully broke up the double play but injured Reese in the process. The Dodgers shortstop was able to stay in the game with a thigh bruise. Joe Collins then hit a fly ball to right fielder Carl Furillo, who "fired the blurred white spec (sic) to the plate" as Rizzuto reversed course and scampered back to third, just beating catcher Roy Campanella's throw.[5] Black was then able to get Irv Noren to ground out to Robinson to end the inning.

Brooklyn's defense was sensational in the fifth inning. After McDougald led off with a walk, Billy Martin looped a single into left. Pafko charged it and fired to third. Billy Cox took the throw and slapped the tag on McDougald for the first out of the inning. McDougald later claimed Cox missed him. "He hasn't tagged me yet," the Yankees third baseman said after the game.[6] Pafko's tremendous throw stood out on the play, as did Cox's play on the receiving end. "The tag that Cox made after Pafko's great throw on Martin's single

in the fifth inning was one of the great plays of the game," Robinson said. "Billy had to come down fast with that tag to get McDougald, and if he hadn't made it that might have been a big inning for the Yankees. They'd have had men on second and third and nobody out."[7] Reynolds grounded harmlessly to Reese for the second out. Pafko then made his second great play in three batters, a "sliding, sitting catch of Hank Bauer's difficult Texas Leaguer" to end the inning.[8]

Collins just missed hitting a two-run home run in the top of the sixth when his deep drive "curved foul by inches."[9] In the bottom of that frame, Duke Snider, who'd already doubled earlier in the game, came up with Reese on base. He sent "the little white ball arching against the blue sky past snapping flags and billowing bunting" over the scoreboard and onto Bedford Avenue, to give the Dodgers a 3-1 lead.[10]

The top of the seventh provided more eye-popping defense from Cox. Black walked Noren to lead off the inning as the Brooklyn bullpen began warming. McDougald hit a groundball to Cox, who made a great stop when it took a bad hop and turned it into an around-the-horn double play. The next batter, Martin, hit a sharp grounder down the third-base line; Cox made a "breath-taking backhand stop" and threw it to first for the out.[11] "You writers call him the best fielding third baseman around," Reese said after the game. "Listen, he's the best fielder, period. I don't care whether he's playing third, second, or shortstop, he's the best fielder in the major leagues no matter where he plays."[12]

Gene Woodling, who didn't start because of a pulled thigh muscle, helped produce another run for the Yankees when he pinch-hit in the eighth inning. Woodling hit a ball off the center-field wall and was able to go into third standing up with a triple. He scored on Bauer's fly ball to cut the Dodgers lead to one at 3-2.

Reese got the run back in the bottom of the eighth. The Dodgers shortstop lined a ball into the left-field seats to put Brooklyn ahead 4-2 and finish the scoring for the day. Black retired the side in order in the ninth, striking out Noren looking to finish the game and give the Dodgers a one-game-to-none lead in the series.

After the game, both managers raved about Brooklyn's amazing glove work. "That fellow at third (Cox) did pretty good in a game that had plenty of good fielding, I'd say," Yankees manager Casey Stengel remarked. "He came up with a couple of nice ones on McDougald and Martin in the seventh."[13] An exuberant Dressen exclaimed, "How about that defensive play of ours? Ever since I've managed this club everybody has talked about how great the hitters are, but nobody said anything about their fielding, which rates with any team in history, if you ask me." He added, "The throw and sliding catch Pafko made. Furillo's throw and Cox's tag on Pafko's throw and those two plays of his in the seventh – going to his left for the double play and spinning around to his right for the third out, they don't come any better than that."[14]

In his complete game, Black allowed two runs on six hits and two walks, while striking out six. He became the first African-American pitcher to win a World Series game. Campanella noted that Black was effective even though he didn't have his best stuff. Black admitted that despite his confidence the day before the game, he felt the pressure of pitching on the big stage. "I was nervous before the game and I stayed nervous," he said. "I've been faster and my control wasn't too sharp but I felt stronger as I went along."[15] Even without his best stuff, the Yankees were impressed with the Dodgers hurler. "You have to hit against him to believe how good he really is," Rizzuto said.[16]

Dressen's strategy of using his recently converted reliever to start Game One had seemingly paid off, with Brooklyn grabbing an early Series lead and his best pitcher ready to pitch again in whatever role his manager asked. "Black will be there tomorrow if I need him," the Dodgers manager said. "He's ready to pitch all the time or any time."[17]

SOURCES

In addition to the sources cited in the Notes, the author consulted Baseball-Reference.com and Retrosheet.org.

NOTES

1 Harold C. Burr, "Pilot Dressen to Play Hunches with Twirlers," *Brooklyn Eagle*, September 29, 1952: 11.

2 Roscoe McGowen, "Joe Black Unawed by Yankee Legend," *New York Times*, October 1, 1952: 41.

3 McGowen.

4 Jimmy Powers, "The Powerhouse," *New York Daily News*, October 2, 1952: 78.

5 Dick Young, "Black, 3 HRs Bash Yanks in 1st, 4-2, Robby, Duke, Reese Circuit for Flock," *New York Daily News*, October 2, 1952: 76.

6 James P. Dawson, "Stengel Praises Dodgers' Power and Pitching but His Yankees Blame Umpire," *New York Times*, October 2, 1952: 37.

7 Roscoe McGowen, "Brooklyn's Defensive Stars Get Big Share of Credit for Victory in Opener," *New York Times*, October 2, 1952: 36.

8 Tommy Holmes, "Erskine Faces Raschi on Hill, Woodling Gets Outfield Call from Yankees," *Brooklyn Eagle*, October 2, 1952: 18.

9 Harold C. Burr, "Sniders's Homer May Set Series Pattern/Reynolds Struck Out Duke Three Times in Series of 1949," *Brooklyn Eagle*, October 2, 1952: 17.

10 Young: 76.

11 Burr, "Snider's Homer May Set Series Pattern."

12 Dave Anderson, "Black Hurling Workhorse," *Brooklyn Eagle*, October 2, 1952: 18.

13 Dawson.

14 Dave Anderson, "Dressen Puts Black on Relief, Joe Available for Emergency Work Today," *Brooklyn Eagle*, October 2, 1952: 18.

15 Anderson.

16 Anderson.

17 Roscoe McGowen, "Brooklyn's Defensive Stars Get Big Share of Credit for Victory in Opener." Black started two more games in the Series, but never pitched in relief. He took the loss in Game Four, even though he allowed only one run on three hits and five walks over seven innings. He also took the loss in Game Seven, when he allowed three runs in 5⅓ innings.

THE BOMBERS BASH "DEM BUMS" BEHIND RASCHI'S THREE-HITTER

October 2, 1952

New York Yankees 7, Brooklyn Dodgers 1 | Game Two of the World Series

by John J. Burbridge Jr.

The 1952 World Series pitted the New York Yankees versus the Brooklyn Dodgers. The Yankees had edged the Cleveland Indians by two games, giving them four consecutive American League pennants. In the previous three years, they were also victorious in the World Series. While leading the National League for almost the entire season, the Dodgers held off a surging New York Giants team to win the National League pennant by 4½ games. In the previous two years, the Dodgers were victimized in their last game of the season by pennant-winning home runs from the bats of Dick Sisler of the Philadelphia Phillies and Bobby Thomson hitting "the shot heard round the world" for the Giants.

Game One of the World Series was played at Ebbets Field in Brooklyn. Joe Black outdueled Allie Reynolds as the Dodgers won 4-2. With his complete-game victory, Black became the first African American pitcher to win a World Series game.[1] Charlie Dressen, the Dodgers' manager, shocked many by starting Black, who was the Dodgers relief ace during the season. Dressen said he was most confident that of all the Dodgers

pitchers, Black could start and win three games.[2] The Dodgers were led by home runs off the bats of Jackie Robinson, Duke Snider, and Pee Wee Reese while Gil McDougald homered for the Yankees. The Dodgers also got sensational defensive support, especially from third baseman Billy Cox.[3]

Game Two was also played at Ebbets Field. Vic Raschi took the mound for the Yankees while Carl Erskine started for the Dodgers. The Dodger faithful were confident the Bums would win both games at Ebbets Field.[4] The game began with Hank Bauer hitting a single to right-center field. He attempted to steal second but was thrown out by catcher Roy Campanella. Phil Rizzuto followed with a walk but Erskine struck out Mickey Mantle. Rizzuto was then thrown out trying to steal second, ending the inning. The Yankees apparently felt they could run on Erskine and Campanella.

Reynolds retired the Dodgers in order in the bottom of the first. The Yankees threatened in the top of the second as Gene Woodling led off with a walk and Yogi Berra singled, putting runners on first and third. Erskine got out of trouble by striking out Joe Collins and McDougald and getting Billy Martin to ground out.

The Dodgers loaded the bases in the bottom of the second. Robinson led off the inning with a walk. Raschi retired the next two hitters but then walked Gil Hodges and Carl Furillo. Fortunately for Raschi, the pitcher's spot was next. Erskine flied to center, ending the inning. In the top of the third, Erskine walked Raschi but got Bauer to hit a double-play grounder to shortstop, and Rizzuto then grounded out.

In the bottom of the third, the Dodgers took a 1-0 lead on Campanella's single scoring Reese. To end the inning, Andy Pafko struck out, leaving runners on first and second. The Yankees quickly retaliated in the top of the fourth as leadoff batter Mantle doubled, went to third on Woodling's groundout, and scored on a Berra fly ball. The Dodgers went out in order in the bottom half of the inning. The Yankees took a 2-1 lead in the top of the fifth as McDougald led off with a walk, stole second, and scored on Martin's single to left. There was no further damage although the Yankees had threatened to score. The Dodgers once again went out in order in the fifth.

The top of the sixth saw the Yankees take a formidable lead, scoring five runs. The inning started with a drag-bunt single by Mantle and a single to center by Woodling. Both runners moved up on a wild pitch by Erskine. After Berra walked, loading the bases, manager Dressen brought in Billy Loes to relieve Erskine. Collins hit a grounder to Robinson who stepped on second, forcing Berra, but his throw to first was mishandled by Hodges for an error. Mantle scored, making the score 3-1. With Woodling on third and Collins on first, McDougald bunted toward first and beat it out for a base hit, scoring Woodling. Martin then finished the scoring with a three-run home run to left field, making the score 7-1.

Once again the Dodgers went out in order in the bottom of the sixth as did the Yankees in the top of the seventh. After Raschi retired the first two hitters in the bottom of the seventh, Rocky Nelson pinch-hit for Loes and walked. Raschi had retired 12 Dodgers in a row before walking Nelson. But Billy Cox's groundout ended the inning. With the Dodgers not scoring in the eighth and ninth innings, the Yankees had tied the series with a resounding 7-1 victory.

Raschi was dominant. He gave up just three hits and struck out nine. He lived up to his reputation as a big-game pitcher as he won his fourth World Series game. He later commented, "I felt good. My control was perfect. You have to throw hard out there all the time. I was mixing them up, fast balls, curves and a let-up with a slider now and then."[5] Yankee players commented that Raschi wasn't wild in the second inning when he walked three hitters; he was just being cautious.[6]

The big hit for the Yankees was Martin's three-run home run. Martin also knocked in the go-ahead run in the fifth with a single, giving him four RBIs. Twenty-year old Mantle was also a big contributor with three hits and two runs scored.

Casey Stengel, the Yankees manager, said, "Of course, we got the break today, but they got it yesterday. Our break came when they flubbed that double play in the sixth. That opened the day for the squeeze McDougald worked and the homer Martin hit."[7] Stengel was commenting on the error by the usually sure-handed Hodges in the sixth inning. Stengel also commented on his two hitting stars and McDougald's bunt in the sixth, "Say, that Martin did all right, didn't he? And that Mickey Mantle was pretty good, too, with his three hits, hey? Another thing, it was McDougald who put on that squeeze. Yes, sir. The hitter himself did it."[8]

As the series moved to Yankee Stadium, the optimism that Brooklyn fans had going into game two had dissipated. A *Brooklyn Daily Eagle* headline said, "Dodger Defense Must Perk Up Or Else ...."[9] However, the Dodgers surprised the baseball world by winning two of the three games in the big ballpark in the Bronx. But in their return to Ebbets Field, they proceeded to lose the final two games of the Series. Billy Martin's ankle-high grab of a wind-blown pop fly off the bat of Jackie Robinson in the bottom of the seventh will long be remembered as the deciding play in Game Seven. The Dodgers had the bases loaded, and if the ball had dropped, two runs would have surely scored, tying the score.

The ball didn't drop and the Yankees went on to win Game Seven, 4-2. With their fourth World Series championship in a row, the Yankees had become a dynasty. Stengel became only the second manager to win for World Series in a row. (Yankees manager Joe McCarthy had won four in a row from 1936 to 1939. Johnny Mize won the Babe Ruth Award as the outstanding player in the 1952 Series although many felt Mantle was more deserving. Mize had 18 plate appearances, hitting .400 in 15 at-bats, while Mantle had a batting average of .345 with two home runs in 29 at-bats, and made several outstanding defensive plays.

The Yankees proved victorious once again in 1953 World Series, giving Stengel his fifth consecutive championship. The Dodgers and the Brooklyn faithful had to wait until 1955 when they finally beat the Yankees in the World Series. The "next year" of "Wait till next year" had finally arrived.

SOURCES

In addition to the sources mentioned in the Notes, the author consulted Baseball-Reference.com.

NOTES

1   Tommy Holmes, "Big Joe and Power Get Dodgers Away," *Brooklyn Daily Eagle*, October 2, 1952: 17.

2   Holmes.

3   Holmes.

4   "Make It A 1-2 Punch!" *Brooklyn Daily Eagle*, October 2, 1952: 1.

5   John Drebinger, "Yanks, Behind Raschi, Rout Dodgers, 7-1, to Tie Series," *New York Times*, October 3, 1952: 1.

6   Drebinger.

7   Drebinger.

8   Drebinger.

9   Harold C. Burr, "Dodger Defense Must Perk Up or Else...." *Brooklyn Daily Eagle*, October 3, 1952: 17.

Mantle and Berra power Yankees
to force Game Seven

October 6, 1952

New York Yankees 3, Brooklyn Dodgers 2 | Game Six of the World Series

by Gregory H. Wolf

For the first time in six World Series appearances, the Dodgers reached Game Six with a chance to capture their first title in franchise history. Coming off a dramatic 6-5 victory in 11 innings over the New York Yankees in the Bronx to take the Series lead, "Dem Bums" returned to Brooklyn and Ebbets Field, where oddsmakers favored them to win the championship, but predicted a loss in Game Six.[1]

In his second season, skipper Charlie Dressen had guided the Dodgers to the best record in baseball (96-57) and their third pennant since Jackie Robinson integrated baseball five years earlier. The club was led by baseball's most potent offense, pacing the majors in scoring (5.0 runs per game) and home runs (153). Its weakness was its pitching staff, opined beat reporter Tommy Holmes, even though it finished with a stellar 3.53 team ERA, second best in the NL.[2] With three-time All-Star Don Newcombe missing the entire season due to military commitments, the Dodgers lacked a bona fide ace. Carl Erskine (14-6) had led the team with 26 starts and was one of five hurlers with at least 10 wins; however,

their most effective pitcher was reliever Joe Black (15-4). After making just two late September starts among his 56 appearances, the NL Rookie of the Year was thrust into the spotlight, starting the Series Opener and Game Four, and was the presumptive starter for Game Seven, if needed. The Dodgers' hopes rested on Dressen's ability to "squeeze enough pitching out of a hurling staff, unorthodox by championship standards," contended Brooklyn sportswriter Harold C. Burr.[3]

Taking the mound for the Dodgers was 22-year-old rookie Billy Loes. The Long Island native, who became known for his wacky personality, went 13-8 with a 2.69 ERA, but found himself embroiled in a mini-controversy on the eve of the World Series when he claimed the Yankees would win it in seven games.[4] His only appearance in the Series thus far had not inspired confidence: In a two-inning relief stint in Game Two, Yogi Berra blasted a three-run home run off him.

The Yankees (95-59) were aiming for their fourth straight World Series title under skipper Casey Stengel. A balanced team, it boasted the

AL's second-highest scoring offense (4.7 runs per game) and a staff with the majors' lowest ERA (3.14) and two aces. Hard-throwing Allie Reynolds, an 11-year veteran with a 156-96 record, led the club with 20 wins and the AL with a 2.06 ERA and six shutouts. He had started Game One, tossed a shutout in Game Four, and was slated to start a possible Game Seven. Stengel tabbed Vic Raschi, who like Reynolds, earned his payday in the pressure cooker of the World Series, and was coming off a three-hit victory in Game Two. After winning 21 games for three consecutive seasons, Raschi had dropped to 16-6 in '52.

Potent offenses notwithstanding, the fall classic had been thus far been a "pitching series," opined sportswriter Dick Young.[5] The two teams had combined for just 35 runs, while four of the five games had been decided by two runs or less. The Dodgers had "scored a great moral victory" in their extra-inning affair in Game Five, submitted Holmes, but several of the team's major contributors were struggling at the plate.[6] Slugger Gil Hodges, who had led the team with 32 home runs and 102 RBIs, was hitless in 14 at-bats; Roy Campanella, whose 22 homers and 97 RBIs trailed only Hodges, was 3-for-20; while catalyst Jackie Robinson was just 3-for-15, but had drawn seven walks. An exception was Duke Snider, the star of the previous game with his second home run of the Series and a game-winning extra-inning double. The Dodgers were without slugger Andy Pafko, who had pulled a muscle in his left leg running out a grounder the day before, and was replaced by George Shuba.[7] Yankee stars were also scuffling. Middle infielders Phil Rizzuto (2-for-19) and Gil McDougald (2-for-16) weren't expected to carry the offense like Mickey Mantle and Berra; however, home-run threat Hank Bauer (1-for-17) was. Stengel shook up the lineup by benching Bauer and replacing him with utilityman Irv Noren.

The potentially biggest game in Dodgers history drew a "disappointing crowd," wrote Dick Young, despite ideal 70-degree weather on a sunny Monday afternoon at Ebbets Field.[8] The "astonishing" attendance of 30,037, considerably less than the 34,861 in Game One (as well as 70,536 in Game Five at Yankee Stadium), noted Arthur Daley of the *Times*, resulted from what he considered the Dodgers' tactical mistake of selling tickets for each game instead of in blocks.[9]

The game emerged as a pitchers' duel. Loes, who had not registered a victory since August 31, held the vaunted Bronx Bombers to two hits and three walks in six scoreless frames. Sportswriter Dave Anderson of the *Brooklyn Eagle* considered it the "best ball of the series."[10] Pitching on three days' rest, Raschi yielded what *Times* sportswriter Roscoe McGowen called a "lucky pop fly" double down the left-field foul line to the first batter he faced, Billy Cox, but stranded him on second.[11] Through five innings, Raschi surrendered only three more hits, all singles, and fanned six.

The bottom of the sixth was filled with "delirious moments," gushed John Drebinger, when Snider led off by spanking Raschi's first pitch over the right-field screen and onto Bedford Avenue to give the Dodgers a 1-0 lead.[12] Raschi retired the next three batters.

When Loes took the mound to begin the seventh, it "looked like the Dodgers were ready to wrap up their first championship," opined Burr.[13] However, the crowd's euphoria dramatically evaporated when Berra tied the game, 1-1, with a leadoff home run to almost the exact same spot as Snider's. Loes looked "visually perturbed," observed Burr.[14] "I tried to get it high and outside," said Loes later about his intent to waste the pitch.[15] After Gene Woodling singled, Loes balked. "I was trying to grip the ball for a curve," said the pitcher.[16] However, the "pitch squirted out," quipped Young, "like a cake of squeezed soap," and Woodling advanced into scoring position.[17] Dressen calmly walked to the mound to speak with his inexperienced hurler, who he claimed had gotten "a little unstrung after that balk"; while Campy told his batterymate to slow down.[18] Loes regained his composure, fanned Noren and retired Billy Martin on a popup. As the midday sun from behind home plate cast long shadows onto the field, Raschi hit a hard grounder back to the mound that ricocheted off Loes' knee and into short right field.[19] Woodling easily scored while right fielder Carl Furillo retrieved the ball.

In the bottom of the seventh, Loes singled with two outs. With a hit-and-run in place, Loes broke for second, but Cox took the pitch. Loes looked like a "cooked goose," sniped Young, but second baseman Martin muffed the throw and Loes was credited with a rare stolen base for a pitcher. Then he was left stranded when Raschi struck out Billy Cox.

Mantle led off the eighth with a towering home run to deep left-center-field to extend the Yankees' lead to 3-1. It was the 13th round-tripper in the World Series, breaking the record of 12 set in the 1925 Series between the Washington Senators and the Pittsburgh Pirates.

Snider rekindled Dodger fans' hope for victory with his second home run of the game, a deep shot to right-field with one out in the eighth. His fourth World Series round-tripper tied a Series record set by Babe Ruth (1926) and Lou Gehrig (1928). Shuba's double brought the Ole Perfessor from the dugout. Raschi "didn't have his best stuff," said Stengel, who called on Allie Reynolds to put out the fire.[20]

In what sportswriter Stan Baumgartner described as a "magnificent" performance, Reynolds showed his grit and tenacity.[21] On his first pitch he brushed back Campanella and ultimately fanned him.[22]

The Yankees threatened again in the ninth with consecutive one-out singles by McDougald and Rizzuto to send Loes to the showers. He was replaced by Preacher Roe, who filled the bases on four straight wide pitches to Mantle, then struck out Joe Collins, a late-inning defensive replacement for Johnny Mize at first base, and retired Berra on a liner to right field.

Reynolds worked around a one-out walk to Furillo in the ninth to secure the Yankees' victory in 2 hours and 56 minutes and force Game Seven. "I didn't have any trouble out there," said Reynolds, who tossed 22 pitches, but also slightly pulled a back muscle falling off the mound. "I used mostly fast stuff."[23]

It was a tough loss for the Dodgers, but no one blamed Loes. "He pitched a fine game," said Campy. "He had a good curve and generally good control and a lot of nerve."[24] More than anything, Loes forced Stengel to use Reynolds, his Game Seven starter, to save the win, causing havoc with his pitching staff. "I honestly don't know now who I'll use," said Stengel. "I ain't trying to be mysterious. ... I'll decide tomorrow morning."[25]

SOURCES

In addition to the sources cited in the Notes, the author accessed Retrosheet.org, Baseball-Reference.com, and SABR.org.

NOTES

1   The Dodgers were made slight favorites, 6-5, to win the World Series in seven games; however, the Yankees were given 8-5 odds to win Game Six. See Tommy Holmes, "Raschi 8-5 Choice Over Loes," *Brooklyn Eagle*, October 6, 1952: 1.

2   Holmes, "Raschi 8-5 Choice Over Loes."

3   Harold C. Burr, "Joe Black Confident on Eve of His Big Day," *Brooklyn Eagle*, September 30, 1952: 1.

4   Jimmy Breslin, "The Dodgers' New Daffiness Boy," *Saturday Evening Post*, August 23, 1953: 116.

5   Dick Young, "Yanks Win HR Duel, 3-1; Ties Series," *New York Daily News*, October 7, 1952: 60.

6   Holmes, "Raschi 8-5 Choice Over Loes."

7   Holmes, "Raschi 8-5 Choice Over Loes."

8   Young.

9   Arthur Daley, "Sports of the Times," *New York Times*, October 7, 1952: 35.

10 Dave Anderson, "Quiet in O'Malley's Alley," *Brooklyn Eagle*, October 7, 1952: 13.

11 Roscoe McGowen, "Brooklyn's Hopes for Series Honors Ride on Trusty Arm of Joe Black," *New York Times*, October 7, 1952: 36.

12 John Drebinger, "Yanks Win, 3-2, Tie Dodgers; Series to Be Decided Today," *New York Times*, October 7, 1952: 1.

13 Harold C. Burr, "Dodgers Ready for Zero Hour in Fall Classic," *Brooklyn Eagle*, October 7, 1952: 17.

14 Burr, "Dodgers Ready for Zero Hour in Fall Classic."

15 Dana Mozley, "Snider HRs Tie Ruth, Lou; Casey Ouija Says 'Gorman,'" *New York Daily News*, October 7, 1952: 61.

16 Associated Press, "Sad Dodgers Replay Loss in Dressing Room," *Chicago Tribune*, October 7, 1952: F2.

17 Young.

18 Anderson.

19 In one of his typically zany comments, Loes calmly explained his miscues in his strong New York City accent and gruff, profanity-ridden language (which sportswriters liberally edited): "I might have had the [expletive] thing if it wasn't for the low sun shining in my face." Tommy Holmes, "High Homers, Low Sun Foil Paleface Kid," *Brooklyn Eagle*, October 7, 1952: 13.

20 Anderson.

21 Stan Baumgartner, "Yankees Bat Dodgers, 3-2, to Even Series," *Philadelphia Inquirer*, October 7, 1952: 1.

22 Harold C. Burr, "Dodgers Ready for Zero Hour in Fall Classic."

23 James P. Dawson, "We'll Give Them Our Best Today; Stengel Searching for Fourth Series in a Row," *New York Times*, October 7, 1952: 35.

24 Holmes, "High Homers, Low Sun Foil Paleface Kid."

25 Ted Smits (Associated Press), "Casey Stengel 'Not Sure' Who Will Oppose Black in Today's Series Finale," *Oneonta* (New York) *Star*, October 7, 1952: 10.

BILLY MARTIN SAVES THE SERIES

October 7, 1952

New York Yankees 4, Brooklyn Dodgers 2 | Games Seven of the World Series

by Stew Thornley

The 1952 World Series was the fourth straight for the New York Yankees and the third in six seasons for the Brooklyn Dodgers. The teams had met in the last Game Seven, in 1947, with the Yankees winning—a familiar outcome. In 1952, New York was looking for its 15th world championship, the Dodgers, seemingly as ever, for their first.

Joe DiMaggio was gone, with Mickey Mantle moving from right field to take his place in center. DiMaggio had played in 10 World Series with the Yankees, but in only one that went to a seventh game. That was still one more than DiMaggio's long-time teammate, Bill Dickey, who had played in eight World Series. He was participating in his first Game Seven in 1952—as a coach.

Another man taking part in his first seventh game was Casey Stengel, the New York manager. Stengel had played in three World Series, two of them against the Yankees, and managed in three, winning all of them, since becoming manager of the team in 1949. Under Stengel, the Yankees beat Brooklyn in five games in 1949, Philadelphia

in four games in 1950, and the New York Giants in six games in 1951.

In 1952, however, the Yankees had a greater challenge and trailed after five games as the Series shifted from Yankee Stadium back to Ebbets Field in Brooklyn. Despite two home runs by the Dodgers' Duke Snider, New York won the sixth game. In doing so, Stengel had to upset his pitching plans, calling on Allie Reynolds—whom he planned to start in the seventh game—in relief of his starter, Vic Raschi. As a result, Stengel was undecided on a starter for the seventh game.

On the other hand, everything remained in place for Brooklyn manager Chuck Dressen and his pitcher of choice for the World Series finale, Joe Black. Black had pitched eight seasons with the Baltimore Elite Giants in the Negro National and Negro American leagues before spending the 1951 season with Montreal in the International League and St. Paul in the American Association. Black became a 28-year-old rookie with Brooklyn in 1952 and was the Dodgers' relief ace, compiling a 14-3 record out of the bullpen. He added a win and a loss as a starter late in the season, part of

Dressen's plan to rely on Black in the World Series. Dressen worked out the timing of Black's starts so that he could be the starting pitcher in the series opener on Wednesday, October 1. Black won that game but was the losing pitcher in the fourth game on Saturday, October 4, despite giving up only one run and three hits in seven innings. Dressen had said he might use Black both as a starter and reliever in the series, and Black warmed up in the bullpen during the fifth game, but didn't come in. He stayed exclusively a starting pitcher.

With the World Series taking place entirely within one city, no travel off-days were necessary, and the series was played on consecutive dates, meaning that Black had only two days of rests between his starts. In the first and fourth games, Black had pitched against Reynolds, and the two would have met again if not for Reynolds's relief stint the day before.

Stengel considered rookie Tom Gorman, who had made one relief appearance in the series, before finally settling on left-hander Eddie Lopat, who had pitched 8 1/3 innings in losing the third game, four days before. Stengel didn't make his decision on a starter until 11:30, fewer than two hours before the game. "I had 55 reasons why I should not start Lopat, but I had 56 reasons why I should," explained Stengel, although the loquacious Case did not follow up with a Stengelese elaboration on those reasons.[1]

The Yankee team bus drew a police escort from Yankee Stadium to Ebbets Field, but partway there, a candy red sports car joined the motorcade. A motorcycle cop in the escort dropped back to tell the driver to buzz off, but it turned out to be Phil Rizzuto, who chose to drive himself from his New Jersey home to his native Brooklyn.

Ebbets Field was full for Game Seven, unlike the sixth game when the attendance was several thousand short of capacity. The Dodgers sold tickets for each game individually instead of in blocks, as the Yankees had done. As a result, Brooklyn found itself with unpurchased tickets for the sixth game. However, when it was clear that the entire Series would come down to one game, long lines of ticket buyers circled Ebbets Field through the evening following the sixth game and on the morning of the seventh game.

Neither team got a runner past first base through the first three innings. Black retired the Yankees in order in the first, walked lead-off hitter Johnny Mize before retiring the next three batters on fly outs in the second, and then put the Yankees down without a runner in the third.

Lopat was equally effective over that span, although he got a couple breaks in the first inning. With one out, Pee Wee Reese reached first on a throwing error by third baseman Gil McDougald. However, had McDougald's throw not struck Brooklyn first-base coach Jake Pitler, Reese likely would have ended up on second. With two out, Jackie Robinson hit a hard liner to left-center. Gene Woodling raced to his left to make the catch and save a run. Lopat allowed a two-out single to George "Shotgun" Shuba in the second and retired the Dodgers in order in the third.

Phil Rizzuto led off the top of the fourth with the Yankees' first hit, a double inside the third-base bag, and went to third on a ground out by Mantle. John Mize stepped up and hit a hard drive to right that hooked foul, then went the opposite way with a line-drive single to bring home Rizzuto. Yogi Berra grounded into a double play to end the inning, but the Yankees had a 1-0 lead.

The lead didn't last long as Lopat was unable to retire a batter in the bottom of the fourth. Snider opened with a single, and Jackie Robinson put down a bunt, intending to sacrifice Snider to second. Robinson's bunt, down the third-base line, was so well-placed that he also reached safely. Roy Campanella followed with the same intention, a bunt designed to move up the runners, and likewise ended up with a hit, filling the bases.

This was enough for Stengel, who brought in the man he had decided not to start, Allie Reynolds, to face the right-handed hitting Gil Hodges. Hodges had endured a miserable series. He was hitless in 17 at-bats through the first six games. He had struck out three times before being lifted for a pinch-hitter in the sixth game and had flied out his first time up in Game Seven. Against Reynolds, Hodges flied out again, but it was deep enough to bring home Snider with the tying run. (Although Hodges got a run batted in, he was charged with an at-bat on the play, as it wasn't until 1954 that the practice resumed of awarding a sacrifice fly—with no at-bat charged—for a run-scoring fly ball.)

In addition to Snider scoring on Hodges' fly, Robinson took third as Reynolds fumbled Woodling's throw to the plate. Robinson stayed at third, though, when Shuba struck out and Carl Furillo grounded to McDougald to end the inning.

Woodling quickly put the Yankees back in front, opening the fifth with a home run onto Bedford Avenue, beyond the right-field fence. Joe Black told reporters, "My curve spun but it didn't move."[2] The Dodgers came back again, tying the score on a one-out double off the fence in right-center by Billy Cox and a single to left by Reese. Cox scored on the hit, and Reese went to second as Woodling uncorked a wild throw. Snider grounded out, sending Reese to third, and Robinson ripped a liner toward left that McDougald speared for the third out to prevent Brooklyn from taking the lead.

Instead, the Yankees got the go-ahead run in the top of the sixth. After Rizzuto lined out, Mantle hit a towering home run to right-center. A single by Mize finished off Black, who gave way to Preacher Roe. With another hit and an error, New York loaded the bases, but Roe got out of the inning without any more damage.

Campanella started the last of the sixth with a single but was wiped out as the hitless Hodges grounded into a double play. Shuba grounded out to end the sixth with the Dodgers down by a run.

New York made it a two-run margin in the seventh, scoring a single run for the fourth inning in a row, as Mantle singled in McDougald from second with two out. Reynolds had been removed for a pinch-hitter in that inning, and Vic Raschi, who had pitched 7 2/3 innings the day before, was on the mound for the last of the seventh. Raschi walked Furillo but got Rocky Nelson, hitting for Roe, to pop out. Cox came through with a single and Reese walked to load the bases. With the left-handed hitting Snider up next, Stengel called for southpaw Bob Kuzava. A year before, against the New York Giants, Kuzava had saved the final game of the World Series, but he had seen little action during the final weeks of the 1952 season.

Snider worked the count full, then popped out when Kuzava handcuffed him with an inside fastball. "The pitch was right down the middle," Kuzava told reporters later. "The type that Snider could powder a mile."[3] With Johnny Sain warming up in the New York bullpen, Kuzava thought he would be lifted. Stengel even started toward the mound, but then changed his mind and returned to the dugout, leaving Kuzava in to face Jackie Robinson. Like Snider, Jackie Robinson popped up. Robinson's fly, however, became anything but routine. "Nobody told me he (Kuzava) could break it off that good," Robinson later said of Kuzava's curve.[4]

First baseman Joe Collins lost sight of ball in the sun, leaving it to second baseman Billy Martin. Collins thought it was a foul ball in the stands. Martin knew otherwise. As Martin moved in for the catch, a gusting wind pulled the ball back to the plate. Martin sped up, lunged, and caught the ball about two feet off the ground, ending the inning. "He ran out from under his hat and almost ran out of his shoes in a breakneck lunge," wrote Arthur Daley in the *New York Times*.[5]

The play was greeted with a lack of sympathy for Collins and Martin. Stengel yelled at Collins, "Wake up out there," while Yankee General Manager George Weiss, sitting in the team's field box, and never a fan of Billy, sneered, "Little show-off. He made an easy play look hard." Martin himself didn't realize how tough the catch was until he saw the films after the game.[6]

Accounts differ as to what the impact would have been had the ball dropped safely. Some versions of the play claim the count to Robinson was 3-2, meaning that the runners would have been going on the pitch and give some credence to the claim that three runs might have scored, giving the Dodgers the lead. Stan Baumgartner, in the 1953 *The Sporting News Baseball Guide*, also said the count was 3-2. However, the game story by Dan Daniel (writing under the byline "Daniel") in the *New York World-Telegram* and Red Smith's column in the *New York Herald-Tribune* both give the count as two balls and two strikes. As for Kuzava, he recalls that the count was 2-2 but that, even with the runners not going on the pitch, "they all would have scored."[7]

Kuzava was correct about the count, confirmed by a full-game broadcast now available. (The pitch sequence to Robinson was foul, ball, ball, foul, foul, pop up.) However, the video also shows Reese just around second when the ball was caught, and it is clear that he would not have scored. Regardless of how many runs would have come home on the play, the Yankees' lead would have been wiped out. But Martin, with his grab, prevented that from happening.

It was the Dodgers' last threat. Hodges got to first on an error with one out in the eighth (his 21st at-bat without a hit in the series), but Kuzava allowed no more baserunners, retiring the final five Dodgers in the eighth and ninth innings, and New York had a 4-2 win, and the World Championship.

Gloomy Dodger fans endured the final innings. After the game, Dodger organist Gladys Gooding serenaded them with a medley of appropriate songs, which included "Blues in the Night," "What Can I Say, Dear, After I Say I'm Sorry," "This Nearly Was Mine," "What a Difference A Day Makes," and finally, "Auld Lang Syne."

Casey Stengel explained the victory in typical fashion: "Them Brooklyns is a little tough in this park," he said. "But I knew we would win today. My men play good ball on the road. Now, you are gonna ask me why I left in the left-hand fella [Kuzava] to face the right-hand fella [Robinson], who makes speeches, with bases full. Don't I know percentages and et cetera? The reason I left him in is the other man [Robinson] has not seen hard-throwing left-hand pitchers much and could have trouble with the break of a left-hander's hard curve, which is what happened."[8]

For Mickey Mantle, who had the game-winning home run, the end of the season meant a return to the mines. "I've had enough excitement for one season," he told the United Press, "so I'm going right back to work in the lead and zinc mines of Oklahoma, where things are a little more quiet."[9] He added that he had seven dependents to care for: three brothers, a sister, his mother, his wife, and a baby due in March.

For Casey Stengel, the win allowed him to join Joe McCarthy as the only manager to win four consecutive World Series. McCarthy did it with New York in 1936 to 1939, the Yankees not even having to go to a seventh game in any of those years.

Stengel topped McCarthy when New York won the World Series again in 1953, once again beating the Dodgers, this time in six games. The Yankees, with 19 pennants and 15 World Series championships since 1921, were in the midst of their greatest dominance. However, they would encounter a few bumps, along with several more Game Sevens, during its dynasty.

SOURCES

In addition to the sources cited in the Notes, the author accessed Retrosheet.org, Baseball-Reference.com, and SABR.org.

NOTES

1   Louis Effrat, "Dodgers' Organist Plays the 'Blues," *New York Times*, Wednesday, October 8, 1952: 38.

2   Cecilia Tan, *50 Greatest Yankees Games in Yankee History*, (Hoboken: Wiley and Sons, 2005), 83.

3   Tan, 84.

4   Tan, 84.

5   Tan, 84.

6   Peter Golenbock, *Wild, High, and Tight: The Life and Death of Billy Martin* (New York: St. Martin's Press, 1994), 72 and 73.

7   Author's interview with Bob Kuzava, September 29, 2002.

8   Roger Kahn, *The Era*, 1947-1957, (New York: Ticknor & Fields, 1993), 308.

9   "Mantle to Return to Peace of Mine" by Mickey Mantle, as told to The United Press, *New York Times*, Wednesday, October 8, 1952: 38.

Dodgers clobber Giants to extend winning streak to 13 games

August 20, 1953

Brooklyn Dodgers 10, New York Giants 0

by John J. Burbridge Jr.

The New York Giants were scheduled to play the Brooklyn Dodgers in the final game of a three-games series at Ebbets Field on August 20, 1953. Eleven days earlier, Charlie Dressen, the Dodgers manager, had proclaimed, "The Giants is dead!"[1] Twenty-nine years before that, in 1934, Giants manager Bill Terry, when asked about the Dodgers at a preseason event, commented, "I haven't heard anything from them; are they still in the league?"[2] The 1934 season ended at the Polo Grounds as the Dodgers played spoiler and deprived the Giants of a National League pennant by winning the final two games of the season before loud and vociferous Dodger fans.[3] The Giants had been tied with the St. Louis Cardinals before the final two games. Giants fans were hoping that Dressen's proclamation would motivate the Giants but this was not to be the case: The Dodgers won the first two games of the series, giving them a 12-game winning streak.

In this final game of the series, Carl Erskine (14-5, 3.72 ERA) was the starting pitcher for the Dodgers and 25-year-old rookie Ruben Gomez (10-6, 3.01) took the mound for the Giants. The Dodgers were led by their Boys of Summer, Jackie Robinson, Duke Snider, Billy Cox, and Roy Campanella.[4] Pee Wee Reese was taking the day off and Bobby Morgan was playing shortstop. They had an 8½-game lead over the Milwaukee Braves in the National League pennant race; the Giants found themselves 22½ games behind the Dodgers. The Giants had Alvin Dark, Don Mueller, and Bobby Thomson in their starting lineup and were managed by Leo Durocher. As long as Leo was managing the Giants, there was the potential for sparks to fly between the two hated rivals.[5] Not in the lineup for the Giants was Willie Mays, who had been drafted into the US Army in 1952. As their performance showed, the Giants were missing the Say-Hey Kid.

Erskine retired the Giants in order in the top of the first. With one out in the bottom half, Morgan walked. Gomez struck out Snider, but Robinson reached first base and Morgan went to second when the Giants shortstop, Alvin Dark, made an error on Robinson's groundball. Campanella followed with a line drive into the left-field corner for a double, scoring Morgan and Robinson with

289

two unearned runs. Campanella went to third on the throw home but Gomez ended the inning by getting Gil Hodges to fly out to left field.

The second inning was uneventful. In the top of the third, the Giants threatened. Wes Westrum and Gomez led off with singles. But Erskine retired Dark, Whitey Lockman, and Hank Thompson on a foul popup and two grounders. The Dodgers lengthened their lead to 5-0 in the bottom of the inning. Morgan walked with one out, Snider singled, and Robinson hit a three-run home run in the lower left-field stands. The Dodgers continued to threaten but with the bases loaded, Erskine flied out to center, ending the inning.

Don Mueller led off the Giants fourth with a single but Erskine retired the next three batters. In the bottom of the inning, Junior Gilliam led off with a home run over the scoreboard in right field onto Bedford Avenue, bringing an end to Gomez's day. He was replaced by Monty Kennedy, who was ineffective. Singles by Morgan and Campanella and a walk to Hodges loaded the bases, and another walk, to Carl Furillo, forced in a run and increased the Dodgers' lead to 7-0. Marv Grissom relieved Kennedy and was greeted by Cox's two-run single. Grissom retired Erskine on a groundball, ending the inning with the Dodgers leading 9-0.

The Giants went out in order in the top of the fifth, but in the Dodgers' half of the inning, Bobby Morgan homered, the Dodgers' third home run of the day. The score was now 10-0. In the Giants sixth, Hank Thompson doubled to right off the scoreboard with one out and took third on Mueller's groundout, becoming the first Giant to reach third. But Bobby Thomson's popup ended the inning.

The remaining innings proved uneventful until with two outs in the top of the ninth, a small boy ran onto the field and raced around the outfield, getting a pat on the back from Snider. He then ran to the scoreboard in right field with a

policeman in pursuit. The boy opened the door in the scoreboard, and he and the policeman disappeared. After the third out, ending the game, the policeman emerged from the scoreboard without the boy. Apparently, the scoreboard tender had hidden the boy.[6]

Erskine allowed only four hits and retired the last 11 Giants in order with Hank Thompson on his sixth-inning double being the last Giants batter to get on base. The win was Erskine's 15th. He had shut out the Giants on August 11, giving him 19 consecutive shutout innings against the Polo Grounders.[7] After the August 20 game, Dressen praised his pitcher: "If the All-Star game is coming up now, I'd start Erskine. I'd start him against anybody. (Robin) Roberts is faster and has better control than Erskine. But Erskine's curve is better and so is his changeup. His changeup is the best in the league."[8] (Dressen also organized a small party in the Dodgers clubhouse after the game. He had 20 pounds of crab fingers shipped up from Vero Beach, Florida, garnished with butter and cocktail sauce. He also provided a few bottles of pink champagne.[9])

The victory was the Dodgers' 13th in a row, increasing their lead over the Braves to nine games. The Giants fell to 23½ games behind the league leaders. Asked whether he was shooting for the winning streak record of 26 games, set by the Giants in 1916, Dressen replied, "We won't think about that. I remember now — that was the year Ferdie Schupp got hot for John McGraw, wasn't it? The Giants didn't win the pennant either."[10] Apparently, Charlie did not want to jinx his team.

While the Dodgers were just halfway to the major-league record, they were only two away from the team record of 15, set by the 1924 Dodgers. The 1947 Dodgers also won 13 in a row.[11]

The day after Erskine's victory, the Dodgers played the Pirates in Pittsburgh and lost, 7-1. Their streak was over.

While the winning streak may have ended, the Dodgers went on to finish first in the

Jackie Robinson and Roy Campanella bashed NL pitchers in 1953. Jackie slashed 12/95/.329 with a .425 on-base-percentage and .502 slugging percentage, while Campy won his second of three NL MVP wards with his best season, setting personal records with 41 home runs, 142 RBIs, and a .611 slugging percentage. (Photo: SABR-Rucker Archive)

National League, winning 105 games. The Giants continued to falter and finished in fifth place with a record of 70-84. Roy Campanella was the National League's Most Valuable Player with a batting average of .312, an on-base percentage of .395, and 142 RBIs. Carl Furillo (.344) emerged as the NL batting champion. On September 6 in a game against the Giants at the Polo Grounds, Furillo was hit by a pitch and went to first base. From first base, he charged the Giants dugout. He was met by Durocher who had been taunting him. During the skirmish, Furillo fractured a bone in his left hand, ending his season.[12] (He had enough at-bats to qualify for the batting title.) Snider and Robinson also had super seasons. Snider led the league in slugging average (.627) and hit 42 home runs. Robinson had a batting average of .329 with an on-base percentage of .425. Erskine led the pitching staff with a 20-6 record.

The Dodgers had high hopes as they once again faced the New York Yankees in the World Series. The Yankees won the first two games, at Yankee Stadium. The Dodgers rebounded to win Games Three and Four, at Ebbets Field, but lost Game Five, 11-7. In Game Six, at Yankee Stadium, the Yankees won the World Series with a 4-3 victory, with Billy Martin knocking in the winning run in the bottom of the ninth.

During the offseason, Dodgers manager Dressen attempted to negotiate a three-year contract. The Dodgers responded by offering another one-year deal. Since Dressen did not back off in the negotiations, the Dodgers named Walter Alston their manager. The Alston era and his consecutive one-year contracts thus began.

With Willie Mays back from military duty, the Giants won the National League pennant and the World Series in 1954. In 1955 the Dodgers finally beat the Yankees in the World Series. "Wait Till Next Year" had finally arrived.

SOURCES

In addition to the sources mentioned in the Notes, the author consulted Baseball-Reference.com.

NOTES

1   Roscoe McGowen, "Erskine's 4-Hitter Marks 10-0 Victory," *New York Times*, August 21, 1953: 11.

2   Fred Stein, "Bill Terry," SABR BioProject, https://sabr.org/bioproj/person/4281b131.

3   "Bill Terry."

4   Roger Kahn, *The Boys of Summer* (New York: Harper and Row, 1972).

5   John J. Burbridge Jr. and John R. Harris, "The Giants-Dodgers Rivalry During 'The Era': The Dark-Robinson Incident," *The National Pastime*, 2017. https://sabr.org/research/dodgers-giants-rivalry-during-era-dark-robinson-incident.

6   McGowen, "Erskine's 4-Hitter Marks 10-0 Victory."

7   "Flock on Victory Swing," *Brooklyn Daily Eagle*, August 21, 1953: 13.

8   Dave Anderson, "Erskine Best Hurler in Loop," *Brooklyn Daily Eagle*, August 21, 1953: 13.

9   Tommy Holmes, "Dodgers Win Streaks – Past and Present," *Brooklyn Daily Eagle*, August 21, 1953: 13.

10 Holmes.

11 Holmes.

12 Louis Effrat, "Durocher and Furillo Stage Battle; Dodger Player Fractures Left Hand," *New York Times*, September 7, 1953: 1.

Brooklyn's bats and Erskine's arm subdue Muggsy's insults

August 30, 1953
Brooklyn Dodgers 20, St. Louis Cardinals 4

by Russ Lake

The Brooklyn Dodgers were as hot as the steamy weather that had ruled New York City boroughs for five days.[1] The talented first-place squad was 88-40 and had a comfortable 10½-game lead over the Milwaukee Braves with four weeks of the season remaining. However, an anonymous letter postmarked from Youngstown, Ohio, and addressed to Dodgers manager Chuck Dressen did not wax kindly toward the Dodgers' season. The text read in part, "What are you trying to do – dominate the National League? If you win the pennant this year, you will be shot. Yours in sports. A Rabid Fan." Dressen surmised, "Fine stuff. If I win the pennant, I'll be shot. If [I] lose it, I'll be lynched. People are unreasonable."[2]

Dressen disclosed that he had received a similar warning communication from north-eastern Ohio before the end of the previous season, and nothing happened.[3] His thoughts turned to the fourth-place St. Louis Cardinals (70-56), who were in town for a three-game series beginning Sunday, August 30, at Ebbets Field. The Cardinals were skippered by combative Durocher disciple and former Dodger Eddie Stanky, whose nicknames included Muggsy and The Brat.[4]

Rookie southpaw Harvey Haddix (16-6, 3.47 ERA), who was 3-0 vs. the Dodgers so far in the season, started against Carl Erskine (16-5, 3.60). The veteran right-hander Erskine had an 11-4 career mark against St. Louis. With a forecast of 90 degrees, many New Yorkers flocked to beaches and elsewhere hoping to cool off.[5] Nevertheless, a crowd of 16,781 made their way into the ballpark.

With the exception of a walk to Stan Musial, Erskine had an easy first inning. It could have been the same result for Haddix, but an error by shortstop Solly Hemus on Pee Wee Reese's grounder extended Brooklyn's chances. Reese went to second on a groundout, swiped third, and scored on a single by Jackie Robinson. Roy Campanella followed with his 34th home run deep into the left-field seats. The Schaefer Beer scoreboard displayed the Dodgers up, 3-0. All three runs were unearned.

The Cardinals stranded two runners in the second when Erskine pitched around a walk and a base hit by Sal Yvars. Carl Furillo opened the

Dodgers' second with a single. Haddix had Furillo picked off, but first baseman Steve Bilko muffed the throw. Furillo advanced to second on Bilko's miscue, and later scored from third on Erskine's fly ball, the Dodgers' fourth unearned run.

After Hemus tripled in the third, Musial put St. Louis on the board with a line drive to right-center that cleared the scoreboard for his 20th home run. Musial's blast not only cut the Cardinals' deficit in half; it expanded his NL record of scoring 100 or more runs to 10 consecutive seasons.[6] Brooklyn responded in its half when Campanella singled home Duke Snider. The Dodgers loaded the bases, but Haddix escaped the jam to keep the score at 5-2.

Both teams went scoreless during the next two frames, and the Cardinals made it 5-3 in the sixth. Enos Slaughter led off with a double, took third on a fly out, and sprinted home on a groundout. The Dodgers answered once again to push their lead to 6-3 when Jim Gilliam singled in Bobby Morgan. Haddix made it through the rest of the frame unscathed, but Stanky decided to lift his southpaw.

St. Louis had scored prolifically in the seventh inning of its last five games, so Stanky hoped his hitters could muster another rally.[7] With one out, Red Schoendienst, the NL batting leader at .340 but nursing an ankle injury, batted for Haddix and grounded out.[8] Erskine put down the Cardinals on three straight infield outs.

Right-hander Eddie Erautt came on to pitch for the Cardinals, and Stanky decided to initiate some entertainment-style bench banter. Jackie Robinson, who had been nursing a sore left knee, moved toward the plate while Muggsy went into his act. First, the St. Louis pilot motioned like an ape in the dugout, and then held onto a knee to get a rise from Robinson.[9] The fans on the first-base side saw what Stanky was doing, and they initially laughed, but then the partisan crowd began to boil with anger and boo the former Brooklynite. After Robinson lost his balance to avoid an inside

pitch while protecting his knee, he and Stanky exchanged barbs. Stanky barked that Jackie could fool himself, but not any ballplayers about the injury. Robinson stepped out and countered, saying that surely Stanky had fooled someone in St. Louis to be awarded a three-year contract.[10]

Erautt struck out Robinson and Stanky continued his insults by tossing towels in derision. Next, the scrappy manager wrapped his right knee (not the left), and limped to the water cooler. After returning to the Brooklyn dugout, Robinson ripped down the posted lineup card and waved it at Stanky. The St. Louis manager had earlier erred twice this season by issuing the wrong batting order to the umpires, thus causing automatic outs for his team.[11]

The roof was about to collapse on the mind-baiting Stanky and his squad. Erautt allowed a single to Campanella, walked Gil Hodges and Furillo, and then went 2-and-0 to Morgan. Stanky trudged out sans towel to bring in left-hander Cliff Chambers. During the parade of walks, Robinson held up a cardboard sign that read "How to Make Up a Lineup, by Eddie Stanky."[12]

Upon Stanky's return to the dugout, Brooklyn fans waved white handkerchiefs and tossed food items at him.[13] Chambers completed Erautt's mid-batter free pass, forcing in a run that made it 7-3, and then gave up a two-run single to Erskine. Another walk and two more hits followed to produce three additional tallies for a 12-3 spread. Out came Stanky again as the crowd was in a frenzy with the rout taking place. Willard Schmidt, a month removed from Triple A, was summoned from the bullpen. As Stanky traipsed back to his bench, a familiar local favorite postured herself next to the visiting dugout. Hilda Chester the cowbell lady, taunted Stanky as part of the hankie-waving swarm.[14]

The right-handed Schmidt fanned Robinson; however Stanky was beyond taking delight, or in conjuring up additional attempts to hex the

Dem Bums taking batting practice in an empty Ebbets Field. The Dodgers led or co-led the NL in home runs in every season from 1949 through 1955. (Photo: SABR-Rucker Archive)

Dodgers. Campanella singled home a pair before Hodges walked again, and Furillo chased both runners home with a double. Morgan hit the next pitch for his sixth homer to increase the assault to 18-3. The carnage finally ended when Erskine struck out, and the scoreboard operator slipped the little-used "12" plate into the slot for the Dodgers' seventh. Brooklyn had sent 15 batters to the plate for a dozen runs on seven hits with Campanella, Hodges, Furillo, and Morgan all scoring twice in the inning. It was the most runs scored during the seventh inning in the NL since 1925.[15] An oddity of the frame was that the ineffective Redbird relievers had actually struck out the side.

St. Louis plated a meaningless run in the eighth, and Brooklyn notched a hollow pair to bring about the eventual 20-4 final. Erskine (17-5) finished off the Dodger pitchers' first complete game in their last eight contests in 3:04, and Haddix (16-7) took the loss. Campanella drove in five runs with his four safeties to move his league-leading RBI total to 122. This tied him with former NL catchers Gabby Hartnett (Chicago Cubs, 1930) and Walker Cooper (New York Giants, 1947). The line score for the Dodgers read 20 runs, 19 hits, no errors, while the Cardinals' numbers showed 4 runs, 8 hits, 2 errors. St. Louis was now 0-for-9 in Brooklyn this season and had been outscored 91-28 in those contests.[16] The Dodgers magic number fell to 15.[17] Still, they nearly lost the day's top billing for a winning margin when the Milwaukee Braves pounded the Pittsburgh Pirates, 19-4, at Forbes Field.

Stanky proved to be a diehard in the clubhouse when he insisted, "The ball is too lively. Too many humpties are hitting home runs." Robinson continued rubbing it in on his former teammate. "Just like Durocher. Everything's lovely as long as they are ahead. When they get behind, they start their yapping," said Robinson.[18]

Days later, Robinson informed a Brooklyn scribe that his "best crack" at Stanky had not been quoted. "One Busch signed another bush," Robinson repeated for publication.[19]

SOURCES

In addition to the sources cited in the Notes, the author accessed Retrosheet.org, Baseball-Reference.com, Baseball-Almanac.com, Newspapers.com, SABR.org/bioproj, and *The Sporting News* archive via Paper of Record.

NOTES

1   David Quirk, "97.3, Year's Hottest; Cool Tuesday, Maybe," *New York Daily News*, August 30, 1953: 74.

2   Tommy Holmes, "Chuck 'On Spot' in Letter from Fan," *Brooklyn Eagle*, August 31, 1953: 11.

3   Roscoe McGowen, "Crank Threatens to Shoot Dressen if Brooklyn Wins," *The Sporting News*, September 9, 1953: 6.

4   Alexander Edelman, "Eddie Stanky," SABR Baseball Biography Project, https://sabr.org/bioproj/person/f33416b9.

5   Quirk, "97.3, Year's Hottest."

6   Bob Broeg, "Something Snaps as Cards Lose, 20-4," *St. Louis Post-Dispatch*, August 31, 1953: 16.

7   Broeg, "Something Snaps as Cards Lose, 20-4."

8   Bob Broeg, "Stanky Throws Open Roster in Pitch to Stimulate Birds," *The Sporting News*, September 9, 1953: 9.

9   Photograph Caption, "Ebbets Field Frolics," *Brooklyn Eagle*, August 31, 1953: 11.

10   Tommy Holmes, "Stanky Incites Flock to Big Spree," *Brooklyn Eagle*, August 31, 1953: 11.

11   Roscoe McGowen, "Bush Burlesque Show in Flatbush," *The Sporting News*, September 9, 1953: 5.

12   McGowen, "Bush Burlesque Show in Flatbush."

13   Holmes, "Stanky Incites Flock to Big Spree."

14   Photograph caption, "Ebbets Field Frolics."

15   Roscoe McGowen, "Only Seven Hits in Dozen Dodger Runs," *The Sporting News*, September 9, 1953: 6. On May 28, 1925, the Chicago Cubs scored 12 runs in the top of the seventh inning during a 13-3 win at Redland Field vs. the Cincinnati Reds. (https://www.retrosheet.org/boxesetc/1925/B05280CIN1925.htm).

16   Broeg, "Something Snaps as Cards Lose, 20-4." The Cardinals lost the next two games of the three-game set, 6-3 and 12-5, to end the '53 season winless at Ebbets Field.

17   "Dodgers Magic Number 15; Yankees 17," *Brooklyn Eagle*, August 31, 1953: 11.

18   Holmes, "Stanky Incites Flock to Big Spree."

19   McGowen, "Bush Burlesque Show in Flatbush."

ERSKINE SETS WORLD SERIES RECORD WITH 14 STRIKEOUTS

October 2, 1953

Brooklyn Dodgers 3, New York Yankees 2 | Game Three of World Series

by Don Zminda

When Game Three of the 1953 World Series began, Carl Erskine was looking for redemption. By the time it had finished, Erskine had not only gotten redemption – he had broken one of the most cherished records in World Series lore.

The 1953 Series marked the seventh World Series appearance for Erskine's Brooklyn Dodgers franchise, and the fifth matchup since 1941 between the Dodgers and the New York Yankees. The Dodgers, who were still looking for their first World Series championship, had come closest in 1952, taking the Yankees to the seven-game limit. Now, in 1953, they faced the Yankees again with one of the strongest teams in franchise history. Its 105 wins in 1953 would be the most for a Dodgers team until the 2019 Los Angeles Dodgers won 106 (the club also won 106 games in 2021), and the '53 team's .682 winning percentage remains the Dodger franchise's best since 1900 except for the .717 mark (43-17) that the club posted in the pandemic-shortened 2020 season.

Erskine had led the 1953 Dodgers mound staff with a 20-6 record, and he was manager Chuck Dressen's choice to start Game One against the Yankees' Allie Reynolds (13-7) at Yankee Stadium. The outing was a total disaster for Erskine; he walked three batters, surrendered two triples, and gave up four runs in the first inning before being lifted for a pinch-hitter in the top of the second. The Dodgers lost, 9-5; after dropping Game Two as well (4-2), the they were desperate for a win as the Series shifted to Ebbets Field for Games Three, Four, and Five.

Despite Erskine's horrid Game One appearance, his manager had not lost faith in him.

"Dressen came to me after that ballgame [Game One]," he recalled, "and he said, 'I know something about you. You've come back on short rest despite the fact that you've had arm trouble. ... I want to bring you back in the third game.' And I was dee-lighted. You don't often get that second shot that quick. And probably never before or since have I had as much determination as I had that day, and I told Duke [Snider] and Campy [Roy Campanella], 'I'm going to pitch every inning like it's my last, and these guys are not going to jump on me early.'"[1]

Erskine started Game Three strongly, striking out Gil McDougald and Joe Collins to begin the game. Hank Bauer grounded out to end the inning. In the second, Erskine issued two walks but got both Mickey Mantle and Phil Rizzuto on called third strikes. He recorded two more strikeouts in a one-two-three third: his mound opponent, Vic Raschi (13-6), and Collins (for the second time). In the fourth he allowed Yogi Berra to reach base via a hit by pitch, but fanned Mantle for his seventh strikeout of the game.

Through four innings Erskine had yet to allow a hit, but Raschi, who had defeated the Dodgers twice in the 1952 World Series, was tough as well, with only two hits allowed in four shutout innings. The Yankees broke through in the top of the fifth; Billy Martin and Rizzuto opened the frame with infield singles; both runners moved up on Raschi's sacrifice bunt, and Martin scored on a hard single by McDougald that was knocked down by Dodgers third baseman Billy Cox. Erskine escaped the jam with no further damage, striking out Collins for the third time and getting Bauer to bounce out to second. The Dodgers tied the game in the bottom of the inning when Jackie Robinson doubled, moved to third when "Jackie, dancing off second, made Vic Raschi balk,"[2] and then scored on a push bunt by Cox. "I did it on my own," said Cox, explaining that the bunt was not a squeeze play. " You don't have to tell Jackie to run when he sees you're going to bunt."[3]

After Erskine held the Yankees scoreless in the top of the sixth (with two more strikeouts, including Mantle for the third time), the Dodgers took a 2-1 lead in the bottom half when Duke Snider singled, Gil Hodges walked, and Robinson drove home Snider with a single to left.

Through six innings, Erskine had recorded 10 strikeouts, only three short of the World Series record set by Howard Ehmke in Game One of the 1929 Series against the Cubs.

In the seventh, an inning in which neither team scored, Erskine failed to record a strikeout

for the first time. He fanned Collins for the fourth time to open the eighth, but then gave up a single to Bauer before hitting Berra with a pitch for the second time in the game to put runners on first and second. Erskine got the second out by fanning Mantle – also for the fourth time – to give him 12 strikeouts in the game, but Gene Woodling singled to center to score Bauer with the tying run.

Raschi retired Hodges to open the bottom of the eighth, bringing up Roy Campanella. The Dodgers catcher had badly bruised his hand in Game Two and had been considered a doubtful starter for the third game. Robinson said later that as Campanella took his stance, Yankees manager Casey Stengel was pointing to his left ear, and he was yelling at Raschi, "Stick it in his ear, stick it in his ear." Instead, wrote Dave Anderson, "Roy stuck Vic Raschi's first pitch into the left field stands"[4] to give the Dodgers a 3-2 lead. "You fellows told me Campanella was dead," Stengel said after the game. "If he's dying I didn't see it out there today. If he had a good hand, he'd a hit that home run ball 80 miles."[5]

Raschi retired the side in the eighth without allowing any more runs, and Erskine took the mound for the ninth inning with a one-run lead, unaware that he was one strikeout short of the single-game World Series record. Don Bollweg, pinch-hitting for Rizzuto, was the first hitter. Erskine, who related that he had faced Bollweg in the Texas League, "struck him out on all fastballs, and I did not know that tied a record, though the crowd was really frenzied by that time."[6] The paid attendance of 35,270 was the largest to ever see a World Series game at Ebbets Field to that point. (The record was broken the next day.)

Johnny Mize, batting for Raschi, was the next hitter. Mize had been a Yankee hero in the 1952 World Series with three home runs off Dodgers pitching – one of them a three-run shot off Erskine, who recalled,

John Mize had a unique quality of being a power hitter and having a very good concept of the strike zone. ... And I was not thinking about strikeouts. I was thinking about giving him my best shot. He took two well-placed curveballs ... and then I almost made a mistake. I wanted to get a fastball up and in on him, and I got it up, but I got it up over the plate, and he had a rip, a really had a cut, but he fouled it back, 'cause I had good stuff that day. I could see John's expression of 'That was it, darn it.' Then we came right back with another overhand curve, probably the worst swing I ever saw Mize have at a ball, and then the crowd erupted, and I will tell you for the first time – and I didn't know why because I didn't know about the record – but I turned and faced center field to gain my composure because I had a sensation about that strikeout that moved me emotionally.[7]

Mize's strikeout gave Erskine the single-game record with 14, but there was still one out to go. Perhaps drained by emotion, Erskine walked pinch-hitter Irv Noren (batting for McDougald) on four pitches. That brought up Collins, who had struck out in each of his four previous plate appearances. Collins later told Erskine that his Yankee teammates were razzing him about getting into the record books with five strikeouts. (Yankees pitcher George Pipgras held the record with five strikeouts in Game Three of the 1932 series against the Cubs.) But after getting to two strikes, Collins tapped to Erskine, who threw him out to end the game.

The 1953 World Series would ultimately last six games. Facing the Yankees for the third time with the Dodgers trailing three games to two, Erskine lasted four innings and allowed three runs in a no-decision; the Yankees won, 4-3, for their fifth consecutive World Series championship. Erskine's strikeout record would be broken in 1963 (by Sandy Koufax with 15); Bob Gibson fanned 17 in Game One of the 1968 series for the all-time World Series mark to date. But for one day in 1953, Carl Erskine had reached the pinnacle.

SOURCES

In addition to the sources cited in the Notes, the author consulted Baseball-Reference.com, Retrosheet.org, and the following:

Daley, Arthur. "Sports of the Times: Fantasy in Flatbush," *New York Times*, October 3, 1953: 21.

Effrat, Louis. "Dodgers Did Most of Their Damage Against Bad Balls, in Raschi's Opinion," *New York Times*, October 3, 1953: 21.

"Game Three: Bums Brace on Erskine's Record 14-Strikeout Feat," *The Sporting News*, October 14, 1953: 11.

Spink, J.G. Taylor. *Baseball Guide and Record Book 1954* (St. Louis: Charles C. Spink & Son, 1954).

NOTES

1   Peter Golenbock, *Bums: An Oral History of the Brooklyn Dodgers* (New York: G.P. Putnam's Sons, 1984), 362.

2   "Robinson Starts to Find Target," *Brooklyn Daily Eagle*, October 3, 1953: 9.

3   "Robinson Starts to Find Target."

4   Dave Anderson, "Campy Has Last Laugh on Stengel," *Brooklyn Daily Eagle*, October 3, 1953: 9.

5   Joe Lee, "Yanks Sing Praises of Erskine's Stuff," *Brooklyn Daily Eagle*, October 3, 1953: 9.

6   Golenbock, 362.

7   Golenbock, 362.

LET'S BE UNMERCIFUL!

October 3, 1953

Brooklyn Dodgers 7, New York Yankees 3 | Game Four of the 1953 World Series

by Alan Cohen

There were other events, including the meanderings of a runaway horse named Red, worthy of ink on the front page of the Brooklyn Eagle on Sunday, October 4, 1953, but after the Dodgers had evened up the World Series the day before, the banner headline, "Let's Be Unmerciful!" expressed the sentiment of the Brooklyn faithful.[1] The Dodgers had stroked 12 hits, including six doubles and a homer, to out-bomb the Bombers of the Bronx, 7-3.

On Saturday, two pitchers from Astoria, Queens, who first appeared at Ebbets Field as teenagers took to the mound for the fourth game of the 1953 World Series. The New York Yankees, leading the Series two games to one, sent left-hander Whitey Ford, who had won 18 games during the season, to the mound. The Brooklyn Dodgers, hoping to even up the Series, countered with righty Billy Loes.

Mental mistakes and sloppy play by the Yankees allowed the Dodgers to take an early lead and withstand a late rally as they evened up the Series, winning 7-3.

With a sense of history, the Dodgers brought back Tommy Leach, who had played for Pittsburgh in the very first World Series, in 1903, to throw out the first pitch.

The Dodgers' predominantly right-handed-hitting lineup figured out Ford early, scoring three runs in the first inning, bringing cheers from most of the record Ebbets Field World Series crowd of 36,775.

"I overran it. There was some wind, but that's no excuse. I don't even think it swerved when it came down. I just overran it."

– Hank Bauer[2]

Junior Gilliam, a switch-hitter batting leadoff for Brooklyn, lifted an opposite-field fly ball toward the right-field corner that appeared playable. However, Hank Bauer overran the ball, and he was standing in foul territory when the ball landed a foot fair and took a sideways bounce into the seats for a ground-rule double. Pee Wee Reese's grounder to first baseman Joe Collins advanced Gilliam to third. Jackie Robinson drove in Gilliam with a single to center field, then was forced at second by Gil Hodges. Roy Campanella was up next for Brooklyn and when Ford's 2-and-0 offering went wild, Hodges advanced to second base. Campanella was walked intentionally. Duke Snider, on a 1-and-0 pitch, drove the ball off the bunting adorning the right-field screen, and his double scored Hodges and Campanella. There was no further scoring as Carl Furillo flied out to Bauer in right, but Brooklyn had an early 3-0 lead, scoring in the first inning for the first time in the 1953 World Series.

Tom Gorman replaced Ford on the mound for the Yankees in the second inning and kept the Dodgers from scoring in the second and third. The only hit in those innings was Gilliam's second double of the game, a pop fly to short left field that eluded shortstop Phil Rizzuto and left fielder Gene Woodling.

Gorman yielded a run in the fourth inning. With one out, Furillo singled to center field and moved to third on a single by Loes. Gilliam with his third double of the game drove in Furillo with the Dodgers' fourth run. With Gilliam at second, Billy Martin took the throw from the outfield and attempted the hidden-ball trick. Dodgers manager Chuck Dressen saw Martin wedge the ball in his glove, called for time, and told Gilliam to stay on the bag. Umpire Bill Stewart asked Martin for the ball, and Billy's attempt at deception was foiled. But Gilliam was stranded as Reese popped up to Martin to end the inning.

Loes was in command on the mound and didn't allow a hit until Yogi Berra singled in the fourth inning. The Yankees halved the Dodgers' margin in the fifth inning when Martin tripled, lunching a curveball to right-center field between Snider and Furillo, and Gil McDougald homered. Not an out had been registered at this point, but Loes was able to retire Rizzuto, pinch-hitter Don Bollweg, and Mickey Mantle. Mantle looked at strike three.

"I've hit 'em harder, but I hit that one good enough"

– Duke Snider[3]

The Dodgers reestablished their four-run lead off Johnny Sain, who entered the game in the sixth inning. Snider homered on Sain's first pitch. Billy Cox doubled and advanced to third on Loes' second single of the game. He scored on a fly ball by Gilliam, just beating Bauer's throw home. Snider's homer was his fifth in World Series competition – most ever by a National League player. He had previously been in a tie, at four, with Mel Ott of the Giants.

Art Schallock, who had originally signed with the Dodgers in 1946, came on to pitch for the Yankees in the seventh inning. With two out, he walked Campanella. Roy scored from first on Snider's double to the left-field corner. The Yankees outfield had been playing the lefty slugger to pull and Campanella had ample time to score. The RBI gave Snider four for the game.

"There is always that feeling of sitting on a powder keg when Loes is pitching."

– Tommy Holmes of the Brooklyn Eagle[4]

The Dodgers took a 7-2 lead into the ninth inning. Loes was unable to survive the inning. Singles by Woodling and Martin and a walk to McDougald loaded the bases with none out. Manager Dressen then called on his bullpen ace, Clem Labine, to wrap things up. After Rizzuto struck out, manager Casey Stengel of the Yankees sent up Johnny Mize as a pinch-hitter. Mize flied to Snider in short center field and the Yankees were down to their last out.

"I sent him in. I thought he'd make it easy. That throw from the outfield was unbelievable"

– Yankees third-base coach Frank Crosetti[5]

Mantle, batting leadoff for the Yankees, came up for the fifth time having gone hitless, striking out twice. When he struck out in the first inning, he set a record with five consecutive strikeouts in World Series competition. Batting left-handed, he singled off the end of his bat, lining the ball over the outstretched glove of Reese into left field, scoring Woodling. Don Thompson, who had replaced Robinson in left field for defensive purposes, gunned down Martin who, given the green light by third-base coach Frank Crosetti, tried to score from second on Mantle's hit.

"I tried to lunge in and knock it loose from [Campanella's] hand but couldn't."

– Billy Martin[6]

Thompson's perfect throw reached Campanella on one hop, and the game was over when Campanella slapped the tag on Martin's shoulder as he came in standing up, trying to bowl over Campanella.

The Series was even up through four games.

After the game, Stengel said he pulled Ford after one inning to have him ready for Game Seven. The matter proved moot. The Yankees went on win the next two games, needing only six games to take their fifth World Series championship in a row.

Snider would build on his home-run record in World Series competition. He played in three more Series with the Dodgers and his total of 11 is still the standard for a National League player.

Martin, despite being thrown out on the final play of Game Four, had his best World Series, going 12-for-24 with eight RBIs. His 12th hit, a single in the ninth inning of Game Six, clinched the game and the Series for the Yankees. It was the second straight year that Martin's last-inning heroics had factored in a Series win. In 1952 he dashed in from second base to grab a popup by Robinson with the bases loaded to save the game and Series for New York.

Loes, after his senior year at Bryant High School, started in a Long Island vs. Brooklyn all-star game at Ebbets Field on July 7, 1948. He pitched the first two innings for the Long Island (Queens, Nassau, and Suffolk Counties) team and struck out five batters. He allowed a couple of doubles in the second inning that resulted in Brooklyn's first run of the game. Off this performance, Loes was selected to represent the *Brooklyn Eagle* in "Brooklyn Against the World" later that summer. He signed with the Dodgers after the *Eagle* team concluded its travels to Washington, D.C., three Canadian provinces, and Providence, Rhode Island.

Ford first appeared at Ebbets Field in Brooklyn Against the World in 1946, playing in right field and going 0-for-4 in the second game of a series between the *Brooklyn Eagle* team and a World team comprising 20 players from cities across the United States, Canada, and Hawaii. He was scheduled to pitch the middle three innings of the game on August 9, 1946, but Dressen, who was managing the Brooklyn kids, did not put Ford in the game. When Whitey took the mound at Ebbets Field for the first time, on October 3, 1953, Dressen was looking on from the opposition dugout.

SOURCES

In addition to the sources cited in the Notes, the author consulted Baseball-Reference.com, Retrosheet.org, and the following:

Broeg, Bob. "Dodgers Win, 7-3, Square Series at 2 Each; Snider Bats in Four Runs with Homer, 2 Doubles," *St. Louis Post-Dispatch*, October 4, 1953: Part 5, 1.

Holmes, Tommy. "Dodgers' 7-3 Win Ties Series," *Brooklyn Eagle*, October 4, 1953: 1, 22, 32.

Kahn, Roger. "Martin's Mad Dash for Home in 9th Humors Dodger Clubhouse," *New York Herald Tribune*, October 4, 1953: B2.

Lee, Bill. "With Malice Towards None," *Hartford Courant*, October 4, 1953: Section 4,1.

Rennie, Rud. "Snider Bats in 4; Loes, Labine Halt Champions," *New York Herald Tribune*, October 4, 1953: B1.

Smith, Red. "Views of Sport," *New York Herald Tribune*, October 4, 1953: B1.

Stockton, J. Roy. "Extra Innings: Dodgers Brush Off Early Defeats," *St. Louis Post-Dispatch*, October 4, 1953: Part 5, 1.

Young, Dick. "Dodgers Tie it Up! Blast Yanks, 7-3," *New York Sunday News*, October 4, 1953: 96.

NOTES

1   *Brooklyn Eagle*, October 4, 1953: 1.

2   Joe Trimble, "Crow Sits on His 'Rock'; Chuck's Mum on Pitcher," *New York Sunday News*, October 4, 1953: 98.

3   John Drebinger, "Dodgers Down Yankees, 7-3, for 2-2 World Series Tie," *New York Times*, October 4, 1953: Section 5, 2.

4   Tommy Holmes, "Dodgers Win 7-3 to Even Series," *Brooklyn Eagle*, October 4, 1953: 32.

5   Ted Smits (Associated Press), "Don Thompson Made Perfect Peg to Plate," *Lancaster* (Pennsylvania) *Sunday News*, October 4, 1953: 32.

6   Trimble, "Crow Sits on His 'Rock.'"

YANKEES BLASTS PROVE TOO MUCH
FOR BROOKLYN TO OVERCOME

October 4, 1953

New York Yankees 11, Brooklyn Dodgers 7 | Game Five of the World Series

by Russ Lake

Baseball fans making their way to Ebbets Field for Game Five of the 1953 World Series were in a festive mood even while a weather prediction of overcast skies took shape.[1] Police officers yearned for a reduction of incidents they had dealt with so far. Patrol force personnel had a two-day total of 22 ticket scalpers being arrested and arraigned at Manhattan Night Court.[2] After Game Four's completion, a roan horse named Red broke loose from behind his stable on 96th Street in Brooklyn. The steed scattered Flatbush pedestrians and enjoyed a two-mile jaunt through jampacked city streets and crowded intersections before being lassoed by a patrolman.[3]

An impostor was escorted off the field during player interviews before Game Five after he clumsily interrupted New York's Johnny Mize. When Mize requested the offender's newspaper affiliation, the fellow declared, "Paper? I ain't with no paper. I'm a barber downtown, and I want to know if you're going to quit next year?"[4]

Yankees manager Casey Stengel had already named his starter, but Dodgers pilot Chuck Dressen remained tight-lipped about his choice.

Stengel tabbed 26-year-old right-hander Jim McDonald, who was 9-7 with 3.82 ERA during the regular season. Dressen informed rookie left-hander Johnny Podres (9-4, 4.23) that he would be the Brooklyn starter right after the just-turned 21-year-old arrived at the ballpark. Dressen reasoned, "I wanted him to get a good night's sleep."[5] Both hurlers would be making their postseason debuts. Speculation arose that Podres might be the youngest player to start a World Series game, but that mark remained with Bullet Joe Bush of the Philadelphia Athletics, who was 20 when he started Game Three of the 1913 World Series.

In honor of the golden anniversary of the fall classic, first-pitch honors went to 77-year-old Otto Krueger, who was on the roster of the 1903 Pittsburgh Pirates during the year of the first World Series. A standing-room-only crowd of 36,775 spectators shoehorned their way into the aged ballpark, equaling the announced attendance of the previous day.[6]

Statistics on Podres informed scribes that he had held the Yankees scoreless for 13 straight innings in a pair of exhibition contests. That streak ended quickly when Gene Woodling drove Podres' fourth pitch high and deep toward the left side of the center-field wall. Duke Snider raced back and made a gallant leap, but the ball landed just over the barrier for a 1-0 New York lead.[7] Woodling's blast was the first time since October 13, 1909, that a World Series contest had opened with a home run.[8] After the rough inauguration of his postseason, Podres settled down and retired the next three batters. McDonald allowed a lead-off single to Jim Gilliam, who moved no farther as the ensuing trio was dispatched.

The Dodgers put runners at first and second on hits from Roy Campanella and Gil Hodges to open the bottom of the second. Carl Furillo grounded to shortstop Phil Rizzuto, who hurried his force toss to Billy Martin and the ball was deflected into center. Campanella scored on the error to tie the game, 1-1, while Hodges raced to third. A big inning for the Dodgers looked probable, but defensive action quickly reversed the flow when Billy Cox lofted a fly to left. Woodling made the catch and fired a no-bounce strike to Yogi Berra as Hodges raced plateward. Berra put the tag on Hodges for a double play.[9] Furillo at first base had gone halfway, then retreated to first.[10] His decision not to advance cost Brooklyn a possible run when Podres singled to center. McDonald retired Gilliam on a groundball to strand the duo.

Rizzuto walked to start the third, and was bunted to second by McDonald. Woodling smashed a hard comebacker that knocked Podres' glove off. In haste, Podres first picked up his mitt, then grabbed the ball to nip Woodling with Rizzuto moving to third. Joe Collins rapped a grounder toward first that bounced waist-high off Hodges' glove, and Rizzuto scored on the miscue to move the Yankees up, 2-1.[11] Podres then hit Hank Bauer with a two-strike pitch.[12]

Berra called time while batting and protested to second-base umpire Ed Hurley that he was being blinded by a glare from beyond center field. Play was halted while workers erected a makeshift tarp across the area.[13] When action resumed, Podres walked Berra to load the bases. With Mickey Mantle up, Dressen decided to lift the youngster. He called for right-hander Russ Meyer, who had warmed up prior to the game, and had openly campaigned for a chance to pitch in the Series. Mantle had fanned six times through Game Four facing right-handers, and had been treated for a freak left-hand injury during batting practice.[14] Stengel had previously told the switch-hitting Mantle to quit pulling everything when he batted left.[15]

Meyer went into his windup and glanced at third before he released an overhand curve that floated to the outside corner of the plate. Mantle leaned to go with the pitch, and drove the ball in a high arc to left. Jackie Robinson acknowledged the deep flight path and retreated a few steps before he simply halted to watch the ball sail into the upper deck. The 21-year-old slugger had increased the Yankees' lead to 6-1 with the fourth grand slam in World Series history.[16] Mantle dashed around the bases and was happily greeted by teammates who had scored ahead of him. Several Yankees also mobbed Mantle as he neared the dugout entrance.[17]

The shell-shocked Dodgers went down in order in the third on four pitches.[18] A rally in the fourth was defused when Rizzuto grabbed Furillo's bouncer up the middle and turned a 6-3 twin-killing. Meyer pitched in and out of trouble from the fourth through the sixth while stranding six New York runners. Cox made several remarkable plays at third base to keep the Yankees from adding to their lead.[19] Brooklyn's high-powered offense had been stifled until the fifth when the Dodgers made it 6-2 on a hit-by-pitch to Gilliam and singles by Pee Wee Reese and Snider.

Martin popped a two-run homer in the seventh for his 10th hit of the Series. Then McDonald, who hit .098 during the regular season with no extra-base hits, delivered a two-out run-scoring double to put the Yankees ahead 9-2. New York increased the mark to 10-2 in the eighth versus reliever Ben Wade. Collins opened with a double, was sacrificed to third, and scored on Berra's deep fly ball.

McDonald tired in the Brooklyn eighth and the Dodgers parlayed four hits into four tallies. The capper came from a three-run home run by Cox to make the score 10-6. After lefty-swinging George Shuba was announced as a pinch-hitter, Stengel motioned to the bullpen. Shuba had belted a two-run pinch homer in Game One at Yankee Stadium. Southpaw Bob Kuzava, who had been the relief hero in Game Seven of the '52 World Series, was summoned. Right-handed batter Dick Williams replaced Shuba, and Kuzava fanned him.

Joe Black was tasked to hold the Yankees in the ninth. He fanned Martin, but gave up a solo home run to Gil McDougald to make the score 11-6. Kuzava came in to close out the Dodgers in the ninth, but Gilliam greeted him with a leadoff homer. It was 11-7. Snider singled with one out and Stengel brought in Game One starter Allie Reynolds to suppress Brooklyn's notion of an uprising. The veteran right-hander coaxed Robinson to hit a hard grounder to the left of the mound. Reynolds reached but could not field it, but Martin swooped over to glove the hot shot. The second sacker flipped the ball to Rizzuto for the force and peg to first to complete the game-ending 4-6-3 double play.[20]

The contest took 3:02 to complete. The teams accounted for a World Series game record of 47 total bases.[21] The Yankees scored 11 runs on 11 hits. The Dodgers scored seven runs on 14 hits, all but two of them singles. Each team committed one error. McDonald was the winner and Podres the loser as the Yankees had earned a three-games-to-two advantage. Three New York hurlers permitted no walks, while four Brooklyn pitchers walked six.

In the clubhouse, Dressen explained his decision to pull Podres: "I had to turn Mantle over. He can kill you right-handed, but we had been getting him out left-handed because he has that bad right knee and can't pivot."[22]

Stengel was photographed signaling one more win as the World Series shifted back to Yankee Stadium for Game Six the next day.[23] Beginning in 1949, the Yankees had not lost a regular-season or postseason series to any team,[24] and they appeared determined to retain that record.

SOURCES

In addition to the sources cited in the Notes, the author accessed Retrosheet.org, Baseball-Reference.com, Newspapers.com, SABR.org/bioproj, and *The Sporting News* archive via Paper of Record.

NOTES

1   "Fifth Game Flickers," *The Sporting News*, October 14, 1953: 16.

2   "Ticket Scalper Arrests Total 22 in Borough," *Brooklyn Eagle*, October 4, 1953: 1.

3   Ken Johnston, "Horse Joins in Dodger Spree," *Brooklyn Eagle*, October 4, 1953: 1.

4   "Jawn Learns Interviewer Is No Scribe, But Barber," *The Sporting News*, October 14, 1953: 16.

5   "Fifth Game Pickups," *The Sporting News*, October 14, 1953: 13.

6   "Fifth Game," *The Sporting News*, October 14, 1953: 13.

7   Dick Young, "Yankees HRs Pop Bums, 11-7, in Fifth Tilt," *New York Daily News*, October 5, 1953: 144, 150.

8   "Fifth Game Flickers," *The Sporting News*, October 14, 1953: 16. Davy Jones of the Detroit Tigers hit a bounce homer off Babe Adams of the Pittsburgh Pirates on October 13, 1909, leading off Game Five of the World Series. https://www.retrosheet.org/boxesetc/1909/B10130PIT1909.htm.

9   Young, "Yankees HRS Pop Bums, 11-7."

10 "Field Day for Second Guessers," *The Sporting News*, October 14, 1953: 16.

11 "Yankees HRS Pop Bums, 11-7."

12 Tommy Holmes, "One Pitch to Mantle and What Happened," *Brooklyn Eagle*, October 5, 1953: 15.

13 "Mirror May Have Annoyed Batters," *Brooklyn Eagle*, October 5, 1953: 15.

14 "Yankees HRs Pop Bums."

15 "Fifth Game Flickers," *The Sporting News*, October 14, 1953: 16.

16 "Fifth Game," *The Sporting News*, October 14, 1953: 16. Players who had hit World Series grand slams before Mantle were Elmer Smith of the Cleveland Indians in 1920, Tony Lazzeri of the Yankees in 1936, and Gil McDougald of the Yankees in 1951.

17 Video of Mantle's Grand Slam, https://www.youtube.com/watch?v=8jLqTK_hQI4.

18 Joe Trimble and Dana Mozley, "On the Block a Year Ago, McDonald Sold Casey" *New York Daily News*, October 5, 1953: 144, 150.

19 Dave Anderson, "Yankees Call Cox's Fielding Tops," *Brooklyn Eagle*, October 5, 1953: 15.

20 Video: A Championship Legacy:1953, https://www.youtube.com/watch?v=DOu_6yjqjGO.

21 "Bombers Again Take Bulge in Battle of Boundary Belts," *The Sporting News*, October 14, 1953: 13.

22 Tommy Holmes, "One Pitch to Mantle and What Happened."

23 Photo Caption, "The One of His Dreams," *New York Daily News*, October 5, 1953: 492.

24 Dan Daniel, "What About Vic Power? First Post-Season Poser for Yanks," *The Sporting News*, October 7, 1953: 7.

Joe Adcock smashes four home runs in historic performance at Ebbets Field

July 31, 1954

Milwaukee Braves 15, Brooklyn Dodgers 7

by Gregory H. Wolf

When one thinks of home-run hitters and the Milwaukee Braves, Hank Aaron and Eddie Mathews immediately come to mind. However, Joe Adcock, the hulking 6-foot-4-inch former basketball player at Louisiana State University, had the reputation of smashing some of the longest home runs ever witnessed. Although measuring the distance home runs travel has historically been an imprecise science, driven by myth and legend, Adcock belongs to a select few sluggers whose feats still inspire awe. On April 29, 1953, Adcock hit the first ball into the revamped center-field bleachers at the Polo Grounds and the first shot over the 83-foot-high grandstand onto the upper-deck roof in left-center field in Ebbets Field (June 17, 1956), and was the first right-hander to smash one over the 64-foot-high scoreboard in right-center field at Connie Mack Stadium (April 14, 1960). Described by Brooklyn sportswriter Tommy Holmes as a "one-man demolition squad," Adcock achieved his most enduring feat during a torrid streak in the summer of 1954 when he whacked four home runs and a double in a wild, record-setting affair at

Ebbets Field.[1] Braves beat writer Lou Chapman hailed Adcock's power punch as the "most powerful individual performance for a single game in modern baseball history."[2]

Skipper Charlie Grimm's third-place Braves (54-45) were on a roll, propelled by an eight-game winning streak, yet trailed the red-hot NL-leading New York Giants by nine games. In Brooklyn as part of a 15-game road swing, the Braves bashed Walter Alston's second place Dodgers (61-40) in the opener of a three-game set, 9-3, led by Adcock's homer, double, and three runs batted in. The Braves, in their second season in Milwaukee since relocating from Boston, and Dodgers were quickly becoming the NL's fiercest rivalry, which sports reporter Bill Paddock characterized as a bitter feud.[3] Vocal, fiery-tempered Adcock was a major reason for that animosity. The 26-year-old right-handed slugger had scorched the Dodgers, hitting .365 (19-for-52) with 4 home runs and 13 RBIs in 13 games thus far in '54, and was the target of "more verbal ridings from the Dodger than any other player in the league," reported the *Brooklyn Eagle's* Dave Anderson.[4]

On a sizzling Saturday afternoon with temperatures in the mid-90s,[5] Ebbets Field drew a modest paying crowd of 12,263, plus an estimated 5,000 children as part of the knothole gang.[6] The Braves had their own cheering section in that hostile environment, as more than 600 fans were bused in from Milwaukee for the showdown.[7]

The Braves came out swinging against starter Don Newcombe (6-5). The former Dodgers ace, who reeled off 56 wins in his first three seasons with Dem Bums (1949-1951), had missed the previous two full seasons while serving in the military and had not regained his top-of-the-rotation form. Mathews, the reigning NL home-run leader with 47 in '53, began what sportswriter Holmes called the Braves' "unprecedented power orgy" with a two-out, first-inning solo blast to deep right field, his 26th of the season. The Dodgers led off the bottom of the first with three straight hits, including Duke Snider's RBI single, off journeyman Jim Wilson, who entered the game undefeated (7-0) and fresh off an All-Star berth.

Adcock led off the second with a deep blast to center field to put the Braves back in front, 2-1. "I broke my bat on the last single in Friday night's game," revealed Adcock, who used teammate Charlie White's stick. "It's the heaviest on the team."[8] Andy Pafko doubled and scored on Johnny Logan's single to send the beleaguered Newcombe to the showers. Reliever Clem Labine retired the first two batters he faced before Bill Bruton lined a double to center to drive in Logan and increase the Braves' lead to 4-1. Wilson, equally as ineffective as Big Newk, loaded the bases with no outs on a double by Sandy Amoros, Jackie Robinson's hit-by-pitch, and Carl Furillo's single, then headed to the dugout. In relief came Lew Burdette, who escaped the fire by fanning Rube Walker and inducing Walt Moryn to hit into a 4-6-3 twin killing.

While Fidgety Lew settled into a groove, yielding only one run – on Don Hoak's sixth-inning home run – over the next five innings, the Braves bashed the Brooklyn boys. In the third inning, Mathews greeted Brooklyn's third reliever, Erv Palica, with a mammoth clout to deep center field. Two batters later, Adcock got under the ball and whistled a screeching liner for a double, then came home on Pafko's single for the Braves' 6-1 lead. After Palica tossed the only one-two-three inning by any pitcher in the game, he faltered in the fifth. With Mathews on via a walk and rookie Hank Aaron on a single, Adcock blasted a towering shot into the upper deck in left-center, extending the Braves lead, 9-1.

Leading 9-2 to start the seventh, the Braves battered 34-year-old rookie Pete Wojey, who had relieved Palica with one out in the fifth. Aaron led off with a double and scampered home on Adcock's line-drive missile into the left-field bleachers. Pakfo followed with his 12th home run of the season to make it 12-2.

In the eighth inning, "Burdette finally wilted in the stifling temperatures," quipped sportswriter Red Thisted.[9] Gil Hodges led off with his 28th home run. Amoros singled and scored two batters later on Furillo's single. The Dodgers' fifth and sixth runs resulted from Rube Walker's round-tripper to deep right-center. Bob Buhl entered in relief but was pulled after surrendering consecutive singles. Dave Jolly walked Don Zimmer to load the bases, but escaped the jam by retiring George Shuba and Hodges.

Adcock led off the top of the ninth facing his fourth different pitcher, Johnny Podres. "I wasn't nervous or pressing," said the muscular slugger. "I didn't have time."[10] Nonetheless, he came to the plate thinking about hitting his fourth home run of the game. "[Coach] John Cooney has been of great help to me all season," said Adcock after the game. "[He] kept telling me I had a chance. Just make sure you get under the ball."[11] Launch angles aside, Adcock connected squarely again and powered the ball into deep center field. An error and two singles loaded the bags for Jolly, who hit into a double play, but not before Jim Pendleton crossed the plate. Roy Smalley scored on Podres' wild pitch to make it 15-6. The Dodgers tacked on a run in the ninth on Hoak's sacrifice fly driving in Amoros, who had led off with a triple.

The game was an "unprecedented power orgy," declared sportswriter Dick Young.[12] Adcock became the seventh player in NL/AL history to hit four home runs in a game and the first since Gil Hodges on August 31, 1950.[13] "If I played for the Dodgers, I'd hit 35 homers a year in this ballpark," said Adcock, who took advantage of the 350-foot fence in left-center field.[14] According to sportswriter Roscoe McGowen, Adcock hit two home runs and his double on the first pitch and his other two home runs on the second pitch.[15] "I hit a fast ball for the first homer," claimed Adcock, "a slider for the second, a curve ball for the third, and another fast ball for the last one."[16] His 5-for-5 performance with 5 runs and 7 RBIs set the big-league record for most total bases (18) in a game. In a contest characterized by "extraordinary slugging,"[17] the Braves (7) and Dodgers (3) combined for 10 home runs to tie an NL record.[18]

While improving his season total slashmark to 19/69/.324, Adcock had already surpassed his home-run total from the previous season (18). His eight home runs at Ebbets Field tied an NL, record for the most home runs in an opponent's park; he eventually tacked on one more home run in Flatbush and finished the season with a 1.231 slugging percentage in Brooklyn. A day after his four-home-run game, Adcock doubled in the third, and then was hit above the left temple in the fourth inning by Clem Labine, in what was described as a "deliberate beaning" by Brooklyn sportswriter Tommy Holmes. Adcock was wearing a protective helmet and was carried off the field on a stretcher.[19] A hard-as-nails player, Adcock was back in the lineup the next day and smashed a double in five at-bats.

SOURCES

In addition to the sources cited in the Notes, the author accessed Retrosheet.org, Baseball-Reference.com, SABR.org, and *The Sporting News* archive via Paper of Record.

NOTES

1   Tommy Holmes, "A Hot Hitter Gets Skulled," *Brooklyn Eagle*, August 2, 1954: 11.

2   Lou Chapman, "Adcock Used White's Club," *Milwaukee Sentinel*, August1, 1954: II, 1.

3   Bill Paddock, "Braves-Bums Feud Revives Over Beaning," *The Sporting News*, August 11, 1954: 13.

4   Dave Anderson, "Adcock's 4 Homers Help Rout Flock," *Brooklyn Eagle*, August 1, 1954: 20.

5   "Weather Table," *Brooklyn Eagle*, August 1, 1954: 1.

6   Roscoe McGowen, "Ten 4-Beggars Hit; Mathews Adds Pair to Adcock's 4," *New York Times*, August 1, 1954: S1.

7   Red Thisted, "Braves Out-Bomb Dodgers, 15-7, for 9th Straight," *Milwaukee Sentinel*," August 1, 1954: II, 1.

8   Lou Chapman, "Adcock Used White's Club."

9   Red Thisted, "Braves Out-Bomb Dodgers."

10 Lou Chapman, "Adcock Used White's Club."

11 Lou Chapman, "Adcock Used White's Club."

12 Dick Young, "Adcock's 4 Belt Flock, 15-7," *New York Daily News*, August 1, 1954: 74.

13 The other players in NL/AL history to hit four home runs in a game are Bobby Lowe (Boston Beaneaters) on May 30, 1894; Ed Delahanty (Philadelphia Phillies) on July 13, 1896; Lou Gehrig (New York Yankees) on June 3, 1932; Chuck Klein (Philadelphia Phillies) on July 10, 1936; Pat Seerey (Chicago White Sox) in 11 innings on July 18, 1948, and Gil Hodges (Brooklyn Dodgers), on August 31, 1950, Rocky Colavito (Cleveland Indians) on June 10, 1959, Willie Mays (San Francisco Giants) on April 30, 1961, Mike Schmidt (Philadelphia Phillies) April 17, 1976, Bob Horner (Atlanta Braves) on July 6, 1986, Mark Whiten (St. Louis Cardinals) on September 7, 1993, Mike Cameron (Seattle Mariners) on May 2, 2002, Shawn Green (Los Angeles Dodgers) on May 23, 2002, Carlos Delgado (Toronto Blue Jays) on Sept. 25, 2003, Josh Hamilton (Texas Rangers) May 8, 2012, and J.D. Martinez (Arizona Diamondbacks) on September 4, 2017.

14 Dave Anderson, "Secret's Out: Adcock Used Borrowed Bat," *New York Daily News*, August 1, 1954: 75.

15 Roscoe McGowen, "Ten 4-Baggers Hit; Mathews Adds Pair to Adcock's 4."

16 Associated Press, "Cooney's Tip, White's Bat Pay off for Joe," *Wisconsin State Journal* Madison), August 1, 1954: 43.

17 Red Thisted, "Braves Out-Bomb Dodgers, 15-7, for 9th Straight."

18 Records according to Dave Anderson, "Adcock's 4 Homers Help Rout Flock."

19 Tommy Holmes, "A Hot Hitter Gets Skulled," *Brooklyn Eagle,* August 2, 1954: 11.

A 13-RUN INNING

August 8, 1954
Brooklyn Dodgers 20, Cincinnati Redlegs 7

by Kevin Larkin

Most of the time the number 13 is considered unlucky. For the Brooklyn Dodgers on this fateful day in August, the number 13 was very, very lucky. Dem Bums were able to get to three Cincinnati Redlegs pitchers for 13 runs in the eighth inning as they won, 20-7. The Dodgers' offensive explosion was their most productive single inning of the 1954 season, in which they finished second in the National League with 778 runs scored. (The sixth-place St. Louis Cardinals led the league with 799 runs scored.)

On August 8 skipper Birdie Tebbetts' Redlegs (52-57) were in sixth place. The Dodgers had lost six of their previous 10 games to fall to 65-44, in second place, and trailed the first-place New York Giants by four games.

Dodgers manager Walter Alston sent seven-year veteran Carl Erskine to the mound. Erskine had won 20 games for first time in his career in 1953 and led the NL with a .769 winning percentage. So far in 1954 he was 12-10. Tebbetts chose second-year major leaguer Fred Baczewski (5-6) to start for Cincinnati.

The *Brooklyn Daily Eagle's* Tommy Holmes wrote, "This was an astounding performance for a somnolent Sunday after 10,884 customers had deserved more than two hours as the Dodgers and their opposition droned through the routine maneuvers."[1]

Bobby Adams, the Redlegs' leadoff hitter, singled. Nino Escalera struck out. A single by Lloyd Merriman sent Adams to second base. Cincinnati's cleanup hitter, Ted Kluszewski, singled to score Adams and give the Redlegs a 1-0 lead.

Brooklyn wasted little time in tying the game. Don Hoak led off the Dodgers' first with a walk and scored when Pee Wee Reese doubled to left.

The Redlegs retook the lead in the top of the third inning. Escalera tripled with one out. Merriman struck out swinging, but Kluszewski and Wally Post walked, and the Redlegs had filled the bases. Chuck Harmon singled to center field to score both Escalera and Kluszewski and the Redlegs had a 3-1 lead.

Brooklyn came back in the fourth inning when Gil Hodges and Carl Furillo led off with singles. Jim Gilliam grounded into a double

312

play that scored Hodges, and Roy Campanella's home run into the left-field stands knotted the score, 3-3.

Karl Drews replaced Baczewski to begin the fifth inning.

"You couldn't picture a game that would end up 20-7 being close at any time – and yet this one was as the Brooks came up for the sixth," observed sportswriter Dick Young.[2] The Dodgers emphatically broke the tie in the sixth inning against the Redlegs' Drews. Jackie Robinson led off with a walk. A single by Hodges sent Robinson to second base. Furillo hit a single to score Robinson and send Hodges to third base. Gilliam atoned for his earlier double-play ball when he hit a Drews 3-and-2 pitch for a home run to right field that gave Brooklyn a 7-3 lead.

The Redlegs got a run back in the seventh inning when Hobie Landrith led off with a single, took second on a wild pitch and third base on a groundout by Ed Bailey, then scored on a sacrifice fly by Bobby Adams.

The Redlegs made it a 7-5 game in the top of the eighth when Kluszewski doubled, went to third base on a single by Wally Post, and scored on a sacrifice fly by Harmon.

The scoreboard official was extremely busy in the bottom of the eighth inning as 19 Dodgers came to the plate. Hodges began the carnage with a triple to right field off of the Redlegs' new pitcher, Howie Judson, and scored on Furillo's fly ball. Gilliam grounded out and it seemed as though the Redlegs would get out of the inning relatively unscathed.

Dodgers beat writer Tommy Holmes noted, "It was at this stage that Howie Judson decided to put Roy Campanella on base and pitch to Labine, one of the game's most harmless hitters. Trouble was he also walked Labine and Don Hoak to fill the bases."[3] Before the third out was attained, four Redlegs pitchers saw 15 consecutive Dodgers batters reach base, filling the bases four times and scoring a total of 12 runs.

Pee Wee Reese reached on an error by Harmon at third base that scored Campanella and Labine, leaving Hoak at third base and Reese at second. Duke Snider got the Dodgers' fourth walk of the inning off the Redlegs' second pitcher of the inning, Jackie Collum, to again load the bases. Robinson hit a line-drive single to right field and all three runners scored. Sandy Amoros ran for Robinson and went to third base on a ground-rule double by Hodges. Furillo singled to center field to score Amoros and Hodges with the seventh and eighth runs of the inning.

Gilliam was hit by a pitch. Campanella's single to left field drove in Furillo. Labine walked to load the bases for the third time in the inning. "The bases were filled and Frank Smith, Cincinnati's ace reliever could not stand it any more," Tommy Holmes reported. He walked from the bench to the mound and after eight warm-up pitches faced Hoak. On a 3 and 2 pitch, Don hit a grand slam home run into the left field seats."[4] Hoak cleared the bases with a grand slam, his first in the majors. Smith stayed in the game. Reese walked, Snider singled, and Amoros got the Dodgers' seventh walk of the inning, loading the bases for the fourth time, and Tebbetts yanked Smith.

Gil Hodges, coming to the plate for the third time in the inning, facing Art Fowler, the Redlegs' fourth pitcher of the inning, flied out to end the damage with Brooklyn now holding a 20-5 lead.

Of the 19 Dodgers who batted in the inning, seven hit safely, seven walked, one was hit by a pitch, and one got on as the result of Chuck Harmon's error that made the last dozen Dodgers' runs unearned. "The 13 runs set an NL record for most runs in the eighth inning and the 12 tied the record for most runs with two outs in one inning," Cincinnati scribe Lou Smith reported. "The Dodgers themselves set the record on May 21, 1952, and against who? The Redlegs of course."[5]

In the ninth, the Redlegs converted three consecutive singles and a sacrifice fly into two

Roy Campanella began his professional baseball career at age 15 with the Negro League Washington Elite Giants in 1937. In 1948 he debuted with the Dodgers and established himself as the NL's most productive catcher, winning three league MVP awards. (Photo: SABR-Rucker Archive)

runs, and made make the final score Brooklyn 20, Cincinnati 7.

Kluszewski led the Redlegs' offense, going 3-for-4 with a double. Hodges had two singles, a double, and a triple in six at-bats while scoring four runs to lead the Dodgers offense. Furillo and Hoak each had four runs batted in. Furillo had three hits, and Hoak, Reese, and Campanella two each.

Despite the runaway score, the Dodgers only outhit the Redlegs by 16 to 12. But Brooklyn was aided by the 11 bases on balls given up by Cincinnati's pitchers. Brooklyn used two pitchers (Erskine and Labine) and a total of 11 players, while the Redlegs used seven pitchers and 20 players in suffering the defeat. Lou Smith's final assessment: "What might have been a routine Red Leg defeat with honor was turned into a rout today when the Dodgers scored 13 runs in the eighth inning to apply a 20-7 crusher on the Cincinnati club at Ebbets Field."[6]

At the end of the season, Brooklyn had 92 wins and 62 losses, placing them five games behind the eventual World Series champion New York Giants. Cincinnati's record of 74 wins and 80 losses put them in fifth place, 23 games behind the Giants.

SOURCES

In addition to the game story and box-score source cited in the Notes, the author consulted the Baseball-Reference.com and Retrosheet.org websites.

NOTES

1   Tommy Holmes, "None-On Intentional Pass Ruins Redlegs – Dodgers Get 13 Runs After Weird Move," *Brooklyn Eagle*, August 9, 1954: 13.

2   Dick Young, "Dodgers Beat Redlegs, 20-7; Rack Up 13 Runs in 8th," *New York Daily News*, August 9, 1954: 20.

3   Holmes.

4   Holmes.

5   Lou Smith, "Extra Point Missed, Dodgers Win, 20-7," *Cincinnati Enquirer*, August 9, 1954: 26.

6   Smith.

KARL SPOONER STRIKES OUT 15 IN DEBUT

September 22, 1954

Brooklyn Dodgers 3, New York Giants 0

by Steven C. Weiner

"Before Sandy Koufax became Sandy Koufax, before Clayton Kershaw was invented, there was Karl Spooner."

– George Vecsey[1]

It was the last week of the 1954 regular season, a disappointing one for the Brooklyn Dodgers. The archrival New York Giants were in town, grabbing the opportunity to clinch the National League title in the opener of the three-game series. They were going to the World Series and the Dodgers were going home in a few days' time. After all, Dodgers fans expected their team to be in pennant contention and this was the earliest September date on which they had been eliminated since 1948.[2]

Now, the Dodgers' job was to halt a season-high five-game losing streak after also losing the second game of the series. A sparse crowd of 3,256 fans decided to spend their afternoon at Ebbets Field, the smallest crowd for any Dodgers vs. Giants game this season. Perhaps they were intrigued by the pitching matchup. It is unlikely that they anticipated what was about to unfold in this bitter rivalry.

The Giants started their All-Star pitcher, Johnny Antonelli (21-6, 2.29 ERA). Desperate for pitching help before the season started, they had chosen "pragmatism over sentiment" and traded Bobby Thomson to the Milwaukee Braves for Antonelli.[3] Antonelli, Billy Klaus, Don Liddle, Ebba St. Claire, and $50,000 went to the Giants for Sam Calderone and Thomson.

It was time for the Dodgers to bring up 23-year-old southpaw Karl Spooner from Fort Worth in the Double-A Texas League. Despite missing a month of the season with a right-knee injury, Spooner (21-9, 3.14 ERA) finished the season with 262 strikeouts (as well as 162 walks) in 238 innings, the most strikeouts in that league since Dizzy Dean's 303 in 1931.

The life in Spooner's fastball was never a question, but his control was. In 1951 and 1952, as he worked his way up the Dodgers' minor-league chain from Class D to Class B, Spooner walked roughly one batter per inning – 284 walks in 289⅔ innings pitched. A stint at Pueblo in the Class A Western League in 1953 showed some encouraging signs – 198 strikeouts and "only" 115 walks in 153 innings – and his pitching line (11-6, 2.53 ERA) included a no-hitter.[4]

The Giants' starting lineup that faced Spooner for his debut was a reasonable match to their expected lineup for the World Series in one week's time, but with little at stake, Giants manager Leo Durocher substituted freely beginning in the second inning.

Spooner's first strikeout couldn't have come at a better time to calm his nerves than in the tense first inning. Two walks and an infield single found him facing Bobby Hofman with two outs and the bases loaded. A swing-and-miss on a full count and the inning was over. Meanwhile, in the bottom of the first, the Dodgers scored the only run they would need. Don Hoak opened with a single to right-center and advanced to second on a groundout. With two outs, Gil Hodges was safe on a throwing error by Giants shortstop Alvin Dark, scoring Hoak for a 1-0 Dodgers lead.

The Dodgers added their final two runs in the third inning. Spooner's first-pitch double to center field in his first major-league at-bat and Antonelli's walk to Hoak started the rally. With one out, Sandy Amoros singled to right, scoring Spooner and advancing Hoak to third. He scored from there on Hodges' double to right, and the afternoon's offense was over for all practical purposes.

Meanwhile, Spooner was piling up strikeouts at an increasing pace as the game progressed. He struck out the side in the fifth, seventh, and eighth innings and at one point struck out six consecutive batters – Hank Thompson, Ray Katt, Marv Grissom, Joey Amalfitano, Billy Gardner, and Bill Taylor. In the ninth inning, after Eric Rodin grounded out, Spooner struck out Monte Irvin for number 14. His control had been exceptional and a walk to Hofman was Spooner's first since the very first inning. Dusty Rhodes pinch-hit for

Thompson having claimed "there isn't a pitcher alive who can throw a ball past me."[5] Spooner's 143rd pitch of the game got Rhodes swinging for strikeout number 15.

Eight of the last nine outs recorded by Spooner were swinging strikeouts. The final pitching line for Spooner's major-league debut was impressive – three hits, three walks, and 15 strikeouts, 11 against right-handed hitters and four against left-handers. His performance beat the first-start record set by the Giants' Cliff Melton, who struck out 13 Boston Braves in a losing cause on April 25, 1937.[6]

What did his catcher think? Roy Campanella was effusive in his praise of Spooner. "He's the greatest young pitcher I've ever seen," said Campy. "I couldn't believe it and, buddy, I put him to the test. I didn't let him rely on his fast ball. I called for the curve and the change-up and he fanned them on them, too."[7]

On the day after Spooner's stellar debut, both sarcasm and rhyme headlined the *Brooklyn Eagle* sports page: "When The Giants Were Doing Us Harm, He Was Down on the Farm. We Needed Spooner Much Sooner."[8] Dodgers general manager Buzzy Bavasi answered the obvious question: "In mid-season, we felt he wasn't ready. He had as many walks as strikeouts. He just wasn't the pitcher he is now."[9]

The Dodgers sent Spooner to the mound again four days later to close out the season against the last-place Pittsburgh Pirates. Fred Haney wasn't convinced by all the hoopla. "All right," said the long-suffering manager of the Pirates, "he struck out 15 Wednesday. He's just as likely to walk 15 today."[10] Spooner had the last word on this day with the help of Hodges' 42nd home run of the season. It was another stellar pitching line for Karl Spooner – four hits, three walks, 12 strikeouts, and a 1-0 shutout.

Spooner became the first National League pitcher to strike out 27 men over a span of successive games.[11] He also joined the Giants'

Al Worthington (1953), the Red Sox' Dave Ferriss (1945), the Athletics' Johnny Marcum (1933), and the Yankees' Joe Doyle (1906) as the only pitchers to open their major-league careers with successive shutouts.[12]

What did those closest to the Brooklyn Dodgers make of Spooner after these first two starts? Rube Walker caught Spooner in his second start, remembering back that a Dodgers' phenom of the 1940s, Rex Barney, was faster. "But this kid's fast ball seems more effective because it's so live," Walker said. "It's really active. Jumps right up on top of you."[13]

The Dodgers' front-office staff responsible for player development under Fresco Thompson were more guarded in their assessment of Spooner than the Dodgers catching duo. Dick Walsh, one of Thompson's assistants, considered Spooner's strikeout/walk ratio in his first two games. "We don't expect that kind of ratio every time, but at the same time we don't think bases on balls will run him out of the league."[14]

It was a story to be pondered, discussed, and debated over the winter. Sportswriter Tommy Holmes, who covered the Brooklyn Dodgers for 33 years, put it best.[15] "Perhaps something remains that wasn't uncovered by the junior varsity Leo Durocher used Wednesday or the bold, bad Buccaneers, who are a jolly last in the race. But that will have to 'wait 'til next year.'"[16] Wait 'til Next Year![17] Indeed!

AUTHOR'S NOTE

SABR author Richard Cohen opened his biography of Karl Spooner with a definition – "meteoric: transiently brilliant, as a meteoric rise to fame."[18] Spooner's journey to major-league baseball fame was most certainly that. It was also short-lived. Barely a year passed and Spooner's major-league career was over. He had sustained a shoulder injury in the early days of spring training in 1955. "I guess I just tried to throw too hard, too soon."[19]

Spooner, 8-6 in the regular season, pitched a solid three innings of one-hit ball in relief against the Yankees in Game Two of the 1955 World Series. That performance earned him the starting nod for Game Six, needing only a Dodgers victory for Brooklyn's first World Series title. It didn't go well. In the first inning, Spooner walked two of the first three batters, yielded run-scoring singles to Yogi Berra and Hank Bauer and a three-run home run to Bill Skowron. He walked off a major-league mound for the last time having given up five runs and retiring only one batter.

SOURCES

The author accessed Baseball-Reference.com for box scores/play-by-play information (baseball-reference.com/boxes/BRO/BRO195409220.shtml) and other data, as well as Retrosheet.org (retrosheet.org/boxesetc/1954/B09220BRO1954.htm).

NOTES

1   George Vecsey, "Instant Memories of a Dodger Phenom," GeorgeVecsey.com, August 13, 2014, accessed September 3, 2019, georgevecsey.com/home/10.

2   "Dodgers' Kayo on Sept. 20 Earliest for Club Since '48," *The Sporting News*, September 29, 1954: 26.

3   Leonard Koppett, *Koppett's Concise History of Major League Baseball* (New York: Carroll & Graf Publishers, 2004 edition), 266.

4   Richard S. Cohen, "Karl Spooner," SABR Baseball Biography Project, sabr.org/bioproj/person/b6f00e89.

5   Dave Anderson, "Wasn't Ready, Says Bavasi – He's a Krazy!" *Brooklyn Eagle*, September 23, 1954: 19.

6   Roscoe McGowen, "Rookie Lifts Bums' 'Next Year' Hopes," *The Sporting News*, September 29, 1954: 26.

7   McGowen.

8   *Brooklyn Eagle*, September 23, 1954: 19.

9   Anderson.

10 Tommy Holmes, "Young Rookie Breaks Record, Ties Another," *Brooklyn Eagle*, September 27, 1954: 14.

11 Holmes. The previous mark of 25 strikeouts was accomplished by Brooklyn's Dazzy Vance in 1926 and again in 1928. Spooner fell one strikeout short of Bob Feller's major-league mark.

12 Bill Roeder, "Brooks Buzz Over Lefty's Whiff Feats," *The Sporting News*, October 6, 1954: 2.

13 Roeder.

14 Roeder.

15 Holmes was posthumously honored with the J.G. Taylor Spink Award from the National Baseball Hall of Fame in 1980.

16 Holmes. It is worth noting that six position players who were in the Giants' starting lineup against Spooner also started Game One of the World Series – Whitey Lockman, Alvin Dark, Don Mueller, Willie Mays, Monte Irvin, and Davey Williams. Spooner recorded only one strikeout (Irvin) against these players. The Pittsburgh Pirates' batters led the major leagues with 737 strikeouts in the 1954 season.

17 The phrase became a euphemism for a baseball season gone awry and nowhere did it receive greater play than in the 1940s and 1950s with the Brooklyn Dodgers and their long-suffering fans.

18 Cohen.

19 Cohen.

THE BUMS FLEX THEIR DOMINANCE IN RECORD-SETTING VICTORY

April 21, 1955

Brooklyn Dodgers 14, Philadelphia Phillies 4

by Luis A. Blandon, Jr.

Few Flatbushers made the effort to attend the game on a cloudy, warm afternoon.[1] Just 3,874 – only 12 percent of Ebbets Field's capacity in 1955 – bore witness to a record-breaking 10th straight win to start the season.[2]

Before the season, Dodgers President Walter O'Malley reminded Brooklyn that the Dodgers had won four pennants in the last eight seasons. But "still our attendance declines,"[3] he said. … "[W]e've already had too much of that wait-'til-next-year-stuff in Brooklyn."[4] He developed a plan for a 52,000-seat multipurpose, column-free Dodger Dome in Brooklyn with a movie theater, a shopping mall, and a retractable roof with plenty of parking.[5]

Second-year Brooklyn manager Walter Alston appeared calm "for a guy on spot after the Brooks lost in '54."[6] The Dodgers were in first place with a record-tying 9-0 start and 2½-game lead over Milwaukee. Even though shortstop Pee Wee Reese was unavailable with a pulled groin muscle, Don Zimmer "seems to have found the range, Pee Wee won't be sorely missed."[7] Jackie Robinson's availability was in doubt after he was hit by a pitch the game before.[8]

The Phillies' rookie manager, Mayo Smith, had a tough job. Upon his hiring in October 1954, *The Sporting News* was ambivalent: "[Roy Hamey][9] grabbed a microphone. … 'This is Mayo Smith, the new manager of the Phillies.'" "Mayo Smith. … Who is he?"[10] The Phillies were 4½ games behind the Dodgers, in fourth place with a record of 4-4. Even with the Dodgers pulling away after only two weeks, Smith believed "it's anybody's race in the National League" and "[T]here's little difference to choose between the clubs."[11] Center fielder Richie Ashburn was unavailable "[a]fter having knee tapped [drained]."[12] The Dodgers were facing the best pitcher in the league in Robin Roberts.[13] Teammate Curt Simmons said, "[Roberts] was like a diesel engine. The more you used him, the better he ran."[14] Though he had a winning record at Ebbets Field, Roberts "hasn't had too much success against the Brooks" with an overall career mark of 17-21 against the Dodgers.[15]

Russ Meyer took the mound for the Dodgers, coming off a two-hit, 6-0 shutout of the Pirates in his second start of the season and his 200th career start.[16] The Phillies drew first blood when

320

leadoff hitter Bobby Morgan hammered Meyer's second pitch into the lower left-field stands for his second homer of the season. Meyers shook off the gopher ball, retiring Earl Torgeson, Del Ennis, and Smoky Burgess. Then Roberts displayed his expected dominance, retiring the Dodgers in order on 10 pitches.

Granny Hamner lined a double off Meyer to start the second, but the Brooklyn pitcher then retired the Phillies on three groundouts. Roberts experienced his first signs of trouble in the bottom of the frame. Gil Hodges led off with a line single to left. Sandy Amorós reached on an error unfairly charged to Roberts when Torgeson apparently thought the grounder hit down the first-base line was foul and neglected to toss promptly to Roberts covering first.[17] Carl Furillo singled to right scoring Hodges and advancing Amorós to third. Roy Campanella delivered an 0-1 pitch sacrifice fly to left field, driving in an unearned run. Zimmer followed with a single to left. With Furillo in scoring position, Roberts struck out Meyer on a foul bunt, then Jim Gilliam grounded out to Hamner at short. The Dodgers were ahead, 2-1.

The Phillies tied the game in the third. Roberts singled to right, then went to third when Morgan doubled to left. Torgeson walked to load the bases. Ennis lofted a sacrifice fly to Duke Snider in center field, scoring Roberts. Meyer uncorked a wild pitch with Burgess at the plate and then intentionally walked him to load the bases. Whereupon Alston signaled in Joe Black.

Black was the 1952 NL Rookie of the Year. His signing "helped the Dodgers prove the success of desegregation."[18] The team tried to make Black a full-time starter. It failed, with Black last pitching in the majors on May 26, 1954.[19] In his first appearance in the majors since then, Black induced an inning-ending double-play ball from Hamner.

Leading off the bottom of the third inning, Robinson "broke the deadlock" with his first homer of the season, into the familiar left-field stands.[20] Then the fourth turned out to be the biggest frame of the young season for the Dodgers, with seven runs and seven hits. Roberts's greatness abandoned him after two outs. Leading off, Furillo singled up the middle on an 0-and-2 pitch. Campanella lined to center for the first out. Zimmer doubled into the left-center gap, scoring Furillo. Black struck out looking. Roberts needed one out to keep the score at a manageable 4-2, but Torgeson butchered a Gilliam grounder at first. An implosion followed: two homers, one double, two singles, and six unearned runs. Robinson singled to right. Zimmer crossed the plate with a run. Snider delivered a three-run blast on a 2-and-0 pitch, driving it deep over the right-field screen. Roberts struggled with Hodges, who doubled. Amorós followed with a two-run homer over the right-field screen. Mercifully, Roberts was replaced by Bob Greenwood, who stanched the bleeding to end the inning. The Phillies were behind 10-2. Roberts departed with "one of the worst trouncings, if not the worst" of his career.[21]

In the fifth Zimmer hit his second homer of the season, leaving him only a triple short of the cycle. The sixth saw both teams score runs. Black allowed two runs. After Burgess doubled and Hamner singled, a balk was called on Black when, starting his delivery, "Joe accidentally hit a knee and dropped the ball" with Willie "Puddin Head" Jones at the plate.[22] Burgess scored. Jones went down swinging but Stan Palys singled to center, scoring Hamner.

The Dodgers followed in the bottom of the inning with three runs on five hits off the ineffective Greenwood. With one out, Hodges doubled. Furillo sliced a grounder through the infield for his fourth hit, scoring Hodges. Campanella advanced Furillo with a line single to left. Zimmer failed to hit for the cycle, doubling for his fourth hit of the game, driving in Furillo. Black hit a "bad-hop single" to third, scoring Campanella.[23] The Dodgers led 14-4.

The final three innings were quiet. By game's end the Dodgers had eviscerated Phillies pitching with 17 hits, including four homers and four doubles. But Ron Mrozinski was effective for the Phillies in a mop-up role, pitching two hitless scoreless innings. Black faced the minimum in the last three innings, giving up only a walk to Ennis in the eighth that was followed by Burgess's double-play grounder. Black earned the victory, his first since August 29, 1953.[24] He was "the fourth Dodger relief pitcher in as many days to turn in a sparkling rescue performance."[25]

With the win, the Dodgers established a new modern record by starting the season with 10 consecutive wins, breaking the record held by the 1918 Giants, 1940 Dodgers, and 1944 Browns. The record of 12 games of the 1884 Giants was next.[26]

The Dodgers were greeted by the sign on a clubhouse blackboard: "The Bums dood it. 10 straight."[27] Alston "wore a broad grin."[28] Furillo saw the Dodgers as a motivated group "because the boys missed the World Series money they didn't get last year."[29] Reese saw the attitude as "a lot different" as the players were more determined, since last season they "just didn't give a damn."[30] Snider tempered expectations: "[H]ell. We still got 144 to play."[31]

The *New York Daily News* printed an ode to Black:

"*A man named Black came in from the pen.*
Time tunnel back and the Dodgers had 'ten.'"[32]

Black did not survive the year, pitching in six games in relief. On June 9 he was sold to the Cincinnati Redlegs.[33] Black noted, "I just couldn't get anybody out."[34]

Immediately at game's end, O'Malley said he would give "suitable mementos" to each of the 3,872 fans who showed up at Ebbets Field to watch the club set its record."[35] Each fan who "showed loyalty" could claim their reward by mailing their ticket stubs to the Dodgers' offices at 215 Montague Street, Brooklyn, 1.[36]

The Phillies finished the season fourth 77-77, 21½ games behind the Dodgers. A decent second half helped Smith to finish second in the NL Manager of the Year voting behind Alston.[37]

The streak ended in the next evening at home when the Giants beat the Dodgers, 5-4. The Dodgers ended the month 14-2 and in first place with a 4½-game lead, never relinquishing the top spot since the third game of the season on April 15. Finishing the season 98-55 with second-place Milwaukee 13½ games behind, Brooklyn defeated the Yankees in seven games for their first World Series title. O'Malley was ebullient: "We kind of like that title, world champions."[38]

SOURCES

In addition to the sources cited in the Notes, the author consulted Baseball-Reference.com, Retrosheet.org, and MLB.com.

NOTES

1   "The Weather Throughout the Nation," *New York Times,* April 21, 1955: 59.

2   Philip Lowry, *Green Cathedrals: The Ultimate Celebrations of All 273 Major League and Negro League Ballparks Past and Present* (Reading, Massachusetts: Addison-Wesley Publishing Company, 1993).

3   Michael Beschloss, "The Tangled Hunt That Led to Los Angeles," *New York Times,* July 15, 2015: SP4.

4   Michael D'Antonio, *Forever Blue: The True Story of Walter O'Malley, Baseball's Most Controversial Owner, and the Dodgers of Brooklyn and Los Angeles* (New York: Riverhead Books. 2009), 178.

5   Tom Meany, "Baseball's Answer to TV," *Collier's,* September 27, 1952: 60-63.

6   Ed Wilks (Associated Press), "Unbeaten Bums Shell Roberts and Phillies for 14-4 Conquest," *Alabama Journal* (Montgomery), April 22, 1955: 20.

7   "Diamond Dust: Jint Series Tix Available," *New York Daily News,* April 22, 1955: 71.

8   "Diamond Dust: Jint Series Tix Available."

9   The Phillies' general manager from 1954 to end of the 1958 season.

10 Stan Baumgartner, "Smith, a Middle-of-the-Roader on First Spin, Phillie Finds," *The Sporting News,* October 27, 1954: 15.

11 Associated Press, "Phils' Pilot Not Sold on Dodgers," *Des Moines Tribune,* April 21, 1955: 39.

12 "Diamond Dust: Jint Series Tix Available." Ashburn won the first of his two National League batting championships in 1955 with a .338 average

13 With a 2-0 record, Roberts was on the way to a sixth consecutive season of 20 wins or more. Roberts ended the 1955 season with a 23-14 record and a 3.28 ERA in 38 starts and 305 innings pitched. It was his last 20-win season.

14 https://baseballhall.org/hall-of-famers/roberts-robin, Accessed February 16, 2020.

15 Ed Wilks (Associated Press), "Brooklyn Takes Number Nine, Faces Robin Roberts Today," *Clarksville* (Tennessee) *Leaf-Chronicle,* April 21, 1955: 6.

16 "Diamond Dust: Jint Series Tix Available."

17 Roscoe McGowen, "Unbeaten Dodgers Break Record With No. 10," *New York Times,* April 22, 1955: 29.

18 D'Antonio, 177.

19 McGowen.

20 McGowen.

21 Associated Press, "Record Set in 14-4 Rout of Roberts," *Washington Post and Times Herald,* April 22, 1955: 63.

22 McGowan. A myth has taken hold that Willie Jones's nickname came from a Rudy Vallee song "Puddin' Head Jones." See: https://archive.org/details/78_puddin-head-jones_rudy-vallee-and-his-connecticut-yankees-rudy-vallee-al-bryan-lou_gbia0040707b.

23 McGowen.

24 Stan Baumgartner, "Brooks Win 10th in Row for Mark, 17 Hits Jolt Phillies, Roberts 14-4," *Philadelphia Inquirer,* April 22, 1955: 43.

25 Associated Press, "Record Set in 14-4 Rout of Roberts."

26 McGowen. Baumgartner.

27 McGowen.

28 McGowen.

29 Joe Reichler (Associated Press), "Brooks See Good Reasons for Streak," *Mount Vernon* (Illinois) *Register-News,* April 22, 1955: 8.

30 Reichler.

31 Ed Wilks, Associated Press, "Unbeaten Bums Shell Roberts and Phillies for 14-4 Conquest."

32 Dana Mozley, "Brooks Bag 10 in a Row to Set Record," *New York Daily News,* April 22, 1955: 80.

33 The Cincinnati Redlegs sent outfielder Bob Borkowski to the Dodgers on June 14, 1955, as part of the deal.

34 Roscoe McGowen, "Dodgers Sent Black to Redlegs for Cash and Unidentified Player," *New York Times,* June 10, 1955: 18.

35 United Press, "Dodgers Faithful to Be Rewarded," *Akron Beacon Journal,* April 22, 1955: 40. The attendance figure in the account was incorrect. The correct figure is 3,874.

36 McGowen, "Unbeaten Dodgers Break Record With No.10."

37 Joe Reichler, "Higgins, Alston Picked As 1955's Top Managers," *Hackensack* (New Jersey) *Record.* November 15, 1955: 31.

38 Beschloss.

DON NEWCOMBE BLASTS TWO HOMERS AND FIRES COMPLETE GAME FOR EIGHTH STRAIGHT WIN

May 30, 1955

Brooklyn Dodgers 8, Pittsburgh Pirates 3 | Second Game of Doubleheader

by Gordon Gattie

The Brooklyn Dodgers and Pittsburgh Pirates were heading in opposite directions on Memorial Day 1955. Entering the day, the National League-leading Dodgers claimed the majors' best record at 30-10, six games ahead of the Chicago Cubs. The cellar-dwelling Pirates were tied with the Baltimore Orioles for the majors' worst record at 13-29. The Dodgers opened the season with a 6-1 victory over Pittsburgh on a chilly afternoon at Ebbets Field[1] that started a 10-game winning streak. They dominated in early 1955, having a 22-2 record after Don Newcombe's one-hit shutout against Chicago on May 10.[2] The Dodgers outclassed the NL; after Newcombe's gem, Brooklyn's road record was 11-0, their winning streak reached 11 games, and both losses were by a single run.[3]

The Dodgers were perennial playoff contenders led by future Hall of Famers Walter Alston, Duke Snider, Roy Campanella, and Jackie Robinson, with All-Stars Carl Erskine anchoring the pitching staff and Gil Hodges solidifying the infield. Brooklyn's core had played together since 1949 and finished first or second every year since. The Dodgers had won at least 92 games every year since 1951; during those seasons, they lost two World Series to the New York Yankees and two close NL pennants to the New York Giants. Brooklyn was seeking its elusive first World Series victory; the Baseball Writers' Association of America favored the Milwaukee Braves to win the NL with the Dodgers finishing second and the reigning champion Giants third.[4]

Pittsburgh experienced challenging times during the early 1950s. The Pirates finished last three consecutive years, accumulating over 100 losses each season. General manager Branch Rickey was optimistic the ballclub would improve in 1955.[5] The Pirates won six straight games from the second game of a May 1 doubleheader through May 6, but an 11-game losing streak from May 11 through 22 erased those gains. After the second game on May 22, the Pirates were one game from tying their modern-day record of 12 consecutive losses.[6] However, there were hopeful glimpses; the Pirates routed the Dodgers 15-1 on May 24 to end their lengthy losing streak.[7]

324

Batterymates Roy Campanella and Don Newcombe. In 1955 Campy won his third NL MVP award, hitting 32 home runs and driving in 107 runs, while Big Newk won 20 games and proved to be a terror with the bat, clubbing seven home runs and batting .359. (Photo: SABR-Rucker Archive)

The teams played a doubleheader that afternoon; Brooklyn won the first game, 8-4, behind a four-run second inning and Campanella's sixth-inning three-run blast. The Dodgers scored the game's first eight runs before Pittsburgh rallied with some late offense.[8]

Newcombe started the second game for Brooklyn. He was attempting to regain his ace status; an All-Star his first three seasons (1949-1951) and winner of the NL Rookie-of-the-Year Award in 1949, he missed the 1952 and 1953 seasons serving in the Army. In early 1955, Alston didn't consider Newcombe the dominant force he was during previous seasons.[9] Newcombe struggled to a 9-8 record and 4.55 ERA in 1954, but rebounded to bring a 7-0 record and 2.83 ERA into the Pittsburgh matchup. He had

pitched a complete game against Pittsburgh four days earlier, allowing one earned run on six hits to earn his seventh victory while also tripling in two runs and stealing home.[10] Newcombe's repertoire included a high fastball, a curveball more akin to a slider, and an effective changeup.[11]

Ron Kline started for Pittsburgh. Kline had pitched one season for the Pirates, and like Newcombe was in the military for two years. After serving in 1953 and 1954, he returned for the 1955 campaign and was 2-6 with a 3.47 ERA in 49⅓ innings. Kline was the starter and loser to Newcombe on May 26, and absorbed his sixth loss when Brooklyn scored four runs in the ninth inning.[12] Kline threw a fastball and curve (later developing a slider and knuckleball).[13]

Newcombe immediately provided highlights for the 26,711 attendees. He struck out rookies Roberto Clemente and Gene Freese swinging. Then Jerry Lynch topped an infield single and stole second. Pittsburgh's leading slugger and All-Star center fielder Frank Thomas followed with his third home run, off the left-field foul pole as Pittsburgh grabbed the lead.[14] Brooklyn fans disputed the home-run call and harassed umpire Hal Dixon for several innings. They shouted and threw debris on the field, nearly hitting Dixon with an empty bottle.[15] Once play resumed, Dale Long singled, then George Freese lined out to end the inning. Pittsburgh led 2-0.

Kline was more effective than Newcombe in the first. Snider's single among three infield outs was all Brooklyn mustered. Pittsburgh threatened in the following frame; with two outs, Kline walked and Clemente singled to place runners at first and second. However, Gene Freese struck out swinging after fouling off two balls with a 2-and-2 count. Brooklyn responded quickly as Sandy Amorós bunted for a hit and Hodges reached on an error by third baseman Freese. Carl Furillo hit into a 6-4-3 double play, moving Amorós to third, but a groundout ended the threat. Newcombe returned the defensive favor in the next inning; Lynch singled, but was forced out at second, and Long hit into a 1-6-3 double play.

Newcombe started the bottom half by hitting a single to center. A groundout moved him to second. Pee Wee Reese doubled off the scoreboard in right-center field, scoring Newcombe and giving Brooklyn its first run. Snider walked, but Kline struck out Campanella and got Amorós to fly out.

In Pittsburgh's fourth, Newcombe benefited again from solid fielding when Dick Groat hit into another 1-6-3 double play. In Brooklyn's half, Hodges singled as the Dodgers placed the leadoff hitter aboard for the third consecutive inning. After a strikeout and groundout, Newcombe blasted a two-run homer over the scoreboard to give Brooklyn the lead. Jim Gilliam was hit on the

first pitch in the next at-bat, then stole second and advanced to third on catcher Jack Shepard's wild throw. A popout ended the inning with Brooklyn leading 3-2.

Newcombe's clout invigorated his pitching; he needed only 10 pitches to strike out Kline, Clemente, and Gene Freese all looking in the next frame. In the bottom half, Kline responded with a popout and a groundout, but his efforts were undone when Amorós walked, stole second, and scored on yet another wild throw by catcher Shepard. Hodges reached base on Pittsburgh's fourth error, this one by shortstop Groat, but didn't advance as the Dodgers led 4-2 after five innings.

Newcombe continued quieting Pittsburgh bats in the sixth. Lynch flied out, then Thomas reached base on a line-drive single. For the third time, Newcombe was involved in a key defensive moment when Long hit a grounder near first base that Hodges threw to Reese at second, who threw to Newcombe at first to complete Brooklyn's third double play.

With one out in Brooklyn's half, Newcombe deposited a Kline offering into the center-field seats, the second time that season he homered twice during a game.[16] Gilliam doubled and advanced to third, but was stranded. The Dodgers were ahead, 5-2.

The Pirates threatened in the seventh when George Freese and Jack Shepard singled. Groat's sacrifice moved the runners up and Pittsburgh had two runners in scoring position for the first time in the game. Newcombe settled down, retiring pinch-hitter Preston Ward on an infield fly and Clemente on a groundout.

Roy Face relieved Kline to start the Brooklyn seventh. Campanella greeted Face with a towering solo shot into the left-field seats. After a strikeout and fly out, Furillo blasted his 10th homer into the same seats. Robinson flied out to deep center field. Brooklyn now led 7-2.

After three strikeouts, Gene Freese reached base with an eighth-inning leadoff single and took second on left fielder Amorós's error. He reached third on a groundout. Thomas struck out on a full count. A Pittsburgh hitter finally made solid contact off Newcombe when Long laced Pittsburgh's second extra-base hit, a double off the wall in right-center scoring Gene Freese. George Freese flied out as Pittsburgh trailed 7-3.

Dodger bats didn't abate during the late innings. After Newcombe grounded out leading off the eighth – his only batted out that afternoon – Gilliam and Reese singled, with Gilliam reaching third. Snider flied out to left, and Gilliam scored. Reese was thrown out at second attempting an advance. Gilliam's run counted as Brooklyn's lead reverted to five runs.

Newcombe returned to the mound for the ninth; Shepard fouled out and Groat flied out. Pinch-hitter Román Mejías walked, and Clemente singled as Pittsburgh grasped for one more rally. Newcombe shrugged off the threat and struck out Gene Freese for the fourth time, giving Brooklyn the 8-3 victory.

The win extended Brooklyn's league-best record while Pittsburgh dropped to 20 games behind the Dodgers. Newcombe became the majors' leading pitcher with an 8-0 record[17] and increased his batting average to .357 with 4 homers and 8 RBIs in 28 plate appearances; Campanella now led the NL with 44 RBIs.[18]

Newcombe demonstrated his prowess on several dimensions that afternoon: winning his eighth consecutive decision with a complete game and nine strikeouts, hitting two homers, and participating in three double plays. He regained his ace status that summer, leading Dodgers pitchers with a 20-5 record and a 3.20 ERA over 233⅔ innings. He set the NL record for the most home runs in a season by a pitcher (7), finished seventh in the MVP voting, and received a championship ring when Brooklyn was crowned World Series winners.

SOURCES

Besides the sources cited in the Notes, the author consulted Baseball-Almanac.com, Baseball-Reference.com, Retrosheet.org, and the following:

Golenbock, Peter. *Bums: An Oral History of the Brooklyn Dodgers* (New York: Putnam Books, 1984).

James, Bill. *The New Bill James Historical Abstract* (New York: The Free Press, 2001).

Kahn, Roger. *The Boys of Summer* (New York: The New American Library, 1973).

Neyer, Rob, and Eddie Epstein. *Baseball Dynasties: The Greatest Teams of All Time* (New York: W.W. Norton & Company, 2000).

Thorn, John, and Pete Palmer, et al. *Total Baseball: The Official Encyclopedia of Major League Baseball* (New York: Viking Press, 2004).

NOTES

1   Dick Young, "B-r-r-ooks Chill Pirates, 6-1; Gilliam, Furillo HR," *New York Daily News*, April 14, 1955: 80.

2   Edward Prell, "Sox Win; Cubs Get 1 Hit, Lose 3-0," *Chicago Tribune*, May 11, 1955: 53.

3   Prell: 57.

4   Carl T. Felker, "Scribes Pick Tribe and Braves for Flags, Drop Giants to Third," *The Sporting News*, April 13, 1955: 6.

5   Branch Rickey, "Bucs Best in Years – Rickey," *Pittsburgh Post-Gazette*, April 14, 1955: 14.

6   Jack Hernon, "Buc Streak Soars to 11 as They Lose 5-2, 5-3," *Pittsburgh Post-Gazette*, May 23, 1955: 18.

7   Jack Hernon, "Bucs Give Bums Rush, End Losing Ways, 15-1," *Pittsburgh Post-Gazette*, May 25, 1955: 18.

8   Jack Hernon, "Dodgers Flex Muscles and Kayo Bucs, 8-4, 8-3," *Pittsburgh Post-Gazette*, May 31, 1955: 14.

9   Russell Bergtold, "Don Newcombe," SABR Biography Project, https://sabr.org/bioproj/person/a79b94f3. Accessed October 14, 2019.

10 Jack Hernon, "Bums Profit on Buc Charity at Home, 6-2," *Pittsburgh Post-Gazette*, May 27, 1955: 20.

11 Bill James and Rob Neyer, *The Neyer/James Guide to Pitchers: An Historical Compendium of Pitching, Pitchers, and Pitches* (New York: Fireside Books, 2004), 323.

12 Hernon, "Bums Profit on Buc Charity at Home, 6-2."

13 James and Neyer, 267.

14 Hernon, "Dodgers Flex Muscles and Kayo Bucs, 8-4, 8-3."

15 Dick Young, "Flock Bops Bucs, 8-4, 8-3; Newk, Campy Homer (2)," *New York Daily News*, May 31, 1955: 108.

16 United Press, "Unbeaten Newcombe Gains Eighth Win as Dodgers Cop Two," *Hartford Courant*, May 31, 1955: 28.

17 Young, "Flock Bops Bucs, 8-4, 8-3."

18 Young.

The Duke smashes three homers in anticipated pitchers' duel

June 1, 1955
Brooklyn Dodgers 11, Milwaukee Braves 8

by Gregory H. Wolf

Sportswriters expected another duel between the starting pitchers, but Duke Snider and his Brooklyn Dodgers teammates changed the script against the visiting Milwaukee Braves. Dem Bums exploded for a team-record six home runs, including three by Snider, who barely missed a fourth one in his last at-bat.

Skipper Walter Alston's Dodgers were rolling over competition in 1955. They started the season on a 22-2 run, and were in first place with the best record in baseball (32-11), 5½ games in front of the Chicago Cubs. Alston's team anticipated adding to that lead against an uncharacteristically sputtering fourth-place Braves squad (21-22) during its 16-game homestand. Despite the teams' seemingly disparate records, the opener of a two-game series was a highly anticipated pitching matchup between right-handers Carl Erskine and Gene Conley. An established star, Erskine possessed a 95-51 career slate (including 6-2, 1.73 ERA thus far in '55); had won 20 games in 1953, the same season he set a World Series record with 14 punchouts; and authored a no-hitter in 1952.[1] Conley, a 6-foot-8 giant who placed his professional basketball career with the Boston Celtics on hold to pursue baseball, had gone 14-9 in his first full season in 1954 and appeared ready to add his name to the list of best hurlers in baseball with a 7-1 slate in '55. The two had engaged in two tense, 12-inning affairs in May, with Erskine tossing a six-hit, 2-0 shutout in the first and Conley emerging victorious, 2-1, on a six-hitter in the second. Sportswriter Dick Young compared the performances to the legendary battles between the Dodgers' Whit Wyatt and the Cardinals' Mort Cooper in late 1941 and 1942.[2]

On a crisp, 60-degree Wednesday evening, 18,380 spectators came to Ebbets Field, 5,000 more than the team's eventual season average and more than three times than the 6,008 of a day earlier, a lackluster 6-3 loss to the lowly Pittsburgh Pirates.[3]

It didn't take long for the game to transform into a "shoot-'em-up," noted Young.[4] Erskine looked wobbly from the beginning against the Braves' formidable lineup, which was without its most dangerous threat, Eddie Mathews, sidelined with appendicitis.[5] After retiring leadoff man

Bill Bruton, Erskine walked Chuck Tanner, and Hank Aaron singled. Big George Crowe smacked a liner to center, driving in Tanner, but Aaron was out on third baseman Danny O'Connell's relay throw home. The potent Dodgers' offense, which easily led the majors with 201 home runs and 857 runs scored in 1955, quickly reclaimed the lead. With one out in the bottom of the first, slumping Pee Wee Reese, just 8-for-42 in his last 11 games, knocked one over the left-field wall. Snider followed with a blast into the lower center-field stands to make it 2-1, Dodgers.[6]

By the beginning of the second inning, both managers had their bullpens working. It looked as if Erskine might not make it through the frame when Bobby Thomson led off with a triple off the center-field wall[7] and tied the game on O'Connell's groundout. Del Crandall doubled and gave the Braves the lead, 3-2, two batters later, scoring on Bruton's single.

Both pitchers regained their composure, retiring a combined 14 of 15 batters, until two out in the bottom of the fourth. Carl Furillo walked and Jackie Robinson, who had doubled and was erased in a twin killing in his last at-bat, smashed his fourth home run of the season to give the Dodgers the lead for good. "Don [Newcombe] watched Conley warm up before the game," said Robinson, "and noticed that he wasn't masking his curve ball. We knew every pitch he was throwing."[8] After Jim Gilliam walked and Erskine singled over the mound, Reese's single made it 5-3 and sent Big Gene to the showers.

Braves skipper Charlie Grimm played the percentages by calling on rookie southpaw Roberto Vargas to face the left-hand-hitting Snider. It seemed like a good decision. The Duke of Flatbush feasted on right-handers throughout his career, but saw his power numbers fall precipitously against southpaws. In 1954, when Snider lost the batting title on the last day of the season to Willie Mays, his slugging percentage dropped almost 200 points (.669 to .477) against lefties,

though he still hit .308 against them. He greeted Vargas with a towering shot that sailed "far over the right field screen," wrote Young, for an 8-3 Dodgers lead. Vargas loaded the bases on walks to Roy Campanella and Gil Hodges sandwiched around a single to Sandy Amoros. He was replaced by Ernie Johnson, who retired Furillo to keep the Braves in the game.

With the Dodgers still leading 8-3, Reese walked to lead off the bottom of the sixth. Snider hit a towering shot over the right-field wall and onto Bedford Avenue, reported the New York Times.[9] The Duke's third home run and sixth RBI of the game gave him the NL lead in both categories (15/48).

The Dodgers' seven-run lead quickly evaporated in the seventh when Erskine unraveled. He loaded the bases on walks to pinch-hitter Joe Adcock and Tanner and a single by Bruton. Reese flubbed a possible double-play grounder by Aaron, leading to the Braves' first run of the frame. After Crowe fanned, Johnny Logan cleared the bases by tripling into the center-field corner niche.[10] Rubber-armed Jim Hughes, who had led the majors with 60 appearances in 1954, took over for Erskine. Thomson's deep fly plated Logan to cut the Dodgers' lead to 10-8.

With the Dodgers still clinging to a two-run lead in the bottom of the eighth, Snider came to bat with one out against left-hander Chet Nichols, the Braves' fifth pitcher of the day, with a chance to make history with his fourth home run. A year earlier, on July 31, 1954, at Ebbets Field, Joe Adcock became the seventh player in NL/AL history to hit four home runs in a game, and narrowly missed another when his deep fly caromed off the left-field wall in the third.

In an electric atmosphere, the Ebbets Field crowd cheered for the Duke while organist Gladys Gooding played the 1920s Al Jolson Broadway hit "California, Here I Come." At the height of his popularity, Snider was in the third year of an impressive five-year run (1953-1957) during

Duke Snider, the Duke of Flatbush, had a phenomenal stretch, blasting at least 40 home runs in five straight seasons (1953-1957) while batting .311 with a .407 on-base percentage and a .618 slugging percentage, yet did not win an MVP award. (Photo: SABR-Rucker Archive)

which he clouted at least 40 home runs every season, averaged 41 homers and 117 RBIs per season, and slashed .311/.407/.618 as one of baseball's most dangerous sluggers. Nonetheless, he never won an MVP Award in that stretch, though he finished as high as second in 1955. However, his teammates Robinson (1949), Campanella (1951, 1953, 1955), and Newcombe (1956) won trophies.

The situation might have conjured up feeling of déjà vu for Snider. In the second game of a twin bill on May 30, 1950, against the Philadelphia Phillies at Ebbets Field, Snider blasted home runs in his first three plate appearances. In his fourth and final at-bat, leading off the seventh, he barely missed his fourth, when his powerful shot "nearly tore the top hamper off the right-field screen," wrote Dodgers beat reporter Harold C. Burr.[11]

Facing an infield shift with the third baseman in the grass in shallow right field,[12] Snider launched a shot to deep right field. "For a minute I thought I had the fourth one," he said after the game. Snider. "I hit it real good but it sort of sunk on me and hit the screen."[13] The Associated Press's Joe Reichler lamented that "two yards of chicken wire" robbed Snider of history, as the ball caromed off the screen for a double.[14] Moments later, Snider was caught stealing. Campanella, who had entered the game leading the NL in home runs (13) and RBIs (46) before giving way to Snider, sent one into the stands in deep center field to set a new Dodgers team record with six home runs in a game.

Hughes worked a scoreless ninth, working around a two-out double by Logan and ending the game in 2 hours and 46 minutes when Thomson flied out.

The Duke was the story in the Dodgers' 11-8 slugfest victory. He went 4-for-5, hit three home runs for the second time, and set a career best with six RBIs.

Epilogue: Both starting pitchers struggled physically as the season wore on. Erskine tossed a four-hit shutout two starts later, but posted an ERA approaching 6.00 for the remainder of the season to finish with 3.79 ERA and an 11-8 record, plagued by shoulder pain. Conley suffered a torn rotator cuff that derailed his promising career. He pitched only once in '55 after July 22 and ended with an 11-7 record and a 4.16 ERA. Snider finished with 42 home runs, and led the majors with 126 runs and 136 RBIs; however, Campanella won his third MVP in five seasons, slashing 32/107/.318. Dem Bums captured their fifth pennant since Jackie Robinson debuted in 1947. Facing the Yankees in each of those series, the Dodgers finally emerged victorious, capturing their first and only title in Brooklyn, in seven games. Snider was one of the heroes, blasting four home runs and driving in seven runs, while 22-year-old Johnny Podres pitched a 2-0 shutout in the clinching game.

SOURCES

In addition to the sources cited in the Notes, the author accessed Retrosheet.org, Baseball-Reference.com, and SABR.org.`

NOTES

1   Erskine's 1952 no-hitter was a 5-0 whitewashing of the Chicago Cubs. He pitched a second no-hitter in 1955 against the New York Giants.

2   Dick Young, "Erskine, Conley Resume Duel at Dusk in B'klyn," *New York Daily News*, June 2, 1955: 92.

3   "Daily Almanac, *New York Daily News*, June 2, 1955: 92: 2.

4   Dick Young, "Flock Sprays Braves, 11-8, with 6 HRs (3 by Duke)," *New York Daily News*, June 2, 1955: 78.

5   Associated Press, "Grimm Shrugs Off Reports His Milwaukee Days Are Numbered," *Elmira* (New York) *Star-Gazette*, June 2, 1955: 39.

6   Roscoe McGowen, "Dodgers Defeat Braves; Six Brook Homers Decide Game, 11-8," *New York Times*, June 2, 1955: 36.

7   McGowen.

8   Fred Down (United Press), "Snider's 3 Homers Defeat Braves, 10-8," *News-Record* (Neenah, Wisconsin), June 2, 1955: 4.

9   McGowen.

10 McGowen.

11 Harold C. Burr, "Dodgers Find Cards Alive and Slugging," *Brooklyn Eagle*, June 1, 1950: 21.

12 United Press, Snider Gives Up Sure Single to Try for Homer Record. Who Wouldn't?" *News-Record* (Neenah, Wisconsin), June 2, 1955: 4.

13 Joe Reichler (Associated Press), "Snider Just Missed 4-HR Bid," *Elmira Star-Gazette*, June 2, 1955: 38.

14 Reichler.

A GAME WITH MORE UPS AND DOWNS THAN THE CYCLONE AT CONEY ISLAND

June 30, 1955

Brooklyn Dodgers 6, New York Giants 5 (11 Innings)

by Alan Cohen

The injury-plagued Dodgers played the Giants at Ebbets Field on June 30, 1955 and emerged with a come-from-behind 6-5 victory. The win brought their record to 20-8 for the month of June and extended their league lead to 13 games over the Milwaukee Braves.

A crowd of 22,434 was kept on edge during a 3-hour and 24-minute roller-coaster ride as the first-place Dodgers played a back-and-forth game with their rivals from Manhattan that went 11 innings and featured three rallies by the home team.

The starting pitchers were Don Newcombe (13-1) for Brooklyn and Jim Hearn (7-8) for the Giants. The Giants broke the ice with two runs in the first inning. Al Dark singled and Whitey Lockman doubled. Dark came home on a groundout by Don Mueller and Lockman scored on a double by Hank Thompson. Newcombe, the only fully healthy member of the Dodgers rotation, then got down to business, striking out the last batter in the first inning, the side in the second inning, and the leadoff batter in the third inning.

The Dodgers tied it in the fourth inning. Pee Wee Reese walked and made the trip around the bases on singles by Duke Snider and Jackie Robinson. Snider, who had advanced to third on Sandy Amoros's force out, scored on a fly ball by Gil Hodges to deep center field to tie the score. The throw home by Willie Mays was deadly accurate and drew cheers from the Giants partisans in the crowd, but it was too late to get the runner.

The Giants pushed across a run when Wayne Terwilliger stole home in the seventh inning to give the visitors a 3-2 lead. The play had been set up when Dodgers pitcher Newcombe threw a potential double-play comebacker into center field. On the play, Terwilliger went from first to third. Dusty Rhodes, pinch-hitting for catcher Ray Katt, had hit the grounder and wound up on first. Bill Taylor came up pinch-hitting for Giants pitcher Hearn. With the count 2-and-1, Rhodes broke for second base. As the throw left catcher Rube Walker's hand, Terwilliger broke for home. Before the throw reached second base, Reese cut it off and threw home, but Terwilliger scored as the throw was just enough off-line to be mishandled

---

334

by the catcher. Terwilliger's hook slide gave the Giants a 3-2 lead. Walker was playing in place of Roy Campanella, who was out of action with a kneecap injury sustained two days earlier.

The Dodgers' injured ranks grew in the eighth inning. Mays singled, knocking Newcombe out of the game. The Dodgers brought in Karl Spooner to face Mueller. Mueller bunted Mays to second, and Thompson walked. The next batter was Gail Harris. A hard grounder to the right side was headed to the gap between first baseman Hodges and second baseman Junior Gilliam. Gilliam darted to his left and fielded the ball. He spun and threw to first to retire Harris. Mays kept running. Hodges gunned a throw to Walker. Mays was out on the play, but he caught Walker's shoulder with his knee as he tumbled over the Dodgers catcher. As the dust cleared and Walker held on to the ball, umpire Stan Landes made the out call. To no avail, Giants manager Leo Durocher and coach Freddie Fitzsimmons argued that Mays was safe on the play. Walker and his banged-up shoulder left the game. Seldom-used Homer "Dixie" Howell, who had not been behind the plate in three years and started the season as Brooklyn's bullpen catcher, finished the game behind the plate for the hosts.

Marv Grissom, who had entered the game to pitch for the Giants in the seventh inning, easily retired Brooklyn in the eighth. No ball left the infield during the first two innings he pitched.

As the ninth inning began, another Dodger was lost to injury. Reese had pulled a thigh muscle rounding third base in the fourth inning and came out of the game after striking out in the bottom of the eighth. He was replaced by Don Zimmer. Spooner retired the Giants in order in the top of the ninth.

The Giants took their 3-2 lead into the bottom of the ninth inning. Singles by Sandy Amoros and Hodges put runners on first and second. Carl Furillo stepped to the plate and the powerful Skoonj bunted the runners over on the first pitch. It was the first of four bunts, each on the first pitch, that the Dodgers used to advance their cause in the last three innings of the game. With first base open, the Giants elected to pitch to Howell, and a fly ball by Dixie brought Amoros home with the tying run.

Rookie Ed Roebuck took the mound for Brooklyn in the 10th inning. A two-run homer by Mays, his 20th of the season, following a single by Dark and a force play looked to clinch the game for the Giants, but Brooklyn, using all of its resources, came from behind to tie the game.

Gilliam opened the Dodgers' 10th with a bunt single off Grissom, who was pitching his fourth inning. After Zimmer struck out, Snider's triple scored Gilliam and brought Robinson to the plate. Durocher brought knuckleballer Hoyt Wilhelm into the game. Dodgers manager Walt Alston ordered a suicide squeeze that Robinson executed to perfection, laying the bunt down the first-base line. Robinson reached first base and Snider scored when Terwilliger was unable to handle Wilhelm's throw to first base. Wilhelm left the game and was replaced by left-hander Windy McCall, who struck out Amoros. With the right-handed Hodges due up, Durocher next brought in Paul Giel, who retired the Dodgers first baseman. The Giants had used four pitchers to get three outs.

The Giants were held scoreless by Roebuck in the top of the 11th inning. Giants pitcher Ramon Monzant, their sixth pitcher of the game (and fifth in as many batters), came on to face Brooklyn in the bottom of the inning after Giel left for a pinch-hitter in the top of the inning. Monzant walked leadoff batter Furillo, who took second on a sacrifice by Howell, and scored the winning run on a single up the middle by George Shuba, batting for Roebuck. Shuba was the 33rd and final participant in the game.

The win went to Roebuck, bringing his record for the season to 5-3. Monzant, with the loss, went to 0-4.

Robinson's two hits raised his batting average to .286. Robinson, in his next-to-last season, played in only 105 games, 84 of them at third base. After June 30, he appeared in only 45 of Brooklyn's remaining 83 games, batting .202 over that stretch. At age 36, he was nearing the end of a career that had begun in 1945 with the Kansas City Monarchs of the Negro American League.

The Dodgers went on to win the National League pennant and defeated the Yankees in five games for their first World Series championship. With the loss, the Giants, the defending World Series champions, slipped to four games below .500 and were in fifth place. They finished the season in third place with an 80-74 record.

Howell, the catcher who took over for Walker, was a capable sub, starting seven of Brooklyn's 10 games between July 1 and 7, sitting out the second game of three doubleheaders when Walker, not quite at 100 percent, started. Howell batted .300 over that span. Campanella returned to action on July 14 and despite missing 31 games during the season, won his third MVP title.

Willie Mays, whose 20th home run of the season gave the Giants the lead in the 10th inning, went on to club a league-leading 51 homers during the 1955 season. He also led the league with 13 triples and finished fourth in the MVP balloting. Mays, who was a streak hitter, was very hot against the Dodgers in the three-game series that concluded on June 30. In the three games he had three homers and 10 RBIs while going 9-for-14 and lifting his batting average from .273 to .293. He brought his hitting streak to five straight games and that streak would grow to 11 straight and 18 out of 19.

For Dodgers starting pitcher Newcombe, his 0-for-2 at the plate on June 30 brought his batting average down to .418. He got his 14th win in his next start and went on to post a 20-5 season record. It was his second 20-win season. The following year Newcombe went 27-7 and won both the Cy Young Award and the MVP, becoming the first player to win both awards in the same season.

SOURCES

In addition to Baseball-Reference.com, the author used the following:

Daley, Arthur. "Sports of the Times: Overheard in Flatbush," *New York Times*, July 1, 1955: 15.

Drebinger, John. "Dodgers Rally to Down Giants in Eleventh Inning on Pinch Single by Shuba," *New York Times*, July 1, 1955: 15.

Lang, Jack. "Bench Strength Keeps Dodgers Flying," *Jersey Journal* (Jersey City), July 1, 1955: 15.

Lundquist, Carl (United Press). "Dodgers Bunting Their Way to Bunting!" *Durham* (North Carolina) *Sun*, July 1, 1955: D-1.

McGowen, Roscoe. "Walker's Left Shoulder Bruised/ Campanella's Replacement Is Injured in Collision with Mays of Giants in Eighth — Howell Will Work Behind Bat," *New York Times*, July 1, 1955: 15.

Morris, Everett B. "Dodgers Come from Behind 3 Times, Beat Giants in 11th, 6-5," *New York Herald Tribune*, July 1, 1955: 17.

Young, Dick. "Shuba Pinch-Single in 11th Nips Re-Tied Giants, 6-5," *New York Daily News*, July 1, 1955: 60, 63.

19-YEAR-OLD KOUFAX TOSSES TWO-HITTER AND FANS 14 TO NOTCH FIRST BIG-LEAGUE VICTORY

August 27, 1955
Brooklyn Dodgers 7, Cincinnati Redlegs 0

by Gregory H. Wolf

Brooklyn Dodgers skipper Walter "Smoky" Alston was on edge. Though his club (80-45) was in first place, leading the Milwaukee Braves by 10 games, they had been playing terribly and had lost 12 of their last 18 contests. To shake up his team, he tabbed 19-year-old Sandy Koufax to start the final contest of a four-game series with the fifth-place Cincinnati Redlegs (64-65) in front of family and friends at Ebbets Field.

It had been thus far a rough rookie season for the Brooklyn-born Koufax. Blessed with a blazing heater and devastating curve ball, the southpaw had whiffed 58 in 32 innings, including 34 in consecutive games, as a freshman the previous year at the University of Cincinnati, where he had enrolled to study architecture; however, he suffered from chronic bouts with wildness. Reds scouts, reported sportswriter Lou Smith of the *Cincinnati Enquirer*, were turned off by the teenager's lack of control and doubted he would ever develop big-league "stuff."[1] The Dodgers swooped in and signed Koufax for $20,000 (including a $6,000 salary), but were required to keep the "bonus baby" on their roster for two full seasons.[2]

It was obvious that Koufax was not ready for the big leagues and many wondered if he might be better suited to Class-A ball, where he'd at least have the opportunity to pitch regularly.

Koufax's season started badly and seemed to get worse. Early on he sprained both ankles within a three-day period and then soon developed acute pain in his left wing and landed on the 30-day disabled list without yet having thrown his first regular season pitch. "All of a sudden, my arm was so sore I couldn't throw at all," he said.[3] He made his major-league debut on June 24, tossing two scoreless innings of relief. About two weeks later he was given his first start, but was pulled after 4⅔ innings having walked eight, yet yielded just a run in the second game of a double header against the Pittsburgh Pirates. Tabbed to make his second start of the season, against the Reds, Koufax had thus far walked more batters than innings (12 to 11⅔) and had not yet earned a decision. "I'd be happier if I could be pitching regularly," he said, fully aware of his lack of experience and bonus status which had the potential to rankle veterans. "But I know I've got a lot to learn before that can happen."[4]

On a warm, summer Friday afternoon, Ebbets Field was packed with 18,133 spectators on Ladies Day, though paid admission was just 7,204.[5] "Dem Bums" were in the middle of a 16-game home stand and had their work cut out for them against skipper Birdie Tebbetts' hard-hitting squad, winners of seven of their last nine games and were making a push to finish in the first division. After Koufax quickly dispatched the first two batters, muscular Ted Kluszewski singled to right. It would be a long time before the Reds connected off the 19-year-old again.

The Dodgers, on the other hand, teed off on Reds starter Art Fowler. In his second season, the 33-year-old right-hander was 9-7 following an impressive rookie campaign (12-10), but was overmatched by Brooklyn's slugging crew. Lead-off hitter Jim Gilliam walloped a double off the scoreboard in rightfield. After a wild pitch sent him to third with one out, Duke Snider walked, and Roy Campanella drove home the first run on a sacrifice fly. Up stepped Carl Furillo, one of the hottest hitters in the league, batting .395 (45-for-114) and slugging .605 in his last 27 games. He sent a line drive "dozen rows back in the lower center-field stands," wrote Dodgers beat reporter Roscoe McGowen, to make it 3-0. It was the Reading Rifle's 22nd home run of the season to set a new career high.[6]

After young Sandy breezed through the second, third, and fourth innings, whiffing five more and issuing a walk to Big Klu, the Jackie Robinson show began. The 36-year-old led off the fourth by beating out a single to deep short. On successive pitches to Gil Hodges he stole second and then third base. Reds reporter Lou Smith took what might be construed as an off-handed dig at Robinson's aggressive baserunning, noting that he reached third by 'nonchalantly kicking the ball out of [Rocky] Bridges hand.'"[7] After Hodges walked, Sandy Amoros hit a tailor-made double-play grounder to shortstop Roy McMillan, but the future two-time All-Star and three-time Gold Glove winner fumbled the ball, according to McGowen, and could only manage to force Hodges at second while Robison crossed the plate. (No error was charged). The Dodgers tacked on another run in the next frame when the Duke and Campy walked with one out to send Fowler to the showers. Furillo greeted reliever Gerry Staley with a single to load the bases, then Robinson drew a walk to force in Snider. The Dodgers threatened to blow the game open, but Hodges' grounder to third forced out Campanella at home and then Amoros whiffed.

By the end of the fifth Tebbetts had seen enough of Koufax, who had whiffed eight. Lou Smith reported that the hard-nosed pilot instructed his batters to play a waiting game to disturb the rhythm of the young twirler. "It failed to disrupt Koufax who continued to mow 'em down with uncanny consistency," continued Smith.[8] The devious strategy nonetheless had an immediate effect. Koufax issued consecutive one-out walks to Johnny Temple and Smoky Burgess in the sixth which drew Alston to the mound for the first and only time in the game. "I thought maybe he might be trying to aim the ball," explained Alston. "I just wanted to tell him to keep throwing it as he had been doing."[9] Koufax's two-out balk sent both runners up a station, but he retired Wally Post on a soft fly to rightfield.

Koufax had another hiccup in the seventh, walking Bridges and McMillan with two outs before emphatically ending the frame by making Chuck Harmon his 11th strikeout victim.

The Dodgers scored their final two runs in the seventh. After McMillan flubbed Furillo's grounder for the only error of the game, Robinson sent the first pitch to him from Rudy Minarcin, the Reds fourth hurler of the afternoon, into the lower left-centerfield stands for a two-run blast, his seventh of the season, for a 7-0 Dodgers lead.

Koufax punched out two more in the eighth and entered the ninth with an outside chance to tie Nap Rucker's team record of 16 strikeouts in a game, set in 1909. That quest became moot when Post grounded to third. Gus Bell, on a tear in his last 23 games, slugging .628 with seven home runs and 21 RBIs, donned the golden sombrero with his fourth strikeout. "The lad had as much stuff as any pitcher I've faced in quite a spell," gushed Bell who couldn't remember whiffing four times in a game, even in high school.[10] Sam Mele, entering the game batting .145, connected for the "hardest hit ball," according to McGowen, a line-drive double to leftfield.[11] Koufax retired Bridges on pop-up to short to end the game in 2 hours and 37 minutes to record his first big-league victory and shutout.

"He had a good curve and his fast ball was good, too," said batterymate Campanella. "His control was all right. He never was wild at any time. Did not ever miss the plate by much."[12] Sportswriter Lou Smith was equally impressed by the teenager, lamenting that the teenager did not play for the Reds. "He had poise, a smooth delivery, along with a changeup that usually takes years for a young hurler to acquire."[13]

Koufax's 14 strikeouts were the most by an NL pitcher in 1955. Combined with the nine strikeouts by Reds pitchers, the game produced 23 punchouts which tied a then-major league record for most in a nine-inning game, matching the mark set by the Boston Braves and Reds in 1901 and matched by the New York Yankees and Washington Senators in 1914.

Continuing his season-long roller-coaster, Koufax was clubbed for five hits and four runs by the Braves in his next appearance, on August 31 at Ebbets Field, then followed that outing by blanking the Pittsburgh Pirates on five hits and fanned six on September 3. He concluded the season with a 2-2 slate and 3.02 ERA, 30 strikeouts and 28 walks in 41⅔ innings for the eventual pennant-winning Dodgers who defeated the Yankees in seven games to capture their only World Series in Brooklyn. Koufax did not pitch in that Fall Classic.

Plagued by excruciating elbow pain, Koufax retired prematurely 12 years later, after winning his third Cy Young Award in four seasons at the age of 30 with 165 wins and 40 shutouts. He was elected to the Baseball Hall of Fame in his first year of eligibility, 1972, becoming at the age of 36 the youngest player to be enshrined.

SOURCES

In addition to the sources cited in the Notes, the author also accessed Retrosheet.org, Baseball-Reference.com, Newspapers.com, and SABR.org.

Box Scores:

https://www.baseball-reference.com/boxes/BRO/BRO195508270.shtml

http://www.retrosheet.org/boxesetc/1955/B08270BRO1955.htm

NOTES

1   Lou Smith, "Koufax Lacks Stuff, Reds Scouts Reported," *Cincinnati Enquirer*," August 28, 1955: 58.

2   Instituted in 1947, the bonus rule required major league teams to retain any player who signed a contract in excess of $4,000 on their 25-man roster for two seasons. This rule went through various iterations until it was abolished in 1965.

3   Roscoe McGowen, "Brooklyn-Bred 'Bonus Baby' Is Coming of Age," *New York Times*, August 29, 1955: 13.

4   Ibid.

5   Roscoe McGowen, "Koufax Is Victor," *New York Times*, August 29, 1955: S1.

6   Ibid.

7   Lou Smith, "Koufax Fans 14 As Dodgers trounce Reds, 7-0," *Cincinnati Enquirer*, August 28, 1955: 55.

8   Smith, "Koufax Fans 14 As Dodgers trounce Reds, 7-0."

9   McGowen, "Koufax Is Victor."

10   Smith, "Koufax Lacks Stuff, Reds Scouts Reported."

11   McGowen, "Koufax Is Victor."

12   McGowen, "Koufax Is Victor."

13   Smith, "Koufax Lacks Stuff, Reds Scouts Reported."

PODRES, DODGERS NARROW YANKEES' WORLD SERIES LEAD

September 30, 1955

Brooklyn Dodgers 8, New York Yankees 3 | Game Three of the World Series

by Steven C. Weiner

After "two days of aimless wandering,"[1] the Dodgers returned home for World Series Game Three in front of the largest crowd of the season at Ebbets Field, 34,209 boisterous fans. There was an enthusiasm among Dodgers fans that belied their 0-2 Series deficit and rather long odds of being able to finally win a World Series.[2] As the starting pitchers began warming up, Gladys Gooding, Ebbets Field organist since 1942, played her rendition of "Happy Birthday to You." Dodgers fans added their voices, realizing that the Dodgers starting left-hander Johnny Podres (9-10, 3.95 ERA) was celebrating his 23rd birthday.[3]

Casey Stengel selected hard-throwing but erratic Bob Turley (17-13, 3.06 ERA) to start Game Three for the Yankees. Stengel was hoping that the Turley with six shutouts and 210 strikeouts for the season would take the mound. Turley led American League pitchers in 1955 with 177 walks.

Podres first pitched against the Yankees as a 20-year-old rookie in the 1953 Mayor's Trophy Game, an annual in-season exhibition game in New York.[4] He pitched seven innings in the Dodgers' 9-0 victory, allowing only four Yankees to reach base.[5] Later that season, Podres made his World Series debut against the Yankees, in Game Five at Ebbets Field. It was an inauspicious outing. In the third inning with the score tied at 1-1, two outs, and Phil Rizzuto on third, a fielding error by first baseman Gil Hodges allowed Rizzuto to score. Perhaps the rookie was unnerved. He hit Hank Bauer and walked Yogi Berra, and his afternoon was over. The Yankees scored five runs in the inning, including a grand slam by Mickey Mantle off Russ Meyer. They won Game Five that afternoon and the World Series on the next day.

Podres' 1955 regular season started well but finished in mediocrity. By mid-June his record stood at 7-3; he had pitched consecutive shutouts against the Cincinnati Redlegs and completed his fifth game of the season. He was bothered with a sore arm and shoulder trouble at various times during the season and didn't throw another complete game after those shutouts. Remarkably, Podres' availability for the World Series was even in doubt in September after a freak accident. The batting cage was being moved off the field. Podres remembered: "They started wheeling that thing and, jeez, they hit me right in the side with it. Banged up my ribs pretty good. For two or three weeks I could hardly breathe."[6]

The Game Three box score reveals that the Dodgers' offensive production was scattered throughout the lineup. Everyone but Gil Hodges had at least one hit; but the bat of Roy Campanella stood out. Campanella was about to become the National League MVP for the third time, but in the first two games of this Series, he was 0-for-8. His two-out home run off Turley in the bottom of the first inning, scoring Pee Wee Reese ahead of him, gave "Dem Bums"[7] a 2-0 lead. Just as they had responded in each of the first two games, the Yankees did it again. Mickey Mantle, starting in his first game since September 16 because of a torn right thigh muscle, clobbered a solo home run to the deepest part of the center-field bleachers to lead off the second inning.[8] Bill Skowron followed with a double down the left-field line. With two outs, Phil Rizzuto singled to left. Campanella moved up the line to get the throw from left fielder Sandy Amoros. Skowron ran straight into Campy, the ball came loose, and the score was tied, 2-2.

The Dodgers had a wild Bob Turley on the ropes in the second and he wouldn't survive. With one out, Jackie Robinson singled and Amoros was hit by a pitch. Turley couldn't field a bunt by Podres and the bases were loaded. When Turley forced in a run by walking Jim Gilliam, Yankees manager Casey Stengel had seen enough. Turley was replaced on the mound by Tom Morgan, who promptly walked Reese for another run and a 4-2 Dodgers lead.

The Dodgers were scoring runs in pairs and continued to do so in the fourth inning against Morgan. Gilliam opened with a single to left field. With one out, Duke Snider walked, already the fifth walk given up by a Yankees pitcher. Campanella singled to left for his third RBI of the

afternoon, scoring Gilliam and advancing Snider to third. Carl Furillo's foul pop fly down the left-field line scored Snider for a 6-2 Dodgers lead.

Meanwhile as the Dodgers kept adding to their lead, Podres was getting stronger. His third and fourth innings were "three up, three down"[9] with three strikeouts. A walk to Phil Rizzuto in the fifth inning was of no consequence. Singles in the sixth by Gil McDougald and Yogi Berra mattered little when Mantle, having difficulty running, grounded into a double play. The Yankees managed to add a run in the seventh inning, when Podres walked Phil Rizzuto with two outs. Pinch-hitter Andy Carey tripled to left, scoring Rizzuto, before Podres struck out Bob Cerv for the third time.

When the Dodgers came to bat after the seventh-inning stretch, it was time to put some icing on Podres' birthday cake. Robinson doubled to left off Tom Sturdivant. When left fielder Elston Howard threw into second base, Robinson scampered to third and scored on Sandy Amoros' single to right. Podres tried to bunt Amoros over but wound up forcing him at second. After Gilliam walked, Pee Wee Reese delivered a single to center for an 8-3 Dodgers lead.

In the ninth inning, Podres yielded an opening single to Skowron, but three infield pop flies later he had the complete game and the victory. Never before had the Dodgers won a World Series game by more than four runs.[10] After the game, Podres credited former Dodgers manager Chuck Dressen with teaching him how to throw a changeup. "It was my changeup that did it. I kept them off balance most of the day with my 'out' ball."[11]

The Dodgers could certainly celebrate key performances throughout their lineup. For example, Jackie Robinson's outstanding play covered the gamut: a single, a double, two runs scored, opportunistic baserunning in the seventh inning and seven assists playing the hot corner. Sandy Amoros' first World Series start was perfection – a single, two walks and a hit-by-pitch – and Junior

Gilliam had two walks and a single. After his dramatic steal of home in the Dodgers' loss in Game One, Robinson said, "Whether it was because of my stealing home or not, the team had a new fire."[12] Was their Game Three victory an indication of that fire?

Appropriately, the afternoon's victory celebration had to conclude with another happy-birthday wish for Podres by Gooding and the remaining fans.[13] Along with a festive mood, there must have been a sense of relief in Brooklyn that, indeed, this World Series was not going to be a one-sided affair.

AUTHOR'S NOTE

On the field in just a few days' time, Johnny Podres went from one of the Dodgers heroes in Game Three to the World Series Most Valuable Player after Game Seven and the Brooklyn Dodgers were champions for the first time.[14] How did Podres do it? Simple. He followed Campanella's advice given as they sat quietly in the clubhouse discussing Yankee hitters minutes before the pregame warmup for Game Seven. "Just get that changeup over like the other day," Campy said. 'Get it over, you got nothing to worry about."[15] He did that for the first three or four innings, "but over the last five I stayed pretty much with the fastball … with the ball flashing from sunlight into shadow."[16] Podres shook off his catcher only once in the entire Game Seven and it was

on the last pitch. "I wanted a fastball," Campy said. "He wanted a changeup. That boy had the last word. He sure did."[17] They both got it right and the wait 'til next year was over.

Baseball was played "between the white lines"[18] at Ebbets Field in the early to mid-1950s against the backdrop of owner Walter O'Malley's relentless drive to find a new home for his Dodgers. In fact on this very day (September 30, 1955), architect Buckminster Fuller, commissioned by O'Malley, revealed design plans for a circular domed stadium intended to replace Ebbets Field.[19] In his World Series diary, sportswriter Dan Daniel added his own prognosis, "I dare say Bob Moses is not likely, now, to oppose the wishes of the people of Brooklyn as regards that new ball park Walter O'Malley wants to build at Flatbush and Atlantic avenues."[20] Soon enough, Dodgers fans of all ages would learn otherwise!

SOURCES

The author accessed Baseball-Reference.com for box scores/play-by-play information (baseball-reference.com/boxes/BRO/BRO195509300.shtml) and other data, as well as Retrosheet.org (retrosheet.org/boxesetc/1955/B09300BRO1955.htm).

NOTES

1   John Drebinger, "Dodgers Win 8-3; Cut Series Lead of Yankees to 2-1," *New York Times*, October 1, 1955: 1.

2   Douglas Jordan, "World Series Situation Winning Probabilities: An Update," *Baseball Research Journal* 48 (2019): 70. Data analyzed as part of SABR research concludes that a team that loses the first two games of a World Series has a 20 percent chance of winning the Series.

3   "Dodgers, Back in Flatbush, Swing Away Behind Podres," *The Sporting News*, October 12, 1955: 22.

4   The game was played at Yankee Stadium on June 29, 1953, in front of 56,136 fans, the largest New York baseball crowd of the season to that point. Wayne Belardi was the MVP, driving in six runs with two home runs and a double.

5   David Krell, "Johnny Podres," SABR Baseball Biography Project, sabr.org/bioproj/person/14288820.

6   Donald Honig, *The October Heroes* (New York: Simon & Schuster, 1979), 210.

7   Paul Dickson, *The Dickson Baseball Dictionary, 3rd Edition* (New York: W.W. Norton & Company, 2009), 250. "Traditional affectionate nickname for the Brooklyn Dodgers, established and characterized by a bewhiskered, cigar-chomping cartoon tramp drawn by Willard Mullin."

8   Drebinger.

9   Paul Dickson, 869. "Said of an inning in which the three batters are retired in order."

10 Drebinger.

11 *The Sporting News*, October 12, 1955: 23.

12 Jackie Robinson, *I Never Had It Made* (New York: Putnam, 1972), 120.

13 Bob McGee, *The Greatest Ballpark Ever* (New Brunswick: Rivergate Books, 2005), 246.

14 Steven C. Weiner, "October 4, 1955: Brooklyn Dodgers win first World Series as 'Next Year' finally arrives," SABR Games Project.

15 Milton Gross, "Podres Greatest Day," *Baseball Digest*, November-December 1955: 41.

16 Honig, 212.

17 Gross, 42.

18 Paul Dickson, 102. "On the field of play, the location of the action of the game itself, as opposed to off-the-field activity."

19 McGee, *The Greatest Ballpark Ever*.

20 Dan Daniel, "Over the Fence: A World Series Reporter Gossips (Tuesday, October 4)," *The Sporting News*, October 12, 1955: 10.

SNIDER'S BAT AND GLOVE PROPEL DODGERS TO TIE SERIES

October 1, 1955

Brooklyn Dodgers 8, New York Yankees 5 | Game Four of the World Series

by Gregory H. Wolf

"It was not a tidy game, but an exciting one," declared *New York Times* sports editor Arthur Daley about the Brooklyn Dodgers' 8-5 victory over the New York Yankees in Game Four to even the World Series at two games each.[1] Described by *Times* sportswriter John Drebinger as a "bruising contest of power hitting," the game featured five home runs while Dem Bums tied a team record for the most hits in a postseason game and set a new one for total bases.[2]

What a difference two days made. Facing the Yankees in the fall classic for the fifth time since 1947, skipper Walter Alston's Dodgers dropped the opening two games at Yankees Stadium, just as they did in 1947 and 1953. No team had ever lost the first two games and won the World Series; nonetheless, the heavy-hitting Dodgers had the advantage when the Series moved about 17 miles south from the Bronx to Brooklyn. Their 8-3 victory in Game Three at Ebbets Field reignited the borough's hope for its team's first title.

The Dodgers (98-55) rolled over opposition with their bats, leading the majors in home runs (201) and runs per game (5.6). Casey Stengel's

Yankees (96-58) matched up well on paper. The Bombers belted an AL-most 175 home runs; however, two of their sluggers were ailing. Mickey Mantle, who suffered a severely strained thigh 10 days before the end of the regular season, retuned in Game Three, but was still severely hobbled; and Hank Bauer had pulled a hamstring in Game Two and could not start.

"[P]itching is our trouble," lamented Stengel, though Alston could have said the same.[3] After leading their respective leagues in ERA (Dodgers, 3.68; Yankees, 3.23), the staffs were unusually thin, forcing each team to use its fourth different starting pitcher in the Series. The Dodgers' ace, 20-game winner Don Newcombe had started Game One, but was suffering from arm problems; consequently, Alston sent Carl Erskine to the mound. The veteran had a stellar 100-57 career slate, but was just 11-8 in '55. His "arm has not been right for months," commented sportswriter Dick Young, and he had won only twice since the All-Star break.[4] Ebbets Field was notoriously difficult for left-handed pitchers, which neutralized one of the Yankees' strengths.

The Ole Perfessor used his southpaw stars Whitey Ford and Tommy Byrne at Yankee Stadium against the Dodgers' right-handed-hitting lineup. Right-handed pitcher Bob Turley's loss in Game Three put Stengel in a bind. He called on Don Larsen (9-2), who had made just 13 starts in '55. A year earlier, Larsen had plodded through a woeful 3-21 season with the St. Louis Browns.

On a cool, cloudy, and windy Saturday afternoon, with temperatures in the 60s, Ebbets Field was packed with 36,242 spectators for Game Four.[5] Erskine looked wobbly from the outset. The second batter he faced, Gil McDougald, crushed a solo home run to deep left field to give the Yankees a 1-0 lead. In the second, Erskine issued a leadoff walk to Joe Collins, who scored three batters later on Phil Rizzuto's single past shortstop Pee Wee Reese to make it 2-0. Alston motioned for his bullpen to warm up.

After breezing through the first and second innings, Larsen led off the third with a walk to Sandy Amoros. With the hit-and-run called, Jim Gilliam smacked a liner over third base and into the Yankees bullpen. Left fielder Elston Howard made a "remarkable peg" to home plate, wrote Young, but Amoros scored on a close play.[6]

The Yankees threatened to blow the game open in the fourth after a leadoff single by Yogi Berra and a walk to Collins. Alston replaced Erskine with Don Bessent. Called up in midseason, the rookie reliever (8-1) was thrust into a "ticklish spot," Drebinger wrote.[7] The Yankees immediately pressured him. He retrieved Howard's sacrifice bunt and threw to third to retire Berra. After Collins swiped third, Billy Martin dropped a bloop single, plating Collins to give the Yankees a 3-1 lead. In what might have been the game's key defensive play and its turning point, Jackie Robinson picked up Rizzuto's grounder to third and started an inning-ending 5-4-3 double play.

Coming off an 11-hit, eight-run explosion in Game Three, "the Brooks power broke loose" in the fourth, wrote Young. Roy Campanella, who slashed 32/107/.318 and was voted National League MVP for the third time in five seasons in '55, led off with what Young described as a "humming liner to the left corner seats."[8] After Carl Furillo singled, Gil Hodges gave the Dodgers a 4-3 lead on a wind-aided home run to deep right-center field and onto the scoreboard.[9] According to sportswriter Jack Hand, fly balls to right field were aided by a "strong wind" all afternoon.[10]

The Yankees threatened in the fifth, but Bessent overcame a "bases-loaded mess," Young noted.[11] In a calculated move, Stengel saved his pinch-hitters for later in the game and let Larsen bat to start the fifth. Adept with the bat despite his .146 average in '55, Larsen grounded weakly to short but only after whacking a foul that landed weakly on Yankees owner Del Webb's head. (Sitting a few boxes away was former President Herbert Hoover.)[12] Singles by Irv Noren and Mantle and a walk to Berra juiced the bags with two outs. Alston called on Clem Labine to put out the fire. Labine, whose 60 appearances in the regular season had tied the Cleveland Indians Ray Narleski for the most in the majors, induced Collins to hit into a force at second to end the threat.

The Dodgers fifth began with a walk to Gilliam, who stole second. Larsen was unceremoniously removed with a 2-and 0 count on Reese and replaced by Johnny Kucks. Reese slapped a routine grounder to first baseman Collins, who pivoted and saw no one to throw the ball to. "He's gotta cover," said an irate Stengel about his rookie pitcher. "If Kucks gets the putout … then I walk Snider."[13]

Coming off yet another exceptional season, the Duke of Flatbush hit 42 home runs, the third time in an eventual five-year stretch of at least 40 round-trippers, led the majors with 136 RBIs and 126 runs scored, and slugged .628. Snider connected on what the *Times's* Daley called a

"Ruthian" home run, a towering three-run shot over the right-field screen, across Bedford Avenue, and into a used-car lot across the street to extend the Dodgers' lead to 7-3.[14] It was his NL-record seventh career home run in the World Series, which trailed only Babe Ruth (15), Lou Gehrig (10), and Joe DiMaggio (8). Campanella followed with a double but was stranded on third when Kucks retired the next three.

Labine "staggered through" the sixth, opined sportswriter Art Morrow.[15] Howard led off with a single followed by Martin's deep blast to center. Snider had played the slap-hitter shallow and misjudged the carry of the ball, reported Young.[16] It sailed over the Duke's head for a double and Howard scored. Two batters later, pinch-hitter Eddie Robinson's single drove in Martin to pull the Yankees to within two runs, 7-5. It was the Yankees' last hit of game, owing in large part to Snider's noteworthy defense.

The Dodgers tacked on their final run in the seventh which began with consecutive singles by Campanella, Furillo, and Hodges off reliever Rip Coleman. "The Dodgers knocked his ears off," quipped Daley about the rookie hurler, who had also yielded two singles in the sixth.[17]

Snider was "all over the lot," raved Jack Hand about the Duke's defensive clinic.[18] After his miscue, he made four putouts, each of which saved a potential extra-base hit. The first two came after Robinson's single in the sixth. In the eighth, Snider singlehandedly "broke the back of the Yankees' resistance," gushed Morrow.[19] In a full sprint, he corralled Martin's screecher for the second out. After Rizzuto's walk, Snider made another sprinting grab, robbing Moose Skowron of a hit and ending the ending.

Labine retired 10 of the final 11 batters he faced and ended the game when a limping Mantle hit a weak grounder back to the mound. Labine's throw to Hodges concluded the game in 2 hours and 57 minutes and tied the series at two games each.

Newspaper reports the next day focused on Snider, Labine, and both teams' offenses. Snider was the star for his home run and athletic catches, while rubber-armed Labine labored through 4⅓ innings, yielding two runs (both earned). He was credited with the victory, even though Bessent had been the Dodgers pitcher when the club took the lead. The game featured 23 hits and 13 runs. The Dodgers' 14 hits off five pitchers equaled a team record for a World Series game; while their 25 total bases set a new club mark. "We're keeping those Yankee pitchers running in and out of the bullpen," raved Campanella.[20] Dodgers reliever Russ Meyer added more fodder to the rivalry, adding, "Suddenly those Yankees don't look so tough anymore."[21]

With no offdays scheduled in the all-New York World Series, the attention of postgame interviews turned to the teams' biggest challenge. Peppered with questions about their starters for Game Five, Alston named rookie midseason call-up Roger Craig while Stengel put his faith in injury-plague Bob Grim, who hadn't started since June 12.

SOURCES

In addition to the sources cited in the Notes, the author accessed Retrosheet.org, Baseball-Reference.com, and SABR.org.

NOTES

1 Arthur Daley, "Sports of the Times," *New York Times*, October 2, 1955: S2.

2 John Drebinger, "Dodgers Beat Yankees, 8-5, for 2-2 World Series Tie," *New York Times*, October 2, 1955: S1.

3 Joe Trimble, "Kucks' Boner Seen as Key Play of Yank Loss," *New York Daily News*, October 2, 1955: 108.

4 Dick Young, "Dodgers Draw Even on 8-5 Win," *New York Daily News*, October 2, 1955: 104, 110.

5 "Cloudy in 60s," *New York Daily News*, October 1, 1955: 25.

6 Young.

7 Drebinger.

8 Young.

9 Young.

10 Jack Hand (Associated Press), "Dodger Homers Sink Yanks, Tie Series," *Binghamton* (New York) *Press and Sun-Bulletin*, October 2, 1955: D1.

11 Young.

12 Drebinger.

13 Trimble.

14 Daley.

15 Art Morrow, "Dodgers Win, 8-5, Even Series," *Philadelphia Inquirer*, October 2, 1955: 1S.

16 Young.

17 Daley.

18 Hand.

19 Morrow.

20 United Press, "Dodgers All Agreed: 'This Is Different,'" *Binghamton Press and Sun-Bulletin*, October 2, 1955: 3D.

21 "Dodgers All Agreed: 'This Is Different.'"

THE DUKE'S BLASTS MOVE DODGERS
TO PRECIPICE OF FIRST TITLE

October 2, 1955

Brooklyn Dodgers 5, New York Yankees 3 | Game Five of the World Series

by Gregory H. Wolf

"It may have been the most thrilling game of the postseason festival," opined sportswriter Arthur Daley of the Brooklyn Dodgers' "brutal clubbing" of the Yankees in Game Five of the World Series.[1] Dem Bums' 5-3 victory completed a "stunning home-ground three-game sweep," declared scribe Dick Young, moving the club to within a game of the franchise's first championship ever.[2] "What a team job," exclaimed Dodgers skipper Walter Alston. "It was a combination of home runs, double plays, and clutch hitting."[3]

It was indeed a dramatic turnaround. After losing the first two games of the fall classic at Yankee Stadium, the Dodgers returned to Brooklyn and Ebbets Field, where they exploded for eight runs in both Games Three and Four to tie the Series. No team had ever lost the first two games of the World Series and won the next three, let alone the title.

Despite an NL-best team ERA (3.68), Alston's pitching staff was reeling. Club ace and 20-game winner Don Newcombe had lost the opener and was suffering from arm and back miseries, and his status for the remainder of

the Series was doubtful.[4] Longtime standout Carl Erskine, plagued by arm pain for months, had been pummeled in Game Four. Holding hard-throwing rookie southpaws Karl Spooner and Johnny Podres in reserve for Yankee Stadium, Alston tabbed Roger Craig to start Game Five in what sportswriter John Drebinger declared a "daring move."[5] A year earlier, the 25-year-old right-hander was pitching in the Class B Piedmont League. After going 10-2 with the Triple-A Montreal Royals in 1955, Craig was added to the Dodgers' injury-riddled staff in mid-July. The lanky hurler made 10 starts among his 21 appearances and posted an impressive 2.78 ERA. He has a "good fast ball, good curve, good change-up and plenty of poise," asserted Roy Campanella, displaying confidence that his young hurler would rise to the occasion few rookies had ever experienced in World Series competition.[6] "[Craig] can throw hard," proclaimed Alston. "The only thing I have to worry about is his control."[7]

Yankees skipper Casey Stengel, whose pitching staff paced the majors with a 3.23 ERA, rolled the dice with his Game Five starter. Instead of

Duke Snider, Clem Labine, Roy Campanella, and Gil Hodges helped Dem Bums finally capture an elusive World Series title in 1955. (Photo: SABR-Rucker Archive)

left-handed staff aces Whitey Ford and Tommy Byrne, who had held the explosive Dodgers' bats in check in Yankee Stadium in Games One and Two, the Ole Perfessor counted on ailing Bob Grim, who hadn't started since June 12. The 25-year-old right-hander had won 20 games and was named the AL Rookie of the Year in 1954, but had struggled most of the '55 season, making just 11 starts among his 26 appearances and posting a disappointing 4.19 ERA. This game marked the first time since 1923, when the World Series was a best-of-eight-format, that each team used a different starting pitcher for the first five games of the fall classic. While both managers juggled their pitching staffs, Stengel's biggest concern was the health of his team. Slugger Mickey Mantle, hobbled by a thigh injury suffered near

the end of the regular season, was unable to play; vocal team leader Hank Bauer couldn't start due to leg injury suffered in Game Two.

On a seasonably warm Sunday afternoon with temperatures in the 60s, Ebbets Field was packed with 36,796 spectators, a record crowd in the bandbox ballpark in the Flatbush neighborhood of Brooklyn, according to New York dailies.[8]

The 300th game in World Series history began tentatively. Craig escaped unscathed from a second-inning jam caused by consecutive leadoff walks. After Gil Hodges collected the game's first hit, a one-out single in the second, the Dodgers' shortest player, 5-foot-7, Cuban-born Sandy Amoros belted a home run over the right-field wall and onto Bedford Avenue to give Brooklyn a 2-0 lead.

After Craig set down the Yankees in order in the third, Duke Snider led off with a blast that landed about where Amoros's had. "[It] was on a punk pitch," said a frustrated Grim. "[A] change-up high that wasn't doing a thing when it got to the plate."[9] Campanella followed with a bullet to center field, but Irv Noren's "headlong plunge," opined Drebinger, robbed Campanella of an extra-base hit.[10] Grim flashed his heater to fan Carl Furillo and Hodges.

Yogi Berra led off the fourth with a single, the Yankees' first hit of the game, followed by Eddie Robinson's walk two batters later. Billy Martin's single drove in Yogi Berra to put Craig on the ropes. Dodgers reliever Don Bessent began warming up, as he had done in the second. With two on and one out and trailing 3-1, Stengel made a chess move. He sent Moose Skowron to pinch-hit for weak-hitting Phil Rizzuto. The plan backfired as Skowron popped up to Campy and Grim lined to short.

The Duke of Flatbush was in a groove when he came to bat with one out and none on in the fifth. In Game Four he smashed a three run-run home and flashed his brilliance in the outfield. As far as Dodgers fans were concerned, Snider was as good as his Yankees counterpart, the injured Commerce Comet, and was coming off yet another Snider-esque season, whacking 42 home runs and leading the majors in RBIs (136) and runs scored (126). Grim pitched Snider carefully, but the 29-year-old Los Angeles native walloped one to deep right-center field to give the Dodgers a 4-1 lead. "[The pitch was] away and low," muttered a perplexed Grim after the game, "breaking about as much as a slider can and catch some of the plate."[11] With that solo shot, Snider became the first major leaguer to hit four home runs in two different World Series (also in 1952); it was also his ninth career home run in the World Series, one more than Joe DiMaggio, and trailed Lou Gehrig (10) and Babe Ruth (15); and it accounted for Snider's NL-record 20th RBI in the World

Series. It was the Dodgers' ninth home run of the World Series, breaking the NL mark they set in 1953. "Snider was the turning point," moaned an exasperated Stengel.[12]

Through six innings Alston looked like a mastermind with his decision to start Craig, who had yielded only a run on three hits and four walks. Bob Cerv, pinch-hitting for Grim to lead off the seventh, connected for a solo shot. After Elston Howard drew a walk to bring the tying run to the plate, Alston replaced Craig with Clem Labine.

The "difference is in the bullpen," observed sportswriter John W. Fox about the Dodgers and Yankees.[13] And no reliever epitomized that difference more than 29-year-old right-hander Labine, who had tied for the majors' lead with a Dodgers-record 60 appearances. Making his fourth appearance in the Series, he was coming off a 4⅓-inning stint in Game Four. With his trademark sinking fastball, he was an ideal hurler for the cozy dimensions of Ebbets Field. Noren chopped his sinker to first. Affected by a "badly swollen right knee," noted sportswriter Dick Young, Noren had no chance as the slick-fielding Hodges initiated a 3-6-3 twin killing.[14]

The Dodgers "took a gamble," opined sportswriter Jim McCalley, in the seventh, when third-base coach Billy Herman held speedy Jim Gilliam at third on Snider's two-out double.[15] Both were left stranded when reliever Bob Turley punched out Campanella to strike out the side.

Herman's decision seemed ill-advised when Berra homered off Labine to lead off the eighth to pull the Yankees to within one run. Two batters later Eddie Robinson singled and was replaced by 19-year-old pinch-runner Tom Carroll. In what might have been the most critical defensive play of the game, Martin hit a bounder to third, where a 36-year-old Jackie Robinson began a soul-crushing 5-4-3 double play.

Jackie Robinson, who set career lows with a .256 batting average and 105 games in an injury-laden campaign, laced a one-out single in the eighth to drive in Furillo for the last run of the game.

It was the Labine show in the ninth. He retired pinch-hitters Andy Carey and Tommy Byrne, and Howard on just four pitches to end the game in 2 hours and 40 minutes.[16] Alston "handled his pitchers with a touch of genius in the last three games," proclaimed sportswriter Jack Hand.[17] Labine's pitching, Snider's slugging, and the team's excellent defense complemented Craig's "stout-hearted" performance.[18]

One win away from the first World Series title in franchise history for the second time in three years, the Dodgers hoped to avoid a repeat of 1952, when they lost Games Six and Seven at Ebbets Field. With no offday, the World Series returned to Yankee Stadium, where the Bronx Bombers had lost only one deciding game, in 1942 against the St. Louis Cardinals.

SOURCES

In addition to the sources cited in the Notes, the author accessed Retrosheet.org, Baseball-Reference.com, SABR.org, and the following articles.

McGowen, Roscoe. "Alston Discovers Questions (and Answers) Are Different After a Victory," *New York Times*, October 2, 1955: S3.

Associated Press, "Play-by-Play Story of the Sixth Series Tilt," *Troy* (New York) *Times Record*, October 3, 1955: 1.

NOTES

1   Arthur Daley, "Sports of the Times," *New York Times*, October 3, 1955: 31.

2   Dick Young, "Dodgers Go 1 Up; Win 5th, 5-3," *New York Daily News*, October 3, 1955: 56.

3   United Press, "Snider Couldn't Kid Yogi," *Binghamton* (New York) *Press*, October 3, 1955: 17.

4   Roscoe McGowen, "Alston Will Send Newcombe or Spooner Against Yankees at Stadium Today," *New York Times*, October 3, 1955: 30.

5   John Drebinger, "Dodgers Triumph, 5 to 3; Lead Yankees, 3-2, in Series," *New York Times*, October 3, 1955: 1.

6   Associated Press, "Alston Picks Boy for Man's Job," *Philadelphia Inquirer*, October 2, 1955: S1.

7   Dick Young, "Dodgers Go 1 Up; Win 5th, 5-3."

8   Associated Press, "Series Weather," *Fort Lauderdale* (Florida) *News*, October 2, 1955: 2-C.

9   John W. Fox, "Happier Snider Still Not Sure if Dodgers' Fans Deserve Title," *Binghamton* (New York) *Press*, October 3, 1955: 17.

10   Drebinger.

11   John W. Fox, "Happier Snider Still Not Sure if Dodgers' Fans Deserve Title," *Binghamton Press*, October 3, 1955: 17.

12   Jack Hand (Associated Press), "Brooks Tops Yanks, 5-3," *Syracuse Post-Standard*, October 3, 1955: 1.

13   John W. Fox, "Happier Snider Still Not Sure if Dodgers' Fans Deserve Title."

14   Dick Young, "Dodgers Go 1 Up; Win 5th, 5-3."

15   Jim McCulley, "'Home Now,' Dodgers Shout; 'Cheap' Home Runs Disgust Yankees," *New York Daily News*, October 3, 1955: 57.

16   Jack Hand (Associated Press), "Brooks Tops Yanks, 5-3," *Syracuse Post-Standard*, October 3, 1955: 1.

17   Hand, "Brooks Tops Yanks, 5-3," *Syracuse Post-Standard*, October 3, 1955: 10.

18   Hand: 10.

ERSKINE'S SECOND CAREER NO-HITTER IS FIRST TO BE BROADCAST NATIONALLY

May 12, 1956
Brooklyn Dodgers 3, New York Giants 0

by Gregory H. Wolf

"Not bad for a junk pitcher, and for nine old men," shouted Jackie Robinson after Carl Erskine's no-hitter.[1] Robinson's ire was directed toward New York Giants scout Tom Sheehan, whose club had just been beaten by the team he considered to be over the hill. Erskine became only the 10th pitcher since 1900 to toss two no-hitters, and his performance was the first nationally televised no-hitter. It aired on CBS's *Game of the Week*, and suggested that the reigning World Series champions weren't ready to roll over just yet.[2]

Jackie's contempt aside, Sheehan's comments seemed to reflect on Erskine, whom Dodgers skipper Smoky Alton had described as a "question-mark pitcher" in spring training.[3] At just 29 years old, Erskine's glory days seemed to be over, though his list of accomplishments was long. He had tossed a no-hitter against the Chicago Cubs in 1952, won 20 games in 1953, set a World Series record (later broken) by fanning 14 batters in Game Three of the '53 fall classic,[4] and earned an All-Star Game berth in 1954. While Dem Bums marched to the pennant in 1955,

Erskine struggled over the last two months of the season, plagued by potentially career-ending bone spurs in his elbow. He was shelled for 27 earned runs in his last 44 innings (5.52 ERA) beginning on August 9 and failed to go beyond five innings in five of his eight starts. His struggles continued in the Dodgers' World Series victory over the Yankees. He was knocked out of Game Three after yielding three earned runs in three innings.

The Dodgers might have played like old men in the first few weeks of the 1956 season, at least compared with a year earlier. Preparing for the second game of a three-game set with the Giants, Alston's squad was 10-9, three games behind the St. Louis Cardinals, in fourth place. In 1955 they had won their first 10 games and 22 of 24 in one of the best starts in big-league history. But in '56 the offense seemed flat and the pitching staff had already been victimized for at least 10 runs in a game on four occasions. The Dodgers had an encouraging sign in their previous game, scoring a season-high eight runs in their win against the Giants. Just 18 months removed from winning

354

the World Series, manager Bill Rigney's club was likewise faltering and in sixth place (9-11).

As the 1956 season commenced, little was expected of Erskine, whom sportswriter Dana Mozley described as "the little gentleman whose heart is often stronger than his arm."[5] The slightly built, 5-foot 10, 165-pound right-hander, who began the season with a 100-57 lifetime record, went nine innings in his first two starts, one of which was a victory against the Giants at the Polo Grounds; however, he felt weak in his last two starts, both losses on the road. Never a hard thrower, he thought his fastball had lost its zip. Taking the advice of two friends, he exercised and warmed up before his start against his crosstown rivals with a stainless steel ball in order to loosen his muscles and stretch his wrist.[6]

On a sunny spring Saturday afternoon with temperatures in the mid-60s and rising at the 2:00 start time, Ebbets Feld was packed with 24,588 fans on Ladies Day (paid attendance was 17,395).[7]

The game pitting rivals unfolded as a tense pitchers' duel. Erskine breezed through the first two innings, yielding only one baserunner, a walk to Willie Mays in the opening frame. In the second, Bill White tagged Erskine for a deep shot that flew over the right-field fence and onto Bedford Avenue, but it was foul by seven or eight feet, according to the Daily News.[8]

On the mound for the Giants was three-year veteran right-hander Al Worthington, back in the majors after spending the entire 1955 season in the minors to work on his control. Through the first six innings, he yielded just two hits, but was undone by his wildness, issuing six walks, including three in the third. In that frame, Pee Wee Reese drew a one-out free pass. Duke Snider raked a single to center field which Mays "fumbled."[9] Reese didn't want to test Mays's arm and held up at second. After Roy Campanella's dribbler in front of home plate advanced both runners, Gil Hodges walked to load the bases,

and Robinson's walk plated Reese with the first run. Sandy Amoros fanned to end the threat.

Staked to a one-run lead. Erskine walked Alvin Dark to lead off the fourth inning, which proved to be his toughest. Mays, who entered the game in a season-long funk batting just .225 (12-for-80), smashed a wicked liner to third base. Jackie Robinson instinctively dived to his left and caught the ball, though he "fell hard, perhaps carried by the momentum of the drive as much as by the effort of his lunge," reported the Daily News.[10] After slumping Dusty Rhodes, homerless in 44 plate appearances thus far in '56 and batting .237, popped up behind the plate to Campanella, Daryl Spencer sent a drive to the deepest part of the ballpark, in right-center field. It looked "good for extra bases," opined sportswriter John Drebinger of the New York Times.[11] Carl Furillo, back after missing the last two games because of a cold, took off and had it played perfectly. The Reading Rifle made a nifty over-the-head, off-balance grab.

Willie Mays's defense saved a run in the sixth. After Furillo drew a two-out walk, Erskine doubled to the left-center-field wall. Rhodes fielded the ball, then flipped it to Mays. According to the Daily News, Mays's 340-foot throw was a bit offline to catcher Ray Katt, who was still able to pick up the ball, dive, and tag a sliding Furillo in what was surely the highlight sequence of the game.[12]

The Dodgers finally solved Worthington in the seventh. Reese laced a one-out single and scored on Snider's double. Campanella's single plated Snider and sent Worthington to the showers. Reliever Marv Grissom set down all five Dodgers he faced.

Erskine retired 18 consecutive batters after walking Dark to lead off the fourth. "I definitely didn't have overpowering stuff," he commented.[13] He relied on his changeup and breaking balls, as well as an occasional fastball to keep the Giants guessing. He was "more confusing than overpowering," opined Mozley.[14] "[Erskine's] speed was gone," read a United Press report, "but his guile and courage carried him through."[15] The Giants pounded Erskine's curves into the dirt for easy rollers and slow bounders, and hit only seven balls to the outfield. He fanned three, all on slow curves for called strikes.[16] "[M]y curveball was my best pitch today," he said "It was fooling them."[17]

Erskine had some good fortune, too. Left-hander Don Mueller, pinch-hitting for Foster Castleman, hit a screeching liner with one out in the eighth. But it was right at Pee Wee Reese at shortstop who barely moved to make the catch.

As Erskine took the mound three outs from a no-hitter, Don Ferrarese of the Baltimore Orioles was trying to do the same at Yankee Stadium. Ferrarese yielded a leadoff single to Andy Carey in the ninth, settling for two-hit shutout. Erskine dispatched pinch-hitter George Wilson on a routine popup to first base. The next batter, Whitey Lockman sent Erskine's first pitch into the right-field stands, but it hooked several feet foul. Lockman sent an 0-and-2 pitch back to Erskine on a tricky hop. "I reached down and swatted at the ball," said Erskine. "I jammed the ball under the glove into the ground."[18] He recovered quickly and threw to Hodges for the second out. Hitting a team-high .329 entering the game, Dark stepped to the plate. "I was more worried about Dark than anyone else," confessed Erskine about the contact

hitter, one of the most difficult batters to strike out. "He slaps the ball and is tough to pitch to."[19] With his 102nd pitch, Erskine induced Dark to hit an easy tapper back to the mound. His throw to Hodges completed his no-hitter in 2 hours and 10 minutes.

Evening his record, 2-2, Erskine's no-hitter was the highlight of his last productive, yet wildly inconsistent season in the majors (13-11; 4.25 ERA in 186⅓ innings). Bombed for six hits and five earned runs in a no-decision in his next start, on May 18 against the Cincinnati Reds, Erskine eventually dropped to 2-6. He then reeled off a career-best nine consecutive winning decisions, despite a 4.14 ERA, profiting from the Dodgers' big bats. He ended the season on a 2-5 skid with a 5.34 ERA, as the Dodges secured their last pennant in Brooklyn on the final day of the season. Erskine spent his final three years as swingman and mop-up artist, retiring after the 1959 campaign with a 122-78 record.

SOURCES

In addition to the sources cited in the Notes, the author accessed Retrosheet.org, Baseball-Reference.com, SABR.org, and *The Sporting News* archive via Paper of Record.

NOTES

1 Dick Young, "Exercise With Steel Ball Relaxes Carl's Muscles," *New York Daily News*, May 13, 1956: 98.

2 "Erskine Received a $500 Check from O'Malley for Pitching Feat," *New York Times*, May 13, 1956: 185.

3 "Erskine Received a $500 Check from O'Malley for Pitching Feat."

4 The record was broken by Sandy Koufax (17 K's) in the 1963 World Series and Bob Gibson (17) in 1968.

5 Dana Mozley, "Erskine Wins His 2d No-Hitter, 3-0," *New York Daily News*, May 13, 1956: 94.

6 Young.

7 Ladies Day attendance from Mozley. Weather from "Daily Almanac," *New York Daily News*, May 13, 1956: 2.

8 Mozley.

9 Mozley.

10 Mozley.

11 John Drebinger, "Two Reach Base," *New York Times*, May 13, 1956: 183.

12 Mozley.

13 "Erskine Received a $500 Check from O'Malley for Pitching Feat."

14 Mozley.

15 United Press, "Carl's 2d No-Hitter 1st on TV," *Bingham-ton* (New York) *Press and Sun-Bulletin*, May 13, 1956: 1-D.

16 Mozley.

17 Young.

18 Mozley.

19 Young. Al Dark fanned just 534 times in 7,833 plate appearances. The ratio was even better vduring Dark's most productive stretch (1951-1955), when he struck out 184 times in 3,244 plate appearances.

BUMS TAKE IVER NL LEAD AFTER DOUBLEHEADER SWEEP OF BUCS

September 29, 1956

Brooklyn Dodgers 6, Pittsburgh Pirates 2 | First Game of Doubleheader
Brooklyn Dodgers 3, Pittsburgh Pirates 1 | Second Game of Doubleheader

by Frederick C. Bush

The Brooklyn Dodgers and Milwaukee Braves were battling down to the wire for the National League crown in 1956 and both teams were having trouble winning on a consistent basis at the end of September. The St. Louis Cardinals gave Brooklyn an opening to move into the pennant lead when they defeated Milwaukee, 5-4, on September 28. The Dodgers seized the opportunity in a September 29 twin bill against the seventh-place Pittsburgh Pirates. Sal "The Barber" Maglie went the distance in the opener and spot-starter Clem Labine followed suit in the nightcap to hand Dem Bums a doubleheader sweep, by scores of 6-2 and 3-1, ensuring that the team would end the regular season in no worse position than a tie with the Braves.

Although the Pirates arrived at Ebbets Field with a record that was 19 games under .500, it was no foregone conclusion that they would be easy fodder for the Brooklynites. Only one week earlier, the Bucs had taken three of four from the Dodgers at Pittsburgh's Forbes Field. A crowd of 34,022 was on hand to see if the Dodgers could respond in kind at their home venue.[1] With the

recent debacle in Pittsburgh fresh in their minds, Brooklyn fans "booed the Pirates when they took the field, booed each man when he was announced in the starting lineup but the biggest boo was saved for (Pirates Game One starter Bob) Friend, the Dodger killer."[2]

Friend had beaten the Dodgers four times in 1956, most recently in a 6-5 triumph just five days earlier. There was irony in the fact that the Dodgers countered with Maglie since he also had been a "Dodger killer" as a member of the New York Giants for most of the 1950s. The Dodgers had purchased the 39-year-old Maglie's contract from the Cleveland Indians on May 15, and he had paid dividends throughout the season, including spinning a no-hitter against the Philadelphia Phillies in his last start, on September 25. Now he planned to make the Pirates walk the plank in Game One as he tried to pitch the Dodgers to the pennant.

If any fans wished that Maglie could duplicate Johnny Vander Meer's feat of tossing consecutive no-hitters, those hopes were dashed in the first inning. Dale Long hit a two-out single and Frank

Thomas clouted his 25th homer for a quick 2-0 Pirates lead. According to one Pittsburgh reporter, "[E]very Dodger fan in the ball park turned pale" at Thomas's blast as they likely thought that the lowly Bucs would dash their team's title hopes.[3]

As it turned out, the denizens of Flatbush needed not worry. Jim Gilliam led off the Dodgers' half of the inning with a single. After Pee Wee Reese and Duke Snider struck out, Gilliam stole second as Jackie Robinson batted. Robinson then drove in Gilliam with a single to center field and Sandy Amorós followed with a two-run homer. Gil Hodges singled but was erased for the third out on Carl Furillo's fielder's choice grounder. Nonetheless, the Dodgers now had a 3-2 lead that they would not surrender.

Amorós's homer not only gave Brooklyn the lead but also provided him with much-needed relief from criticism he had received over the previous three days. On September 26 Amorós had made an error that resulted in three unearned runs scoring as the Dodgers suffered a 7-3 setback to the Phillies, and his miscue had turned him into a scapegoat for both Brooklyn fans and some Dodgers players. Catcher Roy Campanella said, "He feels badly about all that's been said and written about him. … I know his Cuban friends read it to him and I know it hurt him inside. But I try to pep him up. He sort of looks up to me. I'll have a talk with him before the doubleheader."[4] Campy's talk apparently worked wonders as Amorós not only hit the game-winning homer in the opener but also hustled on defense and made a fine play in the third inning of the nightcap when he "ran to the boxes in left field and speared Bill Virdon's fly just as it was going into the seats."[5]

After his first-inning hiccup, Maglie set the Pirates down in order from the second inning through the fifth and allowed only a two-out single to Bob Skinner in the sixth. Friend made it a duel and kept the Dodgers from scoring again until Furillo hit a solo homer in the bottom of the sixth to make it a 4-2 game.

The Pirates tried to mount a rally in the top of the eighth, but the attempt was short-lived. After Virdon hit a two-out single, Skinner hit a long shot to center but was robbed of a hit by Snider who made a "fantastic back-handed catch of [the] low liner" to end Pittsburgh's aspirations of drawing closer or even tying the game.[6]

The Dodgers added the final two runs of the ballgame in the bottom of the inning against Nellie King, Pittsburgh's third pitcher of the day, who had replaced Luis Arroyo with Snider on second and one out in the inning. Randy Jackson, pinch-hitting for Amorós, flied out, but Hodges drove in Snider with the third Dodgers homer of the game for the final 6-2 margin of victory.

Maglie worked around ninth-inning singles by Thomas and Dick Groat and struck out Hank Foiles to end the game. The complete-game victory was The Barber's 13th win in 1956 and gave the Dodgers momentum as they headed into the nightcap of the doubleheader.

Labine's effort in the second game seemed more labored in comparison to Maglie, who had hurled a masterpiece from the second inning onward. However, while Labine retired the side in order only once (in the fifth inning), he did manage to accomplish the more important feat of keeping the Bucs off the scoreboard in all but one inning. When the game was over, Labine had surrendered seven hits, compared with the six Maglie had given up, and had allowed half the number of runs as his fellow moundsman.

Labine was normally a reliever, but he was making his third start in 62 appearances over the course of the 1956 season and had a 9-6 record. His mound opponent for Game Two was Ron Kline, who entered the contest with a 14-17 season ledger.

On this day, Labine wrestled with his control and gave up five walks, which resulted in far more traffic on the bases than Maglie, who had surrendered only one walk, had had to negotiate. The control problems reared their head in the top of the first inning as Labine put himself in a precarious position via walks to Skinner and Thomas. The ever-dangerous Roberto Clemente came up with the two runners on base, but Labine induced a fly out to Furillo in right to end the threat.

Labine and Kline settled into a pitchers' duel in which the only run scored over the first 5½ innings came on Campanella's leadoff home run in the bottom of the third inning. This is not to say that there were no exciting moments over the first half of the game. Indeed, the most important events occurred in the Dodgers' half of the fifth inning "with an amazing crowd demonstration that for a time threatened to cause forfeiture of the game."[7]

Campanella, whose homer had provided the lone thrill to this point, also led off the fateful fifth for Brooklyn. According to the New York Times, "Campanella, no Olympic sprint champion by any stretch of the imagination, topped a ball down the third base line and outgalloped it for a hit."[8] Labine then attempted a sacrifice bunt that Foiles, the Pirates catcher, grabbed and rifled to second in an attempt to force Campanella. Foiles's throw was high and Groat, the shortstop, had to leap off the bag to keep it from sailing into the outfield. Campanella slid into second and appeared to be safe, but umpire Vic Delmore called him out.

As expected, Dodgers manager Walter Alston ran out of the dugout and argued Campy's case vociferously but to no avail. Although the Dodgers finally quit yelling at Delmore, the Flatbush faithful refused to be silent. The crowd "sent up a deafening roar as play was resumed and there was just no let up to it. To add to the confusion, most everyone in the park pulled out a handkerchief and started waving it."[9] Home-plate umpire Stan Landes called time to confer with his fellow arbiters, and crew chief Jocko Conlon had the public-address announcer warn the crowd to cease its demonstration lest the game be called a forfeit.

The Times seemed stunned that the umpires threatened the Dodgers with a forfeit, since they purportedly were only raising a loud ruckus and waving handkerchiefs. It reported that "[a] couple of beer cans rolled on the field back of home plate, but otherwise nothing appeared to be thrown on the field except scraps of paper."[10] The Pittsburgh Press provided a somewhat different account, asserting, "Then the fans started booing and threw objects on the field, including vegetables, beer cans, etc."[11] A neutral-city news account stated, "The Brooklynite crowd protested ... both vocally and by throwing refuse on the field," thus corroborating the Press's account and shedding light on the reason why the umpires resorted to such an extreme threat.[12]

When the Pirates came to bat in the top of the sixth, Clemente stroked a one-out triple to right field and Groat walked. Had Pittsburgh tied the game or taken the lead, it boggles the imagination to wonder how the Brooklyn fans might have reacted. But Labine struck out Lee Walls and induced a popout from Foiles to prevent a potential riot and maintain the Dodgers' 1-0 lead.

What finally quelled any potential fan uprising was the fact that the umpires ran afoul of the Pirates with a call in the bottom of the sixth. Robinson was aboard first after a one-out single, and Amorós was at bat. Landes ruled catcher's interference on Foiles and pointed Amorós to first. Now, it was Pirates manager Bobby Bragan and Foiles who argued long and loud about the latest questionable call to the point that Landes threw them out of the game. Immediately after the Bucs' skipper and catcher were tossed, Hodges shot a triple down the right-field line that drove in Robinson and Amorós. Although Hodges ended up stranded at third, he had extended the lead to 3-0, and his hit provided the winning run in the ballgame.

Just as had been the case in the first game, the Pirates tried to rally in the eighth inning of Game Two. Clemente and Groat led off the frame with singles, with Clemente advancing to third on Groat's hit. Johnny O'Brien grounded into a double play that allowed Clemente to score but that also thwarted any thoughts of a Pittsburgh comeback. Jack Shepard lofted a fly ball to Snider in center for the third out of the inning, and the Dodgers maintained a 3-1 lead.

Friend, who had pitched seven innings in the opener, had entered this game in relief of Kline in the bottom of the seventh inning. Although he kept the Dodgers from adding to their lead, he was no help on the offensive side for Pittsburgh. Thus, after Friend retired the side in order in the bottom of the eighth, he was replaced by pinch-hitter John Powers, who led off the top of the ninth. Powers provided no lift for the Pirates either as he struck out. Skinner gave the Bucs one last hope with a two-out double, but Long grounded out to second base to end the game.

Labine had earned his 10th win of the year with a stellar effort in which he overcame five walks, allowed only one run, and struck out 10 Pittsburgh batters. It was his first complete game since a 6-3 triumph over the Phillies in the second game of a doubleheader on July 4, 1955, and his biggest clutch victory since his 10-0 shutout of the New York Giants in the second game of the 1951 tiebreaker series to determine that season's National League champion.

After St. Louis again beat Milwaukee, 2-1 in 12 innings, on the same evening, the Dodgers were one game in front of the Braves. The next day, Don Newcombe pitched 7⅓ innings of a hard-fought 8-6 victory over the Pirates for his 27th win that clinched the pennant for the Dodgers, who finished the year with a 93-61 record.

SOURCES

In addition to the sources cited in the Notes, the author accessed Retrosheet.org, Baseball-Reference.com, Newspapers.com, and SABR.org.

NOTES

1   John Drebinger, "Brooks Are First: Clinch at Least a Tie for Flag with Final Game Slated Today," *New York Times*, September 30, 1956: S1. The official, paid attendance was 26,340; however, according to the *Times*, "it also was Ladies Day, and the fair sex, plus some 3,000 Knothole youngsters, brought the over-all count to 34,022."

2   Les Biederman, "The Scoreboard," *Pittsburgh Press*, September 30, 1956: 70.

3   Kaspar Monahan, "Dem Brooklyn Fans Has a Lot of Noise," *Pittsburgh Press*, September 30, 1956: 2.

4   Biederman.

5   Biederman.

6   Biederman.

7   Drebinger, S1.

8   Drebinger, S1.

9   Drebinger, S1.

10 Drebinger, S3.

11 Lester J. Biederman, "Brooklyn Game Ahead/Braves Lose," *Pittsburgh Press*, September 30, 1956: 69.

12 Fred DeLuca, "Dodgers Rip Pirates, 6-2, 3-1 in Crucial Doublebill," *Atlanta Daily World*, September 30, 1956: 8.

BROOKLYN DODGERS WIN NL PENNANT
ON FINAL DAY OF SEASON

September 30, 1956
Brooklyn Dodgers 8, Pittsburgh Pirates 6

by Thomas J. Brown Jr.

The reigning World Series champion Brooklyn Dodgers finally made a push to the National League pennant late in the 1956 season. After being 1½ games out of first place following a doubleheader split September 7, the Dodgers charged forward and held a one-game lead on September 30.

Brooklyn had swept the Pirates in a doubleheader on September 29, 6-2 and 3-1. Sal Maglie won the first game. Clem Labine, usually the team's relief ace, started the second game and went the whole way.[1] The second-place Milwaukee Braves, meanwhile, lost 2-1 to the St. Louis Cardinals. Now, it was coming down to the final game of the season. Could Brooklyn win the game and the pennant? A Dodgers loss against Pittsburgh and a Braves win against St. Louis would force a playoff.

Don Newcombe took the mound for Brooklyn against Vern Law. Newcombe brought a 26-7 record into the game. Law, meanwhile, was trying to avoid his 16th loss for the Pirates, who occupied seventh place in the eight-team NL, 26 games out of first.

Newcombe retired the side in order in the top of the first inning The Dodgers jumped on Law in the bottom of the frame. Law walked leadoff batter Jim Gilliam and gave up a single to Pee Wee Reese that sent Gilliam to third. Duke Snider now stepped to the plate. He sent the first pitch from Law over the Ebbets Field outfield wall for his league-leading 42nd home run of the season. Law got the next two batters out, but gave up a single to Gil Hodges. Pirates manager Bobby Bragan had seen enough, although the score was still just 3-0. He replaced Law with Roy Face, who got the third out.

Newcombe kept the Pirates in check in the second inning but faltered in the third. He gave up a single to leadoff batter Jack Shepard and walked Dick Cole. After throwing a wild pitch that allowed Shepard and Cole to advance, Roberto Clemente stroked a two-run single. The score was now 3-2.

In the bottom of the third, Bob Purkey came on in relief for Pittsburgh. Reese grounded out to start the frame; Snider followed up by flying out to center field. Jackie Robinson then hit his 10th home run of the season. It was the 137th homer of his career and also his last.[2]

Newcombe did not have one of his better days on the mound and allowed six earned runs. After giving up the two runs in the third, he held the Pirates to one hit in each of the fourth, fifth, and sixth innings. The Pirates failed to score each time, although they got a runner to third when Lee Walls tripled with one out in the fourth.

Ron Kline took over the pitching duties for the Pirates in the fifth inning. He gave up a leadoff double to Newcombe, who went to third on Gilliam's grounder to first. Newcombe scored when Reese hit a sacrifice fly to left field. Snider followed with his second home run of the game and 43rd of the season. Robinson struck out, and the inning ended with the Dodgers leading 6-2. They padded that lead in the sixth when Sandy Amorós hit a leadoff home run.

The Pirates, down 7-2, scored three runs off Newcombe in the seventh inning. Dick Groat led off with a double to right field. Consecutive singles by Bill Mazeroski and Shepard loaded the bases. Newcombe got two outs and nearly wiggled out of the threat, but Bill Virdon brought home three runs with a double to center field. The Dodgers lead had been to cut to 7-5.

Bob Friend took the mound for the Pirates and held the Dodgers scoreless in the seventh inning. Walls homered off Newcombe in the top of the eighth, cutting the Pirates' deficit to a single run at 7-6 and knocking the Brooklyn starter out of the game. Dodgers manager Walter Alston summoned second-year right-hander Don Bessent from the bullpen.

Bessent had saved eight games in 37 relief appearances on the season. Labine was unavailable after the previous day's work in his third start of the season.[3] Bessent gave up a hit to Groat, and third baseman Robinson made an error on pinch-hitter Gene Freese's grounder. Jack Shepard flew out and Dale Long struck out to end the threat. Amorós gave the Dodgers a little cushion when he led off the bottom of the eighth with his second solo home run of the game.

Clemente opened the ninth with a single off Bessent. Virdon, though, hit into a double play, and Hank Foiles struck out to end the game. The Dodgers were 8-6 victors.

The Braves beat the Cardinals 4-2, but it didn't matter. Brooklyn had won its second straight pennant. Once again, the Dodgers would face the New York Yankees in the World Series. Brooklyn fans looked forward to seeing their "Bums" celebrate in October one more time.

SOURCES

In addition to the sources cited in the Notes, the author also used the Baseball-Reference.com, Baseball-Almanac.com, and Retrosheet.org websites for box-score, player, team, and season pages, pitching and batting game logs, and other pertinent material.

NOTES

1   Bryan Soderholm, "Baseball Historical Insight: Last Day 60 Years Ago, September 30, 1956," brysholm. blogspot.com, September 30, 2016.

2   Soderholm. This was Robinson's final regular-season homer; he retired after the 1956 season. He also homered once in the World Series.

3   Soderholm.

MAGLIE FANS 10, BESTS FORD IN FALL CLASSIC OPENER

October 3, 1956

Brooklyn Dodgers 6, New York Yankees 3 | Game One of the World Series

by Paul Hofmann

The 1956 World Series was the sixth between the New York Yankees and Brooklyn Dodgers in 10 years.[1] The American League champion Yankees clinched the pennant on September 16 and finished the season with a record of 97-57, nine games ahead of the second-place Cleveland Indians. The defending World Series champion Dodgers won a tight, three-team pennant race in the National League. They clinched the pennant on the final day of the season and finished with a record of 93-61, edging out the Milwaukee Braves by a game and the Cincinnati Reds by two.

The temperature was about 70 degrees and the skies were fair when President Dwight Eisenhower, who was in the midst of running for reelection,[2] threw out the ceremonial first pitch in front of a crowd of 34,479.[3] It was the first time a president threw out the first pitch at a World Series game since President Franklin D. Roosevelt "launched the '36 Series between the Yankees and Giants at the Polo Grounds."[4]

The breezy early-autumn Wednesday afternoon featured a Game One matchup between a pair of veteran World Series hurlers. Yankees manager Casey Stengel turned to Whitey Ford. Given Ebbets Field's short porch in left field and the Dodgers' right-hander-dominated lineup, starting the left-handed Ford seemed like a bit of a gamble. The 28-year-old Ford went 19-6 during the regular season and led the American League in ERA (2.47) and winning percentage (.760). He was opposed by veteran Sal Maglie. The Dodgers right-hander bounced back from a subpar 1955 season and went 13-5 with a 2.87 ERA after being acquired from the Cleveland Indians on May 15.

The Yankees got off to a quick start in the top of the first. After Hank Bauer opened the game by grounding out to third, Enos Slaughter reached on an infield single. On the very next pitch, Mickey Mantle, who captured the circuit's Triple Crown with a .353 batting average, 52 home runs and 130 RBIs, and later received the NL's Most Valuable Player Award, homered to deep right to give the Yankees an early 2-0 lead. The home run was the first of three Mantle hit in the seven-game Series. After walking Yogi Berra, Maglie struck out Bill Skowron and Gil McDougald to end the inning.

The Dodgers purchased 39-year-old Sal Maglie from the Cleveland Indians in mid-May 1956. The Barber bolstered a maligned staff, went 13-5, and was named Game One starter in the World Series. (Photo: SABR-Rucker Archive)

After the game Maglie explained Mantle's tremendous home run – some reports said it found its way on to Bedford Avenue beyond the right-field stands[5] – to reporters. Maglie said, "I didn't mean to get it that far over the plate. It was a slider and it broke right smack on his bat."[6]

Ford pitched a one-two-three inning in the bottom of the first and Maglie followed suit in the top of the second.

The Dodgers evened the score in the bottom of the second. Jackie Robinson hit a home run to deep left on Ford's first pitch of the inning. First baseman Gil Hodges followed with a single to center field and scored when right fielder Carl Furillo doubled to left-center. Hodges scored in large part because Mantle, who was not fully recovered from a groin injury, was unable to get over and cut the ball off before it went to the wall. Ford settled down and retired the next three batters to escape further damage. After two innings score stood at 2-2.

Maglie navigated his way out of trouble after a pair of Yankee singles to start the third inning. Ford quickly found himself in more trouble in the bottom half of the frame. Pee Wee Reese reached on an infield single and took second when Duke Snider singled to center. Robinson lined out to center for the second out of inning before Hodges "drove Ford's 1-and-1 fast ball deep into the left-center seats"[7] for a three-run home run that put the Dodgers up 5-2.

The Yankees got one back in the top of the fourth when second baseman Billy Martin hit a one-out home run to left to make the score 5-3. Ford's day ended when Stengel had seldom-used outfielder George Wilson pinch-hit for the Yankees ace.

Ford later dispelled any notions that his early exit might have been precipitated by an injury. "Just didn't have it," Ford explained to reporters. "No excuses of any kind. They hit me hard. I wasn't getting the ball where I wanted it to go."[8] Ford, who took the loss, bounced back three days later and threw a complete-game victory in Game Three at Yankee Stadium.

Right-hander Johnny Kucks came on to start the bottom of the fourth for the Yankees. The 24-year-old enjoyed a career year in 1956. He was named to the American League All-Star team and finished with a record of 18-9 and a 3.85 ERA.

Roy Campanella greeted Kucks with a double to center and the Dodgers catcher scored when left fielder Sandy Amorós singled to center, extending the Dodgers' lead to 6-3. Maglie attempted to sacrifice Amorós to second but instead bunted into a 3-6-4 double play. Jim Gilliam reached on an error by first baseman Skowron and stole second, but the inning ended when Kucks struck out Reese looking.

Kucks retired the Dodgers in order in the bottom of the fifth and was lifted for a pinch-hitter in the top of the sixth. Right-hander Tom Morgan, who was 6-7 with 11 saves and a 4.16 ERA, pitched a scoreless sixth and seventh and right-hander Bob Turley, who had an up-and-down regular season, pitched a one-two-three eighth for the Yankees.

Meanwhile, Maglie continued to keep the Yankees off the scoreboard for the remainder of the game. The 39-year-old "Barber" scattered four hits and three walks over his last five innings of work and got Mantle to ground into a 4-6-3 double play to end the game. The time of the game was 2 hours and 32 minutes.

The story of the game was the pitching of Maglie. He masterfully worked his way out of "crisis after crisis"[9] on his way to the complete-game victory. In fact, Dodgers manager Walter Alston visited the mound and seriously considered pulling Maglie in the fifth. In the end, he stayed with Maglie who gave up nine hits and three runs (all earned) while walking four and striking out 10. The Yankees left six of their nine stranded runners on base in the last five innings.

After the game teammates and Yankees alike praised Maglie. Campanella, Maglie's batterymate, commended the 39-year-old pitcher's curveball. "Sal wasn't at his best, but he still had Public Enemy No. 1 working for him … the old deuce," Campanella said.[10] Yankees right fielder Bauer, who battled Maglie in five plate appearances, said, "He just fights you on every pitch. He works on you and he won't give in. Even when it's 3-and-2 count, he goes for the corner with breaking stuff."[11]

The victory was Maglie's first in postseason play. He had made starts in both the 1951 and 1954 World Series when he was a member of the New York Giants. However, he was the loser in Game Four of the 1951 Series against the Yankees and had a no-decision in Game One of the 1954 Series against the Cleveland Indians.

Five days after this game, Maglie made his second start of the Series in Game Five at Yankee Stadium. He tossed another complete game, yielding only two runs on five hits.[12] However, on that day, Don Larsen was even better, authoring the only perfect game in World Series history as the Yankees went on to win the Series in seven games.

SOURCES

In addition to the sources cited in the Notes, the author consulted Baseball-Reference.com and Retrosheet.org.

NOTES

1   The Yankees and Brooklyn Dodgers also met in the World Series in 1947, 1949, 1952, 1953, and 1955. The Yankees won in 1947, 1949, 1952, and 1953. The Brooklyn ballclub won its only World Series in 1955.

2   Dwight Eisenhower defeated Adlai Stevenson in a landslide election victory one month later.

3   Marty Appel, *Casey Stengel: Baseball's Greatest Character* (New York: Doubleday, 2017), 236.

4   Dana Mozley, "Ike Threw Curve Strike to Open Series: Campy," *New York Daily News*, October 4, 1956: 20.

5   Jim McCulley, "Curves Did It: Roy, Yanks Praise Sal," *New York Daily News*, October 4, 1956: 45.

6   McCulley.

7   Dick Young, "Sal Shaves Yanks in Opener," *New York Daily News*, October 4, 1956: 20.

8   McCulley.

9   Young.

10   McCulley.

11   McCulley.

12   Maglie was credited with a complete game despite being pinch-hit for in the top of the ninth inning by Dale Mitchell. Mitchell, a reserve outfielder for the Dodgers, struck out to become the final out of Larsen's perfect game.

SLUGGING ON THE DIAMOND AND IN THE PARKING LOT

October 5, 1956

Brooklyn Dodgers 13, New York Yankees 8 | Game Two of the World Series

by John Bauer

For the sixth time in 10 years, October baseball was the exclusive preserve of the same two boroughs of New York City: the Bronx and Brooklyn. Once again, the championship would be contested between the New York Yankees and the Brooklyn Dodgers. Until the Dodgers finally bested the Yankees in 1955, every preceding October matchup went to the Yankees. With home-field advantage at their Ebbets Field home, the Dodgers got the jump on turning the success of the previous year into a trend. They won the 1956 Series opener, 6-3, with Sal Maglie outdueling Whitey Ford.

Ebbets Field would serve as the confluence of sport and politics ahead of the coming presidential election. Game One had been attended by President Dwight Eisenhower; his opponent, Adlai Stevenson, would witness Game Two. The plan had been for Stevenson to throw out the first pitch before Game Three at Yankee Stadium but weather would interrupt those plans. With overcast skies and light sprinkles on the morning of the Wednesday, October 4, Commissioner Ford Frick huddled with the managers and the umpires. Based on information from weather agencies, the game was postponed. The domino effect related not just to the presence of presidential candidates; it also affected the preparation of the starting pitchers, particularly Dodgers ace Don Newcombe.

A 27-game winner during the 1956 NL season, Newcombe had pitched in the pennant-clincher against Pittsburgh the prior Sunday. The extra day of rest was not considered a benefit. Dodgers manager Walter Alston said, "With four days his control isn't always so sharp."[1] Newcombe agreed: "I'm better with three days rest than four."[2] For a pitcher whose season would result in the Cy Young and MVP awards, the issue of rest might seem overdone. Newcombe dealt with lingering questions about winning the "big one"; he pitched three times against the Yankees in the 1949 and 1955 World Series, and lost each time. Irritated by the narrative about his prior performances, Newcombe said, "Some people have said I choke up. I've pitched and won a lot of games and why is it that none of 'em is a 'big one'?"[3] Following some pregame clowning in which Alston and Yankees manager Casey Stengel would place their caps atop the dome of the White Sox-supporting Stevenson, Newcombe took the mound against his tormentors, albeit an altered lineup from what Maglie faced.

Stengel shook up his lineup after the Game One loss. First baseman Bill Skowron was benched in favor of Joe Collins. Andy Carey surrendered third base to Billy Martin, who moved over from second base to accommodate Jerry Coleman. The only unchanged position in the Yankees infield concerned shortstop and leadoff hitter Gil McDougald, who ground out to his opposite number Pee Wee Reese for the first out of Game Two. Enos Slaughter slapped a single to right for the game's first hit. Mickey Mantle flied out to Duke Snider in center field, but Newcombe surrendered a two-out walk to Yogi Berra. Collins lined a single to center that plated Slaughter for an early lead. Hank Bauer's popup to second baseman Junior Gilliam ended the top half. New York starter Don Larsen, who went 11-5 with a 3.26 ERA during the regular season, walked Gilliam and Snider in the bottom half, but Jackie Robinson's grounder to Martin started an inning-ending double play.

The Yankees went back to work against Newcombe in the top of the second. Martin started the inning by beating out a throw from Gilliam on his groundball. Coleman's sacrifice to Newcombe moved Martin to second base, from which Martin scored on Larsen's single to left. McDougald also singled, but then was forced at second on Slaughter's grounder to Reese. Larsen was positioned at third, with Slaughter on first, as Mantle strode to the plate. Despite a Triple Crown-winning season that would end with the AL Most Valuable Player Award, there would be no home-run drama for Mantle on this at-bat. That would be saved for Berra. Instead, Mantle walked on four pitches to load the bases for the Yankee catcher. Berra took Newcombe's first pitch for a ball, but crushed his second pitch over

the right-field screen for the fifth grand slam in World Series history. His ace behind early 6-0, Alston relieved Newcombe of his duties in favor of Ed Roebuck. Collins grounded out to Gilliam, and one could have been forgiven for assuming that irreparable damage had been done to the Brooklyn cause.

By the time Brooklyn completed its "ups" in the bottom of the second, the teams were tied. Gil Hodges opened with a single to center. The next play became one of the game's most discussed events. Sandy Amorós hit a bouncer to the usually reliable Collins at first base. Collins collected the ball and pivoted to throw the ball to second. When Collins, up to then error-free in 24 World Series games, reached into his glove, the ball was not there. Collins later said, "I guess it dropped out as I turned to make the throw to second base. I never got my bare hand on it at all. I didn't know I'd dropped it until I saw it rolling on the ground."[4] With the Yankees holding a six-run lead, the damage from this single miscue might have seemed containable. But Larsen walked Carl Furillo to load the bases. Roy Campanella's sacrifice fly to Slaughter scored Hodges for the first Dodgers run. Veteran Dale Mitchell, who had all of 24 plate appearances for Brooklyn after a midseason trade, popped up to Martin in foul territory for the second out. Gilliam walked to load the bases once again, bringing Stengel out of the dugout and Johnny Kucks into the game. Larsen had faced 10 batters and walked four of them; his next outing for the Yankees would prove much different.

After working the count full against Kucks, Reese fouled off the next three pitches before smacking a single to left that scored Amorós and Furillo. The Dodgers had halved the deficit, 6-3, and Snider would close it completely. Stengel opted for veteran lefty Tommy Byrne to face the Brooklyn slugger, a "percentage move,"[5] according to the Yankees manager. Byrne's curve broke sharply for Snider, who flailed at the ball. The next pitch was intended to back Snider off the plate. According to Berra, "It was supposed to be a waste pitch so we could set him up for the curve."[6] Berra added, "We didn't want the pitch to be in the strike zone but it was."[7] Indeed, Snider launched the ball over the right-field screen and across Bedford Avenue for a game-tying homer. Robinson's strikeout ended the inning with the clubs knotted, 6-6.

Don Bessent took the hill for Brooklyn in the third, and would not surrender the mound for the remainder of the contest. Although Bauer opened the third with a single, Martin's double-play ball and Coleman's grounder, both to Reese, ended the half-inning. Tom Sturdivant started the Brooklyn third on the mound for New York. He walked Hodges before striking out Amorós. Furillo singled to left, advancing Hodges to second. Sturdivant struck out Campanella for the second out, but Bessent cracked a run-scoring single to left for Brooklyn's first lead. Stengel made another pitching change after Gilliam walked to load the bases. Fortunately for the Yankees, Reese popped up against Tom Morgan for the final out. Morgan remained in the game to lead off the Yankees fourth, and did so with a single. McDougald's sacrifice and Bessent's wild pitch moved Morgan to within 90 feet of the plate. Slaughter's sacrifice fly to Snider had enough distance to bring Morgan home and tie the game, 7-7.

In the Dodgers fourth, Snider and Robinson opened with back-to-back singles. Hodges "hammered a buzzing liner over Slaughter's head"[8] with such force that it rebounded halfway to the infield after striking the base of the wall. It was McDougald who fielded the ball, but Snider and Robinson crossed the plate on Hodges' two-bagger for a 9-7 lead. This same group increased the Dodgers lead in the fifth. With two outs, Snider walked and Robinson followed with a single on a ball that skipped over McDougald. Hodges blasted another double past a diving Slaughter in left-center, again scoring Snider and Robinson. Down 11-7, Stengel

dipped once more into his bullpen. Right-hander Bob Turley struck out Amorós on a called third strike for the final out. That strikeout proved Turley's only action; Norm Siebern unsuccessfully hit for him in the sixth, requiring another pitching change for New York. Stengel turned to Mickey McDermott, who would make the only World Series appearance of his career. McDermott walked Bessent with two outs in the sixth, and did the same against Robinson and Hodges in the seventh, but he kept the Dodgers from expanding the lead until the eighth.

Furillo opened that home half with a single to left. Campanella lofted a fly ball toward right-center that appeared an easy catch for Bauer, but the Yankees right-fielder muffed the play. Bauer said, "The ball was right in the middle of my glove and jumped out. It was that kind of day."[9] Bessent's sacrifice advanced Furillo and Campanella up a base, and Gilliam's shot over second base brought home both runners for a 13-7 Dodgers lead. Reese's fly out and Snider's strikeout ended the eighth, and Yankees had three outs to close a six-run gap. Slaughter began a nascent rally with a leadoff single. After Mantle flied out to Snider, Berra singled to left and advanced Slaughter to third. Reese fielded Collins's grounder and opted for the force at second, allowing Slaughter to score. Bauer's fly ball to Amorós ended the game, the longest nine-inning World Series game to that point (3 hours 26 minutes), leaving the Yankees with a two-games-to-none deficit.

Pitching and fielding served as the primary talking points in the postgame commentary. Stengel was quick to absolve Collins of responsibility for his error in the second inning. Stengel explained, "That put the second man on base. But who put the first one on? And who didn't get out the others they should've got out? The pitching was to blame, not Collins."[10] The Yankees established a new Series record with seven pitchers. Stengel analyzed the situation: "They're making the wrong pitches. They're throwing exactly what they shouldn't be throwing."[11] It was not just Yankee pitching that made postgame news. The Dodger offense saved Newcombe from another Series loss to the Yankees, but Newcombe literally heard complaints about his performance. Ebbets Field parking-lot attendant Michael Brown made the mistake of heckling Newcombe after the game, asking "What's the matter with you, Don? When things get tough, do you fold?"[12] Newcombe slugged Brown in the stomach, and a patrolman intervened before another blow could be landed. Alston, however, was in a slightly more jovial mood in the Dodgers clubhouse. His two-finger V-salute displayed the achievement to date: two Series wins with only two more required for a second championship.

SOURCES

Besides the sources cited in the Notes, the author consulted Baseball-Reference.com and Retrosheet.org.

NOTES

1   John Drebinger, "Rivals to Stand on Hurling Plans," *New York Times*, October 5, 1956: 28.

2   Roscoe McGowen, "Labine Rated Strong Possibility to Pitch 3d Contest at Stadium," *New York Times*, October 5, 1956: 28.

3   McGowen.

4   Joe Trimble, "Poor Pitching Doomed Yankees," *New York Daily News*, October 6, 1956: 17.

5   Louis Effrat, "Bombers Absolve Collins for Boot," *New York Times*, October 6, 1956: 25.

6   Trimble.

7   "Flatbush Fusillade," *The Sporting News*, October 17, 1956: 21.

8   Dick Young, "Flock 2 Up; Spot Yanks 6, Win, 13-8," *New York Daily News*, October 6, 1956: 16, 19.

9   Trimble.

10 Effrat.

11 Effrat.

12 "Fan Is Reported Hit by Newcombe," *New York Times*, October 6, 1956: 25.

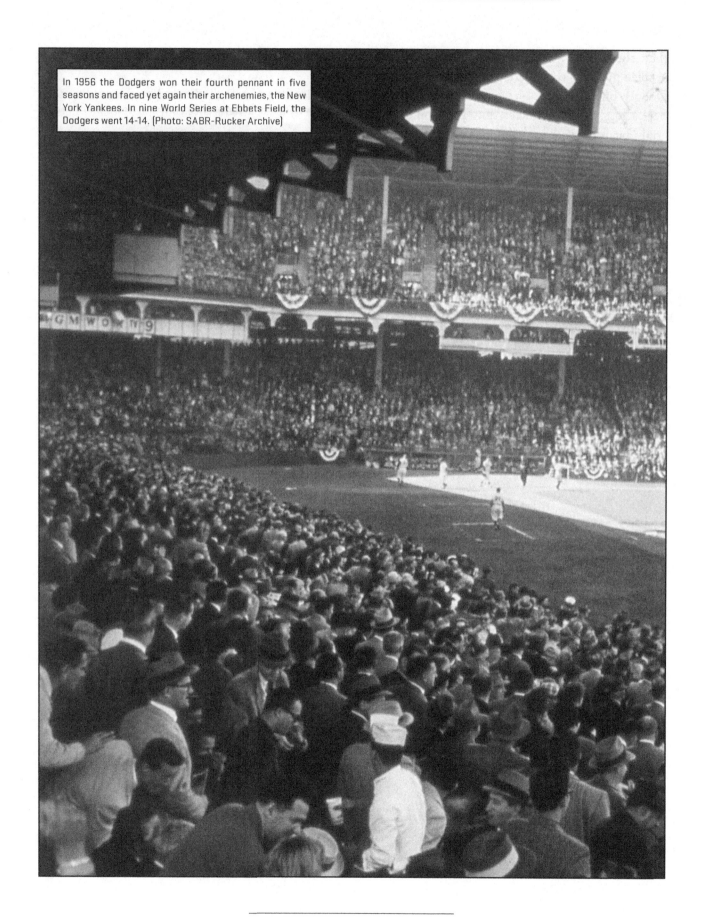

In 1956 the Dodgers won their fourth pennant in five seasons and faced yet again their archenemies, the New York Yankees. In nine World Series at Ebbets Field, the Dodgers went 14-14. (Photo: SABR-Rucker Archive)

LABINE HURLS EXTRA-INNING SHUTOUT TO FORCE GAME SEVEN

October 9, 1956

Brooklyn Dodgers 1, New York Yankees 0 (10 innings)
Game Six of the World Series

by Brian M. Frank

The Brooklyn Dodgers had fallen behind in the 1956 World Series in historic fashion. In Game Five, their hitters came up empty as Yankees hurler Don Larsen threw the first World Series perfect game. Larsen's performance put the defending world champion Dodgers' backs to the wall, trailing in the series three games to two.

Faced with the prospect of elimination, Dodgers manager Walter Alston made an unlikely choice for a Game Six starter in Clem Labine. Labine had pitched in a franchise-record 62 games during the regular season, going 10-6 with a 3.35 ERA; however only three of his 62 appearances had been starts. The veteran right-hander had also pitched in eight World Series games in his career, all in relief. In the 1956 World Series, he'd thrown two innings out of the bullpen in Game Three, allowing one unearned run, and he'd also warmed up in the bullpen behind Sal Maglie during Larsen's Game Five masterpiece. "I had Labine up in the ninth inning," Alston said, "but only with the idea that I'd bring him in if we tied the score. Labine didn't throw hard in his warm-up because he knew he'd have time if we did tie it."[1]

Yankees manager Casey Stengel tapped Bob Turley to try to close out the Series and give the Yankees their seventh championship in the last 10 seasons. After a solid season in 1955, fastballer Turley struggled through the 1956 season, going 8-4 with a 5.05 ERA. He'd pitched in three games in the 1955 World Series, including a rough start in Game Three at Ebbets Field, lasting only 1⅓ innings, allowing four earned runs. But he'd performed better in the postseason in 1956, working in relief in Games One and Two, and striking out three of the four batters he faced. Even with Turley's recent success, Stengel took no chances. He had Johnny Kucks warming up before Turley threw his first pitch. Kucks wouldn't be needed, as Turley was brilliant.

A beautiful blue sky greeted the 33,224 fans on hand at Ebbets Field. The cloudless sky and stiff breeze blowing out to right made it a tough afternoon for outfielders, especially Yankees left fielder Enos Slaughter.

Jim Gilliam hit a high fly ball in the third inning that Slaughter lost in the sun. "Gilliam's ball went up in the sun and stayed there,"

Slaughter said. "I waited for it to come out, but it never did. Sometimes you can play those balls from the side and catch a sight of them when they come out of the sun. This one didn't come out."[2] The ball dropped for a hit, but Slaughter picked up the ball and fired it to second to beat a sliding Gilliam for the second out of the inning.

There were some tense moments in the sixth inning as "Turley's control which was uniformly good all day, momentarily faltered" and the wind and sun played havoc with some popups that would have been routine under normal conditions.[3] Turley walked Gilliam to start the inning, and with one out he walked Duke Snider. Jackie Robinson hit a high popup "into short left, whipping around in the tricky currents as Slaughter and shortstop Gil McDougald drifted uncertainly underneath."[4] The next batter, Gil Hodges, also hit a high popup to the left side of the infield. This time, third baseman Andy Carey and McDougald both staggered under it "in the bright glare" before Billy Martin raced all the way over from second base to make the grab for the final out of the inning.[5]

Labine and Turley continued to dominate as the game remained scoreless. The Yankees threatened in the eighth inning when they put two runners on with one out. Cleanup hitter Yogi Berra stepped to the plate. "I threw him a curve that broke inside," Labine said of the pitch he managed to get Berra out on. "He swung at it, the first pitch, and the Duke came in and got it on the fly in left center."[6] Labine induced Slaughter to ground out to Gilliam to end the inning.

The weather affected play once again in the bottom of the eighth, when Labine hit a ball to left that Slaughter stopped running for because it seemed certain to go foul. "But the strong crosswinds picked up the pill and swept it back. The ball plunked between Slaughter and the railing, no more than a foot fair, then bounced up above the low, white[-]painted bar, and was grabbed by a fan for a ground-rule double."[7] Turley fanned

Gilliam for his 11th strikeout of the afternoon. He then retired Pee Wee Reese on a fly ball for the second out. Stengel ordered Snider intentionally walked, and the strategy paid off when Robinson popped out to end the inning.

As the game moved to extra innings, it was only the second time in World Series history that a game had been scoreless through nine innings, and the first since 1913. To compound matters for the Brooklyn faithful, the Dodgers hadn't scored in 18 innings.

The Dodgers finally broke through in the 10th. Gilliam drew a four-pitch walk. Reese then sacrificed Brooklyn's speedy leadoff hitter to second. With the winning run in scoring position, Stengel used the same strategy that had been successful in the eighth inning. He ordered Turley to intentionally walk Snider and pitch to Robinson with runners at first and second with two down. "He is their longest hitter," Stengel said of Snider. "If he got one into the wind, he'd have won the game. I figured Robinson would be hitting into the wind while anything Snider pulled would be helped by the wind."[8]

This time, Robinson made the Yankees pay. He drove a 1-and-1 pitch to left field, where Slaughter had been struggling to chase down fly balls all afternoon. Slaughter initially took a step in and then "leaped awkwardly but couldn't touch it" as the ball sailed over his head and bounced off the base of the wall, while Gilliam raced home to score the winning run.[9] "I thought when Jackie hit the ball, I might have a chance to catch it," Slaughter said. "But that ball took off, it rose suddenly and hit the base of the wall. I had no chance."[10]

"That was the same pitch Turley got me on in the eighth inning," Robinson said of Turley's sidearm fastball.[11] In the eighth Robinson popped it up to end the inning, but in the 10th he drove it to left to end the game. "I thought that ball would take off. I knew I'd hit it pretty good," Robinson said of his game-winning hit.[12]

"It was a perfect – well almost perfect – pitch," Turley said. "It was fast, it was low, it was in the strike zone. I thought it was tight enough, too, but I guess the ball came in just an inch or so off the spot I wanted. I can't find fault with that pitch, though. I'd try it again if I had to."[13]

The dramatic victory forced the Series to a deciding seventh game and put the Dodgers within one win of a second consecutive world championship. Brooklyn overcame an incredible performance by Turley, who set a Yankees World Series record by striking out 11. In a 143-pitch performance, Turley allowed just four hits, "one legit, two misjudged, and another lost in the air."[14] Stengel proclaimed, "That's the best game he's pitched all year."[15]

But Labine matched Turley pitch for pitch, allowing seven hits and two walks while striking out five over 10 shutout innings. Catcher Roy Campanella said it was the best game Labine had hurled over a prolonged outing. "He's done some amazing things coming in from the bullpen," the Dodgers catcher said, "but he's never been strong over a long route. Curve balls and sinkers; sinkers and curve balls. They killed them."[16] The hero at the plate, Jackie Robinson, said, "I'm awfully happy to have a part in getting that victory for Clem. He has done a wonderful job for us all year. No one deserved to win more."[17]

"It was the longest game I've pitched in the majors," Labine said, "the greatest one, I'd say, and certainly the most important."[18] He also acknowledged the day's other hero, exclaiming, "I never thought they'd ever find that run for me today. When Jackie hit that ball, I could have kissed him."[19]

SOURCES

In addition to the sources cited in the Notes, the author consulted Baseball-Reference.com and Retrosheet.org.

NOTES

1   Roscoe McGowen, "Maglie Discloses Every Bomber Hit Was Made Off a Breaking Pitch," *New York Times*, October 9, 1956: 56.

2   Joe Trimble, "I Never Had a Chance to Catch Drive: Enos," *New York Daily News*, October 10, 1956: 95.

3   John Drebinger, "Dodgers Defeat Yanks in 10th, 1-0, and Even Series," *New York Times*, October 10, 1956: 64.

4   Dick Young, "All Even! Dodgers Win, 1-0, in 10th," *New York Daily News*, October 10, 1956: 96.

5   Drebinger.

6   Roscoe McGowen, "Robinson's Appraisal of Bomber Hurler's Speed Questioned by Team-Mates," *New York Times*, October 10, 1956: 64.

7   Young: 97.

8   Trimble: 101.

9   Young: 94.

10 Louis Effrat, "Turley Is Cheered by Return of Confidence Despite His Defeat by Dodgers," *New York Times*, October 10, 1956: 65.

11 Dana Mozley, "2-Iron Shot Felt Good," *New York Daily News*, October 10, 1956: 95.

12 McGowen, "Robinson's Appraisal of Bomber Hurler's Speed Questioned by Team-Mates."

13 Effrat.

14 Young: 94.

15 Trimble: 95.

16 Mozley.

17 Mozley.

18 Mozley.

19 Mozley.

Johnny Kucks' three-hitter and record-setting home runs give Yankees the title

October 10, 1956

New York Yankees 9, Brooklyn Dodgers 0 | Game Seven of the World Series

by Gregory H. Wolf

It was the "best pitching in my career," exclaimed an elated Johnny Kucks after the struggling pitcher's improbable three-hit shutout in Game Seven of the 1956 World Series.[1] After losing the first two games of the Series, the New York Yankees' 9-0 thrashing of the reigning title-holding Dodgers in Brooklyn was a "loud and emphatic vindication," gushed sportswriter John Drebinger of manager Casey Stengel's strategic moves and belief in a maligned pitching staff supported by a record-setting home-run smashing lineup.[2]

The "Ole Perfessor's" Bronx Bombers cruised to the best record in the majors (97-57) to capture their seventh pennant in eight years. Triple Crown winner Mickey Mantle, Yogi Berra, Hank Bauer, Bill Skowron, and company formed the core of baseball's most formidable offense, led the American League with 190 home runs and 5.6 runs per game. Despite finishing second in the AL in ERA (3.63), the Yankees' pitching staff seemed to be its Achilles' Heel. Other than ace Whitey Ford (19-6), it consisted of a quartet of inexperienced and unpredictable starters. Defying all expectations, that erratic staff proved to be the club's strength when it was in a two-games-to-none hole in the World Series. The starters reeled off four straight complete games for the first time all season, beginning with Ford, Tom Sturdivant, and Don Larsen's perfect game to complete the sweep at Yankee Stadium. Bob Turley's 1-0 loss in a 10-inning heartbreaker in Game Six completed a stretch during which Yankees' pitchers yielded just five earned runs in 36⅔ innings.

Stengel faced a dilemma in the series clincher at Ebbets Field, a notoriously difficult ballpark for left-handed pitchers against the Dodgers' right-handed-heavy lineup. Instead of calling on Ford, Stengel gambled on 23-year-old Kucks. Described by sportswriter Dick Young as a "lanky side-arming sinkerballer," Kucks (18-9) hadn't won a game in more than five weeks and struggled down the stretch.[3] He looked bad in two relief appearances against the Dodgers, yielding three hits and two runs (one earned) in two innings. Stengel recognized the "distinct risk" with Kucks on the mound, opined Young, and had Sturdivant warming up before the game even began.[4]

377

Skipper Walter Alston's Dodgers (93-61) were an aging club that still possessed a daunting pill-bashing lineup, finishing second in the NL in scoring (4.7 runs per game) and home runs (179). Jackie Robinson and Pee Wee Reese were 37; Roy Campanella and Carl Furillo, 34; Gil Hodges, 32, and Duke Snider, 30. Dem Bums were collectively slumping at the most inopportune time. In Games Three through Six, they had scored just six runs and collected only 18 hits. Smoky Alston had a trump card for the deciding game: the 1956 NL MVP and the big leagues' Cy Young Award winner, 30-year-old right-hander Don Newcombe. Big Newk had led the majors with 27 wins and possessed a stellar 112-48 career slate, but also carried some immense baggage. He had been walloped for six runs in 1⅔ innings in Game Two, giving him 16 earned runs allowed in 19 World Series innings dating back to 1949. Newcombe had added pressure: after being pulled in Game Two, he stormed out of the clubhouse while the game was still in progress and was involved in an altercation with a parking attendant.[5] Litigation was pending and Newcombe had sought legal counsel by the time Game Seven took place.

A capacity crowd of 33,782 packed Ebbets Field on Wednesday afternoon with temperatures in the low 50s and an "autumnal tinge" in the air, wrote Drebinger.[6] Few fans could have predicted that they were witnessing the last World Series game played in the venerable ballpark, which opened in 1913.

In addition to Kucks, Stengel "baffled the experts" with other tricks up his sleeve for Game Seven, wrote Irving Vaughn.[7] He replaced 40-year-old Enos Slaughter, who had collected seven hits in the first three Series games, but had gone hitless in the last three, with 27-year-old Elston Howard. Skowron, the 25-year-old slugger, who had been benched after Game One in favor of veteran utilityman Joe Collins, was back at first base for additional power in the bandbox ballpark. And finally, spark plug Billy Martin

batted in the two-hole, up four spots. All four of those moves proved decisive.

The Bronx Bombers' relentless offensive explosion might have led them to victory no matter whom Stengel tabbed to pitch. Bauer led off the game with a single and stole second. Newk fanned Martin and Mantle and had two strikes on Berra, before Yogi "hatched at the high buzzer," quipped Young, and knocked the ball over the right-field fence and into a parking lot off Bedford Avenue to give the Yankees a 2-0 lead.[8] Newcombe fanned Skowron to end the frame. "He had good stuff and threw it hard," said Campanella of his batterymate, but noted that he struggled with location.[9]

In the third, Berra came to the plate with two outs and Martin on first via a single. The heart of soul and the Yankees, Berra was coming off a typical season (30/105/.298), while slugging a career-best .534. Newk had two strikes on him again, but the St. Louis native connected with a low fastball for a "prodigious poke," wrote Drebinger.[10] Berra sent the ball sailing over the scoreboard in right-center to double the score, 4-0. His third round-tripper of the series gave him a record 10 RBIs in the World Series, breaking Lou Gehrig's mark of 9 in 1928.

Howard continued the Yankees' barrage in the fourth with a leadoff home run that landed on top of the scoreboard and sent Newk to the showers while a chorus of boos echoed throughout the park. "I feel sorry for Don Newcombe," said an empathetic Ford after the game. "It is awful the way fans booed him."[11] Despite a warning from Dodgers VP Buzzy Bavasi, a frustrated and angered Newcombe once again showered and left the game while it was in progress. In hindsight, this game was a turning point in Newcombe's career.[12]

Held in check by reliever Don Bessent for three innings, the Yankees savagely whacked Roger Craig, whom Young disparaged as a "pathetic figure."[13] The starter and loser in Game Three faced

378

five batters and all reached base. Martin singled, Mantle walked, and Yogi was intentionally passed after a wild pitch enabled runners to advance. Skowron cleared the bases with a home run to deep left field to extend the lead to 9-0. It marked the first time in World Series history that a team hit two grand slams in the same Series (Berra had one in Game Two). Howard's double mercifully ended Craig's afternoon. Ed Roebuck and Carl Erskine retired the next nine Yankee hitters.

While the Yankees smashed home runs, the Dodgers beat Kucks' sinkers "weakly into the dirt," wrote Young.[14] The opening frame proved to be the right-hander's most difficult inning. With one out Reese walked and Snider singled. Kucks fielded Robinson's slow roller to the mound and fired to second to start a 1-4-3 twin killing. "Jackie howled" at the call at first base, as did the spectators, reported Young, but that was the "last noise the crowd was to make."[15]

Kucks cruised, retiring 19 of the next 21 batters, yielding only a walk in the fourth inning and one in the seventh. "I was nervous until I was helped out of that first-inning jam by that double play. After that I was loose," he said. "I never once shook off a sign from Berra."[16] With one out in the eighth, Furillo singled meekly to center.

"I kept the ball low," said Kucks whose outfielders recorded just two putouts. "You can't pitch high here. I threw about 75 percent fastballs and the rest were sliders and a few curves." His pitching coach, Jim "Milkman" Turner, said: "Kucks made great pitches."[17]

With two outs in the ninth, Kucks surrendered a scratch single to Snider that glazed off his shoulder. He emphatically ended the game by recording his first strikeout, whiffing Robinson, ending the game in 2 hours and 19 minutes.[18]

While the Yankees slugged their way to the 17th title in franchise history, belting a Series-record 12 home runs, and Stengel was lauded for his chess-game moves, the star of the show was Johnny Kucks, whose moment in the national spotlight was brief. Author of one of the best-pitched Game Sevens in postseason history, Kucks won only 28 more games in his career and was out of the majors after the 1960 season with a 54-56 record. But for one day, he was the king of the mound.

"We shouldn't lose to a pitcher like that," quipped a salty Robinson, who went 6-for-24 in the Series. "He's got a good sinker, and that's about all. He's not fast and he has a nickel curve."[19] Reese was more diplomatic. "He beat us and beat us good," he said. "We couldn't even hit the ball."[20] The Dodgers set an unenviable record with the lowest team batting average (.195) in a seven-game Series.

SOURCES

In addition to the sources cited in the Notes, the author accessed Retrosheet.org, Baseball-Reference.com, and SABR.org.

NOTES

1   Louis Effrat, "Ford of Bombers Defends and Sympathizes with Brooklyn's Routed Pitcher," *New York Times*, October 11, 1956: 65.

2   John Drebinger, "Yanks Champions; Kucks' 3-Hitter Tops Dodgers, 9-0," *New York Times*, October 11, 1956: 1.

3   Dick Young, "Yankees Homers Take It All, 9-0," *New York Daily News*, October 11, 1956: C24.

4   Young.

5   Dana Mozley and Joe Trimble, "Newk Walks Out on Pals After Being KO'd Again," *New York Daily News*, October 11, 1956: C24.

6   "The Forecast," *New York Times*, October 11, 1956: 57; Drebinger, "Yanks Champions."

7   Irving Vaughan, "Players Put Over Stengel's Strategy," *Chicago Tribune*, October 11, 1956: Part 6, 1.

8   Young.

9   Dana Mozley, "Don Didn't Choke; Young Hurler OK: Casey," *New York Daily News*, October 11, 1956: 25.

10   Drebinger, "Yanks Champions," *New York Times*, October 11, 1956: 1.

11   Effrat, "Ford of Bombers Defends and Sympathizes with Brooklyn's Routed Pitcher," *New York Times*, October 11, 1956: 65.

12   Seemingly at the top of his game, the NL MVP and major-league Cy Young Award winner had a swift fall. He went just 11-12 in 1957, was involved in a deadly car crash, striking and killing a 4-year old in August, and was charged with assault in December. After the Dodgers' relocation to Los Angeles in 1958, Newcombe began the season 0-6 and was subsequently traded to Cincinnati. Following his MVP season, Newcombe was just 37-42 in four seasons.

13   Young, "Yankees Homers Take It All, 9-0," *New York Daily News*, October 11, 1956: C24.

14   Young.

15   Young.

16   Effrat.

17   Joe Trimble, "Don Didn't Choke; Young Hurler OK: Casey," *New York Daily News*, October 11, 1956: C25.

18   Berra dropped the strike and threw to Skowron to officially end the game. Game Seven also marked the end of umpire Babe Pinelli's career. One of the most respected umpires in baseball history, Pinelli retired after 22 seasons and in excess of 3,400. "Babe was one of the finest umpires ever to work a ball game," said NL President Warren Giles. Dana Mozley and Joe Trimble, "Newk Walks Out on Pals After Being KO'd Again," *New York Daily News*, October 11, 1956: C24.

19   Mozley, "Don Didn't Choke."

20   Mozley.

DODGERS SURVIVE WILD NINTH (12 RUNS!) TO WIN IN 11

July 18, 1957

Brooklyn Dodgers 10, St. Louis Cardinals 9 (11 innings)

by Doug Feldmann

In reviewing the previous day's game at Ebbets Field against the Brooklyn Dodgers, Bob Broeg had much to say of the St. Louis Cardinals' skipper in the July 19, 1957, edition of the *St. Louis Post-Dispatch*: "Red-necked Fred Hutchinson lost the National League lead and his temper. Whether he'll regain either soon is a question as unanswered as the manager's reason for letting a left-hander pitch to a right-handed batter in a crucial moment during yesterday's fiasco in Flatbush."[1]

The right-handed batter was Gil Hodges, who, Broeg reminded his readers, "feeds on left-handers as though they were tender sprouts."[2] Hodges, 0-for-4 to that point on the day, stood at the plate in the bottom of the ninth with the bases loaded and one out, and his Dodgers trailing the Cardinals 9-5. The next moment would unveil the culmination of a wild ninth inning.

That morning, the newspapers listed Hutchinson's Cardinals (48-36) in a virtual tie atop the National League standings with the Milwaukee Braves. The Dodgers (46-37) of Walter Alston, meanwhile – himself a former Cardinal player for his one-day major-league appearance in 1936 – sat a mere game and a half back in fourth place, just behind the Philadelphia Phillies in the tightly-packed midsummer race. Alston's choice for a pitcher was Johnny Podres and his 7-3 mark, slotted against the Cardinals' third-year man Larry Jackson, who also entered the contest with a strong record of 10-5.

The first portion of the afternoon proceeded in relatively nondescript fashion – save for two blows by legendary figures. The Dodgers drew first blood in the bottom of the third, as with two out Duke Snider drove his 21st home run of the season to right field off Jackson. Snider's blast was answered in the top of the fourth by the legend in the other dugout, Stan Musial, who led off with the 600th double of his career to place him sixth all-time behind Paul Waner's 605. Promptly sent home on an RBI single by Del Ennis, Musial was making his last appearance in the ballpark where he garnered his famous nickname in the 1940s, when worried Flatbush faithful began murmuring, "Here comes *that man* to the plate again!"

A close struggle continued into the very last frame, with the Dodgers crafting a 4-2 lead as the Cardinals got ready to take their final turn in the top of the ninth.

After Ken Boyer started the last St. Louis chance with a single, Alston decided Podres was finished and summoned relief specialist Clem Labine from the bullpen. Decades later it would be determined that Labine, with statistics of the era retroactively reconstructed, had "led" the National League in saves in 1956 and was on his way to doing so again in 1957.

Labine permitted another base hit to pinch-hitter Joe Cunningham before retiring the tough Wally Moon on strikes. However, two more hits followed, by Eddie Kasko and another pinch-hitter, Hobie Landrith, for a sudden 5-4 Cardinals lead. Rookie Danny McDevitt replaced Labine and was able to induce Don Blasingame to tap what appeared to be an inning-ending double-play grounder to Hodges; but the first baseman misfired on the throw to second and sent the ball sailing into left field as the deluge of St. Louis runs continued. After Alvin Dark was called out on strikes, a single by Musial, a triple by Ennis, a walk to Boyer, another hit by Cunningham (tying a record with his second pinch-hit in the same inning, most recently achieved by Sid Gordon of the New York Giants 10 years earlier[3]), and a wild pitch by McDevitt followed. It all added up to four additional unearned runs, bringing the grand total to seven in the inning and a stunning 9-4 Cardinal lead.

In the bottom half, Alston attempted to conjure magic from another aging Flatbush hero who, like Snider, Hodges, Pee Wee Reese, and Roy Campanella, was in his final months in Ebbets Field. The manager sent up Carl Furillo to bat for McDevitt. On the mound for St. Louis was Hoyt Wilhelm, pitching in his first season for the Cardinals after five with the Giants. Furillo took a mighty hack at a Wilhelm knuckleball, but was only able to squib the fluttering pitch softly off the end of his bat toward Kasko at third. Furillo hustled down the line and beat the throw, providing Brooklyn with a baserunner. Charlie Neal and Jim Gilliam followed with walks, as the Dodgers were instantly back in business with the bases loaded and nobody out. When southpaw Vinegar Bend Mizell replaced Wilhelm to face the left-handed-batting Snider, the Cards conceded a run with Snider's subsequent groundout to first.

To the surprise of many of his players on the field, Hutchinson permitted Mizell to next face the right-handed Gino Cimoli. Cimoli walked, which loaded the bases again and brought the tying run to the plate in the person of the powerful Hodges. Right-handers Herm Wehmeier and Lloyd Merritt were warming up in the bullpen, but Hutchinson sat unmoved in the visitors dugout.

A hopeful, growing noise echoed in the stands, as early half the crowd at Ebbets that day was a contingent of vocal adolescents who incessantly championed the Dodgers' cause. "When Mizell was pitching in the big ninth," Roscoe McGowen of the *New York Times* noticed, "most of the 9,500 youngsters among the crowd of 22,059 gave Vinegar a roaring chant with each delivery. It may have upset him."[4]

Looking to atone for his critical error in the field, Hodges unloaded. He cannonaded a 1-and-1 pitch for a home run into the left-center-field bleachers, "the most dramatic of his career," wrote McGowen.[5] The blast tied Rogers Hornsby and Ralph Kiner for the most grand slams by a National League player with 12. (Hornsby and Kiner hit their slams for multiple teams, while all of Hodges' came as a member of the Dodgers.) The blow also gave Hodges 999 RBIs for his career — leaving him behind only Musial and Ennis among active National Leaguers at the time.

However, Mizell was not relieved until he failed on yet another batter. After walking Sandy Amoros, Vinegar Bend finally departed the premises as Hutchinson "storming out[,] grabbed the ball from the pitcher and jawed heatedly at him," according to Broeg.[6] Wehmeier doused the blaze in recording the final outs to send the contest into extra innings.

With each team failing to score in the 10th, Snider once again got the home side going in the bottom of the 11th. After leading off with a double, he moved toward third on a bunt by Cimoli. The St. Louis native and rookie Merritt, now pitching in relief of Wehmeier, pounced on the ball and fired a throw to Kasko in an attempt to get Snider; but the third baseman missed the ball completely, allowing Snider to pop up from his slide and ramble home with the winning run.

While spectators in Ebbets Field jumped up and down in jubilation, one of the locker rooms fell silent. "Manager Hutchinson stalked off to lock himself and his ball club in their dressing quarters," Broeg wrote. It was the first time he recalled Hutchinson forbidding writers inside the clubhouse since he became manager. As a result, Broeg and other reporters were unable to get Fred's reasoning behind his questionable late-game decisions. "There was no explanation forthcoming from Hutchinson why he allowed the unpredictable and disappointing Mizell, hammered hard in previous appearances by the Dodgers, to stay in to face the righthanded batters," wondered Jack Herman of the *St. Louis Globe-Democrat*.[7]

St. Louis general manager Frank Lane, traveling with the club, stated that Hutchinson's job was safe despite the lapse in judgment, while nonetheless noting that "it was a tremendous disappointment to lose a game like that, especially when one of the best left-handers, Warren Spahn, never pitches here [in Ebbets] and Johnny Antonelli rarely wins here."[8]

As the Cardinals licked their wounds and got ready to travel to Pittsburgh for the next stop on their road trip, they would make only one more visit to Ebbets Field — a lone contest on August 25, which brought down the East Coast curtain on a heated rivalry that continues today on the shores of the Pacific.

SOURCES

In addition to the sources cited in the Notes, the author accessed Retrosheet.org, Baseball-Reference.com, SABR.org, and *The Sporting News* archive via Paper of Record.

NOTES

1   Bob Broeg, "Stormy Hutch Bars Door in Brooklyn, but Not on Dodgers," *St. Louis Post-Dispatch*, July 19, 1957.

2   Broeg.

3   Jack Herman, "Hutchinson Blames Wilhelm More Than Mizell," *St. Louis Globe-Democrat*, July 19, 1957.

4   Roscoe McGowen, "Homer by Hodges Marks 10-9 Game," *New York Times*, July 19, 1957.

5   McGowen.

6   Bob Broeg, "Stormy Hutch Bars Door in Brooklyn."

7   Jack Herman, "Hutchinson Blames Wilhelm More Than Mizell.".

8   Herman.

MAJOR-LEAGUE FINALE AT EBBETS FIELD

September 24, 1957
Brooklyn Dodgers 2, Pittsburgh Pirates 0

by Rory Costello

"On a cool, clear, September night, only 6,702 attended the funeral of the beloved Dodgers, a hushed and bereaved gathering come to pay respects to a memory ... only 6,702 could muster the courage to bid a fond farewell, perhaps because it hurt too much to say goodbye."

That was Phil Pepe of the *New York Daily News*, reminiscing 30 years later. His sentimental piece compared Ebbets Field to Never-Never Land, Oz, and Shangri-La. Pepe described the sense of loss that Brooklyn fans felt, saying, "For many of us, it was the first sign that nothing is forever."[1]

Another factor kept the crowd down that Tuesday night: The pennant race was already decided. The Dodgers, defending National League champs, entered the game in third place, 10½ games behind the Milwaukee Braves. As late as August 1, Brooklyn was just 1½ games back, but the Braves went on a red-hot streak while the

Dodgers slumped. In another *Daily News* retrospective a few days after Pepe's, Brooklyn pitcher Clem Labine said, "That last year, there was a general foreboding. I think it kind of affected our play. We didn't know anything for sure, but the talk about moving was a thing that was in the back of your mind. And it just didn't go away."[2]

Right fielder Carl Furillo – who died less than two years after the retrospectives – added, "I loved to play, and we always played hard, but those last games in Ebbets Field, I don't think we really cared. I remember that last game. It was cold. And even though we hadn't been told, we knew we were leaving. And we knew we weren't going anywhere in the standings. There was a sadness."[3]

To get the finale started, Tex Rickards, the longtime public-address announcer at Ebbets, read the starting lineups in his "familiar rasping, undeniably Brooklyn voice."[4] Dodgers captain Pee Wee Reese did not take the field at first. He did come in later, as Gil Hodges moved from third base (which he played seldom) to his more familiar post at first base. Hodges and catcher Roy Campanella were the only remaining marquee "Boys of Summer" to start that night. Gino Cimoli played center field, not Duke Snider, whose ailing left knee had ended his season two days before. Veteran Elmer Valo was subbing in right for Furillo, who'd been sidelined with a pulled hamstring since September 18.[5]

The game was a mercifully swift affair, over in 2 hours and 3 minutes. The Dodgers got the only run they needed in the home half of the first inning. Pittsburgh starter Bennie Daniels – making his big-league debut – walked the leadoff man, Jim Gilliam. Daniels then had Gilliam picked off, but made an error on the throw, allowing Gilliam to reach second. One out later, Valo doubled.

Dodgers chronicler Rudy Marzano also described the "funeral-like atmosphere" that night. Gladys Goodding, the ballpark's organist, set the tone with her musical selections. After Brooklyn scored the first run, she played "After You've Gone" and "Am I Blue."[6]

Fifty years later, Dodgers broadcasting legend Vin Scully told Los Angeles Times columnist Jerry Crowe more. By Scully's account, the mood crossed into maudlin because Gladys Goodding – who was "known to take a drink or three" – was indulging. Scully recalled, "The very first song she played was 'My Buddy,' a pretty down song, and it went down from there. ... The music kept getting more depressing every third out."[7]

Brooklyn's starting pitcher was another rookie, lefty Danny McDevitt (a New York City native who'd originally signed with the Yankees). McDevitt was in control throughout the game. He struck out nine, walked only one, and scattered five hits. The Pirates had a mild threat in the second when cleanup hitter Bob Skinner singled and Bill Mazeroski's infield hit advanced him to second one out later. However, Roberto Clemente then grounded into a 5-4-3 double play. Pittsburgh also got the leadoff man on in the third, fourth, and fifth but was unable to cash in. No other Pirates runner besides Skinner got beyond first base all night.

The game's only other run scored in the third. Cimoli led off with a single and, after he took second on Valo's groundout, Hodges brought him home with a single to right. That prompted Gladys Goodding to play "Don't Ask Me Why I'm Leaving."[8] Brooklyn also managed just five hits off Daniels, who went seven innings, and Roy Face.

McDevitt struck out the side in the seventh (Brooklynite Joe Pignatano had entered as his catcher in the fifth) and set the Pirates down one-two-three in the ninth to end it. He whiffed Skinner for the third time, and then got Dee Fondy to ground to shortstop for the final out. Tex Rickards asked the fans not to go on the field, and they complied, quickly and quietly making their way out as Gladys Goodding played "Thanks for the Memories" and Auld Lang Syne."[9] By a later account, however, at least several hundred fans gathered around the Dodger dugout during "Auld Lang Syne," and some of the broken-hearted cried.[10] But there was no official ceremony. As sportswriter Dave Anderson observed, "the Dodgers ... treated it as just another game because, remember, the Los Angeles deal hadn't closed yet."[11]

Phil Pepe added, "Out of respect for the dearly departed, there was no ravaging for souvenirs. The grounds crew methodically covered the infield and the pitcher's mound with tarpaulin, as if there was to be another game the following day."[12]

McDevitt echoed that view in 2007. "It was just another game, as far as I knew," he told Jerry Crowe, "and when I think about it today, I can't believe that was what I thought. All the older guys – Pee Wee and Duke and those guys – seemed to know." McDevitt also recalled that Gladys Goodding played "California, Here I Come" after the game and it struck him as strange.[13]

Yet Roy Campanella refused to give up hope that the team would stay. "Gosh, I hope last night's game wasn't our last one in Brooklyn," said Campy. But Carl Furillo acknowledged, "I'm afraid it was." Snider called it "an eerie feeling."[14]

Two weeks later, on October 8, owner Walter O'Malley made it official, announcing to the National League that he was moving the franchise to Los Angeles.[15]

McDevitt threw two more shutouts during his major-league career, which ended in 1962. He died in 2010. McDevitt's daughter-in-law said the family was constantly amazed by the attention he drew throughout his life for his role in Brooklyn Dodgers history. "No matter how fast you threw a ball or how many games you won, there's no way of doing that again," she said. "Only one pitcher could win that last game."[16]

The original home plate used in that game was later displayed at Dodger Stadium, along with a plaque describing McDevitt's role in the contest.[17] McDevitt himself presented a game ball from the finale to the Hall of Fame in 1965. That event became part of a leaflet that he sent out to autograph seekers, who began to lodge inquiries with him around the early 1990s. It became a rather lucrative income stream for the ex-pitcher.[18]

The Dodgers franchise closed out its last year in Brooklyn with three games on the road at Philadelphia. Yet the action was by no means done at Ebbets Field. Before it was eventually demolished in February 1960, the ballpark had a prolonged twilight of nearly 2½ years, during which it hosted various forms of sporting entertainment – including baseball. This little-known chapter of Ebbets history featured numerous future big leaguers and two Hall of Fame stars: Roy Campanella and Satchel Paige.

NOTES

1   Phil Pepe, "The Day the Music Died at Good Old Ebbets Field," *New York Daily News*, September 24, 1987.

2   Bill Farrell, "The Day 'Dem Bums' Hit the Road," *New York Daily News*, September 27, 1987.

3   Farrell, "The Day 'Dem Bums' Hit the Road."

4   Pepe, "The Day the Music Died at Good Old Ebbets Field."

5   Roscoe McGowen, "Duke Bids Flatbush Adieu as Record-Tying HR King," *The Sporting News*, October 2, 1957: 22.

6   Rudy Marzano, *The Last Years of The Brooklyn Dodgers: 1950-1957* (Jefferson North Carolina: McFarland & Company, 2008), 186.

7   Jerry Crowe, "The Last Pitch at Ebbets Means More to Him Now," *Los Angeles Times*, September 25, 1997.

8   Marzano, *The Last Years of The Brooklyn Dodgers*, 186.

9   Marzano.

10 Farrell, "The Day 'Dem Bums' Hit the Road."

11 Marzano, *The Last Years of The Brooklyn Dodgers*, 186.

12 Pepe, "The Day the Music Died at Good Old Ebbets Field."

13 Crowe, "The Last Pitch at Ebbets Means More to Him Now."

14 "Dodgers Sad at Thought of Leaving Their Bandbox," *Hackensack* (New Jersey) *Record*, September 25, 1957.

15 "Timeline of Baseball's Historic Expansion to the West Coast," Walteromalley.com (https://www.walteromalley.com/en/features/1957-58-timeline-of-expansion-to-west-coast/ October-8-1957).

16 Associated Press, "Former pitcher Danny McDevitt dies," November 24, 2010 (https://www.espn.com/mlb/news/story?id=5847664).

17 "Pitched Last Game Dodgers Played at Ebbets Field."

18 Claire Noland, "Danny McDevitt Dies at 78; Pitched Brooklyn Dodgers' Last Game at Ebbets Field," *Los Angeles Times*, November 24, 2010.

TWILIGHT AT EBBETS FIELD

by Rory Costello

Ebbets Field has been gone for more than half a century, but the place still has a remarkable grip on our consciousness. At least three books have been devoted to the lovable old ballpark in Crown Heights.[1] Yet even these in-depth works don't shine much light on what happened *after* the Dodgers left Brooklyn. They touch briefly on some teasing references to post-Dodger history, but there's more to this period than mere footnotes. It is a buried chapter of stadium lore – featuring two Hall of Fame stars.

This article does not re-examine whether club owner Walter O'Malley or New York City power broker Robert Moses could have kept the club from going west. By late 1957, it was a foregone conclusion. In major-league terms, Brooklyn had been reduced to a bargaining chip or at best a fall-back option in case O'Malley's negotiations with Los Angeles blew up. People like Abe Stark – the local tailor ("Hit Sign, Win Suit") turned City Council president – were hoping against hope.

What many don't recall is how long Ebbets clung to life. Even people who are Brooklyn to the bone, like journalist Pete Hamill, were prone to misty memory. On his website, Hamill once wrote, "Within a year after the Dodgers lammed to Los Angeles, Ebbets Field was smashed into rubble." Not true – the Bums played their last home game on September 24, 1957, but the wrecking ball did not swing until February 23, 1960.

To recap, the Dodgers played the '57 season on the first year of O'Malley's three-year leaseback deal with developer Marvin Kratter, who had bought the property for $3 million on October 30, 1956. Kratter hinted in October '57 that another club might relocate to Ebbets.[2] However, that may have been just a P.R. red herring. In 1958, the new Dodger home was the Los Angeles Coliseum; meanwhile O'Malley was also paying for three other parks: Wrigley Field in L.A., Roosevelt Stadium in Jersey City (where the Dodgers had played seven "home" games in '56 and eight in '57), and Ebbets. The cagey Irishman estimated his carrying costs on the Brooklyn facility at $170,000 a year – $80K in rental, $40K in maintenance, and $50K in real estate taxes.[3] So in an effort to cut his losses, he subleased.

Enter Robert A. Durk, a local homebuilder who thought he saw an opportunity. Durk, aged 36 in early 1958, was the frontman for Ebbets Field Productions. This venture had grand plans for various sporting attractions and other events; rent would be paid on a percentage basis. One such hope was to bring in the Yomiuri Giants, Japan's version of the Yankees, to play a Latin American team.[4]

This idea was years ahead of its time, but it didn't pan out. Instead, a demolition derby paid a visit. Jack Kochman's Hell Drivers apparently were hell – on the Ebbets Field turf. The New Jersey-based troupe put on two performances a day from May 30 through June 1. It replaced the Dick Clark Caravan Tour after bad publicity from an alleged rock 'n' roll riot in Boston caused the host of *American Bandstand* to postpone his shows.[5]

Kochman's Auto Thrill Show survived through 2004, as did the man himself, who died at the age of 97. Yet for better or worse, there are likely no other records of the "Smashing! Crashing! Racing!!" (as the spectacle was billed in a New York *Daily News* ad). Charlie Belknap, who took over the business in 1989, said, "Jack probably would have remembered those shows because they were in the metropolitan area. But he wouldn't have kept programs or anything like that. He'd have said, 'That's clutter – get rid of it.'"[6]

The available evidence shows that Ebbets Field Productions staged only one more event: the Hamid-Morton circus, also booked for two daily performances from June 29 through July 12. Robert A. Durk Associates, Inc. (liabilities: $86,828 – assets: $9,110) declared bankruptcy in August 1958.[7] Durk, who later became an ad man in Connecticut, then faded from the scene. He died in 1988.

The most popular post-Dodger activity at 55 Sullivan Place was soccer. On May 25, 1958, 20,606 spectators braved the rain to see Hearts of Midlothian (Scotland) beat Manchester City (England) 6-5 on a muddy pitch. Had the weather been better, the crowd might have approached capacity. One day short of a year later, Dundee and West Bromwich Albion drew 21,312 – the best turnout of the twilight years. There were 15 programs in 1959, played both in the afternoon and under the lights. New York Hakoah, a Jewish-oriented team in the old American Soccer League (ASL), moved in from the Bronx. A strong array of international squads – from Italy, Spain, Poland, Sweden, and Austria, as well as the U.K. – built the audience for the ASL.

At first it might seem surprising to see what a drawing card this sport was – it did better than a lot of Dodgers games toward the end. But it is less remarkable in view of Brooklyn's historically large and varied immigrant population. Plus, there was an echo of when Dodger fans occasionally crossed the line from avid and boisterous to riotous. Hundreds of unruly Napoli partisans erupted on the field to attack the officials on June 28, 1959. A patrolman was also knocked out with a linesman's flag.[8]

Although Ebbets had hosted a good deal of boxing and American football in its past, neither sport was visible there during 1958-59. Brooklyn was considered a possibility for the AFL as that rival league was forming in 1959.[9] Instead, the New York Titans (later the Jets) went with the Polo Grounds. Other ideas were merely fanciful. In July 1959, Abe Stark – briefly Acting Mayor in Robert Wagner's absence – injected himself into a racial debate over the West Side Tennis Club in Forest Hills. Dr. Ralph Bunche, the eminent statesman and civil rights leader, and his son ran into the club's color barrier. Stark postured against Forest Hills and announced that he had gained permission from Marvin Kratter to use Ebbets free of charge for Davis Cup matches and the National Championship.[10] But the flap died down within a week, and with it Stark's sentimental hope.

At its core, Ebbets Field was still a baseball venue. In the spring of 1958, Long Island University played six home games there and St. John's played four, under the auspices of the Dodgers. LIU coach William "Buck" Lai, a Dodgers scout and instructor at the Dodgertown Camp for Boys in Vero Beach, was instrumental. His wife Mary stated, "Buck knew the O'Malleys well. Therefore he was able to arrange for the Blackbirds to play at Ebbets Field before it was demolished. He was very proud that his college team's home field was a major league field."[11] Then in '59, LIU returned for one more, while St. John's played two.

Unfortunately, these matches weren't much of a draw – especially the first year, most Dodger fans were still in shock or mourning. College ball was a pretty thin substitute.

However, the St. John's roster boasted a future big-leaguer. Brooklyn-born infielder Ted Schreiber hit a game-winning two-run homer at Ebbets on April 24, 1958; in 1963, he made 55 plate appearances for the New York Mets.[12] Decades later, Schreiber (who went to Ebbets three or four times a year growing up) had clear recall:

"I remember it almost like it was yesterday. I just got through basketball season and I was struggling for hits. Most of my career, I never saw the ball hit the bat. But a lefty was pitching, so the angle was good, and the ball was out in front of the plate. My concentration was so keen, I didn't look up, I was running hard to first base. Then I heard a rattle, and I knew it had to be the ball in the seats. The crowd was just a handful, people who loved college ball – that time of year wasn't conducive to real good baseball.

And you know what was special? The field was so smooth! The regular places I played in Brooklyn, the Parade Grounds was good, but get in front of a ball in Marine Park, you deserve combat pay. I was impressed. As soon as you come out of the tunnel, you see the lights and it takes hold. It was very exciting to be on a major-league field."[13]

At least one other future major-leaguer performed at Ebbets during this period: infielder Chuck Schilling of Manhattan College. Rutgers was coached by a former big-leaguer, George Case. Al Ferrara, like Schreiber a Brooklyn boy, went to LIU in 1958 – but never played baseball for the Blackbirds before turning pro in the spring of 1959.[14]

COLLEGE BASEBALL AT EBBETS FIELD, 1958-59

Date	Score
4/5/58	UConn 7, LIU 6
4/9/58	LIU 11, Adelphi 4
4/10/58	Rutgers 4, St. John's 3
4/24/58	St. John's 2, Manhattan 1
4/30/58	St. John's 4, Hofstra 0
5/1/58	NYU 3, St. John's 0

5/2/58	Fairfield 6, LIU 4
5/9/58	LIU 7, Bridgeport 5
5/12/58	LIU 3, NY Maritime 1
5/17/58	LI Aggies 5, LIU 3
4/18/59	Manhattan 5, St. John's 3
4/25/59	St. John's 11, Manhattan 0
5/6/59	LIU 7, Queens College 6

Source: *New York Times; Washington Post, Times Herald*

College and high-school players also took part in drills and some games at Ebbets Field in 1959. These were to select players and tune up for the Hearst Sandlot Classic between the New York Sandlot Stars and the United States All-Stars. (The age limit was 18 and under.) Starting on July 29, 14 practice sessions were held at Ebbets to select the N.Y. Stars, under the direction of former big-league star Tommy Holmes, who'd been named that April to head the *New York Journal-American* sandlot program.[15] Two future big-leaguers made the cut: Billy Ott, who enjoyed two brief stints in the outfield with the Chicago Cubs in 1962 and 1964, and pitcher Larry Bearnarth, another early Met who later became a major-league pitching coach.

In the first tune-up game, on August 11, Holmes's squad faced the Los Angeles Dodgers Eastern Rookie Stars, a touring amateur team managed by scout John Carey. The Dodger Rookies, won, 2-1. Zack Finkelberg, who'd played on the freshman team for Queens College that spring, had their biggest hit. He homered over the 55-foot-high wall in right field, well above the Schaefer beer sign. It landed on Bedford Avenue shortly before noon. The N.Y. Stars were experimenting with three new pitchers and some key players were participating in other tournaments. The box score shows that Ott and Bearnarth did not play at Ebbets on August 11, if indeed they were even present.[16]

The U.S. Stars, managed by Oscar Vitt and Buddy Hassett, played the Dodger Rookies at Ebbets on August 14 and August 15. The U.S. Stars won the first game, 5-4, and the Dodger Rookies won the second, 7-1. Box scores are not presently available, but in one of those games (more likely the first), future big-leaguer Ernie Fazio homered for the U.S. Stars.[17] The U.S. Stars also worked out at Ebbets on August 17, the day before the Classic itself was held at Yankee Stadium.[18] Five other men on that roster besides Fazio eventually reached the majors: Wilbur

Wood, Darrell Sutherland, Fritz Fisher, Glenn Beckert, and Bobby Guindon.

Stepping down another level, high-school games still took place at Ebbets too. The Dodgers conducted tryouts, with Tommy Holmes and various scouts looking over the prospects.[19] They also sponsored the Public School Athletic League finals. On June 23, 1958, Martin Van Buren High of Queens defeated Curtis High of Staten Island 5-3.[20] The Curtis team included a future major-leaguer, catcher Frank Fernandez, plus an infielder named Jack Tracy who made it to Triple A for several years.[21] The next year, on June 5, Roosevelt High (Bronx) was the champ, and Curtis once more the runner-up, in a 6-5 battle before a crowd of 4,000.[22]

Going younger still, there is a nice anecdote about Babe Ruth ball. Paul Jurkoic was born in 1946 and grew up on Governor's Island when it was an Army post. He knew it must have been the summer of 1959 when he came to Brooklyn, representing Fort Jay as part of an "All-Star Grasshopper" game – the basepaths were 90 feet long, not the Little League distance. Jurkoic still had vivid memories of that special day:

"The game was attended only by the family and friends of the players – a very small crowd indeed – maybe a few hundred. I don't remember ever being in the locker room (disappointment!), so I suspect we traveled to and from the game in uniform. What I most remember was that the field was still very well kept, even though the Dodgers weren't there anymore.

The infield grass was very green and healthy, and was mown short – like a golf fairway, and there were no pebbles or other obvious imperfections on the dirt part. This was like playing in heaven for us, because although the Army did a pretty good job of maintaining the field we played on (which was also used by the soldiers, I believe), it was not up to Major League standards. I was struck by the Spartan appearance of the dugout. I had thought that a big-league dugout would be somehow more fancy than it was. I also have an impression about the telephone that the managers used to call the bullpen – it was missing, but the wires were hanging out of the wall where it had been. It was definitely a thrill for all of us to play in a real big league stadium."[23]

That game took place on August 22, 1959, just days after the tune-ups for the Hearst Sandlot Classic. It was a preliminary to a benefit match, held for the family of Charley Russo, a Dodgers scout who had died not long before. The Dodger Rookies were in action again. Assisting manager John Carey was Rudy Rufer, briefly a New York Giant in 1949-50. Hank Majeski was also involved with that team.[24]

The opponents were the Brooklyn All-Stars, another squad of top high school and college youths playing in the local sandlot leagues. Their manager was Steve Lembo, a catcher who'd played in seven games for the Dodgers in 1950 and 1952. The Brooklyn native then became an instructor at Dodgertown (he also scouted for the team for many years). Lembo had at least one future big-leaguer on his squad, pitcher Larry Yellen.[25]

Yet the most intriguing baseball action during the "twilight era" had fallen into total obscurity until research for the original version of this article unearthed it. A team called the Brooklyn Stars played at Ebbets in 1959. Their sponsor was one of "The Boys of Summer" – Roy Campanella, about 18 months after the auto accident that made him a paraplegic.

The Stars first came to this author's attention in 1999 as a side note while writing the history of baseball in the Virgin Islands. One key source, a St. Croix native named Osee Edwards, also mentioned that he played for this semi-pro squad of black and Latin players. Osee worked as an X-ray technician in a Brooklyn hospital. He and his teammates advertised their games around the community, posting flyers in places like barbershops. He talked about Campy as well as facing another Dodger hero of the '50s, Joe Black. Two

years after Joe's last major-league appearance, the first black pitcher to win a World Series game was a schoolteacher in his hometown of Plainfield, New Jersey. But he still hurled on occasion for a local team called the Newark Eagles.[26] That team was a namesake of the Negro League franchise of 1936-48, whose Brooklyn forerunner played one year at Ebbets in 1935.

A letter seeking confirmation went out to Mr. Black shortly thereafter, but his brief reply was a damper. He pooh-poohed the idea that his old batterymate could have been involved. However, the newspaper archives show that his memory was not as clear as Osee's. Roy Campanella was a surprisingly busy man after recovering from his accident. He attended all three Yankees home games during the 1958 World Series.[27] That prompted U.S. Congressman Francis E. Dorn of Brooklyn to suggest a "Campy Day" at Ebbets, featuring a Dodgers-Yankees charity game after the Series ended. However, that appears to have been another bit of wishful thinking.[28]

After Campanella got out of the hospital for good in November 1958, his health was delicate, but he was still tending to his business ventures and the misadventures of his wayward stepson David. He attended spring training at Vero Beach in 1959 and went out to Los Angeles for the big night in his honor at the Coliseum on May 7. He appeared at Yonkers Raceway on July 1. In August, he even acted in an episode of the TV show *Lassie*. The article about the Charley Russo benefit mentioned the possibility that even in his wheelchair, Campy might serve as third-base coach (concrete evidence of this is lacking).[29]

Among all these other activities, Campanella fit in the formation of a ballclub at his old home field.[30] Other Stars opponents included the Gloversville Merchants, who represented the leather-goods town on the southern fringe of Adirondack Park. They and the Newark Eagles met at old Hawkins Stadium in Albany, which by coincidence was also razed in 1960. Campy's club often played in doubleheaders with teams such as the Memphis Red Sox from the Negro American League. The Negro Leagues, another institution on its last legs, would limp on through one more season.

But Ebbets Field had one last pro baseball hurrah – built around a genuine icon. On August 23, 1959, none other than Satchel Paige was the main attraction in a doubleheader that drew 4,000 fans. Barnstorming with the Havana Cubans, he gave his age as "somewhere between 40 and 60." The Kansas City Monarchs topped the Stars 3-1 in the opener. Then Satch – wearing a Chicago White Sox uniform lent to him by former employer Bill Veeck – came on to strike out four in a three-inning start. The master allowed three runs, but only one was earned. He gave up a homer when he got cute and tried to sneak a second blooper pitch by Monarchs player-manager Herm Green.[31]

ROY CAMPANELLA'S BROOKLYN STARS AND THE NEGRO AMERICAN LEAGUE AT EBBETS FIELD, 1959

Date	Action
7/12	Brooklyn Stars vs. Memphis Red Sox Detroit Stars vs. Memphis
7/26	Brooklyn Stars vs. Memphis Red Sox Birmingham Black Barons vs. Memphis
8/2	Brooklyn Stars vs. Detroit Stars Detroit vs. Raleigh Tigers
8/23	Kansas City Monarchs 3, Brooklyn Stars 1 Havana Cubans 6, Kansas City Monarchs 4

Source: *New York Times*

Also in late August 1959, a few dozen teenage boys from Brooklyn had the opportunity to play a game at Ebbets. In 2007, one of them, Donald Reiss, recalled, "'Word spread through the neighborhood... It seemed one of the guys had an uncle who was, or knew, the head of groundskeeping, and it would be arranged to open the park for us.

... We were like kids in a candy store, but this was even better."[32]

The Dodger Rookies returned on September 4, playing the Yonkers Chippewas to a 4-4 tie. The contest had been scheduled for Fleming Field in Yonkers but a conflict forced a switch to Ebbets. The game was called after seven innings to allow the "Chippies" time to get back home for an evening match.[33]

Finally, what may well have been the last baseball game of any kind at Ebbets Field appears to have taken place that month. It featured 12-year-olds in a youth league. The father of one of the boys, an amateur photographer named David Hirsch, took two photos of the lads on the field and seated in the dugout. The photos were inscribed "Sept. 59."[34]

Yet even after the Cubans' victory and the boys' fun had faded into autumn, a flicker of life was still visible. The Hakoah soccer club scheduled a series of four Sunday doubleheaders. As it turned out, though, only three were played. Thus the last known sporting event at Ebbets took place on October 25, 1959.

Literally at the center of the action was Lloyd Monsen, Hakoah's star striker and a member of the National Soccer Hall of Fame. Monsen was born in 1931 to Norwegian parents and grew up in the Bay Ridge section of Brooklyn. He stated, "The Ebbets Field soccer scene was a large part of my career."[35] For example, he scored a goal and two assists in the May 12, 1957 match between Hapoel F.C. of Israel and an ASL all-star squad, which also presented Marilyn Monroe and Sammy Davis, Jr. as entertainers.

A trove of photos and other items remained in Monsen's possession, including a series of ASL newsletters. The November 1, 1959 issue explained what happened to that fourth Sunday outing. The games were originally slated for November 8, but were rescheduled for Thursday the 5th and then canceled.

"Not that the American Soccer League

would like to leave the confines of Ebbets Field, but circumstances beyond our control make it so. For instance, the Sunday blue law that ball games not commence before 2 P.M., the end of Daylight Saving Time and no lights if a twin bill is scheduled, makes it imperative for the ASL to call it quits at the Brooklyn park. Maybe if Ebbets Field is still around next year and not knocked down for a housing project, the ASL will again consider staging shows there next spring."

Monsen added, "Ebbets was better than any of the other stadiums we used. Crowds were in the thousands, quite good for us – but probably not good enough to support business." He further recalled, "The dirt infield was still there in the right-hand corner of the field. The groundskeepers had leveled the mound and removed the rubber."[36]

Indeed, as Ted Schreiber and Paul Jurkoic had observed, the most loyal Brooklyn foot soldiers were still at their posts. The most diehard retainer of them all has received scant mention in the many books about the team. Joseph Julius "Babe" Hamberger started as a clubhouse boy in 1921 and worked his way up to assistant traveling secretary. Although a number of club employees went west, Babe didn't leave the only workplace he'd ever known. In April 1958, he said he'd miss the team, but added philosophically, "Oh well, I still have a job. With five kids, I'm still getting paid. And that puts meat on the table."[37] Hamberger served as superintendent in the twilight phase, along with a skeleton crew that included a part-collie, part-chow watchdog named Angel.

Gay Talese, a sportswriter for the New York Times before becoming a best-selling author, visited Ebbets Field after the L.A. Dodgers won the World Series in October 1959. Always a writer who pursued the offbeat, Talese filed a brief but arresting report that captured the ghostly feel of the place.[38] The decay hastened after the Dodgers declined to pick up the two-year option on their lease in 1960 and the property reverted to Kratter.

There is a visible difference in the number of broken windows on New Year's Day and several weeks later.

As late as January 29, 1960, lawyer William Shea continued to dangle the possibility that Ebbets might host a team from the Continental League, albeit temporarily.[39] (The permanent site in Flushing, Queens – which Robert Moses offered and Walter O'Malley rebuffed – later became Shea Stadium, home of the New York Mets.) Of course, Branch Rickey's would-be third major league never got off the ground. It folded in August of that year. And less than a month after Shea held out that last faint hope, the wreckers descended.

Jane Leavy's biography of Sandy Koufax referred briefly to a charity game played that final morning, when Campy, Carl Erskine, Ralph Branca, Tommy Holmes, 1913 catcher Otto Miller, and 200 fans gathered to bid their old home adieu. However, newspaper accounts don't mention anything of the sort, and it would seem doubtful on a winter day. The closest thing may have been "Oisk" posing with the baseball-painted wrecking ball that also leveled the Polo Grounds four years later.

Relics of Ebbets Field have survived in New York City. Marvin Kratter donated 2,200 seats to the diamond that bore his name at Hart Island, the spooky prison/potter's field site east of the Bronx in Long Island Sound. Downing Stadium on Randall's Island in the East River got the lights. In one of several ironies, that park had been built by Robert Moses, who commanded his city makeovers from the nearby Triborough Bridge Authority headquarters. Over the years, though, nature overran Kratter Field, while the original fixtures at Downing had grown scarce by the time it was demolished in 2000.[40]

Yet the centerfield flagpole (also donated by Kratter Corp.) stood for more than four decades at 1405 Utica Avenue in East Flatbush. That site was a Veterans of Foreign Wars post. The most ardent Dodger supporters had hoped to transplant the pole to Borough Hall in October 2005, as part of the 50-year celebration of Brooklyn's lone World Series championship. In another irony, that spot is just a Carl Furillo throw away from the old location of the Dodgers team offices. Sad to say, though, the former owners allegedly held out for $50,000. Lucre vs. friendly allure – Ebbets Field's past continued to resonate.

That flagpole disappeared from view around 2007, when the Canarsie Casket Company (which succeeded the VFW) was torn down to make way for a church. Brooklyn Borough President Marty Markowitz, a big booster of Brooklyn Dodger memories, alerted Bruce Ratner, owner and developer of the Barclays Center in downtown Brooklyn, that the flagpole was available. It re-emerged in front of the arena in September 2012.[41] Another irony is that Walter O'Malley had hoped to build a replacement ballpark for the Dodgers in that vicinity.

Among those attending a ceremony for the pole in December 2012 was Sharon Robinson, daughter of Dodgers hero Jackie Robinson. She said, "I think it's a beautiful connection to Ebbets Field… I think he'd be very proud… It's right here in the heart of the city, and that would've been very important to him.[42] The little jewel box has continued to enjoy a prolonged afterlife.

SOURCES

This article was originally published in *The National Pastime – A Review of Baseball History*, Society for American Baseball Research, Cleveland, Ohio, Number 26 (May 2006), pages 104-109. It has been updated and amended at various points over time, most recently on April 24, 2018.

Thanks to SABR member Alan Cohen for his input on the Hearst Sandlot Classic.

SOCCER AT EBBETS FIELD, 1958-59

Score	Remarks
Hearts of Midlothian 6, Manchester City 5	Attendance: 20,606. Rainy and muddy. Sir Hugh Stephenson, the British Consul General in New York, handled the kickoff.
Halsingborg (Sweden) 2, Hakoah 2 Prelim: Ukrainian Nationals 4, Brooklyn Italians 2	Attendance: 6,500 Rainy, windy, and muddy.
Dundee 2, West Bromwich Albion 2 Prelim: Newark Portuguese 5, Uhrik Truckers 4	Attendance: 21,312
Legia (Poland) 8, Hakoah 1 Prelim: Empire State Junior Cup semi-finals Hakoah Juniors 1, Segura 1 (2 OT)	Attendance: 5,241
Dundee 3, Legia (Poland) 3 Prelim: Lewis Cup Ukrainian Nationals 2, Hakoah 1	Attendance: 12,429
Napoli 6, ASL All-Stars 1 Prelim: Newark Portuguese 2, Fall River SC 2	Attendance: 14,682 1,000 Napoli supporters run onto field before match to greet their club; dispersed by Babe Hamberger.
Two-game series for Fernet-Branca Cup Rapid (Vienna) 1, Napoli 0 Prelim: Brooklyn Italians 2, Hakoah 2	Attendance: 18,512 Heavily pro-Napoli crowd is in bad temper. Fans spill onto field and fight in first half, causing 10-minute delay. Hundreds more riot after late goal decides game. Three officials and policeman injured.
Napoli 1, Rapid (Vienna) 1 Prelim: Bayside Boys Club 0, Hakoah Juniors 0	Attendance: 13,351 Extra details of city and special police keep crowd subdued in return match, though one chair is thrown from left field stands.
Real Madrid 6, Graz Sports Club (Austria) 2	Attendance: 13,500 P.A. announcements in Spanish, German, and English.
Real Madrid 8, Graz/New York Hungarians Select 0 Prelim: NY Hungarians reserves 10, Austria F.C. 2	Attendance: 9,056

Palermo 5, ASL All-Stars 0	Attendance: 5,457 Steady downpour, muddy turf.
Palermo 2, Rapid Soccer Club (Vienna) 1 Prelim: Bayside Boys Club 2, Hakoah Juniors 1	Attendance: 12,598
Palermo 7, Italia (Toronto) 0 Prelim: Metropolitan League Cup final Colombia S.C. (Bronx) 2, Orsogna F.C. (Astoria) 1	Attendance: 5,000
Hakoah 2, Newark Portuguese 1 Brooklyn Italians 5, Uhrik Truckers 2	Attendance: 1,500
Ukrainian Nationals 2, Brooklyn Italians 1 Hakoah 8, Elizabeth Polish Falcons 2	Attendance: not available
Hakoah 4, Uhrik Truckers 0 Brooklyn Italians 2, Colombo 0	Attendance: not available

Source: *New York Times, American Soccer League-News* (Vol. 26, No. 4, November 1-8, 1959)

NOTES

1   Joseph McCauley, *Ebbets Field: Brooklyn's Baseball Shrine* (Bloomington, Indiana: AuthorHouse, 2004). Bob McGee, *The Greatest Ballpark Ever* (Piscataway, New Jersey: Rutgers University Press, 2005). John G. Zinn and Paul G. Zinn, editors, *Ebbets Field: Essays and Memories of Brooklyn's Historic Ballpark*, 1913-1960 (Jefferson, North Carolina: McFarland & Co., 2013).

2   "'Feeler' Received for Ebbets Field," *The New York Times*, October 17, 1957, 35.

3   Jeane Hoffman, "O'Malley Loaded with Baseball Parks," *The Los Angeles Times*, May 6, 1958, C5.

4   Roscoe McGowen, "Dodgers Sublet Brooklyn Home," *The New York Times*, March 5, 1958, 41.

5   "Kochman Unit Replaces Rock in N.Y. Park," *Billboard*, May 19, 1958, 47. For background on the alleged riot during Allan Freed's Big Beat show at the Boston Arena on May 3 that featured Chuck Berry and Jerry Lee Lewis, see "Rock 'N Roll Banned in Boston After Riot That Probably Never Happened," New England Historical Society website, May 3, 2014.

6   Telephone interview, Charlie Belknap with Rory Costello, 2005.

7   *The New York Times*, August 26, 1958, p. 48. The Polo Grounds was considerably more successful than Ebbets Field after its prime tenant pulled out. The National Exhibition Company (corporate name of the New York Giants) continued to focus on business at the Manhattan stadium under its lease there. Events included mammoth gatherings of Jehovah's Witnesses, as well as long-running stock car racing and rodeo series. See Roscoe McGowen, "Polo Grounds Is Still Profitable to the Giants," *The New York Times*, March 16, 1958, S1.

8   Gordon S. White Jr., "Soccer Fans Riot and Injure Three Officials and Patrolman at Ebbets Field," *The New York Times*, June 29, 1959, 37.

9   William R. Conklin, "New Pro Eleven Needs Field Here," *The New York Times*, August 16, 1959, S6.

10   Philip Benjamin, "Stark Acts to Force Forest Hills to Drop Bias or Cup Matches," *The New York Times*, July 11, 1959, 1.

11   E-mail from Mary Lai to Rory Costello, April 10, 2006.

12   "Schreiber's Two-Run Circuit Drive Enables St. John's to Beat Manhattan," *The New York Times*, April 25, 1958, 38. In a related curiosity, Schreiber's final home at-bat in the majors, on 9/18/1963 (he grounded into a double play) was the last regular-season out in the Polo Grounds. However, the Latin American Players' Game took place there on October 12.

13   Telephone interview, Ted Schreiber with Rory Costello, January 13, 2006.

14   E-mail, Al Ferrara to SABR member Paul Hirsch, March 20, 2013.

15   Morrey Rokeach, "N.Y. Hearst All-Star Team Holds Drills at Ebbetts [sic] Field," *The Sporting News*, July 22, 1959, 38. "Ex-Trip Holmes NY Sandlot Head," *Binghamton* (New York) *Press*, April 8, 1959, 50. Holmes replaced George "Snuffy" Stirnweiss, who'd died in a train wreck the previous September,

16   Al Spitzer, "Finkelberg Hits Homer A-A Snider," *Long Island Star-Journal*, August 12, 1959, 20. Bearnarth went on to have an outstanding college career at St. John's. Ott also attended St. John's briefly but was signed by the Cubs just before the 1960 college season began. Had they been a little older, they could have been on the same team with Schreiber. Previous versions of this article incorrectly indicated that Ott was a member of the 1959 squad.

17   Al Spitzer, "US All-Stars Halt Rookies," *Long Island Star-Journal*, August 15, 1959, 8. "T-U's Moseley Impresses in Short Hill Appearance," *Albany Times-Union*, August 16, 1959, E-4. "S. F.'s Fazio to Start at Short in Hearst Game," *San Francisco Examiner*, August 18, 1959: III-4. The game accounts from the New York papers do not mention Fazio.

18   "Rainka, Moseley on U.S. Stars," *Albany Times-Union*, July 26, 1959, B-7.

19   James L. Kilgallen, "Ex-Dodger, Giant Fans 'Hoiting' Real Bad," International News Service, April 16, 1958.

20   Michael Strauss, "Van Buren Defeats Curtis for P.S.A.L. Title with Rally in Eighth," *The New York Times*, June 24, 1958, 42.

21   Leo J. Callahan, "The Last Homer at Ebbets," *Elysian Fields Quarterly*, Winter 2006 (this article overlooked the home run by Herm Green on August 23, 1959). Andrew Paul Mele, *The Boys of Brooklyn* (Bloomington, Indiana: AuthorHouse, 2008), 182, 185.

22   "Roosevelt Beats Curtis Nine by 6-5," *The New York Times*, June 6, 1959, 16.

23   E-mail from Paul Jurkoic to Rory Costello, February 1, 2005.

24   Jimmy Murphy, "Duel of Strategy Between Scouts of L.A. Dodgers," *New York World-Telegram and Sun*, August 22, 1959, B4. "Rookies Face Westchester Monday," *Yonkers Herald Statesman*, August 8, 1959.

25   Murphy, "Duel of Strategy Between Scouts of L.A. Dodgers."

26 "Memphis to Meet Stars' Nine Today," *The New York Times*, July 12, 1959, S4. This article noted that baseball entertainer "Prince Joe" Henry was scheduled to appear between games that day. However, Mr. Henry stated to Rory Costello (telephone interview, February 1, 2005) that he was a) out of the game in 1959, b) never appeared at Ebbets Field in his career, and c) always appeared in game action, not between games.

27 "Campy a Spectator This Time," *The Sporting News*, October 15, 1958, 20.

28 "Asks 'Campy Day' at Ebbets Field," *Brooklyn Daily*, October 6, 1958, 8. Ebbets Field stood just outside the boundaries of New York's 12th Congressional District as they were then drawn.

29 Murphy, "Duel of Strategy Between Scouts of L.A. Dodgers." Paul Jurkoic (e-mail to Rory Costello, April 23, 2018) was "pretty sure" that Campanella was on site, but Jurkoic did not stay for the feature game and did not remember much besides how well the field was maintained.

30 "Doubleheader at Ebbets Field," New York Post, July 6, 1959, 43. "Negro Twin Bill Today," *The New York Times*, July 26, 1959, S2.

31 "Paige Fans 4 Men and Allows 3 Hits in 3 Innings Here," *The New York Times*, August 24, 1959, 25.

32 Vincent M. Mallozzi, "The Last Boys of Summer," *The New York Times*, March 11, 2007.

33 "Ebbets Field Date for the Chippewas," *Yonkers Herald Statesman*, September 2, 1959, 25. "Chippies Thump Haveys, 6-1; Clinch Mack Title," *Yonkers Herald Statesman*, September 5, 1959, 15.

34 Brett Cyrgalis, "A Little League Game One of Last Memories from Dodgers' Old Home," *New York Post*, May 31, 2009.

35 E-mail from Lloyd Monsen to Rory Costello, March 1, 2005.

36 Telephone interview, Lloyd Monsen with Rory Costello, February 26, 2005.

37 Kilgallen, "Ex-Dodger, Giant Fans 'Hoiting' Real Bad"

38 Gay Talese, "Brooklyn Displays Little Enthusiasm After Dodgers Win," *The New York Times*, October 9, 1959, 34.

39 Joe Reichler, "Buffalo 8th Club in Rickey League," *The Washington Post, Times Herald*, January 30, 1960, 12. Shea was quoted twice floating the same idea in July 1959.

40 Daniel J. Wakin, "Ebbets Lights Dimmed Again," *The New York Times*, September 27, 2000, B1.

41 Rich Calder, "Barclays honors Brooklyn history," *New York Post*, September 22, 2012. At that time, Calder wrote that it was unclear whether it was the center-field pole or another that had graced Ebbets Field. Another story speculated that it was a replica (http://atlanticyardsreport.blogspot.com/2012/09/coming-to-barclays-center-plaza.html).

42 Mike Mazzeo, "Nets hold ceremony for flagpole," ESPN.com, December 11, 2012.

EBBETS FIELD
BY THE NUMBERS

by Dan Fields

1ST

Career pitch faced in which pitcher Clise Dudley of the Brooklyn Robins hit a home run on April 27, 1929. He had three home runs in 173 career at-bats.

1ST

Televised major-league baseball game, on August 26, 1939. Red Barber called the game for W2XBS (which later became WNBC-TV). The Cincinnati Reds beat the Brooklyn Dodgers 5-2 in the first game of a doubleheader.

1ST

Black player to appear in a major-league game in the twentieth century: Jackie Robinson of the Dodgers, on April 15, 1947, at Ebbets Field against the Boston Braves. He went 0-3 but scored a run.

1ST

All-Star Game to include black players, on July 12, 1949, at Ebbets Field. Jackie Robinson started at second base for the National League, and fellow Dodgers Roy Campanella and Don Newcombe also played for the NL. Larry Doby of the Cleveland Indians played for the American League, which won 11-7.

1ST

Major-league win and shutout by 19-year-old Sandy Koufax of the Dodgers, on August 27, 1955, against the Cincinnati Redlegs.

2

Complete-game wins by Pete Alexander of the Philadelphia Phillies on September 3, 1917, in a doubleheader against the Robins.

2

Relief wins by Clyde King of the Dodgers on August 22, 1951, in a doubleheader against the St. Louis Cardinals.

2

Shutouts thrown by Karl Spooner of the Dodgers in his first two major-league games, on September 22 and 26, 1954, both at Ebbets Field.

2ND

Consecutive no-hitter thrown by Johnny Vander Meer of the Cincinnati Reds on June 15, 1938, beating the Dodgers 6-0 at Ebbets Field. It was the first night game at the ballpark. On June 11, Vander Meer had no-hit the Boston Bees at Cincinnati's Crosley Field.

2.22

ERA of the Robins at Ebbets Field in 1916.

3

Consecutive four-hit games by Milt Stock of the Robins on July 1, 2, and 3, 1925, at Ebbets Field. He also had a four-hit game on the road on June 30, for a total of four consecutive four-hit games.

3

Wild pitches thrown in the first inning by Tom Lasorda of the Dodgers in his first major-league start, on May 5, 1955, against the St. Louis Cardinals. He also walked two batters during the inning.

4.56

ERA of the Dodgers at Ebbets Field in 1954.

7

Consecutive batters struck out by Dazzy Vance of the Robins on August 1, 1924, against the Chicago Cubs, and by Van Mungo of the Dodgers on June 25, 1936, in the first game of a doubleheader against the Cincinnati Reds.

7

Nine-inning no-hitters thrown at Ebbets Field, by Dazzy Vance, Brooklyn Robins, September 13, 1925 (first game of doubleheader); Paul Dean, St. Louis Cardinals, September 21, 1934 (second game of doubleheader); Johnny Vander Meer, Cincinnati Reds, June 15, 1938; Ed Head, Brooklyn Dodgers, April 23, 1946; Carl Erskine, Brooklyn Dodgers, June 19, 1952; Carl Erskine, Brooklyn Dodgers, May 12, 1956; and Sal Maglie, Brooklyn Dodgers, September 25, 1956. Roy Campanella caught the last three games.

8

Players who hit for cycle at Ebbets Field: Dave Robertson, Pittsburgh Pirates, August 30, 1921; Bill Terry, New York Giants, May 29, 1928; Babe Herman, Brooklyn Robins, May 18, 1931; Arky Vaughan, Pittsburgh Pirates, June 24, 1933; Dixie Walker, Brooklyn Dodgers, September 2, 1944; Wally Westlake, Pittsburgh Pirates, July 30, 1948; Stan Musial, St. Louis Cardinals, July 24, 1949; and Ralph Kiner, Pittsburgh Pirates, June 25, 1950.

9

World Series played at Ebbets Field, in 1916, 1920, 1941, 1947, 1949, 1952, 1953, 1955, and 1956. Pee Wee Reese played in all but the first two series. The only championship won by Brooklyn was in 1955, when the Dodgers beat the New York Yankees in seven games.

12

Hits allowed by Leon Cadore of the Robins in a shutout against the Boston Braves on September 4, 1920.

12

RBIs by Jim Bottomley of the St. Louis Cardinals on September 16, 1924, against the Robins. He broke the major-league record of 11 set by Wilbert Robinson (Brooklyn's current manager) in 1892.

13-1

Record of Preacher Roe of the Dodgers at Ebbets Field in 1951.

15

Runs scored by the Dodgers during the first inning on May 21, 1952, against the Cincinnati Reds. Pee Wee Reese reached first base three times during the inning. The Dodgers won 19-1.

15TH

Consecutive game won by Dazzy Vance of the Robins on September 18, 1924, in the first game of a doubleheader against the St. Louis Cardinals. He pitched four innings in relief as Brooklyn won 7-5.

16

Age in years of shortstop Tommy Brown of the Dodgers in his major-league debut on August 3, 1944, in the first game of a doubleheader against the Chicago Cubs. He doubled and scored a run.

16-4

Record of Jeff Pfeffer of the Robins at Ebbets Field in 1914. He had a record of 7-8 on the road.

18

Total bases by Joe Adcock of the Milwaukee Braves on July 31, 1954. He hit four home runs and a double in five at-bats against the Dodgers. The total of 18 bases was a major-league record until 2002.

29

Consecutive games with a hit at Ebbets Field by Zack Wheat of the Robins from April 17, 1923, to July 1, 1923. During the streak, he had 50 hits in 113 at-bats (.442) and drove in 29 runs.

29-47-1

Regular-season record of the Brooklyn Superbas at Ebbets Field in 1913. The team's record in its first year at the ballpark would end up being its worst.

29

Consecutive scoreless innings pitched at Ebbets Field by Ralph Branca of the Dodgers from July 26, 1946, to September 25, 1946.

37

Home runs by Stan Musial of the St. Louis Cardinals at Ebbets Field, the most by a visiting player.

49

Age in years of Jack Quinn of the Dodgers when he had his last major-league win, on September 13, 1932, in the first game of a doubleheader against the St. Louis Cardinals. He pitched five innings in relief.

50

Extra-base hits by Babe Herman of the Robins at Ebbets Field in 1930. He hit 23 doubles, 5 triples, and 22 home runs.

60-17

Regular-season record of the Dodgers at Ebbets Field in 1953, the team's best in one season at the ballpark.

219

Total bases by Babe Herman of the Robins at Ebbets Field in 1930.

237TH

Career home run as a catcher by Roy Campanella of the Dodgers on June 11, 1957, to surpass Gabby Hartnett for the NL record.

.246

Batting average of the Dodgers at Ebbets Field in 1938.

.306

Batting average of the Robins at Ebbets Field in 1930.

758-592-10

Regular-season record of Wilbert Robinson as manager at Ebbets Field from 1914 through 1931.

1,685

Total bases by Zack Wheat at Ebbets Field, the most of any player.

1963-1450-34

Regular-season record of the Brooklyn Superbas/ Robins/Dodgers at Ebbets Field from April 9, 1913, to September 24, 1957.

83,831

Regular-season attendance at Ebbets Field in 1918, the least in one season (1,552 per game).

1,807,526

Regular-season attendance at Ebbets Field in 1947, the most in one season (23,173 per game).

CAREER LEADERS AT EBBETS FIELD

BATTING

GAMES

1035	Pee Wee Reese
942	Zack Wheat
802	Carl Furillo
751	Gil Hodges
701	Duke Snider

PLATE APPEARANCES

4422	Pee Wee Reese
3863	Zack Wheat
3122	Carl Furillo
3100	Gil Hodges
2935	Duke Snider

AT-BATS

3704	Pee Wee Reese
3512	Zack Wheat
2823	Carl Furillo
2657	Gil Hodges
2550	Duke Snider

RUNS

615	Pee Wee Reese
534	Zack Wheat
508	Duke Snider
487	Jackie Robinson
470	Gil Hodges

HITS

1154	Zack Wheat
996	Pee Wee Reese
842	Carl Furillo
797	Duke Snider
764	Dixie Walker

DOUBLES

182	Zack Wheat
170	Dixie Walker
153	Pee Wee Reese
152	Duke Snider
143	Carl Furillo

TRIPLES

65	Zack Wheat
60	Hi Myers
40	Jimmy Johnston
36	Dixie Walker
35	Del Bissonette

HOME RUNS

175	Duke Snider
172	Gil Hodges
140	Roy Campanella
98	Carl Furillo
82	Dolph Camilli

RBIS

534	Gil Hodges
525	Duke Snider
516	Zack Wheat
499	Carl Furillo
445	Roy Campanella

WALKS

629	Pee Wee Reese
394	Gil Hodges
368	Jackie Robinson
352	Duke Snider
349	Dolph Camilli

INTENTIONAL WALKS

56	Gil Hodges
53	Dixie Walker
48	Roy Campanella
48	Duke Snider
42	Pee Wee Reese

STRIKEOUTS

458	Gil Hodges
433	Duke Snider
421	Pee Wee Reese
305	Dolph Camilli
224	Roy Campanella

HIT BY PITCH

35	Jackie Robinson
24	Carl Furillo
24	Zack Wheat
18	Jack Fournier
18	Andy Pafko

BATTING AVERAGE (MIN. 1,400 AT-BATS)

.341	Babe Herman
.329	Zack Wheat
.326	Jake Daubert
.325	Dixie Walker
.324	Johnny Frederick

ON-BASE PERCENTAGE (MIN. 1,400 AT-BATS)

.411	Jackie Robinson
.404	Dolph Camilli
.401	Dixie Walker
.400	Babe Herman
.396	Duke Snider

SLUGGING PERCENTAGE
(MIN. 1,400 AT-BATS)

.603	Duke Snider
.570	Babe Herman
.562	Roy Campanella
.528	Gil Hodges
.522	Johnny Frederick

OPS
(MIN. 1,400 AT-BATS)

.999	Duke Snider
.970	Babe Herman
.945	Roy Campanella
.922	Dolph Camilli
.903	Jackie Robinson

STOLEN BASES

120	Pee Wee Reese
110	Jackie Robinson
94	Jimmy Johnston
86	George Cutshaw
73	Zack Wheat

PITCHING

ERA (MIN. 500 INNINGS)

2.42	Jeff Pfeffer
2.43	Rube Marquard
2.69	Dazzy Vance
2.88	Sherry Smith
2.98	Leon Cadore

WINS

106	Dazzy Vance
96	Burleigh Grimes
66	Carl Erskine
65	Jeff Pfeffer
60	Van Mungo

LOSSES

69	Burleigh Grimes
60	Dazzy Vance
48	Van Mungo
45	Watty Clark
36	Curt Davis
36	Jeff Pfeffer

WINNING PERCENTAGE
(MIN. 40 WINS)

.716	Kirby Higbe
.714	Preacher Roe
.702	Carl Erskine
.652	Freddie Fitzsimmons
.646	Don Newcombe

GAMES PITCHED

196	Dazzy Vance
186	Burleigh Grimes
164	Watty Clark
156	Clem Labine
152	Carl Erskine

GAMES STARTED

172	Dazzy Vance
161	Burleigh Grimes
116	Van Mungo
107	Jeff Pfeffer
105	Carl Erskine

COMPLETE GAMES

120	Dazzy Vance
115	Burleigh Grimes
82	Jeff Pfeffer
62	Van Mungo
48	Watty Clark
48	Don Newcombe

SHUTOUTS

20	Dazzy Vance
16	Burleigh Grimes
13	Jeff Pfeffer
10	Don Newcombe
9	Van Mungo

SAVES

28	Clem Labine
20	Hugh Casey
19	Jim Hughes
11	Jack Quinn
9	Joe Black
9	Ed Roebuck

INNINGS PITCHED

1489⅔	Dazzy Vance
1400	Burleigh Grimes
944	Van Mungo
944	Jeff Pfeffer
869⅓	Watty Clark

WALKS

396	Dazzy Vance
388	Burleigh Grimes
364	Van Mungo
314	Carl Erskine
301	Kirby Higbe

INTENTIONAL WALKS

32	Ralph Branca
24	Kirby Higbe
24	Van Mungo
23	Hugh Casey
23	Curt Davis

STRIKEOUTS

1201	Dazzy Vance
561	Burleigh Grimes
546	Van Mungo
499	Carl Erksine
427	Ralph Branca

HOME RUNS ALLOWED

95	Preacher Roe
93	Carl Erskine
87	Don Newcombe
65	Ralph Branca
61	Dazzy Vance

HIT BY PITCH

40	Dazzy Vance
32	Jeff Pfeffer
26	Burleigh Grimes
17	Ralph Branca
17	Larry Cheney

WILD PITCHES

36	Burleigh Grimes
25	Larry Cheney
21	Van Mungo
21	Dazzy Vance
18	Hal Gregg

SINGLE-SEASON LEADERS AT EBBETS FIELD

BATTING

GAMES

79 by Buddy Hassett, 1936; Dolph Camilli, 1940; Dolph Camilli, 1942; Billy Herman, 1942; Pee Wee Reese, 1946; Gil Hodges, 1952

PLATE APPEARANCES

358 by Pee Wee Reese, 1949

AT-BATS

334 by Ivy Olson, 1920

RUNS

82 by Babe Herman, 1930

HITS

120 by Babe Herman, 1930

DOUBLES

28 by Johnny Frederick, 1929

TRIPLES

13 by Hi Myers, 1920

HOME RUNS

25 by Gil Hodges, 1954

RBIS

77 by Duke Snider, 1955

WALKS

76 by Eddie Stanky, 1945

INTENTIONAL WALKS

19 by Pee Wee Reese, 1947

STRIKEOUTS

61 by Dolph Camilli, 1941

HIT BY PITCH

10 by Jackie Robinson, 1952

BATTING AVERAGE

.389 by Babe Phelps, 1936

ON-BASE PERCENTAGE

.474 by Augie Galan, 1944

SLUGGING PERCENTAGE

.715 by Duke Snider, 1955

OPS

1.163 by Duke Snider, 1955

STOLEN BASES

19 by George Cutshaw, 1913; Jimmy Johnston, 1921; Pete Reiser, 1946; Jackie Robinson, 1949

PITCHING

ERA

1.32 by Wheezer Dell, 1915

WINS

16 by Jeff Pfeffer, 1914

LOSSES

12 by Burleigh Grimes, 1925

GAMES PITCHED

31 by Clem Labine, 1955

GAMES STARTED

20 by Jeff Pfeffer, 1914; Burleigh Grimes, 1922; Jesse Petty, 1926; Kirby Higbe, 1941; Hal Gregg, 1945; Carl Erskine, 1953; Carl Erskine, 1954

COMPLETE GAMES

17 by Jeff Pfeffer, 1914

SHUTOUTS

5 by Burleigh Grimes, 1920

SAVES

12 by Jim Hughes, 1954

INNINGS PITCHED

186 by Jeff Pfeffer, 1914

WALKS

76 by Kirby Higbe, 1941

INTENTIONAL WALKS

9 by Hugh Casey, 1946; Kirby Higbe, 1946

STRIKEOUTS

159 by Dazzy Vance, 1924

HOME RUNS ALLOWED

21 by Preacher Roe, 1950

HIT BY PITCH

8 by Boom-Boom Beck, 1933

WILD PITCHES

11 by Larry Cheney, 1916

SINGLE-GAME LEADERS AT EBBETS FIELD
(* = EXTRA-INNING GAME)

BATTING

RUNS

5 by Stan Musial, St. Louis Cardinals, May 19, 1948; Gil Hodges, Brooklyn Dodgers, August 31, 1950; Joe Adcock, Milwaukee Braves, July 31, 1954

HITS

6 by Carson Bigbee, Pittsburgh Pirates, August 22, 1917*; Jim Bottomley, St. Louis Cardinals, September 16, 1924; Hank DeBerry, Brooklyn Robins, June 23, 1929*

DOUBLES

3 on 27 occasions, including by Jim Gilliam of the Brooklyn Dodgers on October 3, 1953, in Game Four of the World Series

TRIPLES

3 by Les Bell, St. Louis Cardinals, September 22, 1926

HOME RUNS

4 by Gil Hodges, Brooklyn Dodgers, August 31, 1950; Joe Adcock, Milwaukee Braves, July 31, 1954

RBIS

12 by Jim Bottomley, St. Louis Cardinals, September 16, 1924

WALKS

4 on 30 occasions

INTENTIONAL WALKS

3 by Zack Taylor, Brooklyn Robins, August 30, 1925 (first game of doubleheader)*; Nick Etten, Philadelphia Phillies, September 19, 1942*; Roy Campanella, Brooklyn Dodgers, August 31, 1952

STRIKEOUTS

4 on 48 occasions

STOLEN BASES

4 by Max Carey, Pittsburgh Pirates, July 28, 1922

PITCHING

INNINGS PITCHED

18 by Jeff Pfeffer, Brooklyn Robins, June 1, 1919*

RUNS ALLOWED

14 by Bull Wagner, Brooklyn Superbas July 3, 1913; Dutch Henry, Brooklyn Robins, July 22, 1923 (first game of doubleheader)

HITS ALLOWED

23 by Jeff Pfeffer, Brooklyn Robins, June 1, 1919*

WALKS

11 by Van Mungo, Brooklyn Dodgers, June 5, 1932

INTENTIONAL WALKS

5 by Ace Adams, New York Giants, June 18, 1945*

STRIKEOUTS

17 by Dazzy Vance, Brooklyn Robins, July 20, 1925*

HOME RUNS ALLOWED

5 by Preacher Roe, Brooklyn Dodgers, September 1, 1953; Harvey Haddix, St. Louis Cardinals, June 27, 1954

HIT BY PITCH

3 by Jeff Pfeffer, Brooklyn Superbas, September 3, 1913 (first game of doubleheader); Ed Appleton, Brooklyn Robins, July 6, 1915 (first game of doubleheader); Leon Cadore, Brooklyn Robins, August 22, 1917*; Johnny Cooney, Boston Braves, May 4, 1926; Dick Errickson, Boston Braves, August 10, 1941 (first game of doubleheader); Steve Ridzik, Philadelphia Phillies, April 20, 1955

WILD PITCHES

3 by Rube Benton, Cincinnati Reds, July 27, 1914; Larry Cheney, Brooklyn Robins, April 12, 1916; Burleigh Grimes, Brooklyn Robins, July 23, 1919 (second game of doubleheader); Roy Parmelee, New York Giants, August 6, 1933 (second game of doubleheader); Ed Heusser, St. Louis Cardinals, July 29, 1936 (first game of doubleheader); Tom Lasorda, Brooklyn Dodgers, May 5, 1955

SOURCES

Society for American Baseball Research. *The SABR Baseball List and Record Book* (New York: Scribner, 2007).

Sugar, Bert Randolph, ed. *The Baseball Maniac's Almanac* (fifth edition) (New York: Sports Publishing, 2019).

Baseball-Reference.com

NationalPastime.com

retrosheet.org/boxesetc/N/PK_NYC15.htm

CONTRIBUTORS

JOHN BAUER resides with his wife and two children in Bedford, New Hampshire. By day, he is an attorney specializing in insurance regulatory law and corporate law. By night, he spends many spring and summer evenings cheering for the San Francisco Giants and many fall and winter evenings reading history. He is a past and ongoing contributor to other SABR projects.

NATHAN BIERMA is president of SABR Southern Michigan. He lives in Grand Rapids, Michigan. The first two major-league ballparks he set foot in as a kid were Tiger Stadium and Wrigley Field, and they forged a lifelong love of baseball and historic ballparks. His writing has appeared in the *Chicago Tribune*, *Chicago Sports Review*, and *Detroit Free Press*, and in SABR's recent books on the greatest games at Wrigley Field and Comiskey Park. He is the author of *The Eclectic Encyclopedia of English: Language At Its Most Enigmatic, Ephemeral, and Egregious*. His website is www.nathanbierma.com.

LUIS A. BLANDON, a Washington, DC, native, is a producer, writer, and researcher in video and documentary film production and in archival, manuscript, historical, film, and image research. His creative storytelling has garnered numerous awards, including three regional Emmys®, regional and national Edward R. Murrow Awards, two TELLY awards and a New York Festival World Medal. He worked as a producer and/or researcher on several documentaries including *Jeremiah*; *Feast Your Ears: The Story of WHFS 102.3*; and *#GeorgeWashington*. Most recently, he was co-producer of the documentary *The Lost Battalion*. He is serving as a consultant on a documentary film project for the United States Naval Academy's Stockdale Center for Ethical Leadership on the Vietnam War POWs and leadership. He was senior researcher and manager of the story development team for two national programs for Retirement Living Television. He has worked as a historian for two public policy research firms, Morgan Angel & Associates and MLL Consulting LLC. He served as the principal researcher for several authors including for *The League of Wives* by Heath Hardage Lee and her current biography project on First Lady Pat Nixon. He has a master of arts in international affairs from the George Washington University.

THOMAS J. BROWN JR. is a lifelong Mets fan who became a Durham Bulls fan after moving to North Carolina in the early 1980s. He was a national-board-certified high-school science teacher for 34 years before retiring in 2016. Tom taught science to ELL students in the last eight years of his career and still mentors many of them. He has been a member of SABR since 1995, when he learned about the organization during a visit to Cooperstown on his honeymoon. Tom became active in SABR after his retirement, writing biographies and game stories, mostly about the New York Mets. He loves to travel with his wife, always visiting major-league and minor-league ballparks whenever possible. Tom also loves to cook and writes about the diverse recipes he makes on his blog, "Cooking and My Family."

JOHN J. BURBRIDGE JR. is currently professor emeritus at Elon University, where he was both a dean and professor. While at Elon he introduced and taught Baseball and Statistics. He has authored several SABR publications and presented at SABR conventions, NINE, and the Seymour meetings. He is a lifelong New York Giants baseball fan. The greatest Giants-Dodgers game he attended was a 1-0 Giants victory in Jersey City in 1956. Yes, the Dodgers did play in Jersey City in 1956 and 1957. John can be reached at burbridg@elon.edu.

FREDERICK C. "RICK" BUSH has written articles for over two dozen SABR books and, together with Bill Nowlin, has co-edited five SABR books about the Negro Leagues, including *When the Monarchs Reigned: Kansas City's 1942 Negro League Champions* (2021), which received the 2022 Robert Peterson Recognition Award.

Rick lives with his wife, Michelle, their three sons – Michael, Andrew, and Daniel – and their border collie mix, Bailey, in the Houston metro area. He has been an educator for over 25 years, the past 18 of which have been spent teaching English at Wharton County Junior College's satellite campus in Sugar Land, Texas, which is home to the Astros' Triple-A franchise.

A lifelong White Sox fan surrounded by Cubs fans in the northern suburbs of Chicago, **KEN CARRANO** works as a chief financial officer for a large landscaping firm and as a soccer referee. He has been a SABR member since 1992, and has contributed to several SABR publications and the SABR Games Project. Ken and his Brewers' fan wife, Ann, share two children, two golden retrievers, and a mutual distain for the blue side of Chicago.

ALAN COHEN has been a SABR member since 2010. He chairs the BioProject fact-checking committee, serves as vice president-treasurer of the Connecticut Smoky Joe Wood Chapter, and is a datacaster (MiLB stringer) with the Double-A Hartford Yard Goats. His essay "Josh Gibson Blazes a Trail," catalogued Gibson's feat of hitting a home run in virtually every big-league ballpark in which he played from 1930 through 1946 — 17 in all, including Ebbets Field. Alan's biographies, game stories, and essays have appeared in more than 60 SABR publications. A major area of his research is Brooklyn Against the World (1946-1950), from which 10 players advanced to the majors. He has four children, nine grandchildren, and one great-grandchild, and resides in Connecticut with his wife, Frances, their cats Ava and Zoe, and their dog Buddy.

RORY COSTELLO has been a Brooklyn resident since 1992. He lives in the Borough of Churches with his wife, Noriko, and son, Kai. He regrets having been born too late to see a game at Ebbets Field.

RICHARD CUICCHI joined SABR in 1983 and is an active member of the Schott-Pelican Chapter. Since his retirement as an information-technology executive, Richard authored *Family Ties: A Comprehensive Collection of Facts and Trivia about Baseball's Relatives*. He has contributed to numerous SABR BioProject and Games Project publications. He does freelance writing and blogging about a variety of baseball topics on his website, TheTenthInning.com, and CrescentCitySports.com. Richard lives in New Orleans with his wife, Mary.

PAUL E. DOUTRICH is professor emeritus at York College of Pennsylvania, where he taught American history for 30 years. He now lives in Brewster, Massachusetts. Among the courses he taught was a one entitled Baseball History. He has written scholarly articles and contributed to several anthologies about the Revolutionary era, and has written a book about Jacksonian America. He has also curated several museum exhibits. His recent scholarship has focused on baseball history. He has contributed numerous manuscripts to various SABR publications and is the author of *The Cardinals and the Yankees, 1926: A Classical Season and St. Louis in Seven*.

ERIC ENDERS is a freelance writer, editor, and former research librarian at the National Baseball Hall of Fame Library in Cooperstown. He is the author of a dozen books, including *Ballparks: A Journey Through the Fields of the Past, Present, and Future* and *Mexican-American Baseball in El Paso*. His writing on baseball has also appeared in the *New York Times*, MLB's World Series programs, and numerous SABR publications. A native of El Paso, Texas, he was inducted into the El Paso Baseball Hall of Fame in 2016.

DOUG FELDMANN is a professor in the College of Education at Northern Kentucky University and a former part-time scout for the San Diego Padres, Seattle Mariners, and Cincinnati Reds. He is the author of 14 books, more information on which is available at dougfeldmannbooks.com.

DAN FIELDS is a senior manuscript editor at the *New England Journal of Medicine* and lives in Framingham, Massachusetts. He has contributed to numerous SABR books.

JAMES FORR is a recovering Pirates fan in the heart of Cardinals country. His book, *Pie Traynor: A Baseball Biography*, co-authored with David Proctor, was a nominee for the 2010 CASEY Award. He is also a winner of the McFarland-SABR Baseball Research Award and has spoken at the Frederick Ivor-Campbell 19th Century Base Ball Conference and the Jerry Malloy Negro League Conference.

BRIAN FRANK is passionate about documenting the history of major- and minor-league baseball. He is the creator of the website The Herd Chronicles (www.herdchronicles.com), which is dedicated to preserving the history of the Buffalo Bisons and professional baseball in Buffalo. His articles can also be read on the official website of the Bisons. He was an assistant editor of the book *The Seasons of Buffalo Baseball, 1857-2020*, and he's a frequent contributor to SABR publications. Brian and his wife, Jenny, enjoy traveling around the country in their camper to major- and minor-league ballparks and taking an annual trip to Europe. Brian was a history major at Canisius College, where he earned a bachelor of arts. He also received a Juris Doctor from the University at Buffalo School of Law.

GORDON J. GATTIE is a lifelong baseball fan and a SABR member since 1998. Currently a civilian US Navy engineer, he includes among his baseball research interests ballparks, historical trends, and statistical analysis. Gordon earned his PhD from SUNY Buffalo, where he used baseball to investigate judgment performance in complex dynamic environments. Ever the optimist, he dreams of a Cleveland Guardians World Series championship. Lisa, his wonderful wife, who roots for the Yankees, and Morrigan, their beloved Labrador retriever, enjoy visiting ballparks and other baseball-related sites. Among their treasured possessions is a brick from Ebbets Field. Gordon has contributed to many SABR publications, including several issues of *The National Pastime*, and the Games Project.

PAUL HOFMANN, a SABR member since 2002, is the associate vice president for international affairs at Sacramento State University and a frequent contributor to SABR publications. Paul is a native of Detroit and a lifelong Tigers fan. He currently resides in Lakeville, Minnesota.

SABR member **MIKE HUBER** is professor of mathematics and dean emeritus at Muhlenberg College in Allentown, Pennsylvania, where he teaches an undergraduate course titled Reasoning with Sabermetrics. He studies rare events in baseball, such as games in which batters hit for the cycle. Mike has published his sabermetrics research in several books and journals, including *The Baseball Research Journal*, *Chance*, and *Base Ball*, and he genuinely enjoys contributing to SABR's Baseball Games Project.

RUSS LAKE lives in Champaign, Illinois, and is a retired college professor. The 1964 St. Louis Cardinals remain his favorite team. He was distressed to see Sportsman's Park (aka Busch Stadium I) being demolished not long after he had attended the last game there on May 8, 1966. His wife, Carol, deserves an MVP award for watching all of a 13-inning ballgame in Cincinnati with Russ in 1971 – during their honeymoon. In 1994 he was an editor for David Halberstam's baseball book *October 1964.*

BOB LEMOINE is a high-school librarian and adjunct professor at White Mountains Community College and Emporia State University. He lives in New Hampshire and has contributed to several SABR projects. Bob is the author of *When the Babe Went Back to Boston: Babe Ruth, Judge Fuchs, and the Hapless 1935 Boston Braves* (McFarland & Co., 2023).

For over 20 years, **KEVIN LARKIN** patrolled the highways and byways of the roads in his hometown of Great Barrington, Massachusetts. When not at work keeping the citizens of his hometown safe, inevitably Larkin was listening to a baseball game on the radio. He has been going to baseball games since he was 5 years old. His baseball life is the only thing he loves more than his children and grandchildren. Larkin has published *Baseball in the Bay State: A History of Baseball in Massachusetts* and *Gehrig: Game by Game*. His latest book, *Big Time Baseball in a Small Berkshire County Town*, led to his heading an effort to erect a historical marker in the town where a semipro team played a number of major-league teams, Black baseball teams and the House of David touring team with the plaque being dedicated on July 6, 2022. Larkin and Jesse Stewart co-host a monthly radio show on WSBS that talks about baseball history with a focus on Berkshire County baseball and its players. He also writes and fact-checks for SABR, an experience he considers the best decision he has ever made.

LEN LEVIN is a longtime newspaper editor in New England, now retired. He lives in Providence with his wife, Linda, and an overachieving orange cat. He now (Len, not the cat) is the grammarian for the Rhode Island Supreme Court and edits its decisions. He also copyedits many SABR books, including this one. He is just down the interstate from Fenway Park, where he has spent many happy hours.

SABR member and Massachusetts native **MIKE LYNCH** is the founder of Seamheads.com and the author of five books, including *Harry Frazee, Ban Johnson and the Feud That Nearly Destroyed the American League*, which was named a finalist for the 2009 Larry Ritter Award and was nominated for a Seymour Medal. His most recent work includes a three-book series, *Baseball's Untold History*, and several articles that have appeared in SABR books. His collaboration with others on Negro Leagues history earned him the 2019 Tweed Webb Lifetime Achievement Award given by SABR's Negro Leagues Research Committee. He lives in Roslindale, Massachusetts, with Catherine and their cats, Jiggs and Pepper.

ANDREW MILNER's maternal grandparents from Brooklyn grew up in the shadow of Ebbets Field. A SABR member since 1984, he has written for *The National Pastime, Baseball: New Research on the Early Game*, and other publications and reference works. His contributions to the *St. James Encyclopedia of Popular Culture* (2000) included an entry on *The Boys of Summer* author Roger Kahn, whom he interviewed at length in 1994. He currently lives in the Philadelphia area, where he can be regularly heard cursing the Phillies bullpen.

BILL NOWLIN has been to well over 1,000 games at Fenway Park, but wishes he could trade in a few of them (Red Sox losses, of course) for one day at Ebbets Field. Bill still lives in his native Boston area. After 50 years in the record business, overlapping with a dozen as a college professor, he's spent most of the last 10 years ramping up his work with SABR, helping to edit books and hopefully encouraging others to research andwrite, too.

BILL PEARCH, a lifelong Chicago Cubs fan, serves as newsletter editor for SABR's Emil Rothe Chapter (Chicago). In 2022 he helped establish SABR's Central Illinois Chapter. Bill has contributed to SABR's publications about old Comiskey Park and the 1995 Atlanta Braves, and has written the biographies of semipro team owner Col. Frank L. Smith and Deadball Era pitcher Eddie Higgins. He is happily married to a Milwaukee Brewers fan. Follow him on Twitter: @billpearch.

J.G. PRESTON lives in Santa Fe, New Mexico, and has written biographies and game stories for numerous SABR publications. He majored in English at Carleton College in Minnesota and has worked in radio, television, and media relations, in addition to being a freelance writer and copy editor. He has been to games at more major-league ballparks that have been demolished (7) than still exist (5).

After being driven from baseball by those damn curveballs, the late **CHRIS RAINEY** turned to teaching and coaching. He was introduced to the world of baseball research by former SABR President Eugene Murdoch around 1976.

THOMAS RATHKAMP, a senior technical writer, is the author of *Happy Felsch: Banished Black Sox Center Fielder* and is working on his second book, which is sadly not about baseball. Thomas has also written for two other SABR ballpark books (Milwaukee County Stadium and Houston Astrodome). Thomas used to cover high-school sports for a local newspaper. He lives in Cedarburg, Wisconsin, with his wife and two children.

STEPHEN V. RICE, PhD, is a native of Detroit and resides in Collierville, Tennessee. From 2013 to 2022 he authored more than 150 articles for the SABR BioProject and Games Project. A computer scientist and software developer for more than 40 years, he currently develops genomics software for cancer diagnosis and research at St. Jude Children's Research Hospital in Memphis.

CARL RIECHERS retired from United Parcel Service in 2012 after 35 years of service. With more free time, he became a SABR member that same year. Born and raised in the suburbs of St. Louis, he became a big fan of the Cardinals. He and his wife, Janet, have three children and are the proud grandparents of two.

PAUL ROGERS is president of the Ernie Banks-Bobby Bragan (Dallas-Fort Worth) SABR Chapter and the co-author of four baseball books, including *The Whiz Kids and the 1950 Pennant*, written with his boyhood hero Robin Roberts, and *Lucky Me: My 65 Years in Baseball*, authored with Eddie Robinson. He is also the co-editor of recent SABR team histories of the 1951 New York Giants and the 1950 Philadelphia Phillies as well as a frequent contributor to the SABR BioProject and Games Project. His real job is as a law professor at Southern Methodist University, where he was dean of the law school for nine years and has served as the university's faculty athletic representative for 35 years.

PETER SEIDEL has been a member of SABR since 2014. A lifelong Yankee fan, Peter grew up a short ride from Yankee Stadium in southern Westchester County. After earning a master's degree from Harvard University, Peter relocated to the Dallas-Fort Worth area with his two children for his day job as a business development executive for AT&T. Peter has contributed to several SABR books starting with the Mike Sandlock book in 2016 as well as many articles for the SABR Games Project. Aside from being a diehard Yankee fan, Peter enjoys spending time with his teenage kids, bicycling, hiking, kayaking, and playing guitar in whatever spare time he has.

GLEN SPARKS has written SABR game stories and biographies and co-edited books about Babe Ruth, Jackie Robinson, and Roberto Clemente. A lifelong Dodger fan, he wrote a recently published book about the Hall of Fame shortstop Pee Wee Reese. Sparks has a bachelor's degree in journalism from the University of Missouri and worked as a newspaper reporter and editor for many years. He and his wife, Pam, take care of three cats and a busy aquarium.

LYLE SPATZ attended several games at Ebbets Field each season from 1947 through 1957. He is a two-time winner of the Ron Gabriel Award for his editing of *The Team That Forever Changed Baseball and America* (the 1947 Dodgers) and his biography of Dixie Walker. He has also written biographies of former Brooklyn players Bill Dahlen, Willie Keeler, and Hugh Casey. He has been a SABR member since 1973 and was chairman of the Records Committee from 1991 to 2016.

MARK S. STERNMAN wrote about the All-Star Game performances of Jackie Robinson for SABR's book on the great Brooklyn Dodger and has also profiled Jimmy Johnston, who played 1266 games for Brooklyn, for SABR. Sternman's father rooted for the Dodgers until the team left Brooklyn.

STEW THORNLEY has been a member of SABR since 1979. He is an official scorer for Minnesota Twins games and is a member of the MLB Official Scoring Advisory Committee.

JOSEPH WANCHO lives in Brooklyn, Ohio, and has been a SABR member since 2005. His latest book was published by McFarland in 2022: *Hebrew Hammer: A Biography of All-Star Third Baseman Al Rosen*.

STEVEN C. WEINER, a SABR member since 2015, is a retired chemical engineer and a lifelong baseball fan starting with the Brooklyn Dodgers of the 1950s. During his undergraduate years at Rutgers University, Steven worked in the sports information office and broadcast baseball and basketball play-by-play on WRSU radio. Steven obtained his doctoral degree in engineering and applied science from Yale University and has been a contributor to the technical literature on hydrogen and fuel cell safety. Steven currently serves as assignments editor for the SABR Games Project with essay contributions in six SABR books, the *Baseball Research Journal*, and *Jackie Robinson 75: Baseball's Re-Integration*. He volunteers as an in-classroom teacher at local schools.

GREGORY H. WOLF was born in Pittsburgh, but now resides in the Chicagoland area with his wife, Margaret, and daughter, Gabriela. A professor of German studies and holder of the Dennis and Jean Bauman Endowed Chair in the Humanities at North Central College in Naperville, Illinois, he has edited more than a dozen books for SABR. Since January 2017 he has been co-director of SABR's BioProject, which you can follow on Facebook and Twitter.

JACK ZERBY, who died in August 2021, was a retired attorney and estates/trust administrator. He grew up in rural western Pennsylvania. A SABR member starting in 1994, Jack wrote more than a dozen SABR biographies and numerous Games Project accounts. After 25 years in Southwest Florida, where he and SABR colleague Mel Poplock founded the Seymour-Mills Regional Chapter, Jack and his wife, Diana, moved to Brevard, North Carolina.

JOHN ZINN is the author of three books about the Brooklyn Dodgers and is a two-time winner of the Ron Gabriel Award for research on the Brooklyn team. A longtime SABR member, he also writes a baseball history blog entitled A Manly Pastime. John is the scorekeeper for the Flemington Neshanock vintage baseball team. He holds BA and MBA degrees from Rutgers University and is a Vietnam veteran.

DON ZMINDA has been a baseball (and devoted White Sox) fan since attending his first game at Old Comiskey in August of 1954. As director of publications for STATS, Inc. (now STATS LLC) from 1988 to 2000, he co-authored or edited a dozen annual sports publications. Don's book *The Legendary Harry Caray: Baseball's Greatest Salesman* was a 2019 CASEY Award nominee; his latest offering, *Double Plays and Double Crosses: The Black Sox and Baseball in 1920*, was published by Rowman & Littlefield in March 2021. A SABR member since 1979, he is retired and has lived in Los Angeles with his wife, Sharon, since 2000.

The SABR Digital Library

Available wherever books are sold

The First Negro League Champion: The 1920 Chicago American Giants

Edited by Frederick C. Bush and Bill Nowlin

Paperback $29.95 244 pages • Ebook $9.99

This book chronicles the team which won the title of champion in the Negro National League's inaugural season. Rube Foster, a Hall of Famer, and his White business partner John Schorling are featured along with biographies of every player on the team include Cristóbal Torriente, a member of both the National Baseball Hall of Fame and the Cuban Baseball Hall of Fame, as well as early Blackball stalwarts Dave "Lefty" Brown, Bingo DeMoss, Judy Gans, Dave Malarcher, Frank Warfield, and Frank Wickware. A comprehensive timeline of the 1920 season and a history of the founding of the Negro National League are included.

We Are, We Can, We Will: The 1992 World Champion Toronto Blue Jays
Edited by Adrian Fung and Bill Nowlin

Forewords by Buck Martinez and Dave Winfield

Paperback US $34.95/Canada $41.95 394 pages • Ebook $9.99

The 1992 Toronto Blue Jays will always be remembered as the first World Series-winning club from Canada. After a near miss in 1991, the 1992 club confidently adopted "We Are, We Can, We Will" as their team motto. This book features biographies of every player who played for the 1992 Toronto Blue Jays including Hall of Famers Dave Winfield, Jack Morris, and Roberto Alomar. Manager Cito Gaston, Hall of Fame general manager Pat Gillick, and radio broadcaster Tom Cheek are also included, as well as a "ballpark biography" of SkyDome. Ten reports describe significant games from the 1992 season illustrating Toronto's championship journey from Opening Day to the last game of the World Series.

From Shibe Park to Connie Mack Stadium: Great Games in Philadelphia's Lost Ballpark
Edited by Gregory H. Wolf
Paperback $39.95 398 pages • Ebook $9.99

This collection evokes memories and the exciting history of the celebrated ballpark through stories of 100 games played there and several feature essays. The games included in this volume reflect every decade in the ballpark's history, from the inaugural game in 1909, to the last in 1970.

Shibe Park was the home of the Philadelphia A's from 1909 until their relocation to Kansas City and the Philadelphia Phillies from 1938 until the ballpark's closure at the end 1970. In 1953 it was renamed Connie Mack Stadium. The ballpark hosted big-league baseball for 62 seasons and more than 6,000 games—over 3,500 games by the A's and 2,500 by the Phillies—and was home to Frank Baker, Del Ennis, Chief Bender, and Robin Roberts.

¡Arriba!: The Heroic Life of Roberto Clemente

edited by Bill Nowlin and Glen Sparks

Paperback $34.95 338 pages • Ebook $9.99

2022 marks the 50th anniversary year of Roberto Clemente's passing. This book celebrates his life and baseball career. Named to 15 All-Star Game squads, Clemente won 12 Gold Gloves, four batting titles, and was the National League's Most Valuable Player in 1966. The first Latino inducted into the National Baseball Hall of Fame, Clemente played 18 seasons for the Pittsburgh Pirates and became the 11th player to reach the 3,000-hit milestone, hitting number 3000 on the season's last day. At the time no one knew he would never play baseball again. Clemente was known for his charitable work. He lost his life on the final day of 1972 while working to provide relief for victims of an earthquake in Nicaragua.

SABR publishes up to a dozen new books per year on baseball history and culture. Researched and written by SABR members, these collaborative projects cover some of the game's greatest players, classic ballparks, and teams.

SABR members can download all Digital Library publications for free or get 50% off the purchase of paperback editions.

Friends of SABR

You can become a Friend of SABR by giving as little as $10 per month or by making a one-time gift of $1,000 or more. When you do so, you will be inducted into a community of passionate baseball fans dedicated to supporting SABR's work.

Friends of SABR receive the following benefits:
- ✓ Annual Friends of SABR Commemorative Lapel Pin
- ✓ Recognition in This Week in SABR, SABR.org, and the SABR Annual Report
- ✓ Access to the SABR Annual Convention VIP donor event
- ✓ Invitations to exclusive Friends of SABR events

SABR On-Deck Circle - $10/month, $30/month, $50/month

Get in the SABR On-Deck Circle, and help SABR become the essential community for the world of baseball. Your support will build capacity around all things SABR, including publications, website content, podcast development, and community growth.

A monthly gift is deducted from your bank account or charged to a credit card until you tell us to stop. No more email, mail, or phone reminders.

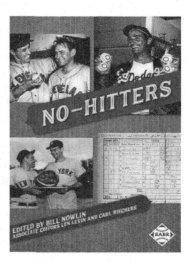

Join the SABR On-Deck Circle

Payment Info: _____Visa _____Mastercard

Name on Card: _____

Card #: _____

Exp. Date: _____ Security Code: _____

Signature: _____

- ○ $10/month
- ○ $30/month
- ○ $50/month
- ○ Other amount _____

Go to sabr.org/donate to make your gift online

44079759R00236